# BEST AMERICAN SCREEN- PLAYS 2

# BEST AMERICAN SCREENPLAYS 2

• COMPLETE SCREENPLAYS •

EDITED BY SAM THOMAS

Crown Publishers, Inc.
New York

The author gratefully acknowledges permission to reprint the following:

*Citizen Kane* by Herman J. Mankiewicz and Orson Welles. Copyright 1941 by RKO Radio Pictures, Inc. Renewed 1968 by RKO General, Inc. All rights reserved. Published by arrangement with Turner Entertainment Co. and The Estate of Orson Welles. *Some Like It Hot* by Billy Wilder and I. A. L. Diamond. Copyright © 1959 by Ashton Productions, Inc. All rights reserved. Renewed © 1986 by MGM/UA Communications Co., formerly known as United Artists Corporation, a successor in interest to Ashton Productions, Inc. Published by arrangement with MGM/UA. *The Treasure of the Sierra Madre* by John Huston. Copyright 1948 by Warner Brothers Pictures, Inc. Renewed 1975 by United Artists Television, Inc. All rights reserved. Published by arrangement with Turner Entertainment Co. *My Man Godfrey* by Morris Ryskind and Eric Hatch. Copyright 1936 by Universal Pictures, a Division of Universal City Studios, Inc. All rights reserved. Published by arrangement with Mrs. Eric Hatch and MCA Publishing, a Division of MCA, Inc. *Judgment at Nuremberg* by Abby Mann. Copyright © 1961 by Roxlom Films, Inc. Published by arrangement with MGM/UA and Abby Mann. *The Lion in Winter* by James Goldman. Copyright © 1968 by James Goldman. All rights reserved. Published by arrangement with James Goldman. *Terms of Endearment* by James L. Brooks. Copyright © 1983 by Paramount Pictures Corporation. All rights reserved. Published by arrangement with Paramount Pictures Corporation and Simon & Schuster Inc. *Julia* by Alvin Sargent. Copyright © 1977 by Twentieth Century-Fox Film Corporation. All rights reserved. Published by arrangement with the Lillian Hellman Estate. *Holy Matrimony* by Nunnally Johnson. Copyright 1943 by Twentieth Century-Fox Film Corporation. All rights reserved. Published by arrangement with Twentieth Century-Fox Film Corporation. *The Sting* by David S. Ward. Copyright © 1973 by Universal Pictures. All rights reserved. Licensed by Merchandising Corporation of America, Inc. Published by arrangement with MCA Publishing Rights, a Division of MCA, Inc., and Mr. David Ward.

Published by Crown Publishers, Inc., 201 East 50th Street, New York, New York 10022
Member of the Crown Publishing Group
CROWN is a trademark of Crown Publishers, Inc.
Manufactured in the United States of America

Library of Congress Cataloging-in-Publication Data

Best American screenplays 2 : complete screenplays / edited by Sam Thomas. — 1st ed.
    p.    cm.
    Contents: Citizen Kane / Herman J. Mankiewicz and Orson Welles — some like it hot / Billy Wilder and I.A.L. Diamond — The treasure of the Sierra Madre / John Huston — My man Godfrey / Morrie Ryskind and Eric Hatch . . . Judgment at Nuremberg / Abby Mann — The lion in winter / James Goldman — Terms of endearment / James L. Brooks — Julia / Alvin Sargent — Holy matrimony / Nunnally Johnson — The sting / David S. Ward.
    1. Motion picture plays. I. Thomas, Sam. II. Title: Best American screenplays two. III. Title: Best American screenplays 2.
PN1997.A1B364    1990
791.43'75'0973 — dc20                                   90-2423
                                                CIP

ISBN 0-517-57463-2

10 9 8 7 6 5 4

# CONTENTS

# BEST AMERICAN SCREEN-PLAYS 2

# INTRODUCTION

On this occasion, the publication of *Best American Screenplays 2*, I want to express my gratification to our readers for their fine support of our premiere and pioneering anthology, *Best American Screenplays*.

Not only did it go into a second printing, but it also was selected by the Doubleday, Literary Guild, and Fireside book clubs as an alternate choice in January 1988, an accolade of which we are very proud.

We now offer a new anthology of outstanding screenplays of which we are equally proud, including *Citizen Kane* by Herman J. Mankiewicz and Orson Welles; *Some Like It Hot* by Billy Wilder and I. A. L. Diamond; *The Treasure of the Sierra Madre* by John Huston; *My Man Godfrey* by Morrie Ryskind and Eric Hatch; *Judgment at Nuremberg* by Abby Mann; *The Lion in Winter* by James Goldman; *Terms of Endearment* by James L. Brooks; *Julia* by Alvin Sargent; *Holy Matrimony,* a lesser-known but fine screenplay, by the gifted writer the late Nunnally Johnson; and last, but certainly not least, David S. Ward's *The Sting*. These fine examples of writing for the screen helped generate dozens of Academy Awards and Academy nominations, their authors being exceptional talents and among the best to have ever worked in the cinema.

Here, as in our first anthology, we present screenplays, which span the last half century and a range in content, that speak well of screenwriters' talent and comment on the American scene, from 1936's *My Man Godfrey* to 1983's *Terms of Endearment*.

We begin with *Citizen Kane*. It is difficult to measure the impact Orson Welles and Herman J. Mankiewicz had upon the cinematic world and beyond when *Citizen Kane* blazed like a brilliant meteor upon the movie screens of the world in 1941. It became a byword and a legend in its own time for excellence of screencraft, not only for its superb screenplay but also its technique, particularly its use of montage. *Citizen Kane* is a metaphor for the rise and fall of an immensely rich, princely power, a thinly veiled portrait of William Randolph Hearst in his fictional counterpart, Charles Foster Kane. It is set in an era when ownership and manipulation of the media meant power to rival the greatest of Machiavellian monarchs in history, who ruled their domains with little interference. Yet what makes Kane something more than Machiavellian are his attempts—in his own self-serving eyes at least—to become the champion of the downtrodden and the powerless. Failing in his attempt to achieve high political office when he is turned down by the voters, and thwarted in his personal relationships, his life becomes a void, a love-parched desert, where at last nothing grows. He is ultimately powerless to control his own life.

Billy Wilder and the late I. A. L. Diamond produced a script for *Some Like It Hot* that bristles with wit and verve, characteristic of the marvelous Wilder-Diamond style that includes some of the most brilliant work for the cinema ever created, with Mr. Wilder directing as well. Using the comic theatrical device of men posing as women, the film is the cream of the genre that includes

*Where's Charley* (1952), which starred Ray Bolger, and, more recently, *Tootsie* (1982), which starred Dustin Hoffman. *Some Like It Hot* surely will forever stand out as one of the most comedic, vital, and successful of this genre.

John Huston's screenplay of *The Treasure of the Sierra Madre*, adapted from the novel by B. Traven, is a treasure trove of some of the finest writing that has ever exploded upon the screen. Other than perhaps Erich Von Stroheim's monumental *Greed* (1925)—initially put together in forty-two reels (which would have required approximately seven hours of continuous showing) and ultimately released in only ten reels—there is no better screen study of avarice than this created with such ruthless realism by Mr. Huston in 1948. In contrast to Von Stroheim's extravagantly large *Greed*, Huston's tale is told with a skillful, exacting economy as lean and spare as a disciplined piece of poetry. It is a masterly work for a film also directed by Mr. Huston.

In Morrie Ryskind and Eric Hatch's *My Man Godfrey*, a work that goes back to the Depression years of the thirties, we have a supremely fine example of comedy with a pungent style and meaningful social content. Underneath the zany characterizations that make sport of the affluent Bullock family is a subtext—a strong feeling of affection for the family, as they are seen as inherently good people, despite the appearance that they are rich and foolish and not very aware of the plight of the poor and homeless.

Also among the extraordinary screenplays that comprise this second anthology, we are very happy to include Abby Mann's *Judgment at Nuremberg*. The screenplay is powerful in its scope and treatment of one of the most important international trials in the history of political jurisprudence, if not the most important up to this time, as it was involved with bringing to trial people other than those who occupied the center stage of Nazi brutality and genocide. The Nuremberg trials were a moral milestone that will be timeless in their impact, as they pose the question: Where were those who could have resisted the horrendous Jacobins and villainous barbarians, who under the guise of citizens of a civilized modern state averted their heads, their hearts, and their consciences and aborted what courage they might have summoned to let the very heart of that supposed civilized state—the right to justice—wither and die on the poisoned vine of Nazism?

Abby Mann's screenplay does great justice, if you will, to the dissection of this fatal cancer in the heart and minds of the German people at that time, held pulsatingly in his hands in full view for us to see, to smell its rottenness, to recoil from its slime in the persona of Ernst Janning, the German judge, so ably played by Burt Lancaster, and ably created by Abby Mann.

James Goldman's *The Lion in Winter* is a superb work in a genre that, when well crafted and performed, never ceases to entertain and enlighten—the study of power struggles among parents with each other and their offspring. This account of family warfare and royal prerogative—in a time when princes were above the law, or who often used it to their own advantage to break, bend, ignore, or abuse it—is fascinating for the parallels found in any age. As Sir Dalberg, the first Baron Acton allegedly once said: "Power tends to corrupt and absolute power corrupts absolutely." Are we more enlightened now in our modern political and economic marketplace with endless investigations and resignations of legislators and financial manipulators?

James L. Brooks, a comparative newcomer to the ranks of fine screenwriters, who honed his writing craft in the world of documentaries prior to his involvement in television sitcoms and theatrical films, adapted Larry McMurtry's novel, *Terms of Endearment,* to the screen. This study of a mother's close relationship with her daughter and of the men in their lives is humanely wrought, and the film is another excellent example of the craft of the writer united with the craft of the director in the same person; and Mr. Brooks served as producer as well.

We welcome the continuation of the trend in recent decades of writers directing their own work, and we hope and trust that Mr. Brooks, as in *Terms of Endearment* and *Broadcast News,* will continue in this vein as have an increasing number of others. This is a most promising trend in the cinema, which we hope will become even more prevalent in the future, as there are more and more noteworthy successors to John Huston and Billy Wilder and company.

Not too many readers may be acquainted with the work of screenwriter Alvin Sargent. In the years he has labored in the Hollywood scene and in television, his scripts have been admired for their craft, precision, and successful marriage of plot and character. *Julia,* a admirable example of these Sargent traits, portrays the close relationship of two women, friends since childhood. Set against a background of early Nazi criminality in Austria, this study of a bond of friendship between two women is among the very best of the genre to appear on the screen.

Although Nunnally Johnson's screenplay for *Holy Matrimony* is probably not very well known among students of the cinema, it has always been a particular favorite of mine. Mr. Johnson was one of the greatest practitioners of his craft and produced a great range of material, from his adaptation of Steinbeck's great novel *The Grapes of Wrath* to *The World of Henry Orient,* one of the best comedic treatments of teenage female adolescents one could ever hope to see.

In *Holy Matrimony,* Mr. Johnson, in his characteristically witty, astringent style, depicts the comforts of old age and the need for companionship that in its own way rivals *On Golden Pond,* which we published in our first anthology. An added pleasure of *Holy Matrimony* is its sly commentary on the methods of talent agents. I trust all readers will take note of Mr. Johnson's skill, his comedic vitality, his invention, and his screenplay's viability as an extremely playable script—the hallmarks of Mr. Johnson's great talent.

Concluding our superb list of screenplays we have David S. Ward's *The Sting,* a work that fascinates with its razor-sharp plot that depicts a great scam. Through twists and turns, the plot spins its web and catches not only the victims in the film but the audience as well.

After we published our first anthology, we received a few inquiries concerning our format of presenting the screenplays and why we did not publish them in their original manuscript form, page by page. Unfortunately, to do so would make our anthology prohibitive both in size and printing cost, which would sharply raise the price of the book. By printing the material in two columns to a printed page, all ten screenplays can be presented in one easily readable and comfortable-to-handle volume.

Nonetheless, for readers who have never seen how a screenplay looks in the original format, we are including here the first page of *The Treasure of the Sierra Madre*.

FADE IN
CLOSEUP LOTTERY LIST

SHOWING the winning numbers drawn in the MEXICAN NATIONAL LOTTERY. AUGUST 5, 1924. CAMERA PULLS BACK to INCLUDE DOBBS. He is slowly tearing a lottery ticket into bits. CAMERA DOLLIES AHEAD of him as he turns away from the list. The tribes of bootblacks that people the streets do not pester Dobbs. He is too obviously on his uppers. His clothes are ragged and dirty and his shoes broken. He hasn't had a haircut in months and there is several days growth of beard on his face. He stops a passing American.

     DOBBS:
   Can you spare a dime, brother?

The American growls, moves on. Dobbs turns, looks after the departing figure. The American flips a cigarette away. Dobbs' eyes follow its flight.

CLOSEUP THE BURNING CIGARETTE
 in the gutter.

CLOSE SHOT DOBBS

He moves half a step toward the gutter, then halts and looks right and left to make sure no one is watching. This brief delay costs him the cigarette. One of the swarm of bootblacks swoops down on it. Dobbs pulls his belt in a couple of notches and continues on up the street. Camera dollies ahead. Something Dobbs sees OUT OF SCENE causes him to increase his pace. He catches up with an American who is dressed in a white suit.

     DOBBS:
   Brother, can you spare a dime?

White Suit fishes in his pocket, takes out a toston and gives it to Dobbs who is so surprised by this act of generosity that he doesn't even say thanks. For several moments he stands rooted looking at the coin in his palm. Then he closes his hand around it, making a fist. Putting the fist in his pocket, he cuts across the street. CAMERA PANS with him to a tobacco stand where he stops to buy a package of cigarettes, then hurries along. CAMERA PANS him to a sidewalk restaurant.

           Dissolve to:

By comparing it to our format, one can see that we still have included all the important stage directions, as well as every word the screenwriter wrote.

Before we close our introduction, we would like to make a comment on a few recent events of the American cinema. The Writers Guild strike of 1988 cost both writers and studios much time, money, and creative energy, but hopefully it will result in a greater, permanent understanding between the two. The new Writers Guild's President's Committee on the Professional Status of Writers has been set up to protect the creative rights of writers whereby problems between writer and studio representatives can be discussed and negotiated in a noninflammatory way. It is hoped that the process of developing scripts will thus be smoother, with an increased, more integral role for writers during the actual shooting of the film. Previously, most writers were left out of this process, during which their skills and advice could have been quite useful.

We expect that 1990 will be a record financial year for American films. In 1987 such films accounted for about half of the world's box office, with receipts of $4.25 billion. This was surpassed in 1988 with a total of $4.38 billion, and it appears that the total will be at least $4.5 billion for 1989. With the immense popularity of home video, we find more interest in films than ever before and a greatly expanded market. Receipts to studios from film cassette rentals and sales now surpass theatrical receipts. And with a growing foreign market, producers now presell video, cable, and foreign rights and, even more than in the past, have joined forces with many foreign entities to share costs, thus reducing some of the huge financial risks that are inherent in filmmaking. We trust that independent filmmakers also will benefit by the expanding world market for films.

And so, we hope you enjoy this second anthology of *Best American Screenplays*. We look forward to a time in the very near future when screenplays will become common reading not only in university and high school film courses, but in English departments as well, alongside the novel, the stage play, and poetry.

SAM THOMAS
*Los Angeles, California*

# CITIZEN KANE

## Screenplay by Herman J. Mankiewicz and Orson Welles

| | |
|---|---|
| JEDEDIAH LELAND | Joseph Cotten |
| SUSAN ALEXANDER | Dorothy Comingore |
| MR. BERNSTEIN | Everett Sloane |
| JIM W. GETTYS | Ray Collins |
| WALTER P. THATCHER | George Coulouris |
| MRS. KANE | Agnes Moorehead |
| RAYMOND | Paul Stewart |
| EMILY NORTON | Ruth Warrick |
| MR. CARTER | Erskine Sanford |
| THOMPSON | William Alland |
| MATISTI | Fortunio Bononova |
| THE HEADWAITER | Gus Schilling |
| MR. RAWLSTON | Philip Van Zandt |
| MISS ANDERSON | Georgia Backus |
| KANE'S FATHER | Harry Shannon |
| KANE II | Sonny Bupp |
| KANE, AGE EIGHT | Buddy Swan |
| KANE | Orson Welles |

Produced and Directed by Orson Welles
Director of Photography: Gregg Toland, A.S.C.
Music by Bernard Herrmann
Special Effects by Vernon L. Walker, A.S.C.
Art Director: Van Nest Polglase
Associate Art Director: Perry Ferguson
Edited by Robert Wise
Recording by Bailey Fesler and James G. Stewart
Costumes by Edward Stevenson
Set Designer: Darrell Silvera
Associate Set Designer: Al Fields

What could one possibly say about the film and the screenplay of *Citizen Kane* that has not been said already? It is undoubtedly a great film and a remarkably inventive screenplay. The script's "March of Time" technique is outstanding, a marvelous achievement. The effect of this "News Digest" sequence, which runs thirty-two pages at the beginning of the screenplay, is overwhelming in its scope and power. It fully achieves what the great Russian director and film theorist Sergei Eisenstein used in his 1925 films *Strike* and *Potemkin:* the successful use of montage—a sequential arrangement of shots in juxtaposition and conflict with each other, which in its cumulative force creates a whole new meaning beyond the individual shots themselves. It is difficult to understand why montage, an intrinsically cinematic and strikingly effective extension of film grammar that goes way beyond cinema's prose narrative language derivation, is so seldom used today.

What controversy still remains over this film, which was conceived and nurtured in dispute over its depiction of William Randolph Hearst as Charles Foster Kane, is concerned with who should be given the major credit for the story and the screenplay. One of cinema's finest critics, Pauline Kael, in her definitive study of the film, *The Citizen Kane Book* (1971), makes a strong case for Herman J. Mankiewicz being the true creative force behind the screenplay, from inception through the final shooting script. Although I agree with her, I feel that Orson Welles's contribution was monumental, and his direction was truly inspired and innovative. And as film is such a collaborative medium, it takes the creative talents of many people to produce such a work. Thus, there is ample glory for both of these men, and all the other creative spirits who contributed to the film.

(George) Orson Welles was born on May 6, 1915, in Kenosha, Wisconsin, and died on October 10, 1985. His father, a wealthy inventor, and his mother, a concert pianist, gave him full reign as a child to express his creative and artistic gifts in writing poetry, painting, acting, playing the piano, and performing magic tricks. His cofounding of the Mercury Theatre with the gifted John Houseman, highlighted his meteoric career in stage and radio that climaxed in film with his masterpiece *Citizen Kane* (1941). After that, his career and personal life suffered. Ironically somewhat like his character Charles Foster Kane, Welles was never again able to attain the great pinnacle of creative power and success that he had achieved with *Kane,* though he did produce some fine works such as *The Magnificent Ambersons* (1942), *The Lady from Shanghai* (1948), *Macbeth* (1948), *Othello* (1955), and *Touch of Evil* (1958).

Herman J. Mankiewicz was born in New York City on November 7, 1897, and died in 1953. He was educated at Columbia University and the University of Berlin, where he began his career as a correspondent for the Chicago *Tribune.* Following a stint as drama editor of the *New York Times* and *The New Yorker* magazine, he went to Hollywood in 1926 to begin his career as a title writer and scenarist. Some of his credits include co-scenarist for *Dinner at Eight* (1933), co-story for *It's a Wonderful World* (1939), and co-scenarist for *Pride of the Yankees* (1942).

PROLOGUE

*Fade In*

*Ext. Xanadu—Faint Dawn—1940 (Miniature)*

*Window, very small in the distance, illuminated*
All around this an almost totally black screen. Now, as the camera moves slowly towards this window which is almost a postage stamp in the frame, other forms appear; barbed wire, cyclone fencing, and now, looming up against an early morning sky, enormous iron grille work. Camera travels up what is now shown to be a gateway of gigantic proportions and holds on the top of it—a huge initial "K" showing darker and darker against the dawn sky. Through this and beyond we see the fairy-tale mountaintop of Xanadu, the great castle a silhouette at its summit, the little window a distant accent in the darkness.

*Dissolve*

(A series of set-ups, each closer to the great window, all telling something of:)

The literally incredible domain of CHARLES FOSTER KANE
Its right flank resting for nearly forty miles on the Gulf Coast, it truly extends in all directions farther than the eye can see. Designed by nature to be almost completely bare and flat—it was, as will develop, practically all marshland when KANE acquired and changed its face—it is now pleasantly uneven, with its fair share of rolling hills and one very good-sized mountain, all man-made. Almost all the land is improved, either through cultivation for farming purposes or through careful landscaping, in the shape of parks and lakes. The castle

itself, an enormous pile, compounded of several genuine castles, of European origin, of varying architecture—dominates the scene, from the very peak of the mountain.

*Dissolve*

*Golf Links (Miniature)*

Past which we move. The greens are straggly and overgrown, the fairways wild with tropical weeds, the links unused and not seriously tended for a long time.

*Dissolve Out*

*Dissolve In*

*What Was Once a Good-sized Zoo (Miniature)*

Of the Hagenbeck type. All that now remains, with one exception, are the individual plots, surrounded by moats, on which the animals are kept, free and yet safe from each other and the landscape at large. (Signs on several of the plots indicate that here there were once tigers, lions, giraffes.)

*Dissolve*

*The Monkey Terrace (Miniature)*

In the f.g., a great obscene ape is outlined against the dawn murk. He is scratching himself slowly, thoughtfully, looking out across the estates of CHARLES FOSTER KANE, to the distant light glowing in the castle on the hill.

*Dissolve*

*The Alligator Pit (Miniature)*

The idiot pile of sleepy dragons. Reflected in the muddy water—the lighted window.

*The Lagoon (Miniature)*

The boat landing sags. An old newspaper floats on the surface of the water—a copy of the New York "Enquirer." As it moves across the frame, it discloses again the reflection of the window in the castle, closer than before.

*The Great Swimming Pool (Miniature)*

It is empty. A newspaper blows across the cracked floor of the tank.

*Dissolve*

*The Cottages (Miniature)*

In the shadows, literally the shadows, of the castle. As we move by, we see that their doors and windows are boarded up and locked, with heavy bars as further protection and sealing.

*Dissolve Out*

*Dissolve In*

*A Drawbridge—(Miniature)*

Over a wide moat, now stagnant and choked with weeds. We move across it and through a huge solid gateway into a formal garden, perhaps thirty yards wide and one hundred yards deep, which extends right up to the very wall of the castle. The landscaping surrounding it has been sloppy and casual for a long time, but this particular garden has been kept up in perfect shape. As the camera makes its way through it, towards the lighted window of the castle, there are revealed rare and exotic blooms of all kinds. The dominating note is one of almost exaggerated tropical lushness, hanging limp and despairing. — Moss, moss, moss. Ankor Wat, the night the last King died.

*Dissolve*

*The Window—(Miniature)*

Camera moves in until the frame of the window fills the frame of the screen. Suddenly the light within goes out. This stops the action of the camera and cuts the music which has been accompanying the sequence. In the glass panes of the window we see reflected the ripe, dreary landscape of MR. KANE'S estate behind and the dawn sky.

*Dissolve*

*Int.     KANE'S     Bedroom—Faint Dawn—1940*

A very long shot of KANE'S enormous bed, silhouetted against the enormous window.

*Dissolve*

*Int.     KANE'S     bedroom—Faint Dawn—1940*

A snow scene. An incredible one. Big impossible flakes of snow, a too picturesque farmhouse and a snow man. The jingling of sleigh bells in the musical score now makes an ironic reference to Indian Temple bells—the music freezes—

KANE'S OLD OLD VOICE. *Rosebud!*

The camera pulls back, showing the whole scene to be contained in one of those glass balls which are sold in novelty stores all over the world. A hand—KANE'S hand, which has been holding the ball, relaxes. The ball falls out of his hand and bounds down two carpeted steps leading to the bed, the camera following. The ball falls off the last step onto the marble floor where it breaks, the fragments glittering in the first rays of the morning sun. This ray cuts an angular pattern across the floor, suddenly crossed with a thousand bars of light as the blinds are pulled across the window.

The foot of KANE'S bed. The camera very close. Outlined against the shuttered window, we can see a form—the form of a nurse, as she *pulls the sheet up over his head. The camera follows this action up the length of the bed and arrives at the face after the sheet has covered it.*

*Fade Out*

*Fade In*

*Int. of a Motion Picture Projection Room*

*On the screen as the camera moves in are the words:*

"MAIN TITLE"

*Stirring brassy music is heard on the sound track (which, of course, sounds more like a sound track than ours.)*

*The screen in the projection room fills our screen as the second title appears:*

"CREDITS"

*Note: Here follows a typical news digest short, one of the regular monthly or bi-monthly features, based on public events or personalities. (These are distinguished from ordinary newsreels and short subjects in that they have a fully developed editorial or story line.) Some of the more obvious characteristics of the "March of Time," for example, as well as other documentary shorts, will be combined to give an authentic impression of this now familiar type of short subject. As is the accepted procedure in these short subjects, a narrator is used as well as explanatory titles.*

*Fade Out*

NEWS DIGEST

NARRATOR. Legendary was the Xanadu where Kubla Kahn decreed his stately pleasure dome—*(with quotes in his voice)* "Where twice five miles of fertile ground With walls and towers were girdled 'round." *(dropping the quotes)* Today, almost as

legendary is *Florida's* XANADU—world's largest private pleasure ground. Here, on the deserts of the Gulf Coast a private mountain was commissioned, successfully built for its landlord. Here in a private valley, as in the Coleridge poem, "blossoms many an incense-bearing tree." Verily, "a miracle of rare device."

U.S.A.
CHARLES FOSTER KANE

*Opening shot of great desolate expanse of Florida Coastline. (1940—DAY)*

*Dissolve*

*Series of shots showing various aspects of Xanadu, all as they might be photographed by an ordinary newsreel cameraman—nicely photographed but not atmospheric to the extreme extent of the Prologue. (1940)*

NARRATOR *(dropping the quotes).* Here for Xanadu's landlord will be held 1940's biggest, strangest funeral; here this week is laid to rest a potent figure of our Century—America's Kubla Kahn—Charles Foster Kane.

NARRATOR. In journalism's history other names are honored more than Charles Foster Kane's, more justly revered. Among publishers, second only to James Gordon Bennett the First: his dashing expatriate son; England's Northcliffe and Beaverbrook; Chicago's Patterson and McCormick;

TITLE:

TO FORTY-FOUR MILLION U.S. NEWS BUYERS, MORE NEWSWORTHY THAN THE NAMES IN HIS OWN HEADLINES, WAS KANE HIMSELF, GREATEST NEWSPAPER TYPCOON OF THIS OR ANY OTHER GENERATION

*Shot of a huge, screen-filling picture of* KANE. *Pull back to show that it is a picture on the front page of the*

*"Enquirer," surrounded by the reversed rules of mourning, with masthead and headlines. (1940)*

*Dissolve*

*A great number of headlines, set in different types and different styles, obviously from different papers, all announcing* KANE'S *death, all appearing over photographs of* KANE *himself. (Perhaps a fifth of the headlines are in foreign languages.) An important item in connection with the headlines is that many of them— positively not all—reveal passionately conflicting opinions about* KANE. *Thus, they contain variously the words, "patriot," "democrat," "pacifist," "war-monger," "traitor," "idealist," "American," etc.*

TITLE:

1895 TO 1940 ALL OF THESE YEARS HE COVERED, MANY OF THESE YEARS HE WAS.

*Newsreel shots of San Francisco during and after the fire, followed by shots of special trains with large streamers: "Kane Relief Organization." Over these shots superimpose the date—1906.*

*Artist's painting of Foch's railroad car and peace negotiators, if actual newsreel shot unavailable. Over this shot superimpose the date—1918.*

NARRATOR *(cont'd)*. Denver's Bonfils and Sommes; New York's late great Joseph Pulitzer; America's emperor of the news syndicate, another editorialist and landlord, the still mighty and once mightier Hearst. Great names all of them—but none of these so loved—hated—feared, so often spoken—as Charles Foster Kane.

NARRATOR. The San Francisco Earthquake. First with the news were the Kane Papers. First with Relief of the Sufferers, First with the news of their Relief of the Sufferers.

NARRATOR. Kane papers scoop the world on the Armistice—publish, eight hours before competitors, complete details of the Armistice terms granted the Germans by Marshall Foch from his railroad car in the Forest of Compeigne.

NARRATOR. For forty years appeared in Kane newsprint no public issue on which Kane papers took no stand.

NARRATOR. No public man whom Kane himself did not support or denounce—often support, then denounce.

NARRATOR. Its humble beginnings a dying daily—

*Shots with the date—1898—(to be supplied)*

*Shots with the date—1910—(to be supplied)*

*Shots with the date—1922—(to be supplied)*

*Headlines, cartoons, contemporary newsreels or stills of the following:*

1. *Woman Suffrage. (The celebrated newsreel shot of about 1914.)*

2. *Prohibition. (Breaking up of a speakeasy and such.)*

3. *T. V. A.*

4. *Labor riots.*

*Brief clips of old newsreel shots of William Jennings Bryan, Theodore Roosevelt, Stalin, Walter P. Thatcher, Al Smith, McKinley, Landon, Franklin D. Roosevelt and such. (Also recent newsreels of the elderly* KANE *with such Nazis as Hitler and Goering; and England's Chamberlain and Churchill.)*

*Shot of a ramshackle building with old-fashioned presses showing through plate glass windows and the name "Enquirer" in old-fashioned gold letters. (1892)*

*Dissolve*

NARRATOR. Kane's empire, in its glory, held dominion over thirty-seven newspapers, thirteen magazines, a radio network. An empire upon an empire. The first of grocery stores, paper mills, apartment buildings, factories, forests, ocean liners—

NARRATOR. An empire through which for fifty years flowed, in an unending stream, the wealth of the earth's third richest gold mine. . . .

NARRATOR. Famed in American legend is the origin of the Kane fortune. . . . How, to boarding-housekeeper Mary Kane, by a defaulting boarder, in 1868 was left the supposedly worthless deed to an abandoned mine shaft: The Colorado Lode.

*The magnificent Enquirer Building of today.*

*1891–1911 a map of the U.S.A., covering the entire screen, which in animated diagram shows the* KANE *publications spreading from city to city. Starting from New York, miniature newsboys speed madly to Chicago, Detroit, St. Louis, Los Angeles, San Francisco, Washington, Atlanta, El Paso, etc., screaming "Wuxtry, Kane Papers, Wuxtry."*

*Shot of a large mine going full blast, chimneys belching smoke, trains moving in and out, etc. A large sign reads "Colorado Lode Mining Co." (1940) Sign reading: "Little Salem, Colo., 25 miles."*

*Dissolve*

*An old still shot of Little Salem as it was 70 years ago. (Identified by cop-per-plate caption beneath the still.) (1870)*

*Shot of early tintype stills of* THOMAS FOSTER KANE *and his wife,* MARY, *on their wedding day. A similar picture of* MARY KANE *some four or five years later with her little boy,* CHARLES FOSTER KANE.

NARRATOR. Fifty-seven years later, before a Congressional Investigation, Walter P. Thatcher, grand old man of Wall Street, for years chief target of Kane Papers' attack on "trusts," recalls a journey he made as a youth. . . .

*Shot of Capitol in Washington, D.C.*

*Shot of Congressional Investigating Committee. (Reproduction of existing J. P. Morgan newsreel.) This runs silent under narration.* WALTER P. THATCHER *is on the stand. He is flanked by his son, Walter P. Thatcher, Jr., and other partners. He is being questioned by some Merry Andrew congressmen. At this moment a baby alligator has just been placed in his lap, causing considerable confusion and embarrassment.*

*Newsreel closeup of* THATCHER, *the sound track of which now fades in.*

THATCHER. . . . because of that trivial incident . . .

INVESTIGATOR. It is a fact, however, is it not, that in 1870 you did go to Colorado?

THATCHER. I did.

INVESTIGATOR. In connection with the Kane affairs?

THATCHER. Yes. My firm had been appointed trustees by Mrs. Kane for the fortune, which she had recently acquired. It was her wish that I should take charge of this boy, Charles Foster Kane.

NARRATOR. That same month in Union Square—

INVESTIGATOR. Is it not a fact that on that occasion the boy personally attacked you after striking you in the stomach with a sled?

*Loud laughter and confusion.*

THATCHER. Mr. Chairman, I will read to this committee a prepared statement I have brought with me— and I will then refuse to answer any further questions. Mr. Johnson, please!

*A young assistant hands him a sheet of paper from a brief case.*

THATCHER *(reading it).* "With full awareness of the meaning of my words and the responsibility of what I am about to say, it is my considered belief that Mr. Charles Foster Kane, in every essense of his social beliefs and by the dangerous manner in which he has persistently attacked the American traditions of private property, initiative and opportunity for advancement, is—in fact—nothing more or less than a Communist."

*Newsreel of Union Square meeting, section of crowd carrying banners urging boycott of* KANE *papers. A speaker is on the platform above the crowd.*

SPEAKER *(fading in on sound track).* —till the words "Charles Foster Kane" are a menace to every working man in this land. He is today what he has always been and always will be—*a Fascist!*

NARRATOR. And yet another opinion—Kane's own.

*Silent newsreel on a windy platform, flag-draped, in front of the magnificent Enquirer Building. On platform, in full ceremonial dress, is* CHARLES FOSTER KANE. *He orates silently.*

TITLE:

"I AM, HAVE BEEN, AND WILL BE ONLY ONE THING—AN AMERICAN."
CHARLES FOSTER KANE

*Same locale,* KANE *shaking hands out of frame.*

*Another newsreel shot, much later, very brief, showing* KANE, *older and much fatter, very tired-looking, seated with his second wife in a night-club. He looks lonely and unhappy in the midst of the gaiety.*

NARRATOR. Twice married—twice divorced—First to a President's niece, Emily Norton,—today, by her second marriage, chatelaine of the oldest of England's stately homes.

NARRATOR. Sixteen years after that,—two weeks after his divorce from Emily Norton, Kane married Susan Alexander, singer, at the Town Hall in Trenton, New Jersey.

TITLE:

FEW PRIVATE LIVES
WERE MORE PUBLIC

*Period still of* EMILY NORTON *(1900). Dissolve*

*Reconstruction of very old silent newsreel of wedding party on the back lawn of the White House. Many notables, including the bridegroom, the bride,* THATCHER, SR., *Thatcher, Jr., and recognizably* BERNSTEIN, LELAND, *et al, among the guests. Also seen in this group are period newspaper photographers and newsreel cameramen. (1900)*

*Period still of* SUSAN ALEXANDER. *Dissolve*

*Reconstructed silent newsreel.* KANE, SUSAN *and* BERNSTEIN *emerging from side doorway of City Hall into a ring of press photographers, reporters, etc.* KANE *looks startled, recoils for an instant, then charges down upon the photographers, laying about him with his stick, smashing whatever he can hit.*

NARRATOR. For wife two, one-time opera singing Susan Alexander, Kane built Chicago's Municipal Opera House. Cost: Three million dollars. Conceived for Susan Alexander Kane, half finished before she divorced him, the still unfinished Xanadu. Cost: No man can say.

*Still of architect's sketch with typically glorified "rendering" of the Chicago Municipal Opera House.*

*Dissolve*

*A glamorous shot of the almost finished Xanadu, a magnificent fairytale estate built on a mountain. (1920)*

*Then shots of its preparation. (1917)*

*Shots of truck after truck, train after train, flashing by with tremendous noise.*

*Shots of vast dredges, steam-shovels.*

*Shot of ship standing offshore unloading into lighters.*

*In quick succession, shots follow each other, some reconstructed, some in miniature, some real shots (maybe from the dam projects) of building, digging, pouring concrete, etc.*

NARRATOR. One hundred thousand trees, twenty thousand tons of marble, are the ingredients of Xanadu's mountain.

Xanadu's livestock: the fowl of the air, the fish of the sea, the beast of the field and jungle—two of each; the biggest private zoo since Noah.

Contents of Kane's palace: paintings, pictures, statues, the very stones of many another palace, shipped to Florida from every corner of the earth, from other Kane houses, warehouses, where they mouldered for years. Enough for ten museums.—The loot of the world.

*More shots as before, only this time we see (in miniature) a large mountain—at different periods in its development—rising out of the sands.*

*Shots of elephants, apes, zebras, etc., being herded, unloaded, shipped, etc. in various ways.*

*Shots of packing cases being unloaded from ships, from trains, from trucks, with various kinds of lettering on them (Italian, Arabian, Chinese, etc.) but all consigned to* CHARLES FOSTER KANE, *Xanadu, Florida.*

*A reconstructed still of Xanadu—the main terrace. A group of persons in clothes of the period of 1917. In their midst, clearly recognizable, are* KANE *and* SUSAN.

NARRATOR. Kane urged his country's entry into one war.—
—Opposed participation in another.—
—Swung the election to one American President at least, was called another's assassin. Thus Kane's papers might never have survived—had not the President.

TITLE:

FROM XANADU, FOR THE PAST TWENTY-FIVE YEARS, ALL KANE ENTERPRISES HAVE BEEN DIRECTED, MANY OF THE NATION'S DESTINIES SHAPED.

*Shots of various authentically worded headlines of American papers since 1895.*

*Spanish-American War shots. (1898)*

*A graveyard in France of the World War and hundreds of crosses. (1919)*

*Old newsreels of a political campaign.*

*Insert of a particularly virulent headline and/or cartoon.*

HEADLINE: "PRESIDENT SHOT"

NARRATOR. Kane, molder of mass opinion though he was, in all his life was never granted elective office by the voters of his country.

Few U.S. news publishers have been. Few, like one-time Congressman Hearst, have ever run for any office—most know better—conclude with other political observers that no man's press has power enough for himself. But Kane papers were once strong indeed, and once the prize seemed almost his. In 1910, as Independent Candidate for Governor, the best elements of the State behind him—the White House seemingly the next easy step in a lightning political career—

*Night shot of crowd burning* CHARLES FOSTER KANE *in effigy. The dummy bears a grotesque, comic resemblance to* KANE. *It is tossed into the flames, which burn up—*

*—and then down. . . . (1910)*

*Fade Out*

TITLE:

IN POLITICS—ALWAYS A BRIDESMAID,
NEVER A BRIDE

*Newsreel shots of great crowds streaming into a building—Madison Square Garden—then shots inside the vast auditorium, at one end of which is a huge picture of* KANE. *(1910)*

*Shot of box containing the first* MRS. KANE *and young* HOWARD KANE *aged five. They are acknowledging*

*the cheers of the crowd. (Silent Shot) (1910)*

*Newsreel shot of dignitaries on platform, with* KANE, *alongside of speaker's table, beaming, hand upraised to silence the crowd. (Silent Shot) (1910)*

NARRATOR. Then, suddenly—less than one week before election—defeat! Shameful, ignominious;—defeat that set back for twenty years the cause of Reform in the U.S., forever cancelled political chances for Charles Foster Kane.

Then in the third year of the great depression. . . . As to all publishers it sometimes must—to Bennett, to Munsey and Hearst it did—a paper closes! For Kane, in four short years: collapse! Eleven Kane papers, four Kane magazines merged, more sold, scrapped—

*Newsreel shot—closeup of* KANE *delivering speech. . . . (1910)*

*The front page of a contemporary paper—A screaming headline—Twin photos of* KANE *and* SUSAN. *(1910)*

*Printed title about depression.*

*Once more repeat the map of the U.S.A. 1932–1939. Suddenly the cartoon goes into reverse, the empire begins to shrink, illustrating the narrator's words.*

*The door of a newspaper office with the signs: "Closed."*

NARRATOR. Then four long years more—alone in his never finished, already decaying, pleasure palace, aloof, seldom visited, never photographed, Charles Foster Kane continued to direct his failing empire. . . . vainly attempted to sway, as he once did, the destinies of a nation that has ceased to listen to him. . . . ceased to trust him. . . .

*Shots of Xanadu (1940)*

*Series of shots, entirely modern, but rather jumpy and obviously boot-legged, showing* KANE *in a bath chair, swathed in steamer rugs, being perambulated through his rose garden, a desolate figure in the sunshine. (1935)*

NARRATOR. Last week death came to sit upon the throne of America's Kubla Kahn—last week, as it must to all men, death came to Charles Foster Kane.

*Dissolve*

*Cabinet Photograph (Full Screen) of* KANE, *as an old, old man. This image remains constant on the screen (as camera pulls back, taking in the interior of a dark projection room).*

*Int. Projection Room—Day—1940*

*(A fairly large one, with a long throw to the screen.) It is dark.*

*The image of* KANE *as an old man remains constant on the screen as camera pulls back, slowly taking in and registering Projection Room. (This action occurs, however, only after the first few lines of ensuing dialogue have been spoken. The shadows of the men speaking appear as they rise from their chairs—black against the image of* KANE'S *face on the screen.)*

*(Note: these are the editors of a "News Digest" short, and of the Rawlston magazines. All his enterprises are represented in the projection room, and* RAWLSTON *himself, that great man, is present also and will shortly speak up.*

*During the entire course of this scene, nobody's face is really seen. Sections of their bodies are picked out by a table light, a silhouette is thrown* on the screen, and their faces and bodies are themselves thrown into silhouette against the brilliant slanting rays of light from the projection room.*

*A* THIRD MAN *is on the telephone. We see a corner of his head and the phone.*

THIRD MAN *(at phone).* Stand by. I'll tell you if we want to run it again. *(hangs up)*
THOMPSON'S VOICE. Well?

*A short pause.*

A MAN'S VOICE. It's a tough thing to do in a newsreel. Seventy years of a man's life—

*Murmur of highly salaried assent at this.* RAWLSTON *walks toward camera and out of the picture. Others are rising. (Camera during all this, apparently does its best to follow action and pick up faces, but fails. Actually, all set-ups are to be planned very carefully to exclude the element of personality from this scene; which is expressed entirely by voices, shadows, silhouettes and the big bright image of* KANE *himself on the screen.)*

A VOICE. See what Arthur Ellis wrote about him in the American review?
THIRD MAN. I read it.
THE VOICE *(its owner is already leaning across the table, holding a piece of paper under the desk light and reading from it).* Listen:—Kane is dead. He contributed to the journalism of his day the talent of a mountebank, the morals of a bootlegger, and the manners of a pasha. He and his kind have about succeeded in transforming a once noble profession into a seven percent security—no longer secure.
ANOTHER VOICE. That's what Arthur Ellis is writing now. Thirty

years ago when Kane gave him his chance to clean up Detroit and Chicago and St. Louis, Kane was the greatest guy in the world. If you ask me—

ANOTHER VOICE. Charles Foster Kane was a . . .

*Then observations are made almost simultaneous.*

RAWLSTON'S VOICE. Just a minute!—

*Camera moves to take in his bulk outlined against the glow from the projection room.*

RAWLSTON *(cont'd)*. What were Kane's last words?

*A silence greets this.*

RAWLSTON *(cont'd)*. What were the last words he said on earth?— Thompson, you've made us a good short, but it needs character—

SOMEBODY'S VOICE. Motivation—

RAWLSTON. That's it—motivation.—What made Kane what he was? And, for that matter, what was he?—What we've just seen are the outlines of a career—what's behind the career? What's the man? Was he good or bad?—Strong or foolish?— Tragic or silly? Why did he do all those things? What was he after?

*(then, appreciating his point)*

Maybe he told us on his death bed.

THOMPSON. Yes, and maybe he didn't.

RAWLSTON. Ask the question anyway, Thompson! Build the picture around the question, even if you can't answer it.

THOMPSON. I know, but—

RAWLSTON *(riding over him like any other producer)*. All we saw on that screen was a big American—

A VOICE. One of the biggest.

RAWLSTON *(without pausing for this)*. But how is he different from Ford? Or Hearst for that matter? Or Rockefeller—or John Doe?

A VOICE. I know people worked for Kane will tell you—not only in the newspaper business—look how he raised salaries. You don't want to forget—

ANOTHER VOICE. You take his labor record alone, they ought to hang him like a dog.

RAWLSTON. I tell you, Thompson— a man's dying words—

SOMEBODY'S VOICE. What were they?

*Silence.*

SOMEBODY'S VOICE *(hesitant)*. Yes, Mr. Rawlston, what were Kane's dying words?

THOMPSON *(with disgust)*. Rosebud!

*A little ripple of laughter at this, which is promptly silenced by* RAWLSTON.

RAWLSTON. That's right.

A VOICE. Tough guy, huh? *(derisively)* Dies calling for Rosebud!

RAWLSTON. Here's a man who might have been President. He's been loved and hated and talked about as much as any man in our time—but when he comes to die, he's got something on his mind called "Rosebud." What does that mean?

ANOTHER VOICE. A racehorse he bet on once, probably, that didn't come in—Rosebud!

RAWLSTON. All right. But what was the race?

*There is a short silence.*

RAWLSTON *(cont'd)*. Thompson!

THOMPSON. Yes, sir.

RAWLSTON. Hold this thing up for a week. Two weeks if you have to . . .

THOMPSON *(feebly)*. But don't you think if we release it now—he's only been dead four days—it might be better than if—

RAWLSTON *(decisively)*. Nothing is ever better than finding out what makes people tick. Go after the people that knew Kane well. That manager of his—the little guy, Bernstein—those two wives—all the people who knew him—who worked for him—who loved him—who hated his guts—

*(pauses)*

I don't mean go through the City Directory, of course—

*The* THIRD MAN *gives a hearty "yesman" laugh.*

THOMPSON. I'll get to it right away, Mr. Rawlston.

RAWLSTON *(rising)*. Good!

*The camera from behind him, outlines his back against* KANE'S *picture on the screen.*

RAWLSTON'S VOICE *(cont'd)*. It'll probably turn out to be a very simple thing. . . .

*Fade out*

*(Note: Now begins the story proper—the search by* THOMPSON *for the facts about* KANE—*his researches . . . his interviews with the people who knew* KANE.*

*It is important to remember always that only at the very end of the story is* THOMPSON *himself a personality. Until then, throughout the picture,—we photograph only* THOMPSON'S *back, shoulders, or his shadow—sometimes we only record his voice. He is not until the final scene a "character." He is the personification of the search for the truth about* CHARLES FOSTER KANE. *He is the investigator.)*

*Fade in*

*Ext. Cheap Cabaret—"El Rancho"—Atlantic City—Night—1940—(Miniature—(Rain)*

*The first image to register is a sign:*

"EL RANCHO"
FLOOR SHOW
SUSAN ALEXANDER KANE
TWICE NIGHTLY

*These words, spelled out in neon, glow out of the darkness at the end of the fade out. Then there is lightning which reveals a squalid roof-top on which the sign stands. Thunder again, and faintly the sound of music from within. A light glows from a skylight. The camera moves to this and closes in. Through the splashes of rain, we see through the skylight down into the interior of the cabaret. Directly below us at a table sits the lone figure of a woman, drinking by herself.*

*Dissolve*

*Int. "El Rancho" Cabaret—Night—1940*

*Med. shot of the same woman as before, finishing the drink she started to take above. It is* SUSIE. *The music, of course, is now very loud.* THOMPSON, *his back to the camera, moves into the picutre in the close f.g.* A CAPTAIN *appears behind* SUSIE, *speaking across her to* THOMPSON.

THE CAPTAIN *(a Greek)*. This is Mr. Thompson, Miss Alexander.

SUSAN *looks up into* THOMPSON'S *face. She is fifty, trying to look much younger, cheaply blonded, in a cheap, enormously generous evening dress. Blinking up into* THOMPSON'S *face, she throws a crink into her mouth. Her eyes, which she thinks she is keeping commandingly on his, are bleared and watery.*

SUSAN *(to* THE CAPTAIN*)*. I want another drink, John.

*Low thunder from outside.*

THE CAPTAIN *(seeing his chance)*. Right away. Will you have something, Mr. Thompson?

THOMPSON *(starting to sit down)*. I'll have a highball.

SUSAN *(so insistently as to make* THOMPSON *change his mind and stand up again)*. Who told you you could sit down here?

THOMPSON. Oh! I thought maybe we could have a drink together.

SUSAN. Think again!

*There is an awkward pause as* THOMPSON *looks from her to* THE CAPTAIN.

SUSAN *(cont'd)*. Why don't you people let me alone? I'm minding my own business. You mind yours.

THOMPSON. If you'd just let me talk to you for a little while, Miss Alexander. All I want to ask you . . .

SUSAN. Get out of here! *(almost hysterical)* Get out! Get out!

THOMPSON *looks at* THE CAPTAIN *who shrugs his shoulders.*

THOMPSON. I'm sorry. Maybe some other time—

*If he thought he would get a response from* SUSAN, *who thinks she is looking at him steelily, he realizes his error. He nods and walks off, following* THE CAPTAIN *to the door.*

THE CAPTAIN. She's just not talking to anybody from the newspapers, Mr. Thompson.

THOMPSON. I'm not from a newspaper exactly. I—

*They have come upon* A WAITER *standing in front of a booth.*

THE CAPTAIN *(to* THE WAITER*)*. Get her another highball.

THE WAITER. Another double?

THE CAPTAIN *(after a moment, pityingly)*. Yes.

*They walk to the door.*

THOMPSON. She's plastered, isn't she?

THE CAPTAIN. She'll snap out of it. Why, until he died, she'd just as soon talk about Mr. Kane as about anybody. Sooner.

THOMPSON. I'll come down in a week or so and see her again. Say, you might be able to help me. When she used to talk about Kane—did she ever happen to say anything—about Rosebud?

THE CAPTAIN. Rosebud?

THOMPSON *has just handed him a bill.* THE CAPTAIN *pockets it.*

THE CAPTAIN *(cont'd)*. Thank you, sir. As a matter of fact, yesterday afternoon, when it was in all the papers—I asked her. She never heard of Rosebud.

*Fade out*

*Fade in*

*Int. Thatcher Memorial Library— Day—1940*

*An excrutiatingly noble interpretation of* MR. THATCHER *himself executed in expensive marble. He is shown seated on one of those improbable Edwin Booth chairs and is looking down, his stone eyes fixed on the camera.*

*We move down off of this, showing the impressive pedestal on which the monument is founded. The words, "Walter Parks Thatcher" are prominently and elegantly engraved thereon. Immediately below the inscription we encounter, in a med. shot, the person of* BERTHA AN- DERSON, *an elderly, mannish spin-*

ster, *seated behind her desk.* THOMP-
SON, *his hat in his hand, is standing
before her.* BERTHA *is on the phone.*

BERTHA *(into phone).* Yes. I'll take
him in now. *(hangs up and looks at
Thompson)* The directors of the
Thatcher Library have asked me to
remind you again of the condition under which you may inspect certain
portions of Mr. Thatcher's un-
published memoirs. Under no circumstances are direct quotations from
his manuscript to be used by you.

THOMPSON. That's all right.

BERTHA. You may come with me.

*Without watching whether he is
following her or not, she rises and
starts towards a distant and im-
posingly framed door.* THOMPSON,
*with a bit of a sigh, follows.*

*Dissolve out*

*Dissolve in*

*Int. the Vault Room—Thatcher
Memorial Library—Day—1940*

*A room with all the warmth and
charm of Napoleon's tomb.*

*As we dissolve in, the door opens in
and we see past* THOMPSON'S *shoulders the length of the room. Everything
very plain, very much made out of
marble and very gloomy. Illumination
from a skylight above adds to the
general air of expensive and classical
despair. The floor is marble, and
there is a gigantic, mahogany table in
the center of everything. Beyond this
is to be seen, sunk in the marble wall
at the far end of the room, the safe
from which a guard, in a khaki uniform, with a revolver holster at his
hip, is extracting the journal of*
WALTER P. THATCHER. *He brings it to*
BERTHA *as if he were the guardian of
a bullion shipment. During this,* BER-
THA *has been speaking.*

BERTHA *(to the* GUARD*).* Pages
eighty-three to one hundred and forty-
two, Jennings.

GUARD. Yes, Miss Anderson.

BERTHA *(to* THOMPSON*).* You will
confine yourself, it is our understanding, to the chapter dealing with Mr.
Kane.

THOMPSON. That's all I'm interested in.

*The guard has, by this time, deliv-
ered the precious journal.* BERTHA
*places it reverently on the table before*
THOMPSON.

BERTHA. You will be required
to leave this room at four-thirty
promptly.

*She leaves.* THOMPSON *starts to
light a cigarette. The* GUARD *shakes
his head. With a sigh,* THOMPSON
*bends over to read the manuscript.
Camera moves down over his shoulder onto page of manuscript.*

*Manuscript, neatly and precisely
written:*

"CHARLES FOSTER KANE

WHEN THESE LINES APPEAR IN PRINT,
FIFTY YEARS AFTER MY DEATH, I AM
CONFIDENT THAT THE WHOLE WORLD
WILL AGREE WITH MY OPINION OF
CHARLES FOSTER KANE, ASSUMING
THAT HE IS NOT THEN COMPLETELY
FORGOTTEN, WHICH I REGARD AS EX-
TREMELY LIKELY. A GOOD DEAL OF
NONSENSE HAS APPEARED ABOUT MY
FIRST MEETING WITH KANE, WHEN
HE WAS SIX YEARS OLD. . . . THE
FACTS ARE SIMPLE. IN THE WINTER OF
1870. . . ."

*The camera has not held on the
entire page. It has been following the
words with the same action that the
eye does in reading. On the last
words, the white page of the paper*

*Dissolves into*

*Ext.* MRS. KANE's *Boardinghouse—Day—1870*

The white of a great field of snow—
(seen from angle of parlor window).
In the same position as the last word
in above Insert, appears the tiny figure of CHARLES FOSTER KANE, *aged
five, (almost like an animated cartoon.) He is in the act of throwing a
snowball at the camera. It sails
toward us and over our heads, out of
scene.*

*Reverse angle—on the house fea-
turing a large sign reading:*

MRS. KANE'S BOARDINGHOUSE
HIGH CLASS MEALS AND LODGING
INQUIRE WITHIN

CHARLES KANE's *snowball hits the
sign.*

*Int. Parlor—*MRS. KANE's *Boardinghouse—Day—1870*

*Camera is angling through the win-
dow, but the window-frame is not cut
into scene. We see only the field of
snow again, same angle as in previous scene.* CHARLES *is manufacturing
another snowball. Now—*

*Camera pulls back, the frame of the
window appearing, and we are inside
the parlor of the boardinghouse.* MRS.
KANE, *aged about 28, is looking out
towards her son. Just as we take her
in she speaks:*

MRS. KANE *(calling out).* Be careful, Charles!
THATCHER'S VOICE. Mrs. Kane—
MRS. KANE *(calling out the window
almost on top of this).* Pull your muf-
fler around your neck, Charles—

*But* CHARLES, *deliriously happy in
the snow, is oblivious to this and is
running away.* MRS. KANE *turns into
camera and we see her face—a strong
face, worn and kind.*

THATCHER'S VOICE. I think we'll
have to tell him now—

*Camera now pulls back further,
showing* THATCHER *standing before a
table on which is his stove-pipe hat
and an imposing multiplicity of
official-looking documents. He is 26
and, as might be expected, a very
stuffy young man, already very expensive and conservative looking,
even in Colorado.*

MRS. KANE. I'll sign those papers—
KANE, SR. You people seem to
forget that I'm the boy's father.

*At the sound of* KANE, SR.'S *voice,
both have turned to him and camera
pulls back still further, taking him in.*

(KANE, SR., *who is the assistant
curator in a livery stable, has been
groomed as elegantly as is likely for
this meeting ever since daybreak.)*

*From outside the window can be
heard faintly the wild and cheerful
cries of the boy, blissfully cavorting in
the snow.*

MRS. KANE. It's going to be done
exactly the way I've told Mr.
Thatcher—
KANE, SR. If I want to, I can go to
court. A father has the right to—
THATCHER *(annoyed).* Mr. Kane,
the certificates that Mr. Graves left
here are made out to Mrs. Kane, in
her name. Hers to do with as she
pleases—
KANE, SR. Well, I don't hold with
signing my boy away to any bank as
guardian just because—
MRS. KANE *(quietly).* I want you to
stop all this nonsense, Jim.
THATCHER. The Bank's decision in
all matters concerning his education,
his places of residence and similar
subjects will be final. *(clears his
throat)*

KANE, SR. The idea of a bank being the guardian—

MRS. KANE *has met his eye. Her triumph over him finds expression in his failure to finish his sentence.*

MRS. KANE *(even more quietly).* I want you to stop all this nonsense, Jim.

THATCHER. We will assume full management of the Colorado Lode—of which you, Mrs. Kane, are the sole owner.

KANE, SR. *opens his mouth once or twice, as if to say something, but chokes down his opinion.*

MRS. KANE *(has been reading past* THATCHER'S *shoulder as he talked).* Where do I sign, Mr. Thatcher?

THATCHER. Right here, Mrs. Kane.

KANE, SR. *(sulkily).* Don't say I didn't warn you.

MRS. KANE *lifts the quill pen.*

KANE, SR. *(cont'd).* Mary, I'm asking you for the last time—anyone'd think I hadn't been a good husband and a—

MRS. KANE *looks at him slowly. He stops his speech.*

THATCHER. The sum of fifty thousand dollars a year is to be paid to yourself and Mr. Kane as long as you both live, and thereafter the survivor—

MRS. KANE *puts pen to the paper and signs.*

KANE, SR. Well, let's hope it's all for the best.

MRS. KANE. It is.—Go on, Mr. Thatcher—

MRS. KANE, *listening to* THATCHER, *of course has had her other ear bent in the direction of the boy's voice.* THATCHER *is aware both of the boy's voice, which is counter to his own,*

and of MRS. KANE's *divided attention. As he pauses,* KANE, SR. *genteelly walks over to close the window.*

*Ext.* MRS. KANE's *Boardinghouse—Day—1870*

KANE, JR., *seen from* KANE, SR.'S *position at window. He is advancing on the snowman, snowballs in his hands, dropping to one knee the better to confound his adversary.*

KANE. If the rebels want a fight boys, let's give it to 'em!

*He throws two snowballs, missing widely, and gets up and advances another five feet before getting on his knees again.*

KANE *(cont'd).* The terms are unconditional surrender. Up and at 'em! The Union forever!

*Int. Parlor—*MRS. KANE's *Boardinghouse—Day—1870*

KANE, SR., *closes the window.*

THATCHER *(over the boy's voice).* Everything else—the principal as well as all monies earned—is to be administered by the bank in trust for your son, Charles Foster Kane, until his twenty-fifth birthday, at which time he is to come into complete possession.

MRS. KANE *rises and goes to the window.*

MRS. KANE. Go on, Mr. Thatcher.

THATCHER *continues as she opens the window. His voice, as before, is heard with overtones of the boy's.*

*Ext.* MRS. KANE's *Boardinghouse—Day—1870*

KANE, JR., *seen from* MRS. KANE's *position at the window. He is now within ten feet of the snowman, with one snowball left which he is holding back in his right hand.*

KANE. You can't lick Andy Jackson! Old Hickory, that's me!

*He fires his snowball, well wide of the mark and falls flat on his stomach, starting to crawl carefully toward the snowman.*

THATCHER'S VOICE. It's nearly five, Mrs. Kane—don't you think I'd better meet the boy—

*Int. Parlor—*MRS. KANE'S *Boardinghouse—Day—1870*

MRS. KANE *at the window.* THATCHER *is now standing at her side.*

MRS. KANE. I've got his trunk all packed—*(she chokes a little)* I've had it packed for a couple of weeks—

*She can't say any more. She starts for the hall door.* KANE, SR., *ill at ease, has no idea of how to comfort her.*

THATCHER. I've arranged for a tutor to meet us in Chicago. I'd have brought him along with me, but you were so anxious to keep everything secret—

*He stops as he realizes that* MRS. KANE *has paid no attention to him and, having opened the door, is already well into the hall that leads to the side door of the house. He takes a look at* KANE, SR., *tightens his lips and follows* MRS. KANE. KANE, *shoulders thrown back like one who bears defeat bravely, follows him.*

*Ext.* MRS. KANE'S *Boardinghouse— Day—1870*

KANE, *in the snow-covered field. With the snowman between him and the house, he is holding the sled in his hand, just about to make the little run that prefaces a belly-flop. The* KANE *house, in the b.g., is a dilapidated, shabby, two-story frame building, with a wooden outhouse. Kane looks* up *as he sees the single file procession,* MRS. KANE *at its head, coming toward him.*

KANE. H'ya, Mom.

MRS. KANE *smiles.*

KANE *(cont'd). (gesturing at the snowman)* See, Mom? I took the pipe out of his mouth. If it keeps on snowin', maybe I'll make some teeth and—

MRS. KANE. You better come inside, son. You and I have got to get you all ready for—for—

THATCHER. Charles, my name is Mr. Thatcher—

MRS. KANE. This is Mr. Thatcher, Charles.

THATCHER. How do you do, Charles.

KANE, SR. He comes from the East—

KANE. Hello. Hello, Pop.

KANE, SR. Hello, Charlie!

MRS. KANE. Mr. Thatcher is going to take you on a trip with him tonight, Charles. You'll be leaving on Number Ten.

KANE, SR. That's the train with all the lights.

KANE. You goin', Mom?

THATCHER. Your mother won't be going right away, Charles—

KANE. Where'm I going?

KANE, SR. You're going to see Chicago and New York—and Washington, maybe . . . Isn't he, Mr. Thatcher?

THATCHER *(heartily).* He certainly is. I wish I were a little boy and going to make a trip like that for the first time.

KANE. Why aren't you comin' with us, Mom?

MRS. KANE. We have to stay here, Charles.

KANE, SR. You're going to live with Mr. Thatcher from now on, Charlie!

You're going to be rich. Your Ma figures—that is—er—she and I have decided that this isn't the place for you to grow up in. You'll probably be the richest man in America some day and you ought to—

MRS. KANE. You won't be lonely, Charles . . .

THATCHER. We're going to have a lot of good times together, Charles . . . Really we are.

KANE *stares at him.*

THATCHER *(cont'd).* Come on, Charles. Let's shake hands. *(extends his hand.* CHARLES *continues to look at him)* Now, now! I'm not as frightening as all that! Let's shake, what do you say?

*He reaches out for* CHARLES'S *hand. Without a word,* CHARLES *hits him in the stomach with the sled.* THATCHER *stumbles back a few feet, gasping.*

THATCHER *(cont'd) (with a sickly grin).* You almost hurt me, Charles. *(moves towards him).* Sleds aren't to hit people with. Sleds are to—to sleigh on. When we get to New York, Charles, we'll get you a sled that will—

*He's near enough to try to put a hand on* KANE'S *shoulder. As he does,* KANE *kicks him in the ankle.*

MRS. KANE. Charles!

*He throws himself on her, his arms around her. Slowly* MRS. KANE *puts her arms around him.*

KANE *(frightened).* Mom! Mom!
MRS. KANE. It's all right, Charles, it's all right.

THATCHER *is looking on indignantly, occasionally bending over to rub his ankle.*

KANE, SR. Sorry, Mr. Thatcher! What that kid needs is a good thrashing!

MRS. KANE That's what you think, is it, Jim?

KANE, SR. Yes.

MRS. KANE *looks at* MR. KANE.

MRS. KANE *(slowly).* That's why he's going to be brought up where you can't get at him.

*Dissolve*

*(1870—night) (stock or miniature) old-fashioned railroad wheels underneath a sleeper, spinning along the track.*

*Dissolve*

*Int. Train—Old-fashioned Drawing Room—Night—1870*

THATCHER, *with a look of mingled exasperation, annoyance, sympathy and inability to handle the situation, is standing alongside a berth, looking at* KANE. KANE, *his face in the pillow, is crying with heartbreaking sobs.*

KANE. Mom! Mom!

*Dissolve out*

*The white page of the* THATCHER *manuscript. We pick up the words:*

"HE WAS, I REPEAT, A COMMON ADVENTURER, SPOILED, UNSCRUPULOUS, IRRESPONSIBLE."

*The words are followed by printed headline on "Enquirer" copy (as in following scene).*

*Int. Enquirer City Room—Day— 1898*

*Closeup on printed headline which reads:*

"ENEMY ARMADA OFF JERSEY COAST"

*Camera pulls back to reveal* THATCHER *holding the "Enquirer" copy, on which we read the headline. He is standing near the editorial round table around which a section of the staff, including* REILLY, LELAND *and* KANE *are eating lunch.*

THATCHER *(coldly).* Is that really your idea of how to run a newspaper?

KANE. I don't know how to run a newspaper, Mr. Thatcher. I just try everything I can think of.

THATCHER *(reading headline of paper he is still holding).* "Enemy Armada Off Jersey Coast." You know you haven't the slightest proof that this—this armada—is off the Jersey Coast.

KANE. Can you prove it isn't?

BERNSTEIN *has come into the picture. He has a cable in his hand. He stops when he sees* THATCHER.

KANE *(cont'd).* Mr. Bernstein— Mr. Thatcher—

BERNSTEIN. How are you, Mr. Thatcher?

THATCHER. How do you do—

BERNSTEIN. We just had a wire from Cuba, Mr. Kane—*(stops, embarrassed).*

KANE. That's all right. We have no secrets from our readers. Mr. Thatcher is one of our most devoted readers, Mr. Bernstein. He knows what's wrong with every issue since I've taken charge. What's the cable?

BERNSTEIN *(reading).* The food is marvelous in Cuba the senoritas are beautiful stop I could send you prose poems of palm trees and sunrises and tropical colors blending in far off landscapes but don't feel right in spending your money for this stop there's no war in Cuba regards Wheeler.

THATCHER. You see! There hasn't been a true word—

KANE. I think we'll have to send our friend Wheeler a cable, Mr. Bern-stein. Of course, we'll have to make it shorter than his, because he's working on an expense account and we're not. Let me see—*(snaps his fingers)* Mike!

MIKE *(a fairly tough customer prepares to take dictation, his mouth still full of food).* Go ahead, Mr. Kane.

KANE. Dear Wheeler—*(pauses a moment).* You provide the prose poems—I'll provide the war.

*Laughter from the boys and girls at the table.*

BERNSTEIN. That's fine, Mr. Kane.

KANE. I rather like it myself. Send it right away.

MIKE. Right away.

BERNSTEIN. Right away.

MIKE *and* BERNSTEIN *leave.* KANE *looks up, grinning at* THATCHER, *who is bursting with indignation but controls himself. After a moment of indecision, he decides to make one last try.*

THATCHER. I came to see you, Charles, about your—about the Enquirer's campaign against the Metropolitan Transfer Company.

KANE. Won't you step into my office, Mr. Thatcher?

*They cross the City Room together.*

THATCHER. I think I should remind you, Charles, of a fact you seem to have forgotten. You are yourself one of the largest individual stockholders.

*Int.* KANE'S *Office—Day—1898*

KANE *holds the door open for* THATCHER. *They come in together.*

KANE. Mr. Thatcher, isn't everything I've been saying in the Enquirer about the traction trust absolutely true?

THATCHER *(angrily).* They're all part of your general attack—your senseless attack—on everything and everybody who's got more than ten cents in his pocket. They're—

KANE. The trouble is, Mr. Thatcher, you don't realize you're talking to two people.

KANE *moves around behind his desk.* THATCHER *doesn't understand, looks at him.*

KANE *(cont'd).* As Charles Foster Kane, who has eighty-two thousand, six hundred and thirty-one shares of Metropolitan Transfer—you see, I do have a rough idea of my holdings—I sympathize with you. Charles Foster Kane is a dangerous scoundrel, his paper should be run out of town and a committee should be formed to boycott him. You may, if you can form such a committee, put me down for a contribution of one thousand dollars.

THATCHER *(angrily).* Charles, my time is too valuable for me—

KANE. On the other hand—*(his manner becomes serious).* I am the publisher of the Enquirer. As such, it is my duty—I'll let you in on a little secret, it is also my pleasure—to see to it that decent, hard-working people of this city are not robbed blind by a group of money-mad pirates because, God help them, they have no one to look after their interests!—I'll let you in on another little secret, Mr. Thatcher. I think I'm the man to do it. You see I have money and property—

THATCHER *doesn't understand him.*

KANE *(cont'd).* If I don't defend the interests of the underprivileged, somebody else will—maybe somebody *without* any money or any property and that would be too bad.

THATCHER *glares at him, unable to answer.* KANE *starts to dance.*

KANE *(cont'd).* Do you know how to tap, Mr. Thatcher?—You ought to learn—*(humming quietly, he continues to dance).*

THATCHER *puts on his hat.*

THATCHER. I happened to see your consolidated statement yesterday, Charles. Could I not suggest to you that it is unwise for you to continue this philanthropic enterprise—*(sneeringly)*—this Enquirer—that is costing you one million dollars a year?

KANE. You're right. We did lose a million dollars last year.

THATCHER *thinks maybe the point has registered.*

KANE *(cont'd).* We expect to lose a million next year, too. You know, Mr. Thatcher—*(starts tapping quietly)*—at the rate of a million a year—we'll have to close this place—in sixty years.

*Dissolve*

*Int. the Vault Room—Thatcher Memorial Library—Day*

THOMPSON—*at the desk. With a gesture of annoyance he is closing the manuscript.*

*Camera arcs quickly around from over his shoulder to hold on door behind him, missing his face as he rises and turns to confront* MISS ANDERSON *who has come into the room to shoo him out. Very prominent on this wall is an over-sized oil painting of* THATCHER *in the best Union League Club renaissance style.*

MISS ANDERSON. You have enjoyed a very rare privilege, young man. Did you find what you were looking for?

THOMPSON. No. Tell me something, Miss Anderson. You're not Rosebud, are you?

MISS ANDERSON. What?

THOMPSON. I didn't think you were. Well, thanks for the use of the hall.

*He puts his hat on his head and starts out, lighting a cigarette as he goes.* MISS ANDERSON, *scandalized, watches him.*

*Fade out*

*Fade in*

*Int.* BERNSTEIN'S *Office—Enquirer Skyscraper—Day—1940*

*Closeup of a still of* KANE, *aged about sixty-five. Camera pulls back, showing it is a framed photograph on the wall. Over the picture are crossed American flags. Under it sits* BERNSTEIN, *back of his desk.* BERNSTEIN, *always an undersized Jew, now seems even smaller than in his youth. He is bald as an egg, spry, with remarkably intense eyes. As camera continues to travel back, the back of* THOMPSON'S *head and his shoulders come into the picture.*

BERNSTEIN *(wryly).* Who's a busy man? Me? I'm Chairman of the Board. I got nothing but time . . . What do you want to know?

THOMPSON *(still explaining).* Well, Mr. Bernstein, you were with Mr. Kane from the very beginning—

BERNSTEIN. From *before* the beginning, young fellow. And now it's after the end. *(turns to* THOMPSON*)* Anything you want to know about him—about the paper—

THOMPSON. —We thought maybe, if we can find out what he meant by that last word—as he was dying—

BERNSTEIN. That Rosebud? Maybe some girl? There were a lot of them back in the early days and—

THOMPSON. Not some girl he just knew casually and then remembered after fifty years, on his death bed—

BERNSTEIN. You're pretty young, Mr.—*(remembers the name)*—Mr. Thompson. A fellow will remember things you wouldn't think he'd remember. You take me. One day, back in 1896, I was crossing over to Jersey on a ferry and as we pulled out there was another ferry pulling in—*(slowly)*—and on it there was a girl waiting to get off. A white dress she had on—and she was carrying a white parasol—and I only saw her for one second and she didn't see me at all—but I'll bet a month hasn't gone by since that I haven't thought of that girl. *(triumphantly)* See what I mean? *(smiles)* Well, so what are you doing about this "Rosebud," Mr. Thompson.

THOMPSON. I'm calling on people who knew Mr. Kane. I'm calling on you.

BERNSTEIN. Who else you been to see?

THOMPSON. Well, I went down to Atlantic City—

BERNSTEIN. Susie? I called her myself the day after he died. I thought maybe somebody ought to . . . *(sadly)* She couldn't even come to the 'phone.

THOMPSON. You know why? She was so—

BERNSTEIN. Sure, sure.

THOMPSON. I'm going back there.

BERNSTEIN. Who else did you see?

THOMPSON. Nobody else, but I've been through that stuff of Walter Thatcher's. That journal of his—

BERNSTEIN. Thatcher! That man was the biggest darn fool I ever met—

THOMPSON. He made an awful lot of money.

BERNSTEIN. It's no trick to make an awful lot of money if all you want is to make a lot of money. *(his eyes get reflective)* Thatcher!

BERNSTEIN *looks out of the window and keeps on looking, seeming to see something as he talks.*

BERNSTEIN *(cont'd)*. He never knew there was anything in the world but money. That kind of fellow you can fool every day in the week—and twice on Sundays! *(reflectively)* The time he came to Rome for Mr. Kane's twenty-fifth birthday . . . You know, when Mr. Kane got control of his own money . . . Such a fool like Thatcher—I tell you, nobody's business!

*Dissolve out*

*Dissolve in*

*Int.* BERNSTEIN'S *Office—Day—1940*

BERNSTEIN *speaking to* THOMPSON.

BERNSTEIN. He knew what he wanted, Mr. Kane did, and he got it! Thatcher never did figure him out. He was hard to figure sometimes, even for me. Mr. Kane was a genius like he said. He had that funny sense of humor. Sometimes even I didn't get the joke. Like that night the opera house of his opened in Chicago . . . You know, the opera house he built for Susie, she should be an opera singer . . . *(indicates with a little wave of his hand what he thinks of that; sighing)* That was years later, of course—1914 it was. Mrs. Kane took the leading part in the opera, and she was terrible. But nobody had the nerve to say so—not even the critics. Mr. Kane was a big man in those days. But this one fellow, this friend of his, Bradford Leland—

*He leaves the sentence up in the air, as we*

*Dissolve*

*Int. City Room—Chicago Enquirer—Night—1914*

*It is late. The room is almost empty. Nobody is at work at the desks.* BERNSTEIN, *fifty, is waiting anxiously with a little group of* KANE'S *hirelings, most of them in evening dress with overcoats and hats. Everybody is tense and expectant.*

CITY EDITOR *(turns to a young* HIRELING; *quietly)*. What about Bradford Leland? Has he got in his copy?

HIRELING. Not yet.

BERNSTEIN. Go in and ask him to hurry.

CITY EDITOR. Well, why don't you, Mr. Bernstein? You know Mr. Leland.

BERNSTEIN *(looks at him for a moment; then slowly)*. I might make him nervous.

CITY EDITOR *(after a pause)*. You and Leland and Mr. Kane—you were great friends back in the old days, I understand.

BERNSTEIN *(with a smile)*. That's right. They called us the "Three Musketeers."

*Somebody behind* BERNSTEIN *has trouble concealing his laughter. The* CITY EDITOR *speaks quickly to cover the situation.*

CITY EDITOR. He's a great guy—Leland. *(another little pause)* Why'd he ever leave New York?

BERNSTEIN *(he isn't saying)*. That's a long story.

ANOTHER HIRELING *(a tactless one)*. Wasn't there some sort of quarrel between—

BERNSTEIN *(quickly)*. I had nothing to do with it.—*(then somberly)* It was Leland and Mr. Kane, and you couldn't call it a quarrel exactly. Better we should forget such things.—*(turning to* CITY EDITOR*)*—Leland is writing it up from the dramatic angle?

CITY EDITOR. Yes. I thought it was a good idea. We've covered it from the news end, of course.

BERNSTEIN. And the social. How about the music notice? You got that in?

CITY EDITOR. Oh, yes, it's already made up. Our Mr. Mervin wrote a swell review.

BERNSTEIN. Enthusiastic?

CITY EDITOR. Yes, very! *(quietly)* Naturally.

BERNSTEIN. Well, well—isn't that nice?

KANE'S VOICE. Mr. Bernstein—

BERNSTEIN *turns.*

*Med. long shot of* KANE, *now forty-nine, already quite stout. He is in white tie, wearing his overcoat and carrying a folded opera hat.*

BERNSTEIN. Hello, Mr. Kane.

*The* HIRELINGS *rush, with* BERNSTEIN, *to* KANE'S *side. Widespread, half-suppressed sensation.*

CITY EDITOR. Mr. Kane, this *is* a surprise!

KANE. We've got a nice plant here.

*Everybody falls silent. There isn't anything to say.*

KANE *(cont'd).* Was the show covered by every department?

CITY EDITOR. Exactly according to your instructions, Mr. Kane. We've got two spreads of pictures.

KANE *(very, very casually).* And the notice?

CITY EDITOR. Yes—Mr. Kane.

KANE *(quietly).* Is it good?

CITY EDITOR. Yes, Mr. Kane.

KANE *looks at him for a minute.*

CITY EDITOR *(cont'd).* But there's another one still to come—the dramatic notice.

KANE *(sharply).* It isn't finished?

CITY EDITOR. No, Mr. Kane.

KANE. That's Leland, isn't it?

CITY EDITOR. Yes, Mr. Kane.

KANE. Has he said when he'll finish?

CITY EDITOR. We haven't heard from him.

KANE. He used to work fast—didn't he, Mr. Bernstein?

BERNSTEIN. He sure did, Mr. Kane.

KANE. Where is he?

ANOTHER HIRELING. Right in there, Mr. Kane.

*The* HIRELING *indicates the closed glass door of a little office at the other end of the City Room.* KANE *takes it in.*

BERNSTEIN *(helpless but very concerned).* Mr. Kane—

KANE. That's all right, Mr. Bernstein.

KANE *crosses the length of the long City Room to the glass door indicated before by the* HIRELING. *The* CITY EDITOR *looks at* BERNSTEIN. KANE *opens the door and goes into the office, closing the door behind him.*

BERNSTEIN. Leland and Mr. Kane—they ain't spoke together for ten years. *(long pause; finally)* Excuse me. *(starts toward the door)*

*Int.* LELAND'S *Office—Chicago Enquirer—Night—1914*

BERNSTEIN *comes in. An empty bottle is standing on* LELAND'S *desk. He has fallen over his typewriter, his face on the keys. A sheet of paper is in the machine. A paragraph has been typed.* KANE *is standing at the other side of the desk looking down at him. This is the first time we see murder in* KANE'S *face.* BERNSTEIN *looks at* KANE, *then crosses to* LELAND. *He shakes him.*

BERNSTEIN. Hey, Brad! Brad! *(he straightens, looks at* KANE; *pause)* He ain't been drinking before, Mr. Kane. Never. We would have heard.

KANE *(finally; after a pause).* What does it say there?

BERNSTEIN *stares at him.*

KANE *(cont'd).* What's he written?

BERNSTEIN *leans over near-sightedly, painfully reading the paragraph written on the page.*

BERNSTEIN *(reading).* "Miss Susan Alexander, a pretty but hopelessly incompetent amateur—*(he waits for a minute to catch his breath; he doesn't like it)*—last night opened the new Chicago Opera House in a performance of—of—" *(looks up miserably)*—I can't pronounce that name, Mr. Kane.

KANE. Thais.

BERNSTEIN *looks at* KANE *for a moment, then looks back, tortured.*

BERNSTEIN *(reading again).* "Her singing, happily, is no concern of this department. Of her acting, it is absolutely impossible to . . ." *(he continues to stare at the page).*

KANE *(after a short silence).* Go on!

BERNSTEIN *(without looking up).* That's all there is.

KANE *snatches the paper from the roller and reads it for himself. Slowly a queer look comes into his face. Then he speaks, very quietly.*

KANE. Of her acting, it is absolutely impossible to say anything except that it represents in the opinion of this reviewer a new low . . . *(then sharply)* Have you got that, Mr. Bernstein? In the opinion of this reviewer—

BERNSTEIN *(miserably).* I didn't see that.

KANE. It isn't here, Mr. Bernstein. I'm dictating it.

BERNSTEIN *(looks at him).* I can't take shorthand.

KANE. Get me a typewriter. I'll finish the notice.

BERNSTEIN *retreats from the room.*

*Quick dissolve out*

*Quick dissolve in*

*Int.* LELAND'S *Office—Chicago Enquirer—Night—1914*

*Long shot of* KANE *in his shirt sleeves, illuminated by a desk light, typing furiously. As the camera starts to pull even further away from this, and as* BERNSTEIN—*as narrator—begins to speak—*

*Quick dissolve*

*Int.* BERNSTEIN'S *Office—Day—1940*

BERNSTEIN *speaking to* THOMPSON.

BERNSTEIN. He finished it. He wrote the worst notice I ever read about the girl he loved. We ran it in every paper.

THOMPSON *(after a pause).* I guess Mr. Kane didn't think so well of Susie's *art* anyway.

BERNSTEIN *(looks at him very soberly).* He thought she was great, Mr. Thompson. He really believed that. He put all his ambition on that girl. After she came along he never really cared for himself like he used to. Oh, I don't blame Susie—

THOMPSON. Well, then, how could he write that roast? The notices in the Kane papers were always very kind to her.

BERNSTEIN. Oh, yes. He saw to that.—I tell you, Mr. Thompson, he was a hard man to figure out. He had that funny sense of humor.—And then, too, maybe he thought by finishing that piece he could show Leland he was an honest man. You see, Leland didn't think so. I guess he showed him all right. You must talk to Leland some time. He's a nice fellow, but he's a dreamer. They were always together in those early days when we just started the Enquirer.

*On these last words, we*

*Dissolve*

*Int. City Room—Enquirer Building—Day—1891*

The front half of the second floor constitutes one large City Room. Despite the brilliant sunshine outside, very little of it is actually getting into the room because the windows are small and narrow. There are about a dozen tables and desks, of the old-fashioned type, not flat, available for reporters. Two tables, on a raised platform at the end of the room, obviously serve the city room executives. To the left of the platform is an open door which leads into the Sanctum.

As KANE and LELAND enter the room an elderly, stout gent on the raised platform, strikes a bell and the other eight occupants of the room—all men—rise and face the new arrivals. CARTER, the elderly gent, in formal clothes, rises and starts toward them.

CARTER. Welcome, Mr. Kane, to the "Enquirer." I am Herbert Carter.
KANE. Thank you, Mr. Carter. This is Mr. Leland.
CARTER *(bowing)*. How do you do, Mr. Leland?
KANE *(pointing to the standing reporters)*. Are they standing for me?
CARTER. I thought it would be a nice gesture—the new publisher—
KANE *(grinning)*. Ask them to sit down.
CARTER. You may resume your work, gentlemen. *(to KANE)* I didn't know your plans and so I was unable to make any preparations.
KANE. I don't know my plans myself.

*They are following* CARTER *to his raised platform.*

KANE *(cont'd)*. As a matter of fact, I haven't got any. Except to get out a newspaper.

*There is a terrific crash at the doorway. They all turn to see* BERNSTEIN *sprawled at the entrance. A roll of bedding, a suitcase and two framed pictures were too much for him.*

KANE *(cont'd)*. Oh, Mr. Bernstein!

BERNSTEIN *looks up.*

KANE *(cont'd)*. If you would come here a moment, please, Mr. Bernstein?

BERNSTEIN *rises and comes over, tidying himself as he comes.*

KANE *(cont'd)*. Mr. Carter, this is Mr. Bernstein. Mr. Bernstein is my general manager.
CARTER *(frigidly)*. How do you do, Mr. Bernstein.
KANE. You've got a private office here, haven't you?

*The delivery wagon driver has now appeared in the entrance with parts of the bedstead and other furniture. He is looking about, a bit bewildered.*

CARTER *(indicating open door to left of platform)*. My little sanctum is at your disposal. But I don't think I understand—
KANE. I'm going to live right here. *(reflectively)* As long as I have to.
CARTER. But a morning newspaper, Mr. Kane.—After all, we're practically closed for twelve hours a day —except for the business offices—
KANE. That's one of the things I think must be changed, Mr. Carter. The news goes on for twenty-four hours a day.

*Dissolve*

*Int.* KANE'S *Office—Late Day— 1891*

KANE, *in his shirt sleeves, at a roll top desk in the Sanctum, is working feverishly on copy and eating a very sizeable meal at the same time.* CAR-

TER, *still formally coated, is seated alongside him.* LELAND, *seated in a corner, is looking on, detached, amused. The furniture has been pushed around and* KANE's *effects are somewhat in place. On a corner of the desk,* BERNSTEIN *is writing down figures. No one pays any attention to him.*

KANE. I'm not criticizing, Mr. Carter, but here's what I mean. There's a front page story in the "Chronicle," *(points to it)* and a picture—of a woman in Brooklyn who is missing. Probably murdered. *(looks to make sure of the name)* A Mrs. Harry Silverstone. Why didn't the "Enquirer" have that this morning?

CARTER *(stiffly).* Because we're running a newspaper, Mr. Kane, not a scandal sheet.

KANE *has finished eating. He pushes away his plates.*

KANE. I'm still hungry, Brad. Let's go to Rector's and get something decent. *(pointing to the "Chronicle" before him)* The "Chronicle" has a two column headline, Mr. Carter. Why haven't we?

CARTER. There is no news big enough.

KANE. If the headline is big enough, it *makes* the news big enough. The murder of Mrs. Harry Silverstone—

CARTER *(hotly).* As a matter of fact, we sent a man to the Silverstone home yesterday afternoon. *(triumphantly)* Our man even arrived before the "Chronicle" reporter. And there's no proof that the woman was murdered—or even that she's dead.

KANE *(smiling a bit).* The "Chronicle" doesn't say she's murdered, Mr. Carter. It says the neighbors are getting suspicious.

CARTER *(stiffly).* It's not our function to report the gossip of house-

wives. If we were interested in that kind of thing, Mr. Kane, we could fill the paper twice over daily—

KANE *(gently).* That's the kind of thing we *are* going to be interested in from now on, Mr. Carter. Right now, I wish you'd send your best man up to see Mr. Silverstone. Have him tell Mr. Silverstone if he doesn't produce his wife at once, the "Enquirer" will have him arrested. *(he gets an idea)* Have him tell Mr. Silverstone he's a detective from the Central Office. If Mr. Silverstone asks to see his badge, your man is to get indignant and call Mr. Silverstone an anarchist. Loudly, so that the neighbors can hear.

CARTER. Really, Mr. Kane, I can't see that the function of a respectable newspaper—

KANE *isn't listening to him.*

KANE. Oh, Mr. Bernstein!

BERNSTEIN *looks up from his figures.*

KANE *(cont'd).* I've just made a shocking discovery. The "Enquirer" is without a telephone. Have two installed at once!

BERNSTEIN. I ordered six already this morning! Got a discount!

KANE *looks at* LELAND *with a fond nod of his head at* BERNSTEIN. LELAND *grins back.* MR. CARTER, *meantime, has risen stiffly.*

CARTER. But, Mr. Kane—

KANE. That'll be all today, Mr. Carter. You've been most understanding. Good day, Mr. Carter!

CARTER, *with a look that runs just short of apoplexy, leaves the room, closing the door behind him.*

LELAND. Poor Mr. Carter!

KANE *(shakes his head).* What makes these fellows think that a newspaper is something rigid, something inflexible, that people are supposed to pay two cents for—

BERNSTEIN *(without looking up)*. Three cents.

KANE *(calmly)*. Two cents.

BERNSTEIN *lifts his head and looks at* KANE. KANE *gazes back at him.*

BERNSTEIN *(tapping on the paper)*. This is all figured at three cents a copy.

KANE. Re-figure it, Mr. Bernstein, at two cents.

BERNSTEIN *(sighs and puts papers in his pocket)*. All right, but I'll keep these figures, too, just in case.

KANE. Ready for dinner, Brad?

BERNSTEIN. Mr. Leland, if Mr. Kane he should decide to cut the price to one cent, or maybe even he should make up his mind to give the paper away with a half-pound of tea—you'll just hold him until I get back, won't you?

LELAND. I'm not guaranteeing a thing, Bernstein. You people work too fast for me! Talk about new brooms!

BERNSTEIN. Who said anything about brooms?

KANE. It's a saying, Mr. Bernstein. A new broom sweeps clean.

BERNSTEIN. Oh!

*Dissolve*

*Int. Primitive Composing and Pressroom—New York Enquirer— Night—1891*

The ground floor with the windows on the street—of the "Enquirer." It is almost midnight by an old-fashioned clock on the wall. Grouped around a large table, on which are several locked forms of type, very old-fashioned of course, but true to the period—are KANE and LELAND in elegant evening clothes, BERNSTEIN, unchanged from the afternoon, CARTER

*and* SMATHERS, *the composing room foreman, nervous and harassed.*

SMATHERS. But it's impossible, Mr. Kane. We can't remake these pages.

KANE. These pages aren't made up as I want them, Mr. Smathers. We go to press in five minutes.

CARTER *(about to crack up)*. The "Enquirer" has an old and honored tradition, Mr. Kane . . . The "Enquirer" is not in competition with those other rags.

BERNSTEIN. We should be publishing such rags, that's all I wish. Why, the "Enquirer"—I wouldn't wrap up the liver for the cat in the "Enquirer"—

CARTER *(enraged)*. Mr. Kane, I must ask you to see to it that this— this person learns to control his tongue.

KANE *looks up.*

CARTER *(cont'd)*. I've been a newspaperman my whole life and I don't intend—*(he starts to sputter)*—if it's your intention that I should continue to be harassed by this—this—*(he's really sore)* I warn you, Mr. Kane, it would go against my grain to desert you when you need me so badly—but I would feel obliged to ask that my resignation be accepted.

KANE. It *is* accepted, Mr. Carter, with assurances of my deepest regret.

CARTER. But Mr. Kane, I meant—

KANE *turns his back on him, speaks again to the composing room foreman.*

KANE *(quietly)*. Let's remake these pages, Mr. Smathers. We'll have to publish a half hour late, that's all.

SMATHERS *(as though* KANE *were talking Greek)*. We can't remake them, Mr. Kane. We go to press in five minutes.

KANE *sighs, unperturbed, as he reaches out his hand and shoves the forms off the table onto the floor, where they scatter into hundreds of bits.*

KANE. You can remake them now, can't you, Mr. Smathers?

SMATHER'S *mouth opens wider and wider.* BRADFORD *and* BERNSTEIN *are grinning.*

KANE *(cont'd).* After the types 've been reset and the pages have been remade according to the way I told you before, Mr. Smathers, kindly have proofs pulled and bring them to me. Then, if I can't find any way to improve them again—*(almost as if reluctantly)*—I suppose we'll have to go to press.

*He starts out of the room, followed by* LELAND.

BERNSTEIN *(to* SMATHERS*).* In case you don't understand, Mr. Smathers—he's a new broom.

*Dissolve out*

*Dissolve in*

*Ext. New York Street—Very Early Dawn—1891*

*The picture is mainly occupied by a large building, on the roof of which the lights spell out the word "Enquirer" against the sunrise. We do not see the street or the first few stories of this building, the windows of which would be certainly illuminated. What we do see is the floor on which is located the City Room. Over this scene newsboys are heard selling the Chronicle, their voices growing in volume.*

*As the dissolve completes itself, camera moves toward the one lighted window—the window of the Sanctum.*

*Dissolve*

*Int.* KANE'S *Office—Very Early Dawn—1891*

*The newsboys are still heard from the street below—fainter but very insistent.*

KANE'S *office is gas-lit, of course, as is the rest of the Enquirer building.*

KANE, *in his shirt sleeves, stands at the open window looking out. The bed is already made up. On it is seated* BERNSTEIN, *smoking the end of a cigar.* LELAND *is in a chair.*

NEWSBOYS' VOICES. CHRONICLE!—CHRONICLE!—H'YA—THE CHRONICLE —GET YA! CHRONICLE!

KANE, *taking a deep breath of the morning air, closes the window and turns to the others. (The voices of the newsboys, naturally, are very much fainter after this.)*

LELAND. We'll be on the street soon, Charlie—another ten minutes.

BERNSTEIN *(looking at his watch).* It's three hours and fifty minutes late—but we did it—

LELAND *rises from the chair, stretching painfully.*

KANE. Tired?
LELAND. It's been a tough day.
KANE. A wasted day.
BERNSTEIN *(looking up).* Wasted?
LELAND *(incredulously).* Charlie?!
BERNSTEIN. You just made the paper over four times today, Mr. Kane—That's all—
KANE. I've changed the front page a little, Mr. Bernstein. That's not enough.—There's something I've got to get into this paper besides pictures and print—I've got to make the "New York Enquirer" as important to New York as the gas in that light.
LELAND *(quietly).* What're you going to do, Charlie?

KANE *looks at him for a minute with a queer smile of happy concentration.*

KANE. My Declaration of Principles—*(he says it with quotes around it)*—Don't smile, Brad.—*(getting the idea)* Take dictation, Mr. Bernstein—

BERNSTEIN. I can't write shorthand, Mr. Kane—

KANE. I'll write it myself.

KANE *grabs a piece of rough paper and a grease crayon. Sitting down on the bed next to* BERNSTEIN, *he starts to write.*

BERNSTEIN *(looking over his shoulder).* You don't wanta make any promises, Mr. Kane, you don't wanta keep.

KANE *(as he writes).* These'll be kept. *(stops for a minute and reads what he has written; reading)* I'll provide the people of this city with a daily paper that will tell all the news honestly. *(starts to write again; reading as he writes)* I will also provide them—

LELAND. That's the second sentence you've started with "I"—

KANE *(looking up).* People are going to know who's responsible. And they're going to get the news—the true news—quickly and simply and entertainingly. *(he speaks with real conviction)* And no special interests will be allowed to interfere with the truth of that news.

*He looks at* LELAND *for a minute and goes back to his writing, reading as he writes.*

BERNSTEIN *has risen and crossed to one side of* KANE. *They both stand looking out.* LELAND *joins him on the other side. Their three heads are silhouetted against the sky.* LELAND'S *head is seen to turn slightly as he looks into* KANE'S *face—camera very close on this—*KANE *turns to him and*

*we know their eyes have met, although their faces are almost in silhouette.* BERNSTEIN *is still smoking a cigar.*

*Dissolve*

*Front Page of the "Enquirer" shows big boxed editorial with heading:*

MY PRINCIPLES—A DECLARATION
BY CHARLES FOSTER KANE

*Camera continues pulling back and shows newspaper to be on the top of a pile of newspapers. As we draw further back, we see four piles, and as camera continues to pull back, we see six piles and go on back until we see a big field of "Enquirers"—piles of "Enquirers"—all 26,000 copies ready for distribution.*

*A wagon with a huge sign on its side reading:*

"ENQUIRER—CIRCULATION 26,000"

*passes through foreground, and we wipe to:*

*A pile of "Enquirers" for sale on a broken down wooden box on a street corner, (obviously a poor district). A couple of coins fall on the pile.*

*The stoop of a period door with old-fashioned enamel milk can and a bag of rolls. Across the sidewalk before this moves the shadow of an old-fashioned bicycle with an enormous front wheel. A copy of the "Enquirer" is tossed on the stoop.*

*A breakfast table—beautiful linen and beautiful silver—everything very expensive, gleaming in the sunshine. Into a silver newspaper rack there is slipped a copy of the "Enquirer". (Here, as before, the boxed editorial reading* MY PRINCIPLES—A DECLARATION BY CHARLES FOSTER KANE, *is very prominent on the front page.)*

*The wooden floor of a railroad station, flashing light and dark as a train behind the camera rushes by. On the floor there is tossed a bound bundle of the "New York Enquirer"—the Declaration of Principles still prominent.*

*Rural Delivery—a copy of the "Enquirer" being put into RFD boxes.*

*Back to Enquirer building, showing copies of "Enquirers" being put into bins, showing state distribution.*

*The railroad platform again. We stay here for four images. On each image the speed of the train is faster and the piles of the "Enquirer" are larger. On the first image we move in to hold on the words* "CIRCULATION-31,000." *We are this close for the next pile which reads 40,000; the next one which reads 55,000, and the last which is 62,000. In each instance, the bundles of newspapers are thicker and the speed of the moving train behind the camera is increased.*

*The entire montage above indicated is accompanied by a descriptive complement of sound—the traffic noises of New York in the 1890's; wheels on cobblestones and horses' hooves; bicycle bells; the mooing of cattle and the crowing of roosters (in the RFD shot), and in all cases where the railroad platform is used—the mounting sound of the railroad train.*

*The last figure "62,000" opposite the word* "CIRCULATION" *on the "Enquirer" masthead changes to:*

*Ext. Street and Chronicle Building—Day—1895*

*Angle up to wall of building—a painter on a cradle is putting the last zero to the figure "62,000" on an enormous sign advertising the "Enquirer." It reads:*

THE ENQUIRER
THE PEOPLE'S NEWSPAPER
CIRCULATION 62,000

*Camera travels down side of building—takes in another building on which there is a sign which reads:*

READ THE ENQUIRER
AMERICA'S FINEST
CIRCULATION 62,000

*Camera continues to travel down to sidewalk in front of the Chronicle office. The Chronicle office has a plateglass window in which is reflected traffic moving up and down the street, also the figures of* KANE, LELAND *and* BERNSTEIN, *who are munching peanuts.*

*Inside the window, almost filling it, is a large photograph of the "Chronicle" staff, with* REILLY *prominently seated in the center. A sign over the photo reads:* EDITORIAL AND EXECUTIVE STAFF OF THE NEW YORK CHRONICLE. *A sign beneath it reads:* GREATEST NEWSPAPER STAFF IN THE WORLD. *The sign also includes the "Chronicle" circulation figure. There are nine men in the photo.*

BERNSTEIN (*looking up at the sign—happily*). Sixty-two thousand—
LELAND. That looks pretty nice.
KANE (*indicating the Chronicle Building*). Let's hope they like it in there.
BERNSTEIN. From the Chronicle Building that sign is the biggest thing you can see—every floor guaranteed—let's hope it bothers them—it cost us enough.
KANE (*pointing to the sign over the photograph in the window*). Look at that.
LELAND. The "Chronicle" is a good newspaper.
KANE. It's a good idea for a newspaper. (*reading the figures*) Four hundred sixty thousand.

BERNSTEIN Say, with them fellows—(*referring to the photo*)—it's no trick to get circulation.

KANE. You're right, Mr. Bernstein.

BERNSTEIN (*sighs*). You know how long it took the "Chronicle" to get that staff together? Twenty years.

KANE. I know.

KANE, *smiling, lights a cigarette, at the same time looking into the window. Camera moves in to hold on the photograph of nine men, still holding the reflection of* KANE's *smiling face.*

*Dissolve*

*Int. City Room—The Enquirer—Night—1895*

*Nine men, arrayed as in the photograph, but with* KANE *beaming in the center of the first row. The men, variously with mustaches, beards, bald heads, etc., are easily identified as being the same men,* REILLY *prominent amongst them.*

*As camera pulls back, it is revealed that they are being photographed—by an old-type professional photographer, big box, black hood and all—in a corner of the room. It is 1:30 at night. Desks, etc. have been pushed against the wall. Running down the center of the room is a long banquet table, at which twenty diners have finished their meals. The eleven remaining at their seats—these include* BERNSTEIN *and* LELAND—*are amusedly watching the photographic ceremonies.*

PHOTOGRAPHER. That's all. Thank you.

*The photographic subjects rise.*

KANE (*a sudden thought*). Make up an extra copy and mail it to the "Chronicle."

*Chuckling and beaming, he makes his way to his place at the head of the table. The others have already sat down.* KANE *gets his guests' attention by rapping on the table with a knife.*

KANE (*cont'd*). Gentlemen of the "Enquirer"! This has, I think, been a fitting welcome to those distinguished journalists—(*indicates the eight men*) Mr. Reilly in particular—who are the latest additions to our ranks. It will make them happy to learn that the "Enquirer's" circulation this morning passed the two hundred thousand mark.

BERNSTEIN. Two hundred and one thousand, six hundred and forty-seven.

*General applause.*

KANE. All of you—new and old—You're all getting the best salaries in town. Not one of you has been hired because of his loyalty. It's your talent I'm interested in. That talent that's going to make the "Enquirer" the kind of paper I want—the best newspaper in the world!

*Applause.*

KANE (*cont'd*). However, I think you'll agree we've heard enough about newspapers and the newspaper business for one night. There are other subjects in the world.

*He puts his two fingers in his mouth and lets out a shrill whistle. This is a signal. A band strikes up a lively ditty of the period and enters in advance of a regiment of very magnificent maidens, as daringly arrayed as possible in the chorus costumes of the day. (The rest of this episode will be planned and staged later. Its essence is that* KANE *is just a healthy and happy young man having a wonderful time.)*

*As some of the girls are detached from the line and made into partners for individual dancing—*

*Dissolve out*

*Dissolve in*

*The "Enquirer" Sign:*

THE ENQUIRER
AMERICA'S FINEST
CIRCULATION
274,321

*Dissolve just completes itself—the image of* KANE *dancing with a girl on each arm just disappears as camera pans down off the Temple Bldg. in the same action as the previous street scene. There is a new sign on the side of the building below. It reads:*

READ THE ENQUIRER
GREATEST STAFF IN THE WORLD

*Camera continues panning as we*

*Dissolve*

*A montage of various scenes, between the years 1891–1900.*

*The scenes indicate the growth of the "Enquirer" under the impulse of* KANE'S *personal drive.* KANE *is shown, thus, at various activities:*

*Move down from sign:*

READ THE ENQUIRER
GREATEST STAFF IN THE WORLD

*to street in front of saloon with parade passing (boys going off to the Spanish-American War)—A torchlight parade with the torches reflected in the glass window of the saloon—the sound of brass band playing "It's A Hot Time." In the window of the saloon is a large sign or poster*

"REMEMBER THE MAINE"

*Insert: Remington drawing of American boys, similar to the parade above, in which "Our Boys" in the expeditionary hats are seen marching off to war.*

*Back of observation car. Shot of* KANE *congratulating Teddy Roosevelt. (The same shot as in News Digest—without flickering.)*

*The wooden floor of the railroad platform again—a bundle of "Enquirers"—this time an enormous bundle—is thrown down, and the moving shadows of the train behind the camera indicate that it is going like a bat out of hell. A reproduction of* KANE *and Teddy shaking hands as above is very prominent in the frame and almost hogs the entire front page. The Headline indicates the surrender of Cuba.*

*Int. Enquirer Office—Cartoon, highly dramatic and very involved as to content—lousy with captions, labels and symbolic figures, the most gruesome and recognizable—"Capitalistic Greed." This cartoon is almost finished and is on a drawing board before which stand* KANE *and the artist himself.* KANE *is grinning over some suggestion he has made.*

*Dissolve*

*The cartoon finished and reproduced on the editorial page of the "Enquirer"—in quite close, with an editorial and several faces of caps shown underneath. The entire newspaper is crushed with an angry gesture and thrown down into an expensive-looking wastebasket reposing on thick Persian carpeting. Into this wastebasket (which is primarily for ticker tape) tape is pouring.*

*Int. Enquirer Office—Cartoonist and* KANE *working on comic strip of "Johnny the Monk."*

*Dissolve*

*Floor of room—Two kids on floor, with newspaper spread out, looking at the same comic strip.*

KANE'S *photographic gallery with photographers, stooges and* KANE *himself in attendance on a very hot-looking item of the period. A sob sister is interviewing this hot number and* KANE *is arranging her dress to look more seductive.*

*Dissolve out*

*Dissolve in*

*The hot number reproduced and prominently displayed and covering almost half a page of the "Enquirer." It is being read in a barber shop and is seen in an over-shoulder shot of the man who is reading it. He is getting a shine, a manicure and a haircut. The sob-sister caption over the photograph reveals:* "I DIDN'T KNOW WHAT I WAS DOING, SAYS DANCER. EVERYTHING WENT RED." *An oval photograph of the gun is included in the lay-out of the pretty lady with a headline which says:* "DEATH GUN."

*Street—shot of bucket brigade*

*Shot of* KANE, *in evening clothes, in obvious position of danger, grabbing camera from photographer. Before him rages a terrific tenement fire.*

*Dissolve*

*Insert: Headline about inadequacy of present fire equipment.*

*Dissolve*

*Final shot of a new horse-drawn steam engine roaring around a street corner (Stock).*

*Dissolve*

*A black pattern of iron bars. We are in a prison cell. The door is opened and a condemned man, with priest, warden and the usual attendants, moves into f.g. and starts up the hall past a group which includes photographers,* KANE'S *sob sister and* KANE. *The photographers take pic-*

*tures with a mighty flash of old-fashioned flash powder. The condemned man in the f.g. (in silhouette) is startled by this.*

*Dissolve*

*A copy of the "Enquirer" spread out on a table. A big lay-out of the execution story includes the killer as photographed by* KANE'S *photographers, and nearby on the other page there is a large picture of the new steam fire engine (made from the stock shot) with a headline indicating that the "Enquirer" has won its campaign for better equipment. A cup of coffee and a doughnut are on the newspaper, and a servant girl—over whose shoulder we see the paper—is stirring the coffee.*

*The Beaux Art Ball. A number of elderly swells are jammed into a hallway. Servants suddenly divest them of their furs, overcoats and wraps, revealing them to be in fancy dress costume, pink fleshings, etc., the effect to be very surprising, very lavish and very very ridiculous. We see, among others,* MR. THATCHER *himself (as Ben Hur) ribbon around his bald head and all. At the conclusion of this tableau, the image freezes and we pull back to show it reproduced on the society page of the "New York Enquirer."*

*Over the "Enquirer"'s pictorial version of the Beaux Art Ball is thrown a huge fish—then coffee grounds—altogether a pretty repulsive sight.*

*The whole thing is bundled up and thrown into a garbage can.*

*Extreme closeup of the words:* "OCCUPATION—JOURNALIST."

*Camera pulls back to show passport open to the photograph page which shows* KANE, *registering Birth,*

Race, and Nationality. Passport
cover is closed, showing it to be an
American passport.

Ext. Cunard Docks—Gangplank
and Deck of Boat—Night—1900

As camera pulls back over shoulder
of official, taking in KANE, LELAND,
and BERNSTEIN, we see the bustle and
noise of departing ocean liner. Behind the principals can be seen an
enormous plain sign which reads:
"FIRST CLASS." From offstage can be
heard the steward's cry, indispens-
able in any Mercury production, the
old familiar cry, "All Ashore That's
Going Ashore!"—gongs, also blasts
of the great whistle and all the rest of
it.

THE OFFICIAL. There you are, Mr.
Kane. Everything in order.
KANE. Thank you.

KANE and LELAND and BERNSTEIN
start up the gangplank.

THE OFFICIAL (calling). Have a nice
crossing!
KANE. Thanks.
BERNSTEIN (shrieking above the
noise of departure—running up the
gangplank after KANE). Have a good
rest, Mr. Kane.
KANE. Thanks.
BERNSTEIN. But please, Mr. Kane,
don't buy any more paintings. Nine
Venuses already we got, twenty-six
Virgins—two whole warehouses full
of stuff—
KANE. I promise not to bring any
more Venuses and not to worry—and
not to try to get in touch with any of
the papers—
STEWARD'S VOICE. All ashore!
KANE. —and to forget all about the
new feature sections—and not to try
to think up any ideas for comic sections.

STEWARD'S VOICE. All ashore that's
going ashore!

KANE leaves LELAND and BERN-
STEIN midway up gangplank, as he
rushes up it, calling back with a
wave:

KANE. Good-bye, gents! (at the top
of the gangplank, he turns and calls
down) Hey!

LELAND and BERNSTEIN, who have
started down to dock, turn back to
him.

KANE (cont'd) (calling down to
them). You don't expect me to keep
any of those promises, do you?

A band on deck strikes up "Auld
Lang Syne." BERNSTEIN and LELAND
turn to each other.

BERNSTEIN. Do you, Mr. Leland?
LELAND (smiling). Certainly not.

They start down the gangplank
together.

Dissolve

Long Shot of the Enquirer Bldg.—
Night

The pattern of telegraph wires,
dripping with rain, through which we
see the same old building but now
rendered fairly remarkable by tremendous outline sign in gold which
reads "THE NEW YORK DAILY ENQUIR-
ER." A couple of lights show in the
building. We start toward the window
where the lights show, as we—

Dissolve

Ext. Outside the Window at BERN-
STEIN'S Desk—Night

The light in the window in the former shot was showing behind the letter
"E" of the Enquirer sign. Now the
letter "E" is even larger than the
frame of the camera.—Rain drips disconsolately off the middle part of the

figure. We see through this and through the drizzle of the window to BERNSTEIN'S *desk where he sits working under a blue shaded light.*

*Dissolve out*

*Dissolve in*

*Same setup as before*

*except that it is now late afternoon and late in the winter of the year. The outline "E" is hung with icicles which are melting, dripping despairingly between us and* MR. BERNSTEIN, *still seated at his desk—still working.*

*Dissolve*

*Same setup as before*

*except that it is spring. Instead of the sad sounds of dripping rain or dripping icicles we hear the melancholy cry of a hurdy-gurdy in the street below. It is spring and through the window and through the letter "E" we can still see* BERNSTEIN *working at his desk. Pigeons are gathering on the "E" and on the sill.* BERNSTEIN *looks up and sees them. He takes some crumbs from his little homemade lunch which is spread out on the desk before him, carries them to the windows and feeds the pigeons, looking moodily out on the prospect of spring on Park Row. The birds eat the crumbs—the hurdy-gurdy continues to play.*

*Dissolve*

*The same setup again*

*It is now summer. The window was half-open before . . . now it's open all the way and* BERNSTEIN *has gone so far as to take off his coat. His shirt and his celluloid collar are wringing wet. Camera moves toward the window to tighten on* BERNSTEIN *and to take in the City Room behind him, which is absolutely deserted. It is*

clear that there is almost nothing more for BERNSTEIN *to do. The hurdy-gurdy in the street is playing as before but a new tune.*

*Dissolve*

*A beach on Coney Island*

BERNSTEIN *in a rented period bathing suit sits alone in the sand, reading a copy of the "Enquirer."*

*Dissolve out*

*Dissolve in*

*Int. City Room—Enquirer Bldg.— Day—1900*

*The whole floor is now a City Room. It is twice its former size, yet not too large for all the desks and the people using them. The windows have been enlarged, providing a good deal more light and air. A wall calendar says September 9th.*

KANE *and* BERNSTEIN *enter and stand in the entrance a moment.* KANE, *who really did look a bit peaked before, is now clear-eyed and tanned. He is wearing new English clothes. As they come into the room,* BERNSTEIN *practically walking sideways, is doing nothing but beaming and admiring* KANE, *quelling like a mother at the Carnegie Hall debut of her son. Seeing and recognizing* KANE, *the entire staff rises to its feet.*

KANE *(referring to the staff; with a smile).* Ask them to sit down, Mr. Bernstein.

BERNSTEIN. Sit down, everybody— for heaven's sake!

*The order is immediately obeyed, everybody going into business of feverish activity.*

BERNSTEIN. So then, tonight, we go over everything thoroughly, eh? Especially the new papers—

KANE. We certainly do. Vacation's over—starting right after dinner. But right now—that lady over there—*(he indicates a woman at a desk)*—that's the new society editor, I take it? You think I could interrupt her a moment, Mr. Bernstein?

BERNSTEIN. Huh? Oh, I forgot—you've been away so long I forgot about your joking—

*He trails after* KANE *as he approaches the Society Editor's desk. The Society Editor, a middle-aged spinster, sees him approaching and starts to quake all over, but tries to pretend she isn't aware of him. An envelope in her hand shakes violently.* KANE *and* BERNSTEIN *stop at her desk.*

BERNSTEIN *(cont'd)*. Miss Townsend—

MISS TOWNSEND *looks up and is so surprised to see* BERNSTEIN *with a stranger.*

MISS TOWNSEND. Good afternoon, Mr. Bernstein.

BERNSTEIN. This is Mr. Kane, Miss Townsend.

MISS TOWNSEND *can't stick to her plan. She starts to rise, but her legs are none too good under her. She knocks over a tray of copy paper as she rises, and bends to pick it up.*

KANE *(very hesitatingly and softly)*. Miss Townsend—

*At the sound of his voice, she straightens up. She is very close to death from excitement.*

KANE *(cont'd)*. I've been away several months, and I don't know exactly how these things are handled now. But one thing I want to be sure of is that you won't treat this little announcement any differently than you would any other similar announcement.

*He hands her an envelope. She has difficulty in holding on to it.*

KANE *(cont'd) (gently)*. Read it, Miss Townsend. And remember—just the regular treatment!

KANE *(cont'd)*. See you at nine o'clock, Mr. Bernstein!

KANE *leaves.* BERNSTEIN *looks after him, then at the paper.* MISS TOWNSEND *finally manages to open the envelope. A piece of flimsy paper, with a few written lines, is her reward.*

MISS TOWNSEND *(reading)*. Mr. and Mrs. Thomas Moore Norton announce the engagement of their daughter, Emily Monroe Norton, to Mr. Charles Foster Kane.

BERNSTEIN *(starts to read it)*. Mr. and Mrs. Thomas Monroe Norton announce—

MISS TOWNSEND *(fluttering—on top of him)*. She's—she's the niece of—of the President of the United States—

BERNSTEIN *(nodding proudly)*. I know. Come on, Miss Townsend—From the window, maybe we can get a look.

*He takes her by the hand and leads her off.*

*Angle toward open window.* BERNSTEIN *and* MISS TOWNSEND, *backs to camera, rushing to the window.*

*Ext. Street Outside Enquirer Bldg.—Day—1900*

*High angle downward—(What* BERNSTEIN *and* MISS TOWNSEND *see from the window).*

KANE *is just stepping into an elegant barouch, drawn up at the curb, in which sits* MISS EMILY NORTON. *She looks at him smilingly. He kisses her full on the lips before he sits down. She acts a bit taken aback, because of the public nature of the scene, but she isn't really annoyed. As the barouche starts off, she is looking at him adoringly. He, however, has turned his head and is looking adoringly at the "Enquirer." He apparently sees* BERNSTEIN *and* MISS TOWNSEND *and waves his hand.*

*Int. City Room—Enquirer—Day— 1900*

BERNSTEIN *and* MISS TOWNSEND *at window.*

BERNSTEIN. A girl like that, believe me, she's lucky! President's niece, huh! Say, before he's through, she'll be a President's wife.

MISS TOWNSEND *is now deweyeyed. She looks at* BERNSTEIN *who has turned away, gazing down at the departing couple.*

*Dissolve*

*Front Page "Enquirer." Large picture of the young couple—*KANE *and* EMILY—*occupying four columns— very happy.*

*Dissolve*

*Int.* BERNSTEIN'S *Office—Enquirer—Day—1940*

BERNSTEIN *and* THOMPSON. *As the dissolve comes,* BERNSTEIN'S *voice is heard.*

BERNSTEIN. The way things turned out, I don't need to tell you—Miss Emily Norton was no rosebud!

THOMPSON. It didn't end very well, did it?

BERNSTEIN *(shaking his head).* It ended.—*(a slight pause)* Then there was Susie.—That ended too. *(shrugs, a pause; then looking up into* THOMPSON'S *eyes)* I guess he didn't make her very happy.—*(a pause)*—You know, I was thinking—that Rosebud you're trying to find out about—

THOMPSON. Yes—

BERNSTEIN. Maybe that was something he lost. Mr. Kane was a man that lost—almost everything he had— *(a pause)* You ought to talk to Bradford Leland. He could tell you a lot.—I wish I could tell you where Leland is, but I don't know myself. He may be out of town somewhere— he may be dead.

THOMPSON. In case you'd like to know, Mr. Bernstein, he's at the Huntington Memorial Hospital on 180th Street.

BERNSTEIN. You don't say! Why I had no idea—

THOMPSON. Nothing particular the matter with him, they tell me. Just —*(controls himself)*

BERNSTEIN. Just old age. *(smiles sadly)* It's the only disease, Mr. Thompson, you don't look forward to being cured of. *(pauses)* You ought to see Mr. Leland. There's a whole lot of things he could tell you—if he wanted to.

*Fade out*

*Fade in*

*Ext. Hospital Roof—Day—1940*

*Close shot—*THOMPSON. *He is tilted back in a chair which seems to me, and is, leaning against a chimney.* LELAND'S *voice is heard for a few moments before* LELAND *is seen.*

LELAND'S VOICE. When you get to my age, young man, you don't miss anything. Unless maybe it's a good drink of Bourbon. Even that doesn't make much difference, if you remember there hasn't been any good Bourbon in this country for twenty years.

*Camera has pulled back, during above speech, revealing that* LELAND, *wrapped in a blanket, is in a wheel chair, talking to* THOMPSON. *They are on the flat roof of a hospital. Other people in wheel chairs can be seen in* the b.g. along with a nurse or two. *They are all sunning themselves.*

THOMPSON. Mr. Leland, you were—

LELAND. You don't happen to have a cigar, do you? I've got a young physician—must remember to ask to see his license—the odds are a hundred to one he hasn't got one—who thinks I'm going to stop smoking. . . . I changed the subject, didn't I? Dear, dear! What a disagreeable old man I've become. You want to know what I think of Charlie Kane?—Well,—I suppose he has some private sort of greatness. But he kept it to himself. *(grinning)* He never—gave himself away—He never gave anything away. He just—left you a tip. He had a generous mind. I don't suppose anybody ever had so many opinions. That was because he had the power to express them, and Charlie lived on power and the excitement of using it.— But he didn't believe in anything except Charlie Kane. He never had a conviction in his life. I guess he died without one—That must have been pretty unpleasant. Of course, a lot of us check out with no special conviction about death. But we do know what we're leaving . . . we believe in something. *(looks sharply at* THOMPSON*)* You're absolutely sure you haven't got a cigar?

THOMPSON. Sorry, Mr. Leland.

LELAND. Never mind.—Bernstein told you about the first days at the office, didn't he?—Well, Charlie was a bad newspaper man even then. He entertained his readers but he never told them the truth.

THOMPSON. Maybe you could remember something that—

LELAND. I can remember everything. That's my curse, young man. It's the greatest curse that's ever been inflicted on the human race. Mem-ory—I was his oldest friend. *(slowly)*—As far as I was concerned, he behaved like a swine. Maybe I wasn't his friend. If *I* wasn't, he never had one. Maybe I was what nowadays you call a stooge—

*Dissolve out*

*Dissolve in*

*Int. City Room—The Enquirer— Night—1895*

*The party (previously shown in the* BERNSTEIN *sequence).*

*We start this sequence towards the end of the former one, but from a fresh angle, holding on* LELAND, *who is at the end of the table.* KANE *is heard off, making a speech.*

KANE'S VOICE. None of you has been hired because of his loyalty! It's your talent I'm interested in. The talent that's going to make the "Enquirer" the kind of paper I want—the best newspaper in the world!

*Applause. During above,* BERNSTEIN *has come to* LELAND'S *side.*

BERNSTEIN. Isn't it wonderful? Such a party!

LELAND. Yes.

*His tone causes* BERNSTEIN *to look at him.*

KANE'S VOICE. However, I think you'll agree we've heard enough about newspapers and the newspaper business for one night.

*(The above speeches are heard under the following dialogue.)*

BERNSTEIN *(to* LELAND*)*. What's the matter?

LELAND. —Mr. Bernstein, these men who are now with the "Enquirer"—who were with the "Chronicle" until yesterday—weren't they just as devoted to the "Chronicle" kind of paper as they are now to—our kind of paper?

BERNSTEIN. Sure. They're like anybody else. They got work to do. They do it. *(proudly)* Only they happen to be the best men in the business.

KANE *(finishing his speech)*. There are other subjects in the world—

KANE *whistles. The band and the chorus girls enter and hell breaks loose all around* LELAND *and* BERNSTEIN.

LELAND *(after a minute)*. Do we stand for the same things that the "Chronicle" stands for, Mr. Bernstein?

BERNSTEIN *(indignantly)*. Certainly not. So what's that got to do with it? Mr. Kane he'll have them changed to his kind of newspapermen in a week.

LELAND. Probably. There's always a chance, of course, that they'll change Mr. Kane—without his knowing it.

KANE *has come up to* LELAND *and* BERNSTEIN. *He sits down next to them, lighting a cigarette.*

KANE. Well, gentlemen, are we going to war?

LELAND. Our readers are, anyway, I don't know about the rest of the country.

KANE *(enthusiastically)*. It'll be our first foreign war in fifty years, Brad. We'll cover it the way the "Hickville Gazette" covers the church social! The names of everybody there; what they wore; what they ate; who won the prizes; who gave the prizes—*(gets excited)* I tell you, Brad, I envy you. *(quoting)* By Bradford Leland, the "Enquirer"'s Special Correspondent at the Front. I'm almost tempted—

LELAND. But there *is* no Front, Charlie. There's a very doubtful civil war. Besides, I don't want the job.

KANE. All right, Brad, all right—you don't have to be a war correspondent unless you want to—I'd want to. *(looking up)* Hello, Georgie.

GEORGIE, *a very handsome madam has walked into the picture, stands behind him. She leans over and speaks quietly in his ear.*

GEORGIE. Is everything the way you want it, dear?

KANE *(looking around)*. If everybody's having fun, that's the way I want it.

GEORGIE. I've got some other little girls coming over—

LELAND *(interrupting)*. Charles, I tell you there is no war! There's a condition that should be remedied—but between that and a—

KANE *(seriously)*. How would the "Enquirer" look with no news about this non-existent war—with Benton, Pulitzer and Hearst devoting twenty columns a day to it?

LELAND. They do it only because you do!

KANE *(grins)*. And I do it because they do it, and they do it—it's a vicious circle, isn't it? *(rises)* I'm going over to Georgie's, Brad—you know Georgie, don't you?

LELAND *nods.*

GEORGIE *(over* KANE'S *next lines)*. Glad to meet you, Brad.

LELAND *shudders.*

KANE. I told you about Brad, Georgie. He needs to relax.

BRAD *doesn't answer.*

KANE *(cont'd)*. Some ships with wonderful wines have managed to slip through the enemy fleet that's blockading New York harbor—*(grins)* Georgie knows a young lady whom I'm sure you'd adore—

wouldn't he, Georgie? Why only the other evening I said to myself, if Brad were only here to adore this young lady—this—*(snaps his fingers)* What's her name again?

*Dissolve out*

*Dissolve in*

*Int.* GEORGIE'S *Place—Night—1895*

GEORGIE *is introducing a young lady to* BRADFORD LELAND. *On sound track we hear piano music.*

GEORGIE *(right on the cue from preceding scene)*. Ethel—this gentleman has been very anxious to meet you—This is Ethel.

ETHEL. Hello, Mr. Leland.

*Camera pans to include* KANE, *seated at piano, with girls gathered around him.*

ONE OF THE GIRLS. Charlie! Play the song about you.

ANOTHER GIRL. Is there a song about Charlie?

KANE *has broken into "Oh, Mr. Kane!" and* CHARLIE *and the girls start to sing.* ETHEL *leads the unhappy* LELAND *over to the group.* KANE, *seeing* LELAND *and taking his eye, motions to the professor who has been standing next to him to take over. The professor does so. The singing continues.* KANE *rises and crosses to* LE-LAND.

KANE. Say, Brad. *(draws him slightly aside)* I've got an idea.

LELAND. Yes?

KANE. I mean I've got a job for you.

LELAND. Good.

KANE. You don't want to be a war correspondent—how about being dramatic critic?

LELAND *(sincerely, but not gushingly; seriously)*. I'd like that.

KANE *starts quietly to dance in time to the music.* LELAND *smiles at him.*

KANE. You start tomorrow night. Richard Carl in "The Spring Chicken." *(or supply show)* I'll get us some girls. You get tickets. A drama critic gets them free, you know. *(grins)* Rector's at seven?

LELAND. Charlie—

KANE. Yes?

LELAND *(still smiling)*. It doesn't make any difference about me, but one of these days you're going to find out that all this charm of yours won't be enough—

KANE *(has stopped dancing)*. You're wrong. It does make a difference to you.—Rector's, Brad? *(starts to dance again)*—Come to think of it, I don't blame you for not wanting to be a war correspondent. You won't miss anything. It isn't much of a war. Besides, they tell me there isn't a decent restaurant on the whole island.

*Dissolve out*

*Dissolve in*

*Int. Rector's—Night—1898*

LELAND, KANE, *two young ladies at Rector's. Popular music is heard over the sound track. Everybody is laughing very, very hard at something* KANE *has said. The girls are hysterical.* KANE *can hardly breathe. As* LE-LAND'S *laughter becomes more and more hearty, it only increases the laughter of the others.*

*Dissolve*

*Ext. Cunard Locks—Gangplank and Deck of Boat—Night—1900*

*(As told by* BERNSTEIN*).* KANE *is calling down to* LELAND *and* BERN-STEIN *(as before).*

KANE. You don't expect me to keep any of those promises, do you?

*A band on deck strikes up "Auld Lang Syne" and further ship-to-shore conversation is rendered unfeasible.*

BERNSTEIN *and* LELAND *on dock.*

BERNSTEIN *(turns to* LELAND*).* Do you, Mr. Leland?

LELAND *(smiling).* Certainly not.

*Slight pause. They continue on their way.*

BERNSTEIN. Mr. Leland, why didn't you go to Europe with him? He wanted you to. He said to me just yesterday—

LELAND. I wanted him to have fun—and with me along—

*This stops* BERNSTEIN. BERNSTEIN *looks at him.*

LELAND *(cont'd).* Mr. Bernstein, I wish you'd let me ask you a few questions, and answer me truthfully.

BERNSTEIN. Don't I always? Most of the time?

LELAND. Mr. Bernstein, am I a stuffed shirt? Am I a horse-faced hypocrite? Am I a New England school-marm?

BERNSTEIN. Yes.

LELAND *is surprised.*

BERNSTEIN *(cont'd).* If you thought I'd answer you different from what Mr. Kane tells you—well, I wouldn't.

LELAND *(good-naturedly).* You're in a conspiracy against me, you two. You always have been.

BERNSTEIN. Against me there should be such a conspiracy some time!

*He pauses. "Auld Lang Syne" can still be heard from the deck of the departing steamer.*

BERNSTEIN *(cont'd) (with a hopeful look in his eyes).* Well, he'll be com-

ing back in September. The Majestic. I got the reservations. It gets in on the ninth.

LELAND. September the ninth?

LELAND *puts his hand in his pocket, pulls out a pencil and small engagement book, opens the book and starts to write.*

LELAND'S *pencil writing on a page in the engagement book open to September 9: "Rector's—8:30 p.m."*

*Dissolve*

*Front page "Enquirer." Large picture of the young couple—*KANE *and* EMILY—*occupying four columns—very happy.*

*Ext. Hospital Roof—Day—1940*

LELAND *and* THOMPSON. LELAND *is speaking as we dissolve.*

LELAND. I used to go to dancing school with her.

THOMPSON *had handed* LELAND *a paper.*

LELAND *(cont'd).* What's this?

THOMPSON. It's a letter from her lawyers.

LELAND *(reading aloud from the letter).* David, Grobleski & Davis— My dear Rawlston—*(looks up)*

THOMPSON. Rawlston is my boss.

LELAND. Oh, yes. I know about Mr. Rawlston.

THOMPSON. He knows the first Mrs. Kane socially.—That's the answer we got.

LELAND *(reading).* I am in receipt of your favor of yesterday. I beg you to do me the courtesy of accepting my assurance that Mrs. Whitehall cannot be induced to contribute any more information on the career of Charles Foster Kane. She has authorized me to state on previous occasions that she regards their brief marriage as a distasteful episode in her life that she prefers to forget. With assurances of the highest esteem—

LELAND *hands the paper back to* THOMPSON.

LELAND *(cont'd)*. Brief marriage! Ten years! *(sighs)*

THOMPSON. Was he in love?

LELAND. He married for love—*(a little laugh)* That's why he did everything. That's why he went into politics. It seems we weren't enough. He wanted all the voters to love him, too. All he really wanted out of life was love.—That's Charlie's story—it's the story of how he lost it. You see, he just didn't have any to give. He loved Charlie Kane, of course, very dearly,—and his mother, I guess he always loved her. As for Emily— well, all I can tell you is Emily's story as she told it to me, which probably isn't very fair—there's supposed to be two sides to every story—and I guess there are—I guess there're more than two sides—

*Dissolve out*

*Dissolve in*

*Newspaper*—KANE'S *marriage to* EMILY *with still of group on White House lawn, same setup as early newsreel in News Digest.*

*Dissolve*

*Screaming headline:*

OIL SCANDAL!

*Dissolve*

*Headline reading:*

KANE TO SEE PRESIDENT

*Dissolve*

*Big headline on "Enquirer" Front Page which reads:*

KANE TO SEE PRESIDENT

*Under this one of those big box signed editorials, typical of* KANE, *illustrated, on subject of the power of the president, expressed in about nine different cases of type, and illustrated by a cartoon of the White House, on which camera tightens, as we—*

*Dissolve out*

*Dissolve in*

*Int. the White House—the* PRES- IDENT'S *Executive Office—Day— 1900*

*This scene is shot so as never to show the* PRESIDENT—*or at least never his face. There is present the* PRES- IDENT'S SECRETARY, *sitting on one side of the desk, intently taking notes.* KANE *is on his feet, in front of the desk, tense and glaring.*

THE PRESIDENT. It is the unanimous opinion of my Cabinet—in which I concur—that the proposed leases are in the best interests of the Government and the people. *(pauses)* You are not, I hope, suggesting that these interests are not identical?

KANE. I'm not suggesting anything, Mr. President! I've come here to tell you that, unless some action is taken promptly—and you are the only one who can take it—the oil that is the property of the people of this country will be turned over for a song to a gang of high-pressure crooks!

THE PRESIDENT *(calmly)*. I must refuse to allow you to continue in this vein, Mr. Kane.

KANE *(screaming)*. It's the only vein I know. I tell the facts the way I see them. And any man that knows the facts—

THE PRESIDENT. I know the facts. Mr. Kane. And I happen to have the incredible insolence to differ with you as to what they mean. *(pause)* You're a man of great talents, Mr. Kane.

KANE. Thanks.

THE PRESIDENT. I understand that you have political ambitions. Unfortunately, you seem incapable of allowing any other opinion but your own—

KANE *(building to a frenzy)*. I'm much obliged, Mr. President, for your concern about me. However, I happen to be concerned at this moment with the matter of extensive oil lands belonging to the people of the United States, and I say that if this lease goes through, the property of the people of the United States goes into the hands of—

THE PRESIDENT *(interrupting)*. You've made your point perfectly clear, Mr. Kane. Good day.

*The* SECRETARY *rises.* KANE, *with every bit of will power remotely at his disposal to control what might become an hysterical outburst, manages to bow.*

KANE. Mr. President.

*He starts out of the office.*

*Dissolve*

*Int. Composing Room—Enquirer—Night—1902*

KANE, REILLY, LELAND *and a composing room* FOREMAN, *in working clothes, bending over a table with several forms of type. They are looking, at this moment, at a made-up headline—but* KANE'S *back is in the way . . . so we can't read it.*

FOREMAN. How about it, Mr. Kane?

REILLY *glances at his wrist watch and makes a face.* KANE *smiles as he notices this.*

KANE. All right. Let her slide!

*He turns away, and we can now read the headline.*

*Insert of the headline, which reads:* "OIL THEFT BECOMES LAW AS PRESIDENT WITHHOLDS VETO"

*Dissolve*

*Here follows a quick montage (presently to be worked out) of no more than four or five images in which the* PRESIDENT, *by means of cartoons, editorials, headlines (all faithfully reproduced from period yellow journalism) is violently attacked. The montage ends on the word* TREASON. *The music cuts.*

*A hand reaches in a side pocket which contains a newspaper—recognizably the "Enquirer." The hand removes a gun. The gun is shot. Many arms seize the hand which is pulled up—gun still firing. As the arm is raised in the air we see that the other arms holding the arm and struggling with it are uniformed, and we see the White House beyond.*

*Dissolve*

*News ticker which is spelling out the words:* "ASSASSINATED 7:45 P.M."

*(Note: Under the following—a down shot, below the "Enquirer," shows a crowd forming, looking angrily up toward the camera. Crowd noises on the sound track under music.)*

*A hand snatches the ticker tape away and as the image of the crowd dissolves out, we pull back to show:*

*Int. of* KANE'S *Office—Night—1902*

*The ticker tape is in* REILLY'S *hand.* REILLY *has a phone to his ear.*

REILLY. —Looks bad for us, Mr. Kane. How shall we handle it?

*Dissolve out*

*Dissolve in*

*Int.* GEORGIE'S *Place—1902*

KANE *in shirtsleeves at phone.*

KANE. It's a news story! Get it on the street!

*Dissolve*

*Headline under "Enquirer" mast-head which reads:*

"PRESIDENT ASSASSINATED"

*A newsboy is crying the headline at the same time. We pull back to show him and—*

*Dissolve*

*Int. Theatre—Night*

*The camera is in tight on a box which contains* EMILY *and distin-guished elderly ladies and gentlemen, obviously family and friends. On the sound-track very limpid opera music. Another elderly gent, in white tie but still wearing an overcoat, comes into the box and whispers to* EMILY. *He has a copy of the "Enquirer" in his hand.* EMILY *rises. He shows the paper to her.*

*Dissolve*

*Ext. Street Outside Enquirer Building—Night—1902*

*An angry crowd seen from the win-dow of* KANE'S *office. They make a deep threatening sound which is aud-ible during the follow scene. Across the heads of the crowd are two great squares of light from the windows above them. One of these disappears as the blind is pulled. As the dissolve completes itself, the second square of light commences to reduce in size, and then the entire street is cut off by a blind which* LELAND *pulls down, covering the entire frame.*

*Int.* KANE'S *Office—Enquirer— Night—1902*

*The staff standing around, worried to death, in their shirtsleeves.*

KANE *(to* REILLY*).* Take dictation— Front page editorial—"This afternoon a great man was assassinated. He was the President of the United States—

LELAND. Charlie—

KANE. Yes?

LELAND. Do you think you're the one who should call him a great man?

KANE. Why not?

LELAND. Why not? Well—no-body's a great man in your estimation until he's dead.

REILLY *(quickly).* Maybe we'd bet-ter wait for more word on the Presi-dent's condition.

KANE *(still looking at* LELAND*).* What do you mean by that?

LELAND *(quietly).* Competition.

REILLY. He may recover—

KANE *(still holding on* LELAND*).* What do you mean by that?

LELAND *(steadily).* Yesterday morning you called the President a traitor. What do you think that crowd is doing down there? They think you murdered him.

KANE. Because the little crackpot who did kill him had a copy of the "Enquirer" in his pocket?

LELAND.—and that copy of the "Enquirer" said the President should be killed.

KANE. I said treason was a capital offense punishable by death—

LELAND. You've said a lot of things about the President in the last few months.

KANE. They're true! Everything I said! Withholding that veto was treason!

LELAND *(interrupting).* Charlie!

KANE *(riding over him).* Oil be-longing to the people of the United States was leased out for a song to a gang of high-pressure crooks—Nobody can blame me because—

LELAND. Look out that window.

KANE *stops—looks at him.*

LELAND *(cont'd).* There are the people of the United States, and they are blaming you—Oh, I know it doesn't make any sense, but at least you can learn a lesson from it.

KANE *(snarling).* What lesson? Not to expose fraud when I see it? Not to fight for the right of the people to own their own property? *(he turns to* REILLY*)* Run it the way I said, Reilly— "This afternoon a great man was assassinated—"

LELAND. Charlie! Now *you're* not making sense.

KANE *(sharply).* I don't have to. I run a newspaper with half a million readers and they're getting a martyred president this morning with their breakfast. I can't help that. Besides they all know I'm married to his niece. I've got to think of her.

LELAND. What?

KANE. I've got to think of Emily—

LELAND *(after a silence).* I'd like to talk to you about that.

KANE. Go ahead.

LELAND *looks back at* KANE, *is conscious of the boys standing around.*

LELAND.—Finish your editorial.

LELAND *walks out into the City Room. More staff members in shirt sleeves in a state of panic.* LELAND *goes to his desk, takes out a bottle, pours himself a very stiff drink. A door opens. A* POLICEMAN *enters with* BERNSTEIN. BERNSTEIN *is badly battered. The boys crowd around.*

LELAND *(worried).* What's happened?

BERNSTEIN *(smiling).* I'm all right, Mr. Leland. Only there was some fellows out front that thought they ought to take things up with me. I learned 'em! Didn't I, officer?

THE COP *(grinning).* You sure did— Say, the Commissioner said I was to stand by and protect Mr. Kane until further orders, no matter how he felt about it. Where is he?

LELAND *(finishing his drink).* In there.

BERNSTEIN. If you hadn't come along and protected me when you did, I'd have killed them fellows.

LELAND *(pouring himself another drink).* Go and get yourself washed up, Mr. Bernstein. *(he looks his face over thoroughly)* There doesn't seem to be any serious injury.

BERNSTEIN. Not to me. But you will let that cop go home with Mr. Kane, won't you?

LELAND. Yes, Mr. Bernstein.

BERNSTEIN *leaves the picture with sympathetic attendance.* LELAND *finishes his second drink.*

*Dissolve*

*Int.* KANE'S *Office—Night—1902*

*The bottle is finished. The door in the Sanctum opens.* REILLY *and the others leave.*

REILLY *(as they go).* Goodnight, Mr. Kane.

KANE *stands in the door, waiting for* LELAND. LELAND *gets up and moves toward the office—goes in, sits down across from* KANE *at the desk. An uncomfortable pause. Then* KANE *smiles ingratiatingly.* LELAND *tries to cope with this.*

LELAND. First of all—*(he can't go on)*

KANE *(not cruelly — genuinely kind).* What's wrong, Brad?

LELAND. I'm drunk.

KANE. I'll get you some coffee. *(He rises and goes to the door.)*

LELAND. First of all, I will not write a good review of a play because somebody paid a thousand dollars for an advertisement in the "Enquirer."

KANE *(gently—opening the door).* That's just a little promotion scheme. Nobody expects you—*(calling)* Mike, will you try and get Mr. Leland some coffee?

MIKE'S VOICE. Sure thing, Mr. Kane.

KANE *turns back to* LELAND. LE-LAND *doesn't look up at him.*

LELAND. Charlie, it's just no go. We can't agree any more. I wish you'd let me go to Chicago.

KANE. Why, Brad?

LELAND. I want to be transferred to the new paper. You've been saying yourself you wish you had somebody to—*(he is heartsick, inarticulate)* That's not what I wanted to talk about.

KANE *goes around behind the desk and sits down.*

KANE. I'll tell you what I'll do, Brad—I'll get drunk too—maybe that'll help.

LELAND. No, that won't help. Besides you never get drunk. I wanted to talk about you and Emily.

KANE *looks at* LELAND *sharply before he speaks.*

KANE *(quietly).* All right.

LELAND *(without looking at him).* She's going to leave you—

KANE *(easily).* I don't think so, Brad. We've just had word that the President is out of danger. *(ruefully)* It seems I didn't kill him after all.

LELAND *(takes his eye).* She was going to leave you anyway—

KANE *takes this in.*

LELAND *(cont'd).* Emily's going South next week with the child. As far as anybody's to know, it's a holiday. When they get back—

KANE *(sharply).* Brad, you *are* drunk.

LELAND. Sure I am. She wants full custody of the child no matter what happens. If you won't agree to that, she'll apply for a divorce regardless of the President's wishes. I can't tell her she's wrong, because she isn't wrong—

KANE. Why *is* she leaving me?

LELAND *(it's very hard for him to say all this).* She hasn't any friends left since you started this oil business, and she never sees you.

KANE. Do you think the "Enquirer" shouldn't have campaigned against the oil leases?

LELAND *(hesitating).* You might have made the whole thing less personal!

*No answer from* KANE.

LELAND *(cont'd).* It isn't just that the President was her uncle—everyone she knows, all the people she's been brought up with, everything she's ever been taught to believe is important—

*Still no answer from* KANE.

LELAND *(cont'd).* There's no reason why this—this savage personal note—

KANE. The personal note is all there is to it. It's all there ever is to it. It's all there ever is to anything! Stupidity in our government, complacency and self-satisfaction and unwillingness to believe that anything done by a certain class of people can be wrong—you can't fight those things impersonally. They're not impersonal crimes against the people. They're being done by actual persons—with actual names and positions and—the right of the American people to own their own country is not an academic issue, Brad, that you debate—and then the judges retire to return a verdict—and the winners give a dinner for the losers.

LELAND. You almost convince me. Almost. *(rising)* I'm just drunk enough to tell you the truth. I have to be a little drunk for that because I'm a coward. You know that. That's why you keep me around. *(smiles)* You only associate with your inferiors, Charlie. I guess that's why you ran away from Emily. Because you can't stand the company of your equals. You don't like to admit they exist— the other big people in your world are dead. I told you that.

KANE *looks at* LELAND, *but* LELAND *can't be stopped now. He speaks very quietly—no poison in his voice—no personal indignation—as though he were explaining the nature of a disease.*

LELAND *(cont'd)*. You talk about the people of the United States as though they belonged to you. When you find out they don't think they are, you'll lose interest. You talk about giving them their rights as though you could make a present of liberty. Remember the working man? You used to defend him quite a good deal. Well,—he's turning into something called organized labor and you don't like that at all. And listen, when your precious underprivileged really get together—that's going to add up to something bigger than—than your privilege and then I don't know what you'll do—sail away to a desert island, probably, and lord it over the monkeys.

KANE. Are you finished?

LELAND. Yes. *(looking down)* Now, will you let me go to Chicago?

KANE *(with a little smile)*. You're not going to like it in Chicago. The wind comes howling in from the lake.

And there's practically no opera season at all—and the Lord only knows whether they've ever heard of Lobster Newburg—

LELAND. That's all right. *(He won't be charmed out of his duty.)* What are you going to do about Emily?

KANE *(his face hardening a little)*. Nothing—if she doesn't love me—

LELAND *has risen. He speaks as he turns away, starting towards the door.*

LELAND. You want love on your own terms, don't you Charlie—*(he stops—his back turned to* KANE*)* Love is something to be played your way, according to your own rules. And if anything goes wrong and you're hurt—then the game stops, and you've got to be soothed and nursed, no matter what else is happening— and no matter who else is hurt!

KANE. It's a little simpler than that, Brad. A society girl can't stand the gaff that's all. Other things are important to her—social position, what they're saying on the front porches at Southampton, is it going to be embarrassing to meet somebody or other at dinner—

LELAND *has turned, taking his eye again. Now* KANE *stops and smiles.*

KANE. She can leave me. As a matter of fact, I've already left her. Don't worry, Brad—I'll live.

LELAND. I know you will.

KANE *(with all his charm)*. Hey, Brad! I've been analyzed an awful lot tonight—let's have another brandy.

LELAND *shakes his head.* KANE *lifts his glass.*

KANE *(cont'd)*. To love on *my* terms. Those are the only terms anybody knows . . . his own.

*Dissolve*

*Ext. Enquirer Building—Night—1902*

KANE, LELAND *and a couple of policemen make their way out of the front toward a hansom cab.*

A VOICE FROM THE CROWD. You moiderer!

*A rock is thrown. It hits* LELAND *on the face. A little blood flows.* KANE *doesn't see it at first. Then when he's in the hansom cab, he turns and notices it.*

KANE. Are you hurt?

LELAND *has a handkerchief to his face.*

LELAND. No.—I wish you'd go home to Emily. She'll be pretty upset by all this—She still loves you—

*The crowd, pushed by the cops, retreats in the background, but still hard by.*

KANE. —You still want to be transferred to the other paper?

LELAND. Yes.

KANE *(leaning out of the hansom cab).* Well, you've been getting a pretty low salary here in New York. It seems to me that the new dramatic critic of our Chicago paper should get what he's worth. *(almost as a question)*

LELAND *(with handkerchief still to his face).* I couldn't possiblely live on as little as that, Charlie. We'll let the salary stay where it is.

*The hansom cab starts up. We hold on* LELAND'S *face as we*

*Dissolve out*

*Dissolve in*

*Int.* KANE'S *New York Home—* KANE'S *Bedroom—Early Morning—1902*

EMILY *is in bed, a damp cloth over her temples.* KANE *is standing at the foot of the bed. The baby's bed is in a corner of the room. The baby's nurse is standing near the crib, a nurse for* EMILY *is near her.* KANE *is looking fixedly at* EMILY, *who is staring tiredly at the ceiling.*

KANE *(to the nurse).* Excuse us a moment, please.

*The nurse looks at* EMILY.

KANE *(cont'd) (peremptorily).* I said, excuse us a moment.

*The nurse, unwilling, leaves.*

KANE *(cont'd).* I've been talking to Leland.—Emily—You can't leave me now—not now—

*Silence.*

KANE *(cont'd).* It isn't what it would do to my changes in politics, Emily—That isn't it—They were talking of running me for governor, but now, of course, we'll have to wait—It isn't that, Emily—It's just—the president is your uncle and they're saying I killed him.

*Still silence.*

KANE *(cont'd).* That story about the murderer having a copy of the "Enquirer" in his pocket—the "Chronicle" made that up out of whole cloth—Emily, please—He's going to be all right, you know, he's going to recover—*(bitterly)* If it will make you any happier, we had nine pages of advertising cancelled in the first mail this morning. Bernstein is afraid to open any more letters. He—

*He stops. He sees that he's getting no place with Emily.*

KANE *(cont'd) (exasperated).* What do you expect me to do? What in the world—

EMILY *(weakly).* Charles.

*He waits for her to continue.*

EMILY *(cont'd).* Do you really think—*(she can't continue)* Those threatening letters, can they really—

*She sits up and looks at the crib. She continues to look at the crib, with almost unseeing eyes.*

KANE *(uncomfortably).* They won't do anything to Junior, darling. *(contemptuously)* Anonymous letter writers—I've got guards in front of the house, and I'm going to arrange—

EMILY *(turning her face toward him).* Please don't talk any more, Charles.

KANE *is about to say something, but bites his lips instead.* EMILY *keeps staring at him.*

EMILY *(cont'd).* Have they heard from father yet? Has he seen—

KANE. I've tried to tell you, Emily. The President's going to be all right. He had a comfortable night. There's no danger of any kind.

EMILY *nods several times. There is an uncomfortable silence. Suddenly there is a cry from the crib.* EMILY *leaps from the bed and rushes to him. She bends over the crib.*

EMILY *(murmuring).* Here I am, darling . . . Darling! . . . Darling, it's all right . . . Mother's here.

KANE. Emily—you mustn't leave me now—you can't do that to me.

EMILY. They won't hurt you, darling. Mother's with you! Mother's looking after you!

KANE, *unwanted, ignored, looks on. Tightening his lips, he walks out.*

*Dissolve out*

*Dissolve in*

*Int.* KANE'S *Office—Night*

*By the desk light,* KANE *is seen working with his usual intensity,* REILLY *standing beside him at the desk.*

KANE. —We'll withdraw support completely. Anything else?

REILLY. Mr. Leland sent back that check.

KANE. What check?

REILLY. You made it out to him last week after he left for Chicago.

KANE. Oh, yes, the bonus.

REILLY. It was for twenty-five thousand dollars.

KANE *is perplexed and worried but we can see in a moment his mind will be on something else.*

REILLY *(cont'd).* He sent it back torn up—all torn up into little bits, and he enclosed something else—I can't make it out.

KANE *doesn't answer.* REILLY *goes on. He has brought out a piece of paper and is reading it.*

REILLY *(cont'd).* It says here, "A Declaration of Principles"—*(he still reads)*—"I will provide the people of this city with a daily paper that will tell all the news honestly"—

KANE *has looked up sharply.* REILLY, *sensing his look, stops reading and meets his eye. Slowly* KANE *reaches out his hand.* REILLY *hands him the piece of paper. Without reading it,* KANE *tears it up, throws it into the wastebasket at his side.*

*Dissolve*

*Int. Madison Square Garden— Night—1910*

*The evening of the final great rally. These shots remind us of and are identical with and supplementary to the "News Digest" scenes earlier. The vast auditorium with a huge picture of* KANE, *cheering crowds, etc.* EMILY *and* JUNIOR *are to be seen in the front of a box.* EMILY *is tired and wears a forced smile on her face.* JUNIOR, *now aged nine and a half, is eager, bright-eyed and excited.* KANE *is just finishing his speech.*

KANE. It is no secret that I entered upon this campaign with no thought that I could be elected Governor of this State! It is now no secret that every straw vote, every independent poll, shows that I will be elected. And I repeat to you—my first official act as Governor will be to appoint a special District Attorney to arrange for the indictment, prosecution and convicition of Boss Edward G. Rogers!

*Terrific screaming and cheering from the audience.*

*Dissolve out*

*Int. Madison Square Garden— Night—1910*

*The Speaker's Platform. Numerous officials and civic leaders are crowding around* KANE. *Cameramen take flash photographs with old-fashioned flash powder.*

FIRST CIVIC LEADER. Great speech, Mr. Kane.

SECOND LEADER (*pompous*). One of the most notable public utterances ever made by a candidate in this State—

KANE. Thank you, gentlemen. Thank you.

*He looks up and notices that the box in which* EMILY *and the boy were sitting is now empty. He starts toward the rear of the platform, through the press of people.* REILLY *approaches him.*

REILLY. A wonderful speech, Mr. Kane.

KANE *pats him on the shoulder as he walks along.*

REILLY (*cont'd*). I just got word from Buffalo, Mr. Kane. They're going to throw you the organization vote—and take a chance maybe you'll give them a break—

*This is said almost inquiringly, as if he were hoping that* KANE *would give him some assurance that McDonald is not making a mistake. There is no answer from* KANE.

REILLY (*cont'd*). On an independent ticket there's never been anything like it! If the election were held today, you'd be elected by a hundred thousand votes—and every day between now and November 7th is just going to add to your majority.

KANE *is very pleased. He continues with* REILLY *slowly through the crowd—a band playing off.* BERNSTEIN *joins him.*

KANE. It does seem too good to be true, doesn't it, Mr. Bernstein?

REILLY. Rogers isn't even pretending. He isn't just scared any more. He's sick. Frank Norris told me last night he hasn't known Rogers to be that worried in twenty-five years.

KANE. I think it's beginning to dawn on Mr. Rogers that I mean what I say. With Mr. Rogers out of the way, Reilly, I think we may really begin to hope for a good government in this state. (*stopping*) Well, Mr. Bernstein?

BERNSTEIN (*clearly not meaning it*). It's wonderful, Mr. Kane. Wonderful. Wonderful.

KANE. You don't really think so?

BERNSTEIN. I do. I do. I mean, since you're running for Governor— and you want to be elected—I think it's wonderful you're going to be elected. Only—(*interrupts himself*) —Can I say something?

KANE. Please, Mr. Bernstein.

BERNSTEIN. Well, the way I look at it—(*comes out with it*)—You want to know what I *really* think would be wonderful?

KANE *indicates he is to proceed.*

BERNSTEIN *(cont'd)*. Well, you're running for Governor and going to be elected—my idea is how wonderful it would be if you don't run at all and don't get elected.

*Dissolve*

*Ext. One of the Exits—Madison Square Garden—Night—1910*

EMILY *and* JUNIOR *are standing, waiting for* KANE.

JUNIOR. Is Pop Governor yet, Mom?

*Just then,* KANE *appears, with* REILLY *and several other men.* KANE *rushes toward* EMILY *and* JUNIOR, *as the men politely greet* EMILY.

KANE. Hello, Butch! Did you like your old man's speech?

JUNIOR. Hello, Pop! I was in a box. I could hear every word.

KANE. I saw you! *(he has his arm around* JUNIOR'S *shoulder)* Good night, gentlemen.

*There are good nights.* KANE'S *car is at the curb and he starts to walk toward it with* JUNIOR *and* EMILY.

EMILY. I'm sending Junior home in the car, Charles—with Oliver—

KANE. But I'd arranged to go home with you myself.

EMILY. There's a call I want you to make with me, Charles.

KANE. It can wait.

EMILY. No, it can't. *(she bends down and kisses* JUNIOR) Good night, darling.

JUNIOR. Good night, Mom.

*The driver is holding the rear door open as* EMILY *guides* JUNIOR *in.*

KANE *(as car starts to drive off).*

What's this all about, Emily? I've had a very tiring day and—

EMILY. It may not be about anything at all.

*A cab has pulled up.*

THE DRIVER. Cab?

EMILY *nods to him.*

EMILY. I intend to find out.

KANE. I insist on being told exactly what you have in mind.

EMILY. I'm going to—*(she looks at a slip of paper in her hand)*—185 West 74th Street.

KANE'S *reaction indicates that the address definitely means something to him.*

EMILY *(cont'd)*. If you wish, you can come with me . . .

KANE *nods.*

KANE. I'll go with you.

*He opens the door and she enters the cab. He follows her.*

*Dissolve*

*Int. Cab—Night—1910*

KANE *and* EMILY. *He looks at her, in search of some kind of enlightenment. Her face is set and impassive.*

*Dissolve*

*Ext. and Int. Apartment House Hallway—Night—1910*

KANE *and* EMILY, *in front of an apartment door.* EMILY *is pressing the bell.*

KANE. I had no idea you had this flair for melodrama, Emily.

EMILY *does not answer. The door is opened by a maid, who recognizes* KANE.

THE MAID. Come in, Mr. Kane, come in.

*They enter,* EMILY *first.*

Int. SUSAN'S *Apartment—Night—1910*

*There is first a tiny reception room, through which an open door shows the living room.* KANE *and* EMILY *enter from the hallway and cross to living room. As they enter,* SUSAN *rises from a chair. The other person in the room—a big, heavy-set man, a little past middle age—stays where he is, leaning back in his chair, regarding* KANE *intently.*

SUSAN. It wasn't my fault, Charlie. He made me send your wife a note. He said I'd—oh, he's been saying the most terrible things, I didn't know what to do . . . I—(*she catches sight of* EMILY)

ROGERS. Good evening, Mr. Kane. (*he rises*) I don't suppose anybody would introduce us. Mrs. Kane, I am Edward Rogers.

EMILY. How do you do? (*pauses*) I came here—and I made Mr. Kane come with me . . . (*she consults the note in her hand without reading it again*) because I received this note—

ROGERS. I made Miss—Miss Alexander send you the note. She was a little unwilling at first—(*he smiles grimly*) but she did it.

SUSAN. I can't tell you the things he said, Charlie. You haven't got any idea—

KANE (*turning on* ROGERS). Rogers, I don't think I *will* postpone doing something about you until I'm elected. (*he starts toward him*) To start with, I think I'll break your neck.

ROGERS (*not giving way an inch*). Maybe you can do it and maybe you can't, Mr. Kane.

EMILY. Charles! (*he stops to look at her*) Your—your breaking this man's neck—(*she is clearly disgusted*) would scarcely explain this note—

glancing at the note) Serious consequences for Mr. Kane—(*slowly*) for myself, and for my son. What does this note mean, Miss—

SUSAN (*stiffly*). I'm Susan Alexander. (*pauses*) I know what you think, Mrs. Kane, but—

EMILY (*ignoring this*). What does this note mean, Miss Alexander?

ROGERS. She doesn't know, Mrs. Kane. She just sent it—because I made her see it wouldn't be smart for her not to send it.

KANE. In case you don't know, Emily, this—this gentleman—(*he puts a world of scorn into the word*) is—

ROGERS. I'm not a gentleman, Mrs. Kane, and your husband is just trying to be funny calling me one. I don't even know what a gentleman is. (*tensely, with all the hatred and venom in the world*) You see, my idea of a gentleman, Mrs. Kane—well, if I owned a newspaper and if I didn't like the way somebody else was doing things—some politician, say—I'd fight them with everything I had. Only I wouldn't show him in a convict suit, with stripes—so his children could see the picture in the paper. Or his mother. (*he has to control himself from hurling himself on* KANE) It's pretty clear—I'm not a gentleman.

EMILY. Oh!!

KANE. You're a cheap, crooked grafter—and your concern for your children and your mother—

ROGERS. Anything you say, Mr. Kane. Only we're talking now about what *you* are. That's what that note is about, Mrs. Kane. Now I'm going to lay all my cards on the table. I'm fighting for my life. Not just my political life. My life. If your husband is elected Governor—

KANE. I'm *going* to be elected Governor. And the first thing I'm going to do—

EMILY. Let him finish, Charles.

ROGERS. I'm protecting myself every way I know how, Mrs. Kane. This last week, I finally found out how I can stop your husband from being elected. If the people of this State learn what I found out this week, he wouldn't have a chance to—he couldn't be elected Dog Catcher. Well, what I'm interested in is seeing that he's not elected. I don't care whether they know what I know about him. Let him keep right on being the Great, Noble, Moral—*(he stresses the word)* Champeen of the people. Just as long as—

EMILY. I think I understand, Mr. Rogers, but I wonder if—*(she leaves her sentence unfinished)*

KANE. You can't blackmail me, Rogers. You can't—

SUSAN *(excitedly)*. Charlie, he said, unless you withdrew your name—

ROGERS. That's the chance I'm willing to give you, Mr. Kane. More of a chance than you'd give me. Unless you make up your mind by tomorrow that you're so sick that you've got to go away for a year or two—Monday morning every paper in this State will carry the story I'm going to give them.

KANE *starts to stare at him intently.*

EMILY. What story, Mr. Rogers?

ROGERS. The story about him and Miss Alexander, Mrs. Kane.

EMILY *looks at* KANE.

SUSAN. There *is* no story. It's all lies. Mr. Kane is just—

ROGERS *(to* SUSAN*)*. Shut up! *(to* KANE*)* I've had a dozen men doing nothing but run this thing down—we've got evidence enough to—well, the evidence would stand up in any court of law. You want me to give you the evidence, Mr. Kane?

KANE. You do anything you want to

do. The people of this State can decide which one of us to trust. If you want to know, they've already decided. The election Tuesday'll be only—

ROGERS. Mrs. Kane, I'm not asking *you* to believe me. I'd like to show you—

EMILY. You don't have to show me anything, Mr. Rogers. I believe you.

ROGERS. I'd rather Mr. Kane withdrew without having to get the story published. Not that I care about him. But I'd be better off that way—*(he pauses)*—and so would you, Mrs. Kane.

SUSAN. What about me? *(to* KANE*)* He said my name'd be dragged through the mud. He said everywhere I'd go from now on—

EMILY. There seems to me to be only one decision you can make, Charles. I'd say that it has been made for you. *(pauses)* I suppose the details can be arranged tomorrow, Mr. Rogers. About the statements by the doctors—

KANE. Have you gone completely mad, Emily?

EMILY *looks at him.*

KANE *(cont'd)*. You don't think I'm going to let this blackmailer intimidate me, do you?

EMILY. I don't see what else you can do, Charles. If he's right—and the papers publish this story he has—

KANE. Oh, they'll publish it all right. But that's not going to stop me—

EMILY. Charles, this—this story—doesn't concern only you. *I'll* be in it too, won't I? *(quickly)* And Junior?

KANE *(squirming a bit)*. I suppose so, but—I'm not afraid of the story. You can't tell me that the voters of this State—

EMILY. I'm not interested in the

voters of this State right now. I am interested in—well, Junior, for one thing.

SUSAN. Charlie! If they publish this story—

EMILY. They won't. Good night, Mr. Rogers. *(she starts out)* There's nothing more to be said, Charles.

KANE. Oh yes, there is.

EMILY. I don't think so. Are you coming, Charles?

KANE. No.

*She looks at him. He starts to work himself into a rage.*

KANE *(cont'd)*. There's only one person in the world to decide what I'm going to do—and that's me. And if you think—if any of you think—

EMILY. You decided what you were going to do, Charles—some time ago. *(she looks at* SUSAN*)* You can't always have it your own way, regardless of anything else that may have happened. *(she sighs)* Come on, Charles.

KANE. Go on! Get out! I can fight this thing all alone!

ROGERS. You're making a bigger fool of yourself than I thought you would, Mr. Kane. You're licked. Why don't you—

KANE *(turning on him)*. Get out! I've got nothing to talk to you about. If you want to see me, have the Warden write me a letter.

ROGERS. I see! *(he starts toward the door)*

SUSAN *(starting to cry)*. Charlie, you're just excited. You don't realize—

KANE. I know exactly what I'm doing. *(he is screaming)* Get out!

EMILY *(quietly)*. Charles, if you don't listen to reason, it may be too late—

KANE. Too late for what? Too late for you and this—*(he can't find the adjective)* this public thief to take the love of the people of this State away from me? Well, you won't do it, I tell you. You won't do it!

SUSAN. Charlie, there are other things to think of. *(a sly look comes into her eyes)* Your son—you don't want him to read in the papers—

EMILY. It *is* too late now, Charles.

KANE *(rushes to the door and opens it)*. Get out, both of you!

SUSAN *(rushes to him)*. Charlie, please don't—

KANE. What are you waiting here for? Why don't you go?

EMILY. Good night, Charles.

*She walks out.* ROGERS *stops as he gets directly in front of* KANE.

ROGERS. You're the greatest fool I've ever known, Kane. If it was anybody else, I'd say what's going to happen to you would be a lesson to you. Only you're going to need more than one lesson. And you're going to get more than one lesson. *(he walks past* KANE*)*

KANE. Don't you worry about me. I'm Charles Foster Kane. I'm no cheap, crooked politician, trying to save himself from the consequences of his crimes—

*Int. Apt. House Hallway—Night— 1910*

*Camera angling toward* KANE *from other end of the hall.* ROGERS *and* EMILY *are already down the hall, moving toward f.g.* KANE *in apartment doorway b.g.*

KANE *(screams louder)*. I'm going to send you to Sing Sing, Rogers. Sing Sing!

KANE *is trembling with rage as he shakes his fist at* ROGERS'S *back.* SUSAN, *quieter now, has snuggled into the hollow of his shoulder as they stand in the doorway.*

*Dissolve*

*The "Chronicle" front page with photograph (as in the "News Digest") revealing* KANE's *relations with* SU-SAN.

*Dissolve out*

*Dissolve in*

*Front page of "Chronicle"—Head-line which reads:*

ROGERS ELECTED

*Dissolve*

*Front page of "Enquirer"—Head-line which reads:*

FRAUD AT POLLS

*Dissolve*

*Int. Living Room—Night—1910*

EMILY *is opening the door for* LE-LAND.

EMILY. Hello, Brad—
LELAND. Emily—

*He pauses.* LELAND *comes in.* EMI-LY *closes the door.*

EMILY. I'm sorry I sent for you, Brad—I didn't—
LELAND. Chicago is pretty close to New York nowadays—only twenty hours—

*She doesn't have anything to say.*

LELAND *(cont'd).* I'm glad to see you.

*She smiles at him and we know that there isn't anybody else in the world for her to smile at. She's too grateful to talk.*

EMILY. Are all the returns in?

LELAND *puts his hand un-consciously on his coat by the news-paper.*

EMILY *(cont'd).* Let me see it.

LELAND *takes the newspaper out of his pocket and hands it to her. She*

takes it. We see the headline, not an insert, but it registers. It reads: "Fraud at Polls." EMILY is looking at the paper with unseeing eyes, and a little smile.

LELAND *(after a pause).* Almost two to one—
EMILY. I'm surprised he got the votes he did.
LELAND. Emily!
EMILY. Why should anyone vote for him? He's made it quite clear to the people what he thinks of them. Chil-dren—to be told one thing one day, something else the next, as the whim seizes him. And they're supposed to be grateful and love and adore him—because he sees to it that they get cheap ice and only pay a nickel in the street cars.
LELAND. Emily, you're being—a little unfair—You know what I think of Charles's behavior—about your personal lives—
EMILY. There aren't any personal lives for people like us. He made that very clear to me nine years ago.—If I'd thought of my life with Charles as a personal life, I'd have left him then—
LELAND. I know that, Emily—
EMILY *(on top of* LELAND*).* Maybe I should have—the first time he showed me what a mad dog he really was.
LELAND *(on the cue "dog").* Emily, you—
EMILY. Brad, I'm—I'm not an old woman yet—
LELAND. It's—all over—

*He stops himself.*

EMILY *(after a pause).* I know it is, Brad—
LELAND. He's paying for it, Emily. These returns tonight—he's finished. Politically—*(he thinks)*—socially—everywhere, I guess. I don't know about the papers, but—

EMILY. If you're asking me to sympathize with him, Brad, you're wasting your time. *(pauses)* There's only one person I'm sorry for, as a matter of fact. That—that shabby little girl. I'm really sorry for her, Brad.

*Dissolve*

*Front page Chicago "Enquirer," with photograph proclaiming that* SUSAN ALEXANDER *opens at new Chicago Opera House in "Thais." (As in "News Digest.")*

*On sound track during above we hear the big expectant murmur of an opening night audience and the noodling of the orchestra.*

*Dissolve*

*Int. Chicago Opera House— Night—Set for "Thais"—1914*

*The camera is just inside the curtain, angling upstage. We see the set for "Thais"—the principals in place—stage managers—stage hands, etc., and in the center of all this, in an elaborate costume, looking very small and very lost, is* SUSAN. *She is almost hysterical with fright. Maids, singing teacher, and the rest are in attendance. Her throat is sprayed. Applause is heard at the opening of the shot, and now the orchestra starts thunderously. The curtain starts to rise—the camera with it—the blinding glare of the foots moves up* SUSAN'S *body and hits her face. She squints and starts to sing. Camera continues on up with the curtain, up past* SUSAN *up the full height of the proscenium arch and then on up into the gridiron into a world of ropes, brick walls and hanging canvas—*SUSAN'S *voice still heard—but faintly. The camera stops at the top of the gridiron as the curtain stops. Two typical stage hands fill the frame. They are looking down on the stage below. Some of the re-flected light gleams on their faces. They look at each other. One of them puts his hand to his nose.*

*Dissolve out*

*Dissolve in*

*Int.* LELAND'S *Office—Chicago Enquirer—Night—1914*

LELAND, *as in the same scene in the* BERNSTEIN *sequence, is sprawled across his typewriter, his head on the keys. The paper is gone from the roller.* LELAND *stirs and looks up drunkenly, his eyes encountering* BERNSTEIN, *who stands beside him (also as in the previous scene).*

BERNSTEIN. Hello, Mr. Leland.
LELAND. Hello, Bernstein.

LELAND *makes a terrific effort to pull himself together. He straightens and reaches for the keys—then sees the paper is gone from the machine.*

LELAND *(cont'd)*. Where is it— where's my notice—I've got to finish it!
BERNSTEIN *(quietly)*. Mr. Kane is finishing it.
LELAND. Kane?—Charlie—? *(painfully he rises to his feet)* Where is he?

*During all this, the sound of a typewriter has been heard off—a busy typewriter.* LELAND'S *eyes follow the sound. Slowly he registers* KANE *out in the City Room beyond. This is almost the same shot as in the previous* BERNSTEIN *story.*

*Int. City Room—Chicago Enquirer—Night—1914*

KANE, *in white tie and shirt sleeves, is typing away at a machine, his fingers working briskly and efficiently, his face, seen by the desk light before him, set in a strange half smile.*

LELAND *stands in the door of his office, staring across at him.*

LELAND. I suppose he's fixing it up—I know I'd never get that through.

BERNSTEIN *(moving to his side).* Mr. Kane is finishing your piece the way you started it.

LELAND *turns incredulously to* BERNSTEIN.

BERNSTEIN *(cont'd).* He's writing a roast like you wanted it to be—*(then suddenly—with a kind of quiet passion, rather than triumph)*—I guess that'll show you.

LELAND *picks his way across the City Room to* KANE'S *side.* KANE *goes on typing, without looking up. After a pause,* KANE *speaks.*

KANE. Hello, Brad.

LELAND. Hello, Charlie—*(another pause)* I didn't know we were speaking.

KANE *stops typing, but doesn't turn.*

KANE. Sure, we're speaking, Brad—You're fired.

*He starts typing again, the expression on his face doesn't change.*

*Dissolve out*

*Dissolve in*

*Ext. Hospital Roof—Day—1940*

THOMPSON *and* LELAND *on the roof, which is now deserted. It is getting late. The sun has just about gone down.*

LELAND. Well, that's about all there is—and I'm getting chills. Hey, nurse! *(pause)* Five years ago he wrote from that place of his down South—*(as if trying to think)*—you know. Shangri-la? El Dorado? *(pauses)* Sloppy Joe's? What's the name of that place? You know . . . All right. Xanadu. I knew what it was all the time. You caught on, didn't you?

THOMPSON. Yes.

LELAND. I guess maybe I'm not as hard to see through as I think. Anyway, I never even answered his letter. Maybe I should have. I guess he was pretty lonely down there those last years. He hadn't finished it when she left him—he never finished it—he never finished anything. Of course, he built it for her—

THOMPSON. That must have been love.

LELAND. I don't know. He was disappointed in the world. So he built one of his own—An absolute monarchy—It was something bigger than an opera house anyway—*(calls)* Nurse! *(lowers his voice)* Say, I'll tell you one thing you can do for me, young fellow.

THOMPSON. Sure.

LELAND. On your way out, stop at a cigar store, will you, and send me up a couple of cigars?

THOMPSON. Sure, Mr. Leland. I'll be glad to.

LELAND. Hey, Nurse!

*A* NURSE *appears.*

NURSE. Yes, Mr. Leland.

LELAND. I'm ready to go in now. You know when I was a young man, there was an impression around that nurses were pretty. It was no truer then than it is now.

NURSE. Here let me take your arm, Mr. Leland.

LELAND *(testily).* All right, all right. *(he has begun to move forward on the* NURSE'S *arm; turning to* THOMPSON) You won't forget, will you, about the cigars? And tell them to wrap them up to look like toothpaste, or something, or they'll stop them at the desk. That young doctor I was telling you about, he's got an idea he wants to keep me alive.

*Dissolve*

*Ext. "El Rancho" Cabaret in Atlantic City—Early Dawn—1940*

*Neon sign on the roof—*
"EL RANCHO"
FLOOR SHOW
SUSAN ALEXANDER KANE
TWICE NIGHTLY

*glows on the dark screen as in the previous sequence early in the script. Behind the lights and through them we see a nasty early morning. Camera as before, moves through the lights of the sign and down on the skylight, through which is seen* SUSAN *at her regular table,* THOMPSON *seated across from her.*

*Very faintly during this, idle piano music playing.*

*Dissolve*

*Int. "El Rancho" Cabaret—Early Dawn—1940*

SUSAN *and* THOMPSON *are facing each other. The place is almost deserted.* SUSAN *is sober. On the other side of the room somebody is playing a piano.*

SUSAN. How do you want to handle the whole thing—ask questions?

THOMPSON. I'd rather you just talked. Anything that comes into your mind—about yourself and Mr. Kane.

SUSAN. You wouldn't want to hear a lot of what comes into my mind about myself and Mr. Charlie Kane.

SUSAN *is thinking.*

THOMPSON. How did you meet him?

SUSAN. I had a toothache.

THOMPSON *looks at her.*

SUSAN *(cont'd).* That was thirty years ago—and I still remember that toothache. Boy! That toothache was just driving me crazy. . . .

*Dissolve out*

*Dissolve in*

*Ext. Corner Drug Store and Street on the West Side of New York—Night—1909*

SUSAN, *aged twenty, neatly but cheaply dressed in the style of the period, is leaving the drug store. (It's about 8 o'clock at night.) With a large, man-sized handkerchief pressed to her cheek, she is in considerable pain. The street is wet—after a recent rain.*

*She walks a few steps towards the middle of the block, and can stand it no longer. She stops, opens a bottle of Oil of Cloves that she has in her hand, applies some to her finger, and rubs her gums.*

*She walks on, the pain only a bit better. Four or five houses farther along, she comes to what is clearly her own doorway—a shabby, old four-story apartment house. She turns toward the doorway, which is up a tiny stoop, about three steps.*

*As she does so,* KANE, *coming from the opposite direction, almost bumps into her and turns to his left to avoid her. His shoulder bumps hers and she turns. As she does so,* KANE, *forced to change his course, steps on the loose end of a plank which covers a puddle in the bad sidewalk. The plank rises up and cracks him on the knee, also covering him with mud.*

KANE *(hopping up and down on one foot, and rubbing his knee).* Ow!

SUSAN, *taking her handerchief from her jaw, roars with laughter.*

KANE *(cont'd).* It's not funny.

*He bites his lip and rubs his knee again.* SUSAN *tries to control her laughter, but not very successfully.* KANE *glares at her.*

SUSAN. I'm sorry, mister—but you *do* look awful funny.

*Suddenly the pain returns and she claps her hand to her jaw.*

SUSAN. Ow!
KANE. What's the matter with you?
SUSAN. Toothache.
KANE. Hmm!

*He has been rubbing his clothes with his handkerchief.*

SUSAN. You've got some on your face.
KANE. If these sidewalks were kept in condition—instead of the money going to some cheap grafter—

SUSAN *starts to laugh again.*

KANE *(cont'd).* What's funny now?
SUSAN. You are. You look like you've been making mud pies.

*In the middle of her smile, the pain returns.*

SUSAN *(cont'd).* Oh!
KANE. You're no Venus de Milo.
SUSAN *(points to the down-stair window).* If you want to come in and wash your face—I can get you some hot water to get that dirt off your trousers—
KANE. Thanks.

SUSAN *starts, with* KANE *following her.*

*Dissolve*

Int. SUSAN's *Room—Night—1909*

*It's in moderate disorder. The Mansbach gas lights are on. It's not really a classy room, but it's exactly what you're entitled to in 1910, for $5.00 a week including breakfast.*

*There is a bed, a couple of chairs, a chiffonier, and a few personal belongings on the chiffonier. These include a photograph of a gent and lady, obviously* SUSAN's *parents, and a few objets d'art. One, "At the Japanese Rolling Ball Game at Coney Island," and—perhaps this is part of the Japanese loot—the glass globe with the snow scene* KANE *was holding in his hand in the first sequence.*

SUSAN *comes into the room, carrying a basin, with towels over her arm.* KANE *is waiting for her. She doesn't close the door.*

SUSAN *(by way of explanation).* My landlady prefers me to keep this door open when I have a gentleman caller. *(starts to put the basin down)* She's a very decent woman. *(making a face)* Ow!

KANE *rushes to take the basin from her, putting it on the chiffonier. To do this, he has to shove the photograph to one side with the basin.* SUSAN *grabs the photograph as it is about to fall over.*

SUSAN *(cont'd).* Hey, you should be more careful. That's my Ma and Pa.
KANE. I'm sorry. They live here too?
SUSAN. No. They've passed on.

*Again she puts her hand to her jaw.*

KANE. Where's the soap?
SUSAN. In the water.

KANE *fishes the soap out of the water. It is slippery, however, and slips out of his hand, hitting him in the chest before it falls to the floor.* SUSAN *laughs as he bends over.*

KANE *(starting to wash his hands).* You're very easily amused.
SUSAN. I always like to see the fun-

ny side of things. No sense crying when you don't have to. And you're so funny. Looking at you I forget all about my toothache.

*Her face distorts in pain again.*

SUSAN (cont'd). Oh!
KANE. I can't stay here all night chasing your pain away.
SUSAN (laughs). I know. . . . But you *do* look so silly.

KANE, *with soaped hands, has rubbed his face and now cannot open his eyes, for fear of getting soap in them.*

KANE. Where's the towel?
SUSAN. On the chiffonier. Here.
KANE (rubs his face dry). Thanks.
SUSAN (on her way to closet). I've got a brush in the closet. As soon as the mud on your trousers is all dry— you just brush it off.
KANE. I'll get these streets fixed, if it's the last thing I do.

SUSAN *comes out of the closet. She holds out the brush with her left hand, her right hand to her jaw in real distress.*

KANE (cont'd) (takes the brush). You are in pain, aren't you, you poor kid?

SUSAN *can't stand it any more and sits down in a chair, bent over, whimpering a bit.*

KANE (cont'd) (brushing himself). I wish there was something I could—

*He stops and thinks.* SUSAN, *her face averted, is still trying hard not to cry.*

KANE (cont'd). I've got an idea, young lady. (there is no response) Turn around and look at me. (there is still no response) I said, turn around and look at me, young lady.

*Slowly,* SUSAN *turns.*

KANE (cont'd). Did you ever see anybody wiggle both his ears at the same time?

*It takes a second for* SUSAN *to adapt herself to this.*

KANE (cont'd). Watch closely! (he wiggles his ears) It took me two solid years at the finest boys' schools in the world—to learn that trick. The fellow who taught me is President of Venezuela now.

*He's still wiggling his ears as* SUSAN *starts to smile.*

KANE (cont'd). That's it! Smile!

SUSAN *smiles, very broadly.*

*Dissolve*

*Int.* SUSAN's *Room—Night—1909*

*Closeup of a duck, camera pulls back showing it to be a shadowgraph on the wall, made by* KANE, *who is now in his shirt sleeves. (It is about an hour later than preceding sequence.)*

SUSAN (hesitatingly). A chicken?
KANE. No. But you're close.
SUSAN. A rooster?
KANE. You're getting farther away all the time. It's a duck.
SUSAN. Excuse me, Mr. Kane. I know this takes a lot of nerve—but— who are you? I mean—I'm pretty ignorant, I guess you caught on to that—
KANE (looks squarely at her). You really don't know who I am?
SUSAN. No. That is, I bet it turns out I've heard your name a million times, only you know how it is—
KANE. But you like me, don't you? Even though you don't know who I am?
SUSAN. You've been wonderful! I can't tell you how glad I am you're here, I don't know many people and—(she stops)

KANE. And I know too many people. Obviously, we're both lonely. (he smiles) Would you like to know where I was going tonight—when you ran into me and ruined my Sunday clothes?

SUSAN. I didn't run into you and I bet they're not your Sunday clothes. You've probably got a lot of clothes.

KANE (as if defending himself from a terrific onslaught). I was only joking! (pauses) This evening I was on my way to the Western Manhattan Warehouses—in search of my youth.

SUSAN is bewildered.

KANE (cont'd). You see, my mother died too—a long time ago. Her things were put into storage out West because I had no place to put them then. I still haven't. But now I've sent for them just the same. And tonight I'd planned to make a sort of sentimental journey—(slowly)—to the scenes of my youth—my childhood, I suppose—to look again at—(he changes mood slightly)—and now—

KANE doesn't finish. He looks at SUSAN. Silence.

KANE. Who am I? Well, let's see. Charles Foster Kane was born in New Salem, Colorado in eighteen six—(he stops on the word "sixty"—obviously a little embarrassed) I run a couple of newspapers. How about you?

SUSAN. Oh, me—

KANE. How old did you say you were.

SUSAN (very bright). I didn't say.

KANE. I didn't think you did. If you had, I wouldn't have asked you again, because I'd have remembered. How old?

SUSAN. Pretty old. I'll be twenty-two in August.

KANE (looks at her silently for a moment). That's a ripe old age.— What do you do?

SUSAN. I work at Seligman's.

KANE. Is that what you want to do?

SUSAN. I wanted to be a singer. (she thinks for a moment) I mean, I didn't. Mother did for me.

KANE (sympathetically). What happened to the singing? You're not in a show, are you?

SUSAN. Oh, no! Nothing like that. Mother always thought—she used to talk about Grand Opera for me. Imagine! An American girl, for one thing—and then my voice isn't really that kind anyway, it's just that Mother—you know what mothers are like.

A sudden look comes over KANE's face.

KANE. Yes—

SUSAN. As a matter of fact, I do sing a little.

KANE (points to the piano). Would you sing for me?

SUSAN (bashful). Oh, you wouldn't want to hear me sing.

KANE. Yes, I would. That's why I asked.

SUSAN. Well, I—

KANE. Don't tell me your toothache is bothering you again?

SUSAN. Oh, no, that's all gone.

KANE. Then you have no alibi at all. Please sing.

SUSAN, with a tiny ladylike hesitancy, goes to the piano and sings a polite song. Sweetly, nicely, she sings with a small, untrained voice. KANE listens. He is relaxed, at ease with the world.

Dissolve

Int. "El Rancho" Cabaret—Early Dawn—1940

SUSAN tosses down a drink, then goes on with her story.

SUSAN. I did a lot of singing after

that. I sang for Charlie—I sang for teachers at a hundred bucks an hour—the teachers got that, I didn't—

THOMPSON. What did you get?

SUSAN (*glares at him balefully*). What do you mean?

THOMPSON *doesn't answer.*

SUSAN (*cont'd*). I didn't get a thing. Just the music lessons. That's all there was to it.

THOMPSON. He married you, didn't he?

SUSAN. He was in love with me. But he never told me so until after it all came out in the papers about us—and he lost the election and that Norton woman divorced him.

THOMPSON. What about that apartment?

SUSAN. He wanted me to be comfortable—Oh, why should I bother. You don't believe me, but it's true. It just happens to be true. He was really interested in my voice. (*sharply*) What are you smiling for? What do you think he built that Opera House for? I didn't want it. I didn't want to sing. It was his idea—everything was his idea—except my leaving him.

*Dissolve*

*Int. Living Room of* KANE'S *House in New York—Day—1913*

SUSAN *is singing.* MATISTI, *her voice teacher, is playing the piano.* KANE *is seated nearby.* MATISTI *stops.*

MATISTI. Impossible! Impossible!

KANE. Your job isn't to give Mrs. Kane your opinion of her talents. You're supposed to train her voice. Nothing more.

MATISTI (*sweating*). But, it is impossible. I will be the laughingstock of the musical world! People will say—

KANE. If you're interested in what people will say, Signor Matisti, I may be able to enlighten you a bit. The newspapers, for instance. I'm an authority on what the papers will say, Signor Matisti, because I own eight of them between here and San Francisco. . . . It's all right, dear. Signor Matisti is going to listen to reason. Aren't you, maestro? (*he looks him square in the eyes*)

MATISTI. Mr. Kane, how can I persuade you—

KANE. You can't.

*There is a silence.* MATISTI *rises.*

KANE (*cont'd*). I knew you'd see it my way.

*Dissolve*

*Int. Chicago Opera House—Night—1914*

*It is the same opening night—it is the same moment as before—except that the camera is now upstage angling toward the audience. The curtain is down. We see the same tableau as before—the terrified and trembling* SUSAN, *the apprehensive principals, the maids and singing teachers, the stage hands. As the dissolve commences, there is the sound of applause (exactly as before) and now as the dissolve completes itself, the orchestra breaks frighteningly into opening chords of the music—the stage is cleared—* SUSAN *is left alone—terribly alone. The curtain rises. The glare of the footlights jump into the image. The curtain is now out of the picture and* SUSAN *starts to sing. Beyond her, we see the prompter's box, containing the anxious face of the prompter. Beyond that, out in the darkness—an apprehensive conductor struggles with his task of coordinating an orchestra and an incompetent singer. Beyond that—dimly white shirt fronts and glistening bosoms for a couple of rows and then deep and terrible darkness.*

*Closeup of* KANE'S *face—seated in the audience—listening.*

*A sudden but perfectly correct lull in the music reveals a voice from the audience—a few words from a sentence—the kind of thing that often happens in a theatre—*

THE VOICE. —really pathetic.

*Music crashes in and drowns out the rest of the sentence, but hundreds of people around the voice have heard it (as well as* KANE*) and there are titters which grow in volume.*

*Closeup of* SUSAN'S *face—singing.*

*Closeup of* KANE'S *face—listening.*

*There is the ghastly sound of three thousand people applauding as little as possible.* KANE *still looks. Then, near the camera, there is the sound of about a dozen people applauding very, very loudly. Camera moves back, revealing* BERNSTEIN *and* REILLY *and other* KANE *stooges, seated around him, beating their palms together. The curtain is falling—as we can see by the light which shutters down off their faces.*

*The stage from* KANE'S *angle*

*The curtain is down—the lights glowing on it—Still the polite applause dying fast. Nobody comes out for a bow.*

*Closeup of* KANE*—breathing heavily. Suddenly he starts to applaud furiously.*

*The stage from the audience again*

SUSAN *appears for her bow. She can hardly walk. There is a little polite crescendo of applause, but it is sickly.*

*Closeup of* KANE*—still applauding very, very hard, his eyes on* SUSAN.

*The stage again*

SUSAN, *finishing her bow, goes out through the curtains. The light on the curtain goes out and the houselights go on.*

*Closeup of* KANE*—still applauding very, very hard.*

*Dissolve*

*Int. Study—*KANE'S *New York Home—Day—1914*

*Some weeks later.* SUSAN, *in a negligee, is at the window. There are the remains of her breakfast tray on a little table.*

SUSAN. *You* don't propose to have *yourself* made ridiculous? What about me? I'm the one that has to do the singing. I'm the one that gets the razzberries. *(pauses)* Last week, when I was shopping, one of the salesgirls did an imitation of me for another girl. She thought I didn't see her but—Charlie, you might as well make up your mind to it. This is one thing you're not going to have your own way about. I can't sing and you know it.—Why can't you just—

KANE *rises and walks toward her. There is cold menace in his walk.* SUSAN *shrinks a little as he draws closer to her.*

KANE. My reasons satisfy me, Susan. You seem unable to understand them. I will not tell them to you again. *(he is very close to her)* You will continue with your singing.

*His eyes are relentlessly upon her. She sees something in them that frightens her. She nods her head slowly, indicating surrender.*

*Dissolve out*

*Dissolve in*

*Front page of the "San Francisco Enquirer" containing a large portrait of* SUSAN *as Thais (as before). It is announced that* SUSAN *will open an independent season in San Francisco in "Thais." The picture remains constant but the names of the papers change from New York to St. Louis, to Los Angeles to Cleveland, to Denver, to Philadelphia—all "Enquirers."*

*During all this, on the sound track,* SUSAN'S *voice is heard singing her aria very faintly and far away, her voice cracking a little.*

*At the conclusion of this above,* SUSAN *has finished her song, and there is the same mild applause as before—over the sound of this, one man loudly applauding. This fades out as we—*

*Dissolve*

*Int.* SUSAN'S *Bedroom—*KANE'S *New York Home—Late Night—1916*

*The camera angles across the bed and* SUSAN'S *form towards the door, from the other side of which voices can be heard.*

KANE'S VOICE. Let's have your keys, Raymond.
RAYMOND'S VOICE. Yes, sir.
KANE'S VOICE. The key must be in the other side. *(pause)* We'll knock the door down, Raymond.
RAYMOND'S VOICE *(calling)*. Mrs. Kane—
KANE'S VOICE. Do what I say.

*The door crashes open, light floods in the room, revealing* SUSAN, *fully dressed, stretched out on the bed, one arm dangling over the side.* KANE *rushes to her.*

KANE *(cont'd)*. Get Dr. Corey.
RAYMOND. Yes, sir.

*He rushes out.* SUSAN *is breathing, but heavily.* KANE *loosens the lace collar at her throat.*

*Dissolve*

*Int.* SUSAN'S *Room—Late Night—1916*

*A little later. All the lights are lit.* SUSAN, *in a nightgown, is in bed, asleep.* RAYMOND *and a nurse are just leaving the room,* RAYMOND *closing the door quietly behind him.* DR. COREY *rises.*

DR. COREY. She'll be perfectly all right in a day or two, Mr. Kane.

KANE *nods. He has a small bottle in his hand.*

DR. COREY *(cont'd)*. The nurse has complete instructions, but if you care to talk to me at any time, I should be only too glad—I shall be here in the morning.
KANE. Thank you. I can't imagine how Mrs. Kane came to make such a silly mistake. The sedative Dr. Wagner gave her is in a somewhat larger bottle—I suppose the strain of preparing for her trip has excited and confused her.
DR. COREY. I'm sure that's it. *(he starts out)*
KANE. There are no objections to my staying here with her, are there?
DR. COREY. Not at all. I'd like the nurse to be here, too.
KANE. Of course.

DR. COREY *leaves.* KANE *settles himself in a chair next to the bed, looking at* SUSAN. *In a moment, the nurse enters, goes to a chair in the corner of the room and sits down.*

*Dissolve*

*Int.* SUSAN'S *Room—Day—1916*

SUSAN, *utterly spent, is lying flat on her back in her bed.* KANE *is in the chair beside her. The nurse is out of the room.*

SUSAN (*in a voice that comes from far away*). I couldn't make you see how I felt, Charlie. I just couldn't—I couldn't go through with singing again. You don't know what it means to feel—to know that people—that an audience don't want you. That if you haven't got what they want—a real voice—they just don't care about you. Even when they're polite—and they don't laugh or get restless or—you know . . . They don't want you. They just—

KANE (*angrily*). That's when you've got to fight them. That's when you've got to make them. That's—

SUSAN'S *head turns and she looks at him silently with pathetic eyes.*

KANE (*cont'd*). I'm sorry. (*he leans over to pat her hand*) You won't have to fight them any more. (*he smiles a little*) It's their loss.

*Gratefully,* SUSAN *with difficulty brings her other hand over to cover his.*

*Dissolve*

*Ext. Establishing Shot of Xanadu— Half Built.*

*Int. the Grand Hall in Xanadu— 1925*

*Closeup of an enormous jigsaw puzzle. A hand is putting in the last piece. Camera moves back to reveal jigsaw puzzle spread out on the floor.*

SUSAN *is on the floor before her jigsaw puzzle.* KANE *is in an easy chair. Behind them towers the massive Renaissance fireplace. It is night and Baroque candelabra illuminates the scene.*

SUSAN (*with a sigh*). What time is it?

*There is no answer.*

SUSAN (*cont'd*). Charlie! I said, what time is it?

KANE (*looks up—consults his watch*). Half past eleven.

SUSAN. I mean in New York.

KANE. Half past eleven.

SUSAN. At night?

KANE. Yes. The bulldog's just gone to press.

SUSAN (*sarcastically*). Hurray for the bulldog! (*sighs*) Half past eleven! The shows have just let out. People are going to night clubs and restaurants. Of course, we're different. We live in a palace—at the end of the world.

KANE. You always said you wanted to live in a palace.

SUSAN. Can't we go back, Charlie.

KANE *looks at her smilingly and turns back to his work.*

SUSAN (*cont'd*). Charlie—

*There is no answer.*

SUSAN (*cont'd*). If I promise to be a good girl! Not to drink—and to entertain all the Governors and the Senators with dignity—(*she puts a slur into the word*) Charlie—

*There is still no answer—*

*Dissolve out*

*Dissolve in*

*Another picture puzzle—*SUSAN'S *hands fitting in a missing piece.*

*Dissolve*

*Another picture puzzle—*SUSAN'S *hands fitting in a missing piece.*

*Dissolve*

*Int. Xanadu—Living Room—Day— 1928*

*Another picture puzzle*

*Camera pulls back to show* KANE

*and* SUSAN *in much the same positions as before, except that they are older.*

KANE. One thing I've never been able to understand, Susan. How do you know that you haven't done them before?

SUSAN *shoots him an angry glance. She isn't amused.*

SUSAN. It makes a whole lot more sense than collecting Venuses.

KANE. You may be right—I sometimes wonder—but you get into the habit—

SUSAN *(snapping)*. It's not a habit. I do it because I like it.

KANE. I was referring to myself. *(pauses)* I thought we might have a picnic tomorrow—it might be a nice change after the Wild West party tonight. Invite everybody to go to the Everglades—

SUSAN *(throws down a piece of the jigsaw puzzle and rises)*. Invite everybody!—Order everybody, you mean, and make them sleep in tents! Who wants to sleep in tents when they have a nice room of their own—with their own bath, where they know where everything is?

KANE *has looked at her steadily, not hostilely.*

KANE. I thought we might invite everybody to go on a picnic tomorrow. Stay at Everglades overnight. *(he pats her lightly on the shoulder)* Please see that the arrangements are made Susan.

KANE *turns away—to* BERNSTEIN.

KANE *(cont'd)*. You remember my son, Mr. Bernstein.

*On the sound track we hear the following lines of dialogue.*

BERNSTEIN'S VOICE *(embarrassed)*. Oh, yes. How do you do, Mr. Kane?

CHARLIE JR'S VOICE. Hello.

*During this, camera holds on closeup of* SUSAN'S *face. She is very angry.*

*Dissolve*

*Ext. The Everglades Camp— Night—1928*

*Long shot—of a number of classy tents.*

*Dissolve out*

*Dissolve in*

*Int. Large Tent—Everglades Camp—Night—1928*

*Two real beds have been set up on each side of the tent. A rather classy dressing table is in the rear, at which* SUSAN *is preparing for bed.* KANE, *in his shirt-sleeves, is in an easy chair, reading.* SUSAN *is very sullen.*

SUSAN. I'm not going to put up with it.

KANE *turns to look at her.*

SUSAN *(cont'd)*. I mean it. *(she catches a slight flicker on* KANE'S *face)* Oh, I know I always say I mean it, and then I don't—or *you* get me so I don't do what I say I'm going to— but—

KANE *(interrupting)*. You're in a tent, darling. You're not at home. And I can hear you very well if you just talk in a normal tone of voice.

SUSAN. I'm not going to have my guests insulted, just because you think—*(in a rage)*—if people want to bring a drink or two along on a picnic, that's their business. You've got no right—

KANE *(quickly)*. I've got more than a right as far as you're concerned, Susan.

SUSAN. Oh I'm sick and tired of

your telling me what I must and what I mustn't do!

KANE *(gently)*. You're my wife, Susan, and—

SUSAN. I'm not just your wife. I'm a person all by myself—or I ought to be. I was once. Sometimes you get me to believing I never was.

KANE. We can discuss all this some other time, Susan. Right now—

SUSAN. I'll discuss what's on my mind when *I* want to. You're not going to keep on running my life the way you want it.

KANE. As far as you're concerned, Susan, I've never wanted anything—I don't want anything now—except what you want.

SUSAN. What *you* want me to want, you mean. What you've decided I ought to have—what you'd want if you were me. But you've never given me anything that—

KANE. Susan, I really think—

SUSAN. Oh, I don't mean the things you've given me—that don't mean anything to you. What's the difference between giving me a bracelet or giving somebody else a hundred thousand dollars for a statue you're going to keep crated up and never look at? It's only money. It doesn't mean anything. You're not really giving anything that belongs to you, that you care about.

KANE *(he has risen)*. Susan, I want you to stop this. And right now!

SUSAN. Well, I'm not going to stop it. I'm going to say exactly what I think. *(she screams)* You've never given me anything. You've tried to buy me into giving *you* something. You're—*(a sudden notion)*—it's like you were bribing me! That's what it's been from the first moment I met you. No matter how much it cost you— your time, your money—that's what you've done with everybody you've ever known. Tried to bribe them!

KANE. Susan!

*She looks at him, with no lessening of her passion.*

KANE *(cont'd)*. You're talking an incredible amount of nonsense, Susan. *(quietly)* Whatever I do—I do— because I love you.

SUSAN. Love! You don't love anybody! Me or anybody else! You want to be loved—that's all you want! I'm Charles Foster Kane. Whatever you want—just name it and it's yours! Only love me! Don't expect me to love *you*—

*Without a word,* KANE *slaps her across the face. They look at each other.*

SUSAN. You—you hit me.

KANE *continues to look at her.*

SUSAN *(cont'd)*. You'll never have another chance to hit me again. *(pauses)* I never knew till this minute—

KANE. Susan, it seems to me—

SUSAN. Don't tell me you're sorry.

KANE. I'm not sorry.

SUSAN. I'm going to leave you.

KANE. No you're not.

SUSAN *(nods)*. Yes.

*They look at each other, fixedly, but she doesn't give way. In fact, the camera on* KANE'S *face shows the beginning of a startled look, as of one who sees something unfamiliar and unbelievable.*

*Dissolve*

*Int.* KANE'S *Study—Xanadu— Day—1929*

KANE *is at the window looking out. He turns as he hears* RAYMOND *enter.*

RAYMOND. Mrs. Kane would like to see you, Mr. Kane.

KANE. All right.

RAYMOND *waits as* KANE *hesitates.*

KANE (*cont'd*). Is Mrs. Kane—(*he can't finish*)

RAYMOND. Marie has been packing since morning, Mr. Kane.

KANE *impetuously walks past him out of the room.*

*Int.* SUSAN'S *Room—Xanadu—Day—1929*

*Packed suitcases are on the floor.* SUSAN *is completely dressed for travelling.* KANE *bursts into the room.*

SUSAN. Tell Arnold I'm ready, Marie. He can get the bags.

MARIE. Yes, Mrs. Kane.

*She leaves.* KANE *closes the door behind her.*

KANE. Have you gone completely crazy?

SUSAN *looks at him.*

KANE (*cont'd*). Don't you realize that everybody here is going to know about this? That you've packed your bags and ordered the car and—

SUSAN. —And left? Of course they'll hear. I'm not saying good-bye—except to you—but I never imagined that people wouldn't know.

KANE *is standing against the door as if physically barring her way.*

KANE. I won't let you go.
SUSAN. You can't stop me.

KANE *keeps looking at her.* SUSAN *reaches out her hand.*

SUSAN (*cont'd*). Good-bye, Charlie.

KANE (*suddenly*). Don't go, Susan.
SUSAN. Let's not start all over again, Charlie. We've said everything that can be said.
KANE. Susan, don't go! Susan, please!

*He has lost all pride.* SUSAN *stops. She is affected by this.*

KANE (*cont'd*). You mustn't go, Susan. Everything'll be exactly the way you want it. Not the way *I* think you want it—but your way. Please, Susan—Susan!

*She is staring at him. She might weaken.*

KANE (*cont'd*). Don't go, Susan! You mustn't go! (*almost blubbering*) You—you can't do this to me, Susan—

*It's as if he had thrown ice-water into her face. She freezes.*

SUSAN. I see—it's *you* that this is being done to! It's not me at all. Not how I feel. Not what it means to me. (*she laughs*) I can't do this to *you!* (*she looks at him*) Oh yes I can.

*She walks out, past* KANE, *who turns to watch her go, like a very tired old man.*

*Dissolve out*

*Dissolve in*

*Int. "El Rancho" Cabaret—Night—1940*

SUSAN *and* THOMPSON *at a table. There is silence between them for a moment.*

SUSAN. In case you've never heard of how I lost all my money—and it was plenty, believe me—

THOMPSON. The last ten years have been tough on a lot of people.

SUSAN. They haven't been tough on me. I just lost my money. But when I compare these last ten years with the twenty I spent with him—

THOMPSON. I feel kind of sorry for him, all the same—

SUSAN (*harshly*). Don't you think I do? (*pause*) You say you're going down to Xanadu?

THOMPSON. Monday, with some of the boys from the office. Mr. Ralston wants the whole place photographed carefully—all that art stuff. We run a picture magazine, you know—

SUSAN. I know. If you're smart, you'll talk to Raymond. That's the butler. You can learn a lot from him. He knows where the bodies are buried.

*She shivers. The dawn light from the skylight above has grown brighter, making the artificial light in the night club look particularly ghastly, revealing mercilessly every year of* SUSIE's *age.*

SUSAN *(cont'd).* Well, what do you know? It's morning already. *(looks at him)* You must come around and tell me the story of *your* life some time.

*Fade out*

*Fade in*

*Int. Great Hall—Xanadu—Night— 1940*

*An open door shows the pantry which is dark.* THOMPSON *and* RAYMOND *are at a table. There is a pitcher of beer and a plate of sandwiches before them.* RAYMOND *drinks a glass of beer and settles back.*

RAYMOND. Yes, sir—yes, sir, I knew how to handle the old man. He was kind of queer, but I knew how to handle him.

THOMPSON. Queer?

RAYMOND. Yeah. I guess he wasn't very happy those last years—he didn't have much reason to be—

*Dissolve*

*Int. Corridor & Telegraph Office— Xanadu—Night—1929*

RAYMOND *walking rapidly along corridor. He pushes open a door. At a desk in a fairly elaborate telegraph office sits a wireless operator named* FRED. *Near him at a telephone switchboard sits a female operator named* KATHERINE *(not that it matters).*

RAYMOND *(reading).* Mr. Charles Foster Kane announced today that Mrs. Charles Foster Kane has left Xanadu, his Florida home, under the terms of a peaceful and friendly agreement with the intention of filing suit for divorce at an early date. Mrs. Kane said that she does not intend to return to the operatic career which she gave up a few years after her marriage, at Mr. Kane's request. Signed, Charles Foster Kane.

FRED *finishes typing and then looks up.*

RAYMOND *(cont'd).* Exclusive for immediate transmission. Urgent priority all Kane papers.

FRED. Okay.

*There is the sound of the buzzer on the switchboard.* KATHERINE *puts in a plug and answers the call.*

KATHERINE. Yes . . . yes . . . Mrs. Tinsdall.—Very well. *(turns to* RAYMOND) It's the housekeeper.

RAYMOND. Yes?

KATHERINE. She says there's some sort of disturbance up in Miss Alexander's room. She's afraid to go in.

*Dissolve*

*Int. Corridor Outside* SUSAN's *Bedroom—Xanadu—Night—1929*

*The housekeeper, Mrs. Tinsdall, and a couple of maids are near the door but too afraid to be in front of it. From inside can be heard a terrible banging and crashing.* RAYMOND *hurries into scene, opens the door and goes in.*

*Int.* SUSAN's *Bedroom—Xanadu— 1929*

KANE, *in a truly terrible and absolutely silent rage, is literally breaking up the room—yanking pictures, hooks and all off the wall, smashing them to bits—ugly, gaudy pictures—*SUSIE'S *pictures in* SUSIE'S *bad taste. Off of table tops, off of dressing tables, occasional tables, bureaus, he sweeps* SUSIE'S *whorish accumulation of bric-a-brac.*

RAYMOND *stands in the doorway watching him.* KANE *says nothing. He continues with tremendous speed and surprising strength, still wordlessly, tearing the room to bits. The curtains (too frilly—overly-pretty) are pulled off the windows in a single gesture, and from the bookshelves he pulls down double armloads of cheap novels—discovers a half-empty bottle of liquor and dashes it across the room. Finally he stops.* SUSIE'S *cozy little chamber is an incredible shambles all around him.*

*He stands for a minute breathing heavily, and his eye lights on a hanging what-not in a corner which had escaped his notice. Prominent on its center shelf is the little glass ball with the snowstorm in it. He yanks it down. Something made of china breaks, but not the glass ball. It bounces on the carpet and rolls to his feet, the snow in a flurry. His eye follows it. He stoops to pick it up—can't make it.* RAYMOND *picks it up for him; hands it to him.* KANE *takes it sheepishly—looks at it—moves painfully out of the room into the corridor.*

*Int. Corridor Outside* SUSAN'S *Bedroom—Xanadu—1929*

KANE *comes out of the door.* MRS. TINSDALL *has been joined now by a fairly sizable turnout of servants. They move back away from* KANE, *staring at him.* RAYMOND *is in the*

*doorway behind* KANE. KANE *looks at the glass ball.*

KANE *(without turning).* Close the door, Raymond.
RAYMOND. Yes, sir. *(he closes it)*
KANE. Lock it—and keep it locked.

RAYMOND *locks the door and comes to his side. There is a long pause—servants staring in silence.* KANE *gives the glass ball a gentle shake and starts another snowstorm.*

KANE *(cont'd).* Raymond—*(he is almost in a trance)*
RAYMOND. Yes, sir—

*One of the younger servants giggles and is hushed up.* KANE *shakes the ball again. Another flurry of snow. He watches the flakes settle—then looks up. Finally, taking in the pack of servants and something of the situation, he puts the glass ball in his coat pocket. He speaks very quietly to* RAYMOND, *so quietly it only seems he's talking to himself.*

KANE. Keep it locked.

*He slowly walks off down the corridor, the servants giving way to let him pass, and watching him as he goes. He is an old, old man!*

*Dissolve*

*Int.* KANE'S *Chapel—Xanadu—Late Afternoon—1939*

*As the dissolve completes itself, camera is travelling across the floor of the chapel past the crypts of* KANE'S *father and mother—(marked:* JAMES KANE—*18— to* 19—; MARY KANE—*18— to* 19—)—*past a blank crypt, and then holding on the burial of* KANE'S SON. *A group of ordinary workmen in ordinary clothes are lowering a very expensive-looking coffin into its crypt.* KANE *stands nearby with* RAYMOND, *looking on. The men strain and grunt as the coffin bangs on the stone floor. The men now place over it a long marble slab on which is cut the words:*

CHARLES FOSTER KANE II.
1907–1938

ONE OF THE WORKMEN. Sorry, Mr. Kane, we won't be able to cement it till tomorrow. We—

KANE *looks right through him.* RAYMOND *cuts him short.*

RAYMOND. Okay.

*The men tip their hats and shuffle out of the chapel.* KANE *raises his head, looks at the inscription on the wall. It is a little to one side of* JU- NIOR'S *grave, directly over the blank place which will be occupied by* KANE *himself.*

KANE. Do you like poetry, Raymond?
RAYMOND. Can't say, sir.
KANE. Mrs. Kane liked poetry—

RAYMOND *is now convinced that the old master is very far gone indeed— not to say off his trolley.*

RAYMOND. Yes, Mr. Kane.
KANE. Not my wife—not either of them.

*He looks at the grave next to his son's—the grave marked* "MARY KANE."

RAYMOND *(catching on).* Oh, yes sir.
KANE *(looking back up at the wall).* Do you know what that is?
RAYMOND *(more his keeper than his butler now).* It's a wall you bought in China, Mr. Kane.
KANE. Persia.—It belonged to a king.
RAYMOND. How did you get him to part with it, Mr. Kane?
KANE. He was dead . . . That's a poem. Do you know what it means?

RAYMOND. No, I don't, Mr. Kane.
KANE. I didn't used to be afraid of it.

*A short pause. His eyes still on the wall but looking through it,* KANE *quotes the translation.*

KANE *(cont'd).* The drunkenness of youth has passed like a fever,
And yet I saw many things,
Seeing my glory in the days of my glory.
I thought my power eternal
And the days of my life
Fixed surely in the years
But a whisper came to me
From Him who dies not.
I called my tributary kings together
And those who were proud rulers un- der me,
I opened the boxes of my treasure to them, saying:
"Take hills of gold, mountains of silver,
And give me one more day upon the earth."
But they stood silent,
Looking upon the ground;
So that I died
And Death came to sit upon my throne.

O sons of men
You see a stranger upon the road,
You call to him and he does not stop.
He is your life
Walking towards time,
Hurrying to meet the kings of India and China.
(quoting)
O sons of men
You are caught in the web of the world
And the spider Nothing waits behind it.
Where are the men with towering hopes?
They have changed places with owls,
Owls who lived in tombs
And now inhabit a palace.

KANE *still stares at the wall, through it, and way beyond it.* RAYMOND *looks at him.*

*Dissolve out*

*Dissolve in*

*Int. Great Hall—Xanadu—Night—1940*

THOMPSON *and* RAYMOND. RAYMOND *has finished his beer.*

RAYMOND *(callously).* That's the whole works, right up to date.

THOMPSON. Sentimental fellow, aren't you?

RAYMOND. Yes and no.

THOMPSON *(getting to his feet).* Well, thanks a lot.

RAYMOND. See what I mean? He was a little gone in the head—the last couple of years, anyway—but I knew how to handle him. *(rises)* That "Rosebud"—that don't mean anything. I heard him say it. He just said "Rosebud" and then he dropped that glass ball and it broke on the floor. He didn't say anything about that, so I knew he was dead.—He said all kind of things I couldn't make out.—But I knew how to take care of him.

THOMPSON *doesn't answer.*

RAYMOND *(cont'd).* You can go on asking questions if you want to.

THOMPSON *(coldly).* We're leaving tonight. As soon as they're through photographing the stuff—

THOMPSON *has risen.* RAYMOND *gets to his feet and goes to the door, opening it for him.*

RAYMOND. Allow yourself plenty of time. The train stops at the Junction on signal—but they don't like to wait. Not now. I can remember when they'd wait all day . . . if Mr. Kane said so.

RAYMOND *ushers* THOMPSON *into*

*Int. the Great Hall—Xanadu—Night—1940*

*The magnificent tapestries, candelabra, etc., are still there, but now several large packing cases are piled against the walls, some broken open, some shut and a number of objects, great and small, are piled pell mell all over the place. Furniture, statues, paintings, bric-a-brac—things of obviously enormous value are standing beside a kitchen stove, an old rocking chair and other junk, among which is also an old sled, the self-same story. Somewhere in the back, one of the vast Gothic windows of the hall is open and a light wind blows through the scene, rustling the papers.*

*In the center of the hall a* PHOTOGRAPHER *and his* ASSISTANT *are busy photographing the sundry objects. The floor is littered with burnt-out flash bulbs. They continue their work throughout the early part of the scene so that now and then a flash bulb goes off. In addition to the* PHOTOGRAPHER *and his* ASSISTANT, *there are a* GIRL *and* TWO NEWSPAPERMEN—*(the* SECOND *and* THIRD MEN *of the projection room scene)—also* THOMPSON *and* RAYMOND.

*The* GIRL *and the* SECOND MAN, *who wears a hat, are dancing somewhere in the back of the hall to the music of a phonograph. A flash bulb goes off. The* PHOTOGRAPHER *has just photographed a picture, obviously of great value, an Italian primitive. The* ASSISTANT *consults a label on the back of it.*

ASSISTANT. No. 9182

*The* THIRD NEWSPAPERMAN *starts to jot this information down.*

ASSISTANT *(cont'd).* "Nativity"—attributed to Donatello, acquired Florence 1921, cost 45,000 lira. Got that?

THIRD NEWSPAPERMAN. Yeah.

PHOTOGRAPHER. All right! Next! Better get that statue over there.

ASSISTANT. Okay.

*The* PHOTOGRAPHER *and his* ASSISTANT *start to move off with their equipment towards a large sculpture in another part of the hall.*

RAYMOND. What do you think all this is worth, Mr. Thompson?

THOMPSON. Millions—if anybody wants it.

RAYMOND. The banks are out of luck eh?

THOMPSON. Oh, I don't know. They'll clear all right.

ASSISTANT. "Venus," Fourth Century. Acquired 1911. Cost twenty-three thousand. Got it?

THIRD NEWSPAPERMAN. Okay.

ASSISTANT *(patting the statue on the fanny).* That's a lot of money to pay for a dame without a head.

SECOND ASSISTANT *(reading a label).* No. 483. One desk from the estate of Mary Kane, Little Salem, Colorado. Value $6.00.

THIRD NEWSPAPERMAN. Okay.

*A flashlight bulb goes off.*

SECOND ASSISTANT. We're all set to get everything. The junk as well as the art.

THOMPSON *has opened a box and is idly playing with a handful of little pieces of cardboard.*

THIRD NEWSPAPERMAN. What's that?

RAYMOND. It's a jigsaw puzzle.

THIRD NEWSPAPERMAN. We got a lot of those. There's a Burmese Temple and three Spanish ceilings down the hall.

RAYMOND *laughs.*

PHOTOGRAPHER. Yeah, all in crates.

THIRD NEWSPAPERMAN. There's a part of a Scotch castle over there, but we haven't bothered to unwrap it.

PHOTOGRAPHER. I wonder how they put all those pieces together?

ASSISTANT *(reading a label).* Iron stove. Estate of Mary Kane. Value $2.00.

PHOTOGRAPHER. Put it over by that statue. It'll make a good setup.

GIRL *(calling out).* Who is she anyway?

SECOND NEWSPAPERMAN. Venus. She always is.

THIRD NEWSPAPERMAN. He sure like to collect things, didn't he?

RAYMOND. He went right on buying—right up to the end.

PHOTOGRAPHER. Anything and everything—he was a regular crow.

THIRD NEWSPAPERMAN. I wonder—You put all this together—the palaces and the paintings and the toys and everything—what would it spell?

THOMPSON *has turned around. He is facing the camera for the first time.*

THOMPSON. Charles Foster Kane.

*Another flash bulb goes off. The* PHOTOGRAPHER *turns to* THOMPSON *with a grin.*

PHOTOGRAPHER. Or Rosebud? How about it Jerry?

THIRD NEWSPAPERMAN *(to the dancers).* Turn that thing off, will you? It's driving me nuts!—What's Rosebud?

PHOTOGRAPHER. Kane's last words, aren't they, Jerry? *(to the* THIRD NEWSPAPERMAN*)* That was Jerry's angle, wasn't it, Jerry? Did you ever find out what it means, Jerry?

THOMPSON. No, I didn't.

*The music has stopped. The dancers have come over to* THOMPSON.

SECOND NEWSPAPERMAN. Say, what did you find out about him anyway, Jerry?

THOMPSON. Not much.

SECOND NEWSPAPERMAN. Well, what have you been doing?

THOMPSON. Playing with a jigsaw puzzle—I talked to a lot of people who knew him.

GIRL. What do they say?

THOMPSON. Well—it's become a very clear picture. He was the most honest man who ever lived, with a streak of crookedness a yard wide. He was a liberal and a reactionary; he was tolerant—"Live and Let Live"—that was his motto. But he had no use for anybody who disagreed with him on any point, no matter how small it was. He was a loving husband and a good father—and both his wives left him and his son got himself killed about as shabbily as you can do it. He had a gift for friendship such as few men have—he broke his oldest friend's heart like you'd throw away a cigarette you were through with. Outside of that—

THIRD NEWSPAPERMAN. Okay, okay.

GIRL. What about Rosebud? Don't you think that explains anything?

THOMPSON. No, I don't. Not much anyway. Charles Foster Kane was a man who got everything he wanted, and then lost it. Maybe Rosebud was something he couldn't get or he lost. No, I don't think it explains anything. I don't think any word explains a man's life. No—I guess Rosebud is just a piece in a jigsaw puzzle—a missing piece.

*He drops the jigsaw pieces back into the box, looking at his watch.*

THOMPSON (cont'd). We'd better get along. We'll miss the train.

*He picks up his overcoat—it has been resting on a little sled—the little*

*sled young* CHARLES FOSTER KANE *hit* THATCHER *with at the opening of the picture. Camera doesn't close in on this. It just registers the sled as the newspaper people, picking up their clothes and equipment, move out of the great hall.*

*Dissolve*

*Int. Cellar—Xanadu—Night—1940*

*A large furnace, with an open door, dominates the scene. Two laborers, with shovels, are shovelling things into the furnace.* RAYMOND *is about ten feet away.*

RAYMOND. Throw that junk in, too.

*Camera travels to the pile that he has indicated. It is mostly bits of broken packing cases, excelsior, etc. The sled is on top of the pile. As camera comes close, it shows the faded rosebud and, though the letters are faded, unmistakably the word "ROSEBUD" across it. The laborer drops his shovel, takes the sled in his hand and throws it into the furnace. The flames start to devour it.*

*Ext. Xanadu—Night—1940*

*No lights are to be seen. Smoke is coming from a chimney.*

*Camera reverses the path it took at the beginning of the picture, perhaps omitting some of the stages. It moves finally through the gates, which close behind it. As camera pauses for a moment, the letter "K" is prominent in the moonlight.*

*Just before we fade out, there comes again into the picture the pattern of barbed wire and cyclone fencing. On the fence is a sign which reads:*

"PRIVATE—NO TRESSPASSING"

*Fade out*

THE END

# SOME LIKE IT HOT

## *Screenplay by Billy Wilder and I. A. L. Diamond*

| | |
|---|---|
| SUGAR | Marilyn Monroe |
| JOE | Tony Curtis |
| JERRY | Jack Lemmon |
| SPATS COLOMBO | George Raft |
| OSGOOD FIELDING III | Joe E. Brown |
| MULLIGAN | Pat O'Brien |
| SWEET SUE | Joan Shawlee |
| LITTLE BONAPARTE | Nehemiah Persoff |
| BIENSTOCK | Dave Barry |
| POLIAKOFF | Billy Gray |
| NELLIE | Barbara Drew |
| FIRST HENCHMAN | Mike Mazurki |
| SECOND HENCHMAN | Harry Wilson |
| TOOTHPICK CHARLIE | George E. Stone |
| DOLORES | Beverly Wills |
| OLGA | Marian Collier |
| ROSELLA | Helen Perry |
| MARY LOU | Laurie Mitchell |
| EMILY | Sandy Warner |
| BELLHOP | Al Breneman |
| JOHNNY PARADISE | Edward G. Robinson, Jr. |
| SECOND OFFICIAL | Tommy Hart |
| WAITER | John Indrisano |
| MOZARELLA | Tito Vuola |
| DRUNK | Fred Sherman |

Produced and Directed by Billy Wilder for Ashton
Productions, Inc.
Cinematographer: Charles Lang, Jr.
Editor: Arthur Schmidt
Music by Adolph Deutsch
Wardrobe: Bert Henrikson
Makeup Artist: Emile La Vigne

Winner of the Writers Guild of America Award for Best Written American
Comedy of 1959, and an Academy Award nominee for Best Screenplay (based
on material from another medium, a story by Robert Thoeren and M. Logan),
this amusing and bright comedy by Billy Wilder and I. A. L. Diamond is
already an American classic.

A fifties vintage film, with more sparkle and finish than any great champagne, *Some Like It Hot* is still remarkable for its effervescence and palatability in 1990, more than thirty years later. Two scenes are especially memorable: the seduction scene between Tony Curtis and Marilyn Monroe on the yacht, and Jack Lemmon dancing the tango with Joe E. Brown.

And who can ever forget the last few lines between Jerry (Jack Lemmon), still dressed as a woman, and Osgood (Joe E. Brown), who's still bent on marrying him:

JERRY. But you don't understand! *(he rips off his wig; in a male voice)* I'm a Man!

OSGOOD *(oblivious)*. Well—nobody's perfect.

In paying tribute to this marvelous team of writers, with Mr. Wilder, the scenarist, working as one with Mr. Wilder, the director, we should note that almost all of the Wilder-Diamond screenplays, including *Some Like It Hot,* were exceptionally and unerringly cast, a testimony to the tremendous talent of Billy Wilder and to the efficacy of the writer-director team at its best in realizing all the potential of a great screenplay.

Billy Wilder was born Samuel Wilder on June 22, 1906, in Vienna. He attended the University of Vienna intending to study law, but he soon quit to become a reporter and later tried to break into cinema as a screenwriter. He collaborated on a number of scripts for German films, but, as a Jew, was forced to leave the country when the Nazis took power. Emigrating to Hollywood, his career took off when he began a rewarding collaboration with screenwriter Charles Brackett, which lasted until 1950. Between them they wrote such hits as *Double Indemnity, The Lost Weekend, Ninotchka, Ball of Fire,* and culminating in *Sunset Boulevard,* with Brackett also assuming the role of producer and Wilder as director. In the mid-fifties Mr. Wilder began a fruitful collaboration with I. A. L. Diamond, which resulted in such redoubtable films as *Love in the Afternoon* and *The Apartment.*

Mr. Diamond, who unfortunately passed away in 1989, was born Itek Dommnici in Ungeny, Romania, in 1920. He attended Columbia University, where he wrote material for the university variety shows, before going to Hollywood. His first collaborative writing venture with Billy Wilder, *Love in the Afternoon,* immediately propelled them into the first ranks of film writers.

Fade in:

City at Night

A hearse of late twenties vintage is proceeding at a dignified pace along a half-deserted wintry street.

Inside the hearse, there are four somber men in black—and a coffin, of course, with a wreath of chrysanthemums on top.

One of the men is driving, another is in the seat beside him. The other two are sitting in the rear of the hearse, flanking the coffin. All four seem fully aware of the solemnity of the occasion.

Now they hear a siren, faint at first, but rapidly growing louder. The driver and the man next to him exchange a nervous glance. The other two men move tensely toward the rear door of the hearse, raise the black curtain over the glass panel, and peek out cautiously.

Through the glass panel, they see a police car bearing down on them, the red light blinking, the siren screaming.

The two men at the rear window gesture to the driver to step on it. He does.

The hearse, obviously a souped-up job, instantly picks up speed, weaves crazily through traffic, the police car in hot pursuit. The hearse careens around a corner at eighty miles an hour, the police car right on its tail.

By this time the policemen are leaning out of their car with drawn guns, firing at the hearse.

The two men in the rear of the hearse, flattened against the sides, pull a couple of sawed-off shotguns out of a hidden overhead rack. Police bullets smash the glass panel and whistle through the hearse. The driver and the man next to him duck, but the hearse continues at the same breakneck speed. The two men in back shove their guns through the shattered glass, fire at the police car.

Despite the hail of lead, the police car—its windshield cobwebbed with bullet holes—gains on the hearse.

Suddenly the car skids out of control, jumps the curb, comes to a screeching stop. Policemen leap out, fire after the hearse.

In the speeding hearse, the last of the police bullets thud into the coffin. Instantly three geysers of liquid spurt through the bullet holes. As the firing recedes, the two men in the back put away their guns, remove the wreath from the coffin, take the lid off. The inside is jampacked with bottles of booze, some of them shattered by the bullets. As the men start to lift out the broken bottles—superimpose:

CHICAGO, 1929

Dissolve to:

Intersection of Streets (Night)

Traffic is light. All the shops are dark except one—a dimly lit establishment, from which drift the mournful strains of an organ. A circumspect sign reads:

MOZARELLA'S FUNERAL PARLOR
24 HOUR SERVICE.

In the window, a sample coffin is on display.

There seem to be some rites going on inside, because a number of mourners, singly and in couples, are hurrying from the cold, windy street into Mozarella's parlor.

Meanwhile, the hearse with the damp coffin draws up to the delivery entrance at the side of the building.

*The driver honks the horn—one long and two short—as the other men step down and start to slide the coffin out. The side-door opens, and a dapper gent emerges. He wears a tight-fitting black suit, a black fedora, and gray spats. The spats are very important. He always wears spats. His name is* SPATS COLOMBO. *He cases the street, motions the men inside. As they carry the coffin past him, he removes his fedora, holds it reverently over his heart. Then he follows the men in, his head bowed.*

*Across the street and around the corner, three police cars draw up silently, and about fifteen uniformed policemen and plainclothesmen spill out. A* CAPTAIN *gives whispered orders, and the men scatter and discreetly take up positions around the funeral parlor.*

*Out of one of the cars steps* MULLIGAN, *a tough Federal Agent—in plainclothes, of course. With him is a little weasel of a man, shivering with cold and fear. They call him* TOOTHPICK CHARLIE *for two reasons—because his name is Charlie, and because he has never been seen without a toothpick in his mouth.*

MULLIGAN *(indicating funeral parlor)*. All right, Charlie—this the joint?

TOOTHPICK CHARLIE. Yes, Sir.

MULLIGAN. And who runs it?

TOOTHPICK CHARLIE. I already told you.

MULLIGAN. Refresh my memory.

TOOTHPICK CHARLIE *(uneasily)*. Spats Colombo.

MULLIGAN. That's very refreshing. Now what's the password?

TOOTHPICK CHARLIE. I come to Grandma's funeral. *(he hands him a folded piece of black crepe)* Here's your admission card.

MULLIGAN. Thanks, Charlie.

TOOTHPICK CHARLIE. If you want a ringside table, tell 'em you're one of the pall bearers.

MULLIGAN. Okay Charlie.

*The* POLICE CAPTAIN *joins* MULLIGAN.

CAPTAIN. We're all set. When is the kickoff?

*As* MULLIGAN *consults his watch,* CHARLIE, *the toothpick working nervously in his mouth, tugs* MULLIGAN'S *sleeve.*

TOOTHPICK CHARLIE. Look Chief— I better blow now, because if Spats Colombo sees me, it's Goodbye Charlie.

MULLIGAN. Goodbye Charlie.

CHARLIE *scoots up the dark street, disappears.*

MULLIGAN *(to* POLICE CAPTAIN*)*. Give me five minutes—then hit 'em with everything you got.

CAPTAIN. You bet!

*They synchronize their watches. Then* MULLIGAN *crosses to Mozarella's parlor, unfolding the black crepe* CHARLIE *gave him. It is a mourning band, and he slips it over the left sleeve of his overcoat.*

*Int. Mozarella's Funeral Parlor (Night)*

*It looks legitimate enough—with potted palms, urns and funeral statuary. A harmless gray-haired man is playing the organ with appropriate feeling. Daintily arranging a funeral spray is the proprietor himself,* MR. MOZARELLA. *His heavyweight build, bashed-in nose and cauliflower ears don't quite jibe with his morning coat, striped pants, ascot and carnation. Dusting one of the marble angels is another funeral director, in the same somber uniform.*

MULLIGAN *enters.*

MOZARELLA *(with grave sympathy).* Good evening, sir.

MULLIGAN. I come to the old lady's funeral.

MOZARELLA *(looking him over).* I don't believe I've seen you at any of our services before.

MULLIGAN. That's because I've been on the wagon.

MOZARELLA. PLEASE!

MULLIGAN *(looking around).* Where are they holding the wake? I'm supposed to be one of the pallbearers.

MOZARELLA *(to* FUNERAL DIREC-TOR*).* Show the gentleman to the chapel—pew number three.

FUNERAL DIRECTOR. This way, sir.

*He leads* MULLIGAN *past the organ toward the black-paneled wall, where there is no evidence of a door.*

*The* ORGANIST, *without missing a note in his playing, reaches over to the end of the keyboard and pulls out a stop. One of the panels slides open, and there is a blast of music from the chapel. It's jazz—and it's "Sweet Georgia Brown."* MULLIGAN *rears back momentarily, then follows the* FUNERAL DIRECTOR *in. The* ORGANIST *pushes the stop in again, and the panel slides shut.*

*Int. Speakeasy (Night)*

*Grandma must have been quite a person, because she left a lot of con-doling friends behind, and they are holding a very lively wake. The chapel is jumping. A small band is blaring out "Sweet Georgia Brown." The musicians are not the slick, well-fed instrumentalists you would find in Guy Lombardo's band—they have all been through the wringer, and so have their threadbare tuxedos. On the stamp-sized dance floor, six girls in abbreviated costumes are doing a* frenetic Charleston. *Crowded around the small tables, mourners in black arm-bands are drowning their sor-rows in whatever they drink out of their coffee cups.*

MULLIGAN *(looking around).* Well, if you gotta go—this is the way to do it.

*The* FUNERAL DIRECTOR *leads* MUL-LIGAN *to a table next to the band-stand. As he moves off, a* WAITER *comes up.*

WAITER. What'll it be, sir?

MULLIGAN. Booze.

WAITER. Sorry, sir, we only serve coffee.

MULLIGAN. Coffee?

WAITER. Scotch coffee, Canadian coffee, sour-mash coffee . . .

MULLIGAN. Make it Scotch. A de-mitasse. With a little soda on the side.

*As the* WAITER *starts away,* MUL-LIGAN *stops him.*

MULLIGAN. Haven't you got an-other pew—not so close to the band? (points to a better table) How about that one?

WAITER. Sorry, sir. That's reserved for members of the immediate family.

*He winks, goes off.* MULLIGAN *scans the room.*

*From a side door comes* SPATS COL-OMBO, *followed by the four hearse-men. They walk cockily toward the table "reserved for the immediate family." A* DRUNK *standing with a cup of booze in his hand, is in their way.* COLOMBO *pushes him aside, and the contents of the cup slop over.* COL-OMBO *freezes in his tracks, glances at his feet. The other four men have also stopped, and stare in the same direc-tion, horrified.*

SPATS COLOMBO'S *immaculate spats are no longer immaculate.*

*There is a whiskey stain on one of them.* COLOMBO *throws his henchmen a sharp look. They grab the offending* DRUNK, *hustle him toward the exit.*

DRUNK (*waving empty cup*). Hey— I want another cup of coffee. I want another cup of coffee.

COLOMBO *proceeds toward the table, seats himself, crosses his legs, takes a handkerchief out of his breast pocket, and meticulously mops the moist spat. His four companions, their mission accomplished, join him at the table.*

MULLIGAN, *who has been studying* COLOMBO, *consults his wrist-watch. The* WAITER *comes up with his order—a demitasse half full of Scotch, and a split of club soda.*

MULLIGAN. Better bring the check now—in case the joint gets raided.

WAITER. Who's going to raid a funeral?

MULLIGAN. Some people got no respect for the dead.

*The* WAITER *moves off.* MULLIGAN *sips from the cup, winces, takes a cigar out of his pocket and starts to light it. His eyes wander to the chorus girls.*

*The girls have gone into a tap-dance. The captain of the chorus looks toward the bandstand, grins and winks at—*

—JOE, *the saxophone player. He winks back.* JERRY, *who is thumping the bass-fiddle behind him, leans forward and taps* JOE *on the shoulder.*

JERRY. Say, Joe—tonight's the night, isn't it?

JOE (*eye on tap-dancer*). I'll say.

JERRY. I mean we get paid tonight, don't we?

JOE. Yeah. Why?

*He takes the mouthpiece out of his saxophone, wets the reed.*

JERRY. Because I lost a filling in my back tooth. I gotta go to the dentist tomorrow.

JOE. Dentist? We been out of work for four months—and you want to blow your first week's pay on your teeth?

JERRY. It's just a little inlay—it doesn't even have to be gold—

JOE. How can you be so selfish? We owe back rent—we're in for eighty-nine bucks to Moe's Delicatessen—we're being sued by three Chinese lawyers because our check bounced at the laundry—we've borrowed money from every girl in the line—

JERRY. You're right, Joe.

JOE. Of course I am.

JERRY. First thing tomorrow we're going to pay everybody a little something on account.

JOE. No we're not.

JERRY. We're not?

JOE. First thing tomorrow we're going out to the dog track and put the whole bundle on Greased Lightning.

JERRY. You're going to bet my money on a *dog*?

JOE. He's a shoo-in. I got the word from Max the waiter—his brother-in-law is the electrician who wires the rabbit—

JERRY. What are you giving me with the rabbit?

JOE (*pulling form sheet out of pocket*). Look at those odds—ten to one. If he wins, we can pay *everybody*.

JERRY. But suppose he loses?

JOE. What are you worried about? This job is going to last a long time.

JERRY. But suppose it doesn't?

JOE. Jerry-boy—why do you have to paint everything so black? Suppose you get hit by a truck? Suppose the stock market crashes?

JERRY, *slapping the bass, is no longer listening. His eyes have strayed to—*

MULLIGAN, *sitting at his table, puffing on the cigar. It isn't drawing too well.* MULLIGAN *reaches under his coat, unpins his Department of Justice badge from his vest. Using the pin of the shining badge, he pokes a hole in the wet end of the cigar.*

JERRY *has stopped playing, and is watching* MULLIGAN'S *operation with morbid fascination.* JOE, *completely unaware, continues talking.*

JOE. Suppose Mary Pickford divorces Douglas Fairbanks?
JERRY *(nudging him).* Hey Joe!
JOE *(paying no attention).* Suppose Lake Michigan overflows?
JERRY. Don't look now—but the whole town is under water!

*He nods toward* MULLIGAN. JOE *looks off. Then, without a word, they both start packing their instruments.*

MULLIGAN *pins the badge back on, checks his wrist-watch.*

MULLIGAN *(to himself).* . . . four, three, two, one . . .

*He glances toward—*

*the door from the funeral parlor. Right on the dot, a pair of police axes smash through the door.*

*Instant pandemonium breaks loose in the speakeasy. Music stops, women scream, customers, chorus girls and waiters scramble toward the side doors. But they too are splintering under the assault of the police axes. The crowd falls back, milling around frantically.*

MULLIGAN *stands up, cups his hands to his mouth, and roars at the top of his voice.*

MULLIGAN. All right, everybody—this is a raid. I'm a federal agent, and you're all under arrest.

*Policemen come streaming through the splintered doors. Carried in on the tide is the* DRUNK *who was just tossed out, reeling unsteadily, and waving his empty coffee cup aloft.*

DRUNK. I want another cup of coffee.

*The policemen start rounding up the customers and employees, and herding them toward the exits.*

*On the bandstand,* JOE *and* JERRY *have packed their instruments, and start to fight their way through the melee, toward some stairs leading up.*

MULLIGAN, *a couple of policemen in tow, comes up to* SPATS *and his henchmen, sitting calmly at their table, with five glasses of white liquid in front of them.*

MULLIGAN. Okay, Spats—the services are over. Let's go.
SPATS. Go where?
MULLIGAN. A little country club we run for retired bootleggers. I'm gonna put your name up for membership.
SPATS. I never join nothin'.
MULLIGAN. You'll like it there. I'll have the prison tailor fit you with a pair of special spats—striped!
SPATS *(to his companions, deadpan).* Big joke. *(to* MULLIGAN) What's the rap this time?
MULLIGAN. Embalming people with coffee—eighty-six proof.
SPATS. Me? I'm just a customer here.
MULLIGAN. Come on, Spats—we know you own this joint. Mozarella is just fronting for you.
SPATS. Mozarella? Never heard of him.
MULLIGAN. We got different information.

SPATS. From who? Toothpick Charlie, maybe?

MULLIGAN. Toothpick Charlie? Never heard of him.

*He picks up* SPAT'S *glass, sniffs it suspiciously.*

SECOND HENCHMAN. Buttermilk!

MULLIGAN. All right—on your feet.

SPATS (*getting up slowly*). You're wasting the taxpayers' money.

MULLIGAN. If you want to, you can call your lawyer.

SPATS (*pointing to his four hoods*). These are my lawyers—all Harvard men.

MULLIGAN *and the two policemen lead* SPATS *and his Harvard men out.*

### Ext. Funeral Parlor (Night)

*Policemen, under the supervision of the captain, are herding customers into a paddy-wagon. Fighting his way out of the wagon is our* DRUNK, *waving his coffee cup in the air.*

DRUNK. I want another cup of coffee.

*He staggers into the alley, toward the side entrance of the speakeasy, camera moving with him. Through the smashed-up side door, policemen are ushering more customers, waiters, musicians and the dancing girls. Camera moves up toward a fire escape on the second floor.* JOE *and* JERRY, *carrying their instruments and overcoats, have just climbed through a window onto the fire escape and are inspecting the scene below. The shot-up hearse is parked directly beneath them. Stealthily they climb down the ladder, drop to the roof of the hearse. Then they scramble over the radiator, steal down the alley away from the street. They stop in the shadows to put on their coats.*

JERRY. Well, that solves *one* problem. We don't have to worry about who to pay first.

JOE. Quiet—I'm thinking.

JERRY. Of course, the landlady is going to lock us out—Moe said no more knockwurst on credit—and we can't borrow any more from the girls, because they're on their way to jail—

JOE. Shut up, will you? I wonder how much Sam the Bookie will give us for our overcoats?

JERRY. Sam the Bookie? Nothing doing! You're not putting my overcoat on that dog!

JOE. I told you—it's a sure thing.

JERRY. But we'll freeze—it's below zero—we'll catch pneumonia.

JOE. Look, stupid, he's ten to one. Tomorrow, we'll have *twenty* overcoats!

*Dissolve to:*

### Ext. Chicago Street (Day)

*The street is covered with snow.* JOE *and* JERRY, *without overcoats, the collars of their tuxedos turned up against the bitter cold, come down the steps of the elevated, carrying their instruments. The only thing that keeps* JERRY *from freezing is that he is boiling over inside. As they proceed along the sidewalk,* JERRY *finally can't hold it any more.*

JERRY. Greased Lightning! Why do I listen to you? I ought to have my head examined!

JOE. I thought you weren't talking to me.

JERRY. Look at the bull fiddle—it's dressed warmer than I am.

*They come up to a building in front of which are gathered several small groups of shivering musicians, also equipped with instruments.* JOE *and* JERRY *exchange frozen waves with their colleagues, start through the entrance.*

*Dissolve to:*

*Int. Corridor of Music Building (Day)*

JOE *moves down the corridor,* JERRY *tagging along grimly beside him. Other job-seeking musicians mill around, and a melange of musical sounds and singing voices issues from the various offices, studios and rehearsal halls.*

JOE *and* JERRY *come up to a door marked:* KEYNOTE MUSICAL AGENCY—BANDS, SOLOISTS, SINGERS. JOE *opens the door, revealing a crummy office, with a* SECRETARY *behind a desk.*

JOE. Anything today?
FIRST SECRETARY. Nothing.
JOE. Thank you.

JOE *shuts the door, and they shuffle along to the next agency, which is marked:* JULES STEIN—MUSIC CORPORATION OF AMERICA. JOE *opens the door. This is like the other office— except a little crummier. There is a* SECRETARY *behind the desk.*

JOE. Anything today?
SECOND SECRETARY. Nothing.
JOE. Thank you.

*He closes the door and starts toward the next office, but* JERRY *stops.*

JERRY. I can't go on, Joe. I'm weak from hunger and I'm running a fever and I got a hole in my shoe—
JOE. If you'd give me a chance, we could be living like kings.
JERRY. Yeah—how?
JOE. There's a dog running in the third race named Galloping Ghost—
JERRY. Oh, no!
JOE. He's fifteen to one. And this is his kind of track—he's a real mudder.

JERRY. What do you want—my head on a plate?
JOE. No—just your bass fiddle. If we hock that and the sax, we can get at least—
JERRY. You out of your mind? We're up the creek—and you want to hock the paddle!
JOE. Okay, so go ahead and starve! Freeze!

*He opens the door to the next agency. On the door it says:* SIG POLIAKOFF—BANDS FOR ALL OCCASIONS. *There is the usual secretary behind the usual desk, and her name is* NELLIE. *She is a brunette, somewhat past her prime, but still attractive.*

JOE. Anything today?
NELLIE (*looking up*). Oh, it's *you!* You got a lot of nerve—
JOE. Thank you.

*He shuts the door quickly, starts to move on.*

NELLIE'S VOICE (*from inside*). Joe— come back here!

JOE *stops in his tracks. With a resigned shrug to* JERRY, *he opens the door again, and the two of them start in.*

*Int. Poliakoff's Outer Office (Day)*

*Beside* NELLIE, *there is another* SECRETARY *pecking away at a typewriter.* NELLIE'*s face is grim as* JOE *and* JERRY *come up.*

JOE. Now look, Nellie—if it's about last Saturday night—I can explain everything.
NELLIE (*to* JERRY; *pointing at* JOE). What a heel! I spend four dollars to get my hair marcelled, I buy me a new negligee, I bake him a great big pizza pie—(*to* JOE)—and where were you?
JERRY. Yeah—where were you?
JOE. With you.
JERRY. With *me?*

JOE. Don't you remember? *(to* NEL-LIE*)* He had this bad tooth—it got impacted—the whole jaw swole up—

JERRY. It did? *(*JOE *throws him a look)* Boy, did it ever!

JOE. So I had to rush him to the hospital and give him a transfusion . . . *(to* JERRY*)* Right?

JERRY. Right. We have the same blood type . . .

JOE. —Type O.

NELLIE. Oh?

JOE. Nellie baby, I'll make it up to you.

NELLIE. You're making it up pretty good so far.

JOE. The minute we get a job, I'm going to take you out to the swellest restaurant—

JERRY. How about it, Nellie? Has Poliakoff got anything for us? We're desperate.

NELLIE *(slyly)*. Well, it just so happens he *is* looking for a bass and a sax—*(to the other* SECRETARY*)* Right? *(she winks at her)*

OTHER SECRETARY *(going along)*. Right.

JERRY *(all excited)*. Did you hear that, Joe?

JOE. What's the job?

NELLIE. It's three weeks in Florida—

JERRY. Florida?

NELLIE. The Seminole-Ritz, in Miami. Transportation and all expenses paid . . .

JOE. Isn't she a bit of terrific? *(busses* NELLIE *on the cheek; to* JERRY*)* Come on—let's talk to Poliakoff.

*They start toward the door of the inner office.*

NELLIE. You better wait a minute, *boys*—he's got some people in there with him.

*That stops them.*

*Int. Poliakoff's Inner Office (Day)*

*The room is small and cluttered, and the walls are covered with photographs of* POLIAKOFF'S *clients—bands, vocalists, trios, radio personalities.*

*Sitting behind the desk, speaking urgently into the phone, is* SIG POLIAKOFF, *a gruff, likeable man in his fifties. Pacing up and down on the other side of the desk is* SWEET SUE, *a flashily dressed broad, who has seen thirty summers and a few hard winters. As she paces, she nervously flips a large white pill from one hand to the other. Slouched in a chair is* BIENSTOCK, *a somewhat prissy man of forty wearing thick glasses. He has a card file on his lap, is thumbing through it.*

POLIAKOFF *(into phone)*. Look, Gladys, it's three weeks in Florida—Sweet Sue and Her Society Syncopators—they need a couple of girls on sax and bass—what do you mean, who is this? Sig Poliakoff. I got a job for you—Gladys, are you there? *(hangs up)* Meshugeh! Played for a hundred and twelve hours at a marathon dance, and now she's in bed with a nervous collapse.

SUE. Tell her to move over.

*She has poured herself a glass of water from a pitcher on the desk, and now she plops the pill into her mouth, washes it down.*

BIENSTOCK *(looking up from file)*. What about Cora Jackson?

POLIAKOFF. The last I heard, she was playing with the Salvation Army, yet. *(consulting list on desk; into phone)* Drexel 9044.

SUE *has wandered over to one of the framed photos on the wall. It shows* SUE *posed in front of her band—sixteen girls, all blonde, all in identical gowns. On the drum it says*

SWEET SUE AND HER SOCIETY SYN-
COPATORS.

SUE. Those idiot broads! Here we are all packed to go to Miami, and what happens? The saxophone runs off with a Bible salesman, and the bass fiddle gets herself pregnant. (*turning to* BIENSTOCK) I ought to fire you, Bienstock.

BIENSTOCK. Me? I'm the manager of the band—not the night watchman.

POLIAKOFF (*into phone*). Hello? Let me talk to Bessie Malone—what's she doing in Philadelphia?—on the level? (*hangs up*) Bessie let her hair grow and is playing with Stokowski.

SUE. *Black Bottom Bessie?*

POLIAKOFF. Schpielt zich mit der Philharmonic.

BIENSTOCK. How about Rosemary Schultz?

POLIAKOFF. Didn't you hear? She slashed her wrists when Valentino died!

SUE. We might as well all slash our wrists if we don't round up two dames by this evening.

*She picks up her handbag.* BIEN-
STOCK *rises, takes his glasses off, puts them in his pocket.*

BIENSTOCK. Look, Sig, you know the kind of girls we need. We don't care where you find them—just get them on that train by eight o'clock.

POLIAKOFF. Be nonchalant. Trust Poliakoff. The moment anything turns up, I'll give you a little tingle.

SUE. Bye, Sig. (*feels her tummy*) I wonder if I have room for another ulcer?

BIENSTOCK *opens the door, and fol-
lows* SUE *into the outer office.* JOE *and* JERRY, *who have been biding their time outside, slip in and shut the door after them.*

JOE. Hey, Sig—can we talk to you?

POLIAKOFF (*into phone*). Nellie, get me long distance. (*to the boys*) What is it?

JERRY. It's about the Florida job.

POLIAKOFF. The Florida job?

JOE. Nellie told us about it.

JERRY. We're not too late, are we?

POLIAKOFF. What are you—a couple of comedians? Get out of here! (*into phone*) Long distance? Get me the William Morris Agency in New York.

JOE. You need a bass and a sax, don't you?

POLIAKOFF. The instruments are right, but you are not. (*into phone*) I want to speak to Mr. Morris.

JERRY. What's wrong with us?

POLIAKOFF. You're the wrong shape. Goodbye.

JOE. The wrong shape? You looking for hunchbacks or something?

POLIAKOFF. It's not the backs that worry me.

JOE. What kind of band is this, anyway?

POLIAKOFF. You got to be under twenty-five—

JERRY. We could pass for that.

POLIAKOFF. —you got to be blonde—

JERRY. We could dye our hair.

POLIAKOFF. —and you got to be girls.

JERRY. We could—

JOE. No, we couldn't!

POLIAKOFF (*into phone*). William Morris!

JERRY. You mean it's a *girls'* band?

JOE. Yeah, that's what he means. Good old Nellie! (*starting toward door*) I ought to wring her neck!

POLIAKOFF (*into phone*). Yes, I'm holding on.

JERRY. Wait a minute, Joe. Let's talk this over. (*to* POLIAKOFF) Why *couldn't* we do it? Last year, when we played in that gypsy tearoom, we wore gold earrings. And you remember when you booked us with that Hawaiian band? *(pantomiming)* Grass skirts!

POLIAKOFF *(to* JOE*)*. What's with him—he drinks?

JOE. No. And he ain't been eating so good, either. He's got an empty stomach and it's gone to his head.

JERRY. But, Joe—three weeks in Florida! We could borrow some clothes from the girls in the chorus—

JOE. You've flipped your wig!

JERRY. Now you're talking! We pick up a couple of second-hand wigs—a little padding here and there —call ourselves Josephine and Geraldine—

JOE. *Josephine and Geraldine! (disgustedly)* Come on!

*He drags* JERRY *toward the door.*

POLIAKOFF. Look, if you boys want to pick up a little money tonight— *(they stop and turn)* At the University of Illinois they are having—you should excuse the expression—a St. Valentine's dance.

JOE. We'll take it!

POLIAKOFF. You got it. It's six dollars a man. Be on the campus in Urbana at eight o'clock—

JERRY *(protesting)*. All the way to Urbana—for a one-night stand?

JOE. It's twelve bucks. We can get *one* of the overcoats out of hock.

POLIAKOFF *(into phone)*. Hello, Mr. Morris? This is Poliakoff, in Chicago. Say, you wouldn't have a couple of girl musicians available? A sax player and a bass?

JERRY *(at the door)*. Look, if William Morris doesn't come through—

JOE. Come on, *Geraldine!*

*He pulls him into the outer office.*

*Int. Poliakoff's Outer Office (Day)*

JOE *leads* JERRY *out.*

JERRY. It's a hundred miles, Joe,— it's snowing—how are we going to get there?

JOE. I'll think of something. Don't crowd me.

NELLIE *(brightly)*. How did it go, *girls?*

JERRY. We ought to wring your neck.

JOE. Please, Jerry—that's no way to talk. *(turning on the charm)* Nellie baby—what are you doing tonight?

NELLIE *(suspiciously)*. Why?

JOE. Because I got some plans—

NELLIE. I'm not doing anything. I just thought I'd go home and have some cold pizza—

JOE. And you'll be in all evening?

NELLIE *(melted by now)*. Yes, Joe.

JOE *(briskly)*. Good! Then you won't be needing your car.

NELLIE. *My car?* Why, you—

JOE *silences her protest with a kiss.* JERRY *shakes his head with mock admiration.*

JERRY. Isn't he a bit of terrific?

*Dissolve to:*

*Ext. Clark Street (Day)*

JOE *and* JERRY, *carrying their instruments, are coming along the snow-covered sidewalk toward a garage entrance, above which is a sign reading:* CHARLIE'S GARAGE. *Their shoulders are hunched up against the cold.*

JERRY. We could've had three weeks in Florida—all expenses paid. Lying around in the sum—palm trees—flying fish . . .

JOE. Knock it off, will you?

*They step over the chain blocking the entrance, start into the garage.*

*Int. Charlie's Garage (Day)*

*There are rows of parked cars, a lube rack and a gas pump. Against the wall, under a naked electric light bulb hanging from a cord, five men are playing. A couple of mechanics, in grease-stained coveralls, are watching the game. The dealer is* TOOTHPICK CHARLIE, *the inevitable toothpick in his mouth.*

TOOTHPICK CHARLIE *(dealing).* King high—pair of bullets—possible straight—possible nothing—pair of eights—

JOE *and* JERRY *come in from the street.* ONE OF THE MECHANICS *notices them, nudges* TOOTHPICK CHARLIE. CHARLIE *looks up, and seeing the instrument cases, leaps to his feet, drawing a gun from his shoulder holster. The other four players also jump up, and pulling their guns, level them at* JOE *and* JERRY.

TOOTHPICK CHARLIE. All right, you two—drop 'em.
JERRY *(stops; puzzled).* Drop what?
JOE. We came to pick up a car.
TOOTHPICK CHARLIE. Oh, yeah?

*He nods to* ONE OF THE MECHANICS, *who steps up to* JOE *and* JERRY, *starts to open the instrument cases.*

JOE. Nellie Weinmeyer's car.
MECHANIC *(as the bass and sax are revealed).* Musicians.
TOOTHPICK CHARLIE. Wise guys!

*He mops his brow with the back of his sleeve, and putting his gun back in the holster, picks up the deck of cards again.*

TOOTHPICK CHARLIE. Let's go. Pair of aces bets.

*The other players resume their seats.* JOE *and* JERRY *follow the* MECHANIC *toward the parked cars.*

JOE. It's a '25 Hupmobile coupe. Green.

*The* MECHANIC *leads them up to the car, which is parked near the gas pump.*

MECHANIC. Need some gas?
JERRY. Yeah. *(takes some coins out of pocket)* Like about forty cents' worth.

*The* MECHANIC *unscrews the cap of the gas tank, inserts the rubber hose from the pump.*

MECHANIC. Put it on Miss Weinmeyer's bill?
JOE. Why not? *(signals* JERRY *to put coins away)* And while you're at it—fill 'er up.

*From the street outside comes the loud squeal of tires.* JERRY *glances off casually toward the entrance.*

*A black Dusenberg bursts the chain hanging across the street entrance, skids into the garage, brakes to a screeching stop some ten feet from the card players.* TOOTHPICK CHARLIE *and his cronies leap up and reach for their guns. Too late. Four men have scrambled out of the car, two armed with submachine guns, the other two with sawed-off shotguns. We recognize them as* SPATS COLOMBO'S HENCHMEN.

FIRST HENCHMAN. All right, everybody hands up and face the wall.

*The frightened poker players start to obey.*

JERRY *is watching the scene, openmouthed.* JOE *grabs his shoulder, pulls him down behind the Hupmobile.*

*The* SECOND HENCHMAN *notices the* MECHANIC *standing petrified beside the gas pump.*

SECOND HENCHMAN *(waving machine gun).* Hey—join us!

*The* MECHANIC *raises his hands,*

*moves reluctantly toward the six men lined up against the wall.*

SECOND HENCHMAN *(continues).* Okay, boss.

*A pair of men's feet step down from the limousine. They are encased in immaculate spats.*

JERRY, *crouching behind the Hupmobile with* JOE, *grabs his arm.*

JERRY *(whispering).* It's Spats Colombo—

JOE *clamps his hand over* JERRY'S *mouth.*

SPATS COLOMBO *joins his armed henchmen, who are covering the seven men facing the wall with their hands up.*

SPATS *(very blase).* Hello, Charlie. Long time no see.

TOOTHPICK CHARLIE *(glancing over his shoulder nervously).* What is it, Spats? What do you want here?

SPATS. Just dropped in to pay my respects.

TOOTHPICK CHARLIE. You don't owe me no nothing.

SPATS. Oh, I wouldn't say that. You were nice enough to recommend my mortuary to some of your friends . . .

*He has strolled over to the table, and picking up the deck of cards, starts to deal out another round to the abandoned poker hands.*

TOOTHPICK CHARLIE *(sweating).* I don't know what you're talking about.

SPATS. So now I got all those coffins on my hands—and I hate to see them go to waste.

TOOTHPICK CHARLIE. Honest, Spats. I had nothing to do with it.

SPATS *deals* TOOTHPICK CHARLIE'S *fifth card, then turns up the hole card.*

SPATS. Too bad, Charlie. You would have had three eights. *(flip cards away)* Goodbye, Charlie!

TOOTHPICK CHARLIE *(knowing what's coming).* No, Spats—no, no, no—*(a scream)* NO!

SPATS *nods, and the two machine-gunners raise their weapons, start to fire methodically at their off-scene victims.*

*Behind the Hupmobile,* JERRY *screws his eyes shut painfully as the steady chatter of bullets continues.*

JERRY. I think I'm going to be sick.

*The machine guns stop firing. There is a moment's silence. Then suddenly, the gas tank of the Hupmobile overflows, and the rubber hose from the pump whips out, gushing gasoline over the floor.*

SPATS *and his* HENCHMEN, *hearing the sound, whirl around and catch sight of* JOE *and* JERRY *squatting behind the car.*

SPATS. All right—come on out of there.

JOE *and* JERRY *emerge quakingly from behind the Hupmobile. They try to raise their hands, but find this rather difficult to manage while holding on to their instruments.* JERRY *darts a horrified glance toward the foot of the wall.*

JOE *(quickly).* We didn't see anything—*(to* JERRY*)*—did we?

JERRY *(to* SPATS*).* No—nothing. Besides, it's none of our business if you guys want to knock each other off—

JOE *nudges him violently with his elbow, and he breaks off.*

SPATS *(studying them).* Don't I know you two from somewhere?

JOE. We're just a couple of musicians—we come to pick up a car—Nellie Weinmeyer's car—there's a dance tonight—*(starting to edge away)* Come on, Jerry.

SPATS. Wait a minute. Where do you think you're going?

JOE. To Urbana. It's a hundred miles.

SPATS. You ain't going nowhere.

JERRY *(quavering)*. We're not?

SPATS. The only way you'll get to Urbana is feet first.

*During this, one of the bodies huddled grotesquely against the foot of the wall begins to stir. It is* TOOTHPICK CHARLIE. *He is covered with blood, but there is still a spark of life in him, and his toothpick is still clutched between his teeth. Painfully, he starts to worm his way across the floor toward a phone on a wooden shelf.*

SPATS *and his gang, facing* JOE *and* JERRY, *are not aware of* CHARLIE'S *activity.*

SPATS. I don't like no witnesses.

JOE. We won't breathe a word.

SPATS. You won't breathe nothin'—not even air.

*He motions lazily to the* SECOND HENCHMAN. *The* HENCHMAN *slowly levels his machine gun at* JOE *and* JERRY, *who stand frozen.*

*At that very moment,* TOOTHPICK CHARLIE *reaches up for the phone. But he is too weak to hold on, and the receiver drops from his limp hand, and clatters to the asphalt floor.*

*Instantly,* SPATS *and his* HENCHMEN *wheel around.* SPATS *grabs the machine gun from the* SECOND HENCHMAN, *and perforates what is left of* CHARLIE *with a hail of lead.*

TOOTHPICK CHARLIE *crumbles in a heap. He is quite dead.* SPAT'S *bespatted foot comes into shot, disdainfully kicks the toothpick out of* CHARLIE'S *mouth.*

JOE *and* JERRY *have taken advantage of this momentary diversion. Like scalded jackasses, they are sprinting toward the entrance, hanging on to their instruments.*

SPATS *and his boys pivot, see the two running. They let go with a salvo of shots, just as* JOE *and* JERRY *scoot through the garage door and disappear down the street.*

*A couple of henchmen start after them. There is the sound of an approaching police siren.*

SPATS. Come on—let's blow. We'll take care of those guys later.

*They all pile into the black Dusenberg. The driver shifts into reverse and the car shoots backwards out of the garage.*

*Ext. Alley (Day)*

JOE *and* JERRY *come skidding around the corner from Clark Street, race down the snow-covered alley. In b.g. there is the sound of squealing tires and police sirens.*

JERRY *(as they run)*. I think they got me.

JOE. They got the bull fiddle.

JERRY *(feeling himself all over)*. You don't see any blood?

JOE. Not yet. But if those guys catch us, there'll be blood all over. Type O.

*They start running even faster.*

JERRY. Where are we running, Joe?

JOE. As far away as possible.

JERRY. That's not far enough. You don't know those guys! But they know *us*. Every hood in Chicago will be looking for us—

*They reach the end of the alley. A couple of motorcycle policemen, their* sirens wailing, flash by in the direction of the garage. The word must have spread, because pedestrians are also running in the same direction. JOE stops, looks around quickly, and seeing a cigar store on the corner drags JERRY inside.

*Int. Cigar Store (Day)*

JOE *hurries to a wall telephone near the entrance.* JERRY *follows breathlessly.*

JOE. Got a nickel?

*He sets the saxophone case down, and taking a coin from* JERRY, *inserts it in the slot.*

JERRY. You going to call the police?
JOE. The police? We'd never live to testify. Not against Spats Colombo. *(into phone)* Wabash 1098.
JERRY. We got to get out of town. Maybe we ought to grow beards.
JOE. We *are* going out of town. But we're going to shave.
JERRY. Shave? At a time like this? Those guys got machine guns— they're going to blast our heads off— and you want to shave?
JOE. Shave our *legs*, stupid.

*Stupid is right.* JERRY *still doesn't get it.*

JOE *(into phone; his voice a tremulous soprano).* Hello? Mr. Poliakoff? I understand you're looking for a couple of girl musicians.

*Now* JERRY *gets it.*

*Dissolve:*

*Ext. Chicago Railroad Platform (Night)*

*Two pairs of high-heeled shoes, unusually large in size, are hurrying along the platform. Camera follows them and pans up gradually, reveal-*

ing rather hefty legs in rolled stockings, short dresses, coats with cheap fur pieces, and rakish cloche hats. One of the pair carries a saxophone case, the other a bull-fiddle case, and each has a Gladstone bag.

*A train, with steam up, is loading for departure. Redcaps, passengers, baggage carts.*

ANNOUNCER'S VOICE. Florida Limited leaving on Track Seven for Washington, Charleston, Savannah, Jacksonville and Miami. All aboard. All aboard.

*Our two passengers accelerate their pace. But evidently they are not too adept at navigating in high heels. Suddenly the one with the bull-fiddle twists her ankle—or we should say his ankle—because it's* JERRY. *He stops and faces his girl-friend—*JOE.

JERRY *(rubbing his ankle).* How can they walk on these things? How do they keep their balance?
JOE. Must be the way their weight is distributed. Come on.

*As they proceed along the platform, a gust of wind sends their skirts billowing.* JERRY *stops again and pulls his skirt down.*

JERRY. And it's so drafty. They must be catching colds all the time.
JOE *(urging him on).* Quit stalling. We'll miss the train.
JERRY. I feel so naked. Like everybody's looking at me.
JOE. With those legs? Are you crazy?

*They are now approaching the Pullman car reserved for the girl's orchestra. Girl musicians, with instruments and luggage, are boarding the car, supervised by* SWEET SUE *and* BIENSTOCK.

JERRY *(stopping in his tracks).* It's no use. We'll never get away with it, Joe.

JOE. The name is *Josephine*. And it was your idea in the first place.

*Just then, a member of the girls' band comes hurrying past them, carrying a valise and a ukulele case. Her name is* SUGAR. *What can we say about* SUGAR, *except that she is the dream girl of every red-blooded American male who ever read College Humor? As she undulates past them,* JERRY *looks after her with dismay.*

JERRY. Who are we kidding? Look at that—look how she moves—it's like jello on springs—they must have some sort of a built-in motor. I tell you it's a whole different sex.

JOE. What are you afraid of? Nobody's asking you to have a baby. This is just to get out of town. The minute we hit Florida, we'll blow this set-up.

JERRY. This time I'm not going to let you talk me into something that . . .

*A* NEWSBOY *approaches along the platform, peddling his papers.*

NEWSBOY. Extra! Extra! Seven Slaughtered in North Side Garage! Fear Bloody Aftermath!

JERRY *(to* JOE, *promptly).* You talked me into it! Come on, Josephine!

JOE. Attagirl, Geraldine.

*They hurry toward the Pullman car, imitating the jello-on-springs movement as well as they can.*

*At the Pullman car,* SUE *and* BIENSTOCK *are checking in the girl musicians as they are boarding.*

SUE. Hi, Mary Lou—Rosella—Okay, Dolores, get a move on—How's your back, Olga?

BIENSTOCK *(checking list).* Clarinet—drums—trumpet—trombone—

JOE *and* JERRY *come mincing up. (Note: From here on in, the two will speak with girls' voices whenever the situation calls for it.)*

JOE. Well, here we are.

SUE. You two from the Poliakoff Agency?

JOE. Yes, we're the new girls.

JERRY. Brand new.

SUE. This is our manager, Mr. Bienstock. I'm Sweet Sue.

JOE. My name is Josephine.

JERRY. And I'm Daphne.

*This is completely out of left field.* JOE *throws him a sharp look.* JERRY *smiles back brightly.*

BIENSTOCK *(checking list).* Saxophone, bass—Am I glad to see you girls. You saved our lives.

JOE. Likewise, I'm sure.

SUE. Where did you girls play before?

JERRY. Oh—here and there—and around.

JOE. We spent three years at the Sheboygan Conservatory of Music.

*From Off comes the voice of the Conductor: "All aboard!"*

BIENSTOCK. You're in Berths 7 and 7A.

JERRY *(his idea of a lady).* Thank you ever so.

BIENSTOCK. You're welcome.

JERRY. It's entirely mutual.

JOE *has already boarded the car. As* JERRY *starts up the steps, he stumbles.* BIENSTOCK *helps him up, with a little pat on the behind.*

BIENSTOCK. Upsy-daisy.

JERRY *(coyly).* Fresh!

JOE *jerks him up into the vestibule before this nonsense gets out of hand.*

BIENSTOCK *(takes off glasses, puts them in pocket)*. Looks like Poliakoff came through with a couple of real ladies.

SUE. You better tell the other girls to watch their language.

*She and* BIENSTOCK *mount the steps of the Pullman. The porter picks up the yellow footstep, hops aboard as the train starts moving.*

*Int. Pullman Car (Night)*

*As* JOE *and* JERRY *come in from the vestibule,* JOE *grabs* JERRY, *holds him against the baggage rack.*

JOE *(an angry whisper)*. DAPHNE?

JERRY. I never *did* like the name Geraldine.

*As* SUE *and* BIENSTOCK *appear from the vestibule,* JOE *lets go of* JERRY, *and they move down the aisle into the Pullman car proper.*

*The girl musicians are all there, except for* SUGAR. *They are removing their coats, settling themselves in their seats, putting away their instruments and baggage. They are all blonde, they are young, and most of them are pretty. They look like a band of angels—but don't you believe it.*

JERRY *(the good neighbor)*. Hello, everybody. I'm the bass fiddle. Just call me Daphne.

JOE. I'm Josephine. Sax.

*There is a slew of general hellos.*

MARY LOU. Welcome to No Man's Land.

GIRLS *(in chorus)*. You'll be sor-ry!

ROSELLA. Take your corsets off and spread out.

JERRY. Oh, I never wear one.

OLGA. Don't you bulge?

JERRY. Oh, no. I have the most divine little seamstress that comes in once a month—and my dear, she's so *inexpensive*—

JOE. Come on, Daphne.

DOLORES. Say, kids, have you heard the one about the girl tuba player that was stranded on a desert island with a one-legged jockey?

JERRY. No—how does it go?

BIENSTOCK *(coming up)*. Now cut that out, girls—none of that rough talk. *(as* JOE *and* JERRY *move off)* They went to a conservatory.

*There is a general horse-laugh from the girls.* JOE *and* JERRY *have now reached their seats, and are taking off their coats.*

JERRY *(in a delighted whisper)*. How about that talent? This is like falling into a tub of butter.

JOE. Watch it, *Daphne!*

JERRY. When I was a kid, I used to have a dream—I was locked up in this pastry shop overnight—with all kinds of goodies around—jelly rolls and mocha eclairs and sponge cake and Boston cream pie and cherry tarts—

JOE. Listen, stupe—no butter and no pastry. We're on a diet!

JERRY *starts to hang his coat across a cord running above the window.*

JOE *(grabbing him)*. Not there—that's the emergency brake.

JERRY *(clutching bosom)*. Now you've done it!

JOE. Done what?

JERRY. Tore off one of my chests.

JOE. You better go fix it.

JERRY. You better come help me.

JERRY *leads the way toward the rest rooms, which are just beyond their seat. Instinctively he heads for the one marked* MEN. JOE *grabs him, steers him back toward the one marked* WOMEN.

JOE. This way, Daphne.

JERRY (*clasping his chest desperately*). Now you tore the *other* one.

JOE *opens the curtain, propels him inside.*

*Int. Women's Lounge*

*There is another customer there—* SUGAR. *She has one leg up on the leather settee, her skirt is slightly raised, and she is about to remove a small silver flask tucked under her garter. As* JERRY *and* JOE *come in, she guiltily pulls her skirt down.*

SUGAR. Oh!

JERRY (*arms folded across chest*). Terribly sorry.

SUGAR (*relieved*). That's all right. I was afraid it was Sweet Sue. You won't tell anybody, will you?

JOE. Tell what?

SUGAR (*taking the flask out and unscrewing the cap*). If they catch me once more, they'll boot me out of the band. (*pours a drink into a paper cup*) You the replacement for the bass and the sax?

JERRY. That's us. I'm Daphne—and this is Josephine.

SUGAR. I'm Sugar Cane.

JOE. Sugar Cane?

SUGAR. I changed it. It used to be Sugar Kowalczyk.

JERRY. Polish?

SUGAR. Yes. I come from a very musical family. My mother is a piano teacher and my father was a conductor.

JOE. Where did he conduct?

SUGAR. On the Baltimore and Ohio.

JOE Oh.

SUGAR. I play the ukulele. And I sing too.

JERRY (*to* JOE). She sings, too.

SUGAR. I don't really have much of a voice—but then it's not much of a band, either. I'm only with 'em because I'm running away.

JOE. Running away? From what?

SUGAR. Don't get me started on that. (*extending flask*) Want a drink? It's bourbon.

*As* JERRY *reaches for it, his bosom starts to slip again, and he quickly refolds his arms.*

JERRY. We'll take a rain check.

SUGAR (*downs cupful of bourbon*). I don't want you to think that I'm a drinker. I can stop any time I want to—only I don't want to. Especially when I'm blue.

JOE. We understand.

SUGAR. *All* the girls drink—but I'm the one that gets caught. That's the story of my life. I always get the fuzzy end of the lollipop.

*She has screwed the cap back on the flask, and now slips it under her garter.*

SUGAR. Are my seams straight?

JERRY (*examining her legs*). I'll say.

SUGAR. See you around, girls.

*She waves and exits into the Pullman car.*

JERRY. Bye, Sugar. (*to* JOE) We been playing with the wrong bands.

JOE. Down, Daphne!

JERRY. How about the shape of that liquor cabinet?

JOE *spins him around, and unbuttoning the back of his dress, starts to fix the slipped brassiere.*

JOE. Forget it. One false move, and they'll toss us off the train—there'll be the police, and the papers, and the mob in Chicago . . .

JERRY (*not listening*). Boy, would I like to borrow a cup of that Sugar.

JOE (*whirling him around, grabbing the front of his dress*) Look—no butter, no pastry, and *no Sugar!*

JERRY (*looking down at his chest, pathetically*). You tore it again!

*Dissolve:*

*Ext. Locomotive Wheels (Night)*

*The wheels are pounding along the track, accompanied by a spirited rendition of Running Wild.*

*Int. Pullman Car (Night)*

*At one end of the car,* SWEET SUE *and her Society Syncopators are beating out "Running Wild." It is a special rehearsal to break in the two new girls, Josephine and Daphne. The other girls, including* SUGAR *on the ukulele, are really swinging. But* JOE *and* JERRY *are playing in a dainty ultra-refined manner, so as not to give themselves away. Sue, who is conducting from the aisle, raps her baton against a seat. The girls stop playing.*

SUE (*to* JOE *and* JERRY.) Hey, She-boygan—you two—what was your last job—playing square dances?

JOE. No—funerals.

SUE. Would you mind rejoining the living? Goose it up a little.

JERRY. We'll try.

SUE *is about to give the downbeat, when her eyes fall on* JERRY'S *bass fiddle. There is a neat row of bullet holes across the face of the instrument.*

SUE. How did those holes get there?

JERRY (*looking down*). Oh—those. I don't know. (*tentatively*) Mice?

JOE (*quickly*). She got it second-hand.

SUE. All right—let's take it from the top. And put a little heat under it, will you?

*She brings the baton down, and the girls start playing again. This time* JOE *and* JERRY *give it both knees—*JOE *going for a wild ride on the sax, and*

JERRY *slapping and twirling the bass like a girl possessed.* SUE *cocks her eyebrows, amazed by the hepness of the two conservatory cats.*

*Now it is time for* SUGAR'S *solo. She steps forward with the ukulele, and starts to sing a hot chorus of "Running Wild." Holding on to the bull-fiddle, Jerry leans forward to get a better view of* SUGAR'S *backfield in motion.*

*As* SUGAR *shimmies through the number, the hidden flask slips out from under her garter, and falls to the floor with a clank. She freezes.* SUE *raps her baton furiously against the seat, stopping the music.*

SUE. BIENSTOCK!

BIENSTOCK, *with his glasses on, is sitting farther back in the car reading Variety. He leaps up.*

BIENSTOCK. Yes, Sue? What is it?

SUE (*pointing at flask*). I thought I made it clear I don't want any drinking in this outfit.

BIENSTOCK (*picking up flask*). All right, girls. Who does this belong to? (*no answer*) Come on, now. Speak up. (*still no answer; his eyes fall on* SUGAR, *who stands there frozen*) Sugar, I warned you!

SUGAR. Please, Mr. Bienstock—

BIENSTOCK. This is the last straw. In Kansas City you were smuggling liquor in a shampoo bottle. Before that I caught you with a pint in your ukulele—

JERRY *has squeezed himself between the girls, and steps forward.*

JERRY. Pardon me, Mr. Bienstock—can I have my flask back?

BIENSTOCK (*automatically*). Sure. (*hands it to him, turns back to* SUGAR) Pack your things, and the next station we come to— (*he does a take, turns to* JERRY) Your flask?

JERRY. Uh-huh. Just a little bourbon.

*He starts to slip it down the neck of his dress.*

BIENSTOCK. Give me that!

*He grabs the flask.* SUGAR *is looking at* JERRY *gratefully.* JOE *glares at* JERRY, *ready to hit him with the saxophone.*

SUE (*to* JOE *and* JERRY; *dryly*). Didn't you girls say you went to a conservatory?

JERRY. Yes. For a whole year.

SUE. I thought you said *three* years.

JOE (*lightly*). We got time off for good behavior.

SUE. There are two things I will not put up with during working hours. One is liquor—and the *other* one is men.

JERRY (*a blinking angel*). Men?

JOE. Oh, you don't have to worry about that.

JERRY. We wouldn't be caught *dead* with men. Those rough, hairy beasts with eight hands—(*looking at* BIENSTOCK) They all want just one thing from a girl.

BIENSTOCK (*drawing himself up*). I beg your pardon.

SUE (*rapping baton*). All right, girls—from the top again.

*Once more the Society Syncopators wade into "Running Wild."* SUGAR, *strumming the ukulele, smiles warmly at* DAPHNE, *a true blue pal;* DAPHNE *smiles back, his mouth watering a little, like a kid in a pastry shop.*

*Dissolve:*

*Ext. Locomotive Wheels (Night)*

*The wheels are still pounding away—but there's no more music.*

*Int. Pullman Car (Night)*

*The berths are made up, and the girls are getting ready for bed.* JOE, *in pajamas, is standing in the aisle beside Lower 7, draping his dress neatly on a hanger.* JERRY, *in a nightgown, is lying in Upper 7 with the curtains open, watching the broads go by. Girls in negligees, in pajamas, in nightgowns, are scurrying with their wash-kits in and out of the ladies' room, climbing into lowers and uppers.*

JERRY (*the young sultan*). Good night, Mary Lou—Dolores dear, sleep tight—Nighty-night, Emily.

EMILY (*climbing into an upper*). Toodle-oo.

JERRY (*to* JOE). How about that toodle-oo?

JOE. Steady, boy. Just keep telling yourself you're a girl.

JERRY (*to himself*). I'm a girl. I'm a girl. I'm a girl—

ROSELLA *and* OLGA *come bouncing past from the ladies' room.*

JERRY (*to* JOE). Get a load of that rhythm section. (*a glare from* JOE) I'm a girl. I'm a girl.

*His eyes stray down the aisle. In Upper 2,* SUGAR *is getting ready for bed. All* JERRY *can see is her legs dangling out of the berth, as she removes her stockings. But that's all the identification* JERRY *needs.*

JERRY (*calling down the aisle*). Good night, Sugar.

SUGAR (*sticking her head out*). Good night, honey.

JERRY (*to* JOE; *enraptured*). Honey—she called me honey.

*Without a word,* JOE *takes the ladder leaning against* JERRY'S *berth, slides it under the lower.*

JERRY. What are you doing?

JOE. I just want to make sure that

*honey* stays in the hive. There'll be no buzzing around tonight.

JERRY. But suppose I got to go—like for a drink of water?

JOE. Fight it.

JERRY. But suppose I lose? Suppose it's an emergency.

JOE (*points to cord running across the back of* JERRY'S *berth*). Then pull the emergency brake!

*Sitting on the edge of Lower 1, ready for bed, is* SUE. *She is looking off intently toward* JOE *and* JERRY, *flipping a stomach pill in one hand and holding a paper cup of water in the other. She turns to* BIENSTOCK, *who is across the aisle in Lower 2, just buttoning his pajama tops.*

SUE. You know, Bienstock, there's something funny about those two new girls.

BIENSTOCK. Funny? In what way?

SUE. I don't know—but I can feel it right here. (*pats tummy*) That's one good thing about ulcers—it's like a burglar alarm going off inside you.

*She swallows the pill, washes it down with water.*

BIENSTOCK. All right, Sue. You watch your ulcers—I'll watch those two. (*rises, claps his hands*) Okay. Everybody settle down and go to bed. Good night, girls.

*The last few girls climb into their berths, lights are being extinguished, curtains are being closed.*

JOE, *standing outside Berth 7, starts to close the curtains of* JERRY'S *berth.*

JOE. Good night, Daphne.

JERRY (*wretchedly*). Good night, Josephine.

JOE *closes the curtains.* JERRY, *in the upper, extinguishes the light. He*

*settles himself back on the pillow, closes his eyes.*

JERRY (*muttering to himself*). I'm a girl—I'm a girl—I wish I were dead—I'm a girl—I'm a girl—

*Ext. Locomotive Wheels (Night)*

*The wheels are pounding along the track in the rhythm of* JERRY'S *I'm a girl, I'm a girl.*

*Dissolve:*

*Int. Pullman Car (Night)*

*There are just a few dim lights illuminating the aisle. Everybody seems to be asleep, all is quiet—except for* BINESTOCK'S *steady snoring in Lower 2.*

*After a moment, the curtains of Upper 2 open, and* SUGAR *peeks out cautiously. She is wearing a negligee over her nightie. Seeing that all is clear, she slips quietly down the ladder, and tiptoes down the aisle.*

*She arrives at Berth 7, and finding no ladder there, takes one from across the aisle, leans it against* JERRY'S *berth, and climbs up.*

JERRY *is asleep in Upper 7, as the curtains part and* SUGAR *leans in.*

SUGAR (a whisper). Daphne . . .

*She taps his shoulders.* JERRY *sits bolt upright, hits his head against the top of the berth.*

JERRY. Oh—Sugar!

SUGAR. I wanted to thank you for covering up for me. You're a real pal.

JERRY. It's nothing. I just think us girls should stick together.

SUGAR. If it hadn't been for you, they would have kicked me off the train. I'd be out there in the middle of nowhere, sitting on my ukulele.

JERRY. It must be freezing outside.

When I think of you—and your poor ukulele—

SUGAR. If there's anything I can do for *you*—

JERRY. Oh, I can think of a million things—

SUGAR, *looking off, sees something in the aisle, quickly climbs into the berth beside* JERRY.

JERRY. And that's one of them.

SUGAR (*finger to her lips*). Sssh. Sweet Sue.

*She peers through the slit in the curtains. Sue, in a wrapper, is padding sleepily down the aisle toward the ladies' room.*

*Back in Upper 7,* SUGAR *turns conspiratorially to* JERRY.

SUGAR. I don't want her to know we're in cahoots.

JERRY. We won't tell anybody—not even Josephine.

SUGAR. I'd better stay here till she goes back to sleep.

JERRY. Stay as long as you like.

SUGAR (*putting her legs under the covers*). I'm not crowding you, am I?

JERRY. No. It's nice and cozy.

SUGAR. When I was a little girl, on cold nights like this, I used to crawl into bed with my sister. We'd cuddle up under the covers, and pretend we were lost in a dark cave, and were trying to find our way out.

JERRY (*mopping his brow*). Interesting.

SUGAR. Anything wrong?

JERRY. No, no.

SUGAR (*putting a hand on his shoulder*). Why you poor thing—you're trembling all over.

JERRY. That's ridiculous.

SUGAR. And your head is hot.

JERRY. That's ridiculous.

SUGAR (*her feet touching his under the cover*). And you've got cold feet.

JERRY (*a wan smile*). Isn't that ridiculous?

SUGAR. Let me warm them a little. (*rubbing her feet against his*) There—isn't that better?

JERRY *has turned his head away, and is now mumbling to himself.*

JERRY. I'm a girl, I'm a girl, I'm a girl—

SUGAR. What did you say?

JERRY. I'm a very sick girl.

SUGAR (*sitting up*). Maybe I'd better go before I catch something.

JERRY (*holding her by the arm*). I'm not *that* sick.

SUGAR. I have a very low resistance.

JERRY. Look, Sugar, if you feel you're coming down with something, the best thing is a shot of whiskey.

SUGAR. You got some?

JERRY. I know where to get some. (*sitting up*) Don't move.

*He climbs across her, and opening the curtains, leans all the way over the edge of the upper berth and down toward the berth below.*

*In Lower 7,* JOE *is asleep, facing the window. The curtains part, and* JERRY, *dangling upside down, reaches toward the suitcase at the foot of the berth. He raises the lid of the suitcase, rummages around till he finds a bottle of bourbon. As he takes it out,* JOE *stirs.* JERRY *freezes, raises the bottle up, ready to conk* JOE *if he wakes up.* JOE *turns over, settles back to sleep, and* JERRY *swings his body through the curtains.*

JERRY, *the bottle clutched in his hand, is hanging upside down, while Sugar in the upper berth holds on to his legs. As* JERRY *tries to raise himself back up, he slips out of* SUGAR'S *grasp, and sprawls in the aisle. He lies absolutely still, afraid that* JOE *may have heard him.*

SUGAR *(a solicitous whisper)*. You all right?

JERRY *(getting up)*. I'm fine.

SUGAR. How's the bottle?

JERRY. Half-full.

*As he hands it up to her, the curtains of Upper 4 part, and* DOLORES, *who has been awakened by the fall, peeks out.*

SUGAR *(to* JERRY*)*. You better get some cups.

JERRY *pads over to the water fountain beside the rest rooms. He punches out a couple of paper cups from a dispenser, flits back to Berth 7, and scurries up the ladder.*

DOLORES *watches all this with great interest.*

*Back in Upper 7,* SUGAR *has already opened the bottle.*

JERRY *(handing her the paper cups)*. I tell you—this is the only way to travel.

SUGAR *(pouring)*. You better put on the lights. I can't see what I'm doing.

JERRY. No—no lights. We don't want anyone to know we're having a party.

SUGAR. I may spill something.

JERRY *(shifting into high)*. So spill it. Spills, thrills, laughs, games—this may even turn out to be a surpise party.

SUGAR. What's the surprise?

JERRY *(coyly)*. Uh-uh. Not yet.

SUGAR. When?

JERRY. We better have a drink first.

SUGAR *(handing him cup)*. Here. This'll put hair on your chest.

JERRY. No fair guessing.

*They drink. The curtains open and* DOLORES, *standing on the ladder outside, sticks her head in.*

DOLORES. This a private clambake, or can anybody join?

JERRY *(turns, startled)*. It's private. Go away.

SUGAR. Say, Dolores—you still got that bottle of vermouth?

DOLORES. Sure.

JERRY. Who needs vermouth?

SUGAR *(to* DOLORES*)*. We have some bourbon—let's make Manhattans.

DOLORES. Okay. *(starts down the ladder)*

JERRY. Manhattans? This time of night?

SUGAR *(calling after* DOLORES*)*. And bring the cocktail shaker.

JERRY *(disgustedly)*. Oh, Sugar. You're going to spoil my surprise.

DOLORES *has crossed the aisle, and getting a foot up on Lower 4, reaches up into her berth for the vermouth. The curtains of Lower 4 open, and* MARY LOU *sticks her head out.*

MARY LOU. What's up?

DOLORES. Party in Upper 7.

MARY LOU. I got some cheese and crackers.

DOLORES. And get a corkscrew.

MARY LOU *gets out of her berth, steps across to Lower 3, wakes up* ROSELLA.

MARY LOU. Party in Upper 7. Got a corkscrew?

ROSELLA *(wide awake)*. No. But Stella has.

MARY LOU. Get some cups.

ROSELLA *hurries toward the water fountain, while* MARY LOU *gets* STELLA *and the corkscrew out of bed. Rapidly, the whole Pullman car springs into action. As silent as mice, the girls slip out of their berths, armed with various provisions. Their nighties billowing, they scuttle down the aisle and up the ladder into Upper 7.*

*In Upper 7, the party is building rapidly, as the mice pile in with their contributions.*

GIRLS. Here's the vermouth. I brought some crackers and cheese. Will ten cups be enough? Can you use a bottle of Southern Comfort?

JERRY *is trying vainly to stem the invasion of gatecrashers.*

JERRY. Please, girls—this is a private party—a party for *two*—go away, no more room—ssh, the neighbors downstairs—you'll wake up Josephine—please, no crackers in bed—go someplace else, form your own party—*be careful with that corkscrew!* Sugar—where are you, Sugar?

SUGAR *is greeting* OLGA, *who has climbed into the berth clutching a hot water bottle.*

OLGA. Here's the cocktail shaker.

SUGAR *starts measuring bourbon and vermouth into it.*

GIRLS. Easy on the vermouth. If we only had some ice—Pass the peanut butter. Anybody for salami?

JERRY *(desperately)*. Thirteen girls in a berth—that's bad luck! *Twelve* of you will have to get out! . . . Please, girls, *no more food!* I'll have *ants* in the morning!

*In Lower 7,* JOE *is stirring restlessly, while subdued noises float down from the party upstairs. The curtains part and* EMILY *sticks her head in and shakes* JOE.

EMILY. Hey—you got any maraschino cherries on you?
JOE *(half-asleep)*. Huh?
EMILY. Never mind.

*She disappears.* JOE *starts to close his eyes, then sits up with a jolt.*

JOE. *Maraschino cherries?*

*Slowly he becomes aware of the sounds of revelry up above. His eyes widen as he sees a girl's bare leg through the curtains. The girl steps on the edge of his berth, hoists herself into the upper.* JOE *throws open the curtains, sees several other pairs of girls' legs dangling down from the upper, and still more legs climbing up the ladder.*

*Frantically,* JOE *jumps out of his berth. He is confronted by a sight which knocks into a cocked hat the principle that two bodies cannot occupy the same space at the same time. In a triumph of engineering, fourteen girls have squeezed themselves into Upper 7—or to be exact, thirteen girls and* DAPHNE—*not to mention the bourbon, the vermouth, the Southern Comfort, the paper cups, the corkscrew, the hot water bottle, the crackers and cheese, and the salami. There is a seething tangle of arms and legs and blonde heads— like a snake pit at feeding time.*

JOE. What's going on here? *(trying to find a needle in the haystack)* Daphne—Daphne—
JERRY *(sticking his head out)*. It's not my fault. I didn't invite them.
JOE *(pleading)*. Break it up, girls! Daphne! Come on, help me!

*He starts to tug at odd arms and legs.*

JERRY *pulls himself back into the berth.*

JERRY. All right, girls. You heard Josephine. Everybody out.

SUGAR *starts to back out of the berth.*

JERRY. Not *you*, Sugar.
SUGAR. I'm just going to get some ice.

JOE *has slipped on his robe as* SUGAR *comes backing out of the berth and down the ladder.*

JOE. Out, out! That's right, Sugar. Now the rest of you.

*As* SUGAR *heads for the water fountain,* JOE *starts to pull the other girls out.*

GIRLS. Aw, don't be a flat tire. Have a Manhattan. Come on in. There's lots of room in the back.

JOE. Ssh. Pipe down. We'll all be fired.

JERRY *sticks his head out, looks after* SUGAR.

JERRY *(plaintively).* Sugar—don't leave me here alone, Sugar.

SUGAR *has pried open the panel under the water fountain, and reaching inside, drags out a huge cake of ice. Not quite knowing what to do with it, she thrusts it into* JOE'S *hands, and turns quickly to the pile of instruments stashed between some empty seats.*

JOE *(unaware of the cake of ice in his hands).* Come on, kids. Give up, will you? The party's over. Everybody go home. *(suddenly notices the ice)* What's this?

*By this time,* SUGAR *has unscrewed a cymbal from the drum, and is holding the drummer's metal brush.*

SUGAR *(beckoning to* JOE*).* Josephine, over here. Before it melts.

*She heads for the women's lounge.* JOE *looks at her, looks at the ice, and not knowing what else to do with it, follows her through the curtains.*

*Int. Women's Lounge (Night)*

SUGAR *comes in, followed by* JOSEPHINE *with the cake of ice.*

SUGAR *(pointing to sunken washbowl).* Put it here.

JOE *(dropping the ice in the bowl).* Sugar, you're going to get yourself into a lot of trouble.

SUGAR. Better keep a lookout.

JOE *crosses to the curtain, peers out.* SUGAR, *using the handle of the metal brush, starts to chop ice into the upturned cymbal.*

JOE. If Bienstock catches you again—What's the matter with you, anyway?

SUGAR. I'm not very bright, I guess.

JOE. I wouldn't say that. Careless, maybe.

SUGAR. No—just dumb. If I had any brains, I wouldn't be on this crummy train with this crummy girls' band.

JOE. Then why did you take this job?

SUGAR. I used to sing with *male* bands. But I can't afford it any more.

JOE. Afford it?

SUGAR. Have you ever been with a male band?

JOE. Me?

SUGAR. That's what I'm running away from. I worked with six different ones in the last two years. Oh, brother!

JOE. Rough?

SUGAR. I'll say.

JOE. You can't trust those guys.

SUGAR. I can't trust myself. The moment I'd start with a new band— bingo!

JOE. Bingo?

SUGAR. You see, I have this *thing* about saxophone players.

JOE *(abandoning his lookout post).* Really?

SUGAR. Especially tenor sax. I don't know what it is, but they just curdle me. All they have to do is play eight bars of "Come to Me My Melancholy Baby"—and my spine turns to custard, and I get goose-pimply all over—and I come to them.

JOE. That so?

SUGAR (*hitting her head*). Every time!

JOE (*nonchalantly*). You know—*I* play tenor sax.

SUGAR. But you're a girl, thank goodness.

JOE (*his throat drying up*). Yeah.

SUGAR. That's why I joined this band. Safety first. Anything to get away from those bums.

JOE (*drier yet*). Yeah.

SUGAR (*hacking the ice viciously*). You don't know what they're like. You fall for them and you love 'em— you think it's going to be the biggest thing since the Graf Zeppelin—and the next thing you know they're borrowing money from you and spending it on other dames and betting the horses—

JOE. You don't say?

SUGAR. Then one morning you wake up and the saxophone is gone and the guy is gone, and all that's left behind is a pair of old socks and a tube of toothpaste, all squeezed out.

JOE. Men!

SUGAR. So you pull yourself together and you go on to the next job, and the next saxophone player, and it's the same thing all over again. See what I mean?—not very bright.

JOE (*looking her over*). Brains aren't everything.

SUGAR. I can tell you one thing— it's not going to happen to me again. Ever. I'm tired of getting the fuzzy end of the lollipop.

OLGA *bursts in through the curtains.*

OLGA. Ice! What's keeping the ice? The natives are getting restless.

JOE *hands her the cymbal piled with ice.*

JOE. How about a couple of drinks for us?

OLGA. Sure.

*She scoots out.* JOE *and* SUGAR *are alone again.*

SUGAR. You know I'm going to be twenty-five in June?

JOE. You are?

SUGAR. That's a quarter of a century. Makes a girl think.

JOE. About what?

SUGAR. About the future. You know—like a husband? That's why I'm glad we're going to Florida.

JOE. What's in Florida?

SUGAR. Millionaires. Flocks of them. They all go south for the winter. Like birds.

JOE. Going to catch yourself a rich bird?

SUGAR. Oh, I don't care *how* rich he is—as long as he has a yacht and his own private railroad car and his own toothpaste.

JOE. You're entitled.

SUGAR. Maybe you'll meet one too, Josephine.

JOE. Yeah. With money like Rockefeller, and shoulders like Johnny Weismuller—

SUGAR. I want mine to wear glasses.

JOE. Glasses?

SUGAR. Men who wear glasses are so much more gentle and sweet and helpless. Haven't you ever noticed?

JOE. Well, now that you've mentioned it—

SUGAR. They get those weak eyes from reading—you know, all those long columns of tiny figures in the Wall Street Journal.

OLGA *is back again, carrying two Manhattans in paper cups on the cymbal. She hands them the drinks, starts to refill the cymbal with ice.*

OLGA. That bass fiddle—wow! She sure knows how to throw a party!

*She dashes out.* JOE *looks after her, worriedly.*

SUGAR *(raising cup).* Happy days.
JOE *(lifting his cup).* I hope this time you wind up with the *sweet* end of the lollipop.

*They drink.* JOE *studies her like a cat studying a canary.*

*Int. Pullman Car (Night)*

OLGA *is climbing up the ladder to Upper 7 with the new supply of ice in the cymbal. The party is now really winging. Amidst the hushed hilarity, the hot water bottle is being passed around, paper cups and crackers are flying, some of the girls are smoking. Despite the absence of* SUGAR, JERRY *is enjoying himself hugely.* DOLORES *has the floor—finishing the joke that* BIENSTOCK *interrupted earlier.*

DOLORES. —so the one-legged jockey said— *(she breaks up in helpless laughter)*
JERRY *(eagerly).* What did he say?
DOLORES. The one-legged jockey said—"Don't worry about *me,* baby. I ride side-saddle."

*To* JERRY, *this is excrutiatingly comical. He puts his hand over his mouth, trying to smother his wild laughter, starts to hiccup.*

JERRY *(Lady Daphne again).* I beg your pardon.

*Another hiccup. And another.*

ROSELLA. Put some ice on her neck!

*She takes a hunk of ice out of the cymbal, rubs it against the back of* JERRY'S *neck.* JERRY *leaps up with a squeal, and the ice slides down into his nightgown. He squirms and wiggles, crying and laughing and hiccuping.*

JERRY. Oooh! Aaah! It's cold! Owwww!

*The girls try to fish the ice from inside his nightie, and suddenly* JERRY *gets a new shock, worse than the ice. His hiccups stop, his eyes widen in panic. His bosoms have torn loose from their moorings again. He folds his arms over his suddenly flat chest, to ward off exposure.*

JERRY *(continuing).* Cut it out, girls. Stop it. Joe—Jospehine—help!
DOLORES. Hey, she's ticklish!

*With that, all the girls pounce on* JERRY, *start to tickle him.* JERRY *flops around like a fish, screaming and laughing and crying. In despair, his eyes fall on the emergency cord. He makes a grab for the cord, pulls it.*

*Ext. Locomotive Wheels (Night)*

*The pounding wheels suddenly lock, and come to a jolting stop.*

*Int. Pullman Car (Night)*

*The abrupt stop sends everybody in Upper 7 tumbling out into the aisle.*

*Int. Women's Lounge (Night)*

SUGAR, *thrown off balance, grabs on to* JOE.

SUGAR. What happened?
JOE. Search me. *(quickly)* I mean— I'll see.

*He sticks his head out through the curtains.*

*Int. Pullman Car (Night)*

*The* GIRLS *heaped in the aisle are extricating themselves and scurrying back as fast as they can into their berths.* JERRY *scrambles up the ladder into Upper 7, pulls the curtains, just as the curtains of Lower 1 are flung open and* SUE *emerges. She glances up the aisle, which is now empty and peaceful-looking.*

SUE (*angrily*). What's going on around here? (*shouting*) Bienstock!

BIENSTOCK *staggers sleepily out of Lower 2.*

BIENSTOCK. Are we in Florida?

*At the entrance to the women's lounge,* SUGAR *has joined* JOE *and the two are peering through the curtains. The door of the car opens, and the* CONDUCTOR *runs in angrily. The two withdraw back into the lounge.*

*The* CONDUCTOR *joins* SUE *and* BIENSTOCK.

CONDUCTOR. All right. Who pulled the emergency brake? Who was it?

BIENSTOCK (*bellowing at the closed curtains*). Come on, girls. *Who was it?*

*Through the curtains of Upper 7,* JERRY'S *head appears timidly.*

JERRY. *I* was it.

SUE. What's the big idea?

JERRY. I'm sorry. I was having a nightmare. (*he hiccups*) Something I ate. I'm not at all well. (*holds out cocktail shaker*) See? Hot water bottle.

CONDUCTOR (*disgusted*). Musicians! The last time we had some on the train, they started a wild, drunken brawl—twelve of them in one berth!

JERRY *clucks his tongue disapprovingly. The* CONDUCTOR *jerks the emergency cord a couple of times, signaling the engineer to start the train again.*

*Ext. Locomotive Wheels (Night)*

*The stalled wheels start to turn over and pick up speed.*

*Dissolve:*

*Int. Pullman Car (Night)*

*The train is moving.* JOE *appears from the women's lounge, signals to* SUGAR, *who is behind him.*

JOE. Okay, Sugar—all clear. You better go back to bed.

SUGAR. I might as well stay in there. I won't be able to sleep anyway.

JOE. Why not?

SUGAR. Bienstock. He snores to beat the band. We cut cards to see who sleeps over him, and I always lose. Wouldn't you know?

JOE. Want to switch berths with me?

SUGAR. Would you mind terribly?

JOE. Not at all.

*He leads her to Lower 7. The curtains of Upper 7 are closed.*

JOE. I can fall asleep anywhere, any time, over anybody.

*He takes his suitcase out, stashes it under the berth.*

SUGAR. Thanks honey.

JOE (*starting away*). Good night, Sugar.

*In Upper 7,* JERRY *is lying on his back with his eyes wide open, listening intently. From OFF comes—*

SUGAR'S VOICE. Good night, Josephine.

JERRY *props himself up on one elbow, a smug grin of anticipation on his face.*

SUGAR *gets into Lower 7, closing the curtains.* JOE *proceeds down the aisle, mounts the ladder to Upper 2.*

*In Upper 2,* JOE *closes the curtains, settles down to sleep. In the berth below,* BIENSTOCK *is snoring away. Unable to take it,* JOE *clamps the spare pillow over his head.*

*In Upper 7,* JERRY *takes a long swig out of the hot water bottle to get his courage up. Then he parts the curtains cautiously, drops to the aisle. He leans toward the closed curtains of Lower 7.*

JERRY *(very softly).* Joe—you asleep, Joe?

*In Lower 7,* SUGAR, *her eyes closed, is drifting off to sleep.*

JERRY, *satisfied that* JOE *is asleep, pussyfoots down the aisle to Berth 2. He listens for a second to* BIENSTOCK *snoring, climbs up the ladder to Upper 2.*

*In Upper 2,* JOE *lies facing the window. The curtains part gingerly, and* JERRY *sticks his head in.*

JERRY *(a honeyed whisper).* Sugar—Sugar baby—

JOE *opens his eyes wide, and is about to turn around, but* JERRY *puts a restraining hand on his shoulder.*

JERRY *(continuing).* Sssh. Don't move. It's me—Daphne. We don't want to wake up Bienstock.

*He slips into the berth, and the curtains close behind him. It's pretty dark now.* JERRY *stretches out on top of the covers, addresses the back of* JOE'S *head.* JOE, *a grim expression on his face, is waiting to see how far* JERRY *will go.*

JERRY *(continuing; the big moment).* You know what I promised you before—that surprise—well, I better break it to you gently. In the first place, I'm not a natural blonde—as a matter of fact, there are all sorts of things about me that are not natural—you see, my friend and I—the reason we're on the train with you girls—well, you know those holes in the bull-fiddle—that wasn't mice—

what I'm trying to say is—my name isn't really Daphne—it's Geraldine—I mean, Jerry—and you know why it's Jerry?—because I'm a boy!

*He sweeps his blonde wig off.* JOE, *who's had enough, makes a move to sit up, but* JERRY *pushes him back gently.*

JERRY *(continuing).* Don't scream, please. Don't spoil it—it's too beautiful. Just think of it, you and I—same berth, opposite sexes—male and female—he and she—the moth and the flame—*(takes* JOE'S *hand, puts it on his heart)* Feel my heart—like a crazy drum. *(starts kissing* JOE'S *hand)* I'm mad for you, Sugar. *(breathing heavily)* What are we going to do about it?

JOE *has had it. Wheeling around, he grabs* JERRY *by the front of his nightgown, starts to shake him like a terrier shaking a rat.*

JERRY *(continuing nonplussed).* Sugar, what are you doing? Don't get sore, baby—

*Beginning to realize something may be wrong,* JERRY *reaches up and switches on the light. There is something wrong.*

JOE *(holding* JERRY *with one hand, cocking the other).* Male and female—the moth and the flame—I ought to slug you!

JERRY *(slapping wig back on his head).* You wouldn't hit a girl, would you?

*Fade out:*

*Fade in:*

*Ext. Seminole-Ritz Hotel (Day)*

*The sprawling gingerbread structure basks in the warm Florida sun, fanned by towering palm trees, and lulled by waves breaking lazily on the exclusive beach frontage.*

*Wintertime and the livin' is easy, fish are jumpin' and the market is high.*

*The hotel bus chugs up the curved driveway toward the main entrance, hauling the Society Syncopators from the station. The rear of the bus is loaded with luggage and instruments. From inside comes the sound of girls' voices, singing "Down Among the Sheltering Palms."*

*On the hotel veranda, creaking in their rocking chairs, are a dozen elderly gentlemen. They are all in resort clothes—white flannels, striped flannels, knickers, Panama hats, white linen caps—and they are all reading the Wall Street Journal. Their combined age must be about a thousand years, and their combined bank balance just about as many millions. As they hear the bus drawing up, they stop rocking, and slowly lower their Wall Street Journals. They are all wearing sunglasses, and leaning forward, they peer through them at the new arrivals.*

*In the driveway, the girls are climbing out of the bus, luggage and instruments are being unloaded.* JERRY *helps* SUGAR *down, while* JOE *gets their instruments out of the pile. He hands the bull-fiddle case to* JERRY, *the ukulele case to* SUGAR.

JERRY (*taking the ukulele from* SUGAR). *I'll* carry the instruments.
SUGAR. Thank you, Daphne.
JOE (*handing* JERRY *the saxophone case*). Thank you, Daphne. (*to* SUGAR) Isn't she a sweetheart?

*He leads her toward the entrance.* JERRY, *loaded down with bass fiddle, ukulele and sax, glares after them an-*

*grily, then follows them, balancing precariously on his high heels.*

*On the veranda, the twelve rich dodos remove their sunglasses to get a better look at the girls. The one nearest to the steps is* OSGOOD FIELDING III. *He is a bit younger than the others, but that still puts him in his late fifties. He wears white plus-fours, argyle socks, two-toned shoes, and a gleam in his eye. He tips his Panama hat rakishly as the girl musicians mount the steps.*

JOE *and* SUGAR *come up the steps.* JOE *nudges her, directing her attention to the old crocks.*

JOE. Well, there they are—more millionaires than you can shake a stick at.
SUGAR. I'll bet there isn't one of them under seventy-five.
JOE. Seventy-five. That's three-quarters of a century. Makes a girl think.
SUGAR. Yeah, I hope they brought their grandsons along.

*As they pass* OSGOOD FIELDING III *and start into the lobby, he tips his Panama jauntily. Then he turns to inspect the next girl.*

*The next girl is* JERRY, *struggling up the steps, loaded with bass fiddle, saxophone and ukulele. He trips on the top steps, loses one of his shoes.* OSGOOD *jumps up gallantly.*

OSGOOD. Just a moment, miss— (*picks up shoe*) May I?
JERRY (*extending his foot regally*). Help yourself.
OSGOOD (*slipping shoe on*). I am Osgood Fielding the Third.
JERRY. I am Cinderella the Second.

*He starts to pull away, but* OSGOOD *holds on to his ankle.*

OSGOOD. If there's one thing I admire, it's a girl with a shapely ankle.

JERRY. Me too. Bye now.

OSGOOD. Let me carry one of the instruments.

JERRY. Thank you. *(loading him up with all the instruments)* Aren't you a sweetheart?

*He starts into the lobby,* OSGOOD *struggling after him with the instruments.*

*Int. Lobby of the Seminole-Ritz (Day)*

*The lobby is very resort-y—potted palms, overhead fans, and a heavy undergrowth of wicker furniture.* OSGOOD, *balancing the instruments, follows* JERRY *in.*

OSGOOD. It certainly is delightful to have some young blood around here.

JERRY. Personally, I'm Type O.

OSGOOD. You know, I've always been fascinated by show business.

JERRY. You don't say.

OSGOOD. Yes, indeed. It's cost my family quite a bit of money.

JERRY. You invest in shows?

OSGOOD. No—in showgirls. I've been married seven or eight times.

JERRY. You're not sure?

OSGOOD. Mama is keeping score. Frankly, she's getting rather annoyed with me.

JERRY. I'm not surprised.

OSGOOD. So this year, when George White's Scandals opened, she packed me off to Florida. Right now she thinks I'm out there on my yacht—deep-sea fishing.

JERRY. Well, pull in your reel, Mr. Fielding. You're barking up the wrong fish.

*They come up to the elevator. The doors are just closing on a load of girl musicians going up.*

OSGOOD. If I promise not to be a naughty boy—how about dinner tonight?

JERRY. Sorry. I'll be on the bandstand.

OSGOOD. Oh, of course. Which of these instruments do you play?

JERRY. Bull fiddle.

OSGOOD. Fascinating. Do you use a bow or do you just pluck it?

JERRY. Most of the time I slap it.

OSGOOD. You must be quite a girl.

JERRY. Wanna bet?

OSGOOD. My last wife was an acrobatic dancer—you know, sort of a contortionist—she could smoke a cigarette while holding it between her toes—Zowie!—but Mama broke it up.

JERRY. Why?

OSGOOD. She doesn't approve of girls who smoke.

*The elevator has come down again, and the doors open.*

JERRY *(reaching for the instruments)*. Goodbye, Mr. Fielding.

OSGOOD. Goodbye?

JERRY. This is where I get off.

OSGOOD *(the naughty boy)*. Oh, you don't get off *that* easy.

*He eases her into the elevator, follows with the instruments.*

OSGOOD *(continuing; to elevator operator)*. All right, driver. Once around the park. Slowly. And keep your eyes on the road.

*The door closes. Camera pans up to the floor indicator. The arrow moves smoothly past the second floor, then stops abruptly, jiggles violently, starts down again. Camera pans down. The elevator door opens.*

JERRY *(outraged womanhood)*. What kind of girl do you think I am, Mr. Fielding!

*He slaps* OSGOOD's *face, takes the instruments from him.*

OSGOOD. Please. It won't happen again.

JERRY. No, thank you. I'll walk.

*He stalks out of the elevator with the instruments, starts indignantly up the stairs.* OSGOOD *stands holding his cheek, looking after him enraptured.*

OSGOOD. Zowie!

*Int. Fourth Floor Corridor (Day)*

*This is the floor on which the girls are billeted.* SUGAR, JOE *and the other Society Syncopators are gathered around* BIENSTOCK *and* SUE, *while bellhops are bringing up the luggage.*

BIENSTOCK *(holding up a list)*. All right, girls—here are your room assignments. *(tapping his pockets)* My glasses—where are my glasses?

*As he continues to search,* SUE *takes the list from him, starts to read it off.*

SUE. Olga and Mary Lou in 412—and Mary Lou, keep your kimono buttoned when you ring for room service—Josephine and Daphne in 413—Dolores and Sugar in 414—

DOLORES. Me and *Sugar?*

SUE. What did you expect—a one-legged jockey?

JOE *and* SUGAR *are moving on toward their rooms.*

SUGAR. I wish they'd put us in the same room.

JOE. So do I. But don't worry—we'll be seeing a lot of each other.

*They reach the door of 414, and* SUGAR *opens it.*

SUGAR *(ruefully)*. 414—that's the same room number I had in Cincinnati—my last time around with a male band. What a heel he was.

JOE. Saxophone player?

SUGAR. What else? And was I ever crazy about him. Two in the morning, he sent me down for knackwurst and potato salad—they were out of potato salad, so I brought coleslaw—so he threw it right in my face.

JOE. Forget it, Sugar, will you? Forget saxophone players. You're going to meet a millionaire—a young one.

SUGAR. What makes you so sure?

JOE. Just my feminine intuition.

*She smiles gratefully at him as she enters 414.* JOE *crosses to the open door of 413, goes in.*

*Int. Room 413 (Day)*

*It's a small room, twin-beds, more wicker, adjoining bathroom. Outside the French windows is a balcony, giving on the ocean.*

*As* JOE *comes in, a* BELLHOP *is just setting down some suitcases—two of them are* JOE's *and* JERRY's, *the third is a somewhat more elegant model in brown cloth with a white stripe down the middle and the initials B.B. The* BELLHOP, *a fresh punk of seventeen, turns to* JOE.

BELLHOP. Are these your bags?

JOE. Yes. And *that* one, too.

BELLHOP. Okay, doll.

JOE. I suppose you want a tip?

BELLHOP. Forget it, doll. After all, you work here—I work here—and believe you me, it's nice to have you with the organization.

JOE. Bye.

BELLHOP *(the young Clark Gable)*. Listen, doll—what time do you get off tonight?

JOE. Why?

BELLHOP. Because I'm working the night shift—and I got a bottle of gin stashed away—and as soon as there's a lull—

JOE. Aren't you a little too young for that, sonny?

BELLHOP. Wanna see my driver's license?

JOE. Get lost, will you?

BELLHOP. That's the way I like 'em—big and sassy. *(at the door)* And get rid of your roommate.

*He pulls out his bow tie, which is on an elastic, lets it snap back like an exclamation point.* JOE *looks after him grimly, then his eyes fall on the suitcase with the stripe, and he shoves it quickly under the bed. The door opens again, and* JOE *whirls around.* JERRY *comes staggering in breathlessly with the instruments, kicks the door shut with his foot.*

JERRY. Why, that dirty old man!

*He throws the instruments disgustedly on one of the beds.*

JOE. What happened?

JERRY. I got pinched in the elevator.

JOE. Well, now you know how the other half lives.

JERRY *(looking in the mirror).* And I'm not even pretty.

JOE. They don't care—just a long as you wear skirts. It's like waving a red flag in front of a bull.

JERRY. I'm tired of being a flag. I want to be a bull again. Let's get out of here, Joe. Let's blow.

JOE. Blow where?

JERRY. You promised—the minute we hit Florida, we were going to beat it.

JOE. How can we? We're broke.

JERRY. We can get a job with another band. A *male* band.

JOE. Listen, stupid—right now Spats Colombo and his chums are looking for us in every male band in the country.

JERRY. But this is so humiliating.

JOE. So you got pinched in the elevator. So what? Would you rather be picking lead out of your navel?

JERRY. All right, all right! *(rips off his hat and wig, tosses them on the bed)* But how long can we keep this up?

JOE. What's the beef? We're sitting pretty. We get room and board—we get paid every week—there's the palm trees and the flying fish—

JERRY. What are you giving me with the flying fish? I know why you want to stick around—you're after Sugar.

JOE *(holier-than-thou).* Me? After Sugar?

JERRY. I watched you two on the bus—lovey-dovey—whispering and giggling and borrowing each other's lipstick—

JOE. What are you talking about? Sugar and me, we're just like sisters.

JERRY. Yeah? Well, I'm your fairy godmother—and I'm keeping an eye on you.

*There is a knock on the door.*

BIENSTOCK'S VOICE. Are you decent?

JOE *pulls* JERRY'S *wig out of the hat, jams it down on his head.*

JOE. Come in.

BIENSTOCK *comes in.*

BIENSTOCK. You girls seen a brown bag with a white stripe and my initials?

JERRY. A what?

BIENSTOCK. My suitcase—with all my resort clothes.

JOE *(glancing down).* No, we haven't.

BIENSTOCK. Can't understand it. First my glasses disappear—then one of my suitcases—

SUGAR *appears in the doorway behind him.*

SUGAR. Where's my ukulele?

BIENSTOCK. —now a ukulele. There must be a sneak thief around here.

*He goes out, shaking his head in puzzlement.*

JERRY *(handing her the ukulele).* Here you are, Sugar.

SUGAR. A bunch of us girls are going for a swim. Want to come along?

JERRY. You betcha.

JOE. Wait a minute, Daphne. You haven't got a bathing suit.

SUGAR. She doesn't need one. I don't have one either.

JERRY *(to* JOE). See? She doesn't have one either—*(to* SUGAR) You don't?

SUGAR. We'll rent some at the bathhouse. How about you, Josephine?

JOE. No, thanks. I'd rather stay in and soak in a hot tub.

*He steps into the bathroom, turns on the faucet.*

JERRY. Yeah—let her soak. Come on.

JOE. Don't get burned, Daphne.

SUGAR. Oh, I have some suntan lotion.

JERRY. She'll rub it on me—and I'll rub it on her—and we'll rub it on each other—bye.

*He ushers* SUGAR *out in high spirits.* JOE *looks after them, then quickly locks the hall door, and stepping into the bathroom, turns off the water. He hurries over to the bed, slides out* BIENSTOCK'S *suitcase, opens it. It's crammed full of resort clothes—and* JOE *takes out a blazer, flannel pants, and a yachting cap, which he perches on his head. Then he lifts his skirt above his knee, plls out* BIENSTOCK'S *glasses from under his garter. He puts them on, peers around myopically. His enlarged eyes are grotesque—but then again, so is his scheme.*

*Dissolve to:*

*Beach (Day)*

*To the accompaniment of "By the Beautiful Sea," several girls from the band, in bathing suits and caps, are running into the surf. The other girls are already in the water, splashing around and frolicking like a school of playful porpoises. There is no sign of* JERRY. SUGAR, *standing up to her waist in water, suddenly lets out a startled squeal, slaps the surface of the water behind her.*

SUGAR. Daphne! Cut that out!

JERRY *comes diving up, spouting water like a dolphin. He is wearing a girl's knitted bathing suit with a short skirt, and a rubber cap.*

SUGAR *(continuing).* What do you think you're doing?

JERRY. Just a little trick I picked up in the elevator.

*A good-sized wave comes rolling in.*

JERRY *(continuing).* Oooh. Here comes a big one.

*He grabs* SUGAR, *holding on to her tightly. The wave breaks over them, sweeps them off their feet. Strolling casually along the beach is* JOE. *He is wearing* BIENSTOCK'S *blazer (crest and eight gold buttons), flannel slacks (bell-bottom), a silk scarf, a yachting cap, and the glasses (which blur his vision considerably). In his hand he carries a rolled-up copy of the Wall Street Journal. He looks off toward the ocean.*

*The girls are scampering out of the water, and some of them start to toss a beach ball around.* SUGAR *and* JERRY *come running up to the beach hand in hand. They take their caps off, and* SUGAR *puts on a short terry-cloth jacket.* JERRY *jumps around on* one foot, his head tilted, shaking the water out of his ear, then starts to rub himself off with a towel.

SUGAR (*studying him*). You know, Daphne—I had no idea you were such a *big* girl.

JERRY. You should have seen me before I went on a diet.

SUGAR. I mean, your shoulders— and your arms—

JERRY. That's from carrying around the bull fiddle.

SUGAR. But there's one thing I envy you for.

JERRY. What's that?

SUGAR. You're so flat-chested. Clothes hang so much better on you than they do on me.

DOLORES' VOICE (*from off*). Look out, Daphne!

*The beach ball comes sailing into shot, and* JERRY *catches it.*

JERRY. Come on, Sugar,—let's play.

*He takes* SUGAR'S *hand, skips off with her to join the other girls.*

JOE, *meanwhile, has come up to a basket chair nearby. Sitting in front of it, sorting sea shells out of a small pail, is a boy of five. A few feet away stands his mother, calling to him.*

MOTHER. Let's go, Junior. Time for your nap.

JUNIOR. Nah. I wanna play.

JOE (*out of the corner of his mouth*). You heard your mudder, Junior. Scram.

*The boy looks up at him, fearfully.*

JOE (*continuing*). This beach ain't big enough for both of us.

*The boy scrambles to his feet, and screaming "Mommy," runs off, leaving the pailful of shells behind.* JOE *settles himself in the chair, peers over* his shoulder toward the girls playing ball.

*The girls,* SUGAR *and* JERRY *among them, are standing in a wide circle, tossing the beach ball around and chanting rhythmically: "I love coffee, I love tea, how many boys are stuck on me? One, two, three, four, five—"*

*There is a wild throw over* SUGAR'S *head, in the direction of* JOE'S *chair.* SUGAR *turns and runs after the ball to retrieve it.*

*This is exactly what* JOE *has been waiting for. As the ball comes rolling past, he unfolds the Wall Street Journal, pretends to be reading it. Just as* SUGAR *runs by,* JOE *extends his foot a couple of inches—enough to trip her and send her sprawling to the sand.*

JOE (*lowering paper; Cary Grant by now*). Oh, I'm terribly sorry.

SUGAR. My fault.

JOE (*helping her up*). You're not hurt, are you?

SUGAR. I don't think so.

JOE. I wish you'd make sure.

SUGAR. Why?

JOE. Because usually, when people find out who I am, they get themselves a wheel chair and a shyster lawyer, and sue me for a quarter of a million dollars.

SUGAR. Well, don't worry. I won't sue you—no matter who you are.

JOE (*returning to chair*). Thank you.

SUGAR. Who *are* you?

JOE. Now, really—

JERRY *and the other girls are looking off toward* SUGAR, *waiting for the ball.*

JERRY. Hey, Sugar—come on.

SUGAR *picks up the ball.*

JOE (*blase*). So long.

*He buries himself behind the Wall Street Journal again.* SUGAR *hesitates for a second, then throws the ball back to the girls. She steps closer to* JOE *peers around the paper, studying him.*

SUGAR. Haven't I seen you somewhere before?

JOE *(without looking up)*. Not very likely.

SUGAR. Are you staying at the hotel?

JOE. Not at all.

SUGAR. Your face *is* familiar.

JOE. Possible you saw it in a newspaper—or magazine—Vanity Fair—

SUGAR. That must be it.

JOE *(waving her aside)*. Would you mind moving just a little? You're blocking my view.

SUGAR. Your view of what?

JOE. They run up a red-and-white flag on the yacht when it's time for cocktails.

SUGAR *(snapping at the bait)*. You have a yacht?

*She turns and looks seaward at half-a-dozen yachts of different sizes bobbing in the distance.*

SUGAR *(continuing)*. Which one is yours—the big one?

JOE. Certainly not. With all that unrest in the world, I don't think anybody should have a yacht that sleeps more than twelve.

SUGAR. I quite agree. Tell me, who runs up that flag—your wife?

JOE. No, my flag steward.

SUGAR. And who mixes the cocktails—your wife?

JOE. No, my cocktail steward. Look, if you're interested in whether I'm married or not—

SUGAR. I'm not interested at all.

JOE. Well, I'm not.

SUGAR. That's very interesting.

JOE *resumes reading the paper.* SUGAR *sits on the sand beside his chair.*

SUGAR *(continuing)*. How's the stock market?

JOE *(lackadaisically)*. Up, up, up.

SUGAR. I'll bet just while we were talking, you made like a hundred thousand dollars.

JOE. Could be. Do you play the market?

SUGAR. No—the ukulele. And I sing.

JOE. For your own amusement?

SUGAR. Well—a group of us are appearing at the hotel. Sweet Sue and Her Society Syncopators.

JOE. You're society girls?

SUGAR. Oh, yes. Quite. You know—Vassar, Bryn Mawr—we're only doing this for a lark.

JOE. Syncopators—does that mean you play that fast music—jazz?

SUGAR. Yeah. Real hot.

JOE. Oh. Well, I guess some like it hot. But personally, I prefer classical music.

SUGAR. So do I. As a matter of fact, I spent three years at the Sheboygan Conservatory of Music.

JOE. Good school! And your family doesn't object to your career?

SUGAR. They do indeed. Daddy threatened to cut me off without a cent, but I don't care. It was such a bore—coming-out parties, cotillions—

JOE. —Inauguration balls—

SUGAR. —opening of the Opera—

JOE. —riding to hounds—

SUGAR. —and always the same Four Hundred.

JOE. You know, it's amazing we never ran into each other before. I'm sure I would have remembered anybody as attractive as you.

SUGAR. You're very kind. I'll bet

you're also very gentle—and help-less—

JOE. I beg your pardon?

SUGAR. You see, I have this theory about men with glasses.

JOE. What theory?

SUGAR. Maybe I'll tell you when I know you a little better. What are you doing tonight?

JOE. Tonight?

SUGAR. I thought you might like to come to the hotel and hear us play.

JOE. I'd like to—but it may be rather difficult.

SUGAR. Why?

JOE (*his eyes on the pail with the shells*). I only come ashore twice a day—when the tide goes out.

SUGAR. Oh?

JOE. It's on account of the shells. That's my hobby.

SUGAR. You collect shells?

JOE (*taking a handful of shells from the pail*). Yes. so did my father and my grandfather—we've all had this passion for shells—that's why we named the oil company after it.

SUGAR (*wide-eyed*). *Shell Oil?*

JOE. Please—no names. Just call me Junior.

*By this time, the ball game is breaking up, and* JERRY *approaches* SUGAR *and* JOE.

JERRY. Come on, Sugar—time to change for dinner.

SUGAR. Run along, Daphne—I'll catch up with you.

JERRY (*a casual glance at* JOE). Okay.

*He takes a couple of steps away from them, freezes, comes back and stares at* JOE *open-mouthed.*

JOE. What is it, young lady? What are you staring at?

JERRY (*points; speechless*). You—you—

JOE (*to* SUGAR). This happens to me all the time in public.

SUGAR (*to* JERRY). I recognized him too—his picture was in Vanity Fair.

JERRY. *Vanity Fair?*

JOE (*waving him aside*). Would you mind moving along, please?

SUGAR. Yes, you're in the way. He's waiting for a signal from his yacht.

JERRY. His *yacht?*

SUGAR. It sleeps twelve. (*to* JOE) This is my friend Daphne. She's a Vassar girl.

JERRY. I'm a *what?*

SUGAR. Or was it Bryn Mawr?

JOE (*to* JERRY). I heard a very sad story about a girl who went to Bryn Mawr. She squealed on her room-mate, and they found her strangled with her own brassiere.

JERRY (*grimly*). Yes—you have to be very careful about picking a room-mate.

SUGAR. Well, I guess I'd better go—

JOE. It's been delightful meeting you both.

SUGAR. And you will come to hear us tonight?

JOE. If it's at all possible—

JERRY. Oh, please *do* come. Don't disappoint us. It'll be such fun. And bring your yacht.

SUGAR. Come on, Daphne.

*She leads* JERRY *away.* JOE *throws them a casual salute.*

*As* JERRY *and* SUGAR *move off,* JER-RY *looks over his shoulder.*

JERRY. Well, I'll be—! How about that guy?

SUGAR. Now look, Daphne—hands off—I saw him first.

JERRY. Sugar, dear—let me give you some advice. If I were a girl—and I *am*—I'd watch my step.

SUGAR. If I'd been watching my step, I never would have met him. Wait till I tell Josephine.

JERRY. Yeah—Josephine.

SUGAR. Will she be surprised. I just can't wait to see her face—

JERRY. Neither can I. Come on— let's go up to her room and tell her— *right now.*

*He grabs her hand, starts to run toward the hotel.*

SUGAR. We don't have to run.

JERRY. Oh yes, we do!

*Dissolve to:*

*Int. Fourth Floor Corridor (Day)*

JERRY, *holding* SUGAR *by the hand, comes running down the corridor from the elevator. He flings open the door of 413, pulls* SUGAR *inside.*

*Int. Room 413 (Day)*

JERRY *and* SUGAR *stop breathlessly, look around. The room is empty.*

JERRY. Josephine—

SUGAR. I guess she's not here.

JERRY That's funny. Josie— (*sees* JOSEPHINE's *dress on a hanger; smugly*) I can't imagine where she can be.

SUGAR. Well, I'll come back later.

JERRY. No, no, Sugar— wait. I have a feeling she's going to show up any minute

SUGAR (*sitting down*). Believe it or not—Josephine predicted the whole thing.

JERRY. Yeah. This is one for Ripley.

SUGAR. Do you suppose she went out shopping?

JERRY. That's it. Something tells me she's going to walk through that door in a whole new outfit.

*He opens the door, peers out into the corridor expecting* JOE *to show up in the yachting outfit. At the same time, through the partly open door of the bathroom, comes* JOSEPHINE's *voice, singing "Running Wild."*

JERRY *does a double-take.* SUGAR *starts toward the bathroom door and opens it.* JERRY *follows her, incredulously.*

*In the bathroom,* JOE *with his wig on, is lying languidly in the tub taking a bubble-bath, up to his neck in white foam.*

SUGAR. Josephine.

JOE. Oh, I didn't hear you come in.

JERRY *looks back toward the windows, trying to figure out how* JOE *got in.*

SUGAR. The most wonderful thing happened—

JOE. What?

SUGAR. Guess!

JOE. They repealed Prohibition?

JERRY. Oh, come on—you can do better than that.

SUGAR. I met one of them.

JOE. One of whom?

SUGAR. Shell Oil, Junior. He's got millions—he's got glasses—and he's got a yacht.

JOE (*beaming*). You don't say!

JERRY. He's not only got a yacht, he's got a bicycle.

JOE (*warningly*). Daphne—(*to* SUGAR) Go on—tell me all about him.

SUGAR. Well, he's young and handsome and a bachelor—and he's a real gentleman—not one of these grabbers.

JOE. Maybe you'd better go after *him*—if you don't want to lose him.

SUGAR. Oh, I'm not going to let *this* one get away. He's so cute— collects shells.

JOE. Shells? Whatever for?

JERRY. You know—the old shell game.

JOE. Daphne, you're bothering us.

SUGAR. Anyway, you're going to meet him tonight.

JOE. I am?

SUGAR. Because he said he's coming to hear us play—maybe.

JERRY. What do you mean, maybe? I saw the way he looked at you. He'll be there for sure.

SUGAR. I hope so.

JERRY. What do you think, Josephine? What does it say in your crystal ball?

JOE *glares at him. Meanwhile,* DO-LORES *has come into the room in her wet bathing suit and carrying a dripping rubber horse. She sticks her head into the bathroom.*

DOLORES. Hey, Sugar, you got the key? I'm locked out and I'm making a puddle in the hall.

SUGAR (*to* JOE *and* JERRY). See you on the bandstand, girls.

*She follows* DOLORES *out, closing the door.* JOE *and* JERRY *are alone now. The atmosphere is tense. They look at each other steely-eyed.*

JOE (*finally*). Wise guy, huh? Trying to louse me up—

JERRY. And what are *you* trying to do to poor Sugar? Putting on that millionaire act—and that phony accent— (*a la Cary Grant*) Nobody talks like that! I've seen you pull some low tricks on dames—but this is the trickiest and the lowest and the meanest—

*His words trail off as he sees* JOE *rise slowly out of the tub. The mystery of his quick change is now solved—he didn't change at all. He is fully dressed in* BIENSTOCK'S *outfit, and is clutching the yachting cap. As he emerges from the bathtub, covered with suds, he looks like some diabolique monster. He advances on* JERRY *menacingly.*

JERRY (*continuing*). I'm not scared of you—(*retreating*) I may be small, but I'm wiry—(*retreating some more*) When I'm aroused, I'm a tiger!

*By this time he is up against the wall.* JOE *is closing in on him.*

JERRY (*continuing; conciliatory*). Don't look at me like that, Joe—I didn't mean any harm—it was just a little joke—don't worry—I'll press the suit myself.

*The phone rings.*

JERRY (*continuing*). Telephone—

JOE *closes in relentlessly.*

JERRY (*continuing*). You better answer the phone—

JOE *slams the sopping cap on* JER-RY'S *head. As* JERRY *coughs and splutters,* JOE *picks up the ringing phone.*

JOE. Hello—(*remembering he is a girl, pitches voice higher*) Hello—yes, this is 413—ship-to-shore?—all right, I'll take it.

*Fantail of the Yacht Caledonia (Day)*

*It is a chic vessel indeed—and so is* OSGOOD FIELDING III, *lounging in a deck chair, speaking into a radio-telephone.*

OSGOOD (*that gleam in his eye*). Hello, Daphne? It's that naughty boy again—you know, Osgood—in the elevator—you slapped my face? Who is this?

*Int. Room 413 (Day)*

JOE *is on the phone. Through the open door of the bathroom we see* JERRY *wiping his face.*

JOE. This is her roommate. Daphne can't talk right now. Is it anything urgent?

OSGOOD—*On phone*

OSGOOD. Well, it is to me. Will you give her a message? I'd like her to have a little supper with me on my yacht after the show tonight.

JOE—*On phone*

JOE. Got it. Supper—yacht—after the show—I'll tell her. *(reacting) Your yacht?*

*Osgood—On phone*

OSGOOD. The New Caledonia. That's the name of it. The *Old* Caledonia went down during a wild party off Cape Hatteras. But tell her not to worry—this is going to be a quiet little midnight snack—just the two of us.

*Joe—On Phone*

JOE. Just the two of you? What about the crew?

*Osgood—On Phone*

OSGOOD. Oh, that's all taken care of. I'm giving them shore leave. We'll have a little cold pheasant—and champagne—and I checked with the Coast Guard—there'll be a full moon tonight—oh, and tell her I got a new batch of Rudy Vallee records—

*Int. Room 413 (Day)*

JOE *(into phone)*. That's good thinking. Daphne's a push-over for him.

JERRY *comes up, still holding the towel.*

JERRY. I'm a push-over for whom? What is it? Who's on the phone?

JOE *(shushing him; into phone)*. Yes, Mr. Fielding—you'll pick her up after the show in your motorboat—goodbye—what's that you said? Oh—zowie! I'll give her the message. *(he hangs up)*

JERRY. What message? What motorboat?

JOE. You got it made, kid. Fielding wants you to have a little cold pheasant with him on his yacht—

JERRY. Oh, he does!

JOE. Just the three of you on that great big boat—you and him and Rudy Vallee.

JERRY. Fat chance! You call him right back and tell him I'm not going.

JOE. Of course, you're not. *I'm* going.

JERRY. You're going to be on the boat with that dirty old man?

JOE. No. I'm going to be on the boat with Sugar.

JERRY. And where's *he* going to be?

JOE. He's going to be ashore with *you.*

JERRY. With *me?*

JOE. That's right.

JERRY. Oh, no! Not tonight, Josephine!

*Dissolve to:*

*Int. Hotel Ballroom (Night)*

*It's a good-sized nightclub of the period, with about 200 guests in formal dress-evening gowns, white dinner jackets—at the tables and on the dance floor. A revolving globe, with a mirrored surface, throws patterns of light and shadow on the dancers.*

*On the bandstand,* SUGAR, *backed by the rest of the orchestra, is singing. The girls in the band,* JOE *and* JERRY *among them, wear uniform evening gowns and long earrings.* SUGAR *and* SUE *wear distinctive gowns.* SUGAR'S *song is "I Want To Be Loved By You"—which she belts across in the style of the Twenties, complete with poop-poop-pa-doop trimmings. As she sings, she scans the room for her bespectacled Prince Charming, but there is no sign of him—naturally, since he is playing the saxophone behind her.*

*In back of* JOE *is* JERRY, *thumping the bass grimly. He looks off, sees—*

OSGOOD FIELDING III, *in a white mess jacket, sitting alone at a table. Catching* JERRY'S *eye, he waves exuberantly, his face beaming with amorous anticipation.*

*On the bandstand,* JERRY *looks away haughtily.*

JOE *(over his shoulder)*. Daphne—your boy friend is waving at you.

JERRY. You can *both* go take a flying jump.

JOE. Remember—he's your date for tonight. So smile.

JERRY *smiles feebly.*

JOE *(continuing)*. Come on, you can do better than that. Give him the teeth—the whole personality.

JERRY *(a frozen smile on his face)*. Why do I let you talk me into these things? *Why?*

JOE. Because we're pals—buddies—the two musketeers.

JERRY. Don't give me the musketeers! How'm I going to keep the guy ashore?

JOE. Tell him you get seasick on a yacht. Play miniature golf with him.

JERRY. Oh, no. I'm not getting caught in a miniature sand trap with *that* guy.

*The fresh young* BELLHOP *we saw earlier comes up beside the bandstand, carrying a large wicker basket full of flowers.*

BELLHOP *(to* JOE). Which of you dolls is Daphne?

JOE. Bull fiddle.

*The* BELLHOP *hands the basket to* JERRY, *nods off toward* OSGOOD'S *table.*

BELLHOP. It's from Satchel Mouth at Table Seven. *(he breaks off one flower, hands it to* JOE). This is from me to you, doll.

JOE. Beat it, Buster.

BELLHOP *(confidentially)*. Never mind leaving your door open—I got a passkey.

*He winks and moves off.* JOE *looks after him contemptuously, then turns to* JERRY, *picks up the basket of flowers.*

JERRY. What are you doing with my flowers?

JOE. I'm just borrowing them. You'll get them back tomorrow.

*He hands* JERRY *the single flower, then looks around, fishes a small envelope out of his decolletage, slips it into the basket.*

SUGAR *finishes her number, returns to her seat next to* JOE. SUE *leads the orchestra into the signature music, "Sweet Sue."*

SUGAR *(to* JOE). I guess he's not going to show up—it's five minutes to one—you suppose he forgot?

JOE. Well, you know how those millionaires are. *(pointing at basket of flowers)* These came for you.

SUGAR. For *me*? *(she opens the note)* It's Shell Oil.

JERRY *(sarcastically)*. No!

SUGAR. Yes. He wants me to have supper with him—on his yacht—he's going to pick me up at the pier.

JERRY. No!

SUGAR. Yes.

JOE *(to* JERRY). You heard her—yes.

SUGAR *(bubbling over)*. Oh, Josephine—just imagine—me, Sugar Kowalczyk, from Sandusky, Ohio, on a millionaire's yacht. If my mother could only see me now—

JERRY *(looking off toward* OS-

GOOD). I hope my mother never finds out.

*At his table* OSGOOD, *catching* JERRY'S *look, blows kisses to him.*

*On the bandstand,* SUE *turns to the audience for her signature spiel.*

SUE. That's it for tonight, folks. This is Sweet Sue, saying good night, and reminding all you daddies out there—every girl in my band is a virtuoso—and I intend to keep it that way.

*Behind her,* SUGAR *picks up her ukulele and the basket of flowers, tiptoes off the stand.* JOE *waves after her, wishing her luck.* SUGAR *hurries toward the staircase, passing* BIENSTOCK, *who is planted near the reservation desk. As* SUE *cuts off the music,* JOE *frantically packs up his saxophone. Then he leaps off the bandstand, and dashing past the bewildered* BIENSTOCK, *starts up the stairs two at a time.*

*Dissolve to:*

*Int. Room 413 (Night)*

JOE *barges in, drops the saxophone case, locks the door. Then he darts into the bathroom, wriggling out of his dress. Camera pans over to the other door of the bathroom as the dress and shoes come flying out. They are immediately followed by* JOE, *now partially dressed as a man. He slips into* BIENSTOCK'S *coat, puts on the yachting cap. Even to a captain he would be a captain now, except for one thing—in his haste, he has neglected to take off his earrings. He opens a window, steps out onto the balcony.*

*Ext. Balcony of Room 413 (Night)*

JOE *moves along the balcony, climbs over the railing, starts to shinny down a post.*

*Ext. Side Entrance of Hotel (Night)*

SUGAR, *a fur boa over the evening gown she wore on the bandstand, comes tripping down the steps, hurries eagerly toward the beach.*

*Hotel Grounds (Night)*

*In the f.g., to one side of the main entrance, a dozen bicycles are parked in rack.* JOE *drops down into the scene, sees the bicycles, pulls one out, mounts it, and pedals off.*

*Standing under a tree in front of the hotel are* OSGOOD *and* JERRY. JERRY *is in his evening gown and is holding the flower in his hand.*

OSGOOD. But it's such a waste—a full moon—an empty yacht—

JERRY. I'll throw up!

OSGOOD. Well, then, why don't we go dancing? I know a little roadhouse down the coast—

JOE *comes whizzing past them on his bicycle.* JERRY *looks after him, open-mouthed.*

JERRY. Well, I'll be—! He *does* have a bicycle.

OSGOOD. Who?

JERRY (*catching himself*). About that roadhouse—

OSGOOD. They've got a Cuban band that's the berries. Why don't we go there—blindfold the orchestra—and tango till dawn?

JERRY. You know something, Mr. Fielding? You're dynamite!

OSGOOD. You're a pretty hot little firecracker yourself.

*He links his arm through* JERRY'S, *leads him down the path.*

SUGAR *is now almost running toward the pier, a look of great expectation on her face. This is the big night of her life.*

JOE *is pedaling desperately to get to the pier before her, oblivious of the earrings dangling incongruously from his ear lobes.*

*Ext. Pier (Night)*

*About a dozen motorboats are tied up to the pier.* SUGAR *hurries across the planking and up the stairs to the deserted pier, stops and looks around for her date. Behind her,* JOE *comes skimming along the planking on his bicycle, swoops under the pier.*

*A disheartened* SUGAR *thinks that she has been stood up.* JOE *dismounts from the bike, ducks underneath the pier, and hops into the motorboat marked Caledonia. Straightening up, he waves to* SUGAR *on the pier above him.*

JOE. Ahoy there!

SUGAR *turns, her face lighting up.*

SUGAR. Ahoy!

*She hurries down the steps toward him.*

JOE *suddenly remembers his glasses. He takes them out of his pocket, puts them on. As he does so, he feels the earrings. He pulls them off, shoves them in his pocket—and not a second too soon, for* SUGAR *has just about reached him.*

SUGAR *(continuing).* Been waiting long?

JOE *(Cary Grant again).* It's not how long you wait—it's who you're waiting for.

*He helps her down into the motorboat.*

SUGAR. Thank you. And thank you for the flowers.

JOE. I wanted them to fly down some orchids from our greenhouse but all of Long Island is fogged in.

SUGAR. It's the thought that counts.

*She settles herself back on the cushioned seat.* JOE *starts fiddling around with the mysterious knobs on the instrument panel. He pushes, pulls twists the knob—finally the motor turns over, but does not catch.*

JOE. I seem to be out of gas.

SUGAR. It's sort of funny—*you* being out of gas—I mean, Shell Oil and everything—

JOE, *working the knobs desperately, does something right, and the motor starts with a roar.*

JOE. Here we go.

*He presses every lever he can find, manages to shift into gear. The boat backs out erratically.* JOE *shifts into neutral, but no matter how hard he tries to find the forward gear, he keeps winding up in reverse.*

JOE *(apologetically).* I just got this motorboat—it's an experimental model.

SUGAR. Looks like they're on the wrong track.

JOE. Do you mind riding backwards? It may take a little longer—

SUGAR. It's not how long it takes—it's who's taking you.

*The motorboat glides off backwards, and as though it were the most natural thing in the world, skims out toward the open water, where the yachts are anchored.*

*Dissolve to:*

*Yacht at Anchor (Night)*

*The Caledonia is bobbing gently on a calm, moonlit sea. The motorboat with* JOE *and* SUGAR *comes in stern-backwards.* JOE, *looking over his shoulder, maneuvers the motorboat to a stop under the landing ladder. (Reams of romantic music under all of this.)*

*Dissolve to:*

*Ext. Deck of Caledonia (Night)*

*As* JOE *helps* SUGAR *aboard. She gazes around, starry-eyed.*

SUGAR. It looked so small from the beach—but when you're on it, it's more like a cruiser—or a destroyer.

JOE. Just regulation size. We have three like this.

SUGAR. Three?

JOE. Mother keeps hers in Southhampton—and Dad took his to Venezuela—the company is laying a new pipe line.

SUGAR. My dad is more interested in railroads. Baltimore and Ohio. Which is the port and which is the starboard?

JOE (*the old mariner*). Well, that depends—on whether you're coming or going—I mean, normally the aft is on the other side of the stern—and that's the bridge—so you can get from one side of the boat to the other—how about a glass of champagne?

SUGAR. Love it. Which way?

JOE. Yes—now let's see—where do you suppose the steward set it up?

*He looks around, confused by the unfamiliar geography, then tentatively opens the nearest door, revealing a flight of stairs leading below deck.*

SUGAR. Oh, you have an upstairs and a downstairs.

JOE. Yes—that's our hurricane cellar.

*He closes the door, opens another one—it's a storage bin, containing mops, pails, coils of rope, etc.*

JOE (*continues*). And another nice thing about this yacht—lots of closet space.

SUGAR, *meanwhile, has stepped up to a lighted porthole, looks inside.*

SUGAR. Oh—in here.

JOE. Of course. On Thursdays, they always serve me in the small salon.

*He opens the door, ushers* SUGAR *inside.*

*Int. Salon of Yacht (Night)*

*It's a very elegant layout—mahogany paneling, shelves of trophies, a stuffed marlin on the wall, a luxurious couch with a table for two set up beside it. On the table are lit candles, cold pheasant under glass, and champagne in a silver ice bucket.*

JOE *and* SUGAR *come in, and as* JOE *takes his cap off,* SUGAR *looks around, dazzled.*

SUGAR. It's exquisite—like a floating mansion.

JOE. It's all right for a bachelor.

SUGAR (*stopping by the stuffed marlin*). What a beautiful fish.

JOE. Caught him off Cape Hatteras.

SUGAR. What is it?

JOE. Oh—a member of the herring family.

SUGAR. A herring? Isn't it amazing how they get those big fish into those little glass jars?

JOE. They shrink when they're marinated.

*During this, he has opened the champagne, filled a couple of glasses.*

JOE (*continues*). Champagne?

SUGAR. I don't mind if I do.

JOE (*toasting her*). Down the hatch—as we say at sea.

SUGAR. Bon voyage.

*As she sips the drink, she glances at the shelves of trophies.*

SUGAR. Look at all that silverware.

JOE. Trophies. You know—skeetshooting, dog-breeding, water polo . . .

SUGAR. Water polo—isn't that terribly dangerous?

JOE. I'll say. I had two ponies drowned under me.

SUGAR. Where's your shell collection?

JOE. Yes, of course. Now where could they have put it? *(looking under the couch)* On Thursdays, I'm sort of lost around here.

SUGAR. What's on Thursdays?

JOE. It's the crew's night off.

SUGAR. You mean we're alone on the boat?

JOE. Completely.

SUGAR. You know, I've never been completely alone with a man before—in the middle of the night—in the middle of the ocean.

JOE. Oh, it's perfectly safe. We're well-anchored—the ship is in ship-shape shape—and the Coast Guard promised to call me if there are any icebergs around.

SUGAR. It's not the icebergs. But there are certain men who would try to take advantage of a situation like this.

JOE. You're flattering me.

SUGAR. Well, of course, I'm sure you're a gentleman.

JOE. Oh, it's not that. It's just that I'm—harmless.

SUGAR. Harmless-how?

JOE. Well, I don't know how to put it—but I have this thing about girls.

SUGAR. What thing?

JOE. They just sort of leave me cold.

SUGAR. You mean—like frigid?

JOE. It's more like a mental block. When I'm with a girl, it does nothing to me.

SUGAR. Have you tried?

JOE. Have I? I'm trying all the time.

*He casually puts his arms around her, kisses her on the lips, lets go of her again.*

JOE *(continues)*. See? Nothing.

SUGAR. Nothing at *all?*

JOE. Complete washout.

SUGAR. That makes me feel just awful.

JOE. Oh, it's not *your* fault. It's just that every now and then Mother Nature throws somebody a dirty curve. Something goes wrong inside.

SUGAR. You mean you can't fall in love?

JOE. Not any more. I *was* in love once-but I'd rather not talk about it. *(takes the glass bell off the cold cuts)* How about a little cold pheasant?

SUGAR. What happened?

JOE. I don't want to bore you.

SUGAR. Oh, you couldn't possibly.

JOE. Well, it was in my freshman year at Princeton—there was this girl—her name was Nellie—her father was vice-president of Hupmobile-she wore glasses, too. That summer we spent our vacation at the Grand Canyon—we were standing on the highest ledge, watching the sunset—suddenly we had an impulse to kiss—I took off my glasses—she took off her glasses—I took a step toward her—she took a step toward me—

SUGAR *(hand flying to mouth)*. Oh, no!

JOE. Yes. Eight hours later they brought her up by mule—I gave her three transfusions—we had the same blood type—Type O—it was too late.

SUGAR. Talk about sad.

JOE. Ever since then—*(indicating heart)*—numb—no feeling. Like my heart was shot full of novocaine.

SUGAR. You poor, poor boy.

JOE. Yes—all the money in the world—but what good is it? *(holding out serving plate)* Mint sauce or cranberries?

SUGAR. How can you think about food at a time like this?

JOE. What else is there for me? *(tears off leg of pheasant)*

SUGAR. Is it that hopeless?

JOE *(eating)*. My family did everything they could—hired the most beautiful French upstairs maids—got a special tutor to read me all the books that were banned in Boston—imported a whole troupe of Balinese dancers with bells on their ankles and those long fingernails—what a waste of money!

SUGAR. Have you ever tried American girls?

JOE. Why?

*She kisses him—pretty good, but nothing spectacular.*

SUGAR. Is *that* anything?

JOE *(shaking his head)*. Thanks just the same.

*He resumes nibbling on the pheasant leg, sits on the couch.*

SUGAR. Maybe if you saw a good doctor . . .

JOE. I have. Spent six months in Vienna with Professor Freud—flat on my back—*(stretches out on the couch, still eating)*—then there were the Mayo Brothers—and injections and hypnosis and mineral baths—if I weren't such a coward, I'd kill myself.

SUGAR. Don't talk like that. I'm sure there must be *some* girl *some* place that could—

JOE. If I ever found a girl that *could*—I'd marry her like that.

*He snaps his fingers. The word "marriage" makes something snap inside* SUGAR, *too.*

SUGAR. Would you do me a favor?

JOE. What is it?

SUGAR. I may not be Dr. Freud or a Mayo Brother or one of those French upstairs girls—but could I take another crack at it?

JOE *(blase)*. All right—if you insist.

*She bends over him, gives him a kiss of slightly higher voltage.*

SUGAR. Anything this time?

JOE. I'm afraid not. Terribly sorry.

SUGAR *(undaunted)*. Would you like a little more champagne? *(proceeds to refill glasses)* And maybe if we had some music—*(indicating lights)*—how do you dim these lights?

JOE. Look, it's terrbly sweet of you to want to help out—but it's no use.

JOE *(pointing)*. I think the light switch is over there—(SUGAR *dims lights*)—and that's the radio. (SUGAR *switches it on*) It's like taking somebody to a concert when he's tone deaf.

*By this time there is only candle-light in the salon, and from the radio comes soft music—"Stairway to the Stars."* SUGAR *crosses to the couch with two champagne glasses, hands one to* JOE, *sits beside him.* JOE *drinks down the champagne, and* SUGAR *hands him the second glass. He drains that, too.*

SUGAR. You're not giving yourself a chance. Don't fight it. Relax. *(she kisses him again)*

JOE *(shaking his head)*. It's like smoking without inhaling.

SUGAR. So inhale!

*This kiss is the real McCoy. As they stay locked in each other's arms—*

*Wipe to:*

*Int. Roadhouse (Night)*

*It is small, dark, and practically deserted. The Cuban band is playing La Cumparsita. Among the dancers on the floor are* OSGOOD *and* JERRY, *easily the most stylish couple in the joint.* JERRY *has the flower tucked in his cleavage. As they tango—*

OSGOOD. Daphne . . .

JERRY. Yes, Osgood?

OSGOOD. You're leading again.

JERRY. Sorry.

*They tango on.*

*Wipe back to:*

*Int. Salon of Caledonia (Night)*

JOE *and* SUGAR *are still in the same embrace. The radio music continues. Finally they break.*

SUGAR *(waiting for the verdict).* Well—?

JOE. I'm not quite sure. Try it again.

*She does. As they break, she looks at him—the suspense is unbearable.*

JOE *(trying to diagnose it).* I got a funny sensation in my toes—like somebody was barbecuing them over a slow flame.

SUGAR. Let's throw another log on the fire.

*Another kiss.*

JOE. I think you're on the right track.

SUGAR. I must be—because your glasses are beginning to steam up.

*She kisses him again.*

*Wipe to:*

*Int. Roadhouse (Night)*

OSGOOD *and* JERRY *have now got the tango by the throat.* JERRY *is dancing with his back to the camera, and as* OSGOOD *whips him around, we see that* JERRY *has the flower clamped between his teeth. They reverse positions again, and* OSGOOD *grabs the flower between his teeth.*

*Wipe back to:*

*Int. Salon of Caledonia (Night)*

*The radio is still on, and* JOE *and* SUGAR *are just coming out of their last kiss.* JOE *removes his glasses, which are now completely fogged up.*

JOE. I never knew it could be like this.

SUGAR. Thank you.

JOE. They told me I was kaputt—finished—washed up and now you're making a chump out of all those experts.

SUGAR. Mineral baths—now really!

JOE. Where did you learn to kiss like that?

SUGAR. Oh, you know—Junior League—charity bazaars—I used to sell kisses for the Milk Fund.

*They kiss again.*

JOE *(going, going, gone).* Tomorrow, remind me to send a check for a hundred thousand dollars to the Milk Fund.

*She doesn't have to kiss him any more—he takes over now.*

*Wipe to:*

*Int. Roadhouse (Night)*

*The chairs are stacked on the tables, and* OSGOOD *and* JERRY *are the only couple on the floor.* OSGOOD *wearing the flower behind his ear, and massaging his behind with a tablecloth, while going with wild abandon around* JERRY. *Suddenly he grabs* JERRY, *bends him over in a dashing dip. They straighten up, dance a couple of steps, and now* JERRY *returns the compliment—he almost breaks* OSGOOD'S *spine with an even more dashing dip.*

*As for the Cuban musicians—we now discover that* OSGOOD *has kept his word. They are all blindfolded.*

*Dissolve to:*

*Yacht at Anchor (Dawn)*

SUGAR *and* JOE *are in the motorboat, gliding away from the Caledonia toward the pier—backwards,* naturally. *It is quite romantic—with the sun about to rise—and the incidental music augmenting the mood.*

*Dissolve to:*

*Ext. Pier (Dawn)*

JOE *and* SUGAR, *his arm over her shoulder, walk dreamily toward the hotel. From the other direction comes* OSGOOD, *twirling the flower in his hand, and humming "La Cumparsita." As he passes* SUGAR *and* JOE, *he waves to them jauntily, then continues toward the same motorboat which just deposited them. He gets in, starts the motor, and leaves.*

*Dissolve to:*

*Ext. Hotel Entrance (Dawn)*

JOE *leads* SUGAR *up to the steps, then stops and faces her.*

JOE. Good night.
SUGAR. Good morning.
JOE. How much do I owe the Milk Fund so far?
SUGAR. Eight hundred and fifty thousand dollars.
JOE. Let's make it an even million.

*He gives her a final kiss.* SUGAR *turns, starts up the steps, then stops and comes back to him.*

SUGAR. I forgot to give you your receipt.

*She kisses him, then floats through the entrance of the hotel.* JOE *watches her till she is out of sight, then takes off his glasses. He hurries up the steps, starts to climb up one of the posts of the veranda.*

*Int. Room 413 (Dawn)*

JERRY, *still in his evening gown, is stretched out on his bed, gaily singing "La Cumparsita" and accompanying himself with a pair of maracas.* JOE

appears over the railing of the balcony, steps through the window into the room.

JOE *(exuberant)*. Hi, Jerry. Everything under control?
JERRY. Have I got things to tell you!
JOE. What happened?
JERRY *(beaming)*. I'm engaged.
JOE. Congratulations. Who's the lucky girl?
JERRY. *I* am.
JOE. *What?*
JERRY *(brimming over)*. Osgood proposed to me. We're planning a June wedding.
JOE. What are you talking about? You can't marry Osgood.
JERRY *(getting up)*. You think he's too old for me?
JOE. Jerry! You *can't* be serious!
JERRY. Why not? He keeps marrying girls all the time!
JOE. But you're not a girl. You're a guy! And why would a guy want to marry a guy?
JERRY. Security.
JOE. Jerry, you'd better lie down. You're not well.
JERRY. Look, stop treating me like a child. I'm not stupid. I know there's a problem.
JOE. I'll say there is!
JERRY. His mother—we need her approval. But I'm not worried—because I don't smoke.
JOE. Jerry—there's *another* problem.
JERRY. Like what?
JOE. Like what are you going to do on your honeymoon?
JERRY. We've been discussing that. He wants to go to the Riviera—but I sort of lean toward Niagara Falls.
JOE. You're out of your mind! How can you get away with this?
JERRY. Oh, I don't expect it to last.

I'll tell him the truth when the time comes.

JOE. Like when?

JERRY. Like right after the ceremony.

JOE. Oh.

JERRY. Then we'll get a quick annulment—he'll make a nice settlement on me—I'll have those alimony checks coming in every month—

JOE. Jerry, listen to me—there are laws—conventions—*it's just not being done!*

JERRY. But Joe—this may be my last chance to marry a millionaire!

JOE. Look, Jerry—take my advice—forget the whole thing—just keep telling yourself you're a boy!

JERRY. I'm a boy—I'm a boy—I wish I were dead—I'm a boy—I'm a boy—*(slaps his wig down on the desk)* What am I going to do about my engagement present?

JOE. What engagement present?

*JERRY picks up a jewel box, opens it, hands it to Joe.*

JERRY. He gave me this bracelet.

*JOE takes* BIENSTOCK'S *glasses out of his pocket, examines the bracelet through one of the lenses.*

JOE. Hey—these are real diamonds.

JERRY. Naturally. You think my fiancé is a bum? Now I guess I'll have to give it back.

JOE. Wait a minute—let's not be hasty. After all, we don't want to hurt poor Osgood's feelings.

*There is a knock on the door.*

JOE *(in girl's voice).* Just a minute.

*They grab their wigs, slap them on.* JOE *dives into bed, pulling the covers up to his chin.*

SUGAR'S VOICE. It's me—Sugar.

JOE. Come in.

SUGAR, *in a negligee, comes in—or rather, floats in.*

SUGAR. I thought I heard voices—and I just had to talk to *somebody*. I don't feel like going to sleep.

JERRY. I know what you need—a slug of bourbon.

*He opens a bureau drawer, takes out the hot-water bottle.*

SUGAR. Oh, no. I'm off that stuff—for good.

JOE. Did you have a nice time?

SUGAR. Nice? *(on a cloud)* It was suicidally beautiful.

JERRY. Did he get fresh?

SUGAR. Of course not. As a matter of fact, it was just the other way around. You see he needs help.

JERRY. What for?

SUGAR. And talk about elegant—you should see the yacht—candlelight—mint sauce *and* cranberries.

JOE. Gee, I wish *I'd* been there.

SUGAR. I'm going to see him again tonight—and *every* night—I think he's going to propose to me—as soon as he gets up his nerve.

JERRY *(looking at* JOE*).* That's some nerve!

JOE *(covering up quickly).* Daphne got a proposal tonight.

SUGAR. Really?

JERRY. From a *rich* millionaire.

SUGAR. That's wonderful. *(suddenly turning to* JOE*)* Poor Josephine.

JOE *(startled). Me?*

SUGAR. Daphne has a beau—*I* have a beau—if we could only find somebody for you.

*The door opens, and in strides the fresh* BELLHOP, *gin bottle in one hand and the passkey in the other.*

BELLHOP. Here I am, doll!

JOE *disappears under the covers.*

*Fade out:*

*Fade in:*

*Int. Lobby Seminole-Ritz Hotel (Day)*

*We are close on a doormat bearing the name Seminole-Ritz hotel. A pair of men's feet step across the mat, the shoes encased in white linen spats.*

*Camera pulls back to reveal* SPATS COLOMBO *entering the lobby, surrounded by his* FOUR HENCHMEN *and followed by bellhops carrying their luggage. The* HENCHMEN *are all dolled up for Florida—knickers, Panamas, two-toned shoes—and one of them is carrying a golf bag.*

SPATS *is somewhat more conservatively dressed in a light gray business suit. They stop and look around.*

*Draped across the rear wall is an impressive banner reading:*

WELCOME DELEGATES
10TH ANNUAL CONVENTION
FRIENDS OF ITALIAN OPERA

SECOND HENCHMAN *(reading banner).* Friends of Eye-talian Opera— hey, that's us!

*A convention* OFFICIAL, *wearing a badge and ribbon identifying him as a committee member, comes up to* SPATS.

FIRST OFFICIAL. Register over there.

SPATS *nods to his boys, and they move toward the registration desk, past other groups of delegates. You would hate to meet any of these mugs in a dark alley, but what makes it heartwarming is that they all have a cauliflower ear for good music.*

*Sitting on a settee is a gentleman reading the Police Gazette. As he lowers the paper, we see it's our friend* MULLIGAN, *the Federal agent.*

*He looks after* SPATS *and his boys with a wry smile.*

*At the desk,* SPATS *and his group are identifying themselves to the registrar. Leaning against a column, supervising the proceedings, is a dark, menacing young hoodlum,* JOHNNY PARADISE. *He is insolently flipping a half dollar in the air.*

SPATS *(to registrar).* Spats Colombo—delegate from Chicago— South Side chapter.

*The registrar pins an identification tag on his lapel.*

PARADISE. Hi, Spats. We was laying eight to one you wouldn't show.
SPATS. Why wouldn't I?
PARADISE. We thought you was all broken up about Toothpick Charlie.
SPATS. Well, we all got to go sometime.
PARADISE. Yeah. You never know who's going to be next. *(jerks his thumb toward screen)* Okay, Spats. Report to the Sergeant-at-Arms.
SPATS. What for?
PARADISE. Orders from Little Bonaparte.

SPATS *has now been joined by the* FOUR HENCHMEN, *who have also received their identification tags, and* PARADISE *motions them behind the screen.*

*Behind the screen, a couple of* OFFICIALS *are waiting.*

SECOND OFFICIAL. Put 'em up, Spats.
SPATS. What's the idea?
SECOND OFFICIAL. Little Bonaparte don't want no hardware around.

SPATS *reluctantly complies and the* OFFICIAL *frisks him.*

SECOND OFFICIAL *(continues).* Okay—you're clean.

SPATS *(tapping official's pocket).* You're not.

*He pulls an automatic out of the* OFFICIAL'S *shoulder holster, tosses it into a wire basket which already holds a large collection of hardware.*

*The* OFFICIAL *glares at him, then turns and runs his hands down the* FIRST HENCHMAN. *He feels something at the bottom of one of his knickers, pulls the elastic cuff. A gun drops out.*

FIRST HENCHMAN. It ain't loaded.

*The* OFFICIAL *pulls the elastic of the other knicker, and several dozen bullets drop to the floor. The* OFFICIAL *kicks them away, faces the* HENCHMAN *with the golf bag.*

SECOND OFFICIAL. What's in here?
SECOND HENCHMAN. My golf clubs. Putter, niblick, number three iron—

*The* OFFICIAL *pulls a submachine gun out of the bag.*

SECOND OFFICIAL. What's this?
SECOND HENCHMAN. My mashie.

SPATS *emerges from behind the screen.*

PARADISE *(still tossing coin).* See you at the banquet, Spats.

SPATS *looks at the young punk contemptuously, snatches the coin out of the air.*

SPATS. Where did you pick up that cheap trick? *(drops the coin in the kid's breast pocket)* Come on, boys.

*He and his* HENCHMAN *start across the lobby toward the reception counter. As they pass* MULLIGAN, *he rises.*

MULLIGAN. Well Spats Colombo— if I ever saw one.
SPATS. Hello, copper. What brings you down to Florida?

MULLIGAN. I heard you opera-lovers were having a little rally—so I thought I better be around in case anybody decides to sing.
SPATS. Big joke!
MULLIGAN. Say, Maestro—where were you at three o'clock on St. Valentine's Day?
SPATS. Me? I was at Rigoletto.
MULLIGAN. What's his first name? And where does he live?
SPATS. That's an opera, you ignoramus.
MULLIGAN. Where did they play it—in a garage on Clark Street?
SPATS. Clark Street? Never heard of it.
MULLIGAN. Ever hear of the Deluxe French Cleaners on Wabash Avenue?
SPATS. Why?
MULLIGAN. Because the day after the shooting you sent in a pair of spats—they had blood on them.
SPATS. I cut myself while shaving.
MULLIGAN. You shave with your spats on?
SPATS. I *sleep* with my spats on.
MULLIGAN. Quit kidding. You did that vulcanizing job on Toothpick Charlie—and we know it.
SPATS. You and who else?
MULLIGAN. Me and those two witnesses whom your *lawyers* have been looking for all over Chicago.
SPATS. You boys know anything about any garage—or any witnesses?
FIRST HENCHMAN. Us? We was with you at Rigoletto's.
MULLIGAN. Don't worry, Spats. One of these days we'll dig up those two guys.
SPATS. That's what you'll have to do—dig 'em up!

*He leads his boys away from* MULLIGAN *toward the reception desk.*

*The elevator door opens, and among the passengers stepping out are* JOE *and* JERRY, *in their summer dresses.* JOE *is carrying their room key.*

JERRY (*indicating diamond bracelet on wrist*). I feel like such a tramp—taking jewelry from a man under false pretenses.

JOE. Get it while you're young. And you better fix your lips. You want to look nice for Osgood, don't you?

JERRY *stops, takes a mirror and a lipstick out of his handbag, starts to touch up his lips.*

JERRY. It's just going to break his heart when he finds out I can't marry him.

JOE. So? It's going to break Sugar's heart when she finds out I'm not a millionaire. That's life. You can't make an omelette without breaking an egg.

JERRY. What are you giving me with the omelette?

JOE. Nag, nag, nag. Look, we got a yacht, we got a bracelet, you got Osgood, I've got Sugar—we're really cooking.

JERRY (*his eyes transfixed by something he sees in the mirror*). Joe—

JOE. What?

*What* JERRY *sees in the mirror is* SPATS COLOMBO *and the* FOUR HENCHMEN.

JERRY. Something tells me the omelette is about to hit the fan.

*He nods in the direction of the reception desk.* JOE *looks, sees what* JERRY *has seen, then—*

JOE. Come on, Daphne.

*With as much grace as they can muster, they hurry back toward the elevator. The doors are just opening, and our* BELLHOP *comes backing out,* *trundling an old man in a wheelchair. The old man wears a Panama hat, dark glasses, and is covered up to his chin with a plaid blanket.* JOE *and* JERRY *almost fall over the invalid in their haste to get into the elevator.*

*Int. Elevator*

JOE *and* JERRY *scramble inside.*

JOE. Going up.

*As the elevator operator starts to close the doors, he is arrested by—*

SPAT'S VOICE. Hold it.

JOE *and* JERRY *freeze as* SPATS *steps into the elevator, followed by the* FOUR HENCHMEN.

SPATS. Three, please.

*The* OPERATOR *shuts the door, and the elevator starts up.* JOE *and* JERRY, *hemmed in by the gangsters, are slowly dying. Noticing them,* SPATS, *removes his hat—and his* HENCHMEN *belatedly do likewise. The* FIRST HENCHMAN *stares at* JOE *and* JERRY, *who are trying to keep their faces averted.*

FIRST HENCHMAN. I don't mean to be forward—but ain't I had the pleasure of meeting you two broads before?

JOE. Oh, no!

JERRY. You must be thinking of two *other* broads.

SECOND HENCHMAN. You ever been in Chicago?

JERRY. Us? We wouldn't be caught dead in Chicago.

SPATS, *his interest aroused, is now also studying the two boys. To their relief, the elevator stops and the operator opens the door.*

OPERATOR. Third floor.

FIRST HENCHMAN (*to the boys*). What floor are you on?

JOE. Never you mind.

*He waves him away with the hand holding the room key. The* HENCHMAN *glances at the numbered tag.*

FIRST HENCHMAN. Room 413—we'll be in touch.

*He follows the others out.*

JERRY *(coyly)*. Don't call *us*—we'll call *you.*

*As the elevator doors start to close,* SPATS *glances over his shoulder toward the boys, frowning thoughtfully. In the elevator,* JOE *and* JERRY *look at each other, swallow hard.*

*Dissolve to:*

*Int. Room 413 (Day)*

JOE *and* JERRY *are frantically dumping their clothes into two open suitcases on the bed.*

JERRY. I tell you, Joe, they're on to us. They're going to line us up against the wall and—(*imitating machine gun*) Eh-eh-eh-eh-eh—and then the police are going to find two dead dames, and they're going to take us to the ladies' morgue, and when they undress us—I tell you, Joe, I'm just going to die of shame.

JOE. Shut up and keep packing.

JERRY. Okay, Joe.

*He picks up an orchid corsage, in a transparent box, from the desk, starts to put it into the suitcase.*

JOE *(grabbing it)*. Not that, you idiot.

JERRY. But they're from Osgood. He wanted me to wear them tonight.

JOE *tosses the corsage box into the waste basket.* JERRY *starts to pack the maracas.*

JERRY. I'll never find another man who's so good to me.

JOE *fishes out* BIENSTOCK'S *yachting cap from under the bed, turns it over in his hand, lost in thought.*

JERRY *(continues)*. Joe, if we get out of this hotel alive, you know what we're going to do? We're going to sell the bracelet, and grab a boat to South America and hide out in one of those banana republics—*(removes bracelet, puts it in jewel case on desk)* The way I figure is; if we eat nothing but bananas, we can live there for fifty years—maybe a hundred years—that is, if we get out of the hotel alive. *(looking around)* Did we forget anything?

JOE *(still studying cap)*. There's our shaving stuff—and there's Sugar.

JERRY. Sugar?

JOE *(picking up phone)*. Get me Room 414.

JERRY. What do you think you're doing?

JOE. Making a telephone call.

JERRY. Telephone call? Who's got time for that?

JOE. We can't just walk out on her without saying goodbye.

JERRY. Since when? Usually you leave 'em with nothing but a kick in the teeth.

JOE. That's when I was a saxophone player. Now I'm a millionaire.

JERRY. Drop her a postcard. Any minute now those gorillas may be up here—

JOE *(into phone, in a Southern female voice)*. Hello, Room 414? This is the ship-to-shore operator—I have a call for Miss Sugar Cane.

*Int. Room 414*

DOLORES, *in a robe and haircurlers, is at the phone.* SUGAR, *in a negligee, is stretched out on her bed, dreamily reading a copy of Vanity Fair.*

DOLORES. Hey, Sugar, it's for you—from the yacht.

SUGAR *jumps up, grabs the phone eagerly.*

SUGAR. Hello?

*Int. Room 413*

JERRY *is watching* JOE *on the phone.*

JOE *(Cary Grant once more).* Hello, my dearest darling. So good to hear your voice again.

JERRY. I *may* throw up.

*He disappears into the bathroom.*

JOE *(into phone).* No, I didn't, darling—to tell the truth, I never closed an eye.

*As he and* SUGAR *continue their telephone conversation, Intercut between the two rooms.*

SUGAR. That's funny—I never slept better. And I had the most wonderful dream. I was still on the yacht, and the anchor broke loose—and we drifted for days and days—you were the captain and I was the crew—I kept a lookout for icebergs, and I sorted your shells, and mixed your cocktails, and wiped the steam off your glasses—and when I woke up, I felt like swimming right back to you.

JOE. Yes. Now about our date for tonight . . .

SUGAR. I'll meet you on the pier again—right after the show.

JOE. I'm afraid not. I can't make it tonight.

SUGAR. Tomorrow night?

JOE. Not tomorrow, either. You see, I have to leave—something unexpected came up—I'm sailing right away.

SUGAR. Where to? South America? Oh. That *is* unexpected.

JOE. You see, we have those oil interests in Venezuela—and I just got a cable from Dad—the board of directors decided on a merger.

SUGAR. A merger? How long will you be gone?

JOE. Quite a while. As a matter of fact, I'm not coming back at all.

SUGAR. You're not?

JOE. It's all rather complicated—what we call high finance—but it so happens that the president of the Venezuelan syndicate has a daughter, and—

SUGAR. Oh—*that* kind of a merger. Is she young? Pretty?

JOE. According to our tax advisers, she's only so-so. But—that's the way the oil gushes. A man in my position has a certain responsibility to the stockholders—all those little people who invest their life savings—

SUGAR. Oh, of course. I understand. At least, I *think* I do.

JOE—*On phone*

JOE. I knew you would.

*He picks up the jewel case with the diamond bracelet from the desk, studies it thoughtfully*

JOE *(continues).* I only wish there were something I could do for you.

SUGAR-*On phone*

SUGAR. But you have. You've given me all that inside information—first thing tomorrow I'm going to call my broker and have him buy fifty thousand shares of Venezuelan oil.

*Int. Room 413*

JOE *(into phone).* Smart move. *(reaches into waste basket, extracts corsage box)* Oh, by the way—did you get my flowers? You know, those orchids from my greenhouse—the fog finally lifted over Long Island, and they flew them down this morning.

*As he talks he opens the corsage box, puts the bracelet in with the orchids, closes it again.*

JOE *(continues)*. That's strange—I sent them to your room—they should have been delivered by now—

*Holding the phone in one hand and the corsage box in the other, he moves toward the hall door.*

*Int. Room 414*

SUGAR *covers the mouthpiece of the phone, turns to* DOLORES.

SUGAR. Hey, Dolores—will you see if there are any flowers outside?

DOLORES *starts toward the hall door.*

*Int. Fourth Floor Corridor (Day)*

*The door of 413 opens.* JOE, *having come as far as the length of the telephone cord will permit, sets the corsage box down, kicks it across the hall to the door of 414. As he closes his door, the door of 414 opens. Dolores reaches out, picks up the corsage box, starts back inside.*

*Int. Room 414*

DOLORES *brings the corsage box to* SUGAR.

SUGAR *(into phone)*. Yes, they're here. *(opening box)* Oh—white orchids. Would you believe it—I haven't had white orchids since I was a debutante. *(finding bracelet)* What's this?

JOE—*On phone*

JOE. What's that? Oh, *that*. Just a little going away present.

SUGAR—*On phone*

SUGAR. Real diamonds. They must be worth their weight in gold. Are you always this generous?

JOE—*On phone*

JOE. Not always. But I want you to know I'm very grateful for what you did for me.

SUGAR—*On phone*

SUGAR. I didn't do anything. It just happened.

*Int. Room 413*

JERRY *emerges from bathroom, carrying their toilet articles and an armful of towels embroidered with Seminole-Ritz Hotel.*

JOE *(into phone)*. Oh. The navigator just came in—we're ready to cast off.

SUGAR—*On phone*

SUGAR. Well, anchors aweigh, and have a bon voyage. And if you need an orchestra to play at your wedding, we'll be through here in a couple of weeks.

*Int. Room 413*

JOE *(into phone)*. Goodbye, my darling.

*He hangs up, stares moodily at the phone.* JERRY *shuts his suitcase.*

JERRY. I don't know about the captain—but the navigator is getting his tail out of here.

JOE *(snapping out of his trance)*. Yeah—let's shove off.

*They start to gather up their instruments and luggage.*

JERRY. Wait a minute—my bracelet. *(picks up jewel case, shuts it, then realizes it's empty)* What happened to my bracelet?

JOE. What do you mean, *your* bracelet? It's *our* bracelet.

JERRY. All right. What happened to *our* bracelet?

JOE. Don't worry. We did the right thing with it.

JERRY. What did we do? Joe, you're not pulling one of your old tricks.

JOE. No tricks, no mirrors, nothing up my sleeve. It's on the level this time.

*The door opens and* SUGAR *comes in. The boys whirl around.*

SUGAR. Where's that bourbon?

*She heads straight for the bureau, starts to open various drawers.* JOE *steps in front of the suitcases to conceal them from her.*

JOE. What's the matter, Sugar?

SUGAR. I don't know. All of a sudden, I'm thirsty.

JOE *fishes the hot-water bottle out of the open suitcase behind him, hands it to* SUGAR. *As she reaches for it,* JERRY *notices the diamond bracelet on her wrist.*

JERRY *(pointing)*. How did you get that bracelet?

SUGAR. You like it?

JERRY. I always did.

SUGAR. Junior gave it to me. It must have at least thirty stones—

JERRY *(promptly)*. Thirty-four.

SUGAR. He's going to South America to marry some other girl—that's what they call high finance.

JERRY. That's what I call a louse! If I were you, Sugar, I'd throw that bracelet right back in his face.

JOE *(admonishingly)*. Daphne—

SUGAR. He was the first nice guy I ever met in my life—and the only one who ever gave me anything.

JOE. You'll forget him, Sugar.

SUGAR. How can I? No matter where I go, there'll always be a Shell station on the corner. *(indicating hot water bottle)* I'll bring this back when it's empty.

*She exits.* JERRY *turns on* JOE *furiously.*

JERRY. You crazy or something? The place is crawling with mobsters—gangrene is setting in—and you're making like Diamond Jim Brady! How are we going to get out of here? How are we going to eat?

JOE. We'll walk. And if we have to, we'll starve.

JERRY. There you go with that *we* again.

*He picks up his suitcase, starts toward the door.* JOE *grabs him and pulls him back.*

JOE. Not that way. *(heading for window)* We don't want to run into Spats and his chums.

*He steps through the open French window onto the balcony.* JERRY *starts to hand out the instruments and luggage to him.*

*Int.* SPATS' *Suite (Day)*

*The* FOUR HENCHMEN, *in dinner clothes are playing cards in the lavishly appointed living room when* SPATS *emerges from the bedroom. He is just slipping into his tuxedo coat, and his spats are unbuttoned.*

SPATS *(to* SECOND HENCHMAN*)*. Your hands clean? *(the* HENCHMAN *extends his hands palms up, then turns them over)* Okay. Button my spats.

*He drops into a chair, and the* SECOND HENCHMAN *kneels, starts to button the spats.*

FIRST HENCHMAN. Say, boss—I been talking to some of the other delegates—and the word is that Little Bonaparte is real sore about what happened to Toothpick Charlie. Him and Charlie, they used to be choir boys together.

SPATS *(drily)*. Stop, or I'll bust out crying.

FIRST HENCHMAN. He even got Charlie's last toothpick—the one from the garage—and had it gold-plated.

SPATS. Like I was telling you— Little Bonaparte is getting soft. *(taps his chest)* He doesn't have it *here* any more. Used to be like a rock. *(shaking his head)* Too bad. I think it's time for him to retire.

SECOND HENCHMAN. Second the motion.

FIRST HENCHMAN. How are we going to retire him?

SPATS. We'll think of something cute. One of these days, Little Bonaparte and Toothpick Charlie will be singing in the same choir again.

*He points up. Outside the window,* JOE *appears, climbing down a post from the floor above. He lands on the balcony, reaches up for the instruments and suitcases which the unseen* JERRY *is passing down to him.*

SPATS. And this time, we'll make sure there are no witnesses.

*The* FIRST HENCHMAN *glances out the window, sees* JERRY *climbing down the post to join* JOE.

FIRST HENCHMAN. Look—it's those two broads from the elevator.

SPATS *turns and looks. The* SECOND HENCHMAN, *beaming, crosses to the open window, calls out.*

SECOND HENCHMAN. Hey—join us!

JOE *and* JERRY, *panic-stricken, peer through the Venetian blinds at* SPATS *and his mob. Then they scramble for their lives over the railing of the balcony and down, their hat and wigs knocked askew.*

SECOND HENCHMAN. What's the matter with those dames?

SPATS. Maybe those dames ain't dames!

*He yanks up the Venetian blinds, steps quickly out onto the balcony, looks down over the railing. Then he picks up the bull-fiddle, drags it through the window into the room.*

SPATS. Same faces—same instruments—*(pointing at bullet holes)*—and here's your Valentine's card.

FIRST HENCHMAN *(catching on).* Those two musicians from the garage!

SPATS. They wouldn't be caught dead in Chicago—so we'll finish the job here. Come on.

*Led by* SPATS, *they all dash out of the room.*

*After a moment,* JOE'S *and* JERRY'S *heads appear cautiously over the balcony railing. Seeing that the room is empty, they climb up, rush in through the open window.*

JERRY. All right—so what do we do now?

JOE. First thing we got to do is get out of these clothes.

*He opens the door to the corridor and they peer out.*

*Int. Third Floor Corridor (Day)*

*There is no sign of* SPATS *and his boys. The elevator door is just opening, and the* BELLHOP *emerges, pushing the old man in the wheelchair.* JOE *and* JERRY *watch as the* BELLHOP *wheels the old man into one of the rooms. They look at each other, as the same idea occurs to them both, nod their heads in agreement. Slipping out of* SPATS' *room, they cross the corridor to the old man's room, start inside.*

*Dissolve to:*

*Int. Lobby (Day)*

*The elevator doors open, and a* BELLHOP *backs out with a man in a wheel chair. As they turn into camera, we discover that the bellhop is* JERRY—*the uniform fitting him much too snugly—and the blanket-covered figure in the wheel chair is* JOE, *dressed in the old man's suit, Panama hat, and dark glasses.*

*As* JERRY *and* JOE *proceed with dignity toward the front door, we see* SPATS *and his* HENCHMEN *deployed in strategic positions around the lobby.* JERRY *wheels* JOE *past* SPATS. SPATS *glances at them casually, then becomes aware of a strange clacking sound. He looks down.*

*There is something decidedly odd about the* BELLHOP—*because his trouser-legs terminate in high-heeled shoes.*

SPATS, *grinning smugly, signals the* TWO HENCHMEN *who are guarding the front door. They start to close in on* JOE *and* JERRY. JERRY *abruptly spins the wheel chair around, trundles it toward the rear of the lobby. The other* TWO HENCHMEN *take up the chase.* JERRY *and* JOE *disappear into a corridor leading toward the rear of the hotel. As the pursuing* HENCHMEN *start to turn into the corridor, the empty wheel chair comes whizzing toward them. The henchmen stumble over it, become momentarily entangled.*

JOE *and* JERRY, *sprinting down the corridor, reach an open door, dart inside. The* HENCHMEN *come racing up, and passing the door, round a bend in the corridor.*

*Int. Pantry*

*In the center of the room stands a huge cake, and two convention officials are decorating it under the watchful eye of* JOHNNY PARADISE, *who leans against the wall monotonously tossing a coin into the air.*

*One of the officials, wielding a confectioner's cone, has almost finished lettering the inscription* HAPPY BIRTHDAY, SPATS.

JOE *and* JERRY *burst in from the corridor, and the three hoods look up, startled. Before they can recover, the boys have scooted across the room and out another door.*

*Int. Banquet Room*

JOE *and* JERRY *come dashing in breathlessly, stop to get their bearings. Dominating the room is a U-shaped table, covered with flowers and about thirty placesettings, with a half grapefruit on each plate. On the wall behind the head of the table is the banner welcoming the Friends of Italian Opera. The boys glance around the empty room; make a beeline for the main entrance. As they reach the door, it starts to open, and voices are heard from the corridor. They turn desperately toward a second door, but that too is opening. Trapped, they duck under the banquet table, disappearing behind the long white tablecloth just as the banqueteers start to troop in. They are the same mugs we saw in the lobby, but they are now dressed in tuxedos or white dinner jackets. Chatting amiably, they move to their places at the table.*

*Under the table,* JOE *and* JERRY *huddle together as the delegates start to seat themselves. Suddenly a pair of legs slide beneath the tablecloth directly in front of them—and the boys recoil when they see that the owner's shoes are encased in spats.*

SPATS COLOMBO *is settling himself at the table, while his* FOUR HENCHMEN *take the seats on either side of him.*

SPATS. What happened?

FIRST HENCHMAN. Me and Tiny, we had them cornered—but we lost 'em in the shuffle.

SPATS (*turning to other* TWO HENCHMEN) Where were *you* guys?

SECOND HENCHMAN. Us? We was with you at Rigoletto's.

SPATS. Why, you stupid—

*He picks up the half-grapefruit in front of him, and is about to ram it in the* HENCHMAN'S *face.*

FIRST HENCHMAN. It's all right, boss—we'll get 'em after the banquet. They can't be too far away.

*Under the table,* JOE *and* JERRY *exchange a panicky look.*

*There is a burst of applause from the delegates as through the door strides* LITTLE BONAPARTE, *accompanied by half a dozen convention* OFFICIALS. LITTLE BONAPARTE *is short, bald, vicious, and wears a hearing aid. As he proceeds toward the head of the table, his pose is Napoleonic—head bowed, hands clasped behind his back.* SPATS *and his* HENCHMEN *pointedly abstain from applauding.* LITTLE BONAPARTE *remains standing at the place of honor while his associates seat themselves.*

BONAPARTE. Thank you, fellow opera-lovers. It's been ten years since I elected myself president of this organization—and if I say so myself, you made the right choice. Let's look at the record. We have fought off the crackpots who want to repeal Prohibition and destroy the American home—by bringing back the corner saloon. We have stamped out the fly-by-night operators who endangered public health by brewing gin in their own bathtubs, which is very unsanitary. We have made a real contribution to national prosperity—we are helping the automobile industry by buying all those trucks, the glass industry by using all those bottles, and the steel industry—you know, all those corkscrews. And what's good for the country is good for us. In the last fiscal year, our income was a hundred and twelve million dollars before taxes—only we ain't paying no taxes.

*The delegates applaud.*

BONAPARTE (*continues*). Of course, like in every business, we've had our little misunderstandings. Let us now rise and observe one minute of silence in memory of seven of our members from Chicago—North Side chapter—who are unable to be with us tonight on account of being rubbed out.

*All the delegates rise and bow their heads—except* SPATS *and his* HENCHMEN.

BONAPARTE (*continues; sharply*). You too, Spats. Up!

SPATS *and his boys get up reluctantly, join the others in silent tribute.*

*Int. Pantry*

*The inscribed top of the cake has been lifted off to reveal a hollow interior.* JOHNNY PARADISE *is climbing inside.*

SECOND OFFICIAL. Easy now. You know when you come out?

PARADISE. Yeah. The second time they sing—(*singing*) For he's a jolly good fel-*low* Which nobody can deny.

SECOND OFFICIAL. Okay. (*handing him a submachine gun*) And don't mess up the cake—I promised to bring back a piece to my kids.

JOHNNY PARADISE *squats down inside the cake. The* OFFICIALS *set the lid back in place.*

*Int. Banquet Room*

*The minute of silence is over, and the delegates are seating themselves.*

LITTLE BONAPARTE *remains on his feet.*

BONAPARTE. Now, fellow delegates, there comes a time in the life of every business executive when he starts to think about retirement.

*There are ad lib cries of "No! No!" from the delegates.* LITTLE BONAPARTE *holds up his hand.*

BONAPARTE (continues). In looking around for somebody to fill my shoes, I've been considering several candidates. For instance, there is a certain party from Chicago—South Side Chapter.

*He glances in the direction of* SPATS. SPAT'S HENCHMEN *turn and look at their boss.*

BONAPARTE (continuing). Now some people say he's gotten a little too big for his spats—but *I* say he's a man who'll go far. Some people say he's gone *too* far—but *I* say you can't keep a good man down. Of course, he still has a lot to learn. That big noise he made on St. Valentine's Day—that wasn't very good for public relations. And letting those two witnesses get away—that sure was careless.

*Under the table,* JOE *and* JERRY *try to make themselves as small as possible.*

SPATS. Don't worry about those two guys—they're as good as dead—I almost caught up with them today.

BONAPARTE (turning on hearing aid). You mean you let them get away twice?

BONAPARTE (cont'd) (clucks his tongue). Some people would say that was real sloppy—but *I* say to err is human, to forgive divine. And just to show what I think of you, Spats—the boys told me you was having a birthday—so we baked you a little cake.

SPATS. My birthday? It ain't for another four months.

BONAPARTE. So we're a little early. So what's a few months between friends? (turning to the others) All right, boys—now all together— (singing) For he's a jolly good fellow. . . .

*The other delegates, including* SPATS' HENCHMEN, *join in the song. The lights are extinguished, and from the pantry come the* TWO OFFICIALS, *pushing a cart on which stands the cake, with candles blazing. They wheel the cake up directly in front of* SPATS, *who eyes it uneasily.* LITTLE BONAPARTE, *meanwhile, is conducting the song with relish. As the singers reach the climactic line, the top of the cake tears open and out pops* JOHNNY PARADISE. *Aiming his machine gun at* SPATS *and his* HENCHMEN, *he starts blazing away.*

*Under the table,* JOE *and* JERRY *cringe.*

LITTLE BONAPARTE *winces, turns down the volume of his hearing aid— he can't stand loud noises.*

SPATS' FOUR HENCHMEN *have slumped across the table.* SPATS *is clutching his chest.*

SPATS. Big joke!

*His eyes close, and he starts to slip out of his chair.*

*Under the table,* JOE *and* JERRY *react as* SPATS' *body comes sliding toward them, feet first.*

JOE. Let's get out of here.

*He grabs* JERRY, *pulls him out from under the table.*

*The delegates, who are watching* JOHNNY PARADISE *scramble out of the cake, are momentarily off guard as* JOE *and* JERRY *streak across the dark-*

*ened banquet room toward the pantry door.*

BONAPARTE. Get those two guys!

*Four of the* OFFICIALS *rush into the pantry after* JOE *and* JERRY. *At the same time, the main door opens, and* MULLIGAN *strides in. Standing in the corridor behind him are several frightened waiters.* MULLIGAN *switches on the lights, looks down at the five corpses.*

MULLIGAN. What happened here?

BONAPARTE *(blandly).* There was something in that cake that didn't agree with them.

MULLIGAN *crosses to the cake, glances inside, then turns to* LITTLE BONAPARTE.

MULLIGAN. My compliments to the chef. And nobody's leaving this room till I get the recipe!

BONAPARTE. You want to make a Federal case out of it?

MULLIGAN *(grabs hearing aid, yells into mike).* Yeah!

*Int. Lobby (Night)*

JOE *and* JERRY *bolt out of the rear corridor, go pounding up the stairs, followed by two of the* OFFICIALS. *As they disappear from sight, Camera pans over to the elevator. The doors open, and out step* JOE *and* JERRY, *wearing their wigs and girls' coats.*

*As the boys mince daintily toward the front door, they see the other* TWO OFFICIALS *coming toward them. They change their course abruptly. The* FIRST TWO OFFICIALS *come hurrying down the stairs.*

FIRST OFFICIAL. They slipped right through our hands.

SECOND OFFICIAL. Don't worry. We got our guys watching the railroad station, the roads, and the airport—they can't get away.

JERRY *(to* JOE, *in a hoarse whisper).* Did you hear that?

JOE. Yeah, but they're not watching yachts. Come on—you're going to call Osgood.

*He steers* JERRY *toward a row of telephone booths near the entrance to the ballroom. There is an easel sign outside announcing that* SWEET SUE AND HER SOCIETY SYNCOPATORS *are appearing nightly in the Peacock Room, and from inside comes the sound of music.*

JERRY. What'll I tell him?

JOE. Tell him you're going to elope with him.

JERRY. *Elope?* But there are laws—conventions—

JOE *(jerking his thumb over his shoulder).* There's a convention, all right. There's also the ladies' morgue.

*He shoves* JERRY *toward a phone booth.* JERRY *reaches under his coat for a coin, revealing the rolled-up trousers of the bellhop's uniform underneath.*

*As he steps into the phone booth,* JOE *becomes aware of the sound of* SUGAR'S *voice drifting up from the ballroom. She is singing "I'm Through With Love." Almost despite himself,* JOE *finds himself drawn toward the ballroom entrance.*

*Int. Ballroom (Night)*

JOE *appears in the vestibule at the top of the stairs, looks down.*

*From his point of view, we see* SUGAR *perched on top of the piano, bathed in a spotlight. She is a little drunk, and more than a little blue, and she is singing the lyrics with heartbreaking conviction.*

JOE, *watching her from the landing, is deeply moved. Slowly, he starts down the steps.*

*On the bandstand,* SUGAR *is winding up the torchy ballad, when suddenly* JOE *steps into the spotlight. Without a word, he takes her in his arms, kisses her.*

SUGAR *(shocked).* Josephine!!

*Nearby,* SWEET SUE *is watching open-mouthed.*

SUE *(screaming).* BIENSTOCK!!

BIENSTOCK, *who is standing near the reservation desk, turns and peers myopically toward the bandstand. At the same time, two of the convention* OFFICIALS *come up behind him.*

SECOND OFFICIAL *(pointing).* Hey—that's no dame!

*He and his companion rush toward the bandstand.*

*On the bandstand,* JOE *is brushing a tear away from* SUGAR'S *cheek.*

JOE *(in a male voice).* None of that, Sugar—no guy is worth it.

*He catches sight of the* TWO OFFICIALS *bearing down on him, and leaping from the bandstand, shoulders his way through the couples on the dance floor. With the* TWO OFFICIALS *on his heels,* JOE *gallops up the stairs.*

*On the bandstand, all is confusion, as the girls stop playing and stand up.* SUGAR *is staring after* JOE *in complete bewilderment.*

SUGAR. *Josephine???*

*Suddenly it dawns on her—that kiss! Her eyes widen, her hand flies to her mouth, and she looks with growing comprehension at the bracelet on her wrist.*

*Int. Lobby (Night)*

JERRY *is just stepping out of the phone booth when* JOE *bursts out of the ballroom entrance.*

JERRY. It's all fixed! Osgood is meeting us on the pier

JOE. We're not on the pier *yet*—

*He grabs* JERRY, *and they take off across the lobby, as their pursuers appear behind them.*

*The boys head for the front door, but finding their way blocked by the* OTHER TWO OFFICIALS, *they reverse their field and hotfoot it toward the rear corridor. The* FOUR OFFICIALS *converge on their trail.*

JOE *and* JERRY *charge down the rear corridor, go skidding around the corner. As the* OFFICIALS *come tooling after them, two ambulance attendants round the turn in the corridor, pushing a wheeled stretcher. On the slab is a body, covered with a sheet that hangs down the sides, and sticking out from the end of the sheet are a pair of spat-covered shoes. The* FOUR OFFICIALS *make way for this grisly cargo, then resume the chase.*

*As the ambulance attendants wheel the stretcher toward the lobby, the trailing sheet lifts up, and* JOE *and* JERRY, *who have been clinging to the undercarriage, hop out. They tear across the lobby and scoot out the front door.*

*Dissolve to:*

*Ext. Pier (Night)*

OSGOOD *is waiting impatiently on the pier. He hears something, looks off toward the beach.*

JERRY *and* JOE, *still wearing their wigs and girls' coats, come scrambling down the steps, race across the planking toward the pier.*

*On the pier,* OSGOOD'S *face lights up.* JERRY *comes puffing up the stairs, followed by* JOE.

JERRY. This is my friend Josephine—she's going to be a bridesmaid.

OSGOOD. Pleased to meet you.

JERRY *(grabbing him)*. Come on!

*He practically drags OSGOOD down the stairs leading to the motorboat.*

OSGOOD *(over his shoulder to JOE)*. She's so eager!

*Swooping down from the beach on a bicycle comes SUGAR, pumping like mad. The bicycle bounces down the steps, and SUGAR pedals across the planking, sounding her horn.*

OSGOOD *and* JERRY *have settled themselves in the front seat of the motorboat, and* JOE *is getting into the rear seat when he hears the sound of the bicycle horn. He looks back.* OSGOOD *starts the motor.* SUGAR *comes racing up the stairs to the pier, leans over the railing.*

SUGAR *(calling down)*. Wait for Sugar!

*She hurries toward the other staircase.*

*In the motorboat,* OSGOOD *turns to* JERRY.

OSGOOD. Another bridesmaid?

JERRY. Flower girl.

SUGAR *comes charging down the stairs, starts to get into the rear seat beside* JOE.

JOE. Sugar! What do you think you're doing?

SUGAR. I told you—I'm not very bright.

JERRY *(clapping OSGOOD on the back)*. Let's go!

*The motorboat takes off with a roar.*

*Motorboat (Night)*

*In the back seat,* JOE *is removing his wig and coat.*

JOE. You don't want me, Sugar—I'm a liar and a phony—a *saxophone* player—one of those no-goodnicks you've been running away from—

SUGAR. I know. *(hitting her head)* Everytime!

JOE. Do yourself a favor—go back where the millionaires are—the *sweet* end of the lollipop—not the cole slaw in the face and the old socks and the squeezed-out tube of toothpaste—

SUGAR. That's right—pour it on. *(twines her arms around his neck)* Talk me out of it.

*She kisses him resoundingly, bending him over backwards till they are both practically out of sight.*

*Up front,* OSGOOD *is blithely steering the boat, keeping his eyes straight ahead.* JERRY *is looking over his shoulder at the activities in the back seat.*

OSGOOD. I called Mama—she was so happy she cried—she wants you to have her wedding gown—it's white lace.

JERRY *(steeling himself)*. Osgood—I can't get married in your mother's dress. She and I—we're not built the same way.

OSGOOD. We can have it altered.

JERRY *(firmly)*. Oh, no you don't! Look, Osgood—I'm going to level with you. We can't get married at *all*.

OSGOOD. Why not?

JERRY. Well, to begin with, I'm not a natural blonde.

OSGOOD *(tolerantly)*. It doesn't matter.

JERRY. And I smoke. I smoke all the time.

OSGOOD. I don't care.

JERRY. And I have a terrible past. For three years now, I've been living with a saxophone player.

OSGOOD. I forgive you.

JERRY *(with growing desperation)*. And I can never have children.

OSGOOD. We'll adopt some.

JERRY. But you don't understand! *(he rips off his wig; in a male voice)* I'm a Man!

OSGOOD *(oblivious)*. Well—nobody's perfect.

JERRY *looks at* OSGOOD, *who is grinning from ear to ear, claps his hand to his forehead. How is he going to get himself out of this?*

*But that's another story—and we're not quite sure the public is ready for it.*

*Fade out*

THE END

# THE TREASURE OF THE SIERRA MADRE

### Screenplay by John Huston
### from the Novel by B. Traven

| | |
|---|---|
| DOBBS | Humphrey Bogart |
| HOWARD | Walter Huston |
| CURTIN | Tim Holt |
| CODY | Bruce Bennett |

Directed by John Huston
Cinematographer: Ted McCord
Music by Max Steiner
Editor: Owen Marks
Set Designer: Fred M. MacLean

In 1948 John Huston won the Academy Awards for Best Screenplay and Best Director for *The Treasure of the Sierra Madre*. His outstanding skills as a writer were particularly demonstrated in the script, as he molded a plot and characters with imagination and ingenuity that played effortlessly well.

This classic, deceptively simple story of cupidity and greed, etched so vividly in the character of Dobbs, as played by Humphrey Bogart, is primitive and basic in its appeal. With no frills and no psychological analyses, it's just as elemental and profound as the Bible in some of its greatest narratives. James Agee, who was an extremely fine film critic and who later collaborated with Mr. Huston on the script of *The African Queen*, called *The Treasure of the Sierra Madre* "one of the most visually alive and beautiful movies I have ever seen." Well, it is that and more.

In his great and colorful career, John Huston was perhaps unique in one respect that is worth noting. Not only was he a superb writer-director of his own work, but he also handled with exquisite care material that wasn't his own. As great as he was in creating entertainment, John Huston's films almost always had exceptional content. He brought a discerning, tasteful, and learned intellectual dimension to most everything he ever touched. Very few writer-directors ever brought to the cinema such a substantial body of accomplished films, many adaptations of fine literary and theatrical works. Consider just a few: *The Maltese Falcon, Key Largo, The Asphalt Jungle, The Red Badge of Courage, Moby Dick, The Misfits, Freud,* and *The Man Who Would Be King*.

One final observation: Take note of Howard's (the old prospector played by the director's father, Walter Huston) dialogue in his last scene with Curtin at the end of the film. There Howard refers to his being fixed for life as a medicine man with the Indian tribe that virtually adopted him, a harbinger of things to come in the thematic material that undoubtedly attracted John Huston to *The Man Who Would Be King*.

Born in Nevada, Missouri, on August 5, 1906, John Huston died on August 28, 1987. Very few writers, directors, or actors—of which he was all three— had as spirited and varied a life. Not only was he a tremendously skilled writer and filmmaker, but he was also a boxer and won the Amateur Lightweight Boxing Championship of California as a youth; a master horseman, who rode in the Mexican Cavalry as a commissioned officer and also performed in Madison Square Garden horse shows; an artist, who studied oil painting in Paris; and a Broadway producer. While in the Signal Corps during World War II, he produced three of the finest documentaries ever created under battle conditions about that conflict. A remarkable man who left much to cinema. We shall miss him.

On a personal note, it was one of the disappointments of my life that I missed a great opportunity to work with John during our country's bicentennial celebration. John was set to direct and I was to produce and write a six-hour drama on the American Revolution for television, which, alas, never came to fruition. A most frustrating experience for both of us with some of the people who then ran network TV.

*Fade in:*

*Closeup lottery list*

*Showing the winning numbers drawn in the Mexican National Lottery. August 5, 1924. Camera pulls back to include* DOBBS. *He is slowly tearing a lottery ticket into bits. Camera dollies ahead of him as he turns away from the list. The tribes of bootblacks that people the streets do not pester* DOBBS. *He is too obviously on his uppers. His clothes are ragged and dirty and his shoes broken. He hasn't had a haircut in months and there is several days growth of beard on his face. He stops a passing American.*

DOBBS. Can you spare a dime, brother?

*The American growls, moves on.* DOBBS *turns, looks after the departing figure. The American flips a cigarette away.* DOBBS' *eyes follow its flight.*

*Closeup the burning cigarette in the gutter.*

*Close shot* DOBBS

*He moves half a step toward the gutter, then halts and looks right and left to make sure no one is watching. This brief delay costs him the cigarette. One of the swarm of bootblacks swoops down on it.* DOBBS *pulls his belt in a couple of notches and continues on up the street. Camera dollies ahead. Something* DOBBS *sees out of scene causes him to increase his pace. He catches up with an American who is dressed in a white suit.*

DOBBS. Brother, can you spare a dime?

WHITE SUIT *fishes in his pocket, takes out a toston and gives it to* DOBBS *who is so surprised by this act of generosity that he doesn't even say*

thanks. *For several moments he stands rooted looking at the coin in his palm. Then he closes his hand around it, making a fist. Putting the fist in his pocket, he cuts across the street. Camera pans with him to a tobacco stand where he stops to buy a package of cigarettes, then hurries along. Camera pans him to a sidewalk restaurant.*

*Dissolve to:*

*Ext. sidewalk restaurant*

DOBBS *at a table. He has just finished eating. The* PROPRIETOR *is serving him with coffee.*

DOBBS. How much?
PROPRIETOR. Trienta centavos.

DOBBS *pays with a toston. Then he takes a black papered cigarette out of the newly purchased pack, lights up and sits back to smoke and enjoy his coffee. A little* BOY, *barefoot, in ragged cotton pants and a torn shirt, enters through the open door of the restaurant brandishing lottery tickets.*

BOY. Michoacan State Lottery, senor.
DOBBS. Beat it. I'm not buying any lottery tickets. Go on, beat it.
BOY. Four thousand pesos the big prize. *(he pulls at* DOBBS' *coat sleeve)*
DOBBS. Get away from me, you little beggar.
BOY. The whole ticket is only four pesos, senor. And it's a sure winner.
DOBBS. I haven't got four pesos.
BOY. Buy a quarter of a ticket for one peso silver.

*The boy pulls at his pant leg.*

DOBBS *(picks up water glass).* If you don't get away from me I'll throw this right in your face.
BOY *(not moving).* Then one tenth of a ticket, senor, for forty centavos.

DOBBS *throws the water into the boy's face. The* BOY *laughs, wipes the water off with his sleeve. The* PROPRIETOR *comes back with the change.* DOBBS *tips him cinco centavos. The* PROPRIETOR *goes back behind his counter.*

BOY *(eyes on the change).* Senor ought to buy one twentieth. One twentieth costs you only twenty centavos. Look, senor, add the figures up. You get thirteen. What better number could you buy? It's a sure winner.

DOBBS *weighs the coin in his hand.*

DOBBS. How soon is the drawing?
BOY. Only three weeks off.
DOBBS. All right. Give me the twentieth so I don't have to look at your ugly face any longer.

*The little merchant tears off the twentieth of the sheet, hands it to* DOBBS *in exchange for a silver coin.*

BOY. It's un numero excelente, senor. *(bites on coin to see if it's good).* Muchas gracias, senor. Come again next time. I always have the winners, all the lucky numbers. Buena suerte, good luck!

*Off he hops, like a young rabbit, after another prospective customer.* DOBBS *finishes his coffee, pushes back his chair and rises. He lets his belt out three notches.*

*Ext. restaurant*

*Camera pans with* DOBBS *across the street to the plaza where he sits down on one of the benches beside another man. He takes out his cigarettes, puts a new one in his mouth and lights it from the old. A bootblack picks up the end he throws away.*

DOBBS *(to his companion on the bench).* Cigarette? *(he extends the pack)*

*The man takes one.* DOBBS *gives him a light with his own.*

CURTIN. Thanks.

CURTIN *takes a long drag, inhales deeply, then blows smoke out of his mouth and nose. He looks to be in his late twenties—about ten years younger than* DOBBS. *He has a strong, hard-bitten face with a slightly crooked nose. Like* DOBBS, *he could use a haircut.*

DOBBS. Hot.
CURTIN. Yeah.
DOBBS. Some town Tampico.
CURTIN. You said it, brother. If I could just land me a job that'd bring in enough so's I could buy me a ticket I'd shake its dust off my feet soon enough you bet.
DOBBS. I beat my way up El Higo last week. There ain't a camp where any work's to be had. I tried 'em all.
CURTIN. You're telling me . . . more companies are closing down all the time. Guys I've known who've worked steady for the past five years are coming back from the fields to town. Why? I don't savvy. The world needs oil. . . .

*A* MAN IN A WHITE SUIT *passes the bench.* DOBBS' *eyes follow him speculatively.*

DOBBS. If I was a Mex I'd buy a can of shoe polish and go into business. They'd never let a Gringo. You can sit on a bench three-quarters starved. You can beg from another Gringo. You can even commit burglary. But try shining shoes in the street or selling lemonade out of a bucket and your hash is settled. You'd never get another job from a white man.
CURTIN. Yeah, and the natives would hound and pester you to death.
DOBBS *(getting to his feet).* It's a hell of a country to be broke in.

CURTIN. Tell me the country that isn't.

DOBBS *turns away from the bench.*

*Close shot shoeshine stand*

*The* MAN IN THE WHITE SUIT *is reading a paper while he gets a shine.* DOBBS *enters scene.*

DOBBS. Brother, can you spare a dime?

WHITE SUIT *takes a toston out of his pocket, gives it to* DOBBS. *For the second time this day,* DOBBS *is surprised into speechlessness. He looks up from the coin in his palm to the white suited man on the wire bootblack stand. The latter's face is hidden by the newspaper.* DOBBS *thrusts the coin into his pants pocket, turns on his heel and marches off.*

*Ext. open-air barber shop close shot* DOBBS

*in barber chair. Laying aside his razor, the* BARBER *pushes a handle and* DOBBS' *position changes from horizontal to sitting. A mirror is put into* DOBBS' *hand. He holds it at various angles, studying the effects of the scissors on the back of his head.*

BARBER. Algo en el pelo, senor? Para que quede bonito. *(he shows* DOBBS *a bottle)*
DOBBS. Cuanto vale?
BARBER. Quince centavos.

DOBBS *frowns slightly, debating with himself whether to indulge in this extravagance.*

BARBER. Muy bonita aroma.
DOBBS. Okay.

*The* BARBER *douses his head liberally, then he combs* DOBBS' *hair.* DOBBS *uses the hand mirror again, the results being much to his liking.*

*His head shines like a nigger's heel. Having performed the final rite of snipping the scissors below each of his customer's nostrils, the* BARBER *unfastens the sheet from around* DOBBS' *neck.* DOBBS *rises from the chair and gives the* BARBER *his one and only toston. He continues to eye himself while the* BARBER *makes change, and it must be that he receives an excellent impression, for he is more than liberal when it comes to tipping.*

BARBER. Gracias, senor. Come again.

DOBBS *issues forth into the street. The change in his manner is rather more noticeable than the change in his appearance. His shoulders are back as he walks, his glance bolder. He allows it to fall on a passing damsel whose swarthiness cannot be hidden by the layers of powder on her face. Returning* DOBBS' *look, her eyes show interest, but this fades as she gives him the once-over and sees the condition of his clothes.* DOBBS *turns to watch her retreating figure. The girl goes into a two-story house, on the front of which is a sign in Spanish:*

CUARTOS AMUEBLADOS

*He tosses the last remaining piece of change out of the toston in his hand. Alas, it is far too little. Returning it to his pocket, he sighs, and continues on down the street. Reaching the corner, he observes a* MAN IN A WHITE SUIT *about to step off the curb.* DOBBS *goes directly up to him.*

DOBBS *(to the* WHITE SUIT*).* Can you spare a dime, mister?

WHITE SUIT *reaches in his pocket, takes out a toston.* DOBBS *reaches for it. But* WHITE SUIT *keeps the piece between his fingers.*

WHITE SUIT. Listen, you. Such impudence never came my way as long as I can remember.

DOBBS *stands utterly perplexed while the stranger continues.*

WHITE SUIT. Early this afternoon I gave you a toston. When I was having my shoes polished I gave you another toston. Now, once again. Do me a favor, will you? Go occasionally to somebody else. This is beginning to get tiresome.

DOBBS. Excuse me, mister. I never realized that it was you all the time. I never looked at your face, only your hands and at the money you gave me. Beg pardon, mister. I promise you I won't put the bite on you again.

WHITE SUIT. This is the last you get from me, understand? *(gives DOBBS the toston)*

DOBBS. Sure, mister—never again will I—

WHITE SUIT. Just to make sure you won't forget your promise, here's another toston so you'll eat tomorrow.

DOBBS *(taking it)*. Thanks, mister, thanks.

WHITE SUIT. But understand—from now on you are to try your best to make your way in life without my assistance.

*And the gentleman goes his way.* DOBBS *clinks the two tostons together thoughtfully, then turns on his heel and starts rapidly up the street he just came down.*

*Ext. waterfront opposite ferry landing dusk*

*Camera dollies with* DOBBS *as he walks slowly along, his eyes on the pavement. He stops outside a cantina, listening to the tinny music of a player-piano. The swinging door opens and two sailors come out.*

DOBBS. Brother, can you spare . . .?

*They push past him and are gone. He is about to start on when the door opens a second time and a man, very tall and bulky, appears.*

DOBBS. Can you spare a dime, brother?

McCORMICK *(interrupting)*. I won't give you a red cent, but if you want to make some money I'll give you a job.

DOBBS. What's the catch?

McCORMICK. No catch. I got a job for you if you want it. Hard work but good pay. Ever rig a camp?

DOBBS. Sure.

McCORMICK. The ferry's making off and one of my men hasn't shown up. I don't know what's happened to him. He's probably filthy drunk in some dive.

DOBBS. What's the pay?

McCORMICK. Eight bucks, American, a day. Grub goes off on your expenses . . . Well, don't just stand there. Make up your mind. You have to come the way you are. No time to get your clothes or anything. The ferry doesn't wait.

DOBBS. I'm your man.

*The huge fellow takes* DOBBS *by the arm. Camera pans as he hurries him across the street toward the ferry landing.*

*About a dozen men*

*standing in the semi-darkness.* McCORMICK *and* DOBBS *enter scene.* McCORMICK *starts counting heads.* DOBBS *recognizes one of the gang as the man with whom he had conversation on the bench during the morning.*

DOBBS. Hello.

CURTIN. Hello yourself.

McCORMICK. Okay, you guys, get aboard.

*They move to obey.*

*Dissolve to:*

*Ext. a clearing in the jungle*

*About fifty men are at work rigging a camp, amongst them* DOBBS *and* CURTIN. *They are engaged in the erection of a derrick.* DOBBS, *one leg snake-fashion around a cable, grabs the heavy boards that are swung up, and bolts them.* CURTIN *helps to bring the boards into position. Sweat is pouring off them. From time to time they groan over their exertions. Over scene a voice: "Come and get it."* DOBBS *and* CURTIN *pull themselves up, straddle a wooden girder and wipe the sweat out of their eyes. Then, hand over hand, they slide down the cable. They start over to where a line of men is forming.* MCCORMICK *falls into step with them.*

MCCORMICK. What's the matter? Can't you two take it?

DOBBS. Must be a hundred and thirty in the shade and there ain't any shade up on the derrick.

MCCORMICK. What the devil. Just figure you're a couple of millionaires in your own private steambath. The sooner we're through the sooner we'll be back in town drinking cold beer. *(he lowers his voice confidentially)* If we finish within two weeks I'm going to give you fellows a bonus.

DOBBS. It's coming to us, working sixteen, eighteen hours a day like we do.

MCCORMICK. Now don't start crying for your mothers. What do you want? I'm paying top salaries . . . and a bonus.

DOBBS. What about our pay anyway? And when do we get it? I haven't seen a single buck out of you yet, Pat.

MCCORMICK. You'll get your dough all right. Don't you worry about that . . . When we get back to Tampico. What would you do with money here anyway except gamble and lose it. You'll get paid as we step off the ferry. . . .

*Dissolve to:*

*Ext. waterfront ferry landing in B.G.*

*Little groups of men, members of* MCCORMICK'S *work gang, are standing around.* MCCORMICK *comes up to one of such group, which includes* CURTIN *and* DOBBS.

DOBBS. What's up, Pat? We were to get our money as we stepped off the ferry.

MCCORMICK. The agent was supposed to be here with it. I don't know what could have happened. Nothing to worry about, though. I'll go over to the office and pick it up myself. *(pulls* DOBBS *aside —lowers his voice)* Supposing I meet you two in about an hour at that cantina right off the Plaza.

DOBBS. Any objection to us going along with you?

MCCORMICK *(suddenly angry)*. What's the matter, don't you trust me? Do you think I'd run out on you?

DOBBS. No, Pat, I don't think you'd do a thing like that, but I haven't got a cent, even to buy me a new shirt, or one glass of beer.

MCCORMICK *(takes some money out of his pocket)*. Here's ten pesos. That ought to hold you for an hour. *(he takes his watch out)* It's a quarter to two. I'll be at that cantino no later than three o'clock.

*He turns and goes abruptly off before there can be any further objections.*

*Dissolve to:*

*Clock over cantina bar*

*It says 5:30.*

BARTENDER'S VOICE *(over scene).* Pat McCormick, si. He comes in here time to time. No see him lately.

*Camera pulls back to include* DOBBS, CURTIN, *the* BARTENDER *and one other* CUSTOMER.

CUSTOMER *(ruggedly built—middle-aged man—slightly drunk).* Pat McCormick? What about Pat McCormick?

DOBBS. He was supposed to meet us here.

CUSTOMER. Does he owe you any money?

DOBBS *nods.*

CUSTOMER. How long you guys been around Tampico anyway?

CURTIN *and* DOBBS *cock their heads at the other man. Scowls appear on their faces.*

DOBBS. What's that got to do with it?

CUSTOMER. Only foreigners and half-baked Americans fall for Pat McCormick's tricks.

CURTIN. How do you mean?

CUSTOMER. I mean he gets dumb guys like you to work for him, and when the time comes for him to pay off, he takes a powder. *(he throws back his head and laughs)*

CURTIN *and* DOBBS *scowl at each other. Then they look at their beer.* CURTIN *murmurs something under his breath that is probably unprintable; then:*

CURTIN. How much we got left out of the ten he gave us, Dobbsie?

DOBBS *takes money out of his pocket; counts it.*

DOBBS. Six-fifty.

CURTIN *(mutters again).* Not even enough for one bed.

DOBBS. I know a joint where we can get cots for fifty centavos a night. It's full of rats and scorpions and cockroaches, but beggars can't be choosers.

*Dissolve to:*

*Int. Oso Negro sleeping quarters*

*Camera dollies ahead of* DOBBS *and* CURTIN *as they move down the narrow aisle between two rows of cots on which men are sitting or lying. We overhear scraps of conversations.*

FIRST MAN. I been in on half a dozen oil booms. It's always the same story. One day the price per barrel goes down two bits. Nobody knows why. It just does. And the next day it's down another two bits. And so on until, after a couple of weeks, jobs that were a dime a dozen ain't to be had, and the streets are full of guys pushing each other for a meal.

DOBBS *and* CURTIN *have found their cots by this time and have begun to undress. Another conversation is taking place in the far corner of the room between three Americans. One, an elderly fellow whose hair is beginning to show white, is lying on his cot. The other two sit, half undressed, on their cots.*

HOWARD *(the old man).* Gold in Mexico? Sure there is. Not ten days from here by rail and pack train, a mountain's waiting for the right guy to come along, discover her treasure and then tickle her until she lets him have it. The question is—are you the right guy . . .? Real bonanzas are few and far between and they take a lot of finding. Answer me this one—will you? Why's gold worth some twenty bucks per ounce?

MAN *(after a pause)*. Because it's a scarce . . .

DOBBS *and* CURTIN, *undressing, listen to the old man.*

HOWARD. A thousand men, say, go searching for gold. After six months one of 'em is lucky—one out of the thousand. His find represents not only his own labor but that of the nine hundred ninety-nine others to boot. Six thousand months or fifty years of scrabbling over mountains, going hungry and thirsty. An ounce of gold, mister, is worth what it is because of the human labor that went into the finding and the getting of it.

MAN. Never thought of it just like that . . .

HOWARD. There's no other explanation, mister. In itself, gold ain't good for anything much except to make jewelry and gold teeth.

*They are silent for a while thinking their thoughts. The old man rolls a cigarette and lights it. Then he resumes:*

HOWARD. Gold's a devilish sort of thing anyway. *(he has a far-away look in his eye)* When you go out you tell yourself "I'll be satisfied with twenty-five thousand handsome smackers worth of it, so help me Lord and cross my heart." Fine resolution. After months of sweating yourself dizzy and growing short on provisions and finding nothing, you come down to twenty thousand and then to fifteen, until finally you say "Lord, let me find just five thousand dollars worth and I'll never ask anything more of you the rest of my life".

FIRST MAN. Five thousand's a helluva lot.

HOWARD. Here in the Oso Negro it seems like a lot. But I tell you, if you were to make a real find, you couldn't be dragged away.

DOBBS *and* CURTIN *have stopped undressing to listen to what the old man is saying.*

HOWARD. Not even the threat of miserable death would stop you from trying to add ten thousand more. And when you'd reach twenty-five, you'd want to make it fifty, and at fifty, a hundred—and so on. Like at roulette . . . just one more turn . . . always one more. You lose your sense of values and your character changes entirely. Your soul stops being the same as it was before.

DOBBS *(unable to restrain himself)*. It wouldn't be like that with me. I swear it. I'd take only as much as I set out to get, even if there was still half a million bucks worth lying around howling to be picked up.

HOWARD *looks at him, examining, it seems, every line in his face. The scrutiny goes on for some time; then he shifts his eyes away and continues as though he had not been interrupted.*

HOWARD. I've dug in Alaska, and in Canada and Colorado. I was in the crowd in British Honduras where I made my boat fare back home and almost enough over to cure me of a fever I'd caught. I've dug in California and Australia . . . all over this world practically, and I know what gold does to men's souls.

SECOND MAN. You talk like you struck it rich some time or other. How about it, Pop, did you?

*The far-away look comes back in* HOWARD'S *eyes, and he nods.*

SECOND MAN. Then how come you're sitting here in this joint—a down-and-outer?

HOWARD. Gold, my young man. That's what it makes of us. Never knew a prospector that died rich. If he makes a fortune, he's sure to blow it in trying to find another. I ain't no exception to that rule. *(he shakes himself as though to throw off past memories)* Sure, I'm an old gnawed bone now, but don't you kids think the spirit is gone. I'm all set to shoulder a pickaxe and shovel again any time somebody's willing to share expenses. I'd rather go all by myself. That's the best way . . . going it alone. Of course, you've got to have the stomach for loneliness. Lots of guys go nutty with it. On the other hand, going with a partner or two is dangerous. All the time murder's lurking about. Hardly a day passes without quarrels—the partners accusing each other of all sorts of crimes, and suspecting whatever you do or say. As long as there's no find, the noble brotherhood will last, but when the piles begin to grow, that's when the trouble starts.

CURTIN. Me, now, I wouldn't mind a little of that kind of trouble.

FIRST MAN. Me neither, brother!

DOBBS. Think I'll go to sleep and dream about piles of gold betting bigger and bigger. . . .

HOWARD *reaches out, turns off the kerosene lamp.*

*Dissolve to:*

*Ext. plaza close shot* CURTIN *and* DOBBS *afternoon*

*On the bench where first they met. It is obvious by their appearance that no luck has come their way.*

DOBBS. Do you believe what that old man who was doing all the talking in the Oso Negro the other night said about gold changing a man's soul so's he ain't the same person he was before finding it?

CURTIN *(after a moment, thoughtfully)*. Guess that depends on the man.

DOBBS. Exactly what I say. Gold don't carry any curse with it. It all depends on whether or not the guy who finds it is a right guy.

CURTIN'S *eyes are caught and held by something out of scene. He is no longer listening to* DOBBS.

DOBBS *(continuing)*. The way I see it, gold can be as much of a blessing as a curse.

CURTIN. Hey, Dobbsie!

DOBBS. Yeah?

CURTIN. Look at who's coming out of the Hotel Bristol. . . . Is that Pat McCormick or am I seeing things?

DOBBS. It's him!

*Cut to include* MCCORMICK *as he strolls in the direction of the Plaza. A Mexican dame by his side is flashing a low-cut dress, a silk parasol and considerable phony jewelry.*

CURTIN. Let's get him. Let's get him hard.

MCCORMICK *stops in his tracks as the two rush toward him.*

MCCORMICK *(grinning)*. Hello, boys. How are you? Want a drink?

*His extreme affability has the effect of keeping the two men from sailing right into him. He addresses the dame.*

MCCORMICK. Perdoni Shlucksy dear, mi vida, I've got some business to attend to with these two gentlemen. You go back into the hotel and wait. I won't be long.

*He steers her back toward the hotel.*

MCCORMICK. Unos minutos nomas, Chiquita.

*She disappears into the lobby. He faces* DOBBS *and* CURTIN.

McCORMICK. Let's have a drink. It's on me.

DOBBS. Okay.

*They step into a cantina.*

McCORMICK *(to the bartender)*. Three shots of rye.

CURTIN. Make mine brandy, 3 Star.

DOBBS. Two brandies.

McCORMICK. Rye is good enough for me.

*The drinks are put down before them.*

McCORMICK. Well, boys, I suppose you're wondering about that money that's coming to you. Fact is I haven't been paid on that contract yet myself. If I had the money, you'd get it first thing. You know that, I'll take you both on my next contract. It'll go through by Monday and we can set out Friday. Glad to have you boys with me again. Well, here's mud in your eyes.

*They all drink.*

CURTIN. We want what's coming to us, and we want it right here and now.

McCORMICK. Didn't I just get through telling you . . .

CURTIN. Better come across, Pat.

McCORMICK. Tell you what I'll do, boys . . . I'll give you twenty-five percent . . . oh, I reckon I can make it thirty. The balance, let's say, the middle of next week.

CURTIN. Nothing doing. Here and now. Every cent you owe us or I swear you won't walk out of here. You'll have to be carried.

McCORMICK. Now let's not stop being friends. How about another drink? *(to the bartender)* Two more Hennesseys for these gentlemen. Put the bottle on the bar.

DOBBS. If you've got any ideas about getting us liquored up . . .

McCORMICK. I'm only inviting you to have a friendly drink with me!

*He reaches for the bottle. Instead of pouring, he hits* CURTIN *on the head with it.* CURTIN *goes down.* McCORMICK *swings at* DOBBS. DOBBS *ducks, then backs away.* McCORMICK *starts after him but* CURTIN, *on the floor, grabs him around the knees.* McCORMICK *tries to kick himself free but* CURTIN *hangs on. Now* DOBBS *plants his fist squarely in the big fellow's face. It's a long fight and a tough one. At times it's* DOBBS *who's down and* CURTIN *who's up. They fight in relays, one carrying on while the other gets over the effects of his punishment. Were it not for their determination, born of hunger,* DOBBS *and* CURTIN *would surely be the losers. But finally the huge hulk of* McCORMICK *collapses and goes down, not to get up again. His eyes are both swollen shut and his face is a misshapen pulp.*

McCORMICK *(begging)*. I'm licked . . . I'm licked.

CURTIN. Give us our money.

DOBBS. Yeah, give us our money.

*They rain kicks on him while he feels blindly for his back pocket, produces his wallet.*

McCORMICK. I can't see. . . .

DOBBS *takes money from the wallet, counts out what's coming to himself and* CURTIN. *Then he throws a bill to the bartender.*

DOBBS *(to the bartender)*. For the use of your cantina. *(to* CURTIN*)* Come on. Let's beat it before the law arrives.

*They stumble out through the rear door.*

*Lap dissolve to:*

*Water fountain*

*Shooting at the reflections of the two men in the water. They are bathing their wounds.*

DOBBS. You know something, Curt?

CURTIN. What?

DOBBS. We ain't very smart if we hang around Tampico waiting for a job. Our money'll get shorter every day until we're right back where we were—on the bum again, pushing guys for dimes and sleeping in freight cars and what have you.

*Camera pulls back to close shot of* DOBBS *and* CURTIN.

CURTIN. That's right. Got any ideas?

DOBBS. Yeah. That old man in the Oso Negro started me thinking.

CURTIN. What about?

DOBBS. Why not try gold digging for a change. It's no riskier than waiting round here for another break. And this is the country where the nuggets of gold are just crying to you to take them out of the ground and make them shine in coins and on the fingers and necks of swell dames.

CURTIN *(catching* DOBBS' *enthusiasm).* One thing, living is cheaper in the open than it is here in Tampico. Our money would last longer and the longer it lasts the greater our chance of digging up something would be.

DOBBS. We'd have to have equipment, of course . . . picks and spades and pans and burros. Wonder how much it would all cost?

CURTIN. The old man would know.

DOBBS. The sooner we leave the better. When we're on our way it'll be like investing our money. That old man could give us some pointers all right. He's too old to take along, of course. We'd have to carry him on our backs.

CURTIN. You can't tell about some of these old guys. It's surprising sometimes how tough they are. . . . I don't know what gold looks like in the ground. I've only seen it in shop windows and in people's mouths. Do you know anything about prospecting?

DOBBS. Not much, come right down to it.

CURTIN. We might have real use for an experienced guy like that old timer.

DOBBS. Maybe you're right. Let's go hunt him up right away.

*Dissolve to:*

*Int. Oso Negro* DOBBS, CURTIN *and the old man are in a huddle*

HOWARD. Will I go? What a question. Course I'll go. Any time, any day. I was only waiting for one or two guys to ask me. Out for gold? Always at your service. *(he takes a pencil and begins scribbling on the back of a magazine)* I've got three hundred American bucks ready cash here in the bank. Two hundred of them I'm all set to invest. It's the last money I have in the world. After it's gone I'm finished up. But, if you don't take a risk you can't make a win. How much dough have you guys got to put in?

DOBBS. I got a hundred and fifty bucks and Curtin here has the same.

*A little* BOY, *barefoot and ragged, is moving down the aisle by the rows of cots, brandishing lottery tickets.*

BOY. Buy a ticket on Loteria National—one hundred thousand pesos—the big prize.

HOWARD. Five hundred bucks— that ain't hardly enough to buy tools and weapons and the most essential provisions.

DOBBS. Weapons? What do we need weapons for?

HOWARD. Meat's one thing. We'll kill our own. And bandits is another . . . We ought to have anyway six hundred bucks between us.

DOBBS. That much, eh?

HOWARD. Can't you dig up any more?

DOBBS. Not a red cent.

*Int. Oso Negro another angle*

*A few feet away from the three men the* BOY *selling lottery tickets stops in his tracks and stares intently at* DOBBS, *then he rushes forward.*

BOY. Give me my money, senor . . . ten percent I get for having sold you the prize-winning ticket.

DOBBS *(misunderstanding)*. Get away from me.

BOY. Please, senor—it is the custom. Whoever draws the lucky number always gives a present to the seller of the ticket. If you don't do it you will have bad luck for the rest of your life. *(he takes hold of* DOBBS' *coat)*

DOBBS. I tell you I don't want any lottery ticket. *(suddenly hearing the kid)* What? What's that . . .?

HOWARD. He says you bought a winning ticket from him.

*A memory flashes through* DOBBS' *mind. He leans forward, peers into the* BOY'S *face, then he begins to dig and claw in his watch pocket. He produces a lottery ticket, unfolds it and holds it toward the* BOY.

DOBBS. Here—is this what you mean?

BOY *(in Spanish)*. Si, senor, si. . . .

DOBBS. You say it's a winner?

BOY *(in Spanish)*. Si, senor—a two hundred peso prize. *(he sorts through the sheets of winning numbers, finds the date he is looking for and holds it out for* DOBBS *to see)* Three—seven—two—one.

DOBBS *(shouts)*. My number!

CURTIN. Sure enough.

DOBBS. Just look at that fat, rich, printed number! Two hundred pesos! That's the sugar Papa likes. Welcome, sweet little smackers. *(he takes a bill out of his pocket)* Here's your present, sonny boy, with my blessing.

BOY *(all smiles now)*. Mucho gracias, Senor. *(he exits on the run)*

*Closer shot* DOBBS *and* CURTIN

DOBBS *(extends his hand to* CURTIN*)*. You want to shake the hand that bought this ticket?

CURTIN *takes* DOBBS *by the hand.*

CURTIN. Congratulations.

DOBBS *(pumping* CURTIN'S *hand)*. Congratulations yourself. You stand to profit by this same as I do.

CURTIN. How do you make that out?

DOBBS. Didn't the old man say we needed six hundred—and that's how much we got now, isn't it? *(he kisses the ticket)*

CURTIN. Yeah . . . but. . . .

DOBBS. But what?

CURTIN. Why should you be putting up for me?

DOBBS. This is an all or nothing proposition. If we make a find we'll be lighting our cigars with hundred dollar bills. And if we don't, the difference between what I'm putting up and you're putting up ain't enough to keep me from being right back where I was half an hour ago, polishing a bench with the seat of my pants. *(once more he holds his hand out)* So put 'er there . . . partner.

*Fade out:*

*Fade in:*

*Ext. long moving shot*

*the arid mountains of Durango. Camera pulls back to:*

*Int. day coach*

*crowded with Indians and Mestizos. Camera moves up the aisle to a close shot of* DOBBS, HOWARD *and* CURTIN. DOBBS *is asleep.* HOWARD *and* CURTIN *are peering at a map the old man is holding on his knees.* HOWARD *is drawing on the map—lines and dots over small sections.*

HOWARD. We'll buy our burros at Perla and head Northeast away from the railroad. It's no use looking anywhere nearby a railroad or any kind of a road at all, because construction engineers make it their business to examine every bit of ground around the roads while they're building them. We have to go where there's no trail—where you can be positive no surveyor or anybody who knows anything about prospecting has ever been before. The best places are those where anybody who's on salary wouldn't go because he wouldn't think it worth his while to risk his hide.

*All of a sudden the brakes of the train are applied, so violently that people are flung out of their seats. Scarcely have they picked themselves up than they are knocked down again. The car wheels scream on the rails. The train stops and a babble of* VOICES *begins.*

VOICES. Que pasará? Parece que chocó el tren.

*Over scene comes the sound of scattered firing.*

VOICES. No es choque. Son bandidos. Están asaltando el tren.

*A number of the women and some of the men begin to pray.* HOWARD *makes a grab for his gun and* DOBBS *and* CURTIN *follow suit.*

HOWARD *(shouts).* Echense al piso, pronto. De barriga, ándenle.

*The natives in the car do as he bids. Almost immediately bullets begin to hit the side of the coach and sing through its windows.*

*Cut to:*

*Long shot ext. train shooting through window*

*The area is strewn with boulders, and from behind those nearby the tracks little puffs of smoke are rising. The partners fire their revolvers whenever they see a sombrero.*

*All at once the bandits are up, racing toward the train. The three partners fire steadily through the train windows and several of the bandits go down. A few reach the coach and are killed or wounded while trying to enter. That the attack will be a failure is apparent almost as soon as it begins. Before they have covered half the distance most of the bandits are hugging the ground or seeking cover.*

*And now the train jolts into motion again. Some horsemen come into view. All but one are dismounted, firing over their saddles. Three horses have been hit and are down. The mounted bandit is wearing a hat painted with gilt that mirrors the sun. He sits boldly upright, firing his rifle from the shoulder. At the moment when our coach is directly opposite him he spurs his horse and gallops alongside the train, firing away. After a hundred yards or so the train, gathering speed, leaves him behind . . . No more bullets are hitting the coach. Presently the sound of firing ceases. People start getting to their feet. It seems nobody has been seriously hurt, at least in this coach. Bullet holes are inspected and commented upon with gusto. The danger through which they have passed serves to unite the passengers and make them all one family. The men slap each other's backs. A bottle of mescal starts making the rounds. Everybody is talking at once.*

DOBBS. I got three of 'em. You can credit me with three. *(to* CURTIN*)* How many did you get?

CURTIN. A couple I guess.

DOBBS. I'm one up on you, Curtin. *(to* HOWARD*)* Bet you didn't get as many as I did, Pop. I got three. Good shooting, eh? *(he points to a groove on the side of the window from which he was firing)* Hey, look! One hit right by my car not two inches away. Close.

CURTIN. The bullets were sure coming thick and fast. For a minute it was like a swarm of bees in this coach.

DOBBS. That bandit in the gold hat who rode his horse along side the train—I had my sights on him nice as you please, but the train gave a jolt and I missed, dammit. Sure wish I'd got him.

*A* PASSENGER *comes in from the next coach and repeats, so everyone can hear, information relayed back from the head of the train:*

PASSENGER. Pusieron una piedra en la vía. Se pegaron chasco los bandidos, porque vienen tropas adelante y atrás. Hubo pocos muertos a bordo. *(in English for* DOBBS' *and* CURTIN'S *benefit)* There was big boulder on the track put there by bandits—that's why the train stop. When bandits board they got big surprise. Soldiers on the train, front and rear, and they were waiting for them. Not many passengers got killed.

HOWARD *has picked the map up from the floor and sat down with it, spreading it across his knees. Out comes his pencil again.*

HOWARD *(as though nothing of moment had happened).* Here's where we're bound for—here abouts. I can't make out properly on this map whether it's mountain, swamp, desert or what, but that shows the makers of the map themselves don't know for sure. Once on the spot all we have to do is wipe our eyes and look round us. Yeah, and blow our noses. Believe it or not, I knew a feller once could smell gold just like a jackass can smell water.

*Dissolve to:*

*Int. general store* DOBBS, HOWARD, CURTIN, STOREKEEPER

*Staple groceries and merchandise are on the shelves lining the walls. Various articles of merchandise hang from the ceiling; pack saddles, rope, etc. Thru the open doorway a pile of boxes can be glimpsed—the equipment which came by train with the three partners.* HOWARD, *his map out, is leaning on the counter conversing in Spanish with the* STOREKEEPER, *a tall, elderly man with graying hair and bronzed face.* CURTIN *stands a little way off, trying to follow what is being said.* DOBBS *roams around the store trying on articles of apparel.*

STOREKEEPER. A cinco días hay un río. Muy caudaloso en el verano, pero seco en el invierno.

HOWARD *draws the river on the map.*

STOREKEEPER *(continuing).* Más allá hay montanas muy altas, más que las nubes. Terreno peligroso. Hay que abrirse paso a machete y hay muchos reptiles y insectos de picada mortal.

Tambien hay tigres muy feroces que pueden arrastrar a un burro y hasta subirlo a un arbol.

DOBBS *brings items he has selected from the stock—a belt with a fancy buckle, a pair of half boots, and a wide brim felt hat—over to the counter, puts them down. The* STOREKEEPER *reckons their value on his fingers.*

DOBBS. Getting any dope?

HOWARD. Five days from here there's a river. It's dry in the winter. Beyond that river the country's very wild and dangerous. Mountains rise above the clouds and we must cut our way through the valleys which are full of deadly insects and huge snakes, and ferocious tigers so big and strong they can climb trees with burros in their mouths . . .

*A* BOY *enters.*

HOWARD *(continues).* Good! . . . I'm pleased to hear tall tales about where we're going, because it means mighty few outsiders have set foot there.

BOY. Aqui está mi primo con unos burros. Quieren verlos?

HOWARD *(to* DOBBS *and* CURTIN*).* There's some burros outside for us to see.

*Pan with them to the door, beyond which a number of burros are standing.*

*Dissolve to:*

*Ext. mountains long shot*

*of the three men and their burros—tiny moving specks in the distance.*

*Dissolve to:*

*Med. shot* HOWARD *climbing a steep slope*

*The old man proceeds at the unwearying gait of one who's accustomed to measuring out endless miles with his legs.*

DOBBS *and* CURTIN

*They are fairly staggering with weariness.* DOBBS *half falls, half sits down, gropes blindly for his canteen, opens it. He raises the canteen, takes a mouthful of water, spits it out, then drinks along.*

DOBBS. If there is any gold in those mountains, how long will it have been there?

CURTIN. Huh?

DOBBS. Millions and millions of years, won't it? . . . So what's our hurry. A couple of days more or less ain't going to make much difference.

CURTIN. Remember what you said back in Tampico about having to carry the old man on our backs . . .

DOBBS. That's when I took him for an ordinary human being and not the son of a goat. Look at him climb, will you?

*Long shot* HOWARD

*moving unwearyingly up the steep slope.*

CURTIN *(grinning).* What gets me is how he can go all day long under this sun without water.

DOBBS. He's part goat I tell you.

CURTIN. If I'd only known what it meant to go prospecting I'd have stayed right in Tampico and waited for a job to turn up. . . . What's the matter?

DOBBS *is peering at the ground where he splattered water. Now he goes down on one knee to examine it more closely.*

DOBBS. Look! Look how it glitters.

CURTIN *kneels down beside him.*

CURTIN *(drawing in his breath).* Yeah.

DOBBS. It's yellow too . . . like . . . like : . .

*He's afraid to say the word.*

CURTIN. . . . like gold.

DOBBS *reaches for the canteen, pours more water out on the ground.*

DOBBS. It's all around . . . *(he pours some water onto a rock)* Look, Curtin, here's a vein of it in this rock.

*They are fairly prancing with excitement now.*

CURTIN *(cups his hands, calls).* Howard! Howard, come back here! We've found something.

*Close shot* HOWARD

*high above the others on a mountain. He turns at the sound of their voices.*

CURTIN'S VOICE *(o.s.).* Come back.

*Without hesitation, he starts back down, running when he can.*

*Cut back to:*

CURTIN *and* DOBBS

DOBBS. What else could it be. Only gold shines and glitters like that. We've struck it, Curtin, or I'm crazy, and from the looks of things we've struck it rich.

CURTIN. Looks like it.

DOBBS *is splashing more water out of his canteen and exclaiming:*

DOBBS. Maybe we've found a whaddya call it—a mother lode.

HOWARD *comes trotting up.* DOBBS *seizes him by the arm.*

DOBBS. Look, Howard, the ground —it's full of gold, and it's in veins in the rocks.

HOWARD *doesn't even bend over. They wait for him to speak, full of expectancy.*

HOWARD *(finally).* This here stuff wouldn't pay you a dinner for a truck load, unless you could dump it right in front of a building under construction. It ain't good for anything but mixing with cement.

*There's a long silence.*

DOBBS. It ain't gold?

HOWARD *(shaking his head).* Nope . . . Not to say there ain't gold here about. We've walked over it four or five times. There was a place yesterday looked like rich diggings but water for washing the sand was eleven miles away. Too far. The other times there wasn't enough gold to pay us a good day's wages.

DOBBS *wears a forlorn expression.* CURTIN *looks sheepish.* HOWARD *inspects the packs on the burro, tightens a couple of hitches.*

HOWARD *(continuing).* Next time you strike it rich holler for me before you go splashing water around. Water's precious. Sometimes it can be even more precious than gold. *(he cuts a burro across its quarters with a willow switch)* Get up.

*The pack train starts moving.*

*Dissolve to:*

*Small campfire night*

HOWARD *has cooked hardtack in the skillet and is eating. Over scene the yip-yipping of coyotes halts while a wolf gives out with his long-drawn, mournful howl.*

HOWARD. Hey, you fellers. How about eating!

*But neither of the inert bodies lying with their backs to the fire show any sign of life.* HOWARD *shakes* CURTIN *by the shoulder.*

HOWARD. How about eating!

CURTIN. Don't want to eat . . . want to sleep.

HOWARD. Hey! Dobbs!

DOBBS' *only answer is a snore. The coyotes start up again. Old man* HOWARD *finishes his piece of hardtack, wipes his mouth and takes a harmonica out of his pocket. The music he makes is even more lonely sounding than the howling of the coyotes.*

*Dissolve to:*

*Med. long shot burro train and three men*

*As before, the old man is in the lead. They are travelling into different kind of country now. Low, sandy hills, dotted with cactus. A wind is blowing.* HOWARD *stops, holds up his hand, testing the wind for direction. He squints at the horizon, then hurriedly begins to take the packs off the burros.* DOBBS *and* CURTIN *come up.*

DOBBS. What's up?

HOWARD. A Norther, looks like.

CURTIN. A Norther? What's a Norther?

*Even as he asks the question a blast of wind starts the desert sands flying.*

HOWARD. Big winds from the North this time of year. When they blow hard enough this desert country stands right up on its hind legs.

*He pulls his bandana up so it covers his nose and mouth.* DOBBS *and* CURTIN *do likewise. The figures of men and beasts become vague shapes behind the curtain of flying sand, then they are obscured entirely.*

*Long shot wild, desolate country*

*First we see no sign of life whatever, but presently there's a movement and a stir in the thick underbrush.*

*Med. shot*

*of the three wielding machetes trying to open a trail over which the burros, with their heavy loads, may pass. Even the old man is showing wear and tear. His face is scratched and sweat and blood mingle to form big drops that drop off the end of his nose and chin each time he strikes with his machete. But he at least works his blade to some purpose. The two others strike out aimlessly, their muscles, out of weariness, no longer obedient. Observing their distress,* HOWARD *lowers his machete. It is a signal for* CURTIN *and* DOBBS *to sink groaning to the ground.* HOWARD *seizes the moment to take out makings and roll a cigarette. But the other two simply lie gasping for breath. Their eyes have that animal dumbness to them.*

HOWARD *(lighting his cigarette).* I reckon there's only a few hundred yards more of this heavy stuff. Pretty soon we ought to be getting up to where it's rocks and nothing else.

*Two or three drags finish the cigarette.* HOWARD *grinds it out, then raises his machete. Hearing the ring of the steel as the blade strikes,* CURTIN *tries blindly to imitate the old man. He strikes twice, feebly. There is a sound from* DOBBS. *He looks around.* DOBBS *is crying, adding tears to the mixture of sweat and blood that gets into his eyes and rolls off his chin.*

*Dissolve to:*

*A high rocky place*

*far below which flows an unending sea of brush.*

DOBBS. You want to know what I'm thinking? I'm thinking we ought to give up—leave the whole outfit—everything behind and go back to civilization.

HOWARD. What's that you say? Go back . . . Well tell my old grandmother I've got two very elegant bedfellows who kick at the first drop of rain and hide in the closet when thunder rumbles. My, my, what great prospectors—two shoe clerks reading in a magazine about prospecting for gold in the land of the midnight sun or south of the Border or west of the Rockies or . . .

DOBBS *(howling)*. Shut your trap.

*He picks up a rock, waves it, threateningly.* HOWARD *begins to dance a goatish kind of jig.*

DOBBS *(continuing)*. I'll smash your head flat.

HOWARD *(dancing)*. Throw it, baby, throw it. Go ahead, just do it. You'd never leave this wilderness if you did. Without me you two would die here. . . . more miserable than sick rats.

DOBBS *takes a step forward, but* CURTIN *restrains him.*

CURTIN. Leave the old man alone—can't you see he's nuts.

HOWARD. Nuts, eh? *(he laughs in a satanical way, kicking a rock in his dance)* Nuts am I. I'll just tell ya something, my two fine bedfellows. . . . You're so dumb there's nothing to compare you with. You're dumber than the dumbest jackass. Look at each other . . . you two. Did ya ever see anything like yourselves for being dumb specimens? *(he laughs and kicks his heels together)*

DOBBS *and* CURTIN *do look at each other, then they look back at* HOWARD. *They are puzzled as to whether the old man has really lost his mind.*

HOWARD. Why you two are so dumb you don't see the riches you're treading on with your own feet.

*They don't get* HOWARD's *meaning right away. He kicks a stone then picks it up, throws it up, catches it, all in the course of his dance.* DOBBS *and* CURTIN *look at each other, mouths agape. Suddenly they drop to their knees, start scratching at the rocky earth.*

HOWARD. Don't expect to find nuggets of molten gold. It's rich but not that rich. It's only heavy dirt and here ain't the place to dig. It comes from somewhere further up. *(he points up toward the mountain crest)* Up there's where we have to go . . . up there . . .

*Camera pans up to a high mountain peak, wearing in its majesty a crown of clouds.*

*Dissolve to:*

*Insert of a pan*

*the water turning in it. Camera pulls back to show* HOWARD *panning dirt. They are near the crest of the mountain now, at the place* HOWARD *pointed to in the previous scene.* DOBBS *and* CURTIN *look on at what* HOWARD *is doing, their faces sober and intent.*

DOBBS. So that's the way the stuff looks, is it . . . not much different from sand . . . plain sand.

HOWARD. Gold ain't like stones in a river bed. It don't call out to be picked up. You got to know how to recognize it. And the finding ain't all. Not by a long shot. You got to know how to tickle it so it comes out laughing. *(sifting some dirt through his fingers)* Mighty rich dirt. It'll pay good.

DOBBS. How good?

HOWARD. Oh, this dirt ought to run about twenty ounces to the ton.

CURTIN. At some twenty dollars an ounce! . . .

*The old man nods.*

DOBBS. How many tons will we able to handle a week?

HOWARD. That depends on how hard we work . . . We better pitch our camp a mile or two away.

DOBBS. Why, if here is where we're goin' to dig?

HOWARD. In case anybody happens by we can tell 'em we're hunters and get away with it maybe . . . We'll cut bushes and pile 'em around the mine itself so it can't be spotted from below.

DOBBS. I'd sure hate to play poker with you, old timer.

HOWARD. Every so often one of us will have to go to the nearest village after provisions. Whoever goes first ought to go all the time. That way they'll figure only one man's up here. If they find out there's more than one they're liable to get suspicious. Hunters usually work alone.

CURTIN. Wouldn't it be a lot easier to file a claim?

HOWARD. Easier, maybe, but not very profitable. It wouldn't be no time till an emissary from one of the big mining companies turned up with a paper in his hand showing we haven't any right to be here. (*squatting there, he picks up some of the dirt, sifts it through his fingers. Then he grins at* DOBBS *and* CURTIN) How does it feel, you fellers, to be men of property . . .?

*Fade out:*

*Fade in:*

*Full shot—water wheel*

*A construction designed to draw water from a tank and, by means of cans and cases, raise it to an upper tank from whence upon opening a lock, the water is to run back down a wooden sluice to the original tank. The power that turns the wheel is a burro. The final nail has just been driven and the moment has arrived when the handiwork of the three partners is to be tested.* HOWARD *harnesses the burro to the wheel and kicks it in the rear, setting the wheel and system of tin cans and boxes into motion.* CURTIN *climbs to the upper tank, pacing himself according to the speed of the crude machine.*

DOBBS (*pumps* HOWARD'S *hand*). My hat's off to you. From now on it's your show, old timer. Whatever you say goes far as I'm concerned.

HOWARD. The tanks'll leak some at first till the boards swell and close the seams.

DOBBS. I sure had some cockeyed ideas about prospecting for gold. It was all in the finding I thought. Once you found it you just picked it up and put it into sacks and carried it to the nearest bank. (*he laughs uproarously at his former innocence*)

HOWARD. We might burn some lime out of the rocks and build a tank that wouldn't lose a drop of water.

DOBBS (*laughing*). I'd hate to think what would've happened to Curtin and me if we'd gone it alone. Even if we'd found the stuff we wouldn't have known how to get it out.

HOWARD. You're learning. Pretty soon I won't be able to tell you anything. You'll know it all.

*If there is any irony in* HOWARD'S *voice it escapes* DOBBS.

HOWARD (*to* CURTIN). Tank full yet?

CURTIN. Right to the top.

HOWARD. Then open up the sluice gate.

CURTIN. Right.

*He obeys and the water starts running down the sluice.*

*Following* HOWARD'S *lead,* DOBBS *begins to wash the sand, trying his* best to imitate the actions of the old man.

HOWARD. Like this—do it.
DOBBS. I get it.

CURTIN *joins them.*

DOBBS *(to* CURTIN*).* This is how it's done—see.
CURTIN. Yeah—I get it.

*Individual closeups of the three men*

*—as they separate the sand from the gold.*

*Tiny flakes of gold*

*—as the sand is washed away.*

*Dissolve to:*

*Camp closeup of* DOBBS*—night*

*His eyes, reflecting the light of the campfire, glitter in their sockets. He leans forward and we see a Mexican calendar tacked to the wall. Lines have been drawn across all the dates up to October 21.*

*Closeup of a scale*

*—as the proceeds of the day's work are weighed. Camera pulls back to a close shot of the three men.* HOWARD *measures dust onto the scale.*

CURTIN. How much do you figure it is now.
HOWARD. Close on to five thousand dollars worth.
DOBBS. When're we going to start dividing it?

HOWARD *looks at him keenly.*

HOWARD. Any time you say.
CURTIN. Why divide it at all. I don't see any point. We're all going back together, when the time comes. Why not wait until we get paid for the stuff, then just divide the money?

HOWARD. Either way suits me. You fellers decide.
DOBBS. I'm for dividing it up as we go along and leaving it up to each man to be responsible for his own goods.
HOWARD. I reckon I'd rather have it that way, too. I haven't liked the responsibility of guarding your treasure any too well.
DOBBS. Nobody asked you.
HOWARD *(smilingly).* That's right—you never asked me. I only thought I was the most trustworthy among us three.
DOBBS. You? How come?
HOWARD. I said the most trustworthy. As for being the most honest, no one can say.
DOBBS. I don't get you.
HOWARD. Well, let's look the thing straight in the face. Suppose you were charged with taking care of the goods. All right, I'm somewhere deep in the brush one day getting timber and Curtin here is on his way to the village for provisions. That'd be your big chance to pack up and leave us in the cold.
DOBBS. Only a guy that's a thief at heart would think me likely to do a thing like that!
HOWARD. Right now it wouldn't be worthwhile. But when our pile has grown to—let's say three hundred ounces—think of such things, you will . . .
CURTIN. How's about yourself?
HOWARD. I'm not quick on my feet any longer. You fellers are a lot tougher than when we started out. And by the time the pile is big enough to be really tempting I won't be able to run half as fast as either one of you. You'd get me by the collar and string me up in no time. And that's why I think I'm the most trustworthy in this outfit.

CURTIN *grins.*

CURTIN. Looking at it that way I guess you're right. But perhaps it would be better to cut the proceeds three ways every night. It'd relieve you of a responsibility you don't like.

HOWARD. Swell by me. After we've gotten more than a couple hundred ounces it'll be a nuisance to carry it around in little bags hanging from our necks, so each of us will have to hide his share of the treasure from the other two. And having done so he'll have to be forever on the watch in case his hiding place is discovered.

DOBBS. What a dirty filthy mind you have.

HOWARD. Not dirty, baby. No, not dirty. Only I know what sort of ideas even supposedly decent people can get in their heads when gold's at stake.

*Dissolve to:*

*Full shot of the mine*

*There are two tunnels now into the rocky shoulder. Over scene the sound of picks. Camera moves into the interior of one of the tunnels.* HOWARD *puts down his pick, starts shoveling the rocky debris out of the cave into the open. Camera moves to the opening of the other tunnel.* DOBBS, *some twenty feet in, is swinging away with his pick.*

*A crack in the ceiling of the tunnel over* DOBBS' *head.*

DOBBS' *pick biting into the rock*

*Over scene we hear* DOBBS' *VOICE.*

DOBBS' VOICE *(he grunts).* Whew! Hot! Geez . . . hot.

*Cut back to:*

*Crack in ceiling*

*It lengthens by half an inch.*

*Ext. tunnel*

—*as* CURTIN *drives his burro up the trail. He is hauling water for the tank. He unloads the burro, pours the water into the tank, then starts back down the trail.*

*Int. tunnel*

DOBBS' *swinging his pick.*

*Crack in ceiling*

*It is twice as long now as before, and with each blow from the pick it gets wider.*

CURTIN

—*starting his burro down the trail. He takes a few strides, hesitates, turns back up toward the tunnels. At the mouth of the first tunnel he calls to the old man.*

CURTIN. Hey, Howard, want me to spell you?

HOWARD. Thanks, not right yet, baby. I'm just getting my second wind. *(he turns around; with a movement of his arm he wipes the sweat and grime out of his eyes)*

CURTIN *moves on to the next tunnel. There has been a cave-in. The ceiling is hanging so low at the opening that there is not enough room for a body to pass through:* CURTIN *doesn't take time to yell for* HOWARD *but starts clawing rubble aside. When he has made a big enough opening he wriggles into the tunnel.*

*Int. tunnel*

DOBBS *is lying unconscious, half covered with rock.* CURTIN *works* DOBBS' *body free, then starts pulling him out. It is an inch by inch proposition getting the unconscious man through the narrow opening, but at last he succeeds.*

CURTIN *(shouting).* Howard! Howard.

HOWARD'S VOICE *answers hollowly from inside the tunnel.*

HOWARD'S VOICE. Yes?

*The ring of* HOWARD's *pick against the stones stops.*

CURTIN. Come quick. Howard!

*The old man comes on the run. One look at* DOBBS' *tunnel tells him what has happened. He immediately goes to work on* DOBBS.

HOWARD *(presently)*. He's coming around.

DOBBS *groans. His eyelids flicker, then open.*

HOWARD. Lie still for a minute till you get your senses back.
DOBBS. What happened?
HOWARD. Tunnel caved in on you.
DOBBS *(remembers)*. Yeah . . . I tell you I heard the harps playing sure enough. *(he sits up now, tests his arms and legs)*
HOWARD. Nothing broken.
DOBBS. Guess I'm almost good as new. Who pulled me out?
HOWARD. Curtin did.

*There is the sound of falling rubble and the three men turn in time to see the tunnel sealed off for good.* DOBBS *shivers, then he stretches out his hand to* CURTIN.

DOBBS. I owe you my life, partner.
CURTIN. Forget it.

*Dissolve to:*

*Night*

HOWARD *is measuring out the yellow sand into three equal parts.* CURTIN *and* DOBBS *follow his every move. Presently it is divided.*

DOBBS *takes up his share and leaves the circle of light the campfire*

*makes to go off into the dark. The old man takes out his harmonica, begins to play softly.*

CURTIN. What are you going to do with your hard earned money, old timer, when you get back and cash in?
HOWARD. I'm getting along in years. Oh, I can still hold up my end when it comes to a hard day's work, but I ain't the man I was once, and next year, next month, next week, by thunder, I won't be the man I am today. Reckon I'll find me some quiet place to settle down. Buy a business maybe . . . a grocery or a hardware store, and spend the better part of my time reading the comic strips and adventure stories. One thing's for sure . . . I ain't going to go prospecting again and waste my time and money trying to find another gold mine. . . . How's about yourself? What are your plans, if any?
CURTIN. I figure on buying some land and growing fruit—peaches maybe.
HOWARD. How'd you happen to settle on peaches?
CURTIN. One summer when I was a kid I worked as a picker in a peach harvest in the San Joaquin Valley. It sure was something. Hundreds of people—old and young—whole families working together. After the day's work we used to build big bonfires and sit around 'em and sing to guitar music, till morning sometimes. You'd go to sleep, wake up and sing and go to sleep again. Everybody had a wonderful time . . .

DOBBS *comes back into the light of the campfire.*

CURTIN *(continuing)*. . . . Ever since, I've had a hankering to be a fruit grower. Must be grand watching your own trees put on leaves, come into blossom and bear . . . watching the fruit get big and ripe on the bough, ready for picking . . .

DOBBS. What's all that about?

HOWARD. We've been telling each other what we aim to do when we get back.

DOBBS. Me now, I got it all figured out what I'm going to do.

CURTIN. Tell us, Dobbsie.

DOBBS. First off I'm going to the Turkish bath and sweat and soak till I get all the grime out of my pores. Then I'm going to a barber shop and after I've had my hair cut and've been shaved and so on, I'm going to have 'em douse me out of every bottle on the shelf. Then I'm going to a haberdasher's and buy brand new duds . . . a dozen of everything. And then I'm going to a swell cafe—and if anything ain't just right, and maybe if it is, I'm going to raise hell, bawl the waiter out, and have him take it back . . . *(he smiles, thoroughly enjoying this imaginary scene at table)*

CURTIN. What's next on the program?

DOBBS. What would be . . . a dame!

CURTIN. Only one?

DOBBS. That'll all depend on how good she is. Maybe one—maybe half a dozen.

CURTIN. Dark or light?

DOBBS *(the liberal)*. I don't care what her nationality is just so long she's kind of small and plump . . . you know . . . *(his hands describe an hourglass)* . . . with plenty of wiggle in 'er.

HOWARD. If I were you boys I wouldn't talk or even think women. It ain't too good for your health.

DOBBS. Guess you're right, seeing the prospect is so far off.

HOWARD. You know what. We ought to put some kind of limit on our take. Agree between ourselves that when we get exactly so much we pull up stakes and beat it.

CURTIN. What do you think the limit ought to be?

HOWARD. Oh, say twenty-five thousand dollars worth apiece.

DOBBS. Twenty-five thousand? That's small potatoes.

CURTIN. How much do you say?

DOBBS. Fifty thousand anyway. Seventy-five's more like it.

HOWARD. That'd take another year at least . . . if the vein held out, which wouldn't be likely.

DOBBS. What's a year more or less when that kind of dough's to be made.

HOWARD. Twenty-five's plenty far as I'm concerned. More'n enough to last me out my life time.

DOBBS. Sure, you're old. But I'm still young. I need dough and plenty of it.

CURTIN. Twenty-five thousand in one piece is more'n I ever expected to get my hands on.

DOBBS *(snorts)*. Small potatoes!

CURTIN. No use making hogs of ourselves.

DOBBS. Hog am I! Why, I'd be within my rights if I demanded half again what you get.

CURTIN. How come?

DOBBS. There's no denying, is there, I put up the lion's share of the cash?

CURTIN. So you did, Dobbsie—and I always meant to pay you back.

DOBBS *(pointedly)*. In civilized places the biggest investor always gets the biggest return.

HOWARD. That's one thing in favor of the wilds.

DOBBS. Not that I intend to make any such demand, you understand, but I'd be within my rights if I did. Next time you go calling me a hog, remember what I could'a done if I'd'a wanted . . .

HOWARD. I think you're wise not to put things on a strictly money basis, partner. Curtin might take it into his head he was a capitalist instead of a guy with a shovel and just sit back and take things easy and let you and me do all the work.

*While the old man talks,* CURTIN *uses the scales to weigh out a portion of his dust.*

HOWARD (*continuing*). He'd stand to realize a tidy sum on his investment without so much as turning his hand over. If anybody's to get more, I reckon it ought to be the one who does the most work.

CURTIN (*giving the dust to* DOBBS). There you are, Dobbsie. What I owe you with interest.

DOBBS (*he takes the dust, weighs it in his hand, then, with a sudden gesture, flings it away so that it falls, a little shower, into the fire*). I just don't like being told I'm a hog, that's all.

HOWARD (*addressing* DOBBS). Other things aside, there's a lot of truth in what you were saying about being younger than me and needing more dough therefore. I'm willing to make it forty thousand apiece. (*to* CURTIN) What do you say, partner?

CURTIN. How long will it take?

HOWARD. Oh, another six months, I reckon.

CURTIN (*after a moment's debate*). Make it forty thousand or six months.

HOWARD. Suits me. Okay, Dobbs?

DOBBS (*sourly*). Okay.

HOWARD. Let's shake on it then.

*The three men shake hands solemnly. Then* CURTIN *gets up, starts away from the fire to hide his goods.*

*Dissolve to:*

*Night int. tent close shot on* DOBBS

*sleeping, a bar of moonlight across his face. Over scene the scream of a tiger. He stirs, turns over. The* scream *is repeated.* DOBBS *opens his eyes. Then he sits up, leaning on an elbow.*

HOWARD'*s blankets*

*They're empty. Camera pulls back to full shot interior tent.* CURTIN *is in his blankets sound asleep.* DOBBS *frowns. After a moment* DOBBS *sits all the way up, throws back his blankets, reaches for his shoes and puts them on. Then, picking up his revolver, he moves silently out of the tent and heads across the campsite. He's gone perhaps a dozen steps when he hears* HOWARD *coming. He draws back into the shadows. When* HOWARD *is scarcely three feet away,* DOBBS *steps out, suddenly confronting him.*

DOBBS. That you, Howard?

HOWARD (*startled*). You oughtn't to go jumping out at me like that. I might've let you have it.

DOBBS. Out for a midnight stroll?

HOWARD. There's a tiger around. I went to see if the burros were all right.

DOBBS (*grunts skeptically, then:*). So!

HOWARD. What's the matter, Dobbsie?

DOBBS. Think I'll make *sure* the burros are all right.

HOWARD. Help yourself.

*He walks away in the direction of the tent.*

*Int. tent*

*as* HOWARD *enters.* CURTIN *stirs.*

CURTIN (*to* HOWARD, *sleepily*). What's up?

HOWARD. Nothing's up.

CURTIN *sees that* DOBBS' *blankets are empty.*

CURTIN. Where's Dobbs?

HOWARD. Poking around in the dark out there.

DOBBS

*taking sacks of the precious dust out of his hiding place—a hole underneath a rock. He is counting the sacks aloud.*

DOBBS. Three—four—five—six.

*He gives a satisfied grunt, then starts putting them back.*

*Int. tent*

HOWARD *has got back in his blankets.*

CURTIN. He's sure taking a long time . . .

CURTIN *throws his blankets off, puts on his shoes.*

CURTIN *(continuing).* I'm going to have a look-see.

*Ext. tent*

*Camera pans with* CURTIN *to his hiding place—a hollow tree. He begins to pick out his sacks of gold.*

*Int. tent*

*as* DOBBS *enters. He starts to take his shoes off then notices* CURTIN'S *absence.*

DOBBS *(sharply).* Where's Curtin?
HOWARD. Out there some place. He said something about having a look-see.

*Again* DOBBS' *brow becomes furrowed with suspicion. He puts his shoe back on, gets up and is about to leave the tent when* CURTIN *enters. He and* DOBBS *survey each other wordlessly.*

HOWARD. It's come around to me again, but I won't take my turn if you guys'll quit worrying about your goods and go to bed. We got work to do tomorrow.

DOBBS *grunts, turns back into the tent.* CURTIN *drops down on his blankets.*

*Dissolve to:*

*Ext. the mine—close shot—*DOBBS

*at the sluice, washing sand and talking to himself.*

DOBBS. You can't catch me sleeping . . . Don't you ever believe that. I'm not so dumb. The day you try to put anything over on me will be a costly one for both of you.

*At the over scene sound of hoofs on rock,* DOBBS *stops talking. Camera pulls back to show* CURTIN *driving two of the burros.* DOBBS *keeps his face averted and* CURTIN *passes without any words being exchanged. As the sound of the hoofs fades,* DOBBS *resumes his monologue.*

DOBBS. Any more lip out of you and I'll pull off and let you have it. If you know what's good for you, you won't monkey around with Fred C. Dobbs.

CURTIN *at a turn of the trail. He comes upon the old man repairing a tool.*

CURTIN. You ought to get a load of Dobbsie. He's talking away to himself a mile a minute.
HOWARD *(shaking his head).* Something's eating him. I don't know what. He's spoiling for trouble.

CURTIN *grunts, proceeds on down the trail.*

DOBBS

DOBBS *(mimicking* HOWARD'S *voice).* We're low on provisions, Dobbsie. How about you going to the village. *(then as* DOBBS *again)* Who does Howard think he is ordering me around?

HOWARD'S VOICE *(over scene)*. What's that, Dobbsie?

DOBBS *looks up in surprise. Camera pulls back to a close shot of* HOWARD *and* DOBBS.

DOBBS. Nothing.

HOWARD. Better look out. It's a bad sign when a guy starts talking to himself.

DOBBS *(angrily)*. Who else have I got to talk to? Certainly not you or Curtin. Fine partners, I must say.

HOWARD. Got something up your nose?

DOBBS *doesn't answer.*

HOWARD. Blow it out. It'll do you good.

DOBBS *(shouts suddenly)*. Don't get the idea you two are putting anything over on me.

HOWARD. Take it easy, Dobbsie.

DOBBS *(still louder)*. I know what your game is.

HOWARD. Then you know more than I do.

DOBBS *(railing)*. Why am I elected to go to the village for provisions— why me instead of you or Curtin? Don't think I don't see through that. I know you've thrown together against me. The two days I'd be gone would give you plenty of time to discover where my dust is, wouldn't it?

HOWARD. If you have any fears along those lines, why don't you take your dust along with you?

DOBBS. And run the risk of having it taken from me by bandits.

HOWARD. If you were to run into bandits, you'd be out of luck anyway. They'd kill you for the shoes on your feet.

DOBBS. So that's it. Everything is clear now. You're hoping bandits'll get me. That would save you a lot of trouble, wouldn't it? And your consciences wouldn't bother you either!

HOWARD. Okay, Dobbs, you just forget about going. Curtin or I'll go.

DOBBS *turns on his heel, stalks off.*

*Pan shot of* CURTIN

*Something he sees out of scene causes him to stop.*

*A gila monster*

CURTIN *picks up a rock, but before he can heave it the big yellow and black lizard has disappeared under a boulder.* CURTIN *drops the rock, picks up a piece of timber, runs one end underneath the rock making a lever. He leans his weight on the end of the timber.*

DOBBS' VOICE *(over scene)*. Just like I thought.

CURTIN *turns. Camera pulls back to show* DOBBS *covering* CURTIN *with his gun.*

CURTIN. What's the idea?

DOBBS. Put your hands up.

CURTIN *obeys.* DOBBS *takes* CURTIN'S *gun away from him.*

DOBBS. I got a good mind to pull off and pump you up, chest and belly alike.

CURTIN. Go ahead and pull, but would you mind telling me first what it's all about?

DOBBS. It won't get you any where playin' dumb.

CURTIN *(comprehension dawning on his face)*. Well, I'll be—so that's where your dust is hidden, Dobbsie?

HOWARD *comes up.*

HOWARD. What's all the hollerin' for?

CURTIN. Seems like I stumbled accidentally on Dobbs' treasure.

DOBBS *(snorts)*. Accidentally! What were you trying to pry up that rock for? Tell me that!

CURTIN. I saw a gila monster crawl under it.

DOBBS. Brother, I got to hand it to you. You can sure think up a good story when you need one.

CURTIN. Okay. I'm a liar. There isn't any gila monster under there. Let's see you stick your hand in and get your goods out. Go ahead.

DOBBS. Sure I will. But don't you make a move or I'll . . .

CURTIN. Don't worry. I'll stand right where I am. I want to see this.

DOBBS *goes down on one knee beside the boulder. He starts to put his hand in, hesitates, then bends forward to look into the hole.*

CURTIN. Reach right in and get your goods. If you don't we'll think you're plain yellow, won't we, Howard?

DOBBS *sneaks his hand forward toward the opening beneath the rock.*

CURTIN. They never let go, do they Howard, once they grab onto you— gila monsters. You can cut 'em in half at the neck and their heads'll still hang on till sundown, I hear, but by that time the victim don't usually care anymore because he's dead. Isn't that right, Howard?

HOWARD. I reckon.

CURTIN. What's the matter, Dobbs, why don't you reach your hand right in and get your treasure? It couldn't be you're scared to, could it, after the way you shot off your mouth. Show us you aren't yellow, Dobbsie. I'd hate to think my partner had a yellow streak up his back.

DOBBS *(sweat showing on his face —the sweat of fear. He springs to his feet, aims wildly at CURTIN, shouting).* I'll kill you, you dirty, thieving . . .

*But before he can pull the trigger* HOWARD *has knocked up his arm. Then both men close in on him.* CURTIN *gets the gun away from him.*

CURTIN. Okay, Howard, I got him covered. Dobbs, another bad move out of you, and I'll blow you to kingdomcome. Hey, Howard, turn that rock over, will you.

HOWARD *obeys. Leaning his weight on one end of the timber until the rock rolls over. The camera moves into a closeup of a gila monster, its body arched, hissing, atop DOBBS' treasure. Over scene the sound of a shot. The slug bores through the lizard's head, its body rises, its tail threshes.*

*Closeup DOBBS*

*his face is white, his eyes are staring.*

*Cut back to:*

*Closeup the gila monster*

*lying belly up on DOBBS' treasure, his arms clawing at the air.*

*Slow dissolve.*

*A typical Durango village*

*A scattering of adobe huts, a church, a cantina, and a general store. Entering the village behind his two burros,* CURTIN *sees that something is going on in the square. The townspeople make a circle around a half dozen Federales whose* LIEUTENANT *is talking to two Mestizos, tough-looking fellows in big hats and blankets such as the bandits that attacked the train were. From the edge of the crowd,* CURTIN *sees the* LIEUTENANT *open a billfold, take out money and a small rectangle of cardboard. He holds up the cardboard for everybody to see. All the talk is in Spanish so* CURTIN *doesn't know for sure what's happening.*

LIEUTENANT *(opening billfold).* No hay ninguna duda, ustedes son, despues del asalto al tren les seguimos la pista. Miron, que más pruebas, la cartera con el boleto. La misma fecha. Ya verán lo que les va a pasar por bandidos.

CURTIN *ties his burros to the hitching post outside the general store, then addresses the* STOREKEEPER *who stands in his doorway watching the proceedings in the square.*

CURTIN. Buenos dias, amigo.
STOREKEEPER. Como está usted, Senor?
CURTIN. What is going on?
STOREKEEPER. Son de los bandidos que han estado asaltando trones. Mire, el Teniente le encontró a ese una cartera robada con un boleto de ferrocarril.

CURTIN *shakes his head, unable to understand.*

STOREKEEPER *(continuing).* Ese par ya tiene dias aquí tomando tequila como aqua, escandalizando y sembrando el miedo por todas partes.

*Over scene another voice speaks.* CURTIN *turns in surprise for the words are English with an American accent.*

CODY'S VOICE. The Lieutenant just found a railroad ticket in a woman's purse the big fellow had on him. The ticket has on it the date of the Agua Caliente train robbery.

*Camera pulls back to:*

*Med. shot* CODY

*in f.g. He is about thirty-five, tall, but not husky. His manner, well-bred, but decisive.*

CODY *(continuing).* Between them they had a diamond ring, two pearl earrings, and quite a lot of money. It seems they've been here in this village several days drinking and shooting off their cannons so that the villagers are afraid to stick their noses out of their huts.

*The* LIEUTENANT *now addresses a small boy upon whom the honor of holding the* LIEUTENANT'S *horse has been bestowed. The boy points. The* LIEUTENANT *motions with his head for the two bandits to move along in the direction the boy pointed. Then he mounts and follows. The Federales and townspeople bring up the rear.*

CURTIN. What'll they do with them now? Where are they taking them?
CODY. To the cemetery.
CURTIN. Oh. *(he enters the store)*

*Int. store*

*The* STOREKEEPER *goes around behind his counter.*

CODY *(who has followed* CURTIN *in).* The Federales are very efficient in their way. It may not be our American way. They aren't fingerprint experts, that is, but they can follow any trail, and against them no hideout's any use. They know all the tricks of the bandits. You can bet your sweet soul that they'll run down every last one of those groups that attacked the train. It'll take time—months—maybe—but they'll do it.

CURTIN *doesn't want to prolong the conversation which may lead to questions he doesn't wish to answer. At the same time he doesn't want to awaken, by his reticence, the other man's curiosity. He "hmmmmms" politely, turns to the* STOREKEEPER *and begins to point out various articles on the shelves—salt, coffee, corn meal, soap, etc.*

CODY. Not many Americans get around this way. You're the first I've bumped into for a long time.

CURTIN. That so.

CODY. Mighty rough country hereabouts.

CURTIN. Yep.

CODY. My name's Cody. I'm from Texas. *(he puts out his hand)*

CURTIN *(shakes hand).* Curtin.

CODY. What's your game?

CURTIN. I'm a hunter.

CODY. Professional?

CURTIN. Yep.

CODY. What all do you hunt?

CURTIN. Oh, tiger cats—anything with a hide of commercial value.

CODY. I should think you'd do better west of here—on the Rio Conchos, for example. Lot better hunting ground over that way.

CURTIN. I'm doing all right.

CODY. How long'd you say you'd been in these mountains?

CURTIN. Few months.

CODY. Seen anything that looks like pay-dirt?

CURTIN *shakes his head "No."*

CODY *(continuing).* I've got an idea there's truck loads of the real goods up in those mountains.

CURTIN. Well, I know the whole landscape around, and if there was a single grain of gold you can bet I'd sure seen it. No, there's nothing doing here for gold.

CODY. Listen, brother, I can look at a hill five miles away and tell you whether it carries an ounce or a ship load. If you haven't found anything up there yet I'll come along with you and put your nose in it. There's in-dications in this valley, lots of indications, and by tracing the rocks I found that they come from the ridge up there, washed down by the tropical rains.

CURTIN. You don't say so.

CODY. Yes, I say so.

*Over scene the sound of a volley.*

CODY. So much for those bandits. You got to hand it to the Mexicans when it comes to swift justice. Once the Federales get their mits on a criminal they know what to do. They put shovels in their hands and tell 'em to dig and when they've dug deep enough they tell 'em to put their shovels down and have a cigarette and say their prayers. And in another five minutes they're being covered over with the earth they dug out.

*Through the open doorway the Federales, led by their* LIEUTENANT, *can be seen departing on horseback.*

CURTIN. Yep, you got to hand it to 'em all right.

*The* STOREKEEPER *counts on his fingers, then tells* CURTIN *the amount owed.* CURTIN *pays him, carries the sacks and tins out of the store.*

*Ext. store*

*as* CURTIN *goes about loading up the burros.* CODY *comes out of the store.*

CODY. I meant what I said about going along with you. These are my two mules. I'm all packed up and ready to start if you'll let me come with you back to your camp. . . .

CURTIN. Thanks just the same, but I prefer going it by myself. *(he tightens the hitches on the burros, unties the lead rope, and starts off. Without looking back he calls:)* Good luck.

*Pan shot* CURTIN

*as he passes the cemetery. The townsmen are throwing dirt into the graves.*

*Dissolve to:*

*Long shot desert plain*

*that leads up to the mountains. Far in the distance six moving specks, three widely separated from three.*

*Dissolve to:*

*Close shot* CURTIN *and his burros*

CURTIN *turns around, frowns. Below him and some distance behind another man with pack animals is following in his tracks.* CURTIN *proceeds another dozen yards then stops. The frown becomes a scowl.*

*Long shot*

*The first three dots are not moving. The second three remain in motion for a time. Then they also stop. After a brief period the first three start again, then sure enough, the second three also start.*

*Dissolve to:*

*Med. shot* CURTIN

*as he turns into a rocky defile. He advances some dozen yards then pulls his burros into a draw, ties them to a sapling and turns back to the entrance of the defile. He takes a position behind a rock. Presently the sound of hooves can be heard, then* CODY's *figure, beating his two mules, comes into scene.* CURTIN *takes out his revolver, twirls the chamber to see that it's working smoothly, then he waits for* CODY *to come abreast. When that occurs he steps out from behind the rock.*

CURTIN. What's the idea you following me. Don't make me sore, you mug, or you may get hurt. I don't go butting into your business, and you better not into mine. Believe me, mug, I could take care of you any day of the week if you were twice your size. So if you know what's healthy for you, you better lay off and quit following me.

CODY. I didn't mean to bother you. I only want to be in the company of an American for a change and sit for a few nights by a fire and smoke and talk.

CURTIN. Well, I don't want to talk, see. And I've heard all the talking out of you I want to, so turn around and start the other way.

*Seeing he means business,* CODY *obeys.* CURTIN *goes back to his burros, waits until the footfalls of* CODY's *mules can no longer be heard, then unties his own burros and starts on.*

*Dissolve to:*

*The campsite* HOWARD, DOBBS *and* CURTIN *night*

*around the campfire—supper is cooking.*

CURTIN. . . . . I went way around and kept on hard ground which wouldn't show tracks. I even drove the burros through long stretches of brush to get the mug off my trail. But whenever I reached a high point and looked back I could see he was coming right along. I guess it's only a matter of time until he shows up here.

DOBBS. I move we tell him straight off to beat it. And if he don't then we fill his belly up with plums too hard for him to digest.

HOWARD. That'd be foolish. He'd sit around for an hour playing the innocent and then go and report us to the officials. Once they were here we couldn't stay any longer. And we couldn't take our goods with us when we left.

DOBBS. All right. Then there's nothing else to do but pull the trigger the minute he appears.

HOWARD *stirs a pot that is on the fire.*

HOWARD. It's no crime to visit these mountains. He may be a guy that just likes to roam around. We can't shoot him for that, and besides if we were to shoot him it might come out.

DOBBS. We don't have to shoot him necessarily. We could push him off a rock and claim it was an accident.

HOWARD. And just who's going to do the pushing? You, Dobbie?

DOBBS. We could play odd man . . .

HOWARD. Brother, count me out!

DOBBS. You're sure he was trailing you, are you?

CURTIN. Absolutely.

DOBBS. How come?

CURTIN *makes a gesture with one hand and glances toward an opening in the bushes where the path leads.*

CURTIN. Because there he is.

HOWARD *and* DOBBS *are so bewildered that for a few seconds they cannot bring themselves to look around.*

DOBBS. Where?

CURTIN *nods toward the path.* HOWARD *and* DOBBS *finally turn around and there in the deep shadows of the falling night, uncertainly lighted by the flickering campfire, stands the stranger between his two mules.*

CODY *(finally after a long silence).* Hello.

*Presently* DOBBS *rises. With long slow strides he crosses to the stranger. Then, hands in his pants pockets, he looks him up and down.*

DOBBS. Come over to the fire.

CODY. Thank you, friend.

*He comes close to the fire, starts taking the packs off his mules. None of the others offer to help him.* DOBBS *drops down by the fire.* HOWARD *takes the pot of potatoes from the fire, shakes it, and tests the potatoes with a knife to see whether they are cooked enough.* CURTIN *gets up and brings more wood, then puts on the coffee can.* DOBBS *simply lies sprawled out watching every move* CODY *makes. The silence becomes interminable.*

CODY *(suddenly).* I know quite well, you fellows, that I'm not wanted around here. (*no one denies this; he addresses himself to* CURTIN) But even after what you told me on the trail I simply couldn't resist the desire to sit around and jaw with an American.

DOBBS. Then why don't you go where there are Americans that might want to talk to you. Durango isn't so far off. All the American clubs you could hope for are there.

CODY. I'm not after that. I've got other things on my mind—more important.

DOBBS. So've we. And don't you make any mistake. Our biggest worry right now is your presence here. We've no use for you. We don't even want you for a cook or a dishwasher. We're full up. No vacancy. Understand! If I haven't made myself clear, let me tell you I think you'll be doing yourself a big favor if you saddle up first thing in the morning and go where you came from and take our blessing with you.

*The newcomer remains silent. He watches the three partners dealing the meat and potatoes out on the plates and fall to eating.*

CURTIN *(over his half-emptied plate).* Help yourself, partner, to a plate and spoon and knife and fork.

DOBBS. Sure. We're no misers. We don't let guys starve to death. Help yourself. Tonight you're welcome. But beginning tomorrow look out. No trespassing around here. You know— dogs! Get me.

DOBBS *gives* CURTIN *a long wink, then:*

DOBBS *(Cont.).* I got five foxes and a lion while you were away to the village.

CURTIN. Good hides?

DOBBS. Pretty good.

CODY *(without emphasis).* Excuse me for butting in, but there's no game here worth going after. It wouldn't take one week for a real hunter to clean up all around for five miles in each direction.

DOBBS *is on his feet instantly, his right hand hovering around the butt of the revolver that is stuck inside his waistband.*

HOWARD *(sharply).* You're right. There's no good hunting here. That's why we've made up our minds to leave this ground inside a week and look for something better. Yep, stranger, you're dead right. This here's awful poor ground. It took us some time to find it out.

CODY. Poor ground, you say? Depends on what you're hunting for. For game, yes. But it's very good ground for something else.

HOWARD. And what might that be?

CODY. Gold.

DOBBS' *hand closes around his revolver butt.* HOWARD *shoots him a fierce look.*

HOWARD. Gold, did you say. Ha-ha—that's a good one.

CURTIN. I told you at the village, mister—there's no gold hereabouts.

HOWARD *(laughs).* My boy, if there were one single ounce, I'd have seen it. Believe me I would.

CODY. If you haven't found any gold here then good night, sir. You aren't as smart as you appear to be.

*This last serves to confound the partners.* HOWARD *clears his throat, then he nods.*

HOWARD. Maybe . . . maybe you're right. Who knows. We never had a thought about gold. Gives me an idea. I'll sleep over it. *(he stretches)* Guess I'll hit the hay.

CURTIN. Me too. *(he gets up)* Until tomorrow, mister.

CODY *doesn't answer.*

CURTIN. G'night.

CODY *whistles. In a few moments his two pack mules come hobbling up. He gives each a handful of corn which he takes from his pack, then after patting their necks, he kicks them lightly and they return to the shadows. Going a little way off from the fire,* CODY *spreads his blankets and lies down to sleep. Only then does* DOBBS *leave the campfire and enter the tent.*

*Int. tent*

*The other two are already stretched out.*

DOBBS. I can't figure that bird out. Is he wise to us or ain't he?

HOWARD. Whether he is or not, he looks fairly harmless to me.

DOBBS. Looks can be mighty deceiving.

HOWARD. There's no denying that.

DOBBS. I'm of the opinion we ought to get rid of him—the quick way. How about me starting a quarrel with him. Make him boil over and then as soon as he draws, all of us blast away at him.

CURTIN. That don't sound too pretty, the way you put it.

DOBBS. For all we know he might have it in his head to murder us all in our sleep this very night.

HOWARD. Anything's possible.

DOBBS *(excitedly)*. Well then?

HOWARD. Tell you what. You guys go to sleep. I'll be watch-dog for a couple of hours. Then you and Curtin can have your turns.

DOBBS. Okay. Is your gun handy?

HOWARD. Yep. *(his hands are tranquilly folded across his chest)*

DOBBS *crawls into his blankets. Over scene the voice of the coyotes yip-yipping.*

*Closeup* DOBBS

*as he goes to sleep, begins to snore.*

*Closeup* HOWARD

*This is all he's been waiting for; hearing* DOBBS *snore he closes his eyes and falls asleep.*

*Dissolve to:*

*Early morning*

*The braying of a jackass awakens* DOBBS. *He looks at* CURTIN *and* HOWARD, *sees they are both asleep, then plunges out of the tent. The stranger is by the fire, making coffee.*

CODY. Good morning, friend.

DOBBS *(ignoring the greeting).* Where'd you get the water to make coffee?

CODY. I just took it from the bucket.

DOBBS. Oh you did, did you. Well, that water wasn't carried up here so's you could make coffee, see.

CODY. I'm sorry. I didn't know water was so hard to get.

DOBBS. Well you know it now.

CODY. I'll go fill the bucket up for you.

CURTIN, *followed by* HOWARD, *comes out of the tent, observes* DOBBS' *belligerent attitude.*

CURTIN. What's up.

DOBBS. This mug has been stealing our water. *(to* CODY) Let me catch you at it once again and I'll let it out of you in little round holes.

CODY. I thought that perhaps I was among civilized men who wouldn't begrudge me a little fresh water.

DOBBS. Who ain't civilized?

*Without waiting for an answer he plants his fist in the stranger's face with such force that* CODY *drops full length as if felled by a heavy club. Then* DOBBS *busies himself at the fire as do* CURTIN *and* HOWARD. *It takes* CODY *some time to come to. When he does, he rises and shakes his head to discover whether his neck is broken. Then he comes close to* DOBBS.

CODY. I could easily do the same to you, and it isn't settled yet who'd come out on top. This time I took it. Thanks for your kind attention.

*The stranger's words and his manner of speaking embarrass* DOBBS *and make him feel ashamed. He shifts awkwardly.*

HOWARD. If I was you, mister, I'd saddle up and go while the going's good.

CODY. But I mean to stay right here.

DOBBS *and* CURTIN *(together).* How's that?

CODY. The brush and the mountains are free, aren't they?

HOWARD. That's right, friend, to whoever is first on the spot.

CODY. That holds for hunters, but not for gold miners. Unless, of course, they've registered their claim. I take it you guys haven't registered yours.

CURTIN. Who said we had a claim to register?

CODY. Whatever you say or don't say, tomorrow I start to dig for gold here.

*Unseen and unheard, another presence joins the now silent group—murder is amongst them. Solid and real as if made of flesh and bone. All their thoughts are upon this new companion in their midst. The problem of what to do about* CODY *is insignificant compared to the decision each of the partners must now make—to kill or not to kill.* CODY, *fully realizing that his life hangs by the most delicate thread, takes a deep breath, begins to talk.*

CODY. Oh, I know quite well you can bump me off any minute you wish, but that's a risk worth running, considering the stakes. Let's lay all our cards on the table. As I see it, you fellows have got to do one of three things: kill me; run me off; or take me in with you as a partner. Let's consider the first. Another guy might show up tomorrow, or maybe a dozen guys. If you start bumping people off, how far are you prepared to go with it? Ask yourselves that. Also, don't forget that the one actually to do the bumping off would forever be in the power of the other two . . . the only safe way would be for all three of you to pull your canons and bang away at the same instant like a firing squad. (*he indicates* DOBBS) He'd be all for that I'm sure, but you two haven't the look of born executioners.

HOWARD. We wouldn't stop at anything in protecting our interests.

CODY. I claim killing me isn't it. But of course, that's for you to decide. As for choice number two, if you chase me off I might very well inform on you.

HOWARD. We'd get you if you did that. We'd go all the way to China to get you. There'd be no quarter.

CODY. Nevertheless, you'd still come off losers.

HOWARD *nods, then:*

HOWARD. Wouldn't the knowledge that we'd follow you till Doom's Day make you think twice before informing on us?

CODY. I'd think twice all right. But that doesn't say I wouldn't turn you in. Twenty-five percent of the value of your find is the reward I'd get paid and that would be mighty tempting—mighty tempting.

CURTIN. That's a pretty strong argument in favor of our doing number one, mister.

CODY. I don't deny it, but let's see what number three has to offer. If you take me in as a partner you don't stand to lose anything. I will not ask to share in what you've made so far . . . only in the profits to come. Well, what do you say?

*The three partners sit silently for several moments. Then:*

HOWARD. Would you mind, stranger, letting us three thrash this out alone among ourselves.

CODY. Not at all. Go ahead. I have to look after my mules anyway.

*The camera pans* CODY *away.*

*Close shot of the three*

*watching him go.*

DOBBS (*when the stranger is out of earshot*). Where does he get off pushing his way in here after all the work we've done. Soft pickings for him, ain't it. Whoever else happens along —are they to be invited in too? Is it a come one come all proposition?

HOWARD. Sending him away is out of the question, all right. Either we bump him off or make him a partner.

DOBBS. Do the mug in I'd say. He himself told us the way. All three of us let him have it so there won't be any question of its being held over anybody's head in time to come.

*Med. shot* CODY

*moving across a high rock. Something out of scene makes him slow his pace and finally stop.*

*Long shot onto the plain below the mountain*

*A dozen or so dots are moving toward the mountain and the camera. The dots are men on horseback.*

*Close-up* CODY

*watching intently.*

*Camp* DOBBS, HOWARD, CURTIN

HOWARD. What's your feelings in the matter, Curtin?

CURTIN. I'm all for protecting our interests, but what do we gain by bumping him off? Nothing, so far as I can see. If he was asking to share in what we've made so far it'd be a different story.

DOBBS. Fred C. Dobbs ain't a guy who likes being taken advantage of.

HOWARD. I don't mind being taken some advantage of so long as it ain't money out of my pocket. What the devil . . . we can throw all the dirty jobs at him.

CODY'S VOICE *(over scene)*. Come up here! Come quick!

*The partners look around in surprise.*

CODY'S VOICE. Come on. Hurry!

*The three start running in the direction of the rock. But before they've gone about a dozen yards,* DOBBS *stops suddenly.*

DOBBS. Wait. Maybe he's up to something—a trick—like rolling a rock down on us or something. You go that way, Howard; and you, Curtin, that way. If he's pulling a trick we'll all let him have it.

DOBBS *takes his revolver out, starts up toward the rock, moving slowly.*

CODY *on the rock*

*He calls again.*

CODY. Hurry up.

HOWARD *is first to appear on top of the rock.*

CODY *(pointing)*. Look!

HOWARD *squints his eyes.*

HOWARD. I can't make out what they are.

CURTIN *is next, followed after an interval by* DOBBS.

HOWARD *(Cont.)*. Must be soldiers.

DOBBS *turns on* CODY, *draws his gun and cocks the hammer with his thumb.*

DOBBS. So that's your stinking game, is it. All right—take what's coming to you. *(he points the gun to* CODY'S *chest)* I knew you were an informer. I knew it all the time. If you know a prayer, you rat, say it now and make it snappy.

CODY *(in a quiet voice)*. You're wrong, partner. This means all our funerals, my own included.

CURTIN. What's that?

CODY. If I'm right in what I'm thinking then may the Lord be with us. They're not soldiers. Bandits— that's what they are. And they aren't after gold but guns and ammunition . . . The villagers must have told them about the American hunter up here.

CURTIN. They don't look like soldiers to me either, but just what he says—a bunch of dirty, ragged bandits.

HOWARD. We're in a hole, I tell you. With soldiers we'd at least have a chance to explain before an official. But with bandits . . .

DOBBS. I still think you're an informer . . .

CURTIN. Shut up, Dobbs. Leave him alone. We've got to think and work fast now.

DOBBS *(on his single track)*. . . . not an informer for the government—an informer for the bandits.

CODY. Wrong again, brother. And if you don't lay off me you may find yourself short one full grown man. Inside an hour or so you're going to need not only every man here but every hand and every gun.

HOWARD. We better start thinking about a way to defend ourselves. We might try hiding in the rocks but then we'd lose the burros and our whole outfit so I guess the best thing is to make a fight of it. *(he points at a ravine, narrow and not very deep, that lies between the rock on which they stand and the camp)* That ravine is a good natural trench. If we make our stand there they can't attack from the rear and they can't flank us. They'll have to pass over the camp site and we'd get some good shots at them. Cody, you seem to have good eyes—you stay up here on this lookout for the time being and watch their movements. You, Curtin, round up the burros and herd them into that thicket over there. Dobbs, let's you and me wrap up all our belongings and dump 'em into the trench.

*They hasten to the task of preparing for the assault that is to come.*

DOBBS

*filling buckets with water and carrying them to the trench.*

CURTIN

*getting the burros.*

CODY

*on the rock, watching the approach of the bandits.*

HOWARD

*piling rocks in front of the trench.*

CODY *(over scene)*. They're turning onto the trail up here.

HOWARD *(calls)*. How many of them are there?

CODY

*watching the approach of the bandits.*

*Long shot bandits*

*riding the trail that leads to the camp.*

*Closeup* CODY

*as he calls:*

CODY. Sixteen of 'em.

*Close shot* HOWARD

*He calls to* CODY.

HOWARD. Come on down, friend. I guess we're about as ready for 'em as we ever will be, so we might as well have something to eat. They'll be the best part of an hour getting here.

*He starts laying a fire. The partners,* CODY *included, gather around.*

CODY. One of 'em's wearing a hat painted gold. It reflects the sunlight . . .

CURTIN. A hat painted gold. Hear that, Dobbs, Howard! Remember the bandit in the gold hat?

DOBBS. Sure, on the train!

HOWARD. Him—Huh!

*Dissolve to:*

*The four men in the trench*

*They have just finished eating.*

HOWARD. If nobody objects, I'll take command. Right by you, partners?

CURTIN. Right.

CODY. No objection.

DOBBS. Sure.

HOWARD. I'll take the left center. You, Cody, take the right. Dobbs, your station is the left corner, and Curtin, you take the right corner. The left corner is the most important. A guy could sneak through that crack in the rocks over there.

*They go to their various posts. Presently there comes sound of hooves. Finally the bandits appear, one after the other, coming up the trail. They carry guns of different types and caliber. All are in rags and are unwashed and unshaven. A few have boots, half ripped open and with torn soles. Some wear leather pants like rancheros. They dismount. Two of the bandits venture forward into the campsite. They observe where the tent has been pitched and they point to the remnants of the fire. They call to the others who come forward and begin walking around the place, peering behind bushes and rocks. A discussion commences in the middle of the camp. There seems to be very little discipline. Each man has his own opinion and talks louder than the next.*

AD LIBS.

FIRST MAN. Hace poco acamparon aqui.

SECOND MAN. Miren muchachos, vengan aqui.

THIRD MAN. No vamonos, aqui nos embotellan.

FOURTH MAN. Los que estaban aqui ya se fueron este es un magnifice escondite.

HOWARD (*to* CURTIN *in a whisper*). They think whoever was here is gone. Some of them want to go back down the mountain and some want to stay up here and use this site as a headquarters from which to raid villages in the valley.

CURTIN. How about pouring it into them and bumping off as many as we can right away fast.

HOWARD. Hold your horses.

*Two of the men begin to build a fire. One exploring for wood leaves the others and comes straight across the camp toward* DOBBS' *station. He is looking upward at a growth of saplings so that he is hardly five feet away from* DOBBS *before he sees him. For a moment his jaw hangs in surprise, then he turns around and shouts:*

BANDIT. Miren muchachos, vengan todos. Pronto . . . Una pajarita echada en su nido. Que cosa mas bonita.

*The others all rise and come hurrying toward him. When they are halfway across the camp* DOBBS *shouts.*

DOBBS. Stop or I shoot.

*They obey.*

FIRST BANDIT. Ya, Ya, esta bueno. Espere. No tire, hombre.

*He walks backwards, making no attempt to reach for the heavy revolver at his side. The bandits hold a rapid-fire consultation, speaking in lowered tones so that the men in the trench cannot make out a word. Then* GOLD HAT *steps forward, thumbs close together in front of his belt to indicate that he does not mean to go for his weapon.*

GOLD HAT. Oiga, senor. Listen, we are no bandits. You are mistaken. We are Federales; you know, the mounted police. We are looking for the bandits to catch them. The ones who robbed the train you know.

DOBBS. All right. If you're the police, where are your badges?

GOLD HAT. Badges? We got no badges. We don't need badges. I don't have to show you any stinking badges.

*Again he starts forward. Four or five of the others move to follow their leader.* DOBBS *yells.*

DOBBS. You better not come any closer if you want to keep your health.

GOLD HAT. No sea malo, hombre. We don't want to do you any harm. No harm at all. Why can't you be a little more polite. We mean well. Give us your gun and we'll leave you in peace. Sure we will.

DOBBS. I need my gun myself.

GOLD HAT. Throw that old iron over here and we'll pick it up and go on our way.

DOBBS. Nothing doing. You better go without my gun—and go quick before I lose my temper.

DOBBS *waves his gun over the rim of the trench. The bandits retreat a few steps and then hold council again.*

HOWARD. They'll be playing some kind of a trick now.

*Sure enough.* GOLD HAT, *the leader, and another stand up move toward* DOBBS. *The second bandit has a gold watch dangling by a chain in his outstretched hand. He is slightly in advance of* GOLD HAT.

GOLD HAT. Look here, amigo, you got the wrong idea. I don't want to have your gun for nothing. I want to

buy it. Here I have a genuine gold watch with genuine gold chain made in your own country. That watch and chain is worth at least two hundred pesos. I'll exchange it for your gun. Good business it is for you. You better take it.

*The other bandit swings the watch on its chain around his head.*

DOBBS. You keep your watch. I'll keep my gun.

GOLD HAT. Oh you will. You'll keep it, oh. We won't get it. I'll show you, you. . . .

*There is a shot. The bandit with the watch throws up both hands so that the watch and the revolver fly through the air.*

BANDIT *(in Spanish).* Estoy herido. I am hit.

*Grabbing at his side he falls and begins crawling back to the others.*

HOWARD

*He is looking through his peek-hole over the sights of his rifle. It was he who fired the shot.*

*Bandits*

*All of the bandits, including* GOLD HAT, *look in the direction from which the shot came. It wasn't* DOBBS *who had fired. At the opposite corner of the trench a faint cloud of blue smoke still hangs in the air. The bandits all move backward toward the bushes.*

*Med. long shot—bandits*

*They are squatting on their heels, having another discussion. Suddenly* GOLD HAT *gets up, laughing.*

GOLD HAT *(he calls to* DOBBS*).* Hey, senor. You there. You cannot play such tricks on us. We know that you had your rifle over there . . . and that by means of a long string you pulled the trigger from where you are. We do the same when hunting ducks at the lakes. Don't try this on us.

*With a rapid move all the men have their guns up.*

GOLD HAT *(Cont.)*. And now come out of your dirty hole. No stalling any longer. Come. Vamanos or we'll drag you out like a rabbit. And when we get you out we will tear open your mouth to your ears.

*The men drop to the ground and, guns in hand, start crawling toward the trench. Hardly have they advanced six feet when there are four shots from the trench, each from a different gun. All the bandits turn around without getting up and crawl back into the bushes. There are shouts in Spanish back and forth between them. The bodies of two of the bandits remain where they fell in the area between the trench and the campsite.*

HOWARD *(to* CURTIN*)*. That'll keep 'em for a while. We've won a breathing space I figure. (*he leaves his position and goes to* CODY). Good work, Cody.

CODY. Do you think we've beat them off for good?

HOWARD. Hardly. Now that they know that there's at least four guns here, they'll be more determined than before.

CODY. What do you suppose they'll pull next?

HOWARD. They'll probably attack just before morning.

*He leaves* CODY *and moves back past his own station to* DOBBS.

DOBBS. We got 'em on the run now. How about us attacking?

HOWARD. Nope. It's better not to give away our number. For all they know there's a dozen of us. We're pretty safe here in this trench. If we prayed to the Lord things couldn't be better. The moon, for instance. It'll be full. The camp site will be flooded with moonlight so's even a cat can't cross without our seeing. We'd better change our stations for the night and stay in two groups. Cody and I'll take the right section and you and Curtin the left so's one can nap and the other watch. As soon as things start to happen, you just kick the sleeping guy in the ribs and he'll be up. I'm positive there won't be any move on the other side for the next six hours. It'll be different around four in the morning. Why don't you take your sweet slumber now?

*Dissolve to:*

*Night*

*as* CODY *shakes* HOWARD *awake.*

CODY *(in a hushed voice)*. I think they're coming.

HOWARD *moves quickly to* DOBBS' *and* CURTIN'S *post. They are both awake.*

HOWARD. Hold your fire till four men reach the middle of the camp. Then shoot to kill.

*He goes back to his post.*

*Med. long shot on camp*

*as the bandits move over the ground. Four shots ring out. There are groans and cries of Holy Mother. The bandits keep on coming. One of the bandits springs upright and charges the trench. He has a revolver in one hand, a machete in the other. He reaches the trench where* CODY *is before he falls. None of the others ever get so close to the trench. Their reception is too hot. The night attack is a failure. Once again they crawl back on their bellies toward the bushes.*

HOWARD. Looks like we won that round.

CODY, *at his post, doesn't answer.*

HOWARD. Hey, Cody.

*He turns to him.* CODY *is dead, a bullet through his neck*

*Dissolve to:*

*Morning all men at their posts*

*including* CODY, *toward whose body the others look somberly now and again. Over scene the sound of wood being chopped.*

DOBBS. I wonder what dirty business they're hatching right now.

HOWARD. I got a pretty good idea.

DOBBS. What?

HOWARD. They're making barricades that move. It's an old Indian trick. They crawl along pushing the barricades before them. You can't see where to shoot. Brother, I'd be willing to trade our gold mine right now for three or four hand grenades. If that's what they're up to, and I'm dead sure it is, we haven't a Chinaman's chance.

DOBBS. All we can do is sell our lives at the highest price possible. I mean to take as many of 'em as I can to hell with me.

HOWARD. Don't forget to save one last bullet for yourself. God forbid any of us fall alive into the hands of those we wounded. If you can't shoot yourself, try to stab yourself to death.

CURTIN. Maybe if we offer them our goods and our guns they will let us off.

DOBBS. Not a chance, baby boy. They'd torture us just the same to find out if there isn't more than we offered them. Then they'd kill us just the same. They don't know what mercy is.

HOWARD. Know why? Because they've never been shown any. If our people in the States had lived in poverty under all sorts of tyrannies for hundreds of years they'd have bred a race of bandits too, every bit as cruel and bloodthirsty. Come right down to it we are bandits of a kind. What right have we got to go looting their mountain anyway? About as much right as the foreign companies that take their oil without paying for it . . . and their silver and their copper.

*Over scene beyond the campsite an excited voice calls:*

VOICE. Compadre, compadre. Muy pronto.

DOBBS. What's up I wonder.

*Over scene the voices of the bandits mingle in rising excitement. The sound of the chopping leaves off.*

CURTIN. Something's happening all right.

*Over scene the sound of the bandits saddling their horses and mounting.* CURTIN *starts to climb out of the trench.*

DOBBS. Wait, pal, this may only be a trick to lure us out and get us.

HOWARD. I don't think so. They aren't good enough actors for this to be a trick.

CURTIN, *not heeding* DOBBS' *warning, leaves the trench and climbs up to the high place where* CODY *first saw the bandits.*

*Long shot what* CURTIN *sees*

*In the far distance a marching squadron of cavalry.*

CURTIN *(calls)*. Hey, partners, up here. Here's a sight if there ever was one.

DOBBS *and* HOWARD *climb rapidly up to* CURTIN.

DOBBS. Soldiers, look at 'em. I could kiss every one of them.

CURTIN. They must have got it from the villagers that bandits had gone up this mountain to rob the Gringo hunter of his guns and provisions.

DOBBS. I can't get it why the bandits are leaving. Why don't they wait for the soldiers up here.

HOWARD. Because they're old fighters who know all the tricks, that's why. With us at their backs and the soldiers facing them they wouldn't have a chance. Their only hope is to get out of this canyon before the soldiers enter.

DOBBS. Anyway they're doing us a big favor by leaving in such a devilish hurry. It wouldn't have been too healthy for us to have soldiers up here. They could be a real nuisance to us fellas if they started asking questions and nosing around.

*Long shot the bandits*

*riding hard. They reach the mouth of the canyon, turn to the right. They are caught sight of by the column of cavalry which goes into a gallop.*

DOBBS. Go get 'em! Sic 'em Tige! Chew 'em into bits and don't spit 'em out—swallow 'em. . . . Am I happy, am I. Fellers, tell you the truth I was already chewing dirt.

CURTIN. Too bad they didn't arrive before what's-his-name got his.

HOWARD. Reckon we couldn't have held out the night without his assistance. I'd say providence had sent him to us except . . .

DOBBS. Except what?

HOWARD. Why should providence put a smaller value on his life than on one of ours?

CURTIN. I wonder who he is and if he's got any folks?

DOBBS. Supposin' he has.

CURTIN. We ought to notify them.

HOWARD. Let's take a look at his belongings.

HOWARD *shakes himself out of his thoughts. The three start back down from the high place.*

*Close shot of the dead* CODY

*lying face down in the same defensive position he held when alive.* HOWARD's *hands come into scene and turn him over. They feel in* CODY's *pockets, bring out a wallet and some letters.*

*Close shot of the three*

*as* HOWARD *opens the wallet.*

HOWARD *(examining the contents).* Couple hundred dollars. Name's James Cody. This here driver's license was issued in Dallas, Texas. Letter's from Dallas too, so that must be his home. *(he takes a snapshot out of the wallet)* Real pretty, ain't she. His girl, I reckon.

DOBBS. Let me see.

*Snapshot in* DOBBS' *hand*

*Young woman with a tender, smiling face.*

*Scene*

*There is something about the way* DOBBS *is looking at the picture that* CURTIN *doesn't like.*

DOBBS. Not bad, not bad.

CURTIN *reaches out and takes the snapshot from* DOBBS' *hand.* HOWARD *has removed the letter from the envelope and is scanning it.*

HOWARD *(reading)*.

Dear Jim: Your letter just arrived. It was such a relief to get word after so many months of silence. I realize, of course, that there aren't any mail boxes that you can drop a letter in out there in the wilds, but that doesn't keep me from worrying about you. Little Jimmy is fine, but he misses his Daddy almost as much as I do. He keeps asking, "When's Daddy coming home?" You say if you do not make a real find this time you'll never go again. I cannot begin to tell you how my heart rejoices at those words if you really mean them. Now I feel free to tell you. I've never thought any material treasure, no matter how great, is worth the pain of these long separations.

The country is especially lovely this year. It's been a perfect spring— warm rains, hardly any frost. The fruit trees are all in bloom. The upper orchard looks aflame and the lower like after a snow storm. Everybody looks forward to big crops. I do hope you are back for the harvest.

Of course, I'm hoping that you will at last strike it rich. It is high time for luck to start smiling upon you, but just in case she doesn't remember we've already found life's real treasure.

> Forever yours,
> Helen

*He holds out the letter for the others to read.*

*Insert—postscript*

*A child's scrawl, big letters and little letters and things that are like letters but aren't. Then a hieroglyphic "Jimmy."*

*Scene*

CURTIN *gives him back the snapshot.* HOWARD *puts it into the wallet and he puts the wallet and the letter back into his pocket. Then he picks up a spade from the pile of equipment at the bottom of the trench. He climbs out of the trench, stands looking around for a moment, selecting a proper site, then he starts digging a grave.*

*Fade out:*

*Fade in:*

*Campfire night*

*The old man is measuring out the gold into three parts as we have seen him do before.*

HOWARD. Only seven penny-weight thirteen grains.

DOBBS. Less than we did yesterday.

HOWARD. If you want my opinion it's going to keep getting less from now on. We've taken about all the gold this here mountain has.

DOBBS. How much do you figure we've made to date?

HOWARD *(wets the end of his lead pencil, figures on a piece of paper)*. Not as much as we were aiming to collect—not forty thousand—Not that much.

CURTIN. I'm willing to lower my hindsights.

HOWARD. We got upwards of thirty-five thousand apiece—and we ought to be plenty thankful.

DOBBS. Sure—let's call it quits and pack up and leave.

HOWARD. It's going to be a lot harder trip going back than it was coming. The burros' loads are heavier and accidents will be more likely to happen on the trail. There's always the danger of bandits, of course, but added to that there's another hazard that wasn't there before—the Federales. If we were to meet up with them they might get kind of curious about what we're carrying in our packs. Oh, we got the goods all right, but I don't figure it's really ours until we pass it over the counter at the bank.

CURTIN. We been mighty lucky so far. Here's hoping our luck holds.

DOBBS. Yeah, here's hoping. Sooner we leave the better, as far as I'm concerned. I don't want to keep that dame waiting, whoever she is.

HOWARD. It'll take us another week to break down the mine and put the mountain back in shape.

DOBBS. Do what to the mountain?

HOWARD. Make 'er appear like she did before we came.

DOBBS *(mystified)*. I don't get it.

HOWARD. We've wounded this mountain and it's our duty to close her wounds. It's the least we can do out of gratitude for all the wealth she's given us. If you guys won't help me I'll do it alone.

CURTIN *(laughs)*. You talk about the mountain like it was a real person. . . .

*Dissolve to:*

*Full shot Ext. mine*

*or rather what was once the mine.* HOWARD'S *wishes have been carried out and the place looks almost the same as before the three men came to take the mountain's gold. The water system—wheel, vats and sluices—is afire. The burros stand patiently while the three men load them up.*

HOWARD. Well, I reckon that's about everything. Go get your goods, boys, and I'll get mine and we'll be off.

*Each man goes to the hiding place of his gold, gets it out and, staggering under its weight, brings it back to where the burros are. They go about loading on the sacks and covering them with hides.*

HOWARD. I reckon each man's burro with his goods better be his own responsibility.

*The others nod.*

DOBBS. Let's get going.

*They start,* CURTIN *in the lead, across the campsite area. Coming to the spot where* CODY *is buried,* CURTIN *slows down but doesn't stop. When they reach the opening in the brush where the trail begins* HOWARD *turns and looks back.*

HOWARD *(waves)*. Goodbye, mountain, and thanks.

DOBBS *(imitates* HOWARD'S *gesture)*. Yeah, thanks, mountain.

CURTIN *(waving at the mountain)*. Thanks.

*Dissolve to:*

*Long shot desert*

*It is not the flat mesquite-littered kind of desert but an arid rocky wasteland full of gullies and ledges with an occasional giant cactus standing sentinel. The heat-waves rising from the ground distort the air so that the whole tortured landscape swims constantly before the eyes of the three men. They move at a slow pace, timing their steps to those of the heavily-loaded burros. Something frightens the lead burro who shies suddenly and begins to back.* HOWARD *looks out of scene.*

*A rattlesnake*

*coiled a few yards ahead.* HOWARD *leads his burro off to the right, giving the snake a wide enough berth. He makes no move to destroy the snake nor do the others who simply follow in* HOWARD'S *steps.*

DOBBS *(calls to the snake over his shoulder)*. This is your domain. No argument, brother. We're trespassing. We don't like being here any more than you like having us. You just tell us a shorter way out and we'll take it.

*Dissolve to:*

*Ext. the wilds twilight*

*The three partners are around a campfire preparing their evening meal. The hobbled burros are grazing near by. The bags of gold are in three separate stacks. The food is on the fire and* DOBBS *and* CURTIN *are stretched out doing nothing beyond listening to* HOWARD'S *harmonica. There is something lonely and haunting about its music.*

CURTIN. I been thinking about her— Cody's widow, I mean—and the kid. You know what . . .? We'd ought'a give 'em a fourth just as if he'd been partners with us from the start.

DOBBS *(his jaw drops, then)*. You mean a fourth of all our goods?

CURTIN. Yeah, that's right.

DOBBS. Are you crazy?

CURTIN. If it hadn't been for Cody we wouldn't 've walked away from that mountain. Ask Howard.

HOWARD. Yep, the buzzards would've got fat on us all right.

DOBBS. It might just as well've been one of us. That it wasn't is our good luck and his bad.

CURTIN. Whatever you guys do I'm going to give a fourth.

HOWARD. What the devil—I got more than I need anyhow. Half what I got is enough to last me out. A fourth—sure.

DOBBS. You guys must've both been born at revival meetings.

HOWARD *has lowered his harmonica. Now, head cocked in an attitude of listening, he sits staring into the surrounding bush.*

HOWARD. Pipe down.

DOBBS *(after a brief silence, whispers)*. What's up?

HOWARD *takes out his revolver, twirls the chamber, then moves away from the fire into the shadows. He motions to the others and they do likewise. Then all at once* FOUR INDIANS *appear. They are unarmed and of innocent appearance. One of them addresses the partners in Spanish.*

FIRST INDIAN. Buenas noches, senores. Podemos sentarnos cerca lumbre? descansar poquito. Favor?

HOWARD *(To the* INDIANS*)*. Con mucho gusto, como no, amigos. Quieren tomar cafe con nosotros?

INDIAN. Si, Muchas gracias, senores.

HOWARD *(to* DOBBS *and* CURTIN*)*. Whatever they want they mean no harm.

*He gestures and* CURTIN *offers them a cup. The* INDIANS *help themselves, all drinking out of the same cup.* DOBBS *produces his tobacco pouch. This they also accept, each taking a pinch of tobacco and rolling it in corn leaves which they carry on them. In return they offer the partners tobacco of their own.*

DOBBS. We give them tobacco and they give us tobacco. I don't get it. Why not everybody smoke his own?

HOWARD. Take some and thank them.

DOBBS *and* CURTIN *obey, saying "Muchas gracias."*

HOWARD. They're after something. It'll take them awhile to come to the point. To say what you want right off the bat isn't considered polite among Indians.

*A long silence ensues, during which the* INDIANS *drink their coffee and smoke their cigarettes. Each time they raise the cup they smile at the white men. Finally, the speaker among them begins:*

INDIAN. Pues vera usted senor. Mi hijito se cayo al agua y lo sacamos tan pronto como pudimos. No se mueve, ni nada y no quiere revivir, pero yo creo que no esta muerto. Nocesitamos ayuda, por favor.

HOWARD. Cuando sucedio esto a su hijito?

INDIAN. Esta tarde, senor.

HOWARD *(to the partners).* His little boy fell into the water. They fished him out but he won't come to. He isn't dead. He just won't come to.

HOWARD *gets to his feet.*

HOWARD. I'll go and have a look at the boy and get back here as soon as I can, before morning probably. Watch after my goods while I'm gone. *(he turns again to the* INDIANS*)* Bueno, amigos, yo voy con ustedes. No se si podre ayudar, Pero hare todo posible. Vamonos.

*The* INDIANS *all get up, politely take leave of* DOBBS *and* CURTIN. *They lead* HOWARD *to the horse which he mounts, then leading the way they run off on foot.*

*Int. adobe hut*

*A palm mat is spread over a table upon which a small boy lies motionless. The room is crowded with* IN-DIANS, *both men and women.* HOW-ARD *enters behind the boy's father. The* INDIANS *stand aside making a pathway to the table.* HOWARD *goes to the boy, stands over him silently for a time, trying to decide what the treatment should be. With his thumb he raises the child's eyelids, then, ear to chest, he listens for a heartbeat. He tries artificial respiration. This treatment makes a deep impression on the* INDIANS *who look at each other and murmur approvingly.*

HOWARD. Quiero aqua caliente. Unas toallas. Tambien un espejo y un poco tequila *(to four* INDIANS*)* Ustedes frotando mucho manos y pies, pronto.

*While these things are being produced,* HOWARD *instructs four of the* INDIANS *on how to rub the boy's hands and feet so that the blood is sent toward the heart. When the hot towels are ready he places them on the boy's belly, after which he forces open the boy's mouth and pours into it a teaspoonful of tequila, Presently he listens again for the heartbeat. His eyes light up. There is life in the little body.*

HOWARD. Dame el espejo.

*He holds it to the boy's mouth. Sure enough it shows a faint mist. A murmur runs through the room.* HOWARD *goes on with the artificial respiration. After a little while the boy coughs. The murmur is repeated. It is hardly a murmur—it is rather that slight sound which accompanies a quick intaking of breath. The on-lookers believe they are seeing a miracle performed. Shouting or any other sign of jubilation would be unseemly. They act as if they were under a spell. And now the boy opens his eyes. No single word is uttered by anyone present. They simply look at the awakened boy and at* HOWARD *in awe.*

HOWARD *helps the little boy to sit up. The child looks around him, wonderingly, at all the faces, his eyes finally resting on the strange bearded face of the white man. Then his mouth puckers up and he begins to cry. Except for the crying of the child, there is no other sound in the room, not even the shuffling of feet.* HOWARD *puts his hand briefly on the little boy's head then turns to go.*

HOWARD. Buenas noches.

*No answer is made. Again the way is cleared for him. The eyes of the* INDIANS *turn with him as he passes, and they are full of awe.*

*Dissolve to:*

*Ext. mountains day*

*Full shot of the partners and their burros*

*moving along the trail.*

HOWARD. Artificial respiration did it and some Boy Scout tricks. I think it was more shock than drowning. He hadn't swallowed much water. Maybe he was stunned when diving.

*Over scene from a distance, the sound of a voice—a man's voice in a long drawn out call.*

DOBBS. Now what!

CURTIN. We've got something on our heels.

*Looking in the direction of the call they see a number of horsemen come into view. Again they reach for their weapons and make ready to defend themselves, but when their pursuers arrive they are the* INDIANS *of the night before. The partners put their weapons aside and greet them. As before, it is the father of the little boy who does the talking.*

INDIAN. Porque se van tan pronto, senores?

HOWARD. Tenemos negocios importantes en Durango.

INDIAN. Pero senores, no se vayan tan pronto. Queremos que esten con nosotros aunque sea unas semanas.

HOWARD. Muchas gracias por la invitacion. Pero necesitamos estar en Durango en una semana.

INDIAN. Pero senor, usted salvo la vida a mi hijito. Si lo dejo que se vaya sin mostrarle gratitud no tendre perdon de Dios.

DOBBS (*to* HOWARD). What's up.

HOWARD. He's insisting that we return with him to his village and be his guests. He wants to pay off his debt to me for saving his son's life, by feasting and honoring us. Otherwise he believes he'll burn in Hades.

DOBBS (*laughing*). Tell him to forget it. He don't owe you a thing.

HOWARD (*to the* INDIAN). Mi mayor recompensa fue el gusto que senti cuando el nino abrio los ojos.

INDIAN. Pero senor, tengo que pagarle mi deuda. Si no se me enojarian todos los Santos del Cielo. Venga por favor.

HOWARD (*to his partners who are laughing at him*). This is no laughing matter. I'm afraid he's determined to show his gratitude even if it means taking us back to the village as prisoners.

DOBBS (*cutting in*). Sabe, hombre. No poder quedar. No. No. Imposible, sabe?

DOBBS *pushes through the* INDIANS, *roughly. They let him pass, but from a determined circle around* HOWARD.

INDIAN (*to* DOBBS). Usted o el no importa. (*pointing at* CURTIN) Este Senor si importa.

CURTIN. What did he say?

HOWARD (*anxiety showing plainly on his face*). It makes no great difference what you two do, but I have to come.

DOBBS. So it's like that. They only want you.

HOWARD. Looks like it.

DOBBS. Okay. Go with 'em. Stay a few days, then follow us to Durango. We'll meet you there.

HOWARD. What about my packs?

CURTIN. Take them along with you.

DOBBS. I'm against that. If they were to discover what's in them they might forget you were their honored guest and rob you or even kill you. In any case, word would get out and then no trail would be safe for you to travel alone.

HOWARD *(at a loss)*. All right. What'll I do—spill my goods out right here on the ground?

CURTIN. We'll take 'em with us if you want us to and wait for you in Durango. If you're held up longer than a week or so we might go on to the port and deposit your goods at a bank there.

HOWARD *(after a pause)*. I reckon that's about the only solution there is.

CURTIN *takes out a piece of paper and a pencil.*

CURTIN. If we don't meet at Durango your goods'll be deposited in the Banking Company. We'll tell the manager you hold this receipt. We'll leave our signatures with him to identify you. Here's a receipt. Okay?

HOWARD. Okay. Maybe after I've stayed with 'em a little while these fellows will let me have a horse to ride to Durango. I may get there only a day or two behind you.

CURTIN *gives him the receipt.*

CURTIN. That'll be fine. Good luck, old man.

*First* CURTIN, *then* DOBBS *shake hands with* HOWARD.

DOBBS. Yeah, all the luck in the world. We'll sure feel lonesome without you, but like my Sunday school teacher said, "We have to swallow disappointments in this sad life."

CURTIN. Hurry up and join us.

DOBBS. Don't go getting mixed up with any of those Indian dames. Pretty smart some of 'em are. Look out a squaw don't marry you.

*He slaps* HOWARD'S *back.*

HOWARD *(trying to joke)*. Maybe I'll do just that. Pick me out a good-looking squaw and marry her. They're easy to feed and dress and entertain. And they don't nag at you either. So long, partners.

*He turns away so that they don't see the mist in his eyes. The* INDIAN *indicates which horse* HOWARD *is to ride. After the old man has mounted, the* INDIAN *gets up behind him in the saddle. Shouting joyfully, they start back toward the village.*

DOBBS *and* CURTIN *(together)*. See you in Durango.

DOBBS *and* CURTIN *turn to the burros and start the train once more on its way.*

*Dissolve to:*

*Ext. the village*

*as the troop of* INDIANS *enter with* HOWARD. *It's an occasion for great celebration. Young and old people are awaiting him. They cheer him as though he had returned from some victory in foreign lands for the greater glory of their village.* HOWARD'S *dismounting is the cue for the fiesta to begin. He is in the center of everything. It is to him the musicians play and the singers sing; for him the dancers dance.*

*Dissolve to:*

*Ext. mountains a high steep pass*

DOBBS *and* CURTIN, *their breath coming in agonizing gasps, struggle up the trail, beating the burros, pushing them on, shoulder to quarters. Every few yards they have to halt to give their pounding hearts a rest.*

DOBBS *(raises the water bottle to drink)*. Isn't it always his burros that won't march in line and stray off and smash their packs against the trees and rocks. I wish they'd break off the trail and drop down a few thousand feet of gorge and crash their bones. What was in your head when you offered to carry his goods? As if he couldn't manage by himself. He knew what he was doing when he turned them over to us. Mighty cute of him, wasn't it.

CURTIN. What's the use of railing against the old man. It won't do any good. Save your breath for that next piece of trail.

DOBBS. I'm stopping here for the night. If you want to go on it's okay by me, only take the old man's burros with you. They ain't my responsibility.

CURTIN (looking at the sun). It's still early. We might make four or five miles more before dark.

DOBBS. No one's ordered you to camp here. You can go twenty miles more for all I care.

CURTIN (losing his temper). Ordered me? You? Who's ordering who to do anything. You talk like you were boss of this outfit.

DOBBS. Maybe you are. Let's hear you say it. (he looks as though he were ready to spring upon CURTIN)

CURTIN. Okay, if this is as far as you can go.

DOBBS. Who says it is? (he advances a step on CURTIN; his face is dark and wicked looking in his anger) Don't make me laugh. I can go four times as far as a mug like you. I don't want to go any further that's all. I could but I don't want to. See, mug!

CURTIN. What's the good of hollering. We're started on something. Like it or not, we got to finish it. All right, let's camp here.

DOBBS. That was my idea in the first place.

*He begins to unload the burro standing next to him.* CURTIN *comes close and gives him a hand at the job.*

*Dissolve to:*

*Night*—DOBBS *and* CURTIN *by the campfire*

CURTIN. I wonder what the old man's doing now?

DOBBS. Finishing a meal of roast turkey and a bottle of tequila most probably.

CURTIN. This is the first day we've had to handle everything without his help. Once we get the hang of it, it'll be lots easier.

DOBBS. How far from the railroad do you think we are?

CURTIN. Not so far as the crow flies.

DOBBS. But we ain't crows.

CURTIN. I figure we can make the high pass in two days more. Then it'll be three or four days before we get to the railroad. That's figuring no hard luck on the trail.

CURTIN *puts more wood on the fire.* DOBBS *sits staring into space. All at once he laughs.*

CURTIN (looks around at DOBBS). What's the joke?

DOBBS *laughs again, louder this time.*

CURTIN. Won't you let me in on it, Dobbsie?

DOBBS. In on it? Sure I will. Sure. (he keeps on laughing)

CURTIN. Well, go ahead. Spill it. What's so funny?

DOBBS. It just came to me what a bonehead play that old jackass made when he put his packs in our keeping.

CURTIN. How do you mean?

DOBBS. Figured to let us do his sweating for him, did he? We'll show him! (he laughs again)

CURTIN. What are you getting at?

DOBBS. Man, can't you see. It's all ours now. We don't go back to the port, savvy. Not at all.

CURTIN (*unable to believe his ears*). I don't follow you, Dobbsie.

DOBBS. Don't be such a sap. Where'd you grow up? All right, to make it plain to a dumb-head like you—we take all the goods and go straight up north leaving the old jackass flat.

CURTIN. You aren't serious are you? You don't really mean what you're saying?

DOBBS. I never say anything I don't mean.

CURTIN *puts another stick of wood on the fire then he gazes up at the clear night sky.*

CURTIN (*finally*). As long as I can stand on my two legs you won't take a single grain from the old men's goods. You understand?

DOBBS (*craftily*). Sure, babe. Sure I do. I see very plainly what you mean. You want to take it all for yourself and cut me out.

CURTIN. No, Dobbs. I'm on the level with the old man. Exactly as I'd be on the level with you if you weren't here.

DOBBS (*takes up his pouch and starts filling his pipe*). Maybe I don't need you at all. I can take it alone. I don't need no outside help, buddie. (*he laughs*)

CURTIN (*looks him over from head to foot*). I signed that receipt.

DOBBS. So did I. What of it. I've signed many receipts in my life.

CURTIN. I guess I've signed things, too, which I forgot about before the ink was dry, but this case is different. The old man worked like a slave for what he got. It was harder on him old as he is then it was on us. I don't respect many things in life, but one thing I do respect—a man's right to what he's worked and slaved for honestly.

DOBBS. Get off your soapbox, will you. You only succeed in sounding funny out here in the wilderness . . . Anyway, I know you for what you are. I've always had my suspicions about you. Now I know I've been right.

CURTIN. What suspicions are you talking about?

DOBBS. You can't hide anything from me, brother. I see right through you. For some time you've had it in your mind to bump me off at the first good opportunity and bury me somewhere out here in the bush like a dog so's you could make off not only with the old man's goods but with mine in the bargain.

CURTIN *shakes his head in a dazed way. His pipe drops from his fingers.*

DOBBS (*continuing*). When you reach the port safely you'll laugh like the devil, won't you, to think how dumb the old man and I were not to guess what was brewing. I'm wise to you, babe.

CURTIN *looks into* DOBBS' *eyes, at once fascinated and terrified by the malignancy he sees. He tries to pull his eyes away from* DOBBS—*cannot. To cover his agitation he bends down to pick up his pipe.* DOBBS, *mistaking this for hostile, draws his gun.*

DOBBS. Another move, brother, and I pull the trigger. Get your hands up. (*shouting*) Up, up!

CURTIN *raises his hands.*

DOBBS. Higher.

CURTIN *obeys.* DOBBS *smiles, satisfied, nods his head.*

DOBBS. Was I right or was I? You and your Sunday school talk protecting other people's goods. You. *(yells suddenly)* Stand up and take it like a man.

CURTIN *rises slowly, his hands still in the air.* DOBBS *reaches for* CURTIN'S *gun. As he does so his own gun goes off. For a fraction of a second he is surprised.* CURTIN, *instinctively sensing his opportunity, lands* DOBBS *a hard blow on the jaw, knocking him to the ground. He throws himself upon* DOBBS *quickly and disarms him. Then he springs up and steps a few paces back.*

CURTIN *(two guns pointed at* DOBBS*).* The cards are dealt the other way now, Dobbsie.

DOBBS. So I see.

CURTIN *(calmly).* Listen to me. You're all wrong. Not for a moment did I ever intend to rob you or do you any harm. Like I said, I'd fight for you and yours just as I'd fight for the old man.

DOBBS. If you really mean what you say then hand over my cannon.

CURTIN *waves the gun in his hand, then breaks it open and empties the cartridges out. He throws it up in the air, catches it cowboy fashion, then holds it out toward* DOBBS. DOBBS *looks at it sneeringly.*

DOBBS. My pal.

*He spits, then retires to his former place by the fire. A long silence follows, broken only by* CURTIN.

CURTIN. Wouldn't it be better, the way things stand, to separate tomorrow—or this very night?

DOBBS. That would suit you fine, wouldn't it.

CURTIN *(perplexed).* Why me more than you?

DOBBS. So you could fall on me from behind, sneak up and shoot me in the back.

CURTIN. I'll go ahead.

DOBBS. And wait for me on the trail and ambush me? My pal.

CURTIN. Why shouldn't I do it here and now if I meant to kill you.

DOBBS. I'll tell you why. You're yellow. You don't dare pull the trigger while I'm looking at you in the eye that's why.

CURTIN *(shakes his head again).* If you think that, I can't see any way out but to tie you up every night.

DOBBS *(sneering).* Come on and try to tie me up.

CURTIN *and* DOBBS *sit looking at each other. Both men are exhausted after the hardships of the day.* CURTIN *knows he is in for a night of horror. He cannot afford to go to sleep even if* DOBBS *does for how is he to know if* DOBBS *is really asleep. Or, on the other hand, if* DOBBS *is not feigning, what is to keep him from waking up.* CURTIN *yawns.*

DOBBS *(laughs).* I'll make you a bet. Three times thirty-five, is a hundred and five. I bet you a hundred and five thousand dollars you go to sleep before I do.

*He laughs again.*

*Dissolve to:*

*Exterior the trail day*

*The pack train on the move,* DOBBS *in the lead.* CURTIN *walks like a man in a trance, stumbling every so often out of exhaustion brought on by the sleepless night.*

*Now his eyes are actually closed. He is holding on to one of the burro's packs, letting the animal guide his steps. Observing this,* DOBBS *halts and stands aside on the trail, letting the train pass. Some instinct causes* CURTIN *to open his eyes just before coming abreast of* DOBBS.

CURTIN *(reaching for his gun).* Get up there ahead of the train.

*Grinning,* DOBBS *obeys.*

*Dissolve to:*

*Campfire off the trail night*

*As on the night before, the two men sit a few feet apart, facing each other.* CURTIN'S *eyes finally begin to blink. He gets up, walks back and forth.* DOBBS *never stops looking at him. Presently* CURTIN *sits down again. It is not long before his head drops forward.* DOBBS *starts to crawl over to him.* CURTIN *jerks awake and draws his gun.* DOBBS *laughs.*

DOBBS. A born night watchman. I have to hand it to you. You should try for a job at a bank.

DOBBS *stretches out full length, lies on his side, looking at* CURTIN. CUR-TIN'S *eyes start blinking again. Each time he opens them it is a greater effort. It is as though heavy weights are attached to each lid. Finally they remain closed. Not that* CURTIN *is asleep—it is simply that his eyes need a few seconds rest. He is determined not to go to sleep—determined. Both fists are clenched with the effort. Even after his head has dropped forward on his chest the knuckles show white.*

*When* CURTIN'S *breathing is deep and regular* DOBBS *gets up, goes over to him and relieves him of his gun. Then he kicks* CURTIN *hard in the ribs.*

DOBBS. The cards are dealt once more—another way, and this is the last time. No more shuffling.

CURTIN *(tries to rise; mumbles).* What cards do you mean?

DOBBS. Stay where you are. I'm going to finish things up right now. No more orders from you such as I had to swallow today. Get me?

CURTIN *(he is too sleepy to com-prehend all that is going on about him; voice thick).* You mean you're going to murder me?

DOBBS *kicks him again to arouse him.*

DOBBS. No, brother, not murder. Your mistake. I'm doing it to save my life which you'd be taking the first instant I stopped looking at you.

CURTIN. Don't forget the old man. He'll catch up with you. Just wait and see.

DOBBS. Yeah? Will he? Well, I got the answer for that when the time comes. You want to know what I'll tell him? I'll tell him you tied me to a tree and made your getaway with all the goods—yours, mine and his. Then he'll be looking for you, not for me.

*He laughs as if this were the best joke he'd ever heard.* CURTIN, *fighting to keep awake, tries to shake the sleepiness out of his system, but fails.* DOBBS *kicks him again.*

DOBBS. Up now, and march where I tell you. Today I had to march to your music—now you're to march to mine.

CURTIN *(lurches upright).* Where to . . . march?

DOBBS. To your funeral.

CURTIN *moves in a dream.* DOBBS *grabs him brutally by the collar, pushes him ahead into the brush.*

DOBBS. Keep going.

CURTIN. Please, let me have just another hour's sleep. I'm all in. I can't march any longer. And let the burros have another hour too. The poor beasts—they're all over-worked and their backs are sore. *(he falls)*

DOBBS *(kicks* CURTIN*).* Get up.

Keep going. You'll have time enough to sleep in a minute.

CURTIN *staggers again, with* DOBBS *close behind, pushing and kicking. When they are far enough in the bush to suit* DOBBS, *he draws his pistol and shoots.*

CURTIN *goes down like a felled tree.* DOBBS *stands over him for a few seconds, pistol in hand. Then he bends down and listens briefly. Hearing no sigh and no moan, he rises and, putting his pistol back in the holster, returns to the campfire where he sits and stares into the flames. Presently he turns his face around toward the bush where* CURTIN *is. It's as though he expected* CURTIN *to appear out of the darkness.*

DOBBS *(to himself).* Maybe I didn't bump him off. Maybe he only staggered and dropped to the ground without being hit.

*His eyes turn back to the fire where they remain staring. Suddenly he jumps up, takes a thick piece of burning wood out of the fire to use as a torch and rushes back into the bush.*

CURTIN *is lying motionless in the same spot where* DOBBS *had left him.* DOBBS *leans over, goes to put his hand against the breast of his victim, then jerks his hand away. He holds the burning stick near* CURTIN'S *face, moving it back and forth, but there is not even the flicker of an eyelash.*

DOBBS *straightens up and turns away again, but before he goes ten feet he pulls out his gun, squares around and lets* CURTIN *have another shot to make absolutely sure. Having fired the gun, he looks at it.*

DOBBS *(to himself).* It'll look better this way. *(he throws the gun toward where* CURTIN *lies; mutters)* It's his

anyhow. *(then he goes back to the fire and resumes his former position; he shivers, then:)* This fire don't give any real heat. I'd ought to've brought more sticks in before dark. I won't go back into the bush now and get them. *(he gets his blanket and rolls up in it)* They won't find him. I'll dig a hole first thing in the morning.

*He closes his eyes. Suddenly they are open and he is sitting up, staring into the surrounding bush; then he laughs to himself.*

DOBBS. Conscience. Conscience. What a thing. If you believe you've got a conscience, it'll pester you to death. But if you don't believe you've got one, what can it do to you? Makes me sick so much talking and fussing about nonsense. *(assuming a matter-of-fact tone)* Time to go to sleep.

*He closes his eyes, but not for long. After a few seconds they're open again and he is staring into the fire.*

*Dissolve to:*

*Morning*

DOBBS *is just finishing the loading of the burros which is not easy without the help of a second man. His shirt is drenched with sweat and his impatience amounts to rage. He kicks one of the beasts savagely when a pack slips, as though it were the burro's fault. By the time the pack train is ready to start, the sun is high in the heavens. But there is one more task awaiting* DOBBS. *He has left a spade on the ground in anticipation of it. He picks up the spade and starts into the bush, but he only goes a step or two before stopping.*

DOBBS. Might be better to leave him where he is. Ain't very likely anybody would happen on him in there. If they did they'd just as like to find a grave as a body. Bandits wouldn't have buried him. In a week's time the tigers and wild pigs and the buzzards and the ants will have done away with him entirely.

*While he is standing thus, irresolutely arguing with himself, there is a cry from not far distant; shrill as a woman's scream. It cuts into* DOBBS *like a knife. His hands start trembling and he totters in his tracks.*

DOBBS. What's getting into me? That was only a tiger.

*He pulls himself together and, in an attempt to shake off his fear, takes another step forward into the bush. Again he falters.*

DOBBS. No. What if his eyes were open. I don't dare look at his eyes. Best thing is to hurry and try and reach the railroad soon as possible.

*He leaves the bush, goes back to the burros, shouts at them. The train is once more on its way. But immediately trouble begins. A burro goes out of his way to scrape against a rock. The pack shifts on his back so that its weight is all on one side of the animal, who staggers, then falls.* DOBBS *must unhitch the burro, get him back on his feet and do the whole job of packing him up over again. While he is about this, the other animals scatter. At last he succeeds in rounding them up and getting them all onto the trail again. But his difficulties have only started. When he marches at the head of the train, the animals in the rear stray off and when he is at its rear, the leader either stops or goes off the trail. He has to run up and down the train like a dog keeping a flock of sheep together. But presently, through* DOBBS' *strenuous*

*efforts the animals are all in single file and going in the right direction.*

DOBBS (*resuming the argument with himself*). Better not to bury him. I did right. Yeah. The chance of anybody happening on him inside a week is a mighty slim one . . . and there won't be much of anything left of him by then. Only his clothes . . . What I should've done maybe . . . undressed him and buried his clothes and left him for the wild pigs and the ants and the buzzards. . . .

*He stops suddenly. An appalled expression comes over his face.*

DOBBS. . . . buzzards! They'll be seen circling overhead. Everybody around'll know something's dead . . . something bigger'n a coyote. (*he looks up at the sky then groans with relief*) They ain't spotted him yet. Lucky for me.

*He is some time in getting the animals turned on the trail and headed back toward last night's campsite. Upon reaching it he ties a rope around the neck of each burro, fastens it to the burro ahead. Then he ties the lead burro to a tree. He takes the spade out of one of the packs and moves quickly to the task before him. Reaching the bush he hesitates again briefly, then plunges ahead. Camera dollies ahead of* DOBBS *as he pushes his way through, disregarding the brambles which tear his face and hands. Then he gets to the place,* CURTIN'S *body isn't there.* DOBBS *cannot believe his eyes. He rubs them, then looks again.*

DOBBS. This was the place right here. I know it was.

*Nevertheless, he begins to look around, crawling through the underbrush, spreading open the foliage, peering left and right and becoming more excited every second.*

DOBBS. He couldn't have flown away!

*His nervousness mounts to the point of hysteria.*

DOBBS *(calls).* Curtin. Where are you? Curtin.

*His voice comes bouncing back at him from a canyon wall—"Curtin. Where are? Curtin." The echo causes him a moment of real terror.*

DOBBS *(to himself).* I gotta get hold of myself. Mustn't lose my head. One thing, certain, he ain't here.

DOBBS' *mind delves gropingly into the problem. Finally he comes up with a solution.*

DOBBS. I got it. The tiger. It dragged him off, that's what, to its lair. Very soon not even a bone will be left to tell the tale. Done as if by order.

*The camera pans with him, laughing delightedly, as he starts out of the bush on back toward the campsite.*

*Pack animals*

*as* DOBBS *comes up. Miraculously no accident has occured in his absence. They are all in line waiting for the kicks that will set them into motion. These* DOBBS *delivers.*

DOBBS. Curtin didn't cry when I shot him. Not a sound out of him. He just dropped like a tree falls. *(after a moment)* Funny the way his legs and arms were twisted around. I could have laughed right out. *(he chuckles)* Just to think, one slug and finished. A whole life. *(he chuckles again; after a moment)* Tiger got him all right. Took him up in his jaws and carried him off. Must have been a big tiger—a royal tiger. They can jump over a fence with a cow in their mouths. *(suddenly)* His gun—it wasn't there either. No tiger would've taken that gun away . . . Maybe he's crawling around in the bush. If he reaches a village. . . . nearest village is twenty miles. Take him two days anyway. That's all the start I need . . . Vamos! Vamos! Pronto!

*Dissolve to:*

*Ext. Nightfall deep in the bush*

*An* INDIAN *charcoal burner is tending his fire. A sound that is different from the other noises of the wilderness, causes him to pause in his work and listen. Locating the sound, he picks a burning brand from the fire, reaches for his machete and with cautious movements, goes to investigate. The* INDIAN *pushes aside a heavy bough, revealing, in the flickering transient light of his torch, the figure of* CURTIN, *all in rags and with a bloody head.* CURTIN *looks at the* INDIAN *but does not seem to see. He keeps on crawling forward. After several moments, the* INDIAN *recovers from his initial bewilderment and calls for help.*

INDIAN. Hidalgo, ven pronto aqui. Ven a ayudarno.

*Then he goes to the aid of* CURTIN.

INDIAN. Pero que le pasó, senor? Lo atacó un tigre, o qué?

*He raises* CURTIN'S *body, gets an arm over his shoulder, supports him out of the thicket. A* SECOND INDIAN *appears from the bush on the opposite side of the charcoal fire. He also is dumbfounded at the bloody spectacle the white man makes.*

FIRST INDIAN. Mira a este pobre hombre, parece extranjero y que lo atacó un tigre. Ayudame a llevarlo a la rancheria, ándale.

*They carry* CURTIN *to the fire, lower him to the ground, then hurriedly set about cutting saplings to make a litter. As they are lifting* CURTIN *onto the litter—*

*Dissolve to:*

*Ext. trail Med. shot pack train day*

DOBBS *is driving the animals at a desperate pace, kicking them along and beating them with the flat side of his machete. The inevitable finally happens. One of the poor beasts goes down and cannot rise despite the blows* DOBBS *rains upon it. Even after his pack is removed, he will not get up. The other burros are too heavily loaded to take on the extra weight of what was in the fallen burro's pack, so everything in excess of the sacks of gold, a few hides, and a little water, must be discarded.*

DOBBS. I can't be more than three days from the railroad track. One water skin ought to see me through.

*He goes to work rearranging the packs.*

*Dissolve to:*

*Ext. adobe hut* HOWARD

*ensconced on a hammock. The old man has obviously been leading the life of Riley. An Indian girl of fifteen or sixteen waves a leafy branch at him, keeping off the flies. There is a bottle of tequila beside him on the box. Without ever opening his eyes,* HOWARD *feels for it, finds it, and raises it to his lips, thereby rinsing down the last of a whole roast chicken. Over scene the sound of hoof-beats. Presently* HOWARD'S *host appears with the* INDIAN *who dis-*

*covered* CURTIN *in the bush. He points at* HOWARD *saying: "El senor es un gran Doctor."*

HOWARD *(still not opening his eyes).* Que dice, amigo?

HOST. Oiga, senor Doctor. Este hombre es de un poblado lejano y tiene algo de interés que contarle.

*The* INDIAN *squats down in the sand beside* HOWARD'S *hammock while the host continues the act.*

HOST. Lázaro, aquí, es carbonero. Andaba trabajando cuando oyó algo on la maleza. Creyó que sería un tigre pero al fijarse vió que era un hombre que se arrastraba, cubierto de sangre y casi muerto.

HOWARD *(sitting up with a bound).* Como es ese hombre?

INDIAN. Tiene el pelo castano y ojos azules. Es muy alto y parece extranjero.

HOST. Creo es uno de sus companeros.

INDIAN. Está muy malo. Perdió mucha sangre. Si usted me acompaña pronto puede que le salve la vida.

HOWARD. Me prestan un caballo?

HOST. Seguro, y hasta vamos con usted.

*Camera pans with* HOWARD *and his host on their way to the corral. The host calls:*

HOST. Vamos todos a Zapupa, a donde está herido el amigo del gran Doctor.

*They're on the horses in no time at all, and riding off agallop.*

*Dissolve to:*

*Ext. wild and rocky wasteland*

DOBBS *gets down on his hands and knees studying the map. His face is haggard; the cheekbones are more prominent than before and there is a frightened, haunted look in his eyes.*

DOBBS. I don't get it. *(he looks around him)* Where's the Rio de la Saucella? According to this map I'm sitting on its banks with my feet in the water.

*He takes the canteen off one of the burros, weighs it in his hands and drinks sparingly. After he has screwed the cap on again and hung the canteen back in place he looks around. A litter of brush and dead-wood are piled up on either side of a narrow winding gully.* DOBBS *frowns. His mind is dull and he is slow to comprehend the meaning of what he sees. When he does he grunts, then whines slightly like someone who's been hit a hard blow in the stomach.*

DOBBS. This is the Saucella! . . . All dried up. The river that don't have any water in it in the winter.

*He picks up the map with trembling hands, stares at it.*

DOBBS. Forty miles to Porla. *(he turns back to the canteen, weighs it again in his hands, giving it a circling motion)*

*The next instant he is kicking the burros savagely and shouting at the top of his lungs.*

DOBBS. Get on, damn you. Vamos!

*Dissolve to:*

HOWARD

*examining* CURTIN, *washing his wounds, pouring tequilla in him.* CUR-TIN'S *condition is greatly improved.*

CURTIN *(smoking a cigarette as he talks).* I came to in the middle of the night. My gun was beside me on the ground. He must've left it there to make it look like suicide. There were four empty shells in it—only one live bullet. I figured he'd come back again in the morning to see if I still had a flicker of life. I thought of waiting for him and letting him have it, but there was a good chance, in my condition, I might miss, so I decided to crawl away like a poisoned dog.

HOWARD. Take it easy, son. You're talking too much.

CURTIN. Don't you worry about me. I'll pull out of this if only to get that guy.

HOWARD. So it appears our fine Mr. Dobbs has made off with the whole train and is on his way north.

CURTIN *growls.*

HOWARD *(continuing).* Well, I reckon we can't blame him too much.

CURTIN. What do you mean by that?

HOWARD. I mean he's not a real killer as killers go. I think he's as honest as the next fellow—or almost. The mistake was in leaving you two alone in the depths of the wilderness with more'n a hundred thousand between you. That's a mighty big temptation, believe me, partner.

CURTIN. He shot me down in cold blood and after I was down, shot me a second time to make absolutely sure.

HOWARD. If I were still young and I had been alone with you or him out there, I'd have been tempted too. Maybe I wouldn't have fallen, but I reckon I'd've been sure enough tempted. *(he's put on the last bandage)* There. You're almost as good as new. Now to go and find that thief and get our goods back. *(he turns to the IN-DIANS)* Si no llego a Durango para mañana noche perdere toda mi fortuna. Presteme un caballo. Se lo devolvere.

INDIAN. Un caballo? Seguro que si. Y vamos ir con usted para que no le pase algo como a su companero.

HOWARD (to CURTIN). Not only are they giving me a horse but they are coming along to keep me from any harm.

CURTIN, *sitting up, reaches for his clothes.*

HOWARD. You ain't coming.

CURTIN. Who says so?

HOWARD. We'll have some hard riding to do and you wouldn't be up to it. You're too weak.

CURTIN. You aren't leaving me behind, see (*he gets to his feet, stands swaying in his weakness*)

HOWARD. Look at you . . . weak as a newborn kitten. Don't worry. I'll do all in my power . . .

CURTIN (*interrupting*). I'm going.

HOWARD (*looks him up and down, then*). I reckon you're going.

*He starts out of the room;* CURTIN *follows.*

*Dissolve to:*

*Long shot pack train*

*The trail has turned into a dirt road covered with fine dust. A plume of dust set up by* DOBBS *and the animals hangs in the air.*

*Close shot*

DOBBS *at the head of the train.*

*The dust rises each time he puts a foot down. He is the same color all over—face, clothes, hands—the pale gray of the road. Only his eyes are different, appearing darker by contrast. Every so often a burro brays.*

DOBBS *is moving in a nightmare. At times the landscape revolves as though he were the center of a great turning wheel. Every so often the* ground he is walking on rushes up at him and deals him a vicious blow in the face. Whenever this happens he must spit and blow to get rid of the dust that gets into his mouth and nose. Now and then he mumbles incoherently—his dry and thickened tongue and swollen lips are incapable of forming the sounds that make words. He is almost to the place before he knows: a clump of trees by a pool of brackish water. At first he thinks it is a trick of his mind— something conjured up out of his suffering. He rubs his forehead with the back of his hand then, moving slowly, he leaves the road and passes into the cooling shade. The burros are before him to the water, their legs spread wide and their muzzles submerged.* DOBBS *gets down on his knees and drinks beside them. He splashes the water over himself. It's as though it had miraculous powers. He laughs with delight. It is only a little time before the madness goes out of his eyes.* DOBBS *addresses his reflection in the water.*

DOBBS. Made it. I made it.

*The reflection of another face shows in the pool above* DOBBS'. *The ugly, grinning face of a man wearing a palm leaf hat painted gold.* DOBBS *turns slowly around and gets to his feet. Behind* GOLD HAT *two others are standing and they too are grinning.*

GOLD HAT. Tiene un cigarro, hombre? Have you got a cigarette?

DOBBS (*attempting nonchalance*). No I haven't, but I've got a few pinches of tobacco if that will do.

GOLD HAT. And paper to roll it in?

DOBBS. I've got a bit of newspaper. (*he takes a piece out of his pocket and hands it together with his tobacco pouch to* GOLD HAT)

GOLD HAT. Matches. *(it's an order)*

DOBBS *hands him a box of matches.* GOLD HAT *lights up, then:*

GOLD HAT. Going to Durango?

DOBBS. Yes. That's where I'm headed. I'm going to sell my burros. I need money. I haven't got a red cent.

DOBBS *thinks he is being very clever in answering thus.*

GOLD HAT. Money? We need money too.

GOLD HAT *gives him back his tobacco pouch.* DOBBS *leans against a tree and fills his pipe. He takes plenty of time. He is trying to appear in no way worried or afraid.*

DOBBS. I could use a good mule driver—or two or three.

GOLD HAT *(laughs).* Could you?

*Whenever* GOLD HAT *laughs the other two do also, even though they don't understand English.*

GOLD HAT. How much is the pay?

DOBBS. Two pesos apiece. Of course I can't pay in advance. I'll pay you when we get to town and I get some cash.

GOLD HAT. Sure. . . . Are you alone?

DOBBS *hesitates, then:*

DOBBS. Oh no, I'm not alone. Two of my friends are coming on horseback. They'll be here any minute now.

GOLD HAT. That's funny . . . a man all by himself in bandit country with a string of burros, his friends behind him on horseback. *(he addresses his two companions in Spanish)* Pablo, asomate al camino y ve si vienen dos jinetes.

*The* SECOND BANDIT *gets up slowly, goes over to the road and looks toward the mountains.*

SECOND BANDIT. Han de estar mas lejos de lo que el cree. Ni siquiera el polvo se divisa.

GOLD HAT *(to* DOBBS). Your friends must be very far behind you. Pablo cannot see any dust even from their horses. What have you got in the packs? *(he walks over to the burros and with his fists pushes and pokes the packs)* Seems to me like hides.

DOBBS. It is hides. You're right.

GOLD HAT. Ought to bring quite a lot of money.

DOBBS *goes to one of the burros, tightens the straps, then he turns to another and pushes against its pack to see if it's still holding fast. Finally he tightens his own belt, pulling his pants higher up, this to indicate he is ready to make off.*

DOBBS. I guess I'll have to beat it now. How about it? Do you want to come along with me and help with the burros?

*Instead of answering,* GOLD HAT *winks at his companions.* DOBBS *sees the wink. His breath stops for a second, then he kicks the lead burro, starting the train toward the road. The three* BANDITS *edge in among the remaining burros and take them by their halters.*

DOBBS *(shouts).* Get away from my burros.

GOLD HAT. We can sell these burros for just as good a price as you'd get.

DOBBS. Get away from those burros I tell you. *(he draws his gun)*

GOLD HAT. You can't frighten even a sick louse with that. *(he points at the gun)* You can only shoot one and he won't mind much because the Federales are after him anyway, so what with your gun—we take that chance.

DOBBS. Get back there from my burros.

*Without waiting for the* BANDITS *to obey he aims at* GOLD HAT *and pulls the trigger. But the gun clicks cold . . . twice . . . three times . . . five times.* DOBBS *stares at the gun in amazement. So do the three* BANDITS. *While* DOBBS *is remembering about the gun, one of them bends slowly down, picks up a heavy stone.* DOBBS *looks around frantically for another means of defense or escape. His glance falls upon the machete that is tied to the side of one of the burros. He leaps for it and grasps its haft but as he goes to pull it out of its scabbard the stone crashes against his forehead.* DOBBS *falls. Before he can rise* GOLD HAT *has the machete.* GOLD HAT *springs at the fallen* DOBBS, *the machete upraised. The rest we see reflected in the brackish waters of the pool: The stroke of the machete, then the figures of the three* BANDITS *standing, eyes downward, looking at something on the ground. The water in the pool begins to darken.* GOLD HAT *looks up from the ground to the machete in his hand. He touches his thumb and forefinger to the tip of his tongue, then he tests the cutting edge of the blade. The waters of the pool are growing darker and darker. In the excitement over stripping the body, the* BANDITS *forget about the burros who, paying no heed to what has happened, march off toward town.* GOLD HAT *struts and swaggers around the pool admiring himself in* DOBBS' *pants, held up by* DOBBS' *belt. The other two are having an argument. Each has a shoe in his hand.*

SECOND BANDIT. Dame ese zapato, sinvergüenza. Es mio. Yo lo vi primero.

THIRD BANDIT. A mi no me importa quien lo vio primero. Yo fui el que le dio el piedrazo que lo tumbo. A ti no te toca nada.

GOLD HAT. Silencio, ladrones habladores. Vale mas que se callen porque usare el machete por segunda . . . y por tercera vez tambien. *(Looking around he sees that the burros have gone off; he begins to roar)* Donde estan los burros. . . . Ya se fueron al demonio. Andenle a trerlos, bandidos inutiles. Si llega uno al pueblo nos metera en un cochino lio.

*The burros*

*moving briskly in the direction of the village, where they know from past experience food awaits them and much needed rest. The shadows are lengthening now and the evening wind is blowing in. When the three* BANDITS *finally catch up to the burros the sun has disappeared behind the rim of the mountains to the west and night is beginning to fall. They drive the pack train off the road into a thicket of mesquite and get busy. The burros are unloaded and the packs are opened up. What they discover is a great disappointment to them.*

GOLD HAT. Estas pieles no sirven. Estan llenas de agujeros. Estan dadas a la desgracia. Si nos dan viente pesos por todas sera mucho.

*The* SECOND BANDIT *has found a number of bags made of rags and old sack cloth. Looking at them, he scratches his head.*

SECOND BANDIT. Que demonios seran estos? Mira . . . *(He pours the contents of one out onto the ground)* Uuh . . . es arena . . . pura arena cochina. . . . Para que diablos andaba cargando toda esta arena? *(He opens one bag after another, spilling the stuff out)*

GOLD HAT, *taking up a handful of it, looks at it closely and then tosses the stuff into the air. He shakes his head, makes a circling gesture with his forefinger at his temple.*

*Closeup the yellow sand*

*spilled on the ground, the wind blowing it.*

*Dissolve to:*

*Ext. trail* HOWARD, CURTIN *and* IN-DIANS *night all on horseback*

*Two* INDIANS *riding ahead of the others rein in. When* HOWARD *and* CURTIN *come up to them they discover, lying on the trail, a dead burro and the equipment* DOBBS *discarded. They exchange a significant look, then:*

HOWARD. How are you holding up?
CURTIN. My shoulder's stinging some but I'm okay.

*They ride on.*

*Dissolve to:*

*Ext. Plaza village early morning*

*The three* BANDITS *appear with their pack train.* GOLD HAT *hails an* INDIAN *youth crossing the plaza and goes up to him. It is the same boy who, long months before, when the partners were just starting out, came into the general store to tell them there were some burros outside for them to look at.*

GOLD HAT. Oye muchacho. Sabes quien quiera comprar unos burros?

*He walks around the burros inspecting the brands, then casually he looks at the high boots which the* SECOND BANDIT *is wearing.*

*Close up*

*The high boots.*

INDIAN

*looking at them. Now his gaze shifts to* GOLD HAT.

*Close up*

*The belt with the silver buckle.*

INDIAN

YOUTH *(when he is through with his inspection).* Pues puede que mi tio se los compre, si los vende baratos. *(he waves for them to follow him)* Vengan a la tienda de mi tio.

*Camera pans as they proceed across the plaza to the general store. The youth hails the* STOREKEEPER *who comes out.*

YOUTH. Oiga tio, estos hombres quieren vender estos burros.

*The* STOREKEEPER *approaches the three strangers with dignity.*

GOLD HAT *(with a flourish).* Son magnificos burros, senor. Le garanti-zo que no los encontrara mejores en ninguna parte.

*The* STOREKEEPER *examines them with the utmost care, and while doing so he discreetly notes the attire of the three Mesitsos. Camera cuts from the boots to the uncle's sharp eyes, then to the trousers on* GOLD HAT. *Camera moves up to a close up of the belt buckle.*

STOREKEEPER. Y cuanto pide por estos burros?
GOLD HAT *(in Spanish; smiles craft-ily, narrows his eyes, trying to give the impression that he is a sly old horse trader well acquainted with all the tricks).* Doce pesos cada uno. . . . Una ganga, entre caballeros.
STOREKEEPER. Pues yo no puedo comprarlos todos, pero ya vera. An-gel, llama a la gente del pueble, pro-nto. Usted podra venderlos al mejor precio. Asi les ira bien a todos. *(Angel gets up and leaves the group)* Mien-

tras tanto pueden descansar *(he calls into the house)* Zeferina, trainos agua y unos cigarrillos.

GOLD HAT *and his companions squat down on their heels. A young girl brings out a pitcher of water, tobacco and papers.*

*While they are rolling their cigarettes the villagers begin to arrive. Oddly enough they all wear firearms or are carrying machetes. Observing this, the three companions glance nervously at each other. Not until the circle is complete and the three companions surrounded does the* STOREKEEPER *speak.*

STOREKEEPER. Amigos, aqui estan tres individuos que vienen del valle a vender sus burros.

*The three so introduced rise and greet the villagers.*

BANDITS. Buenas tardes, senores.
STOREKEEPER *(suddenly to* GOLD HAT*)*. Y tienen fierro estos burros?
GOLD HAT. Naturalmente que todos tienen fierro.

*He looks around the burros to read the brand, but the villagers are standing in a way that covers them up.*

STOREKEEPER *(quietly)*. A ver . . . Como es?
GOLD HAT *(uncomfortably)*. El fierro? . . . Pues es. . . . Bueno, usted sabe . . . es una rueda . . . con una raya, asi *(he makes a sign with his fingers)*
STOREKEEPER *(to one of the villagers)*. A ver si es cierto.
VILLAGER. No compadre, nunca.

*The villagers laugh as though* GOLD HAT *had got off a very good joke.*

GOLD HAT. Valgame, que memoria. . . . Sera el calor . . . quise decir . . . es una cruz con un circulo *(he also makes this sign in the air with his fingers)*.
STOREKEEPER. A ver si es cierto, amigos.
VILLAGER. No compadre, menos.

*This time there is louder laughter and more of it.* GOLD HAT *looks around at his partners. His mouth is open and the sweat is pouring off him.*

STOREKEEPER *(taking a step forward)*. Usted no sabe el fierro porque no son suyos. Son de tres Americanos. Y como se hizo de esas botas y los pantalones?

GOLD HAT *reaches back to his holster to pull his gun or rather the gun that had once been* DOBBS'. *To his surprise he finds the holster empty. The weapon is in the hands of the villager standing behind him. Again there is laughter and general merriment.*

GOLD HAT *(swings both fists and looks at the men around him as if he were threatening them all)*. Esto es demasiado, pues de que se trata? Ni que fueramos bandidos.
STOREKEEPER. Pues precisamente, eso deben ser. A poco no son los bandidos que asaltaron el tren, fueron capturados y despues se escaparon?

*The three do not wait for the next sentence. With one jump they break through the circle of villagers. They don't get very far. The villagers are after them instantly and the three companions are caught before they reach the line of adobe houses on the other side of the plaza. The villagers start tying them up.*

STOREKEEPER. Esto compete a las autoridades militares. A ver, Angel, ve a avisar a la Guarnicion, inmediatamente.

*Dissolve to:*

*Ext. the dusty road outside the village*

*The camera pans with* HOWARD *and* CURTIN *and their* INDIAN *escort. Over scene the sound of a volley being fired. The troop of riders rein their horses in and listen.*

CURTIN. Shooting.

HOWARD. Yeh—a volley. Execution probably.

INDIAN. Si, son los rifles do los Federales.

*They ride on, spurring their horses into a gallop. Camera pans them into the village. The plaza is deserted. They ride to the other end of the plaza and take a dirt road leading up to higher ground where a crowd has collected.*

*Graveyard*

*Men and boys are shovelling dirt into three graves. Those gathered look up at the approach of* CURTIN, HOWARD *and the* INDIANS. *A voice hails them.*

VOICE *(over scene).* Ah . . . senores Americanos . . . Cuanto gusto de volver a verlos bien.

*It is the* STOREKEEPER, *who comes forward with outstretched hands.* HOWARD *and* CURTIN *dismount and greet him.*

STOREKEEPER. Siento tenerles muy malas noticias. Cerca de aqui le paso algo terrible a su companero. Lo asaltaron tres bandidos y lo asesinaron para robarle la ropa, los burros y su carga.

CURTIN. What's he saying?

HOWARD. Dobbs is dead. Murdered by bandits.

STOREKEEPER. Sin embargo, sus cosas estan en lugar seguro; las pieles estan en mi tienda y los burros en el corral. Aunque esto es poco consuelo por la perdida de su companero.

HOWARD *(to* CURTIN*).* It seems all our goods are safe in his store but he realizes, of course, that that is poor consolation for the loss of our dear brother.

STOREKEEPER. Favor de pasar a mi tienda.

*He leads the way and they follow.* CURTIN *and* HOWARD *exchange a long look. The younger man raises his right hand.* HOWARD *sees that the fingers are crossed.*

*The general store*

*as he comes into view, followed by* CURTIN *and* HOWARD. *On reaching the doorway the* STOREKEEPER *waves them inside.*

*Interior store*

*In one corner there is a pile of saddles, hides, canvas coverings, an empty canteen, and several lengths of rope.*

STOREKEEPER. Creo que no les faltara nada.

HOWARD *and* CURTIN *go to the corner, and start burrowing in the pile. When they do not immediately find what they are looking for they begin to fling things helter-skelter in the search.*

CURTIN *(finally).* Not here . . . not here.

HOWARD. Keep your shirt on.

*He turns to the* STOREKEEPER.

HOWARD. Sabe algo sobre unos costalitos, como asi. . . .? *(he shows with his hands)* . . . y muy pesados?

*The old man shakes his head slowly.*

STOREKEEPER. No. De eso no se nada.

*The youth who originally encountered the bandits in the plaza and led them to the* STOREKEEPER *steps forward from the group in the doorway.*

ANGEL. Dice usted, unos costalitos de lona?

HOWARD. Si, si, donde estan?

ANGEL. Pues no se. No los vi. Yo solo se lo que dijeron los bandidos.

CURTIN (*to* HOWARD). What's he saying?

HOWARD *ignores the question.*

ANGEL. Dijeron que habia unos costalitos con arenita que creyeron que eran para que pesaren mas las pieles cuando las vendieran

CURTIN (*wild*). What does he say? Tell me!

HOWARD (*to* CURTIN). The bandits thought they were bags of sand hidden in among the hides to make them weigh more when our dearly beloved brother went to sell them in Durango.

CURTIN (*shouting*). But where are they. . . . Where?

HOWARD. Don't you understand? They poured our goods out on the ground. The wind has carried all of it away—all of it to the four corners of Mexico. (*he begins to laugh*)

STOREKEEPER. Todo esta alli, verdad? Solo falta la arena?

HOWARD (*laughing*). Si . . . *s o l o* falta la arena.

CURTIN. What's that?

HOWARD. He wanted to know if everything else wasn't there, and I told him yes, only the sand was gone.

HOWARD *lets out such a roar of Homeric laughter that the* INDIANS *are startled by it, but after a moment, supposing that he is overjoyed by something, they fall in with him and laugh as heartily as he does.*

HOWARD. Laugh, Curtin, old boy, it's a great joke played on us by the

Lord or fate or by nature . . . which ever you prefer, but whoever or whatever played it, certainly has a sense of humor. The gold has gone back to where we got it. Laugh, my boy, laugh. It's worth ten months of labor and suffering—this joke is.

*Still laughing,* HOWARD *strolls out the door. After a moment* CURTIN *moves after him.*

CURTIN. Well, what now?

HOWARD. Far as I'm concerned I'm fixed for life—as a Medicine Man. I'll have three meals a day, five if I want 'em and a roof over my head, and every now and then a drink to warm me up. I'll be worshipped and fed and treated like a high priest for telling people things they want to hear. A good medicine man is born, not made. Come visit me some time, my boy; even you will take off your hat when you see how respected I am there. Only the day before yesterday they wanted to make me their Legislature—the whole Legislature. I don't know what they mean by that but it must be the greatest honor they can bestow. Yep, I'm taken care of for the rest of my natural life. How about you now? What do you aim to do?

CURTIN *rolls a cigarette, stands looking off into space.*

CURTIN. I dunno. Wish I did.

HOWARD (*slaps him on the back*). Buck up. You're young—in years anyway. You got plenty of time to make three or four fortunes for yourself.

CURTIN. The worst ain't so bad when it finally happens. Not nearly as bad as you figure it will be before it's happened. (*he draws on his cigarette*) I'm no worse off than I was in Tampico. All I'm out is a couple hundred bucks, come right down to it. Not very much compared to what Dobbsie lost. *(nods)* Too bad about Mrs. Cody—I'm sorry about our not being able to do like we planned.

HOWARD. There's no place you're especially set on going to is there?

CURTIN. It's all the same to me where I go.

HOWARD. Tell you what. You can keep my share of what the burros and hides'll bring if you use the money to buy a ticket to Dallas. Seeing her in person and telling her what happened would be a lot better than writing a letter . . . Besides, it's July and there might be a job for you in the fruit harvest . . . Well, what do you say?

*The idea appeals to* CURTIN.

CURTIN. I'll do it.

HOWARD *takes the wallet and letter out of his pocket, gives them to* CURTIN. *Then,* HOWARD *shakes hands with him briefly.*

HOWARD. Well, good luck.
CURTIN. Same to you, old man.

*They stand for a moment, hands joined, each trying to think of something further to say. Just about everything has been said.* HOWARD *lets go of* CURTIN's *hand and turns to his horse and climbs into the saddle. His* INDIAN *companions also mount.*

CURTIN *watches them ride away. Once* HOWARD *turns and waves at him.* CURTIN *waves back.*

HOWARD *and the* INDIANS

*walking their horses along the dusty road outside the village. Something blowing along the road catches his eye and he bends down from the saddle and picks it up. It is a canvas sack, torn and empty.* HOWARD *looks at it briefly, then throws it away. The camera follows it as the wind picks it up and carries it off. Overscene the sound of a harmonica.*

*Fade out.*

THE END

# MY MAN GODFREY

*Screenplay by Morrie Ryskind and Eric Hatch*
*Based on the Novel by Eric Hatch*

| | |
|---|---|
| GODFREY | William Powell |
| IRENE BULLOCK | Carole Lombard |
| ANGELICA BULLOCK | Alice Brady |
| CORNELIA BULLOCK | Gail Patrick |
| ALEXANDER BULLOCK | Eugene Pallette |
| MOLLY | Jean Dixon |
| TOMMY GRAY | Alan Mowbray |
| CARLO | Mischa Auer |
| MIKE | Pat Flaherty |
| FAITHFUL GEORGE | Robert Light |

Produced by Charles R. Rogers
Directed by Gregory La Cava
Film Editors: Ted Kent and Russell Schoengarth
Cinematographer: Ted Tetzlaff
Art Director: Charles D. Hall
Music Director: Charles Previn

This screenplay of *My Man Godfrey,* as written by Morrie Ryskind and Eric Hatch, is in the great tradition of zany comedies that came out of Hollywood a generation ago. In its vivacity and insouciance it ranks as high as any of them.

Nominated for Best Screenplay in 1936, this charming and deft work—which features as suave and appealing a butler as anyone would hope to have (could he or she afford one)—flits about its antics with grace and laughter, peopled with an array of eccentric characters, all of them as likable as they are bizarre.

In this Depression-era comedy, the spoiled, rich Bullock offspring, their kooky mother, and their indulgent head-of-the-household father, are not portrayed as the uncaring, capitalist exploiters one might find in other Depression literature. There is no class warfare here; Godfrey simply shows the Bullocks the error of their ways in a far gentler fashion as he brings them around and affectionately sets them on the right path.

Godfrey is not only one of the great butlers in the Hollywood tradition, but, as portrayed by the elegant William Powell, he emerges as an unforgettable character in his own right.

Equally interesting and worth noting is the approach of the authors toward "the forgotten man," which is what Godfrey represents when Irene Bullock, on a scavenger hunt, finds him in New York City's shantytown. Contrast this to

Robert Riskin's "forgotten man" in his script for director Frank Capra's *Meet John Doe,* which we published in our first anthology. Godfrey, a former Harvard graduate from a prominent family, is down and out because of an unhappy love affair, while Long John Willoughby (played by Gary Cooper) is truly hungry, homeless, and friendless, except for one buddy.

Although Godfrey is as comedic as Long John is serious, both, despite being Depression stories coming from different directions, have much in common. They are alike in that each has the same central idea—all will be well and America will get out of the Depression if people will look out for each other on a personal basis, with personal involvement. The two just go about playing it in different ways. Comedy, you see, if skillfully applied, often can achieve the same results as drama.

Eric Hatch, who wrote the novel from which this film was adapted, started out as an investment banker. Born in New York City in 1902, he began to write short stories while working on Wall Street. After the success of a number of his novels, including *My Man Godfrey,* Mr. Hatch moved to Hollywood, where he collaborated with Morrie Ryskind. He died in 1973.

Morrie Ryskind was born in New York City on October 20, 1895, and was educated at Columbia University. Involved in the theater soon afterward, he collaborated with George S. Kaufman, and together they created a string of hit Broadway musical comedies. He shared a Pulitzer Prize for the stage musical *Of Thee I Sing* (1931–32), which he wrote with Mr. Kaufman and Ira Gershwin. (This was the first "Best Play" Pulitzer Prize ever awarded a musical.) His film credits as a screenwriter include *The Cocoanuts* (1929), *Animal Crackers* (1930), *A Night at the Opera* (1935), and *Room Service* (1938)—all for the Marx Brothers. Mr. Ryskind passed away on August 24, 1985.

PART ONE

*A panoramic view of a city dump discloses a man standing by a fire. This dissolves, amid a noise of falling junk, to the end of a truck, from which cans are being dumped. Then shabby men are seen searching the ground for something of value—a bridge over a river, from which boat whistles are heard, forming an indistinct background. Miserable shacks are in the foreground, with makeshift fires in front of them. And now two men dimly appear, one of them approaching the fire at which the other is seated.*

MIKE. Hello, Duke.

GODFREY. Hello, Mike. Any luck today?

MIKE. Well, I figured out a swell racket and everything was going great—till the cops came along.

*A close-up of* GODFREY, *a bearded young man, shows him smoking a pipe.*

GODFREY. Too bad it didn't work.

MIKE'S VOICE. If them cops would stick to their own racket and leave honest guys alone, we'd get somewhere in this country without a lot of this relief and all that stuff.

GODFREY. Well, Mike, I wouldn't worry—prosperity is just around the corner.

MIKE *(starting out)*. Yes, it's been there a long time. I wish I knew which corner. Well, Duke, I'm going to turn in. Bon soir.

GODFREY *(sitting down)*. Bon soir, Mike.

*A long view of the dump,* GODFREY *by the fire in the foreground, shows two cars coming along the street at the top of the dump, and stopping.*

*Following this we see a street:* CORNELIA *and her escort,* GEORGE, *alight,*

*a second car stopping back of the first one.*

*Then a close view at the car shows* CORNELIA, *a proud, beautiful young woman, and* GEORGE, *looking off, following which a pretty girl,* IRENE, *gets out of the second car, and comes forward.*

CORNELIA. This is the place, all right. That looks like one of them sitting outside that shack.

GEORGE. It looks like a pretty tough joint to me.

CORNELIA. You stall, Irene. I'll talk to that fellow. *(She goes out.)*

IRENE. I don't think it's fair of you and Cornelia! I told you about this place.

GEORGE. Well, we got here first.

IRENE. Well, she's not going to get ahead of me. *(She follows after her.)*

*At the dump, a bearded, shabby man is crouching by a fire.* CORNELIA *comes down to him,* IRENE *following. The man,* GODFREY, *rises; there is dignity and intelligence in his demeanor.*

CORNELIA. Good evening.

GODFREY *(removing his hat)*. Good evening.

CORNELIA. How'd you like to make five dollars?

GODFREY. How'd—I didn't quite catch what you said.

CORNELIA. How would you like to make five dollars?

IRENE *(seen in a close-up)*. stands waiting—impatient—angry.

GODFREY'S VOICE. Five dollars?

CORNELIA'S VOICE. Five dollars.

*We see next* CORNELIA *and* GODFREY, *with* IRENE *beyond them.*

GODFREY. I don't want to seem inquisitive—but what would I have to do for it?

CORNELIA. Oh—all you have to do is go to the Waldorf-Ritz Hotel with me and I'll show you to a few people and then I'll send you right back.

GODFREY. May I inquire just why you should want to show me to people at the Waldorf-Ritz?

CORNELIA. Oh, if you must know. It's a game—you've probably heard about it—a scavenger hunt. If I find a forgotten man first I win. Is that clear?

*We see a close-up of* IRENE, *watching as a steamer whistle is heard.*

GODFREY *and* CORNELIA *come into view again, standing and talking, the steamer whistle sounding again.*

GODFREY. Yes—quite clear. Shall I wear my tails—or shall I come just as I am?

CORNELIA. You needn't be fresh. Do you want the five dollars or don't you?

GODFREY. Madam, I can't tell you how flattered I am by your very generous offer.

*A close view in front of the shack discloses* CORNELIA *looking for help as she backs away.*

CORNELIA. George!

GODFREY *(following her,* IRENE *in the background watching).* However, I am afraid I'll have to take the matter up with my board of directors.

CORNELIA. Don't you touch me!

GODFREY. No matter what my board of directors advise, I think you should be spanked.

GEORGE *approaches, and* IRENE *moves out of sight.* CORNELIA *backs over to an ash pile as* GODFREY *talks and she suddenly sits down.* GEORGE *helps her up.*

CORNELIA. George—do something!

GEORGE. Are you in the habit of hitting ladies?

GODFREY. Maybe. But I am in the habit of hitting gentlemen also—if that would interest you.

CORNELIA. Aren't you going to do anything?

GEORGE. Yes. Let's get a policeman. *(And they disappear.)*

GODFREY *turns back, the scene moving over to the shack. He suddenly sees* IRENE *there.*

GODFREY. Who are you?

IRENE. I'm Irene. That was my sister Cornelia you pushed in the ash-pile.

GODFREY. How would you like to have me push Cornelia's sister into an ash-pile?

IRENE. Oh, I don't think I'd like it.

GODFREY. Well, you'd better get out of here then.

IRENE. You bet.

GODFREY. Wait a minute! Sit down!

IRENE *and* GODFREY *sit down on the dump, while some men in the background call to him.*

IRENE. I'm sitting.

BOB. What's up, Duke? Need some help?

GODFREY. No thanks, boys. I've got everything under control. *(To* IRENE*)* Are you a member of this hunting party?

IRENE. I was—but I'm not now. Are they all forgotten men, too?

GODFREY. Yes, I guess they are maybe. But why?

IRENE. It's the funniest thing. I couldn't help but laugh. I've wanted to do that ever since I was six years old.

GODFREY. You wanted to do what?

IRENE. Push Cornelia in something—a pile of ashes or something. You know—that was Faithful George with her. It isn't really his name, but we call him that, because he gets in everybody's hair. His father's a broker.

GODFREY. That's funny.

IRENE *(laughing)*. Cornelia thought she was going to win and you pushed her into a pile of ashes.

GODFREY. Do you think you could follow an intelligent conversation for just a moment?

IRENE. I'll try.

GODFREY. Well, that's fine. Do you mind telling me just what a scavenger hunt is?

IRENE. Well—a scavenger hunt is just exactly like a treasure hunt, except that a treasure hunt is where you find something you want and in a scavenger hunt you try to find something that nobody wants.

GODFREY. Hmm—like a forgotten man.

IRENE. That's right—and the one that wins gets a prize—only there really isn't a prize. It's just the honor of winning, 'cause all the money goes to charity—that is—if there's any money left over. Only there never is.

GODFREY. Well—that clears the whole matter up beautifully.

IRENE. Yes—well, I've decided I don't want to play any more games with human beings as objects. It's kind of sordid when you come to think of it—I mean when you think it over.

GODFREY. Yes—I—I don't know. I haven't thought it over.

IRENE. I don't like to change the subject, but will you tell me why you live in a place like this when there are so many other nice places?

GODFREY. You really want to know?

IRENE. Oh, I'm very curious.

GODFREY. It's because my real estate agent thought the altitude would be very good for my asthma.

IRENE. Oh, my uncle has asthma.

GODFREY. No? Well—now there's a coincidence.

IRENE. Well—I suppose I should be going, shouldn't I?

IRENE *and* GODFREY *start walking along. She takes his hand, and they start away.*

GODFREY. It's a good idea.

IRENE. I want to see who won the game—Cornelia, I suppose, again. She's probably got another forgotten man by this time.

GODFREY. You mean—if you took me along with you, that you would win the game? Is that the idea?

IRENE. Well, I might if I got there first—but after seeing what you did to Cornelia, I'm not saying anything.

GODFREY. But you'd win if you got back first with me?

IRENE. It would be awfully nice of you, but I don't like to ask.

GODFREY. Let's beat Cornelia.

IRENE. It wouldn't be asking too much?

GODFREY. You see, I've got a sense of curiosity, the same as you have. I'd really like to see just what a scavenger hunt looks like.

IRENE. But I told you!

GODFREY. Yes—but I'm still curious.

IRENE. Well—come on!

*The scene dissolves to a hotel ballroom full of chatter, with people passing back and forth, men at a bar in close view. A well-dressed man, BLAKE, moves forward and offers his hand to BULLOCK, another well-dressed man. They talk and drink.*

BLAKE. My name is Blake.

BULLOCK. My name is Bullock.

BLAKE. This place slightly resembles an insane asylum.

BULLOCK. Well—all you need to start an asylum is an empty room and the right kind of people.

*We get a close travelling view of the ballroom as an elderly woman,* ANGELICA, *and her young, exotic-looking escort,* CARLO, *appear moving forward through the crowd. She is leading a nanny goat and talks constantly. They stop and talk to other couples.*

ANGELICA. Oh, good evening, Mrs. Dawson. Look what I found up in the Bronx.

MAN. A goat—a real goat! *(The people chatter.)*

*At the bar we again see* BLAKE *and* BULLOCK *talking.* BULLOCK *looks around.*

BLAKE. Take a look at that dizzy old gal with the goat.

BULLOCK. I've had to look at her for twenty years. That's Mrs. Bullock.

*There follows a close view of* AN-GELICA, CARLO *and others with the goat, as she moves off; and then a full view of the ballroom, noisy with chatter, includes the two men at the bar in the foreground, poeple rushing about,* ANGELICA *half-way down the room—shouting.*

BLAKE. I'm terribly sorry.

BULLOCK. How do you think I feel?

ANGELICA. Oh, Alexander! Come here!

BULLOCK *(going to her)*. All right—all right, Angelica!

BULLOCK *approaches her, while several young men come on with a vegetable cart and go out of sight with it.*

ANGELICA. Look at this lovely goat. Carlo and I found him up in the Bronx. Isn't he the sweetest little thing?

BULLOCK. He doesn't smell very sweet.

ANGELICA *(to* CARLO, *explaining breezily)*. Alexander never did like animals.

ANGELICA, *with the goat and the rest of her party, moves to the foreground; then the view moves back and down the steps into the next room—* ANGELICA *leading the goat and a kid. People are passing all sorts of things to the counter where men are receiving them. An old corset is handed to one of the receivers—everybody trying to talk louder than the rest.*

ANGELICA. Come on Go-go-go-go! Come on!

BULLOCK. Are you talking to me or to that animal!

ANGELICA *(as the others keep on talking and shouting)*. I have a goat! I have a goat!

*A close view of the crowd shows* ANGELICA *and* CARLO *trying to be heard.*

CARLO. She has a goat.

ANGELICA. I have a goat.

*A man behind the counter is trying to make himself heard as a* MAN *(closely seen) comes on with an old spinning wheel. It breaks. Then* AN-GELICA *and* CARLO, *with the goat, again appear.*

ANGELICA. I have a goat! A goat!

CARLO. She has a goat.

*We get a close-up of a* MAN, *the receiver, in the foreground talking— the crowd in the background; the* MAN *makes notes.*

MAN. I know you have a goat. Henry, will you come here and get Mrs. Bullock's goat?

HENRY *comes on, takes the goat, and leaves with it.* ANGELICA *picks up the kid, as she talks.*

ANGELICA. I have a little baby goat, too.

*The two receivers are talking as the kid is being held up. Startled, the MAN gives it to a bellhop, who goes out with the kid.*

ANGELICA. Is there anything else we have to get?

*The receiver, checking the goods received, looks up.*

MAN. All you have to get now is one forgotten man and a bowl of Japanese goldfish.

ANGELICA. What? Be still, everybody. What?

MAN *(raising his voice)*. I said a forgotten man and a bowl of Japanese goldfish.

ANGELICA *(repeating after the MAN)*. A forgotten man and a bowl of Japanese goldfish.

*At this CARLO laughs, and they turn to pass through the crowd. Then they appear pushing through the crowd, with BULLOCK close to ANGELICA as a man comes in with snowshoes.*

ANGELICA. A forgotten man—a bowl of Japanese goldfish—A Japanese—I can't remember—

BULLOCK *(to her)*. I'm going home!

ANGELICA. Oh, what are you talking about?

BULLOCK. I'm talking about going home!

ANGELICA. We've only got two more things to get—A bowl of Japanese men and a forgotten goldfish. What was it, Carlo?

CARLO. Goldfish.

BULLOCK *(leaving, angrily)*. I don't know anything about goldfish—but if you want a forgotten man—you'll find me home in bed.

ANGELICA. I can't stop to talk to you now. A bowl of Japanese goldfish. (CARLO *and she go out.)*

*Near the entrance of the ballroom as men and women are passing, we see IRENE coming forward with GODFREY. She leads him up the steps, the view moving with them.*

GODFREY. Are all these people hunters?

IRENE. Oh, no. We work in groups—some are hunters and some are receivers.

GODFREY. Sounds like bankruptcy proceedings.

IRENE. You know, I never thought of that.

GODFREY. Who receives me?

IRENE. I have to take you to the committee. But you don't mind, do you?

GODFREY. I can hardly wait.

ANGELICA *(out of sight)*. Wait a minute! Wait a minute! What have you got?

IRENE *(as they stop in the doorway, meeting ANGELICA)*. Oh, this is Godfrey. Has Cornelia got back yet?

ANGELICA. I haven't seen Cornelia. Where did you find him?

*In a close view of one side of the room IRENE appears with GODFREY, people watching her. ANGELICA follows her. The view moves to the receiving counter, where she reports to the receiver. (A monkey jumps about, annoying the man at the counter. As they pass a man with sandwiches on a tray, GODFREY takes some.)*

IRENE *(answering ANGELICA's question)*. Oh, he's a forgotten man.

ANGELICA. Irene! Irene!

IRENE. Oh, Mr. Guthrie! Mr. Guthrie! Mr. Guthrie—I've got a forgotten man.

GODFREY *curiously watches her as she talks.*

IRENE. Oh, Mr. Guthrie! This is Godfrey—he's a forgotten man!

MAN *(who hears her amid the*

*shouting).* Listen, Guthrie, he's the forgotten man.

IRENE. His name is Godfrey.

GUTHRIE *(understanding at last).* A forgotten man? Ladies and gentlemen, please—quiet! Quiet. Miss Bullock has the forgotten man. Would you mind stepping up on the platform, please?

*A close view in the room shows* IRENE, GODFREY, ANGELICA, CARLO *and others,* IRENE *talking—the kid on the counter in the foreground.*

IRENE. Will you go right up on the platform, Godfrey?

*The view moves with* GODFREY *as he gets up on the platform—still eating a sandwich.*

GUTHRIE *(to* GODFREY*).* Would you mind if I ask you a few questions?

GODFREY. Fire away.

GUTHRIE *(seen in a close-up).* What is your address?

GODFREY *(now seen in a close-up).* City Dump Thirty-Two—East River—Sutton Place.

GUTHRIE'S VOICE. Hmm—rather fashionable over there, isn't it?

GODFREY. In spots.

GUTHRIE *(in a close-up amid much talking).* Is that your permanent address?

GODFREY. Well, the permanency is rather questionable. You see, the place is being rapidly filled in.

GUTHRIE *and* GODFREY *are now eating amid much chatter.*

GUTHRIE. May I ask you a personal question?

GODFREY. If it isn't too personal.

GUTHRIE. Are those whiskers your own?

GODFREY *(whimsically).* No one else has claimed them.

GUTHRIE. I must ask that question because one group tried to fool the committee the early part of the evening by putting false whiskers on one of their own group. May I—

GODFREY. It's a pleasure.

GUTHRIE. One more question. Are you wanted by the police?

GODFREY *(dryly).* That's just the trouble—nobody wants me.

IRENE *(in a close-up) is smiling with pleasure. She claps her hands approvingly.*

GUTHRIE'S VOICE. What a good answer.

IRENE. Splendid, Godfrey.

*Now we see* GODFREY, IRENE *and her mother,* ANGELICA, *in the foreground.*

ANGELICA. You mean nobody wants him—nobody at all.

GODFREY. Nobody.

ANGELICA. Oh, that's too bad!

*Next* GODFREY *and* GUTHRIE *appear on a platform—*IRENE, *her mother* ANGELICA, *and* CARLO *with their backs turned in the foreground.* IRENE *gets up beside* GODFREY.

GODFREY. On the contrary, I sometimes find it a great advantage.

GUTHRIE. The committee are satisfied. Miss Irene Bullock wins twenty points for the forgotten man and fifty points extra for bringing in the first one.

CROWD. Speech! Speech!

GUTHRIE. Group Ten wins the silver cup!

IRENE *(receiving the cup).* They want a speech! Turn around, Godfrey.

GODFREY. My purpose in coming here tonight was two-fold. Firstly, I wanted to aid this young woman. Secondly, I was curious to see how a bunch of empty-headed nit-wits conducted themselves. *(Amid the shouting that arises)* My curiosity is satisfied.

*There is now a close-up on the platform showing* IRENE *standing beside* GODFREY, GUTHRIE *behind them.*

GODFREY *(amid more shouting).* I assure you it will be a pleasure for me to return to a society of really important people. *(He goes out.)*

ANGELICA *and* CARLO *are left standing and taking, as* IRENE *goes off past them.*

ANGELICA. What did he call us?
CARLO. Nit-wits.
ANGELICA. Nit-wits—what are they?

*We see* GODFREY *passing through the crowd. He passes through the doorway into the next room,* IRENE *running after him.*

MAN. The man's perfect! I've been wanting to say that all night, but I didn't have the nerve.
IRENE *(catching up with him).* Oh, Godfrey! Godfrey! Oh, Godfrey! I'm terribly sorry.

IRENE *clings to* GODFREY *as they move through the room,* ANGELICA *following them.*

GODFREY. Oh, that's all right.
IRENE. I'd never have brought you here if I had thought they were going to humiliate you. I'm terribly thankful. It's the first time I've ever beaten Cornelia at anything, and you helped me do it.
GODFREY. Well, that makes me a sort of Cornelia beater, doesn't it?
IRENE. You've done something for me. I wish I could do something for you.
GODFREY. Why?
IRENE *(naively).* Because you've done something for me. Don't you see?
GODFREY. No—I don't see. I can

use a job if you've got one hanging around loose.
IRENE. Can you buttle?
GODFREY. Buttle?
IRENE. Yes. We're fresh out of butlers. The one we had left this morning.
ANGELICA *(who has been following them; out of sight).* Irene!

ANGELICA *appears at the steps and the moving view follows her over to a pillar where* IRENE *and* GODFREY *are standing.*

ANGELICA. They're calling for you in the game room. Don't you want your nice cup?
IRENE. They can keep their cup. I don't want it.
ANGELICA. You can't stand here talking to this man. What will people think?
IRENE. I don't care what they think. Godfrey's going to be our butler.
ANGELICA. He's going to be whose butler?
IRENE. He's going to work for us.
ANGELICA. Why, it's ridiculous! You don't know anything about him. He hasn't any recommendations.
IRENE. The last one had recommendations and stole all the silver.
ANGELICA. Oh, that was merely a coincidence.
GODFREY. People that take in stray cats say they make the best pets, Madam.
ANGELICA. I don't see what cats have got to do with butlers. You mustn't pay any attention to my daughter. She is very impulsive.
IRENE. I'm not impulsive!
ANGELICA. And don't shout at your mother.
IRENE. I will shout—

*A woman comes past them, and* AN-GELICA *turns to her, embarrassed.*

ANGELICA. Oh, Mrs. Merriwell! Irene has—*(She continues talking excitedly.)*

MRS. MERRIWELL. You mean it is all over?

ANGELICA. Irene always shouts when she wins. *(The woman leaves them excitedly.)*

ANGELICA *(impatiently)*. Well, run along, my good man, just run along. Thank you so much for coming. Thank you so, so much.

IRENE *(firmly)*. He will not—

*At the entrance we now see* CORNELIA *coming on with* GEORGE *and a* MAN. *They stop.*

IRENE *(completing her sentence)*. —run along.

GODFREY. I think I'd better—

ANGELICA. My word! There's Cornelia—and she has another one.

*We again see, at the entrance,* CORNELIA, GEORGE *and the* MAN, *with other people in the background, and then see the three standing at the pillar, with* CORNELIA *approaching, followed by* GEORGE *and the* MAN, *a tramp.*

IRENE. You're a little late, Cornelia. I've won the game.

CORNELIA *(taken aback)*. Oh, you have.

MAN. Now, when do I get my five bucks?

ANGELICA. Your five? *(To* CORNELIA) Will you talk to your sister? She wants—

*A close-up of* GODFREY *shows him smiling with amusement.*

ANGELICA'S VOICE. —to hire this man as a butler.

CORNELIA *(seen in a close-up; looking at him with interest)*. Why not? He might make a very good butler.

GODFREY *(seen in a close-up, smiling faintly)*. I am sure I would make a very good butler.

MAN *(seen in a close-up, impatient)*. Say, where do I get my five bucks?

ANGELICA *and* GEORGE *go to him.*

ANGELICA. What's he talking about?

MAN. My five bucks.

CORNELIA. Oh, I promised him five dollars.

ANGELICA. Give him the five dollars and the bucks, too, and get him out of here, before your sister hires him as a chauffeur. *(GEORGE gets out the money and pays the* MAN, *who leaves quickly.)* Why did I have to wait till now to find out there is insanity on your father's side of the family. Come along, Cornelia. *(She leaves them.)*

CORNELIA *stops before* IRENE *and* GODFREY.

CORNELIA. I hope Godfrey is very good at shining shoes. *(She leaves them.)*

GODFREY. I think we'd better drop the whole idea.

IRENE. I should say not. You're going to make the best butler we ever had. *(Putting money in his pocket)* And here—you need some clothes and things.

GODFREY *(embarrassed)*. Oh, well, I—

*A roll of bills, and silver, fall on the floor at their feet.*

*Both look down—startled.* GODFREY *shows her the holes in his pocket and stoops down.*

GODFREY. I told Jeeves to lay out my other coat—

*We see* GODFREY *(in a close-up) picking up the money, and then both* IRENE *and* GODFREY:

IRENE. You have a wonderful sense of humor.
GODFREY. Thank you. Well then—good night.

*People appear passing as* GODFREY *starts to leave* IRENE.

GODFREY *(coming back)*. Oh! I forgot one question.
IRENE. What—
GODFREY. Where do you live?
IRENE.     Oh—1011   Fiftieth—funny—I never thought of that.
GODFREY. No, you didn't. 1011 Fiftieth.
IRENE. Yes.
GODFREY. Well, good-night again,.
IRENE. Good-night, Godfrey. *(He leaves and the scene fades out.)*

## PART TWO

*A kitchen fades in. A young woman,* MOLLY, *is seated, reading, as footsteps are heard, and soon* GODFREY *enters, bag and overcoat in hand. He comes forward, and sets down his bag.* GODFREY *is no longer bearded, and looks trim.*

GODFREY. Good morning.
MOLLY. Good morning.
GODFREY. I'm the new—
MOLLY. I know. You're the new—

*A close view of* GODFREY *shows him looking puzzled.*

MOLLY *(out of sight; her voice heard)*. —butler.
GODFREY. How did you know?
MOLLY *(seen in a close-up; seated)*. Oh, there's one every day at this hour. They're dropping in and out all the time.

GODFREY *now comes toward* MOLLY.

GODFREY. Why is that?
MOLLY. Some get fired and some quit—
GODFREY. Is the— *(Puzzled, as he is now seen in a close-up.)* —family that exacting?
MOLLY *(seen in a close-up; holding a paper and a pencil)*. No! They're that nutty.

GODFREY *is now seen standing—* MOLLY *seated.*

GODFREY. May I be frank?
MOLLY. Is that your name?
GODFREY. My name is Godfrey.
MOLLY. All right—be frank.
GODFREY *(in a close-up)*. You're quite an enthusiast—
MOLLY *(seen in a close-up, busy with paper and pencil)*. Don't worry about me. I'm a seasoned campaigner.

GODFREY *now offers his hand, and shakes hands with her.*

GODFREY.    Well—may   we   be friends?
MOLLY. I'm friends with all the butlers. Sit down. What's a three-letter sea-bird with an "E" in the middle?
GODFREY. Oh—I—I don't know.
MOLLY. You're no help. Say, where did you get the trick suit?
GODFREY. What's the matter with it?
MOLLY. Well, it might look better if you took the rental tag off the coat.
GODFREY. Thanks. Does the butler have quarters here in the house or is it necessary?
MOLLY. You won't need any quarters. Just hang your hat near the door so you can get it quickly— *(The buzzer is heard.)*

*We see a bell above a panel—the number 8 is up.*

MOLLY *(out of view; continuing).* —on your way out.

*As the buzzer continues ringing,* GODFREY *rises.*

GODFREY. What's that?

MOLLY *(rising hastily).* That's the old battle-axe. She usually rings about this time.

GODFREY. The old battle-axe?

MOLLY. Mrs. Bullock—she's the mother type.

GODFREY. Don't you do anything about it?

MOLLY. Mrs. Bullock or the buzzer?

GODFREY. The buzzer.

MOLLY. Not the first time. If she has a hangover—and she usually has—she'll ring again in a minute in no uncertain terms. Then, brother, you'd better grab her tomato juice and get going. *(As the buzzer sounds again, she goes over to the refrigerator.)* Aw!—there she goes! Now, Cupid, this is your big opportunity.

MOLLY *is now pouring tomato juice into a tall glass.*

GODFREY. Shall I take it to her?

MOLLY. You might as well know the worst, and I want to warn you she sees pixies.

GODFREY. Pixies?

MOLLY. You know—the little men. *(The buzzer sounds again.)*

GODFREY. Oh those! Well, I know how to take care of those. Have you any Worcestershire? Yes—here it is.

MOLLY. What are you going to do with that?

GODFREY *gets the bottle from the refrigerator and puts some into the glass as they talk. She gives him a tray, and they go to the door.*

GODFREY. Do unto others as you would have them do unto you.

MOLLY. What do you want to do—scorch her windpipe?

GODFREY. There's nothing like a counter irritant in the morning. Where do I find her?

MOLLY. Better go this way—it's quicker. The upper landing to the left.

*We see the service hall,* MOLLY *holding the door as* GODFREY *moves forward with the tray. Then the view moves along the stairway to the main hall as* MOLLY *and* GODFREY *appear. (The buzzer can still be heard.)*

GODFREY *(as he mounts the stairs).* Just which is her——

MOLLY *(pointing).* That's her cage up there. The first door.

GODFREY. Wish me luck.

MOLLY. Happy landing.

*The bedroom door is opened by* GODFREY, *holding the tray, and he looks around as the view moves across to the bed, revealing* AN-GELICA, *while a tinkle of prisms is heard and soon also music. Then a close-up at the windows reveals a lamp with prisms on a table—prisms tinkling—swaying. And now a close view at the bed shows* ANGELICA *in it—*GODFREY *approaching with a tray and taking the buzzer cord from her hand.*

ANGELICA. What day is it, Molly?

GODFREY. I am not Molly.

ANGELICA. Who isn't?

GODFREY. I'm not.

ANGELICA. Stop jumping up and down so I can see who you are.

GODFREY. I am not jumping.

ANGELICA. That's better. What's your name?

GODFREY. Godfrey.

ANGELICA. Are you someone I know?

GODFREY. We met last night at the Waldorf-Ritz.

ANGELICA. Oh yes—you were with Mrs. Maxton's party at the bar—or were you?

GODFREY. I'm the forgotten man.

ANGELICA. So many people have bad memories.

GODFREY. So true.

ANGELICA *(seen in a close-up; frowning as the music is heard again)*. Why do they keep playing that same tune over and over again?

GODFREY *(a close-up showing him standing, tray in hand)*. Why do they?

ANGELICA *(while the music continues)*. Do they?

GODFREY *(looking around)*. Oh— yes—yes. I do—

*At the windows a close views shows the prisms tinkling on the lamp.*

GODFREY'S VOICE. In a way—but—

*We see the room as* GODFREY *offers her the glass.*

ANGELICA. Always the same tune— over and over again.

GODFREY. May I?

ANGELICA. May you what? Where are you? What's that?

GODFREY. Pixie remover.

ANGELICA *(taking the glass)*. Oh— then you see them, too?

GODFREY. We're old friends.

ANGELICA. You mustn't step on them. I don't like them, but I don't like to see them stepped on.

GODFREY *(seen in another close-up, standing)*. I'll be very careful. I wouldn't hurt them for the world.

ANGELICA *(holding the glass)*. What am I supposed to do with this?

GODFREY'S VOICE. Drink it.

*The bedroom comes in to view again as* GODFREY *goes to the window. He closes the shutters, then returns to the bed.*

GODFREY. —and they'll go away very quickly—very, very quickly. You must never be rough with them. You must always send them away quietly. Is that better?

ANGELICA. Yes. You're a great help.

GODFREY *is standing at the bed with the tray:*

ANGELICA *(suddenly)*. Go away— go away—shoo shoo— Oh but— Oh—you haven't told me who you are.

GODFREY. I am Godfrey—the forgotten man. I'm the new butler.

ANGELICA. Are you that ugly man with the beard?

GODFREY. The same.

ANGELICA. My, you've changed. I should never have known you.

GODFREY. Thank you.

ANGELICA. You are very comforting. I hope I'll see more of you. Maybe I'd better not drink any more of this. Then you might go away, too. *(He leaves.)*

*We see* GODFREY *on the upper landing closing the door and the view moves with him as he goes down the stairs.* MOLLY *meets him there with a large tray.*

MOLLY. Well, I put your hat and valise at the foot of the stairs. You can go out the front way—it's closer.

GODFREY. I think I won the first round.

MOLLY. You mean you're still working here?

GODFREY. I haven't heard anything to the contrary.

MOLLY. Well, you just got by the cub. Try the lioness.

GODFREY. Oh—which is she?

MOLLY. Her name's Cornelia. She's a sweet-tempered little number.

GODFREY. Oh yes, I met her last night.

MOLLY *(giving him the tray)*. You've got a treat coming. You never met her in the morning. Second door.

*He goes up the other stairs, carrying the tray, opens the door, stops, and looks in. We see* MOLLY *on the stairs listening as* CORNELIA *is heard speaking irritably.*

CORNELIA'S VOICE. Who are you and what are you doing in here? If I want you to bring my breakfast I'll—

*A close view of the upper landing, as the noise of things being thrown is heard, shows* GODFREY *in the doorway with the breakfast tray. He closes the door, comes forward, and the view moves with him along the stairs as* GODFREY *descends and meets* MOLLY.

CORNELIA *(off scene)*. Get out! You won't come in here again if you know what's good for you!

GODFREY. I'm afraid I lost the second round.

IRENE'S VOICE *(now heard)*. Hey, Molly! Cut out all the noise and bring me some breakfast.

MOLLY. Opportunity never stops knocking in this house. Do you want to try again?

GODFREY. And how is *she* in the morning?

MOLLY. She's not as violent, but she's more insidious.

GODFREY. Okay. *(He goes up again, to the first door, and opens it.)*

MOLLY *(out of sight)*. I'll leave your things right up here so you won't forget them.

IRENE'S *bedroom: The door opens,* GODFREY *enters, and the view moves with him over to the bed where* IRENE *is lying.*

GODFREY. Good morning. I brought your breakfast.

IRENE *(startled)*. Are—are you the new butler?.

GODFREY *(holding the tray)*. Don't you remember last night?

IRENE *(a close-up showing her looking around, puzzled)*. But—what happened to Godfrey?

GODFREY. I'm Godfrey.

IRENE *(the close-up showing her troubled)*. Oh—you look so different. What happened to those nice whiskers?

GODFREY *put the tray on the bed—* IRENE *looking at him.*

IRENE. Turn around and let me look at you. You're the cutest thing I've ever seen.

GODFREY *(turning)*. Thank you. Will there be anything else?

IRENE. Yes. Sit down and talk to me. I like to talk in the morning when your head is clear—especially if you've been somewhere the night before.

GODFREY. Don't you think it would be better if I talked standing?

IRENE. No. Because, if you're uncomfortable, I'd get uncomfortable and forget what I have to say.

GODFREY *(starting to sit down on the bed)*. If you insist.

IRENE *is pleased as* GODFREY *sits down—they talk.*

GODFREY. —but it doesn't seem very good form for a butler.

IRENE. You're more than a butler. You're the first protégé I ever had.

GODFREY *(in the foreground)*. Protégé?

IRENE. You know—like Carlo.

GODFREY. Who is Carlo?

IRENE *(now in the foreground)*. He's mother's protégé.

GODFREY. Oh.

IRENE. You know, it's awfully nice Carlo having a sponsor, because he doesn't have to work and he gets more time to practice—but then, he never does and that makes a difference.

GODFREY *(again in the foreground)*. Yes, I imagine it would.

IRENE. Do you play anything, Godfrey? I don't mean games or things like that. I mean the piano—and things like that.

GODFREY. Well, I—

IRENE. It doesn't really make any difference. I just thought I'd ask. It's funny how some things make you think of other things.

GODFREY. Yes, it is very peculiar.

IRENE. It makes me feel so mature and grown up.

GODFREY. Er—what does?

IRENE. Having a protégé. You're the first one I ever had.

GODFREY. You've never had any others?

IRENE *(in a close-up with him, in the foreground; naively)*. No—you're the first one and it's terribly thrilling. Not only does it occupy my mind, but I think it's character building, too.

GODFREY. Uh-huh. Just what does a protégé have to do?

IRENE. Oh—you just go on buttling and I sponsor you. Don't you see?

GODFREY *(with IRENE in the foreground)*. It's getting clearer.

IRENE. It's really not much work. It gives you something to think of. It's going to be such fun.

GODFREY *(now in the foreground)*. I'm sure it's going to be heaps of fun.

IRENE. You see, if Cornelia gets mean or anything, you don't have to do anything about it. You see, I take care of everything. You see, I'm your sponsor and I'll just take a sock at her.

GODFREY. Oh, I hope that's not going to be necessary.

IRENE. I just wanted to give you the idea.

GODFREY. That's fine, but—you see, a protégé has certain responsibilities also. For instance if someone should ring for me now and I didn't answer, that would reflect upon you because you're my sponsor. Don't you see?

IRENE. Yes, I suppose it would. I never thought of that. you don't know how nice it is having some intelligent person to talk to.

GODFREY. It's been very enlightening to me, too.

IRENE. Oh, I just thought of something else. Do you know what you are?

GODFREY. I'm not quite sure.

IRENE *(brightly—in a close-up)*. You're my responsibility.

GODFREY *(bowing)*. That's very nice.

IRENE *(as he is at the door now)*. See you in church.

GODFREY *opens the door and starts to go out, bowing.*

*Down the lower hall* BULLOCK *is seen coming forward, and looking off. As viewed from the upper landing leading to the lower hall* GODFREY'S *coat appears on the railing and his bag below it, as he closes the door,* BULLOCK *watching from down stairs.* GODFREY *takes his things and descends the stairs.*

GODFREY *(to* BULLOCK*)*. Good morning.

BULLOCK *(scowling)*. Good morning.

GODFREY. Fine morning, sir.

BULLOCK *(descending the lower stairs with him)*. Yes— it is a fine morning. Don't be in a hurry. You see, I'm the old fashioned type and I was also middle weight champion when I was in college. I thought you might like to know that before this thing starts. *(He stops him from leaving.* BULLOCK *removes his coat and vest.)*

GODFREY. Well, you see, sir, I'm the new butler. I just served Miss Irene her breakfast.

BULLOCK. Do you always take a change of wardrobe when you serve breakfast?

GODFREY (*as* MOLLY *enters*), Well—I—I think this young lady can explain.

MOLLY. He really is the new butler, Mr. Bullock. I can't imagine how his things got in the hallway.

BULLOCK. Well, I still don't get it, but if you are the new butler—why didn't you say so?

GODFREY. I'm very sorry, sir. May I? (*He holds* BULLOCK'S *coat for him.*)

MOLLY. There's a man at the door to see you. I think it's a process server.

BULLOCK (*leaving*). Another one?

MOLLY. Yes, sir.

*At the door:* BULLOCK *opens it, and admits a* MAN *who gives him a paper.*

MAN. Well, here I am, Mr. Bullock, with a little present for you.

BULLOCK. Yes—I've heard all that before. Which one of the family is it this time?

MAN. Miss Cornelia. It seems she was feeling pretty gay last night and on the way home she busted up a few windows along Fifth Avenue. I'm sorry to give you that, but girls will be girls.

BULLOCK (*closing the door*). Good-bye.

*The lower hall:* GODFREY *and* MOLLY *stand watching.* BULLOCK *comes in; he is plainly angry.*

BULLOCK. Life in this family is just one subpoena—

MOLLY. Mr. Bullock, there's a hansom cab driver waiting to see you in the kitchen.

BULLOCK. What's he want?

MOLLY. He wants fifty dollars and his horse.

BULLOCK. What horse?

MOLLY. The one Miss Irene rode up the front steps last night.

BULLOCK. Where is his horse? I haven't got it.

MOLLY. It's in the library, where Miss Irene left it.

BULLOCK *opens the library door. He looks in, and is startled at hearing a horse neighing. In the hall* GODFREY *and* MOLLY *look at each other with understanding as the horse neighs again.*

MOLLY (*triumphantly as she leaves*). Well—do you begin to get the idea?

*The scene fades out and then the drawing room fades in, showing* GODFREY *turning on the lights. He comes forward, as music is heard, and turns on a table light as* CORNELIA *enters.*

CORNELIA. Come here, my man. (*Music continues throughout.*)

*A close-up next shows them near the window:*

CORNELIA. Do you like your place here—I mean, so far as you've gone?

GODFREY. I find it very entertaining.

CORNELIA. Yes. We are a very entertaining family. You really think you're going to like it here? (*She is definitely provoked.*)

GODFREY. I must admit it's more desirable than living in a packing case on a city dump.

CORNELIA. Oh, that's where I met you, isn't it?

*She moves through the room,* GODFREY *watching her.*

CORNELIA. Yes—I remember now. We were playing a sort of a game—a scavenger hunt I think we called it.

GODFREY *(in a close-up) is seen closely observing* CORNELIA.

CORNELIA'S VOICE. We needed a forgotten man. I asked you to go to the Waldorf-Ritz Hotel with me and—*(now seen standing close)*—I am just a little bit hazy as to just what happened after that.

GODFREY. I pushed you onto an ash pile.

CORNELIA *(blandly)*. Oh, of course you did. It was very amusing. They were nice clean ashes.

GODFREY *(bowing)*. I am very sorry, Miss.

CORNELIA *(seated now, laughing)*. I didn't mind at all. It was very amusing. Have you a handkerchief?

GODFREY *takes out a handerchief, looking at* CORNELIA, *who is now out of sight.*

CORNELIA'S VOICE. There is a spot on my shoe. Will you see what you can do about it?

*They look at each other intently (in close-up), then we see* CORNELIA *seated—*GODFREY *kneeling—wiping her shoe with his handkerchief.*

CORNELIA. I could have you fired you know, but I like to see things wriggle. When I get through with you, you will go back to your packing case on the city dump and relish it. People don't make a practice of pushing Cornelia Bullock into ash piles.

*A close view at the doorway discloses* IRENE, *who is listening to* CORNELIA'S *voice.*

CORNELIA'S VOICE. I'll make your life so miserable—

*We see* CORNELIA *leaning forward and* GODFREY *on one knee. They look off at the doorway where* IRENE *appears again gazing at the scene and moving forward.*

GODFREY *is now standing—putting his handkerchief in his pocket.* CORNELIA *rises as* IRENE *approaches and sits down.*

IRENE. Hello, Godfrey.

GODFREY. Good evening, Miss Irene.

IRENE. I like your new monkey suit.

GODFREY. Thank you for picking it out.

IRENE. You know, it fits you very well for a hand-me-down.

GODFREY. I'm more or less standard, Miss.

IRENE. How do you like my new pajamas?

GODFREY. I think they're very nice.

GODFREY *goes out.* IRENE *turns to* CORNELIA.

IRENE. I heard what you said to Godfrey.

CORNELIA. So what?

IRENE. So what—you leave him alone.

CORNELIA *(rising)*. So who's going to make me leave him alone?

IRENE. If you don't you'll get a good sock from me.

CORNELIA. Oh, the physical type.

*The sisters move about the room as they quarrel.*

IRENE. What I say goes.

CORNELIA. Since when did you start falling in love with butlers?

IRENE *(she and* CORNELIA *both looking furious)*. I'm not falling in love with him. He's my protégé.

CORNELIA. Oh, your protégé. That's why you're picking out his suits for him. Suppose father hears about this. How long do you think Godfrey will last?

IRENE. Father isn't going to hear about it.

CORNELIA. You seem terribly sure of everything.

IRENE. If father hears about Godfrey, he's going to hear about you and that sappy college boy.

CORNELIA. I don't know what you're talking about, but if father does hear about it, I'm likely to do a little socking myself.

CORNELIA *moves away;* IRENE *follows and faces her as* CORNELIA *sits down. Soon* CARLO *appears in the background.*

CORNELIA. So little Red Riding Hood didn't have enough feminine charm to trap a wolf her own age, so she fell in love with the butler and lived happily every after on the ash pile—if you know what I mean.

IRENE. I know what you mean—if you know what I mean.

CARLO *now appears, standing, book in hand.*

CARLO. May I come in?

CORNELIA. You're in, aren't you?

CARLO. I've just been reading a very interesting book, "The Greeks of The Middle Ages."

CORNELIA. Irene would like that. You love the middle ages, don't you, dear?

*At this point* ANGELICA *(out of sight) is heard talking baby talk. Then she appears with a dog in her arms, and approaches* CARLO.

CARLO *(kissing her hand).* Marta Gratia.

ANGELICA. Oh, Carlo! Who's giving the concert tonight?

BULLOCK *enters the drawing room.*

CARLO. The great Koraninski.

ANGELICA. Pianist, isn't he?

CARLO. No—cellist.

ANGELICA. What's the difference? It's all music, isn't it? Oh! It's so nice to see you two girls having a pleasant chat. Or is it a pleasant chat?

BULLOCK. Well, well, well! Imagine the Bullocks gathered together all in one room.

ANGELICA. Oh, you mustn't forget Carlo.

BULLOCK *(in an expressive close-up—meaningfully).* I'm not going to forget Carlo.

CARLO *(now standing behind the seated* ANGELICA*).* Don't bother about me. I feel like one of the family.

IRENE *starts toward the doorway.* BULLOCK *stops her.*

BULLOCK. Don't you go away. *(In a close-up, to* CARLO*)* You don't mind if I discuss a few family matters, do you, my boy?

CARLO. Oh no, not at all.

ANGELICA. Oh, Alexander—you're not going to bring up those sordid business matters again, I hope.

BULLOCK *(angrily).* I've just been going through the last month's bills and I find that you people have confused me with the Treasury Department.

CORNELIA. Oh, don't start that again, Dad.

BULLOCK. I don't mind giving the government sixty percent of what I make, but I can't do it when my family spends fifty percent.

IRENE. But why should the government get more money than your own family?

ANGELICA. That's what I want to know. Why should the Government get more than your own flesh and blood?

BULLOCK *(dryly—he knows he couldn't possibly explain to them).* Well, it's just a way they have of doing things.

*We see* CARLO *standing back of* ANGELICA *in a close view. He drops his book, and cries out:*

CARLO. Oh, money, money, money! The Frankenstein monster that destroys souls.

BULLOCK, *looking at him, is startled.* ANGELICA *rises.* CARLO *has his hand over his face.*

ANGELICA. Please don't say anthing more about it. You're upsetting Carlo.

BULLOCK, *angry, crosses over to* ANGELICA, *while* CARLO *is raving.*

BULLOCK. We've got to come to an understanding right now. Either Carlo leaves or I am!

CARLO *goes to the windows in the background.*

ANGELICA. And what?

BULLOCK. Well, one of us has got to and that's all there is about it!

ANGELICA. Alexander, you're inebriated. You don't know what you're talking about.

BULLOCK'S *face shows that he is furious.*

BULLOCK. Well, who would know what they're talking about, living with a bunch like this. There is one thing I do know—what this family needs is discipline. I've been a pretty patient man—but when people start riding horses up the front steps and parking them in the library, that's going a little bit too far.

BULLOCK *has crossed to the doorway and addresses himself at this point to* IRENE.

IRENE. Horses?

ANGELICA *(rising).* Are you insinuating that I rode a horse up the front steps last night?

BULLOCK. Maybe that wasn't a horse I saw in the library this morning.

ANGELICA *(holding the dog, sits down).* Well, I'm positive I didn't ride a horse into the library because I didn't have my riding costume on and I hope you're not insinuating that I should ride a horse into the library without my riding costume on.

CORNELIA *(now seen in a close-up; seated).* It was Irene who rode the horse—up the front steps.

IRENE. What horse?

CORNELIA *(again, visible, in a close-up).* Don't try to be innocent. I begged you not to do it.

IRENE *walks angrily over to* CORNELIA.

IRENE *(accusingly).* I didn't ride a horse—but if I did ride a horse—Who broke those windows on Fifth Avenue?

CORNELIA. What windows?

IRENE. You know what windows. And how about the college sap? Yah! Yah! Yah!

BULLOCK *(going over to them).* And I don't care who broke the horse or rode the windows up the steps or who yah-yah-yahed—*(seen in a close-up now; excited).*—This family has got to settle down!

CARLO. Ooooh!

ANGELICA *(out of sight).* Will you stop bellowing! *(Seen standing; indignantly)* Look what you're doing to Carlo.

BULLOCK *(furious).* Hang Carlo!

IRENE *is now watching* GODFREY *at the doorway as he brings a tray. She stops him and takes something from the tray.*

IRENE. Did you make those yourself, Godfrey?

GODFREY. I helped.

IRENE. Oh, they must be wonderful. I'd like to help some time, if you'll let me.

GODFREY. I'd feel honored.

*Now as the family is seated and standing about,* GODFREY *comes forward*—IRENE *following. They come to* CORNELIA, *while* BULLOCK *and* ANGELICA *are arguing in the background.*

BULLOCK *(out of sight).* You might as well face the situation right now. I've been losing a lot of money lately.

ANGELICA *(out of sight).* You have?

BULLOCK *(now in the scene).* Yes, I have!

ANGELICA *(sitting down).* Maybe you left it in your other suit.

BULLOCK. If things keep on the way they're going now, it won't be long till I won't have another suit. *(He starts to go out.)*

IRENE *is watching as* GODFREY *serves* CORNELIA.

CORNELIA. Which one's poisoned? Thank you.

*We see* GODFREY *with* IRENE *and* CORNELIA; *and the view expands as he brings the tray to* BULLOCK *and* ANGELICA.

CORNELIA. While we're on the subject, how about the business of certain people picking up anybody they find on the city dump and dragging them into the house? For all we know, we might all be stabbed in the back some night and robbed.

*We are a close-up of* IRENE—*startled, angry.* GODFREY *is then seen serving* ANGELICA *from the tray.*

ANGELICA. Who's going to stab who?

*We see a close-up of* CORNELIA *seated—talking.*

CORNELIA. We don't know anything about certain people. Someone should speak to Irene about her habit of picking up strays.

GODFREY *is still serving* ANGELICA.

ANGELICA. What's a stray?

*We see* IRENE *(in a close-up)—furious.*

IRENE. You shut up!

*While* GODFREY *is holding the tray near* ANGELICA, *she looks up—startled.*

ANGELICA. Me?

IRENE *(in a closeup)* whirls around.

IRENE. No. Cornelia.

CORNELIA *(out of sight).* I will not shut up.

CORNELIA *is seen seated as* IRENE *comes over to her.*

CORNELIA. My life is precious to me.

IRENE. Well, it won't be in a minute.

*As* GODFREY *is waiting before* ANGELICA, CARLO, *standing in the background, starts toward* GODFREY.

ANGELICA. Now, now, children—Come, Carlo, come and get some nice hors d'ouvres.

IRENE *is standing near* CORNELIA, *who is talking insolently.*

CORNELIA. I think we should get our help from employment agencies.

BULLOCK *(in a close-up; looking toward* GODFREY). I don't know but what I agree with Cornelia.

GODFREY *(in a close-up) looks sideways at* BULLOCK. *Then we see* IRENE *(in a close-up) ready to cry.*

ANGELICA *(out of sight).* Whatever are you all talking about?

CORNELIA *looks delighted.* IRENE, *half crying, crosses the room to her father, and falls crying into his arms.*

*Now* ANGELICA *puts down the dog, goes to* BULLOCK *and* IRENE, *and embraces her, while* CARLO *continues eating, undisturbed.*

ANGELICA. You've upset Carlo and now you're upsetting Irene. Don't you remember her breakdown last summer?

CORNELIA *(in a close-up)*. I certainly do. That's why I'm not paying any attention to this.

GODFREY *is now serving* CARLO *in the background.*

IRENE. Well, if mother can sponsor Carlo, why can't I sponsor Godfrey?

CORNELIA *(out of sight)*. Godfrey knows I'm not being personal, but after all, none of us would like to wake up some morning stabbed to death.

ANGELICA *(as* GODFREY *moves forward with the tray,* CARLO *following him for more food)*. You mustn't come between Irene and Godfrey. He's the only thing she's shown any affection for since her Pomeranian died last summer.

IRENE *drops down on the couch. Her mother picks up the dog and the view moves to* CARLO *seated on the opposite couch.* IRENE *is still crying.*

ANGELICA *(going to* CARLO *and giving him the dog)*. Now, Irene, you mustn't have a spell. Carlo, quick! quick! A sofa cushion—here. *(She takes a cushion from* CARLO.*)* Come darling. Lift up your head now.

CORNELIA *(as* GEORGE *approaches in the background)*. She's not having a spell. That's old stuff.

*As* ANGELICA *is still bending over* IRENE, IRENE *cries out.*

IRENE. Ooooh!

ANGELICA. Now, darling.

BULLOCK. What is all this nonsense?

ANGELICA *is worried over* IRENE, *who is now sobbing.*

ANGELICA *(to* BULLOCK)*. Please be quiet. You never did understand women. Why don't you get the doctor?

IRENE. I don't want a doctor.

ANGELICA. Do you want an icebag?

IRENE. I don't want an ice-bag. I want to die!

ANGELICA. You mustn't do that now.

CORNELIA *(to* GEORGE)*. She makes me ill. Let's get out of here.

CARLO *is now seated before the fireplace, reading, while* ANGELICA *is fussing over* IRENE.

ANGELICA. Carlo—do the gorilla for Irene—it always amuses her, Carlo.

CARLO. I'm not in the mood.

ANGELICA. Stop eating hors d'ouvres and get in the mood. Here.

CARLO *(pettishly)*. All right. I'll do it, but my heart won't be in it.

ANGELICA. Irene, be a good girl.

*We see* BULLOCK *watching with utter amazement.*

ANGELICA *(out of sight)*. Sit up and look at Carlo. You know it always amuses you.

ANGELICA *is now watching* CARLO *as he puts on his monkey act.*

IRENE *(out of sight)*. Ooooh!

ANGELICA. Go ahead!

*We get a close view of* BULLOCK *watching—disgusted.*

ANGELICA'S VOICE. Go on, Carlo.

*The group before the fireplace comes into view,* BULLOCK *watching as* CARLO *puts on the monkey act—* IRENE *lying on the couch, her mother in the background.*

ANGELICA. Look Irene—look at Carlo! Ain't that lovely. Isn't he clever, Irene? Come on—

*And in successive close-ups we see: CARLO jumping on the couch; IRENE sitting up and staring; CARLO making funny noises; BULLOCK standing there, still more disgusted. This is followed by a full view of the room, with CARLO doing the monkey act and the others watching.*

ANGELICA. Father, sit down now. *(Standing up)* Isn't that clever?

*Now CARLO is jumping over tables and chairs amid ANGELICA's laughter as GODFREY enters from the hall, carrying a tray with decanter and glasses. Next, CARLO jumps toward IRENE as she lies on the couch, following which he races around and starts toward the door.*

IRENE. Ooooh!

ANGELICA *(out of sight)*. Look! Ain't that funny? He's going to climb up the door! Look!

CARLO *climbs the doors in the background, swinging like a monkey, laughing.*

IRENE. He frightens me.

ANGELICA. No, no, darling. You mustn't be frightened. He isn't a real gorilla—he's just playing.

CARLO *drops, comes into the room passes BULLOCK and GODFREY and goes toward ANGELICA.*

ANGELICA *(laughing)*. Darling— look at Carlo!

CARLO *picks up her dog and begins looking comically for fleas on the animal amid more laughter.*

ANGELICA *(out of sight)*. Look darling, isn't he clever?

*But IRENE is again crying and AN- GELICA bends over her solicitously. Finally BULLOCK, who has been standing with GODFREY, bursts out in disgust.*

BULLOCK. Why don't you stop imitating a gorilla and try to imitate a man?

*We see CARLO suddenly looking toward him and dropping the dog.*

ANGELICA. You wouldn't know an artist if one came up and bit you.

BULLOCK *addresses himself to GOD- FREY as he takes the cocktail tray from him, and starts to leave the room.*

BULLOCK. This family don't need any stimulant. I'll be in my room and you can repeat this order in thirty minutes. Some day I'm going gorilla hunting—and I won't miss.

*We see CARLO at the couch putting on his shoes, and then ANGELICA bending over IRENE, who has stopped crying.*

IRENE. Has Cornelia gone?

*At the doorway GODFREY turns to leave.*

ANGELICA *(out of sight)*. Yes, darling, She's gone.

IRENE *(also out of sight)*. Where's Godfrey?

ANGELICA'S VOICE. He's right here. Don't go away, Godfrey. *(GODFREY starts back.)*

CARLO *(standing up)*. We'll be late for the concert.

ANGELICA. Get my things. I'll be right with you. Godfrey's right here, darling. Godfrey! Come over here so Irene can look at you.

GODFREY *approaches IRENE.*

ANGELICA. Here's Godfrey, darling.

IRENE. Where?

ANGELICA. Right here—look! Say hello to Irene so she'll know who you are.

GODFREY. Hello.

IRENE. Oh, hello. Godfrey.

ANGELICA. And he's promised to stay on, haven't you, Godfrey?

GODFREY. If I'm wanted.

ANGELICA. Of course you're wanted. Isn't he, Irene?

IRENE. Yes. Go away.

ANGELICA. Yes, darling—I'm going. Take good care of her. Yes, Carlo, I'm coming. Good-bye, darling—good-bye.

IRENE (*whispering to* GODFREY). I'm not really having a spell.

GODFREY. I beg your pardon.

IRENE. I'm not really having a spell.

GODFREY. I'm sorry, but I couldn't quite hear.

*He bends close to her as she whispers.*

IRENE. I said—I'm not really having a spell. (*She kisses him.*)

GODFREY *straightens up, bows, and leaves. She looks after him.*

*We get a close view in the pantry of* MOLLY *busy with glasses as she sends them down the dumbwaiter. She opens the door and addresses the unseen cook.*

MOLLY (*calling out*). Hey, cook, you'd better put this back on the fire. It looks like we've lost most of our customers.

*She closes the door as* GODFREY *enters at the next door.*

MOLLY. What's the matter, handsome. Did something frighten you?

GODFREY. What kind of a family am I up against?

MOLLY (*dryly*). There's some things even I can't answer.

GODFREY. Do they go on this way all the time?

MOLLY (*blandly*). Oh—this is just a quiet evening.

GODFREY. A quiet evening?

MOLLY (*carelessly as he goes out*). If I were you I'd get rid of that lip rouge. It makes you look a little like Cupid.

IRENE *comes in.*

MOLLY. You'll find Godfrey in his room.

IRENE. How did you know I wanted to see Godfrey?

MOLLY (*airily*). I don't know. It just came over me. (IRENE *goes out.*)

*A close view in* GODFREY'S *room shows* GODFREY *wiping his mouth.* IRENE *enters.*

GODFREY. You—you can't come in here.

IRENE (*moving across the room;* MOLLY *seen in the background*). Why not? It's our house, isn't it? And after all—one room is just like any other room—besides, I want to talk.

GODFREY *appears embarrassed.*

GODFREY. I'm terribly sorry but we—we can't talk here.

IRENE *is now seated on his bed.*

IRENE (*pettishly*). Don't you think it's rather indecent of you to order me out after you kissed me?

GODFREY. After I kissed you—did you say?

IRENE (*blithely*). It's funny. This morning you were sitting on my bed and now I'm sitting on yours.

GODFREY. We'll overlook that startling coincidence. (*Pointing to a chair*) will you—er—sit over here?

IRENE. If the bed's not very comfortable to sit on, I'll get you another.

GODFREY *(uneasily)*. We'll have our talk here.

IRENE *(sitting down)*. Now that I'm your sponsor, if you want a new bed you can have it.

GODFREY *(standing; embarrassed)*. The bed's very comfortable, thank you. Much more so than I am at the moment.

IRENE. Any time you're uncomfortable—you just let me know.

GODFREY *(wondering at her)*. Er—thank you. Hasn't anyone ever told you about—certain proprieties?

IRENE. Oh, you use such lovely big words! I like big words. What does it mean?

GODFREY. Well, I'll try to simplify it. Hasn't your mother or anyone ever explained to you that some things are proper and some things are not?

IRENE. No. She hasn't. She rambles on quite a bit, but then she never says anything.

GODFREY. Then—you want me to remain on here as butler—don't you?

IRENE. Oh, of course!

GODFREY. Well, I want to justify your faith in me by being a very good butler—and in time perhaps filling the void created by the death of your late lamented Pomeranian.

IRENE. Oh, I've forgotten all about him. He had fleas anyway. Besides you're different. You use big words and you're much cuter.

GODFREY. May I tell you a story?

IRENE. I'd love it.

GODFREY. Once there was a very sentimental little girl, with a very kind heart. And she helped a man who was very grateful. Then she became a nuisance and undid all the fine work she had done.

IRENE. Is it someone you know?

GODFREY *rising from beside her,* IRENE *rises and follows him to the door.*

GODFREY. Her name is Irene Bullock. And if she were a smart little girl, she would pick out some nice young chap in her own social set and marry him and live happily ever after—and never, never, never enter the butler's room again.

IRENE. You mean I never can come in here again?

GODFREY. Never.

IRENE. But when can we talk?

GODFREY. When I am serving breakfast in the morning, I can say, "Good morning, Miss Irene"—and you can say "Good morning, Godfrey"—but you must never come into my room again.

IRENE *(furiously)*. Oh! You'll be sorry!

GODFREY. I'm only trying to be helpful. *(He gets her out of his room, and closes the door.)*

IRENE *(now out of sight)*. You're being mean. You're being mean! I'll do something—you just wait and you'll be sorry—you'll be sorry!

As GODFREY *listens to her voice, the scene fades out.*

## PART THREE

*A close view in the living room fades in, disclosing* CARLO *seated at the piano in the foreground playing and singing,* ANGELICA *seated in the background.*

CARLO. Otchi tchornia! Otchi tchornia! Otchi tchornia!

*A closeup of* ANGELICA *shows her seated, knitting, and looking toward him, enchanted.*

CARLO *(again seen playing)*. Otchi tchornia! Otchi tchornia!

ANGELICA *(now again seen)*. That's a very pretty tune, Carlo. What's the name of it?

CARLO *(seen in a close-up; explaining)*. Otchi tchornia! Otchi tchornia—Otchi tchornia.

ANGELICA'S VOICE. Oh! That's the name, too. *(In a close-up)* I thought it was just the words. *(Then as we see them both)* I like it because the words are all the same. It makes it so easy to remember. That's probably why the Star Spangled Banner is so confusing. Nobody seems to know the words.

GODFREY *enters carrying a box of roses and a vase, and looks around.*

ANGELICA *(out of sight)*. Except Godfrey. He seems to know everything. *(Seeing him)* Do you know the words, Godfrey?

GODFREY *comes forward carrying flowers and vase as the view moves with him through the room to ANGELICA. We now see CORNELIA and GEORGE seated in the background.*

GODFREY. The words?

ANGELICA *(out of sight)*. Yes, yes. The star Spangled Banner. Nobody seems to know the words. Do you know them, Godfrey?

GODFREY. I suppose I know as many as the average person.

ANGELICA. Oh, I feel ashamed of myself. I should know them all of course, because after all, my ancestors came over on a boat—not the Mayflower, but the boat after that. What did your ancestors come over on, Godfrey?

GODFREY. As far as I know they've always been here.

ANGELICA. They weren't Indians, Godfrey?

GODFREY. One can never be sure of one's ancestors.

ANGELICA. Well, you know, you have rather high cheekbones.

GODFREY. Yes, ma'am—thank you, ma'am— These flowers came— *(As IRENE comes forward, stops, and looks)* for Miss Irene. Where shall I put them?

ANGELICA. You'd better ask her. There she is. Carlo! Did you notice his cheek bones?

GODFREY *(now close to IRENE, the two of them in a close-up)*. These flowers just came for you, Miss. Where shall I put them?

IRENE. What difference does it make where one puts flowers, when one's heart is breaking.

GODFREY. Yes, Miss. Shall I put them on the piano?

IRENE. Life is but an empty bubble.

ANGELICA *(out of sight)*. You don't sound very cheerful *(now seen, mildly disturbed)* for a girl who is giving a tea party.

CORNELIA *and* GEORGE *now appear seated in the foreground playing backgammon,* IRENE *standing in the background.*

IRENE. Why should anyone be cheerful?

CORNELIA. Oh, is Irene giving a tea party?

IRENE *(coldly)*. You're not invited.

CORNELIA. I'll invite myself. *(Gaily to GEORGE)* Let's stick around, George. *(We see GODFREY arranging the roses as though absorbed in his work.)*

GEORGE *(out of sight)*. Sure—why not?

IRENE *(standing by the grill; meaningfully)*. All I have to say is that some people will be sorry some day.

ANGELICA *(out of sight)*. Naturally, everybody will be sorry some day.

CARLO, *who has been playing all the time and continues to play, is seen at the piano.*

CARLO. For what?

IRENE. Some people will know for what—and then—it will be too late.

CARLO *(helplessly, plaintively)*. This conversation is very confusing.

ANGELICA. Now, now, Irene—you mustn't confuse Carlo—(*now out of sight, since we see only* GODFREY *putting roses in the vase*)—he's practicing.

CORNELIA *(laughing suddenly)*. Do you know any good funeral music, Carlo?

IRENE. Shut up!

CORNELIA. Are you acting for anybody in particular? Godfrey might be interested if he would only turn around and look. I remember that pose so well.

*We get a close view of* IRENE *posed by a pillar—tragically.* GODFREY, *studiously ignoring them, continues to arrange the roses in the vase.*

CORNELIA'S VOICE. I learned it in dramatic school. It's number eight, isn't it?

GEORGE *(also out of sight at this point)*. Yeah—that's number eight, all right.

CORNELIA'S VOICE *(as we see* GODFREY *going about his work indifferently)*. Am I spoiling your act, dear?

IRENE *comes to* CORNELIA *and* GEORGE *angrily.*

IRENE. I'll spoil something of yours some day—and it won't be your act. *(She moves angrily away.)*

GODFREY *has the roses in the vase, and the view moves with him across the room as he speaks to* ANGELICA, IRENE *in the background.*

GODFREY. Do you suppose Miss Irene would like sandwiches served in here or shall I create a sort of buffet?

ANGELICA. Where do you want the sandwiches served, Irene?

IRENE *(disconsolately)*. What is food?

ANGELICA (IRENE *now at the doorway,* GODFREY *moving away from* ANGELICA). Something you eat, silly. Do you want the sandwiches served in here or don't you?

GODFREY *approaches her, then passes her, and goes out.*

IRENE. What difference does it make? Some people do just as they like with other people's lives and it doesn't seem to make any difference. (CORNELIA, *out of sight, laughs.*)

ANGELICA *laughs.* IRENE, *at the doorway, looks off, following* GODFREY'S *departure, and the scene dissolves into a close view of the room with men and girls leaning on the piano, and a man and a girl playing. The scene then enlarges to include* ANGELICA *and others seated at a card table in the foreground.*

ANGELICA. What did I call?

GUEST. Five hearts.

ANGELICA. Oh, was it hearts? I meant spades. I can't change, can I. That music has me so confused. Carlo, please.

IRENE *comes to the foreground among the guests.* VAN RUMPEL *approaches and puts his arm about her.*

VAN RUMPEL. Hi yah, Irene. Why the shroud?

IRENE. Listen, Van Rumpel, just because some people have a million dollars doesn't mean that they can put their arms around other people.

VAN RUMPEL *(affecting a mock chill)*. Brrr! Where's the bar?

*We see* CORNELIA *and* GEORGE *seated on the couch as* GODFREY *comes in, serves them sandwiches and leaves them.*

CORNELIA (to VAN RUMPEL; *cattily*). Don't take her seriously, Charlie. She's been having servant problems lately.

GODFREY *comes past* IRENE *carrying the tray.*

IRENE. No, thank you. I'm not hungry. (*She follows him as he goes off.*)

*Men and girls are seen leaning on the piano—talking, laughing,* GODFREY *serving them.* IRENE *approaches him, watching.* GODFREY *presents the tray again.*

IRENE. No, thank you.

GODFREY *comes over to see the bridge players,* IRENE *following him.*
WOMAN PLAYER. Four clubs.
ANGELICA. No—just a minute Godfrey. By—

*At the crowded doorway to the hall, a young man,* TOMMY GRAY, *enters, stops and calls, and looks around.*

TOMMY. Hello, everybody!
PEOPLE. Hello, Tommy!

ANGELICA *looks past* GODFREY *as he leans toward her with his tray.*

ANGELICA. Oh! Tommy Gray! (GODFREY *looks around—startled.*) What's happened to you, Godfrey? Are you ill?

*We see* GODFREY *serving other guests, moving about, as* TOMMY *approaches* ANGELICA.

ANGELICA. Come over here, Tommy, and give Angelica a hug. How's everything in Boston? All the beans and things?
TOMMY (*kissing her hand*). We're rounding them up and putting them in cans as rapidly as possible.
TOMMY (*as* IRENE *is seen standing near the card players*). Hello, Irene, how are you?

IRENE (*morosely*). What does it matter how I am? The—(*out of sight as we see* GODFREY *serving the guests but glancing around at the group at the card table*)—whole thing is only— (IRENE *seen again, being held by the friendly* TOMMY)—a delusion.
TOMMY. What thing?
IRENE. You wouldn't understand. (*And she moves away.*)
TOMMY (*bringing a chair over and sitting down*). How about something to eat?
ANGELICA. Oh, Godfrey! Godfrey! Bring Mr. Gray a sandwich.

GODFREY *brings the tray up behind* TOMMY.

ANGELICA (*annoyed*). Oh, come around here. Mr. Gray's not an acrobat. Whatever has come over you? You're beginning to act like the rest of the family.

ANGELICA *questions* GODFREY *as he leans over with the tray.* TOMMY *looks up, and is startled as he recognizes* GODFREY, *who looks meaningfully at* TOMMY *and leaves.*

TOMMY. Hey! Wait a minute!
ANGELICA. What's the trouble?

TOMMY *without answering, looks around, calls after* GODFREY, *rises and follows him.* TOMMY *stops* GODFREY *in the doorway.*

TOMMY. Godfrey Parke! You old mug.
ANGELICA (*looking after* TOMMY). You know Godfrey?
TOMMY (*standing by* GODFREY). Know him? We went to Harvard together.

*A close-up of* IRENE *shows her staring at them—startled.*

GODFREY'S VOICE. I'm afraid you've confused me with someone

else, sir. I'm Smith. *(Meaningfully)* Remember.

TOMMY. Sure you're Smith—but we did go to college together—

CORNELIA *(seen sitting with* GEORGE; *amused)*. Imagine a butler with a college education.

*A close-up shows* ANGELICA *and the man who sits by her side staring.*

TOMMY'S VOICE. He's not really the butler?

CORNELIA'S voice. And a very good one.

TOMMY *(as* GODFREY *stands by him, looking embarrassed)*. You mean this is not a gag just for my benefit?

GODFREY. Mr. Gray neglected to tell you that when we were in Harvard together—I was his—*(out of sight, as we see* CORNELIA, *amused, starting forward)*—his valet.

CORNELIA. Was he a good servant, Tommy?

*A close-up shows the two men whispering,* TOMMY *amused and puzzled.*

TOMMY. Excellent. *(to* GODFREY) What's the idea?

GODFREY *(bowing)*. I'll tell you later. Mr. Gray never complained.

TOMMY. When? *(Recovering)* No. I had very few complaints about Godfrey's work.

GODFREY *(whispering to him)*. Tomorrow. That's my day off.

CORNELIA *(coming over to them)*. Strange you never gave Mr. Gray as a reference.

GODFREY. Well, I left Mr. Gray under very unusual circumstances.

ANGELICA *(calling from the table; curious)*. What circumstances?

GODFREY. I'd rather Mr. Gray told you about that.

ANGELICA'S VOICE. Well, come here. Don't go away—don't go away. Come here and tell us all about it. *(In a close-up; concerned)* You know, Tommy, Godfrey is a very mysterious person.

*We get a close-up of* IRENE *looking on, smiling.*

ANGELICA'S VOICE. Nobody seems to know anything about him. Don't go away, Godfrey. *(We see the two men and* CORNELIA *standing.)*

TOMMY. No, don't go away, Godfrey. You see, I—I didn't want to say anything about this, but you see Godfrey had been working for us as a butler and—what not—and things had been going along very well, when—*(out of sight, as we see* IRENE *watching)*—when all of a sudden—it happened. *(As we see the group moving along)* Just like that. You're sure you want me to tell all this, Godfrey? Well, you see, as I said, he'd been working—*(out of sight as we see* ANGELICA *and the man listening eagerly)*—for us for some time when one day, he came to—*(we see* IRENE *listening)*—me and said—*(stalling)* Mr. Gray he said—*(TOMMY is now seen in the group that watches him)*—I trust my work has always been satisfactory, he said. I said—*(out of sight, as we see* ANGELICA *deeply interested and the man by her side very much amused)*—I said, I've never had more satisfactory—*(IRENE watching)* —work in all my life. *(We see* TOMMY *with* GODFREY *trying to keep his countenance.)*—He said, Thank you, Mr. Gray. He was always a very courteous man.

ANGELICA. Godfrey is still extremely courteous. Especially in the morning.

CORNELIA *comes to them, a light in her eyes.*

TOMMY. It's not much of a story—maybe we'd better skip it.

CORNELIA *(brightly)*. Oh, Tommy,

come on and finish it. You can't stop in the middle.

TOMMY (*at sea, uncomfortably*). Let me see. Where was I?

CORNELIA (*sweetly*). You were telling us how very polite Godfrey was.

ANGELICA. Yes—and that's where I said that Godfrey was still very polite.

GODFREY. Thank you, Mrs. Bullock. It's a pleasure to have you say so publicly.

ANGELICA (*contentedly*). That's my nature, Godfrey. I'll never say anything behind your back that I won't say in public.

TOMMY. That's what I admire about you, Angelica, very much. . . . Well, anyhow, Godfrey came up to me and said, "I trust my work has been satisfactory." That was about the gist of it, wasn't it, Godfrey?

GODFREY. Those may not have been my exact words, but that was about the gist of it.

CORNELIA (*impatiently, as some men in the background laugh*). All right. We'll settle for that. You said he was very satisfactory and he said "thank you" and then what?

TOMMY. Naturally I had to take an attitude.

ANGELICA. You don't make sense. What kind of an attitude?

TOMMY'S VOICE (*as we see* IRENE *watching eagerly*). It was the only kind I could take toward a faithful servant—(*We see him talking very seriously.*)—but Godfrey decided in favor of his wife and five children.

*A close-up shows* IRENE *terribly startled.*

ANGELICA'S VOICE. Five children?

*A close-view shows* GODFREY *startled, and looking in the direction of* IRENE.

ANGELICA'S VOICE. What?

IRENE *starts to go toward them.*

TOMMY. Five.

ANGELICA. My—my! Was his wife an Indian woman?

TOMMY. I believe she was rather dark. We used to take her on hunting trips to stalk the game.

IRENE *goes to* GODFREY—*horrified.*

IRENE. Why Godfrey! Why didn't you tell me you had five children?

ANGELICA. Well, why shouldn't Godfrey have five children? If a woman in Canada can have five children, why can't Godfrey? (*Amid laughter from the guests*) So, you see!

GODFREY (*to* IRENE). I owe the creation of my family to Mr. Gray's generosity.

IRENE. Well, if other people can have five children, so can other people.

ANGELICA. Of course they can, but I think two are plenty. And strangely enough—Bullock agrees with me.

IRENE (*having made up her mind; she is shocked and intense*). Listen, everybody. I want to make an announcement. I want to announce something.

GEORGE. Well, what are you going to announce?

IRENE. I want to announce my engagement. I'm going to be married.

GUESTS. Married? To whom? You're going to be married? Married? etc. etc.

IRENE. You'll find out soon enough.

GIRL. Not to Charlie Van Rumpel?

IRENE. Yes. Charlie Van Rumpel. Where is he?

GUESTS. No? Where's Charlie? With all that money! Ooooh!

GIRL. He's at the bar, Let's go and get him.

IRENE. I'm not marrying for money.

*We see* CHARLIE *and others drinking as two men come to him.*

CHARLIE *(to the men).* I've had my arms around her plenty of times before, but this is the first time I ever felt that chill September breeze.

VOICES. Paging Van Rumpel! Paging Van Rumpel!

MAN. Congratulations, old boy.

CHARLIE. Congratulations about what?

MAN. Your engagement, you slug.

CHARLIE. What engagement?

MAN. Why, you're engaged to Irene, aren't you?

CHARLIE. Am I?

MEN. Aw, come on—don't play gaga! Come on!

*Now* TOMMY *is standing by the card table, men and girls crowding around* IRENE *and* CHARLIE, IRENE *clinging to him. He is dazed, puzzled.*

CHARLIE. I hear we're engaged.

IRENE. You said it.

CHARLIE. When did it happen?

IRENE. Just now.

ANGELICA *(to* TOMMY*).* What's all the excitement about? What did she say?

TOMMY. I think she's gone and got herself engaged.

ANGELICA *(calmly).* Oh—has she—again? It must be that nice boy in the brown suit. Let's congratulate them.

ANGELICA *goes over to a slender boy.*

ANGELICA. This is thrilling. You're a lucky boy. *(The boy looks at her, speechless.)*

*In a group we see one man mightily amused as the scatter-brained* ANGELICA *is talking to another man.*

MAN. I know I am—I'm not Van Rumpel.

ANGELICA. You're not? Which one is he?

MAN. There he is.

ANGELICA. You'll forgive me, I hope.

IRENE *and* CHARLIE *are now being congratulated by a crowd as* ANGELICA *comes to them.*

ANGELICA. You're Van Rumpel, aren't you?

CHARLIE. Oh, yes—yes.

ANGELICA. Well, you'll take good care of her, won't you?

CHARLIE. I imagine so. My mind's a little cloudy, Irene. I don't even remember proposing.

IRENE. You're always proposing.

CHARLIE. Which one did you take me up on?

IRENE. All of them *(The crowd laughs uproariously.)*

*Now* CORNELIA *faces* IRENE *and* CHARLIE, *the others listening.*

CORNELIA. How do you suppose Godfrey will feel about your engagement?

IRENE. What's Godfrey got to do with it?

CORNELIA. I wonder.

IRENE *(angrily).* You mind your own business.

*We see* GODFREY *carrying a tray with glasses into the room as the crowd moves to the next room. A man takes the tray from him and carries it to the crowd as* GEORGE *speaks to* GODFREY.

GEORGE. All right, Godfrey, let's have those. Come on, everybody. All aboard that's going aboard.

CORNELIA. Aren't you going to congratulate Irene, Godfrey? She just got herself engaged.

GODFREY. I'd be very happy to.

ANGELICA. Godfrey!

GODFREY *passes* CORNELIA, *and the moving scene brings him through the crowd to* IRENE.

ANGELICA'S VOICE. Congratulate Irene!

GODFREY *(solemnly)*. May I congratulate you, Miss Irene. I wish you all the happiness in the world.

IRENE *goes through the hall crying, runs up the stairs, and sits down.*

ANGELICA'S VOICE *(coming over)*. Just let her alone. She'll be all right in a minute.

*Then* CHARLIE *and* ANGELICA *appear, talking in the crowd.*

CHARLIE. Is she mad at me?

ANGELICA. She's not mad at anyone. Don't you know women always cry at their own engagements and other people's weddings.

CHARLIE. Why?

ANGELICA *(going out)*. I don't know why—but they just do.

IRENE *is seated on the stairs as* ANGELICA *comes to her.* BULLOCK *enters a moment later.*

ANGELICA. Irene is so peculiar. She always shouts when she wins and cries when she's happy. Oh, Alexander! You missed all the excitement.

BULLOCK. What's going on?

ANGELICA. Let me think. I knew what it was I wanted to tell you but it slipped my mind.

BULLOCK. What's the matter with Irene?

ANGELICA. Oh yes. That's it. Irene has got herself engaged.

BULLOCK. To whom?

ANGELICA. I don't know—Van something. I think it's that boy with his arm around that girl in pink. He's got lots of money.

BULLOCK. He'll need it.

*We see* TOMMY *and* GODFREY *talking in the crowd,* CORNELIA *watching them closely.*

TOMMY. Well, Godfrey, let's you and I have a good cry. How about lunch at my hotel tomorrow?

GODFREY. I guess so. *(Carefully, as he is being observed)* Would you prefer a soda or giner ale?

TOMMY. Both. Twelve o'clock?

GODFREY. Very good, sir.

BULLOCK *and his wife are talking in the hall as* GODFREY *comes through and goes out and* IRENE, *seen through the balustrade on the stairs, is crying.*

BULLOCK. Well, if you can just make up your mind just who she is going to marry, I'd like to meet the guy.

ANGELICA. I don't know, Alexander. It's one of those boys in there. Come along.

BULLOCK. All right.

*The scene fades out.*

## PART FOUR

*A close view in the breakfast room fades in, disclosing* BULLOCK *seated at the table as* GODFREY *enters.*

GODFREY. You're not eating well this morning, sir.

BULLOCK. You notice everything.

GODFREY. Business troubles, sir?

BULLOCK. What made you ask that?

GODFREY. Well sir, butlers can't help picking up scraps of news, shall we say.

BULLOCK *(eating)*. We shan't say anything about it.

GODFREY. I thought I might be of some help, sir. I dabbled in the market at one time.

BULLOCK *(dryly)*. One dabbler in the family is enough.

GODFREY. Very good, sir. Eggs?

BULLOCK. No, thank you. Godfrey, you seem to be a pretty good sort. Have you noticed anything queer about me lately?

GODFREY. Nothing particularly, sir.

BULLOCK. I sometimes wonder whether my whole family has gone mad or whether it's me.

GODFREY. I know just how you feel, sir. I've felt that way many times since I've been here.

BULLOCK. Then, why do you stay here? I have to—you don't.

GODFREY. It's much more comfortable than living in a packing box on the city dump, sir—Besides—I'm rather proud of my job here.

BULLOCK. You're proud of being a butler?

GODFREY. I'm proud of being a good butler, sir. *(Starting to pour coffee)* And I may add, sir—a butler has to be good to hold his job here.

BULLOCK *(puzzled)*. Say—who are you?

GODFREY. I'm just a nobody, sir. More coffee?

*The scene dissolves to a cocktail bar,* TOMMY *seated in the foreground as* GODFREY *approaches.*

TOMMY. Godfrey! here I am. (GODFREY *sees him.*) Turned up at last, eh? I'd begun to think you'd fallen down the kitchen sink.

GODFREY *(shaking hands)*. Sorry I'm late, Tommy. It's hard to make beds when they're full of people. *(He sits down.)*

TOMMY. Waiter! You seem to do everything but put out the cat.

GODFREY. I'd do that, too, only we have no cat.

TOMMY *(as the waiter arrives)*. The same for me. *(Jovially)* What will you have, Jarvis, my man?

GODFREY. Make it a rousing old lemonade.

TOMMY *(facetiously)*. Lemonade? You've sure you can handle it?

GODFREY. Oh yes. I'm the type that can take it or leave it alone. You see, I'm a working man and I have to keep my wits about me.

TOMMY. I'm beginning to wonder if you've got any left at all. Don't avoid the issue. I've been sitting here like a snoopy old maid with her ears flapping in the breeze, waiting to hear the dirt.

GODFREY. What dirt would you like to hear?

TOMMY. Well, when I wander into a Fifth Avenue asylum and see one of the Parke Parkes of Boston serving hors d'houvres, I think I'm entitled to a pardonable curiosity.

GODFREY. Why tell you something that you won't understand? Tommy— you've fallen off so many polo ponies that your brains are scrambled.

TOMMY. But I still want to know why you're buttling when your family is telling everybody that you're in South America doing something about rubber, or sheep or something.

GODFREY. The family has to say something to save its face. You know the Parkes disgrace very easily.

TOMMY. I'd like to see their faces when they find out that you're a butler.

GODFREY. They're not going to find it out.

TOMMY. All right, they're not going to find it out—but come to the point.

GODFREY *(thoughtfully)*. Well, there isn't much of a point. You remember the little incident up in Boston?

TOMMY. You still have that woman on your mind?

GODFREY. No, not any more—but I was pretty bitter at the time, so I gave her everything I had—and just disappeared. You know, the Parkes were never educated to face life. We've been puppets for ten generations.

TOMMY. And?

GODFREY. Tommy, it's surprising how fast you can go down hill when you begin to feel sorry for yourself. And boy—did I feel sorry for myself! So I went down to the East River one night, thinking I'd just—slide in and get it over with. I met some fellows living there—on the city dump. They were people who were fighting it out and not complaining. I never got as far as the river.

*A close-up at the bar shows* CORNELIA *and* GEORGE *seated. She looks off and turns to* GEORGE.

CORNELIA. Will you do me a big favor?

GEORGE. Who do you want killed?

CORNELIA. I'll do my own killing. Just go around the corner and telephone this place and ask for Tommy Gray. When you get him on the wire, keep him there.

GEORGE *(rising)*. What's this all about?

CORNELIA. Don't ask too many questions.

GEORGE. Okay. *(He goes out.)*

*A close-up at the table shows* TOMMY *and* GODFREY *seated—smoking.*

TOMMY. And so, out of the ruins of Godfrey Parke a new edifice has sprung up in the form of Godfrey Smith.

GODFREY. And I may add—the edifice is going to keep on springing.

TOMMY. You intend to remain a butler?

GODFREY. No. I have some other ideas in mind, but you wouldn't understand those, either, so we won't go into that.

TOMMY. Will you do me a favor?

GODFREY. Maybe.

TOMMY. I have a friend in town—a very eminent brain specialist—I'd like him to examine you.

GODFREY. I'll submit to an examination—if you will also.

TOMMY *(shaking hands)*. That's a bet.

*A waiter approaches the table.*

WAITER. Are you Mr. Gray?

TOMMY. Yes.

WAITER. You're wanted on the phone.

TOMMY. The phone—what the— Back in a minute, Godfrey.

TOMMY *rises from the table, leaving* GODFREY *seated, and goes down the stairs.* CORNELIA *comes up the stairs and sits down beside* GODFREY.

CORNELIA. Well, the mystery is solved.

GODFREY. Mystery?

CORNELIA. Yes. Now I know what a butler does on his day off. When you worked for Mr. Gray, were the two of you always so chummy?

GODFREY. You see—I worked for Mr. Gray a long time and—we got to be—er—

CORNELIA. That was under the name of Smith, wasn't it? Or—did I hear him mention the name of Parke?

GODFREY. He may have said that— we used to take long walks in the park. It was a sort of a custom.

CORNELIA. Oh, I see. Well, if you can be so chummy with the Grays, why can't you be chummy with the Bullocks?

GODFREY. I try to keep my place.

CORNELIA. Why? You're very attractive, you know.

GODFREY. As a butler?

CORNELIA. No—as a Smith. You're a rotten butler.

GODFREY. Sorry.

CORNELIA (*smiling*). Are we going to be friends?

GODFREY. I feel that on my day off, I should have the privilege of choosing my friends.

CORNELIA. You can't go on like this forever. You really like me and you're afraid to admit it.

GODFREY. Do you want me to tell you what I really think of you?

CORNELIA. Please do.

GODFREY. As Smith or—as a butler?

CORNELIA. Choose your own weapons.

GODFREY. You won't hold it against me?

CORNELIA. It's your day off.

GODFREY. Very well—You fall into the unfortunate category I would call the Park Avenue brat—a spoiled child who has grown up in ease and luxury, who always had her own way and whose misdirected energies are so childish that they hardly deserve the comment even of a butler—on his off Thursday.

*They rise as* TOMMY *comes from the stairs.*

CORNELIA (*rising; furious*). Thank you for a very lovely portrait.

TOMMY. Hey! Cornelia—what are you doing here?

CORNELIA. Godfrey and I were discussing tomorrow's menu. (*She starts to leave.*)

TOMMY. Don't run away.

CORNELIA. I'm in an awfully big hurry. Good-bye. I'll see you down by the ashpile. (*She leaves them.*)

TOMMY. What did she mean by that?

GODFREY. That's a little joke we have between us.

TOMMY. Oh, I see—a joking butler. What's the matter with that stuff—did it turn your stomach.

GODFREY. No. I think I'll switch. I'm more in the mood.

TOMMY. Now we're getting somewhere. Waiter! Another one of those.

*The scene dissolves to the kitchen, with* MOLLY *seated—darning—as footsteps are heard.* IRENE *enters, carrying a vase of flowers.*

IRENE (*coming forward*). He's not back yet, is he?

MOLLY. Not yet.

IRENE. Would you mind putting these flowers in his room? I can't go in there any more.

MOLLY. I can't either.

IRENE. You won't tell him they're from me, will you?

MOLLY. If you don't want me to.

IRENE. I don't want him to know. It's his—do you always sew his buttons on?

MOLLY. Sometimes.

IRENE. I'd like to sew his buttons on sometimes when they come off. I wouldn't mind at all.

MOLLY. He doesn't lose very many.

IRENE. He's very tidy, isn't he?

MOLLY. Yes. He's very tidy.

IRENE *sits down by* MOLLY.

IRENE. What does he do on his day off?

MOLLY. He never tells me.

IRENE. Oh, he's probably sitting somewhere with some woman on his lap. He's the meanest man I know.

MOLLY (*feelingly*). I think he's very mean.

IRENE. I suppose he's sitting somewhere with somebody on his lap that doesn't care for him at all. As far as I know maybe his children are there too, calling him—calling him.

*We see* MOLLY *with* IRENE, *crying.*

IRENE Oh, I can't bear it.

MOLLY (*going into the pantry*). Please don't.

*In the pantry:* MOLLY *appears first, she is crying.* IRENE *follows her—crying. A shadow appears at the door. There is a sound of whistling. Then* GODFREY *enters whistling. He is drunk and cheerful.*

IRENE. You too? Oh, Molly, I know exactly how you feel.

GODFREY. Good evening. How about a quartette?

*The girls are crying. When they see him,* MOLLY *goes out.* GODFREY *sings and dances—as* IRENE *also runs out. The scene moves with him as he goes across to his door.*

GODFREY (*singing blithely*). Ladies! "For tomorrow may bring sorrow So tonight let us be gay!"

*We see* ANGELICA *in the living room, settled by the fireplace and sewing as* CARLO *is reading aloud to her.*

CARLO (*reading*).
" 'Courage!' he said,
And pointed toward the land,
'This mounting wave will roll us shoreward soon.'
And in the afternoon they came unto a land
In which it seemed always afternoon."

IRENE *enters and sits down crying.*

ANGELICA. Carlo!

CARLO (*continuing to read*).
"All round the coast the languid air did swoon—"

ANGELICA. What's the matter, darling?

IRENE. Nothing.

ANGELICA. She's been out in the kitchen eating onions again.

CARLO. I like onions. They make me sleep.

ANGELICA. Irene loves onions. When she was a little girl she was always stealing onions from the icebox. Do you know, sometimes I wonder if my children are all there.

CARLO (*resuming his reading*):
"And like a downward smoke,
The slender stream
Along the cliff to fall and pause and fall did seem."

IRENE *rises and goes out, and the scene dissolves to* GODFREY'S *room. We see him (in a close-up) at the mirror fixing his tie and whistling. The scene expands as he goes to the door—drunk—and opens it. The view follows him through the next room, where he puts things on a large tray. At this point* CORNELIA *appears at the stairs in the background; we see her look in his direction and back up the stairs. Then we see her watching in the pantry—partly hidden—as* GODFREY, *fixing a cocktail tray, carries it whistling.*

GODFREY. Good evening. (*He opens the door and goes out.*)

*A close view of a corner of a room shows* GODFREY *entering with a large tray, whistling. He removes glasses as* CORNELIA *enters behind him.*

CORNELIA (*rudely*). I thought I told you to send that gray satin evening dress to the cleaners?

GODFREY. Gray satin?

CORNELIA. Why can't you do as you're told?

GODFREY. 'S a pleasure. (*He goes out. She starts to the door.*)

*The drawing room:* ANGELICA *is seated with a paper as* GODFREY *enters.* CARLO *is on the couch, with a paper over his face.*

ANGELICA. It seems to me that every time you pick up a paper, somebody is being murdered or something.

Imagine a man drowning his wife in the bathtub?

CARLO. Maybe it's the only way he could get her to take a bath.

ANGELICA (*as* GODFREY *moves forward; dotingly*). If anyone ever drowned my "booful" in the bath tub, his mama would be very, very cross, yes she would.

GODFREY *turns on the light at the table.*

GODFREY. Will there be anything else, Madam?

ANGELICA. Well, I haven't asked for anything, so I don't see how I could want anything else.

GODFREY. I beg your pardon. I thought you were Miss Cornelia.

ANGELICA. You thought *I* was Cornelia?

GODFREY. I hope you'll forgive me, madam, but you seem to be looking younger every day, if I may say so.

ANGELICA Well—you certainly may. Thanks very much, Godfrey.

*A close view of the side of a room shows* CORNELIA *at the door looking out. Then the view moves with her over to* GODFREY'S *door as footsteps are heard.* CORNELIA, *entering his room, closes the door, hurriedly crosses the room and hides something under the mattress on the bed. Then she runs back to the door and listens as more footsteps are heard.*

*Next* CORNELIA *appears in the hall, stops in the doorway, and sees* GODFREY *descend the main staircase carrying her gown and going out with it, whistling.*

*In the living room where* ANGELICA *is seated in the foreground, we now see* CORNELIA *entering and addressing her mother.*

CORNELIA. Did you send Godfrey upstairs for anything?

ANGELICA. Did I? No, I'm quite sure I didn't. Why?

CORNELIA. Oh—I just wondered.

*The scene dissolves to the dining room with the family seated at the table as* GODFREY *enters—serving.*

*A close view at the table shows* GODFREY *serving* ANGELICA, IRENE *watching him. Then the view moves around the table to* CORNELIA *as* GODFREY *offers something to* IRENE, *then moves to* CORNELIA.

CORNELIA (*intently*). I was in the Sherry Bar today. That place is getting all run down. They're catering to a very low class of people.

ANGELICA. Then you shouldn't go in there, my dear. Irene, what's the matter? You're not eating.

CORNELIA *is amused as* IRENE *rises, jealous, as* GODFREY *serves the others.*

IRENE. Nobody cares if I starve myself to death.

BULLOCK (*out of sight*). What's the matter with you, Irene?

IRENE. I don't mind dying if other people don't.

CORNELIA. She's in love. Haven't you heard?

ANGELICA. It's probably her engagement. You know, several of my girl friends acted just like that. It has something to do with your chemistry.

CARLO. Maybe her stomach is upset.

IRENE (*abruptly*). Nobody asked you.

*There is a crash and* GODFREY *goes behind a screen—all are startled at the crash of broken dishes. He looks around the screen.*

BULLOCK. There go the profits.

GODFREY (*going out*). I beg your pardon.

ANGELICA *(puzzled)*. I don't know what's the matter with Godfrey. He's been so peculiar lately. But he did pay me a nice compliment.

IRENE. He's always paying other people compliments.

ANGELICA. Darling—why don't you eat something? Look at Carlo.

*We see* CARLO *eating ravenously.*

ANGELICA *(out of sight)*. He had two helpings of everything.

BULLOCK. Let her alone. Carlo is eating enough for both of them.

ANGELICA'S VOICE *(admonishing)*. Now, Alexander.

BULLOCK. He ought to be strong enough pretty soon to give that concert.

ANGELICA *(as* IRENE *looks sulky)*. You can't rush genius.

BULLOCK. He could give a bang-up concert right now with a knife and fork.

CARLO *leaves the table and goes out.*

ANGELICA *(rising angrily)*. Why do you always pick on Carlo? Why don't you pick on someone else for a change? *(She follows* CARLO.*)*

ANGELICA *is going after* CARLO *and* CORNELIA *stops her mother.*

CORNELIA. Wait a minute, Mother. Come here, Dad. Something terrible has happened.

BULLOCK *(rising)*. What is it—what's happened?

ANGELICA. You frighten me. You're as white as a sheet.

CORNELIA *(cautiously)*. Let's go into the living room where we won't be overheard. *(They start out.)*

*The living room:* CARLO *is seen seated when the others come in.*

ANGELICA. Cornelia, what has come over you? What is it? Aren't you feeling well? Come, sit down here. Let me get you an aspirin or something.

CORNELIA. I'm all right.

BULLOCK. What is it—what's troubling you?

CORNELIA. You remember the pearl necklace I got for my birthday last year?

ANGELICA. Why, yes!

BULLOCK. What about it?

CORNELIA. It's disappeared.

CARLO. Maybe somebody stole it.

BULLOCK. Will you fill your gob full of chicken and keep out of this discussion?

CARLO. I'm only trying to help.

BULLOCK. We don't need your help. *(to* CORNELIA) When did you find out about this?

CORNELIA. I put it on my dressing table this afternoon. I went upstairs just now and it was gone.

ANGELICA. My! My! And it cost such a lot of money!

BULLOCK. I'll say it did.

ANGELICA. Well, what are we going to do?

BULLOCK. I'll go call the police.

CORNELIA. Never mind, Dad. I've already called them.

ANGELICA. Oh!

*The scene dissolves to a close view of a* DETECTIVE, *his hat on his head, standing with* CORNELIA *as the scene expands to include the others in the room.*

DETECTIVE. Uh-huh— Well, what I want to know is—when did you miss the pearls?

CORNELIA. During dinner I went to my room and they were gone.

IRENE *(anxiously)*. She probably lost them. She's always leaving them around.

DETECTIVE. Nobody asked you anything, lady.

ANGELICA. If you're going to be

rude to my daughter, you might at least take off your hat.

DETECTIVE. When we're on criminal cases, lady, we keep both hands free.

*Now we see the two* DETECTIVES *and the family.* CARLO *enters, eating, and one of the officers looks in his direction.*

ANGELICA. Do you mean to imply that I'm a criminal?

DETECTIVE. All I know is that it's an inside job.

DETECTIVE *(to* BULLOCK*).* Who's that?

IRENE. It's mother's protégé.

DETECTIVE. No wise cracks. Is that your son?

BULLOCK *(sitting down).* That? Say, listen. I've made a lot of mistakes in my life, but I'll be hanged if I'll plead guilty to that.

CARLO, *in a close-up, looks at them uncomprehendingly.*

ANGELICA *(out of sight).* Stop picking on Carlo.

MOLLY *brings in the tray to the family.*

BULLOCK. He wouldn't have time to steal anything. He's always too busy eating.

DETECTIVE. Who are You?

MOLLY *(pertly).* Guess.

ANGELICA. Where's Godfrey?

MOLLY. He isn't feeling very well. *(to the* DETECTIVE*)* Who are you staring at?

*The* DETECTIVE *follows* MOLLY *and stops her. The* SECOND OFFICER *joins them.*

DETECTIVE. Just a minute, sister.

MOLLY. If I thought that were true, I'd disown my parents.

DETECTIVE. So you've got a passion for jewelry, huh?

MOLLY. Yes—and I've got a passion for socking cops.

DETECTIVE. Where are they?

MOLLY. Most of them in the cemetery.

DETECTIVE. Where's the necklace?

MOLLY. Maybe I swallowed it.

ANGELICA *(coming over).* You mustn't accuse Molly. She's been with us a long time.

MOLLY. That, in itself, is some recommendation.

ANGELICA. Thank you, Molly.

MOLLY. You're welcome, If you don't mind, flat-foot, I'll turn down the beds. *(She goes out.)*

DETECTIVE. Who is this Godfrey?

IRENE. He's the best butler we ever had.

CORNELIA. Oh, I'm sure Godfrey didn't take them—although we don't know much about him.

IRENE. Godfrey wouldn't touch those old pearls of yours with a fork.

SECOND DETECTIVE *(to* CORNELIA*).* Just a minute. What do you mean you don't know much about him?

CORNELIA *(blandly).* You see, we didn't get him from an employment agency. My sister found him on a city dump.

DETECTIVE. Oh, I see.

IRENE *(furiously).* Are you accusing Godfrey?

CORNELIA. I'm not accusing anyone. I want my necklace.

ANGELICA. It's silly to think of Godfrey wearing a pearl necklace.

DETECTIVE. Where is this butler?

CORNELIA. He's probably in his room.

DETECTIVE. Where's that?

CORNELIA. Right this way.

CORNELIA *leads the officers out,* BULLOCK *following them.*

IRENE *(running after them).* Oh!

*In the pantry:* CORNELIA *comes on, followed by* OFFICERS *and others.* IRENE *enters at another door and runs to* GODFREY'S *room. She pounds on the door.*

CORNELIA. That's his room over there.

IRENE. Godfrey! Hide 'em if you've got 'em, Godfrey! Hide 'em if you've got 'em! Godfrey!

DETECTIVE (*approaching*). Hey, what kinda joint is this?

IRENE. Look out, Godfrey! Here they come! (*A* DETECTIVE *pushes her back and opens the door.*)

*The bedroom:* GODFREY *is seen asleep on the bed as they open the door and turn on the light.*

GODFREY. Come in. (*They come forward.*)

*One of the* DETECTIVES *bends over* GODFREY.

DETECTIVE. Where are they?

GODFREY. Where?

DETECTIVE. That's what I said—where?

GODFREY (*sings*). "Where oh where has my little dog gone?"

DETECTIVE. Come on—snap out of it! (*The* SECOND OFFICER *comes over, and they pull at* GODFREY *in the bed.*)

CORNELIA. I suppose you notice he's been drinking?

IRENE. He has not been drinking.

BULLOCK. I don't blame him if he has. This family has probably gotten to him, too.

GODFREY *is now sitting up. The officer standing near him, searches.*

DETECTIVE. Do you mind if we search your room, Godfrey?

GODFREY. Is somebody lost?

DETECTIVE. There seems to be a pearl necklace missing. Do you know anything about it?

GODFREY (*rising and helping them search*). We must look for it. That's too bad.

CORNELIA. It's too bad for you.

BULLOCK. I wouldn't be too cocksure of everything. This is a serious matter.

CORNELIA (*out of sight*). Well, the pearls couldn't just get up and walk away.

GODFREY *goes to the dresser and searches through the drawers. He throws the clothing on the floor. A close-up of* IRENE *shows her looking at the scene, indignant.*

IRENE. She probably threw them out of a taxi like she did last summer.

GODFREY *staggers a bit, the detective searching the dresser, the family watching.*

GODFREY. Listen. Look under the rug. Maybe that's where I put it.

DETECTIVE. We'll do the searching, Godfrey, old boy.

GODFREY (*looking at the shirt he is holding*). 'S a pleasure.

ANGELICA. It's all very silly. I can understand a woman stealing pearls, but what would Godfrey do with them?

CORNELIA. Look under the mattress.

GODFREY. Yes—there's a dandy place.

*We see a close-up of* CORNELIA *looking on and sneering. Now the group is watching as the* DETECTIVES *tear the bed to pieces.* GODFREY, *in the background, is looking in a vase of flowers. The bed clothes are being thrown about. The* DETECTIVE *turns down the mattress. And now we see* CORNELIA *startled as she hears:*

DETECTIVE (*out of sight*). Well, they're not here.

CORNELIA. But they must be there.

*She steps up to the* DETECTIVE, *while* GODFREY, *now seated, watches her ironically.*

DETECTIVE. Just a minute, lady. What makes you so sure they ought to be under the mattress?

CORNELIA. Why, I—I read that's where people put things when they steal them.

BULLOCK *is frowning—angry. He moves forward.*

DETECTIVE'S VOICE. Oh, yeah?

BULLOCK *approaches* CORNELIA *and the* DETECTIVE.

BULLOCK. Say, what are you up to? I'd like to talk to you boys outside, for just a minute, if you don't mind. *(He takes the* DETECTIVES *out with him.)*

*A close view at the open door shows* ANGELICA *and* IRENE *dazed as* BULLOCK *and the two* DETECTIVES *leave the room.*

BULLOCK *(looking back).* I'm terribly sorry, Godfrey.

*A close-up shows* GODFREY *seated, a rose in his hand.*

IRENE *(out of sight).* I told you so.

*A close-up of* CORNELIA *shows her sullen and angry.*

ANGELICA'S VOICE. We're all terribly sorry, Godfrey. Come, Cornelia.

CORNELIA, *sullen—angry—starts to leave. She looks back as she starts to close the door, and* IRENE *taunts her as they leave.*

IRENE. Yah! Yah! Yah!

*A close-up in the room shows* GODFREY *seated—rose in hand—looking off. He tosses the rose aside.*

*In the hall we see* BULLOCK *coming forward with the two men.* ANGELICA *runs past.* CORNELIA *enters and lis-*tens, IRENE *following her, smiling—triumphant.*

BULLOCK. I'm terribly sorry, boys. I want to apologize for my family. They're all slightly hysterical.

DETECTIVE. Yeah. We sorta got an idea of what you're up against.

BULLOCK. I'd like to let the whole matter drop. She's probably mislaid her necklace. As a matter of fact, I'm not certain she ever had one.

DETECTIVE. There's something phoney about the whole thing.

BULLOCK. It's all a mistake. If you don't mind, I'd like to send a little check around tomorrow for the pension fund.

DETECTIVE. Okay, Mr. Bullock. Thanks very much.

BULLOCK *(shaking hands).* Good night.

DETECTIVE. Good night. The whole thing's forgotten.

BULLOCK *(shaking hands).* Good night, boys. *(They go out.)*

BULLOCK *turns and faces* CORNELIA *furiously.*

BULLOCK. Now, just what have you got to say for yourself?

CORNELIA. Aren't they going to do anything about it?

BULLOCK. No! And it's probably a good thing for you that they're not. And there's something else I want to tell you—if you don't find your necklace, the joke's on you—because it's not insured. *(He goes out.)*

IRENE *(gloating).* Cornelia lost her pearls and I've got mine. Cornelia lost her pearls and I've got mine! Cornelia lost her pearls and I've got mine!

*The scene fades out.*

## PART FIVE

*The city dump fades in, disclosing men about—washing, working, searching while trucks are dumping loads on the pile.*

*While the noise of trucks is heard, we see some buildings,* TOMMY GRAY *getting out of a car and coming forward. He is followed by* GODFREY.

GODFREY. Here we are, Tommy— the village of forgotten men.

GODFREY *and* TOMMY *walk down the path on the dump as men watch them passing.*

GODFREY. How do you like it?

TOMMY. I don't know but what I prefer Newport.

GODFREY. It's a matter of choice. Unfortunately, these men have no choice. Come along.

TOMMY. I still prefer Newport. What is that delightful aroma?

GODFREY. That's old man river. You get used to it after awhile. *(They disappear near the bottom of the path.)*

*A close view of the foot of the dump shows them in the foreground. A dump truck is unloading above them. They stop by the shack* GODFREY *had lived in.*

TOMMY. You mean to say that people really live in this place?

GODFREY. Well, they go through the motions. Tommy, observe yon shack on your left. That was the birthplace of the celebrated butler, Godfrey Smith.

TOMMY. And where are the ashes of Godfrey Parke?

GODFREY. Scattered to the winds!

MIKE *appears and shakes hands with* GODFREY.

MIKE. Hello, Duke! Well, well!

GODFREY. How are you, Mike?

MIKE. How's tricks?

GODFREY. Meet Mr. Gray, Mr. Flaherty.

MIKE. How are you, Mr. Gray, Pardon my wet paw. I was just washing out my lingerie.

TOMMY. That's okay.

MIKE. Hey, Bob, look who's here.

*A close-up reveals a man watering a plant in a tin can.*

GODFREY *(out of sight)*. Hello, Bob!

BOB *(looking around, smiling as he starts forward)*. Well, bust my G string.

BOB *comes over and shakes hands with* GODFREY.

MIKE *(moving away)*. Say, thanks for the beans, Duke. They got here just in time.

BOB. If it ain't old Duke himself. The beans was marvelous. Thanks. We ate everything but the cans.

GODFREY. Don't thank me. Thank Mr. Gray. He's got a corner on the bean market.

*We see* MIKE *hanging things on a line as he talks in their direction.*

MIKE. Say, is that the same corner prosperity's just around?

*We see at the shack the four men standing, talking and laughing. Another man approaches; he carries a bundle of wood under his arm.*

TOMMY. No. That's another one.

GODFREY. Hello, Arthur.

BELLINGER *(shaking hands with* GODFREY*)*. Hello, Duke.

GODFREY. Meet Mr. Gray—Mr. Bellinger.

BELLINGER. You look as though you had a job, too. What is this, an epidemic?

A MAN *(out of sight, calling)*. Hey, Mike! Let's get going.

MIKE. Well, Duke, we've got to run along. This is moving day.

BELLINGER. We've got to help some of the boys move their shacks. The dump trucks are crowding in on us a little. We ought to be in the river by early spring. (MIKE *and he leave the group*.)

BOB. Cheer up. We might be able to float by that time.

*We see a long view of "shacktown" as the men leave* TOMMY *and* GODFREY.

BOB *(also leaving)*. See you again, Duke.

GODFREY. Right.

*In a close-up of the shack,* GODFREY *looks at* TOMMY.

GODFREY. That little fellow with the bundle of wood under his arm is Bellinger of the Second National. When his bank failed he gave up everything he had so that his depositors wouldn't suffer.

TOMMY. Not really.

GODFREY. Really. You see, Tommy, there are two kinds of people. Those who fight the idea of being pushed into the river—and the other kind.

TOMMY. Well, after all, things have always been this way for some people. These men are not your responsibility.

GODFREY. There are different ways of having fun.

TOMMY. You have a peculiar sense of humor.

GODFREY. Over here we have some very fashionable apartment houses— over there is a very swanky night club, while down here men starve for want of a job. How does that strike your sense of humor?

TOMMY. What is all this leading to?

GODFREY. Tommy, there's a very peculiar mental process called thinking. You wouldn't know much about that, but when I was living here I did a lot of it. One thing I discovered was that the only difference between a derelict and a man was a job. Sit down

over here and rest your weary bones. I'll tell you what I wanted to talk to you about.

*The two men sit down.*

TOMMY. I'll listen, but I still think you belong in a psychopathic ward.

GODFREY. Maybe you're right, but let me tell you my plan, and listen with both ears. I have an idea—

*The scene fades out; then a close view of a magazine cover—*GOTHAM GOSSIP *50 cents fades in, as music is heard. The cover is turned, disclosing a picture of* IRENE *and a paragraph. As the paragraph is seen closer, we read:*

PARK AVENUE CHATTER
by Hatton Mann

THE MISSES BULLOCK *have returned from a long sojourn in Europe where the younger daughter,* IRENE, *(so it is rumored) was sent to forget her latest broken engagement. If Park Avenue knew the name of her beloved, would everybody be leffing. Cupid strikes in strange places, or words to that effect . . . and heigh-ho . . ."*

*This dissolves to a close view of the living room, with* ANGELICA, CORNELIA *and* CARLO *seated;* CORNELIA *playing with the dog.*

CARLO. Did you and Irene have a good time while you were in Europe?

CORNELIA. As good a time as anyone could have with Irene.

ANGELICA. You should be more civil to Carlo.

CORNELIA. Why?

CARLO. Oh, I don't mind. As the French say, "Cherchez la femme."

ANGELICA *(beaming)*. That will hold you. Carlo always has a clever answer for everything.

IRENE *enters, and next we see her seated with* ANGELICA, CARLO *standing near them.*

ANGELICA. Darling, won't you have some coffee?

IRENE. No, thank you.

CARLO. She didn't eat any dinner, either.

IRENE. *You* had plenty.

CARLO. I can't say anything.

IRENE. You never do.

ANGELICA. Oh darling, what's come over you? We spend good money sending you abroad to forget an engagement and you come back worse off than when you left.

CARLO *(out of sight)*. Her liver is probably upset.

ANGELICA. You'd better take a liver pill then.

IRENE. I don't want a liver pill.

ANGELICA. You mustn't get so upset about a broken engagement. You've broken many before and you've never been this way.

*We see* CORNELIA *seated before the fireplace, amused. She rises.*

CORNELIA. It's not her broken engagement. She's upset because Godfrey didn't fall down in a faint when we got in today.

ANGELICA. Why should Godfrey fall down in a faint?

CORNELIA *sits down and looks at the magazine.*

CORNELIA. He didn't make enough of a fuss over Irene to suit her.

ANGELICA. But Godfrey's not the fussing kind. Shh!

GODFREY *enters.*

ANGELICA. Oh Godfrey, I was just telling my daughters that you missed them both very much while they were away.

GODFREY. Oh, I did, very much indeed.

CORNELIA. We missed you, too, Godfrey didn't we, Irene?

IRENE. Yes.

GODFREY. Thanks. I missed you, too.

ANGELICA. Well, it's so nice for everybody to miss everyone else, because then it makes it so nice when they get together again. There, there, darling. It's nice to see you cheerful again. You do have a way about you Godfrey, you really do.

GODFREY *goes out as* CARLO *puts* ANGELICA's *wrap about her.*

ANGELICA. You know, there's no use denying the fact that Godfrey has a way with him. Well, we must be getting on. Cornelia, cheer her up, like a dear. *(They move on.)*

CORNELIA *(looking at the magazine)*. I'm a cinch. Do you feel better now that you know Godfrey missed us?

IRENE. He missed me more than he did you. I could tell by the light in his eyes.

CORNELIA. Why didn't you throw yourself in the man's arms and get it over with?

IRENE. You can't rush a man like Godfrey.

CORNELIA. You're getting pretty old, you know. It's your last chance to get a husband.

IRENE. He's really in love with me. He's just hard to break down.

CORNELIA. I could break him down in no time at all.

IRENE *(rising, angrily)*. He wouldn't have anything to do with you.

CORNELIA. How do you know?

IRENE. Because he wouldn't. Don't you try anything.

CORNELIA. I'm not saying I will— and I'm not saying I won't. Come to think of it—Godfrey and I have a little unfinished business.

IRENE (*going out*). Well, you'd better leave it unfinished, unless you want to be wearing a lamp for a hat.

*A close view in the pantry shows* GODFREY *washing dishes as* IRENE *enters. He turns to her.*

IRENE. Did you mean it when you said you missed me?

GODFREY (*laughing.*) Of course I did.

IRENE. I mean did you miss Cornelia and me or just me?

GODFREY. Well, I missed both of you, I guess.

IRENE. Not just me?

GODFREY. Oh, I may have missed you a little more than I did Cornelia. Why?

IRENE. I'm glad—because if you missed Cornelia more, you probably would have missed me less.

GODFREY. Well, that sounds very logical.

IRENE. That's all I wanted to know. You look so cute in that apron.

GODFREY. I'm not trying to look cute. Molly has a cold and I'm doubling for her. (IRENE *laughs.*)

GODFREY. What's funny about that?

IRENE. She hasn't got a cold.

GODFREY. No?

IRENE. She's got the same thing I've got; only you won't let me talk about things like that, so I won't because you lose your temper.

GODFREY. No—not seriously.

IRENE. Will you let me do something if I ask you?

GODFREY. What do you want to do?

IRENE. Wipe

GODFREY. Oh—all right. And you can tell me about your trip.

IRENE. You won't get mad.

GODFREY. Why should I?

IRENE. Because every place I went, everybody was Godfrey—

GODFREY. Every?—I don't want to seem dull, but I do seem to have a little trouble in following you at times.

IRENE. For instance, whenever I'd go into a restaurant in Paris or any place, I'd close my eyes and the waiter was Godfrey, and I'd say, I'm home and Godfrey is serving me. It made everything taste better.

GODFREY. Why?

IRENE. Haven't you any sense?

GODFREY. I'm afraid I haven't.

IRENE. And when I'd get in a cab I'd say the driver is Godfrey, and this is a chariot and he's taking me up through the clouds to his castle on the mountain.

GODFREY. Suppose you come down out of the mountains and tell me about your trip.

IRENE. Well, we went to Venice and one night I went for a ride in one of those row boats that the man pushes with a stick—not a matador—that was in Spain, but something like a matador.

GODFREY. Do you by any chance mean a gondolier?

IRENE *is now wiping the dishes—* GODFREY *washing them.*

IRENE. That was the name of the boat, and the man that pushed it sang. It was a beautiful song. I didn't understand it—but it was beautiful.

GODFREY. I see. So you closed your eyes and the man was Godfrey.

IRENE. It was wonderful. I didn't even mind the smells.

GODFREY. It's very convenient to take a trip abroad—without leaving the kitchen.

IRENE. Oh, you have a wonderful sense of humor. I wish I had a sense of humor, but I never can think of the right thing to say until everybody's gone home.

GODFREY. Do you mind if I talk for a little bit while you catch your breath?

IRENE. I'd love it.

GODFREY. While you were away, I've been doing some things also. I've been trying to do things that I thought would make you proud of me.

IRENE. I was proud of you before I went away.

GODFREY. Yes—but I mean—prouder still. You see, you helped me to find myself—and I'm very grateful.

IRENE. You'd make a wonderful husband.

GODFREY. I'm afraid not. You see—I know how you feel about things—

IRENE. How?

GODFREY. Well—you're grateful to me because I helped you to beat Cornelia—and I'm grateful to you because you helped me to beat life—but that doesn't mean that we have to fall in love.

IRENE. If you don't want to—but I'd make a wonderful wife.

GODFREY. Not for me, I'm afraid. You see—I like you very much, but I had a very bitter experience—but I won't bore you with that.

IRENE. Maybe she wasn't in love with you.

GODFREY. Well, maybe not—but that's beside the point. You and I are friends and I feel a certain responsibility to you. That's why I wanted to tell you first.

IRENE. Tell me what?

GODFREY. Well, I thought it was about time I was moving on.

IRENE *(sitting down, startled)*. Godfrey!

GODFREY. Now please.

IRENE *is turning away from him—half crying.*

IRENE. I won't cry. I promise.

GODFREY. That's fine. After all—I'm your protégé and you want me to improve myself, don't you?

IRENE. Yes.

GODFREY. You don't want me to be just a butler all my life, do you?

IRENE. I want you to be anything you want to be.

GODFREY. That's very sweet.

IRENE. When are you leaving?

GODFREY. Pretty soon. I'll call you up every now and then. We'll have long chats, and I'll tell you how I'm getting along and we'll have lots of fun together.

IRENE. Are you going back to her?

GODFREY. To whom?

IRENE. That Indian woman.

GODFREY. Indian— Oh! She was just a fabrication.

IRENE. Oh! Then you weren't married to her?

GODFREY. No. She was just a product of Tommy Gray's imagination.

*The two now busy themselves washing dishes;* IRENE *looks greatly relieved.*

IRENE. Then there wasn't—

GODFREY. No.

IRENE. Then there couldn't have been five children?

GODFREY. Well, naturally.

IRENE. That makes a difference. *(They burst into laughter.)*

*The scene dissolves to a close view of the living room, where* CORNELIA *is seated on the couch as* GODFREY *enters.*

GODFREY. Did you ring, Miss?

CORNELIA. You needn't be so formal when we're alone.

GODFREY. Shouldn't that rather increase a butler's formality?

CORNELIA. But you're not a butler.

GODFREY. I'm sorry if I've disappointed.

CORNELIA (*rising*). You might drop that superior attitude for the moment. There's a little matter I've wanted to talk over with you for quite awhile—called, the mystery of milady's necklace or—what happened to the pearls.

*We see a close-up of* GODFREY *and* CORNELIA *standing and facing each other.*

GODFREY. Pearls? Necklace? Oh, you mean the ones that disappeared last fall?

CORNELIA. The same.

GODFREY. Didn't they ever turn up?

CORNELIA. Oh yes, of course—but not in *my* possession. I know the first part of the story, but I wondered what you might know about the second part.

GODFREY. I can't imagine.

CORNELIA. I know another story that might interest you. I met some people on the boat coming over, a Boston family—quite distinguished. They know a great deal about a family called—the Parkes. An old Mayflower crowd—very upper crust, too, mind you. Never been a breath of scandal connected with the family.

*A close-up in the doorway shows* IRENE *standing—looking at the scene and listening.*

CORNELIA (*out of sight*). It would be a shame if they were made the laughing stock of Boston, wouldn't it?

GODFREY. I should hate to see anyone made the laughing stock of any place.

CORNELIA. Let's you and I take a long taxi ride out Van Cortlandt way.

IRENE, *listening, looks very hurt.*

CORNELIA'S VOICE. We could exchange secrets.

GODFREY (*angrily*). Is that a command?

CORNELIA. As you like. I'll be waiting around the corner.

GODFREY (*pointing*). Which corner? This one or that one?

CORNELIA (*going out*). This corner. It's impossible to exchange intimate secrets here.

*Now* IRENE *has her back turned and* CORNELIA *comes toward her.*

CORNELIA. This traffic is almost as heavy as at the Grand Central Station. Don't forget, darling—fifteen minutes.

GODFREY *turns and comes to* IRENE *as the view moves closer to them. She stops him—crying.*

IRENE. Please, Godfrey. You can't go with Cornelia.

GODFREY. But I didn't say I was going any place with Miss Cornelia.

IRENE. But you will. She always gets her own way. She makes everybody do just as she likes.

GODFREY. Why should you care whether I meet her or not?

IRENE. But I do care. That's why. Cornelia's the one who doesn't care!

GODFREY. But I think I should decide those things for myself.

IRENE. I don't want to be annoying, Godfrey, but I— Ooooh! (*She wilts suddenly and faints in his arms.*)

GODFREY (*looking around; desperately*). See here—you—you can't do that. Please—snap out of it. Oooh! This is the craziest family— (*He picks her up and goes out.*)

*We see him carrying* IRENE *in the hall across to the stairs. He runs up with her and opens the door at the head of the stairs. Then we see him entering her room and dropping her on a couch.*

GODFREY (*bending over the unconscious girl*). Now, see here, stop this nonsense. Do you hear? If you're faking one of your spells to keep me from meeting Cornelia, you're on the wrong track—do you hear? Do you hear?

IRENE *on the couch*, GODFREY *looks off, goes to the dressing table and looks for restoratives.* IRENE *is reflected in the mirror as he smells of the salts. He sees her sitting up—whereupon she drops back onto the couch.*

*He puts down the smelling salts, goes over to her, and slaps her cheek.*

GODFREY. Are you feeling better? No? Godfrey knows how to take care of little Irene—yes, indeed. (*He turns and goes to turn on the lights in her bathroom.*)

*A close view in the bathroom shows* GODFREY *opening the shower stall and putting a stool inside the stall. Then he moves toward her.*

GODFREY. Just lie there quietly and Godfrey will take care of everything.

GODFREY *comes to her—picks her up—talking—puts her over his shoulder and carries her into the bathroom.*

GODFREY. Godfrey knows just how to take care of those nasty old faints. That's the girl. Come right up here—there you are. Godfrey will soon fix Irene—yes, indeed. Just leave everything to Godfrey. Godfrey will take care of everything. Now just sit right down there like a good girl—and in just a minute you'll forget that you had any trouble.

*He puts her in the shower stall and puts her down on the stool. He turns on the water, and backs out.*

IRENE (*coming to with a scream*). Ooh! Godfrey!

*We see* IRENE *in the shower stall wriggling under the spray, as he moves away.*

GODFREY. I thought so. Let that be a lesson to you.

IRENE. Godfrey!

*Now* IRENE *runs after him and grabs him.* GODFREY, *angry, tries to get away from her.*

IRENE. Oh Godfrey, don't go away! Oh, Godfrey! Now I know you love me.

GODFREY. I do not love you and you're getting me all wet.

IRENE. You do or you wouldn't have lost your temper.

ANGELICA *appears in the doorway and moves into the room as* IRENE *is clinging to* GODFREY. IRENE *runs to her mother, excited.*

ANGELICA. What is the meaning of this, may I ask?

IRENE. Oh, Mother, Godfrey loves me. He put me in the shower!

ANGELICA. Whatever are you talking about?

IRENE. Godfrey loves me! Godfrey loves me!

ANGELICA. Godfrey, I demand an explanation.

IRENE (*jumping up and down the couch*). Godfrey loves me! Godfrey loves me!

GODFREY (*coming past* ANGELICA). I think, madam, that I had better resign.

ANGELICA (*stopping him*). I think you'd better. That's a very good idea. What do you suppose your father will say to all this?

IRENE. Godfrey loves me! I don't care what anybody says—Godfrey loves me.

ANGELICA. See here, young lady. You take a bath and put on some dry clothes and come downstairs immediately. Do you hear?

IRENE *(running to the bathroom; singing)*. Godfrey loves me! Godfrey loves me!

ANGELICA. I never heard of anything like this in all my life!

IRENE *(out of sight)*. Godfrey loves me!

*Following this, there is a close view at the piano of* CARLO *playing, eating, and singing.*

CARLO *(singing)*. Otchi tchornia— otchi tchornia!

*Then there appears a full view of the room, as* BULLOCK *enters.*

CARLO. Otchi tchornia! Otchi tchornia!

BULLOCK *puts down his hat, notices him, and speaks angrily.*

BULLOCK. Shut that thing off!— *(Out of sight, as we get another close view of* CARLO, *who looks at him)*—I feel gloomy enough as it is.

BULLOCK *sits down.* ANGELICA *enters, excited, as* CARLO *rises from the piano.*

ANGELICA. Alexander, something terrible has happened!

BULLOCK. What?

ANGELICA. Godfrey pushed Irene into a cold shower.

BULLOCK. What's so terrible about that?

ANGELICA. And besides, he's in love with her or thinks he is or something. I can't make head or tail out of the whole thing.

BULLOCK. I can't make head or tail out of what you're saying.

ANGELICA. The only thing to do is to send him back where he came from. He never should have come here in the first place. Imagine falling in love with a butler.

BULLOCK *(dryly)*. If you're going to feel sorry for anyone, feel sorry for Godfrey.

ANGELICA. Alexander!

BULLOCK. Don't Alexander me— stop fluttering and come to rest. *(She sits down.)* I've got something more important that I want to talk about.

ANGELICA. Don' tell me you're going to talk about those sordid money matters again?

CARLO *(in the background)*. Oh, money—money—money!

BULLOCK. Yes, I am—but before I start I'm going to have a little talk with Carlo.

ANGELICA. What are you going to do, Alexander?

ANGELICA *watches as* BULLOCK *goes to* CARLO.

BULLOCK. This is very private— just for Carlo's ears.

*A close-up at the grill shows* CARLO *uneasy as* BULLOCK *approaches.*

BULLOCK. You don't mind if we have a little chat—Carlo, old boy? You know, for some time, Carlo, I've—*(He leads him out of the room.)*

*Next there is a crash outside.* ANGELICA *looks up, startled—frightened. Another crash follows. Then* BULLOCK *comes in, and goes to her.*

ANGELICA. What happened? What did you say to Carlo?

BULLOCK. I said good-bye.

ANGELICA *(absentmindedly)*. Did he go?

BULLOCK. Yes. He left hurriedly.

GODFREY *and* CORNELIA *appear at the doorway.*

BULLOCK *(continuing)*. —by the side window.

ANGELICA *(out of sight)*. Side window? Side window? Where is he going?

BULLOCK *(out of sight)*. I don't know—but he won't be back.

GODFREY *and* CORNELIA *are standing.* BULLOCK *makes his wife and daughter sit down.*

BULLOCK. Now you sit down and do some listening.

ANGELICA. I've never seen you act like this before.

BULLOCK. Sit down!

ANGELICA. What's come over you, Alexander?

BULLOCK. And you're just in time to sit down and do some listening?

CORNELIA. Do you want Godfrey to listen?

BULLOCK. Yes. I want Godfrey to listen. This concerns him, too. You might as well all know, point-blank, we're about broke.

ANGELICA. You mean—we haven't any money left?

BULLOCK. We've got this house—a few odds and ends and that's about all. Not only that—I've lost all of my stock in the Bullock Enterprises—

*A close-up at the doorway shows* GODFREY *standing—waiting—a small packet in his hand.*

BULLOCK'S VOICE. Not only that—I've borrowed some of the stockholders' money trying to recoup my losses.

*A close view of the side of the room shows the two women seated—* BULLOCK *standing.*

BULLOCK. I don't know where I'm going to end—maybe in jail.

ANGELICA. Oh, Alexander!

BULLOCK *(sitting down)*. But if I do end up in jail, it will be the first peace I've had in twenty years—and I don't want any of you to chortle about Godfrey.

*A close-up at the doorway shows* GODFREY *smiling.*

BULLOCK'S VOICE. You may all be on the city dump before you're through.

ANGELICA'S VOICE. What are we going to do?

GODFREY *(bowing)*. May I intrude, sir?

*We see* BULLOCK *and the two women seated as* GODFREY *comes forward.*

GODFREY. I'm afraid things are not as bad as you make out.

BULLOCK. What do you know about it?

GODFREY. Well, sir— *(He hands the packet to* BULLOCK.*)* I've known for a long time that the Bullock interests were in rather a bad way—I offered to help you once, but you declined that help, so I took the liberty of dabbling in the market on my own account. Here, sir—

*A close-up of* CORNELIA *shows her watching—startled.*

BULLOCK'S VOICE. What's this?

GODFREY *(out of sight)*. That's most of your stock.

BULLOCK *examines the contents of the packet.*

GODFREY. I knew it was being dumped on the market, so I sold short.

ANGELICA. I don't understand— you sold short. You mean gentlemen's underwear?

BULLOCK *(rising)*. Wait a minute. Do you mean that you've been making money while I was losing it?

GODFREY. I did it in your interests, sir. The stock has been indorsed over to you.

BULLOCK *(examining papers)*. I don't understand. You did this for me?

GODFREY. Well, sir, there comes a turning point in every man's life—a time when he needs help. It happened to me, also and—*(as* BULLOCK *sits down, relieved to the point of exhaustion)* This family helped me. I hope I've repaid my debt. And, if I may add, some of the money went into a project of my own—I hope you won't mind, sir.

ANGELICA. You mean that you did all that on one hundered and fifty dollars a month?

GODFREY *(taking* CORNELIA'S *pearls out of his pocket)*. Well, hardly. You see, with the aid of Tommy Gray I was able to transmute a certain trinket into gold—then into stock and then back into pearls again. *(Giving them to her)* Thank you, dear lady, for the use of the trinket.

ANGELICA *(rising)*. Godfrey! Then you did steal them after all?

GODFREY. Well—I—perhaps Miss Cornelia had better explain to you.

CORNELIA. You win.

ANGELICA. What is this all about anyway?

CORNELIA. I put the pearls under Godfrey's mattress.

BULLOCK *stares at them.*

GODFREY. Thank you, Miss Cornelia. I wanted you to say that.

ANGELICA. But why?

CORNELIA. You wouldn't understand, Mother. Here, Godfrey, these are rightfully yours.

GODFREY. No, thank you. I've repaid my debt and I'm grateful to all of you.

CORNELIA. If anyone's indebted we are, after the way some of us have treated you.

GODFREY. I've been repaid in many ways. I learned patience—*(out of sight, as we see* BULLOCK *sitting, dazed)*—from Mr. Bullock.

GODFREY *(now seen with* CORNELIA*)*. I found Mrs. Bullock at all times, shall we say—amusing?

ANGELICA. That's very complimentary of you, Godfrey. Don't forget that you said I looked as young as Cornelia.

CORNELIA. What good did you find in me—if any?

GODFREY. A great deal. You taught me the fallacy of false pride—you taught me humility.

CORNELIA. I don't understand you.

GODFREY. Miss Cornelia, there have been other spoiled children in the world. I happened to be one of them myself. You're a high-spirited girl. I can only hope that you'll use those high spirits in a more constructive way. And so—good day.

*We see the doorway to the hall, the curtains blowing, then a close up of* CORNELIA, *holding the pearls—looking after him. Suddenly she throws aside the pearls and starts to cry.*

ANGELICA *is watching* CORNELIA *as she cries and* BULLOCK *sits with his head bowed.*

ANGELICA. You know, I hate to see Godfrey go. He's the only butler we ever had who understood women.

GODFREY *enters the pantry, and crosses to* MOLLY, *who is standing at the table. He picks up his hat and coat.*

GODFREY. Well, Molly, you told me to leave my hat near the door—remember?

MOLLY. I hate to see you leave, Godfrey.

GODFREY *(kissing her)*. Molly, you've been swell.

MOLLY. The house will seem empty.

GODFREY. Well, I guess the best of friends have to part. Will you say goodbye to Miss Irene for me? I don't think I can go through that ordeal right now. You're sweet, Molly. Good-bye. *(She opens the door for him, and he goes out.* MOLLY *is crying now.)*

IRENE *comes through the hall into the living room as* CORNELIA *goes past her, crying.* IRENE *stares at her as* CORNELIA *goes by.* IRENE *comes to her father and mother; they are seated and look very doleful.*

IRENE. What is it? What's the matter with Cornelia? What's the matter with everybody? Mother, what's the trouble?

ANGELICA *(dolefully)*. He's gone.

IRENE Who's gone?

ANGELICA. Godfrey.

IRENE. Where?

ANGELICA. And Carlo's gone—out the window. Everybody's gone!

*The pantry:* IRENE *enters—runs across to* MOLLY, *who is crying at the door, and runs back across the room.*

IRENE. Oh, Molly, has he gone? Oh, poor Molly. He's not going to get away from me. Order the car—I'll be right down.

*The scene dissolves to the dump where people are arriving in cars. We see the bridge over the river in the background. (Music is heard throughout the scenes that follow.) Then a close view at a car in front of the "night club" (a building on the dump area) shows a doorman taking bags from a chauffeur.* GODFREY *alights,*

*and we see him at close range as he talks to the doorman, who turns out to be* MIKE.

MIKE. Hello, Duke.

GODFREY. Business looks pretty good tonight.

MIKE. I'll say it is. Mayor Courtney's here with a big party.

GODFREY. Well!

MIKE. I'll have one of the boys bring these down, Duke.

*The night club, with people at tables and at the bar, music playing.* GODFREY *comes down the stairs, looks around as he passes between tables, and stops at the door to the office and speaks to a man who turns out to be* BOB.

BOB. Hello, Duke.

GODFREY. Well, Bob. We can't complain about this.

BOB. Say, we've got the Mayor here with us tonight.

GODFREY. So I heard.

BOB. Big stuff.

GODFREY. Yep. *(He opens the door to the office and starts to go out.)*

*The office, where* TOMMY GRAY *is seated at a desk and* BELLINGER *is standing as* GODFREY *enters.*

TOMMY. This is all Greek to me. Here's our wandering butler now. Explain it to him.

BELLINGER *(picking up plans)*. Hello, Duke.

GODFREY. Hello, Arthur.

BELLINGER. I've got an estimate from the contractor on your housing plan for the winter.

GODFREY. Yes?

BELLINGER. He figures he can partition off our present building into compartments to take care of at least fifty people. It will cost fifty-eight hundred dollars, but that includes steam heat.

TOMMY. Forgotten men with steam. That sounds like something that ought to be on the menu.

GODFREY. I'll talk with you about it later, Arthur.

TOMMY. Say, I've still got an interest in this company. When do you start paying dividends?

GODFREY. Well, we're giving food and shelter to fifty people in the winter and we are giving them employment in the summer. What more do you want in the way of dividends?

TOMMY. You're the most arbitrary butler I've ever met.

GODFREY. Ex-butler. I quit. I felt that foolish feeling coming on again.

TOMMY. You mean Irene?

GODFREY. What do you know about that?

TOMMY. Nobody knows anything about her love except all of New York and Lower Manhattan.

GODFREY *rises and gives* TOMMY *a pen.*

GODFREY. Looks like I got out just in time.

TOMMY. Why don't you marry the girl?

GODFREY. No thank you. I've had enough of matrimony.

TOMMY. What's wrong with butlers—lots of society girls run away with their chauffeurs.

GODFREY. Never mind about that. Write me out a check for five thousand dollars.

TOMMY (*sitting down at the desk*). For what?

GODFREY. A new dock, so we'll get some of the yachting trade.

TOMMY. Well, how about an airplane landing? Have you thought of that?

*While* TOMMY, *seated at the desk, is writing a check,* GODFREY, *going to the back, looks out of the big window.*

GODFREY. We'll come to that later.

*A view of the night club and river with people moving about as* MIKE, *the doorman, appears: A car stops in the foreground. As* MIKE *opens the door of the car (now seen closely),* IRENE *gets out, and her chauffeur, getting out, goes around the car to* IRENE *and* MIKE.

IRENE. Say, Mister, what happened to the city dump that was here?

MIKE. Well, Lady, most of it's been filled in.

IRENE. But what happened to all the forgotten men?

MIKE. Forgotten men? We got most of 'em out in time.

IRENE. Don't be fresh. Where's Godfrey?

MIKE. You mean Mr. Godfrey Smith?

IRENE. Yes.

MIKE. Well, lady, his office is right over there where it says "Office."

IRENE (*remembering the shack*). Oh, just where it used to be. Thank you. Come on, Clarence.

MIKE *watches as* IRENE *and* CLARENCE *enter,* CLARENCE *carrying two big baskets of food.* MIKE *stops him.*

MIKE. Hey, wait a minute! What is this—a basket party? (IRENE *goes on.*)

IRENE *enters the house, walks past the tables, and sees the* MAYOR.

IRENE. Good evening, Mr. Courtney.

MAYOR. Good evening, Miss Bullock.

IRENE. Lovely evening, isn't it? Good evening. (*She goes to the office.*)

*The office:* TOMMY *rises.*

TOMMY. Well, there you are. Business is fine—I'm stuck—you're nuts and I'm going back to Boston before I disgrace my family.

GODFREY. Good riddance.

TOMMY *opens the door, and, behold,* IRENE *walks in, smiling.*

TOMMY *(smiling at her).* Oh, Godfrey—company has come.

GODFREY *looks around from the window.*

GODFREY. What are you doing here?

TOMMY. Yes, what are you doing here? Don't let him off the hook.

IRENE. I won't.

TOMMY. You must leave at once, do you hear me?

TOMMY *pushes* IRENE *away from the door into the office as* GODFREY *comes forward.*

TOMMY *(blithely).* Well, we got rid of her in a hurry. If I can help you in any way, be sure and let me know. (TOMMY *goes out, closing the door.*)

IRENE. *(moving about and looking around).* Oh, my, how you fixed this place up, Godfrey! It's much nicer than when I was here before.

GODFREY. Oh, you noticed that?

IRENE. Are the forgotten men having a party?

GODFREY. It's their annual reunion.

IRENE. I saw the mayor out there. Is he one of them, too?

GODFREY. He's the guest of honor.

IRENE *(going to the window).* It's a lovely view! You can see the bridge and everything. Is it always there?

GODFREY. Most always.

IRENE *(opening doors).* Oh, you have a kitchen. I'm going to like this place very much. What's over here? Is this where you sleep?

GODFREY. That's the general purpose of the room. Any observations?

IRENE *turns from the door.*

IRENE. Oh, I think it's very cute, but we'll have to change the wallpaper.

GODFREY. What do you mean—*we'll* have to change the wallpaper?

IRENE *(going to him).* I don't like green wallpaper—it makes me bilious.

GODFREY. Well, you won't have to look at it. You're going home right now.

IRENE. But I can't go home.

GODFREY. Why not?

IRENE. I can't go home after what happened.

GODFREY. What happened?

IRENE. You know what happened just as well as I do.

GODFREY. Now, see here—

IRENE. Oh, go on and lose your temper again. I love it when you lose your temper.

GODFREY. Why can't you let me alone? *(He sits down.)*

IRENE. Because you're my responsibility and someone has to take care of you.

GODFREY. I'll take care of myself.

IRENE *(seated near him).* You can't look me in the eye and say that. You love me and you know it. There's no sense in struggling with a thing when it's got you. It's got you and that's all there is to it—it's got you.

IRENE *and* GODFREY *look up as they hear a knock at the door.*

IRENE. That's Clarence. *(She rises—opens the door—*CLARENCE *enters loaded down with baskets of food.)*

CLARENCE. I'm sorry I was delayed, Miss Irene—but I had to go all the way around the back way.

*A close-up at the seat shows* GODFREY *seated—smoking his pipe—curious.*

IRENE. Put the wood over there.

CLARENCE *follows her with the basket through the room.*

CLARENCE. Hello, Godfrey.

IRENE. You can put the groceries right there in the kitchen. Right there, Clarence.

GODFREY. What's the idea?

IRENE. I brought some wood and I brought some food. It ought to last us for a week anyway.

GODFREY. It's a wonder you didn't have the foresight to bring a minister and a license.

IRENE. It's funny. I never thought of that.

IRENE *is seen standing before* GODFREY *as the* MAYOR *enters.*

MAYOR. May I come in?

IRENE. Oh, Mr. Courtney!

MAYOR. Mr Gray said there were a couple of people over here who wanted to get married.

*A closeup of* GODFREY *shows him startled—his pipe in hand.*

MAYOR'S VOICE. Are you it?

IRENE. Yes, we're it. Can you marry us without a license?

GODFREY *is flabbergasted.*

MAYOR'S VOICE. Without a li—Well, it may get me into trouble—but—I guess I've known your family long enough to take a chance. Who are you going to marry?

IRENE. Godfrey.

*She points at* GODFREY. *The* MAYOR *goes to him and shakes hands.*

IRENE. Oh, this is Godfrey.

MAYOR. How do you do, Godfrey? Er—does your father know about this?

IRENE. Everybody knows about it except Godfrey.

MAYOR. Well, I guess we'd better have a witness.

IRENE (*as* CLARENCE *enters*). Oh, sure! Oh, use Clarence. Clarence, you be the witness. Come down here. Stand right here. (*Pulling* GODFREY *to his feet*) Come on, Godfrey. Now, we're all set.

MAYOR. Join hands, please. Join the right hands.

IRENE (*grasping his hand*). Stand still, Godfrey, it'll all be over in a minute.

*The scene fades out.*

# JUDGMENT AT NUREMBERG

## *Screenplay by Abby Mann*

| | |
|---|---|
| JUDGE DAN HAYWOOD | Spencer Tracy |
| ERNST JANNING | Burt Lancaster |
| COLONEL LAWSON | Richard Widmark |
| MME. BERTHOLT | Marlene Dietrich |
| HANS ROLFE | Maxmilian Schell |
| IRENE HOFFMAN | Judy Garland |
| RUDOLPH PETERSEN | Montgomery Clift |

Produced and Directed by Stanley Kramer
Camera: Ernest Laszlo
Film Editor: Fred Knudson
Music by Ernest Gold

It is extremely interesting to consider the moral judgment made in this work by screenwriter Abby Mann—that there were those, particularly the four German judges on trial here, who uniquely knew or should have known what was at stake when the perversion of justice took place in Nazi Germany. Weigh that judgment against the information that came out just a few years ago in connection with the trial of Klaus Barbie in France for his war crimes—that he was being protected from being brought to justice by the CIA and others in high places so that he could assist them in their battle against Soviet communism. Thus, the adoption of the dictum that "the end justifies the means." An anomaly or a general practice?

An anomaly, I believe. A moment of aberration, of misguided patriotism and zeal at a time when Soviet communism was the archenemy of democracy. Understandable. Nonetheless, it is also a warning. A warning that a state that sets a high moral tone in a proceeding such as the Nuremberg Trials cannot relax its vigilance one iota. Otherwise, one would have to agree with Barbie's lawyer, Jacques Verges, that the trial and conviction of this infamous Nazi criminal was merely "victor's justice, a prime example of Anglo-Saxon hypocrisy"—which, by the way, in Mr. Mann's screenplay is the essence of the defense put forth by Rolfe, the attorney for Janning, the judge who tried to deceive himself until the very end that he was not responsible for Hitler and the mockery that had been made of German justice under his regime.

An able and important screenplay, *Judgment at Nuremberg* is just as timely today as it was when Mr. Mann began to write it as a teleplay in the fall of 1957 for its first showing on television in April of 1959. In the winter of 1960, Mr. Mann was contacted by Stanley Kramer to adapt it to be shot as a feature film.

In 1961 Mr. Mann won an Academy Award for Best Screenplay (based on material from another medium), an honor well deserved.

Mr. Mann was born in Philadelphia in 1927 and educated at Temple University and New York University. During the golden era of live television, he wrote and made substantial contributions to shows such as "Studio One," "Alcoa Goodyear Theater," and "Playhouse 90." Two of his early scripts were adapted from his own successful teleplays—one, of course, was *Judgment at Nuremberg,* and the other *A Child Is Waiting* (1963). Among his other films are *Ship of Fools* (1965) and *Report to the Commissioner* (1975). Mr. Mann also wrote the TV script for "Kojak," upon which that popular series was based. Mr. Mann currently resides in Beverly Hills.

*Fade in*

*Exterior. Nuremberg Stadium, 1933
—Actual newsreel shots*

The height of the Nuremberg rally, 1933. The spotlight picks up ADOLF HITLER *out in the midst of the tremendous Nuremberg stadium field. He looks down the field to the steps leading to the podium. The drums are beating. The regiment of choruses are singing. The swell increases as he walks up the steps to the podium. It is a moment before he speaks; The "Sieg Heils" are tremendous. He begins extolling the glories of the fatherland and the coming thousand-year Reich.*

*Exterior. Nuremberg Stadium, 1946
—Actual newsreel shots*

The voice of Hitler continues over the scene. Exhorting hate, fatherland love, sentiment. The voice is always emotional and terribly, terribly sincere. Underneath his voice is the sound of the regiment of choruses singing a marching song. It is sentimental and buoyant, never grim. The camera moves up to the swastika on top of the Nuremberg stadium. There is an explosion. The swastika splits into smithereens.

*Exterior. Street scenes*

Devastation. Skeletons of buildings. Buildings with gaping holes where windows should be. Rubble piled high. Devastation as far as the eye can see. Hitler's voice continues over the rubble. He is extolling the glories of the thousand-year Reich. The regiment of choruses is continuing.

*Exterior. Nuremberg, 1948—Day*

The entrance to Nuremberg. Devastation and destruction everywhere. Rubble as far as the eye can see it. Sometimes one can get a glimpse of a building still partially standing. Of what life must have been in that building. Family pictures still hanging from the walls. A bath-tub seeming to hang in mid-air. Tattered lamps swinging in the breeze. Hitler's voice continues over the scene, ringing over the devastation with its promises, hate, and hysteria. A car appears on the landscape. It is a large, black Mercedes-Benz.

*Interior. Car—Day*

A German Driver (SCHMIDT) *sits in the front seat.* HAYWOOD *and* SENATOR BURKETTE *are in the back seat.*

*Close-up—*HAYWOOD

His face mirrors the devastation. HAYWOOD *is the "vanishing American." The body of a battered buffalo with great sensitivity underneath. A man of humble origin whose father participated in the railroad strikes of the early twenties. He thought the most wonderful thing in the world would be to be a judge and he has paid dearly for it. He has had to sit hard and to kow-tow to political forces which he sometimes hated because it was the only way to remain a judge. He is like many men in their fifties trying to find their identity. A judge who has never contributed to his profession greatly because he has never had the chance. A man with far greater capacities than he realizes. Earl Warren was thought by many to be a professional party hack until he was on the Supreme Court and showed how he could grow—the seeds had been in him all the time.* HAYWOOD *is such a man, also.*

*Full shot*

SENATOR BURKETTE *is a smooth-looking personable man in his fifties. He can be a man of great charm. He* can also be a deadly enemy. He is above all a marvellous manipulator. Hitler's voice continues over scene until HAYWOOD speaks.

HAYWOOD (quietly). I didn't know it was so bad.

SENATOR BURKETTE (matter-of-factly). A few incendiaries and these old houses go up like cellophane.

HAYWOOD nods absently. Continues to look out window.

Exterior. Nuremberg—HAYWOOD'S point of view—from the car

The old section of Nuremberg. We get a look at the people of Nuremberg as the car goes on. They are dressed badly, of course, and they look hungry. The women are dressed mostly in blouses and skirts that do not match. Some of the men are dressed in knickerbockers. Many of them are carrying briefcases. Their lunches are in the briefcases. Despite the enormity of what has happened, there is still very much in evidence a rhythm to their life. A compulsion, not intellectualized at all, to rebuild what has been destroyed. Everyone seems to be in a hurry. A tram-car stops at a corner. There are not enough seats for all the people in line, or even enough standing room. The people crowd in regardless. Until every last one in the line is on the tram-car. Some of them hang four deep on the outside of the tram-car perilously.

SENATOR BURKETTE. This is the old section of Nuremberg. Some of it is still standing. There's a wall separates the old from the new. Goes back to—how far does it go back, Schmidt?

SCHMIDT. 1219, Sir.

SENATOR BURKETTE. 1219.

HAYWOOD nods absently. Continues to look out window.

HAYWOOD. This is the place where they used to hold the Nazi party rallies, wasn't it?

SENATOR BURKETTE. They all came here. Hitler. Goebbels. The whole crew. Thousands from all over Germany.

HAYWOOD. I remember it from the newsreels.

Interior. Car—Day

The German driver in HAYWOOD'S car is in a hurry, too. He blows his horn loudly whenever pedestrians try to cross in front of the big Mercedes-Benz. HAYWOOD feels self-conscious in the big car in the midst of so much hunger and want. But the natives do not even seem to notice the car. They are used to foreign visitors and their big, black cars.

The German driver blows his horn loudly again speeding across the road.

HAYWOOD. Does he have to blow the horn so much?

SENATOR BURKETTE (to driver). It is not necessary to blow the horn so much, Schmidt.

They drive on a moment. SCHMIDT blows horn automatically at a women and child crossing the street, just missing them. HAYWOOD winces at the grossness of the German driver toward his fellow Germans.

Exterior. Castle on hill in Ludenstrasse, a suburb of Nuremberg—Day

Beautiful baronial house with large grounds and a lake on the farther side. The car pulls up in front.

Interior. Castle—Day

HAYWOOD, SENATOR BURKETTE have entered, followed by SCHMIDT. MR. and MRS. HALBESTADT are standing in the entrance with CAPTAIN BY-

ERS, *in his twenties, pleasant-looking, West Point.*

SENATOR BURKETTE. Hello, Captain. *(to* HAYWOOD*).* This is Captain Byers . . . Judge Haywood. Byers here will be your aide. *(pause)*

HAYWOOD My what—!

CAPTAIN BYERS *(laughingly).* Clerk. General guide. Liaison. Any capacity you wish to use me in.

HAYWOOD. Oh. . . .

CAPTAIN BYERS. This will be your staff, Sir. Mr. and Mrs. Halbestadt.

MRS. HALBESTADT *(warmly).* Good afternoon.

HAYWOOD. Hello.

HALBESTADT *(smiles, nods).* Good afternoon, Your Honor.

CAPTAIN BYERS. You already met your driver, Schmidt.

SCHMIDT. I am at your service any time you need me, Sir. Any time, day or night.

HAYWOOD *looks at him, thinking of their hectic ride through Nuremberg.*

HAYWOOD *(dryly).* Thanks.

*The three of them stand there, just waiting and smiling.*

SENATOR BURKETTE *(mechanically).* Let's show him around.

SENATOR BURKETTE *and* HAYWOOD *follow* CAPTAIN BYERS *through the house.*

*Interior. Reception room—Day*

CAPTAIN BYERS *(matter-of-factly).* Reception room.

*An enormous, once elegant room with high-ceilinged walls. Portrait by Albrecht Dürer staring down from the wall.* CAPTAIN BYERS *keeps walking.* SENATOR BURKETTE *and* HAYWOOD *following him.*

*Interior. Living-room—Day*

CAPTAIN BYERS *(matter-of-factly).* Living-room. Your study is in there. There are two bedrooms on this floor and three upstairs.

*Stolid, heavy German furniture. Enormous chandelier. There is a moment.* HAYWOOD *walks to window. Looks out. From* HAYWOOD'S *point of view we see rolling hills and a lake reflecting the greenery.*

CAPTAIN BYERS. Quite a view, isn't it, Sir?

HAYWOOD *(finally).* Senator. I don't need all this.

SENATOR BURKETTE *(laughs a little).* When the United States' Government does something, it does it right. You know that, Dan.

HAYWOOD *starts back into the house slowly. He goes over to a Bechstein piano, and stares at it.* SENATOR BURKETTE *and* CAPTAIN BYERS *follow him in.*

*Interior. Living-room*

HAYWOOD. Who used to live here?

CAPTAIN BYERS. General Bertholt and his wife. *(then, seeing the concern on* HAYWOOD'S *face, smiles a little)* They were important Nazi Party members, Sir.

*Close-up—*HAYWOOD'S *Face*

*As he stares at the Bechstein piano. Nazis actually lived here. In this house.*

*Full group shot*

SENATOR BURKETTE. Let's see. What else is there that Judge Haywood ought to know?

CAPTAIN BYERS. Are there any questions, Sir?

HAYWOOD. You're West Point, aren't you, Captain?

CAPTAIN BYERS. Yes, Sir.

HAYWOOD. What's your first name?

CAPTAIN BYERS. Harrison. *(smiles a little)* Harry.

HAYWOOD Well, Harry, you see I'm not West Point and this formality kind of gets me down, and not to say, ill-at-ease.

Do you think it would be too much an infraction of rules for you to call me "Judge" or "Dan" or something?

CAPTAIN BYERS *(smiles a little)*. Okay, Judge.

*There is a little laughter.*

CAPTAIN BYERS. We do all our shopping at the Army commissary. There isn't enough food at the local markets for the Germans. The driver knows where the commissary is. *(takes paper out of folder)* Here's a copy of the indictment in the case. I thought you might want to look it over. *(smiles a little)* I hope you'll be comfortable here . . . Judge.

HAYWOOD. I think the whole state of Maine would be comfortable here, Captain.

CAPTAIN BYERS *(laughs)*. My office is next to yours at the Palace of Justice—if you need anything, Senator—

CAPTAIN BYERS *exchanges a smile with* HAYWOOD.

CAPTAIN BYERS *goes. There is a pause.* HAYWOOD *looks around the house somewhat restively.*

HAYWOOD. I don't really need three servants, do I? It makes me feel like a damn' fool.

SENATOR BURKETTE. It helps them out as well as you. Here they eat.

HAYWOOD *(dryly)*. Well. I guess I need three servants.

SENATOR BURKETTE *(smiles a little)*. Good to have you here, Dan. Good to have a man of your stature here.

HAYWOOD *(dryly)*. I'm sure I was the only one in America qualified for this job.

SENATOR BURKETTE *looks at* HAYWOOD *carefully not quite knowing how to evaluate this.*

HAYWOOD *(continuing)*. Well . . . listen, Senator. I wasn't the first choice for this job. Or even the tenth. You know it. I know it. *(pause)*

SENATOR BURKETTE. What do you mean?

HAYWOOD. Let's face it. Hitler's gone. Goebbels is gone. Göring committed suicide before they could hang him. Now we're down to trying the businessmen, the doctors and the judges. A lot of people think they shouldn't be tried at all. *(pause)*

SENATOR BURKETTE. So?

HAYWOOD. So it's made for a hell of a lack of candidates for this job. *(pause)* You even had to beat the backwoods of Maine to come up with a hick like me.

HAYWOOD *continues to look at* SENATOR BURKETTE *steadily.*

SENATOR BURKETTE *lowers his eyes a little.*

SENATOR BURKETTE. I hope you're not sorry you came. *(pause)*

HAYWOOD *(quietly)*. No, I'm not sorry I came. *(pause)* I just wanted you to know I know where the body is buried. *(pause)* I think the trials ought to go on. And particularly, the trial of the German judges. *(pause)* I hope I'm up to it.

SENATOR BURKETTE *(quietly trying to reassure him)*. You're up to it. *(there is an awkward pause)* Relax. Enjoy this place while you still can. You're going to be a pretty busy fellow.

HAYWOOD. Thanks, Senator. Thanks for everything.

SENATOR BURKETTE. See you tomorrow, Judge.

*As the* SENATOR *leaves,* HAYWOOD *walks back into reception room. Looks at the surroundings apprehensively. Feeling more out of place than he ever has in his life. Suddenly he has a thought—goes to a suitcase, and takes out his wife's picture which he places on the piano—stares at it. He is interrupted by the servants standing in the doorway.*

MRS. HALBESTADT *(indicating luggage).* Shall we take these upstairs, Sir?

HAYWOOD. Yes. Thank you.

MR. *and* MRS. HALBESTADT *immediately begin to take up the luggage.*

MRS. HALBESTADT *picks up one of the big suitcases.*

HAYWOOD *(concerned; going after her).* I can take that.

HAYWOOD *goes after* MRS. HALBESTADT. *Tries to take a heavy suitcase from her. There is a compulsion in her voice as she looks at him.*

MRS. HALBESTADT. Your Honor. Let me take it. Please.

HAYWOOD *looks at her understanding that this is something she must do. A compulsion to serve. He watches her helplessly as she tugs the big suitcase up the stairs. There is a moment. He looks about the huge room becoming more aware momentarily that he has been separated more than geographically from the people that live here. He looks about the room with wonder. Puts his hands in his pockets. Whistles a little nervously. Then sits down in chair. Opens indictment in the case absently. Looks at snapshot inside it attached to indictment.*

*Close-up—Snapshot*

*It is the face of* ERNST JANNING.

*Interior. Palace of Justice, Prison Office—Day—close up—*ERNST JANNING

*He is standing with three other men.* EMIL HAHN, FRIEDRICH HOFSTETTER, WERNER LAMMPE. *A half-dozen men in American uniforms around them.* COLONEL MAGUIRE *looks at them. His manner is polite and crisp.*

COLONEL MAGUIRE. I want to give you the rules we have here in Nuremberg. They're much the same as they were at Mondorf, except a little stricter. I think you know the reason for that. *(pause)* There have been a number of suicides. It is incumbent upon us to try to prevent any more. *(pause)* You will not be allowed any sharp utensils in your cells of course. Your belts will be given to your guard upon entering your cell. You will place all your writing materials and possessions on a table in the center of the cell upon entering it. You will exercise in the courtyard depending upon weather conditions, for a total period of not less than one hour daily, divided into two periods, one for morning and afternoon. If you wish to work around the prison, the garden or the library, you may tell the prison psychologist, Dr. Joseph. You can give him a note if there is any request you have to make of me. He will be around to see you in the morning. Prisoners are permitted to receive spiritual guidance. *(pause)* Now. May I have your kits, please?

LAMMPE, HOFFSTETTER, HAHN *and* JANNING *hand the guards their kits.*

COLONEL MAGUIRE. Here are your clothes, and the personal possessions you are permitted to retain. *(he looks into the face of each man as he steps forward)* Number One—Werner Lammpe.

WERNER LAMMPE *steps forward and accepts his clothing.*

COLONEL MAGUIRE. Number Two —Emil Hahn.

EMIL HAHN *steps forward and looks at his clothing as though with disgust.*

COLONEL MAGUIRE. Number Three —Friedrich Hofstetter.

FRIEDRICH HOFFSTETTER *steps forward and accepts his clothing.*

COLONEL MAGUIRE. Number Four —Ernst Janning.

ERNST JANNING *steps forward and accepts his clothing.*

COLONEL MAGUIRE. Any questions?

HAHN *(abruptly).* What about tobacco?

COLONEL MAGUIRE. We'll see what we can do. You will be able to smoke in the courtyard.

HOFFSTETTER. Will we be able to write letters to our families?

COLONEL MAGUIRE. Yes. Of course.

HOFFSTETTER. Thank you.

COLONEL MAGUIRE. Any other questions?

*There is no answer.*

COLONEL MAGUIRE *(continuing).* That's all.

*The men are taken out of the office by the guards.* COLONEL MAGUIRE *stares after them, wondering about them.*

*Interior. Palace of Justice, corridor—Day*

*Camera follows the prisoners as they are led through the prison to their cells. The prison is a three—story structure with a wide corridor running the length of the ground floor. Camera follows* JANNING, HAHN, HOFFSTETTER, LAMMPE *and the guards up the circular stairway. The stairway is screened on either side to prevent any suicide leaps. Camera follows* JANNING *as he is taken by the guard to his cell first. The guard gestures towards* JANNING'S *belt.* JANNING *takes off his belt and hands it to the guard. He steps into the cell. The door closes behind him.*

*Interior. Palace of Justice, prison cell—Day*

JANNING *looks around cell. The cell from* JANNING'S *point of view. It is terribly bare and perfunctory. A steel cot fastened to one side of the door. He looks at the cracked plaster on the walls. The small window and the bars. The toilet without covering. He slowly takes out a picture of his son and wife and places it on a table.*

*Fade out*

*Fade in*

*Exterior. Palace of Justice*

*There is mostly bicycle traffic and a few Mercedes cars for official purposes and—everywhere M.P.s.*

*Interior. Palace of Justice, Courtroom—Day*

*The courtroom is a large affair with rows of spectators. Microphones before each of the judges' chairs. Interpreters' booths for German and English. The courtroom includes spectators, translators, Press, defendants, lawyers. In the audience is* BRIGADIER-GENERAL MATTHEW MERRIN. MERRIN *is a clean-cut man in his fifties. To the right sit the defendants in the dock. Seated first in the dock is* ERNST JANNING. *In front of him are*

ROLFE *and other defense lawyers in black robes. There are three other men in the dock with* JANNING. *To the left is the prosecution table. At the head of it is* COLONEL THADDEUS LAWSON. MAJOR ABE RADNITZ *is seated beside* COLONEL LAWSON. MAJOR RADNITZ *is a short, wiry man in his early forties. Also at the table are a battery of men and women. Most of them in Army uniform.* CAPTAIN BYERS *sits at a small desk to the right of the judges' bench. The judges enter.* HAYWOOD *leads followed by two other men in black robes.* CAPTAIN BYERS *rises. All the courtroom rises.*

CAPTAIN BYERS. The Tribunal is in session. God save the United States of America and this Honorable Tribunal.

*The judges are seated. All in the court are seated.* HAYWOOD *looks about the Tribunal. It is obvious that he feels a responsibility to this position greatly. And he feels a self-consciousness as he first speaks.*

HAYWOOD. The Tribunal will arraign the defendants. The microphone will now be placed in front of the defendant Emil Hahn.

*Erect,* HAHN *stares out at the Tribunal as though he were the accuser instead of the accused.*

HAYWOOD *(continuing).* Emil Hahn. Are you represented by counsel before this Tribunal?

HAHN *rises abruptly.*

HAHN. Not guilty. *(pause)*

*There is tension in the courtroom.*

HAYWOOD. The question is, are you represented by counsel before this Tribunal?

HAHN *(abruptly).* I am represented.

HAYWOOD. How do you plead to the charges and specifications set forth in the indictment against you—guilty or not guilty?

HAHN. Not guilty on all counts.

HAYWOOD. You may be seated.

*The microphone is placed before the next man.*

HAYWOOD *(continuing).* Friedrich Hoffstetter. Are you represented by counsel before this Tribunal?

HOFFSTETTER *looks at* HAYWOOD *anxiously. His manner is courteous, straightforward and sincere.*

HOFFSTETTER. Yes, Your Honor. I am represented by counsel.

HAYWOOD. How do you plead to the charges and specifications set forth in the indictment against you—guilty or not guilty?

HOFFSTETTER. Not guilty, Your Honor.

HAYWOOD. You may be seated.

HOFFSTETTER *is seated. The microphone is placed before the next man.*

HAYWOOD *(continuing).* Werner Lammpe. Are you represented by counsel before this Tribunal?

WERNER LAMMPE *looks about the courtroom in confusion. His voice quavers tremulously as he speaks into the microphone.*

LAMMPE. Counsel? . . . Yes.

HAYWOOD. How do you plead to the charges and specifications set forth in the indictment against you—guilty or not guilty?

LAMMPE *looks about in confusion. It would seem to be the confusion of a man of old age, but it is deeper than that. It is the confusion of a man who refuses to look at the issues that are being presented before him.* LAMMPE'S *defense counsel rises and whispers in his ear.*

LAMMPE *(he nods slowly, then looks toward* HAYWOOD; *his lips tremble).* Not guilty.

HAYWOOD. You may be seated.

LAMMPE *sits down. Microphone is placed before* ERNST JANNING.

HAYWOOD. Ernst Janning. Are you represented by counsel before this Tribunal?

ERNST JANNING *remains seated. The expression on his face is beyond that of not having heard what* HAYWOOD *has said. Beyond that of not having any interest in what he has said.*

*There is a moment.*

HAYWOOD. Ernst Janning. Are you represented by counsel before this Tribunal?

ROLFE *rises in front of* JANNING.

ROLFE I represent the defendant, Your Honor.

HAYWOOD. *(Addressing* JANNING). How do you plead to the charges and specifications set forth in the indictment against you—guilty or not guilty?

*There is a moment.*

*The M.P. behind* JANNING *brusquely raises him to his feet and snaps the earphones over his ears. Whether it is the indignity of the position or whether he can't bring himself to make a plea for himself before these foreigners,* JANNING *refuses to speak. There is an instant.* ROLFE *rises again.*

ROLFE *(anxiously).* Your Honor. May I address the court. *(pause)*

HAYWOOD. Yes.

ROLFE. The defendant does not recognize the authority of this Tribunal and wishes to lodge a formal protest in lieu of pleading.

*There is a moment. The tension in the courtroom builds.*

HAYWOOD. A plea of not guilty will be entered. The prosecution will make its opening statement.

*There is a moment.*

MAJOR RADNITZ *(quietly).* Slow and easy, Junior.

COLONEL LAWSON *rises, flashes a look at* GENERAL MERRIN *and goes to the microphone in the center of the room. As he does so, the newsmen snap pictures of* COLONEL LAWSON. *They poise their pencils to get ready for what he is going to say. It is obvious that he is the star attraction of the proceedings as far as the newspaper men are concerned. This is the first time we see him in action. It is not difficult to see why he has been spoken of as a man with a political future. He has at his fingertips a complete command of the legal procedure, and a hard-hitting, precise sense of delivery. Add to this an erect, handsome presence. Yet there is something else beneath the surface of the man. A weariness. A weariness akin to sickness. He has looked into a great deal of evil in man. It has affected him. It has robbed him of a basic buoyancy and optimism. One has only to look beyond the appearance of* THADDEUS LAWSON *to see that it has affected him. Yet withal he makes an impressive figure, with his sense of decorum and legal fervor; like a man trying to hold water in his hand while running at the same time. He stops short before the microphone at the center of the courtroom. He looks down at the paper he has placed on the stand before him only intermittently. He begins in his precise clipped manner.*

COLONAL LAWSON. The case is unusual in that the defendants are charged with crimes committed in the names of the law. *(looks over at dock)* These men, together with their deceased or fugitive colleagues, are the embodiment of what passed for justice during the Third Reich. The defendants have served as judges during the period of the Third Reich. *(pause; looks back at* HAYWOOD *and others on the bench)* Therefore, you, Your Honors, as judges on the bench will be sitting in judgment of judges in the dock. *(pause)* This is as it should be. For only a judge knows how much more a court is than a courtroom. It is a process and a spirit. It is the House of Law. *(looks over at dock)* The defendants knew this too. They knew courtrooms well. They sat in their black robes. And they distorted and they perverted and they destroyed justice and law in Germany.

*Close up—*JANNING'S *face*

*It is obvious he is not listening to what* COLONEL LAWSON *is saying.*

*Full Shot—The Courtroom*
ROLFE *tense in front of* JANNING.

COLONEL LAWSON *(continuing).* This, in itself is undoubtedly a great crime. But the prosecution is not calling the defendants to account for violating constitutional guarantees or withholding due process of law. It is calling them to account for *(he hits every one of the words as if it were a hammer)* murder, brutalities, torture, atrocities.

*Camera moves to the faces of the spectators. It is obvious that* COLONEL LAWSON *is hitting harder than they thought he would. That he is "going for the money" against these men who were once thought to be some of the most respected in the German community. Camera moves back to* COLONEL LAWSON. *He is staring over at*

the defendants in the dock. The hatred and contempt he feels for them are in his eyes.

COLONEL LAWSON *(continuing).* They share with all the leaders of the Third Reich responsibility for the most . . . malignant . . . the most calculated, the most . . . devastating crimes in the history of mankind. *(pause; looks back at the judges on the bench)* They are perhaps more guilty than some others. They had attained maturity long before Hitler's rise to power. Their minds were not warped at an early age by Nazi teachings. They embraced the ideologies of the Third Reich as educated adults. They, most of all, should have valued justice. *(looks over at the dock once more)* Here they will receive the justice they denied others. They will be judged according to the evidence presented in this courtroom. The prosecution asks nothing more.

*The camera moves to the faces in the courtroom.* LAWSON *returns to his seat at the prosecution table.* RADNITZ *winks at him approvingly.*

HAYWOOD. Herr Rolfe will make the opening statement for the defense.

ROLFE *rises slowly and goes to the microphone in the center of the room. He is a vital-looking young man in his late twenties. He stands before the Tribunal. He looks at the judges on the bench with piercing, arresting eyes. Not allowing their attention to waver for an instant. A word about* ROLFE'S *background. He was once a Hitler youth leader. His studies as a law student were interrupted when he had to join the Army at a very early age. His manner is of decorum and politeness before the Tribunal. Underneath, one sees his scorn of the trials. His conviction that they are unfair, that they are no more than the*

*trial of the vanquished by the vic-
tors, covered by hypocritical, high-
sounding verbiage. Very much appearing in his action, too, is his intention of taking the game at its own
price, to hoist the trials up by their
own petard. But he is even more
deeply involved than that. He is, himself, on trial although he is not fully
aware of it.*

ROLFE. May it please the Tribunal.
*(waits until he has the attention of the
judges completely)* It is not only a
great honor but also a great challenge
for an advocate to aid this Tribunal in
its task. For this is not an ordinary
trial by any means of the accepted
parochial sense. The avowed purpose
of this Tribunal is broader than the
visiting of retribution on a few men. It
is dedicated to the reconsecration of
the Temple of Justice. *(pauses a moment)*

*Camera moves to* HAYWOOD'S *face.*

*Full Shot—The Courtroom*

ROLFE *(continuing).* It is dedicated
to finding a code of justice the whole
world will be responsible to. *(pause)*
How will this code be established? *(he
looks over at* COLONEL LAWSON*)* It
will be established *(pause)* in a clear,
honest evaluation of the responsibility
for the crimes in the indictment stated
by the prosecution. In the words of
the great American jurist, Oliver
Wendell Holmes, "This responsibility
will not be found only in documents
that no one contests or denies. It will
be found in consideration of a politial
or social nature. It will be found, most
of all, in the character of men."
*(pause)* What is the character of Ernst
Janning? Let us examine his life for a
moment. *(pause)*

*Camera moves to* ERNST JANNING'S
*face.*

ROLFE'S VOICE. He was born in
1895. Received the degree of Doctor
of Law in 1917. Became a judge in
East Prussia in 1924. Following
World War One, he became one of
the leaders of the Weimar Republic
and was one of the framers of its
democratic constitution. In subse-
quent years, he achieved international
fame. Not only for his work as a great
jurist, but also as the author of legal
text-books which are still used in uni-
versities all over the world. He became Minister of Justice in Germany
in 1935. A position the equivalent of
the Attorney-General of the United
States. Finally, in a Reichstag speech
of 26 April 1942, Hitler attacked
Janning and forced him to resign.
*(pause)*

*Camera returns to* ROLFE. *He waits
until he has the complete attention of
the judges, arresting them with his
eyes.*

ROLFE *(continuing).* If Ernst Janning is to be found guilty, certain implications must arise. *(pause; sharply)*
A judge does not make the law. He
carries out the laws of his country.
*(pause; with emphasis)* The statement, "My country right or wrong."
was expressed by a great American
patriot. It is no less true for a German
patriot. *(his eyes pierce the judges;
then he looks at* COLONEL LAWSON
*sitting at the prosecution table)*
Should Ernest Janning have carried
out the laws of his country? Or should
he have refused to carry them out and
become a traitor? This is the crux of
the issue at the bottom of this Trial.
*(pause; smiles a little at the judges)*
The defense is as dedicated to finding
responsibility as is the prosecution.
For it is not only Ernst Janning who is
on trial here. It is the German people.

ROLFE *bows politely and goes back
to his seat in front of the dock. He*

*looks over at* COLONEL LAWSON, COL-
ONEL LAWSON *looks over at him. The
two of them stand evaluating each
other. The battle is enjoined.*

*Interior. Palace of Justice, Judges'
Chambers—Day*

HAYWOOD, NORRIS, *and* IVES *enter.
They begin taking off their black
robes. Ives is a handsome-looking
man with imposing presence, in his
late sixties.* NORRIS *is a soft-spoken
man from the South, who is dean of a
law school in Louisiana. His manner
is quiet, observant.* IVES *is talking as
they enter, and takes off his robe.*

IVES. This is interesting. The window looks over the courtyard. You
can see some of the prisoners, coming
out for exercise sometimes.

HAYWOOD *goes to window and
looks out absently.*

NORRIS. It was quite a damning
speech by Colonel Lawson, wasn't it?
*(pause)* I wonder if the men in the
dock can really be responsible for the
things he listed in the indictment.

IVES. I've been here two years.
Once you've been here that long, you
find that responsibility isn't a cut-and-
dried thing. Say, what are you fellows
up to this week-end?

NORRIS. My wife and I are going to
Liège. *(pause)*

IVES *looks at him curiously.*

IVES. There's nothing in Liège. I've
been there.

NORRIS. My son was in the 101st.
He is buried in the American cemetery outside Liège. *(pause)*

IVES. Oh. I'm sorry.

NORRIS. That's all right.

IVES. Well. I guess there's nothing
more here for the moment. Coming
my way, Haywood? *(pause)*

HAYWOOD. No. I'll stay here for a
moment. I'm waiting for some reports
from Byers.

IVES. I'll see you later.

HAYWOOD *(absently).* Yes. Of
course.

HAYWOOD *walks to window and
looks out.*

*Exterior. Prison Courtyard—*
HAYWOOD'S *Point of View from
Chambers*

HAHN, LAMMPE, HOFSTETTER *and*
JANNING *have come out into the yard.
They walk a moment,* HAHN *talking
agitatedly to* HOFFSTETTER *who listens, seemingly confused.* LAMMPE *is
trying to keep up with them.* JANNING
*walks alone. He seems to pay no
attention to the other men. He sits
down on a bench in the courtyard.
The guard stands near him.*

*Interior. Judges' Chambers—Day*

HAYWOOD *stands looking out the
window, watching* JANNING, *wondering about him.* CAPTAIN BYERS *enters.*

CAPTAIN BYERS. Here are the reports you asked for, Sir.

HAYWOOD *(takes them absently).*
Thank you. *(he pauses)* Captain. Do
you think you can get me a copy of
the books that Ernst Janning wrote?

CAPTAIN BYERS. There are quite a
few of them.

HAYWOOD. I'd like to have all of
them, if I can . . . and a copy of the
Weimar Constitution. Do you think
you can get that?

CAPTAIN BYERS Yes. Of course
*(stares at* HAYWOOD *a moment; sensing something).*

*There is a moment.* HAYWOOD
*walks back to the window.*

HAYWOOD. How long have you
been here, Captain?

CAPTAIN BYERS. Two years.

HAYWOOD. Two years. It's a long time.

CAPTAIN BYERS (*quietly*). Yes, Sir.

HAYWOOD. Have any friends here? (*pause*)

CAPTAIN BYERS. Sure.

HAYWOOD. German friends? (*pause*)

CAPTAIN BYERS. Yes.

HAYWOOD. A girl—?

CAPTAIN BYERS. Yes.

HAYWOOD *smiles a little.* (*pause*)

CAPTAIN BYERS (*adds*). Her parents were Nazis. But she was eight years old when they came in. (*pause*)

HAYWOOD. I didn't ask that.

CAPTAIN BYERS. I know. But maybe you were thinking it. It's natural to think about it. (*dryly*) I thought if anybody was going to indoctrinate her, it might as well be me.

*The two of them laugh.*

CAPTAIN BYERS. Is there anything else?

HAYWOOD. I think I'll take a look at the town.

*Exterior. Palace of Justice—Day*

HAYWOOD *comes out of entrance. There are G.I.s and M.P.s everywhere.* HAYWOOD *continues to walk.*

*Exterior. Market Square—Day*

*There are a man and a woman in costume in front of a small, partially bombed-out café. Dancing in costume. Camera pans to* HAYWOOD *sitting at a table. Beer and sausage in a roll in front of him.*

HAYWOOD *is looking at dancers. There is a charm in the music and in the dancing.* HAYWOOD *smiles as he watches them, but the events of the past have not been forgotten by him either.*

*Superimposed over Dancers*

*The feet of German soldiers marching. For a moment, the charming minuet becomes a striding marching song with the heavy black boots of the S.S. Camera returns to the man and woman dancing.*

*Exterior. Nuremberg Field, Nuremberg—Day*

HAYWOOD *walks along the remnant of the stadium. It is still fairly much intact. The only thing that disfigures it seems to be the cracks in the steps, faded paint and the blasted swastika on top of the stadium. His is the lone figure as he walks to the podium where we have seen Hitler speaking at the opening of the film.* HAYWOOD *looks out over the field. Camera explores the field. It is now covered with weeds.*

*Close-up—*HAYWOOD'S *Face*

*Visualizing it as it must have been. The field of brown and scarlet troopers he has seen in newsreels. The voice of Hitler and the "Sieg Heils." We are beginning to hear them as he hears them.* HAYWOOD'S *eyes roaming the field. The "Sieg Heils" are tremendous, as we heard them at the opening of the film. Hitler's voice with his exhortations to hate and sentiment. Camera moves to the top of the stadium to the remnant of the swastika.*

*Exterior. Palace of Justice, Prison Courtyard—Day. Close-up—Rose*

JANNING *is holding it and looking at it in the meager garden.* DR. JOSEPH *approaches him slowly. Speaks to him cautiously.*

DR. JOSEPH. Good afternoon.

JANNING. Good afternoon, Doctor.

DR. JOSEPH. How are you this afternoon?

JANNING. Fine, thank you.

DR. JOSEPH (*dryly*). The other defendants seem to have been cut up about Colonel Lawson's speech. I hope it didn't upset you too much. (*pause*)

JANNING (*pause*). Doctor. The Colonel said we could work around the prison if we want to. I wonder if I could try my hand at the garden? (*pause*)

DR. JOSEPH (*smiles a little*). It's not much of a garden.

JANNING (*smiles a little*). Yes, I know. But I used to work in one at home. I even made a rock garden out of some old bricks. Maybe we could do something like that here. (*pause*)

DR. JOSEPH. I'll speak to the colonel. (*pause*)

JANNING (*quietly*). Thank you. Thank you very much. (*pause*) I'm sorry if I was rude when you asked me about the trial. (*pause*) But the truth is, Doctor, that the trial has no reality for me. No reality at all.

JANNING *continues to stare at flower.* DR. JOSEPH *looks at him, stunned. An* M.P. *comes out to the courtyard. He shouts.*

M.P. Janning! Janning!

JANNING *turns with some irritation at the way he is being called.*

JANNING. Yes.

M.P. *comes over to him.*

M.P. There's someone to see you.
JANNING. Who is it?

M.P. I don't know, but I have to take you to the Visitors' Room right away. (*pause*)

JANNING *begins to follow* M.P. *back into the prison.*

*Interior. Palace of Justice, Prison Waiting-Room—Day*

OSKAR ROLFE *sits on one side of the wire netting in the room.* JANNING *sits down facing* ROLFE *across the netting. Guard remains close by. There is a moment before* ROLFE *speaks.*

ROLFE. Are they treating you all right?

JANNING (*quietly*). Yes. They're treating me all right.

ROLFE. We still have some friends who have contact with the American authorities. I can tell them if they're not treating you all right.

JANNING. They're treating me all right. (*pause*)

ROLFE. Herr Janning. (*pause*) We are both in an embarrassing position. (*pause*) I know you didn't want me as your consel. I know you didn't want anyone. (*pause*) I want to tell you something. Will you listen to me? (*pause*)

JANNING *nods as though not really looking at* ROLFE. ROLFE *speaks nervously as though ill-at-ease in the presence of this eminent figure. But with obviously great compassion. In contrast to his confidence in manner in the courtroom, he seems to be ill-at-ease here.*

ROLFE. I intend to represent your case with complete dignity. (*pause*) There will be no appeal to sentiment. There will be no placing yourself at the mercy of the court. (*pause*) There will be a clear and honest evaluation of responsibility. The game will be played according to their own rules. (*pause*) We will see whether they have the courage to sit in judgment on a man like you. (*pause; thinking*) The way I see it, the most important elements in the case are the sterilization decrees and the Feldenstein-Hoffmann affair.

*Close-up*—JANNING

At the mention of the names Feldenstein and Hoffmann, his face seems to freeze.

*Close-up*—ROLFE

*Looking at him, catching only what he perceives to be his refusal to cooperate. He continues to look at* JANNING, *moved by the sight of this man who has meant so much to the legal profession, in prison clothing and behind the wire netting.*

ROLFE *(continuing)*. Herr Janning. I have followed your career since I was a boy studying at the university. It was because I thought I might be able to achieve some of the things that you did that saw me through the war. You have been a shining light to all of us.

*There is a moment.* ROLFE *sits waiting for* JANNING *to speak.*

JANNING *(speaks finally)*. Are you finished?
ROLFE. Yes.
JANNING *(without any emotion; just a formality)*. Thank you. *(goes)*

ROLFE *looks after him.*

*Interior. Palace of Justice, Courtroom—Day*

DR. KARL WIECK *is on the stand. He is a distinguished-looking man in his seventies. He speaks precisely and slowly.* COLONEL LAWSON *stands before him.*

COLONEL LAWSON. Do you know the defendant, Ernst Janning? *(pause)*
DR. WIECK. Yes, I know him.

*There is a wealth of drama as* DR. WIECK *looks over at his former law student in the dock.*

*Close-up*—DR. WIECK

*Close-up*—JANNING

*Neither one of them really looks into the other's eyes.*

COLONEL LAWSON. Will you tell us in what capacity?
DR. WIECK. We served in the Ministry of Justice together from 1929 to 1935.
COLONEL LAWSON. Did you know him before that?
DR. WIECK. Yes. He was a law student of mine.
COLONEL LAWSON. Did you know him well?
DR. WIECK. Yes.
COLONEL LAWSON. Was he a protégé of yours?
DR. WIECK. Yes.
COLONEL LAWSON. Why?
DR. WIECK *(pause; not looking at* JANNING*)*. He was always a man of great intelligence. He was a man born with the qualities of a great legal mind.
COLONEL LAWSON. Dr. Wieck, will you tell us, from your own experience, the position of the judge in Germany prior to the advent of Adolf Hitler?
DR. WIECK. The position of the judge was one of complete independence.
COLONEL LAWSON. Now. Would you describe the contrast, if any, after the coming to power of National Socialism in 1933?
DR. WIECK *(pause)*. Judges became subject to something outside of objective justice. They became subject to what was "necessary for the protection of the country."
COLONEL LAWSON. Would you explain this, please?
DR. WIECK. The first consideration of the judge became the punishment of acts against the State rather than the objective consideration of the case against the defendant.

COLONEL LAWSON. What other changes were there?

DR. WIECK. The right to appeal was eliminated. The Supreme Court of the Reich was replaced by Peoples' and Special Courts. The concept of race was made a legal concept for the first time.

COLONEL LAWSON. What was the result of this?

DR. WIECK. The result was to hand over the administration of justice into the hands of the dictatorship.

HAYWOOD. I would like to ask a few questions. *(pause)* Did the judiciary protest at these laws abridging their independence?

DR. WIECK. A few of them did. Those who did resigned, or were forced to resign. Others . . .

*He looks over at defendant in dock.*

DR. WIECK *(continuing)*. . . . others adapted themselves to the new situation.

HAYWOOD. Do you think that the judiciary was aware of the consequences to come?

DR. WIECK *sits thinking a moment.*

DR. WIECK. At first, perhaps not. *(pause)* Then it became clear to anyone who had eyes and ears.

HAYWOOD. Thank you.

COLONEL LAWSON. Would you describe for us the changes, if any, in criminal law?

DR. WIECK. It was characterized by the ever-increasing inflation of the death penalty. Sentences were passed against defendants just because they were Jews or politically undesirable. *(pause)* Novel National Socialist measures were introduced, among them sexual sterilization for those who were categorized as "asocial."

COLONEL LAWSON. Dr. Wieck, did it become necessary for judges to wear any distinctive mark on their robes in 1935?

DR. WIECK. Yes. The so-called "Führer's Decree" required judges to wear the insignia of the swastika on their robes.

COLONAL LAWSON. Did you wear such an insignia?

DR. WIECK. No. *(pause)* I would have been ashamed to wear it.

COLONEL LAWSON *(pause)*. Did you resign in 1935?

DR. WIECK. Yes.

COLONEL LAWSON. Did Ernst Janning wear a swastika on his robe?

DR. WIECK. Yes.

COLONEL LAWSON. That's all. Thank you.

COLONEL LAWSON *goes to the prosecution table.* ROLFE *rises slowly from the dock and goes to the witness stand. He stares at the man before him. His attitude toward* DR. WIECK *is careful . . . recognizing the eminent position of* DR. WIECK. *But underneath one can sense hatred. The feeling of one countryman for another. ("You are testifying against your countryman in the presence of the invaders.") He stares at* DR. WIECK *a moment. Then speaks.*

ROLFE. Dr. Wieck, you used the phrase, "what was necessary for the protection of the country." *(pauses significantly)* Would you explain for the Tribunal the conditions in Germany at the time National Socialism came to power.

DR. WIECK *(pause; coolly)*. What conditions?

*There is a moment.* ROLFE *smiles a little.*

ROLFE *(crisply)*. Would you say there was widespread hunger?

DR. WIECK *(pause)*. Yes.

ROLFE *(pause)*. Would you say there was internal disunity?

DR. WIECK *(pause)*. Yes.

ROLFE. Was there a Communist party?

DR. WIECK. Yes.

ROLFE. Was it the third largest party in Germany?

DR. WIECK *(pause)*. Yes.

ROLFE *(significantly)*. Would you say that National Socialism helped to cure some of these conditions?

DR. WIECK *(pause)*. Yes. But at a terrible price.

ROLFE *(smiles a little)*. Dr. Wieck, please confine yourself to answering the questions only. *(pause; significantly)* Therefore, was it not possible that a judge might wear a swastika and yet work for what he thought was best for his country?

DR. WIECK *(pause)*. No. It was not possible.

ROLFE. Dr. Wieck, you were not in the administration from the years 1935 to 1943 by your own admission. Is it not possible that your view of the administration might be distorted?

DR. WIECK *(pause)*. No. It is not.

ROLFE *(pause; calmly)*. How can you testify to what was going on in the administration if you were not there?

DR. WIECK *(pause)*. I had friends in the legal administration. There were books and journals.

ROLFE *(meaningfully)*. From books and journals. I see.

*There is a moment.* ROLFE *continues calmly.*

ROLFE *(continuing)*. Dr. Wieck, you referred to "novel National Socialist measures introduced, among them sexual sterilization." Dr. Wieck, are you aware that this was not invented by National Socialism, but had been advanced for years before as a weapon in dealing with the mentally incompetent and the criminal.

DR. WIECK. Yes. I am aware of that.

ROLFE. Are you aware that it has advocates among leading citizens in many other countries?

DR. WIECK. I am not an expert on such laws.

ROLFE *(crisply)*. Then permit me to read one to you.

ROLFE *signals the clerk in the dock to bring him a book. The clerk comes forward and hands it to him.*

ROLFE *(continuing)*. This is a High Court opinion upholding such laws in existence in another country. "We have seen more than once that the public welfare may call upon the best citizens for their lives. It would be strange, indeed, if it could not call upon those who already sapped the strength of the State, for these lesser sacrifices, in order to prevent our being swamped by incompetence. It is better for all the world, if, instead of waiting to execute degenerate offsprings for crime or to let them starve for their imbecility, society can prevent their propagation by medical means in the first place. Three generations of imbeciles are enough." Do you recognize it now, Dr. Wieck?

DR. WIECK *(with emphatic distaste)*. No, Sir, I don't.

ROLFE *(smiles a little)*. Actually, there is no particular reason why you should, since the opinion upholds the sterilization law in the State of Virginia, in the United States, and was written and delivered by that great American jurist, Supreme Court Justice Oliver Wendell Holmes.

*Close-up*—HAYWOOD

*In reaction.*

*Full Shot—The Courtroom*

ROLFE *puts down the book.* ROLFE *hands the book to the clerk and turns to* DR. WIECK.

ROLFE. Now, Dr. Wieck. In view of what you have just learned, can you still say that this was a "novel National Socialist measure"?

DR. WIECK *(pause).* I can say it because it was never before used as a weapon against political opponents.

ROLFE *(pause).* Do you personally know of a case where someone was sterilized for political reasons?

DR. WIECK. I know such things were done.

*There is an instant.* ROLFE *leans forward.*

ROLFE *(with emphasis).* Please answer the question. Do you know of a case?

DR. WIECK *(pause).* I do not know of a specific name, or of a specific date—

ROLFE *(interrupting).* I am asking you if you have any first-hand, personal knowledge of such a case!

DR. WIECK *(pause).* No. I have no such personal knowledge.

*There is a moment.* ROLFE *makes the most of the moment.*

ROLFE. Dr. Wieck you are aware of the charges in the indictment against Ernst Janning?

DR. WIECK *(pause).* Yes.

ROLFE *(pause).* Can you honestly say he is responsible for them?

DR. WIECK *(quietly).* Yes. I can.

*Pause.* ROLFE *stands staring at* DR. WIECK, *aware of what he must do now.*

ROLFE. Dr. Wieck, do you consider yourself free of responsibility? *(pause)*

DR. WIECK *looks at* ROLFE *in surprise.*

DR. WIECK. Yes, I do.

ROLFE *(pause).* Dr. Wieck, did you ever swear to the Civil Servant Loyalty Oath of 1934?

COLONEL LAWSON *(on his feet).* Your Honor, I object. The witness does not have to answer that question. He is not on trial.

ROLFE *turns to* HAYWOOD

ROLFE. All Germany is on trial, Your Honor. This tribunal placed it on trial when it placed Ernst Janning on trial. *(pause)*

*Close-up—*HAYWOOD

*In reaction.*

*Full Shot—The Courtroom*

ROLFE. If responsibility is to be found, the widest latitude is to be permitted.

*There is a moment.*

HAYWOOD. Objection overruled.

ROLFE *turns back to the stand.* COLONEL LAWSON *remains standing.*

ROLFE. Did you ever swear to the Civil Servant Loyalty Oath of 1934?

DR. WIECK *(pause).* Everyone did.

ROLFE. We are not interested in what everyone did. We are interested in what you did.

*He turns to dock. Speaks to* CLERK.

ROLFE *(continuing).* Would you read the oath from the *Reich Law Gazette,* March 1933?

*The* CLERK *rises in the dock and reads from the journal.*

CLERK. "I swear that I shall be obedient to the leader of the German Reich and people, Adolf Hitler; that I shall be loyal to him; that I will observe the laws; and that I will conscientiously fulfil my duties, so help me God."

*There is a moment. All eyes turn to* DR. WIECK.

DR. WIECK *(finally, as though in explanation)*. Everyone swore to it. It was mandatory.

*Pause.* ROLFE *smiles a little.*

ROLFE *(with emphasis)*. Yes. But you're such a perceptive man, Dr. Wieck. You could see what was coming. You could see that National Socialism was leading Germany to disaster. "It was clear to anyone who had eyes and ears."

*Camera moves up close to* DR. WIECK'S *face as* ROLFE *continues.*

ROLFE *(continuing)*. Didn't you realize what it would have meant if you, and men like you, had refused to swear to the oath? *(there is a moment)* It would have meant that Hitler could never have come to absolute power.

*Close-up*—DR. WIECK

*He sits there trying to think, trying to give a reason for that half-forgotten instant.*

ROLFE'S VOICE. Why didn't you, Doctor? *(pause)* Can you give us an explanation? *(pause)* Did it have something to do with your pension?

*Full Shot—Courtroom*

COLONEL LAWSON *is on his feet at the prosecution table.*

ROLFE. Did your pension mean more to you than your country?

COLONEL LAWSON. Your honor!

ROLFE. No further questions.

DR. WIECK *looks up at* HAYWOOD *as though there were words of justification he would speak. But he knows there is nothing to say now. He looks about as though puzzled, then starts from the stand. The man who thought he had had no part in what happened.*

*With a blemish on his record now. Most importantly, a blemish he will never be able to erase from his own mind.* COLONEL LAWSON *watches him go, moved by what has happened to him on the stand and angered by what he believes to be a breach of legal procedure.*

COLONEL LAWSON *(coming to stand)*. Your Honor, I object to the entire line of questioning and ask that it be stricken from the record!

ROLFE *(as though innocently)*. I thought prosecuting counsel was dedicated to finding responsibility.

COLONEL LAWSON *(impatiently)*. Your Honor, I made an objection.

ROLFE *(as though innocently)*. Prosecution is not interested in finding responsibility?

COLONEL LAWSON *(turning to* ROLFE*)*. There is responsibility for more here than swearing to a Loyalty Oath and you know it!

ROLFE. There is indeed. There is responsibility for heinous crimes. Crimes that have been charged against some of the most eminent men—

COLONEL LAWSON *has heard the word "eminent" so often that it is coming out of his ears.*

COLONEL LAWSON *(heatedly)*. They are all eminent men. Every man who has been in the dock has been an eminent man!

ROLFE *(simultaneously)*. Prosecution has stated it will prove responsibility by evidence—

COLONEL LAWSON *(simultaneously)*. Defense counsel may be speaking that way because he knows no one who was in the administration will step forward and speak the truth.

ROLFE *(objecting)*. Your Honor!

COLONEL LAWSON *(continuing)*.— There is one thing that even the German machine with its monumental efficiency has been unable to destroy—

HAYWOOD *bangs gavel*.

HAYWOOD *(firmly)*. Order!

COLONEL LAWSON.—All the victims. More victims than the world has ever known. They will walk into this courtroom—

HAYWOOD *(firmly)*. Tribunal will now admonish both counsel. It will tolerate nothing like this again. We are not here to listen to outbursts of this kind, but to serve justice. It will not be served by emotions of this kind.

COLONEL LAWSON *(heatedly)*. Your Honor, I made an objection!

HAYWOOD *(firmly)*. Objection overruled! *(bangs gavel)* Court is adjourned until tomorrow morning.

COLONEL LAWSON *stands staring at* HAYWOOD, *then starts to the prosecution table. As he does, he pauses at* ROLFE *in the dock.* ROLFE *smiles at him sardonically.*

*The Dock—Close-up—*JANNING

*He is looking at* ROLFE. *He is not smiling.*

*Interior.* HAYWOOD'S *Quarters, Living-Room—Night*

IVES *and* NORRIS *are sitting on chairs in the living-room.* HAYWOOD *sits on a stool. He has a book in his hand.*

HAYWOOD. Did you ever read any books by Ernst Janning?

*Pause.*

NORRIS. No. I don't think so.

HAYWOOD *goes to bookshelf. Takes out book. Hands it to* IVES.

IVES *(reading title)*. The Meaning of the Law.

NORRIS. How is it? Interesting?

HAYWOOD. All the books by Janning are interesting. They're more than that. They're the picture of an era, its hopes, its aspirations. They weren't very different from ours, really. Listen to this—on the signing of the Weimer Constitution: "Now we can look forward to a Germany without guns and bloodshed. A Germany of justice where men can live instead of die. A Germany of purpose, of freedom, of humanity. A Germany that calls for the best in men." Now how could a man who wrote words like these be part of sterilizations and murders? How could he be?

NORRIS *(pause)*. Dan, there are a lot of things that happened here that nobody seems able to understand.

HAYWOOD. Maybe. But the prosecution is going to have to prove every inch of its allegation against a man like Janning if I'm to pronouce sentence on him.

IVES. Well. I'm on my way. Coming, Ken?

NORRIS. Right.

HAYWOOD. There's just this business on the curtailment of rights.

IVES. It's going to have to wait. I've found after two years in Nuremberg that there's nothing that can't wait here.

*There is an awkward moment.* HAYWOOD *and* NORRIS *exchange an embarrassed look. As they start to walk . . .*

IVES *(continuing)*. Dan, my wife is planning a little get-together at the Grand Hotel tomorrow night. She wants you to come.

HAYWOOD *(pause)*. All right.

IVES. She'd like to fix you up with some kind of female companionship. She has a feeling you might be lonely here.

HAYWOOD. I don't think so, Curtiss.

IVES *looks at* NORRIS.

IVES *(smiles)*. You know how these wives are. Love to play Cupid.

HAYWOOD. Just the same, I just think I'll keep it stag.

IVES. That's up to you. Good night, Dan.

HAYWOOD. Good night.

NORRIS *(smiles)*. Good night.

HAYWOOD *watches them go. Looks around large, empty room. Goes to book by* JANNING *absently. Looks at it again. Puts it down, troubled. Goes into kitchen.*

*Interior.* HAYWOOD'S *Quarters, Kitchen—Night*

*Camera follows* HAYWOOD *as he enters.*

HAYWOOD. Mrs. Halbestadt, I wonder if I could have some—

*He stops as he sees another woman with* MRS. HALBESTADT. *The* WOMAN *is in her forties. Tall, attractive in a rather athletic way. In spite of her capable and athletic look, there is something above all fragile about her. Her clothes are well tailored but they are obviously old. There is a box on the floor before her. It is a large box filled with items.* MR. AND MRS. HAL-BESTADT *start as they see* HAYWOOD, *as though ill-at-ease and apprehensive.*

HAYWOOD *(continuing, quietly)*. Hello.

WOMAN. Hello.

MRS. HALBESTADT *(ill-at-ease)*. Your Honor, this is Mrs. Bertholt. This is His Honor, Judge Haywood. Mrs. Bertholt . . . this is her house . . . she came to get some of her belongings from the basement. I didn't know she was coming tonight or—

MRS. BERTHOLT *speaks quickly, gracefully, assuming responsibility*.

MRS BERTHOLT. It's my responsibility, Mrs. Halbestadt. *(to* HAYWOOD*)* I have just been storing some things in the basement until I could get a room big enough to keep them. I hope you don't mind.

HAYWOOD *doesn't quite know how to relate to this woman. He remembers vaguely what* JUDGE IVES *and* CAPTAIN BYERS *said about her. He is surprised to find her so attractive and delicate a woman. There is also a tremendous charm about* MRS. BERT-HOLT, *and tremendous winsomeness and poignance.*

HAYWOOD. No. No. Not at all.

MRS. BERTHOLT. You can check what I have here if you like.

HAYWOOD. No. No. Of course not.

MRS BERTHOLT. Thank you. I'll just take these out. Thank you, Mrs. Halbestadt.

*She tries to cope with the box.* MRS. HALBESTADT *doesn't help her in the fear that it might bring displeasure to* HAYWOOD. *There is a moment as* HAYWOOD *watches the struggle with the box. His instincts come to the fore.*

HAYWOOD. Here. Let me help you with that.

MRS. BERTHOLT. It's perfectly all right. I can manage.

HAYWOOD *takes box from her.*

HAYWOOD. I'll take it out to the car. I'll tell the driver to take you home.

MRS. BERTHOLT. It's perfectly all right.

HAYWOOD. Please.

HAYWOOD *continues to carry the package out.*

*Exterior.* HAYWOOD'S *quarters— Night*

HAYWOOD *and* MRS. BERTHOLT *start walking toward garage.*

MRS. BERTHOLT *(gracefully and apologetically).* It's heavy. It's full of books and pictures and I don't know what. *(without sentiment)* Things that mean nothing to anyone except me.

HAYWOOD *(calls out to garage).* Mr. Schmidt!

SCHMIDT, *who is polishing the Mercedes-Benz in the garage, anxiously comes over to* HAYWOOD *as soon as he hears his voice.*

SCHMIDT. Your Honor.

*He takes box from* HAYWOOD.

HAYWOOD. Would You take Mrs. Bertholt to her home?

SCHMIDT. Yes, Your Honor.

*He lifts his hat quickly and in perfect form in spite of the heavy box he is carrying.*

SCHMIDT *opens car for* MRS. BERTHOLT.

SCHMIDT. Madame. . . .

MRS. BERTHOLT *(continuing).* Thank you. One-fifteen Karolinenstrasse, please.

*She gets into car.*

MRS. BERTHOLT *(continuing; to* HAYWOOD *without sentiment).* I hope you are comfortable here.

HAYWOOD *(awkwardly).* Yes. I am. Very.

MRS. BERTHOLT. My favorite spot was always the garden. Remind Mr. Halbestadt to take good care of the rock garden. You'll get a great deal of pleasure out of it in the summer. Good night.

HAYWOOD. Good night.

*Car drives off.* HAYWOOD *watches as it goes, then walks slowly back into the house.*

*Interior.* HAYWOOD'S *Quarters, Kitchen—Night*

HAYWOOD. Mrs. Halbestadt, you worked for Mrs. Bertholt, didn't you?

MRS. HALBESTADT *(warily).* Yes, Your Honor.

HAYWOOD *(pause).* How long did she live here?

MRS. HALBESTADT. Mrs. Bertholt? Mrs. Bertholt and her family have lived here for generations, Your Honor.

HAYWOOD. Thanks.

*He stands there thinking.*

MRS. HALBESTADT. Your Honor, you came in here for something—

HAYWOOD. Yes. I was going to make myself a sandwich.

MRS. HALBESTADT. We will make it for you, Your Honor. We will make you anything you want.

HAYWOOD *(embarrassed).* No. It's nothing. I always did it for myself back home.

MRS. HALBESTADT *(stolidly).* What would you like? We have some ham and some tongue and some liver sausage.

HAYWOOD. Liver sausage will be fine.

MRS. HALBESTADT *opens refrigerator and starts preparing the sandwich.* HAYWOOD *watches her.*

HAYWOOD *(continuing; quietly).* That's very kind of you.

*There is a moment,* HAYWOOD *looks at* MR. AND MRS. HALBESTADT *with an agonized expression.*

HAYWOOD *(continuing).* Mr. Halbestadt, what was it like to live under National Socialism?

MR. AND MRS HALBESTADT *exchange a look with each other. A frightened look.*

MRS. HALBESTADT. What was it like?

HAYWOOD. What was it like day-to-day? I know people like you back home. You're good people. I believe that. What was it like for you to live under Hitler?

MRS. HALBESTADT. We were not political. Mr. Halbestadt and I are not political.

HAYWOOD *(pause)*. I know, but you must have been aware of some of the events that were going on.

*Pause.* MRS. HALBESTADT *looks at* MR. HALBESTADT. *They both look, as though blankly, at* HAYWOOD.

HAYWOOD *(with feeling)*. A lot of things were going on, Mr. Halbestadt. There were parades going on. Hitler and Goebbels used to come here every year.

*Pause.* HALBESTADT *and* MRS. HALBESTADT *do not answer.*

HAYWOOD *(continuing)*. What was it like?

MRS. HALBESTADT *(pause)*. We never attended meetings. Never.

HAYWOOD. I'm not putting you on trial, Mrs. Halbestadt. I just would like to know.

MRS. HALBESTADT *finishes making the sandwich. She places it before* HAYWOOD *with a glass of milk.*

HAYWOOD *(continuing)*. Thank you.

MRS. HALBESTADT *(quietly)*. You are welcome, Your Honor.

*There is a moment.* HAYWOOD *speaks in a strained manner.*

HAYWOOD. For instance, there's a place called Dachau. It's eighty miles from here. Did you know anything about it?

MRS. HALBESTADT. We knew nothing about it. Nothing about it. How can you ask if we knew anything about it?

*She seems on the point of tears.* HAYWOOD *looks from* HALBESTADT *to* MRS. HALBESTADT. *Her manner seems very genuine. So genuine that he is filled with a pang.*

HAYWOOD. I'm sorry.

*There was a pause.* HAYWOOD *tries to eat the sandwich.*

MRS. HALBESTADT. Is the sandwich all right, Your Honor?

HAYWOOD. Yes. It's fine. Thank you.

*There is a moment.* HALBESTADT *finally speaks.*

HALBESTADT. Your Honor, we are just little people. We lost a son in the war. We lost a daughter in the bombing. We went hungry during the war. It was terrible for us.

HAYWOOD *(with feeling)*. I'm sure it was.

MRS. HALBESTADT. Hitler did some good things. I won't say he didn't do some good things. He built the Autobahn. He gave more people work. We won't say he didn't do some good things. But the bad things—the things they say he did to the Jews and the rest. We didn't know about such things. Very few Germans knew.

*Pause.* HAYWOOD *sits thinking a moment. He takes another bite out of the sandwich.*

HALBESTADT. And if we did know, what could we do?

*There is a moment.* HAYWOOD *catches something in his voice.*

HAYWOOD. But Mrs. Halbestadt said you didn't know.

*There is a moment.* HALBESTADT *and* MRS. HALBESTADT *exchange a look. It is a moment before* HAYWOOD *continues quietly.*

HAYWOOD *(continuing)*. Mrs. Bertholt. What was Mrs. Bertholt's reaction to all of this?

*Pause.* HALBESTADT *and* MRS. HALBESTADT *look at one another.*

MRS. HALBESTADT. Mrs. Bertholt. Mrs. Bertholt is a very fine woman. Your Honor.

HAYWOOD *(pause)*. What about her husband?

MRS. HALBESTADT *(cautiously)*. He was in the Army.

HAYWOOD *(pause)*. Oh? What happened to him?

HALBESTADT *(cautiously)*. He was a defendant in the Malmedy Case, Your Honor.

HAYWOOD *(realizing)*. Of course . . . General Bertholt. Karl Bertholt.

HALBESTADT *and* MRS. HALBESTADT *look at each other as though not understanding.*

MRS. HALBESTADT *(quietly)*. He was executed, Your Honor.

HAYWOOD. Yes . . . I know that.

*Close-up*—HAYWOOD

*Interior. Palace of Justice, Courtroom—Day*

COLONEL LAWSON *is presenting documents to* CAPTAIN BYERS *who sits at a small table near the judge's bench. He is presenting the documents before the Tribunal.*

COLONAL LAWSON *(looking at documents)*. Prosecution presents affidavit Document No. 448 which concerns the seamstress, Annie Meunch. Document reads as follows: "District Court of Frankfurt am Main has decided the following: the seamstress Annie Meunch, daughter of Wilhelm Meunch, is to be sterilized. She is therefore requested to present herself within two weeks at one of the hospitals mentioned below. If she does not take herself voluntarily, she will be taken by force." Next, Document No. 449, interrogatories in the English and German Text, concerning the farmer's helper, Meyer Eichinger—

ROLFE *(rises from dock)*. Your Honor, defense objects to introduction of these documents. According to the ruling of the first Tribunal, such documents are not admissible unless supported by independent evidence of their authenticity.

*Pause.* HAYWOOD *confers with other judges.*

HAYWOOD *(finally)*. Objection sustained.

COLONEL LAWSON *smiles a little. He has been expecting this objection by* ROLFE.

COLONEL LAWSON. Your Honor, may I ask the defense a question? *(turns to* ROLFE*).* Would evidence on sterilization be acceptable if there were a witness?

*Pause.* ROLFE *rises again. An apprehension flashes through his mind.*

ROLFE. Yes. It would.

COLONEL LAWSON *(pause)*. Prosecution calls the Witness, Rudolf Petersen.

*A man gets up from the rear of the auditorium. All eyes turn to him. He starts up the aisle. The man is in his thirties. Suit worn but carefully pressed. Hair carefully combed.*

CAPTAIN BYERS. Will you raise your right hand and repeat after me the following oath? I swear by God the Almighty and Omniscient that I will speak the pure truth and will withhold and add nothing.

*Pause.* PETERSEN *repeats the oath. As he does, the camera moves to* ROLFE *in the dock.* ROLFE *leans back and looks at* JANNING's *face, trying to get a clue from something there.* JANNING *stares ahead at* PETERSEN *without recognition. Camera moves back to* COLONEL LAWSON *and his witness.*

COLONEL LAWSON *(begins gently).* Will you please tell the court your full name and place of residence?

PETERSEN. Rudolf Petersen. Frankfurt am Main. Gretweg No. 7.

COLONEL LAWSON. When were you born, Mr. Petersen?

PETERSEN. On 20 May 1915, in Limburg.

COLONEL LAWSON. What is your occupation?

PETERSEN. Baker's helper. I'm a baker's helper.

COLONEL LAWSON. Are your parents living?

PETERSEN. No. They are not.

COLONEL LAWSON. What were the causes of their deaths?

PETERSEN *looks at* COLONEL LAWSON *as though he doesn't quite understand the question.* COLONEL LAWSON *persists gently.*

COLONEL LAWSON *(continuing).* Were they natural causes?

PETERSEN. Yes. Natural causes.

COLONEL LAWSON. Mr. Petersen, what political party did your father belong to?

PETERSEN. The Communist party.

COLONEL LAWSON. Now, Mr. Petersen, do you remember anything unusual that happened to you and your family in 1933 before the Nazis came to power? I mean anything of a violent nature?

PETERSEN. Yes.

COLONEL LAWSON. How old were you at the time?

PETERSEN. Seventeen.

COLONEL LAWSON. Would you tell the court what happened?

PETERSEN. Some S.A. men broke into our house. They broke the windows and doors. They called us traitors and tried to attack my father.

COLONEL LAWSON. What happened then?

PETERSEN. My brothers and I went to help my father. We drove them out of the house. There was a fight in the street. We beat up the S.A. men and turned them over to the police.

COLONEL LAWSON. Did the police do anything about the matter?

PETERSEN. No.

COLONEL LAWSON. Why not?

PETERSEN. They had elections, then—at that time.

COLONEL LAWSON. The time the National Socialists came to power?

PETERSEN. Yes.

COLONEL LAWSON *(pause).* Will you tell the Tribunal what happened after 1933—after the Nazis came to power.

PETERSEN. I got a job on a farm, but for the work it was necessary to drive a truck. I went to the town hall to apply for a license.

COLONEL LAWSON. What happened?

PETERSEN. They took me to an official.

COLONEL LAWSON *(pause).* Did you ever have any dealings with this official before?

PETERSEN. Yes. He was one of the men who had broken into our house.

COLONEL LAWSON *(pause).* What did he say to your application?

PETERSEN. He said an examination there would have to be.

COLONEL LAWSON. Where was the examination to take place?

PETERSEN. In the district court of Stuttgart.

COLONEL LAWSON. Who was the presiding justice in the court?

PETERSEN. Justice Hoffstetter.

*Camera moves to* HOFFSTETTER *in dock. He looks at* PETERSEN *as though confused.*

COLONEL LAWSON. What happened in the courtroom?

PETERSEN. They asked me for my name and so forth.

COLONEL LAWSON. What else did they ask you?

PETERSEN. They asked me, "When was Adolf Hitler and Dr. Goebbels born?"

COLONEL LAWSON. What was your reply?

PETERSEN. I told them I didn't know and I didn't care either.

*There is a ripple of laughter in the courtroom. It seems to buoy up* PETERSEN'S *confidence a little. He smiles at the spectators in the courtroom who have laughed.*

COLONEL LAWSON. Were there any other questions?

PETERSEN. No. They told me I would hear from them within ten days.

COLONEL LAWSON *goes to the prosecution table.* RADNITZ *hands him a paper.*

COLONEL LAWSON. Mr. Petersen. Do you recognize this piece of paper?

*He hands it to* PETERSEN. PETERSEN *looks at it.*

PETERSEN. Yes. Yes.

COLONEL LAWSON. Would you read it for the Tribunal?

PETERSEN *seems to have difficulty reading.*

PETERSEN. "District Court of Stuttgart decided the following: the baker, Rudolf Petersen, born 20 May 1915, son of railway employee Hans Petersen, is to be sterilized."

COLONAL LAWSON. Would you read the last paragraph?

PETERSEN *(with difficulty reading).* "You are therefore requested to present yourself within two weeks to one of the hospitals mentioned below. If you do not betake yourself voluntarily, you will be taken by force."

COLONAL LAWSON *(pause).* Would you read the signature at the bottom?

PETERSEN. "Presiding Justice Friedrich Hoffstetter."

COLONEL LAWSON *(pause; with emphasis).* Now, would you read what is written below the signature?

PETERSEN. "By authority of Ernst Janning, Minister of Justice."

*Camera moves to* HAYWOOD'S *face. The surprise on it is clearly indicated there.*

*Full Shot—The Courtroom*

ROLFE *rises from the dock.*

ROLFE. Your Honor, may the defense see the document?

COLONEL LAWSON. Yes. You may.

AIDE *comes from dock. Takes document from* COLONEL LAWSON. *Brings it to* ROLFE *who reads it constantly during the following scene.*

COLONEL LAWSON *(continuing).* What did you do after you received the letter, Mr. Petersen?

PETERSEN. I ran away. I stayed at the farm of a friend.

COLONEL LAWSON. What happened after you returned subsequently?

PETERSEN. The police came. The police came.

COLONEL LAWSON. Where did they take you?

PETERSEN. To the hospital. *(pause)*

HAYWOOD *bending over on bench.*

HAYWOOD. Excuse me. Would you mind speaking a little louder?

PETERSEN. To the hospital.

COLONEL LAWSON. What happened at the hospital?

PETERSEN. They kept me there. *(pause)* The nurse came in to prepare me for the operation. She told me she thought the whole thing was terrible. *(pause)* The doctor came in who was supposed to do it. He said it was a disgrace.

COLONEL LAWSON *(pause)*. Were you in fact sterilized?

PETERSEN *(pause)*. Yes.

COLONEL LAWSON *(pause; gently)*. Thank you, Mr. Petersen, That's all.

COLONEL LAWSON *goes back to the prosecution table. He looks at* ROLFE *as though to say, "Now let's see you get out of this one." There is a moment. All eyes go to* ROLFE. ROLFE *rises slowly from the dock. He goes to the witness stand. He stands there staring at* PETERSEN *a moment before speaking. He smiles a little. He bows a little formally.*

ROLFE. Mr. Petersen. *(politely, almost gently; probing, almost as if he doesn't know what he is probing for)* You worked as a baker's helper. *(pause)*

PETERSEN. Yes. *(pause)*

ROLFE. What other occupations have you held? *(pause)*

PETERSEN. I have worked for my father.

ROLFE. What did your father do?

PETERSEN. He was a railroad worker. *(pause)*

ROLFE. What did he do?

PETERSEN. He carried signal cards on the railroads. *(pause)*

ROLFE. Mr. Petersen. You spoke about your brothers. How many brothers do you have?

PETERSEN. Five.

ROLFE. How many sisters?

PETERSEN. Four.

ROLFE. Four. *(conversationally, in a friendly, intimate manner)* Then you are a family of ten.

PETERSEN. Yes. Ten.

ROLFE. What occupation do your brothers have?

PETERSEN. They are all laborers.

ROLFE. Laborers. I see. *(pause)* Mr. Petersen . . . *(pause)*. You say the court at Stuttgart asked you two questions. Birth dates of Hitler and Dr. Goebbels.

PETERSEN *(pause)*. Yes.

ROLFE *(pause)*. What else did they ask you?

PETERSEN *(pause)*. Nothing else.

ROLFE. Are you sure your recollection is correct?

COLONEL LAWSON *is on his feet immediately.*

COLONEL LAWSON. Your Honor, objection! The counsel has no right to suggest that the witness's memory is inaccurate.

HAYWOOD *(pause; firmly)*. Objection sustained.

ROLFE. *(amending his tone)*. Mr. Petersen, I mean, are you sure there were no questions about your schooling?

COLONEL LAWSON *is on his feet. He snaps out. . . .*

COLONEL LAWSON: Objection, Your Honor. The witness has already answered that question.

HAYWOOD *(firmly)*. Objection sustained.

ROLFE *(pause)*. Could I ask you how long did you attend school, Mr. Petersen?

PETERSEN. Six years.

ROLFE. Six years. *(pause)* Why not longer?

PETERSEN *(pause)*. I didn't want to attend longer. I had to go to work.

*Pause.* ROLFE *smiles a little.*

ROLFE. Would you consider yourself a very bright fellow at school?

PETERSEN *(pause; flustered)*. School? That's so long ago I—

ROLFE *stares at* PETERSEN *realizing by* PETERSEN'S *reaction that he has hit something here. He continues steadily.*

ROLFE. Are you sure you were not able to keep up with the others and that is why you did not continue?

COLONEL LAWSON *is on his feet.*

COLONEL LAWSON. Your Honor. Objection. The witness's school record has nothing to do with what happened to him.

ROLFE *(quietly)*. It was the job of the Health Court to sterilize the mentally incompetent.

HAYWOOD. Objection overruled.

*Pause.* PETERSEN *stares at* ROLFE *with terror now.*

ROLFE *(continuing)*. You say your parents died of natural causes.

PETERSEN *(pause)*. Yes.

ROLFE *(pause)*. Would you describe in detail that illness your mother died of?

PETERSEN *(pause)*. She died of heart disease.

ROLFE *(pause)*. During the last stages of her illness, did your mother show any mental peculiarities?

PETERSEN *(pause; with emotion)*. No!

ROLFE. In the decision that came down from Stuttgart, it is stated that your mother suffered from hereditary feeble-mindedness.

PETERSEN *(pause; cries out)*. It's a lie!

ROLFE *(pause; calmly)*. Could you give us some clarification as to how the Hereditary Health Court at Stuttgart arrived at that decision?

*Pause.* PETERSEN *speaks with emotion, trying to think.*

PETERSEN. It was just something they said to put me on the operating table.

*He speaks to Tribunal, as though trying to convince them.*

PETERSEN *(continuing)*. It was just something they said!

ROLFE *(pause)*. Mr. Petersen, there was a simple question that the Health Court always asked. Form a sentence out of the words; *hare, hunter, field;* perhaps you can do it for us now.

COLONAL LAWSON *is on his feet.*

COLONEL LAWSON *(simultaneously)*. Your Honor, objection!

*Camera moves to* HAYWOOD'S *face. His face is pained for* PETERSEN, *feeling for him. Camera moves back as* HAYWOOD *speaks to* PETERSEN, *gently.*

HAYWOOD. Mr. Petersen, was the court at Stuttgart constituted like this?

PETERSEN *looks at* HAYWOOD *without understanding.* HAYWOOD *speaks gently.*

HAYWOOD *(continuing)*. Was there an audience?

PETERSEN. Yes. There was an audience.

*There is a moment.*

HAYWOOD *(quietly)*. Objection overruled.

ROLFE. *Hare—hunter—field,* Mr. Petersen. *(pause)* Take your time.

*There is a moment. Camera moves to* PETERSEN'S *face. He sits there as though trying to come to terms with the single fact. Hitting against it time and again.*

PETERSEN *(trying)*. Hare . . . hunter . . . field. *(pause)* Hare . . . *(but the enormity of what was done to him doesn't let him. He begins to talk in a confused fashion, lacking clarity)* They had made up their minds before I walked into court. They had made up this minds! *(his emotions run over him like a roaring ocean, covering everything else)* And then they put me in the hospital just like a criminal. Just like a criminal. And I couldn't say anything. I just had to lay there *(trying to come to terms with something again)* My mother. My mother was a servant woman who worked hard all her life. *(with emotion)* It's not fair to say things about a woman like that. It's not fair! *(digs into his pocket. Comes out with worn picture)* I have her picture here with me. I would like to show it to the Tribunal. I would like them to look at it. *(offers it to* HAYWOOD*)* I would like them to judge whether she was feebleminded. I would like them to judge.

*He sits there. Holding out a worn picture in his hand. There is a dead silence in the courtroom, then* PETERSEN *realizes himself that he has been talking irrationally. He stares at the picture in his hands.*

ROLFE *(finally)*. I feel it is my duty to point out to the Tribunal that the witness is not in control of his mental processes. *(pause)*

PETERSEN *(bursts out)*. I am not! I know I am not! I never have been since that day! Since that day—since that day I am half of what I've ever been before! *(pause)*

ROLFE *(quietly)*. The Tribunal does not know how you were before. It can never know. It has only your word.

ROLFE *walks slowly from the stand back to the dock. There is no pride in his walk.*

*Close-up—*PETERSEN

PETERSEN *looks out into the courtroom for reassurance. Eyes look back. Wondering. Uncertain.* PETERSEN *realizes that* ROLFE *is right: they will never know.*

*Close-up—*HAYWOOD

*Feeling for* PETERSEN. *Torn with emotion.*

*Close-up—*ROLFE

*He doesn't look up. We know he isn't proud of what he has done.*

*The Bench—Close-up—*HAYWOOD

*Torn with emotion. Aghast at what has happened in the court to* PETERSEN. *Feeling tremendous compassion for him. Yet, not wanting to believe that* JANNING *could have been part of these events that the prosecution alleges. He rises slowly.*

*Interior. Grand Hotel, Bar—Night—The Stage*

*A* MAN *in black robe and white hair made up to resemble* HAYWOOD *in court is singing a song to the audience. A* WOMAN *is at the piano. The* MAN *begins to sing softly in broken English. The style is reminiscent of the old Brecht-Weill cabaret style. But the content is quite different. For the* MAN *sang under the Nazis as well. The theme of his song is justice. The theme that the victors will always be the judges of the vanquished. As he sings on, it is obvious underneath the satire how bitterly he feels about the Tribunal and the infidels. As he sings on, the Camera wanders around the ballroom. While most of the customers laugh, there is an uneasiness underneath the laugh. For Americans are traditionally uncomfortable in the role of occupiers of another country. And they feel perhaps there is some truth to the* MAN'S *pointed barbs. Camera explores the ballroom. The Grand Hotel ballroom has the atmosphere of people trying hard to enjoy themselves outside the courtroom. Mostly populated by people who work on the staff of the Trials. Many men in uniform. Some women in uniform. Camera goes to table where* HAYWOOD, JUDGE IVES, *and* MRS. IVES *are seated.* MRS. IVES *is a pretty, soft woman in her late sixties. She has a very pronounced New England twang.*

IVES. I don't think they should be allowed to sing stuff like that. As a matter of fact I think it constitutes contempt—

HAYWOOD *(smiles a little).* What difference does it make if it's what they're thinking anyway. *(pause)*

IVES *(smiles).* I guess you're right. *(looks around, spots someone)* Hey, Max! *(turns to* HAYWOOD, *explaining)* Max Perkins. He's with the U.P. here.

*Camera moves to* MAX PERKINS *at the entrance to the ballroom. He is accompanied by a woman who we cannot see clearly yet and is talking to the maître d'hôtel. As he hears* IVES'S *voice he turns and takes the lady's arm. We see now that the lady he is accompanying is* MRS. BERTHOLT. *They start toward* IVES'S *and* HAYWOOD'S *table.* IVES *and* HAYWOOD *rise as* MRS. BERTHOLT *and* PERKINS *approach.*

IVES. Max, what are you doing here?

PERKINS *(dryly).* I thought you might kick up a row or something.

IVES. I haven't had that much to drink yet.

PERKINS. I'm sorry. This is Judge Ives. Mrs. Ives. Judge Haywood. Mrs. Bertholt.

MRS. BERTHOLT *(quietly).* We've met.

HAYWOOD. Yes. We have.

IVES. Won't you join us for a drink?

PERKINS *looks at* MRS. BERTHOLT.

MRS. BERTHOLT. Thank you. We'd like to very much. *(they sit down)*

IVES. Waiter. *(then calls grossly)* Herr Ober!

MRS. IVES. Curtiss, your German is terrible.

IVES. I thought it was getting better.

MRS. BERTHOLT *and* PERKINS *laugh a little.*

IVES *(changing the subject gracefully).* Doing a story on the feature trials, Max?

PERKINS *(laughs).* I'll tell you something frankly, Judge. At the moment, I couldn't give a story away on the Nuremberg trials. *(pause)*

HAYWOOD. What do you mean, Mr. Perkins?

PERKINS *(looks at him).* The American public just isn't interested any more. *(pause)*

HAYWOOD *(looks at him. Quietly).* Mr. Perkins. The war's only over three years.

PERKINS *(shrugs realistically).* That's right.

*There is a moment.* WAITER *comes over.*

WAITER. Can I take your order?

IVES. What will you have, ladies? How about some more beer, Dan? It's wonderful here.

HAYWOOD *(quietly. Smiles a little).* I've had my fill of beer for the moment. I wonder if I could order something else?

MRS. BERTHOLT. Why don't you try some Sonnenberg or Schalbenwinkel? (HAYWOOD *looks at her bewildered. Smiles*) It's the local wine.

HAYWOOD *(repeats with a little difficulty).* Sonneberg or Schal—

MRS. BERTHOLT *(smiles).* Schalbenwinkel.

HAYWOOD *(looks at* WAITER*).* I'll try some Schalbenwinkel. *(the capricious sound of the name intrigues him)*

MRS. BERTHOLT. The same, please.

IVES *(with a nod to* PERKINS*).* We'll stay with the beer.

WAITER *(nods and bows).* Thank you. Thank you, ladies and gentlemen. *(he goes)*

*There is a pause.*

HAYWOOD *(smiles at* MRS. BERTHOLT*).* I hope you got home all right that night.

MRS. BERTHOLT. Yes, I did. Thank you. I don't know how I would have managed without the car.

HAYWOOD. You speak English very well, Mrs. Bertholt.

MRS. BERTHOLT. My husband and I spent some years in America.

*There is an awkward moment.*

MRS. BERTHOLT *(continuing; she covers it by continuing).* I hope you've been able to see some of Nuremberg.

HAYWOOD *(laughing a little).* Mainly the road from my house to the Palace of Justice. And the parts that deal with the case, of course. *(pauses awkwardly)* The historical aspects. *(pause)*

MRS. BERTHOLT *(smiles a little).* The Nazi aspects. You should see some of the other parts of Nuremberg. It's been here a long time. Long before Hitler.

HAYWOOD. I was in the old section . . . once. We've just been so busy. *(pause)* What would you suggest?

MRS. BERTHOLT. There's the Market Square. And there are many beautiful things in the old part of Nuremberg. There are even some museums we're trying to rebuild. *(pause)* There is a piano concert next week at the old opera house. Arthur Reiss. He was a refugee from Hitler in the early days. We persuaded him to come back. It ought to be quite an evening. Would you all like to come?

IVES *(making a little joke at his own expense).* I'm afraid John Philip Sousa is about our speed.

MRS. BERTHOLT *(to* HAYWOOD*).* Would you like to come?

HAYWOOD *(finally).* Yes. I would.

MRS. BERTHOLT *(smiles a little to* HAYWOOD*).* I'll tell them to leave a ticket at the box office for you. I'm on the committee. *(pause)*

HAYWOOD. Thank you very much, Mrs. Bertholt.

MRS. BERTHOLT *(quietly).* It's nothing. You see, I have a mission with Americans, as Mr. Perkins can tell you.

MRS. IVES. What is that, Mrs. Bertholt?

MRS. BERTHOLT. To convince you that we're not all monsters.

*At this point,* COLONEL LAWSON *comes by accompanied by* MAJOR RADNITZ. *He walks unsteadily. He has obviously had a few drinks and is feeling the effects of the events of the courtroom that afternoon and the bitter disappointment he has shared with* PETERSEN. *He is greeted by* HAYWOOD *who spots him.*

HAYWOOD. Good evening Colonel.

*There is an immediate tension at the table.*

COLONEL LAWSON (*it is apparent that he is a little unsteady on his feet*). Good evening, Mrs. Bertholt, Mrs. Ives.

MRS. BERTHOLT (*quietly. Color draining from her face*). I hope you'll excuse me. (*starts to rise*)

HAYWOOD (*rises: with some surprise*). But you've just come, Mrs. Bertholt.

MRS. BERTHOLT. I must go. Please excuse me. It was very nice meeting you. (*to* IVESES) Good-bye. (*then to* HAYWOOD) If you really want to hear the concert, the ticket will be at the box office for you.

HAYWOOD. Thank you.

PERKINS (*quietly*). Good night.

HAYWOOD. Good night.

*There is a moment.* MAJOR RADNITZ *watches* COLONEL LAWSON *warily, knowing his feelings, sensing tension at the table.*

MAJOR RADNITZ (*meaningly*). We have to be going, too.

COLONEL LAWSON *sits down at the table. There is an uneasy moment.*

COLONEL LAWSON. Mrs. Bertholt doesn't harbor a burning passion for me. I prosecuted her husband.

IVES. There are many people who think that a death sentence wouldn't be passed against General Bertholt today. (*pause*)

COLONEL LAWSON (*heatedly*). I'm sure there are. I'm sure there are people who think that all the prisoners in Nuremberg should be free today.

MAJOR RADNITZ *covers his eyes with his hands mercifully.*

COLONEL LAWSON (*continuing: catches himself before he goes further*). I've had one or two too many, as might be painfully obvious to you gentlemen. The spectacle this afternoon with Mr. Petersen put me off my feed. Sorry.

WAITER *brings drinks.* COLONEL LAWSON *takes one of the extra glasses and drinks from it without further ado.*

COLONEL LAWSON (*continuing*). Prosit. Beer is good. They make it good in this country. (*pause. Looks at* IVES *and* HAYWOOD *a moment*) There's one thing about Americans. We're not cut out to be occupiers. We're new at it and we're not very good at it. We come here. We see this beautiful country—and it is beautiful—we see the culture that goes back hundreds of years. We see its *gemütlich* charm and the charm of people like Mrs. Bertholt. We have a built-in inferiority complex. We forgive and forget easy. We give the other guy the benefit of the doubt. That's the American way. (*pause*) We beat the greatest war machine since Alexander the Great—and now the Boy Scouts take over.

IVES. The trouble with you, Colonel, is that you'd like to indict the whole country. That might be emotionally satisfying for you, but it's not exactly practical. And hardly fair.

COLONEL LAWSON *looks at* IVES. *He speaks quietly, bitterly.*

COLONEL LAWSON. *Hare, hunter, field.* Let's be fair. (*quietly*) The hare was shot by the hunter in the field. It's really quite simple. (*pause*)

HAYWOOD *quietly smiles a little, understanding* LAWSON's *feelings, but firmly.*

MAJOR RADNITZ (*dryly*). Colonel, I think we'd better be going. (LAWSON *waves him aside*)

HAYWOOD. We really shouldn't be discussing this, Colonel.

COLONEL LAWSON (*dryly*). No. We're fair Americans and true blue. We mustn't do anything that's out of order. (*scathingly, to* HAYWOOD) There are no Nazis in Germany. Didn't you know that, Judge? The Eskimos invaded Germany and took over. That's how all those terrible things happened. It wasn't the fault of the Germans. It was the fault of those damn' Eskimos!

*There is a moment. He looks at the judges realizing how far he has gone.* MAJOR RADNITZ *shakes his head slowly.* COLONEL LAWSON *goes, a little unsteadily, followed by* MAJOR RADNITZ *whose face expresses only the greatest misgivings.*

IVES (*to* HAYWOOD). You know, that's one problem with the prosecution. It's filled with young radicals like Lawson.
HAYWOOD (*smiles a little*). Is that what Colonel Lawson is, a radical?
IVES. He was a personal protégé of F.D.R. (*pause*)
HAYWOOD (*jocularly*). F.D.R. had a few friends who weren't radicals.
IVES. Name one.
HAYWOOD (*with humor*). Wendell Willkie, for one.
IVES. Willkie. . . . (*snorts*) Is that your idea of a Conservative?

HAYWOOD *laughs a little.*

IVES (*looks at him*). As a matter of fact, I've been wondering how you stand, Dan.
HAYWOOD. I'll clarify that for you, Curtiss. I'm a rock-ribbed Republican who thinks Roosevelt was a great man.
IVES (*dryly*). Oh. One of those.

*An American* CAPTAIN *has made his way into the ballroom. He goes to the platform interrupting the* SINGER.

*There is a moment as the audience begins to buzz with speculation. He goes to the microphone.*

CAPTAIN (*into microphone*). I'm sorry to interrupt the entertainment but I have to request that the following officers report to their units: Major McCarthy, Major Citron, Major Cantor, Captain Byers, Captain Connell.

*Camera moves to table with* HAYWOOD, JUDGE IVES *and* MRS. IVES. *They watch the* CAPTAIN *on the platform speculatively. There are sounds of trucks moving outside.*

CAPTAIN (*continuing*). Captain Douglas, Captain Wolff, Major Booth, Major Rice. Thank you. The dancing will continue now.

*But there is too much confusion for the entertainment to continue.* CAPTAIN *walks from platform and starts out of the ballroom. Other* OFFICERS *who have been called walk out of the ballroom. Among them is* CAPTAIN BYERS *with an attractive young german* GIRL *in her early twenties.* HAYWOOD *hails* CAPTAIN BYERS.

HAYWOOD. Harry!

CAPTAIN BYERS *pauses at their table.*

HAYWOOD (*continuing*). What is it?
CAPTAIN BYERS. The Russians have made their move in Czechoslovakia. (*pause. There is tension at the table*) There's a rumor Masaryk has committed suicide. We're sending some units up there.
IVES. What do you think's going to happen?
CAPTAIN BYERS. I really don't know, Sir. (*starts, then stops awkwardly*) Oh. (*looks at* JUDGE HAYWOOD) This is Elsa Scheffler.

HAYWOOD *smiles at* ELSA SCHEF-FLER *who mumbles "good evening" in German. They exit.*

IVES *(quietly).* This is it. *(dryly)* The end of the grand alliance.

MRS. IVES. What are you getting so excited about, Curtiss?

IVES *(bursts out).* What do you mean—what am I getting so excited about? The Czech border's only sixty miles away. Supposing they decide to come over the border?

HAYWOOD. Nobody's coming over the border, Curtiss. Not yet, anyway.

IVES. How do we know? Nobody thought they'd take over Czechoslovakia. *(pause)* Dan, let's face it. The Russians are in Czechoslovakia. The real fight for Germany is on.

*Close-up—*HAYWOOD'S *face*

*Exterior. Palace of Justice, Prison Courtyard—Day*

HAHN *has a copy of the Stars and Stripes in his hand. He is reading it to the others.* JANNING *is working on the rock garden. He gives no indication of hearing what* HAHN *is reading.*

HAHN. "The Secretary of State stated in a speech in Stuttgart today that the time has come for us to help the German people to the plane of self-independence. President Truman responded to the crisis by calling for an extension of Military Training. He stated that he is deeply concerned with the survival of the Western nations in face of the threat from the East." *(pause. Lowers paper)* Threat from the East . . . Survival of the Western nations. *(quietly)* Just as Hitler said. Just as Hitler said. The clash for survival between West and East. He knew. He knew. *(pause)* They'll see we knew what we were doing all the time. *(pause. With eyes burning)* We must stand together now. The

most crucial part of the case is coming up now. *(pause)* They cannot call us criminals and at the same time ask us to help them. *(pause)*

*Camera goes to close-up—*HOFF-STETTER. *He nods solemnly.*

*Close-up—*LAMMPE

*He looks at* HAHN *raptly.*

*Close-up—*JANNING

*He seems not to have heard* HAHN'S *words. He continues to put the bricks around the garden.*

HAHN. Herr Janning. Did you hear this? (JANNING *does not answer*) Herr Janning. Did you hear what is in the paper?

JANNING *(finally. As he works on garden).* I'm not interested in what is in the paper.

HAHN. You must stand with us. It is not good for Germans to turn on one another. It is not good for them to see that now.

JANNING *stops a moment. Then turns. Looks at* HAHN. *Begins slowly.*

JANNING *(finally).* We have fallen on good times, haven't we, Herr Hahn? In the old times it would have made your day if I had deigned to say "good morning" to you. Now that we are in this place together, you feel obliged to order me what to do with my life.

HAHN *(stolidly).* We must stand together now. We have common ground now.

JANNING. What do I have in common with you? What do I have in common with you and the rest of the Party hacks like you? Listen to me, Herr Hahn. There were terrible things that may have happened to me in my life, but the worst thing that has ever happened is that I find myself in the company of men like you. What do I have in common with you?

HAHN (*stolidly*). You have something in common. You were part of the same régime. You stood by that régime the same as the rest of us. (*pause*) There is something else you have in common. You are a German.

*Close-up*—JANNING

*He realizes the truth of this. He looks at* HAHN, *realizing that his only defense can be the defense of men like* HAHN.

*Interior. Opera House—Night*

*A burst of music from the stage.* ARTHUR REISS, *a sensitive musician with white hair is playing at the piano. Camera probes the faces of the German people listening to the music from the stage of the auditorium. They are sitting in their overcoats because there is no heat in the auditorium. They are obviously deeply moved by the music. They are listening to it with the knowledge of people who know the next bar of music that is coming up. Camera moves to* HAYWOOD *sitting in audience. He looks about to locate* MRS. BERTHOLT. *He sees her finally and turns his attention back to the stage.*

*The Stage*

*The pianist continues, the music growing in climax.*

*Interior. Auditorium*

HAYWOOD *turns to look at the people in the audience again. They are deeply moved.*

*Interior. Lobby—Night*

MRS. BERTHOLT *stands talking to friends.* HAYWOOD *waits in a corner of the lobby with the driver,* SCHMIDT.

*Finally,* MRS. BERTHOLT *approaches* HAYWOOD. HAYWOOD *looks at* MRS. BERTHOLT'S *evening gown. It is obviously pre-war. Her somewhat gallant attempt to add a touch of faded elegance to the evening moves* HAYWOOD.

MRS. BERTHOLT (*smiles*). Did you like it?

HAYWOOD (*self-consciously*). Yes. I did. I did. Very much.

*There is an awkward pause.*

MRS. BERTHOLT. My house is just a few blocks from here. I was going to walk. (*pause*) Would you like to go for a walk? (*pause*)

HAYWOOD (*self-consciously*). All right. (*speaks to* SCHMIDT) I won't be needing the car right now, Mr. Schmidt. I'm going to walk with Mrs. Bertholt.

SCHMIDT. Do you want me to wait for you, Your Honor?

HAYWOOD. No. It's all right. I can get a cab.

SCHMIDT (*stolidly*). I'll wait for you, Your Honor. (*pause*)

HAYWOOD. Thank you.

*Exterior. Street—Night*

HAYWOOD *and* MRS. BERTHOLT *walk. From a beer hall down the street come the sounds of voices singing. It is a rousing drinking song.* MRS. BERTHOLT *swings a white glove as she walks. She sings a snatch of the song. Her voice is charming and unprofessional.*

MRS. BERTHOLT (*smiles a little*). The German people love to sing, no matter what the situation.

HAYWOOD (*quietly; smiles*). Yes. I noticed that.

MRS. BERTHOLT *sings another snatch of the song.*

MRS. BERTHOLT. Do American people sing in bars too? I don't remember.

HAYWOOD *(smiles a little).* No. We're rather sullen in bars.

*They walk on an instant.*

MRS. BERTHOLT. What is life like in America? Do you have a family? *(pause)*

HAYWOOD. Yes, I do. I have a daughter. *(smiles a little)* She has four children. *(pause)*

MRS. BERTHOLT. Four. You must be proud of them.

HAYWOOD *(smiles a little).* I am. I must admit.

MRS BERTHOLT. Where's Mrs. Haywood? *(pause)*

HAYWOOD. She died a few years ago. *(awkward pause)*

A BLACK MARKETEER, *carrying a large brown briefcase—the badge of the black marketeer—comes out of the shadows of a store front.*

BLACK MARKETEER (quietly). Cigarettes?

HAYWOOD *and* MRS. BERTHOLT *continue to walk. The* BLACK MARKETEER *disappears into the shadows of the store front.*

HAYWOOD. How about you? Do you have children?

MRS. BERTHOLT. No, I don't.

*They walk on.*

MRS. BERTHOLT *(quietly).* What kind of position do you hold in America, Judge? Is it important?

HAYWOOD *(quietly, smiles).* No. No. Not very important at all. I'm a District Court Judge, that's all. *(pause)* And for the last year or so, I haven't even been that.

MRS. BERTHOLT. You are retired?

HAYWOOD *(smiles a little).* Forcibly. By the electorate. *(pause)*

MRS. BERTHOLT *(quietly).* You elect judges in the United States?

HAYWOOD. Yes. We do. In some states.

MRS. BERTHOLT. I didn't know that.

HAYWOOD. It's either one of the virtues of our judiciary system or one of the defects. *(smiles. Dryly)* I thought it was one of the virtues until I was defeated last year. *(pause)*

MRS. BERTHOLT *(lightly).* I am sure it was the electorate's fault, not yours.

HAYWOOD *(smiles a little).* There seems to be a difference of opinion about that.

HAYWOOD *and* MRS. BERTHOLT *pause before the building. It is obviously a once-respectable building now partially bombed, giving it a rather decayed atmosphere. A* G.I. *is on the corner with a* FRÄULEIN. *The* FRÄULEIN *is unattractive, in her thirties.*

G.I. How much do you want?

FRÄULEIN. I told you. I do not do that.

G.I. How many cigarettes? I'll give you ten cigarettes.

HAYWOOD *looks at* MRS. BERTHOLT, *embarrassed for her. But she gives no sign of having heard the conversation.*

MRS. BERTHOLT. Would you like to come in? Would you like some coffee? *(gauging expression on* HAYWOOD's *face)* Perhaps you'd rather not. *(pause)*

HAYWOOD *(finally).* Yes. I'd like to. Thank you.

*Interior. House—Night*

*Partially bombed-out. One can see where it was once quite respectable. Upper middle-class. Part of the banister is missing. They walk up the steps—camera following.* HAYWOOD *walking slowly behind* MRS. BERT-HOLT *observing the house.*

*Interior.* MRS. BERTHOLT'S *room—Night*

*It is fairly bare but whatever furniture there is is very tasteful. It is also very clean. There has obviously been very much done with very little.* MRS. BERTHOLT *enters, followed by* HAYWOOD. *Close-up of* HAYWOOD'S *face looking at the small room, obviously struck by the fact that* MRS. BERTHOLT *is living in this small room while he is living in her old house with such enormous space. She turns up the electric stove to heat a pot of coffee on a small table to one side.*

MRS. BERTHOLT. Let me have your coat. *(smiles a little)* It's a little warmer here than in the auditorium.

HAYWOOD *gives her his coat.* MRS. BERTHOLT *hangs it up in small closet. Her attitude as she speaks about the room is quite sincere. Unlike* ROLFE'S *there is no undercurrent in it. This is important to understand. She gestures toward room.*

MRS. BERTHOLT *(continuing; without sentiment and without resentment).* It's pretty threadbare at the moment but I've really just started. *(gestures toward corner of the room)* I'm going to have the dining-room in the alcove. I'm going to get a small piano and put it over there.

*Gestures toward other side of the room. Close-up of* HAYWOOD *thinking of the beautiful Bechstein piano in his quarters that probably once belonged to her.*

MRS. BERTHOLT *(continuing).* I have a beautiful painting by Feininger. I just have to find the right place to put it. *(pause. Smiles a little depreciatingly)* But then, Germans are always talking about their possessions, aren't they? *(she touches the coffee pot)* It will be ready in a moment.

HAYWOOD *looks about the room. He goes to the bookcase. Close-up copies of books. Copies of Shakespeare, Goethe, Schiller. Walks about the room a moment.*

*Then he sees a large portrait hanging from the wall. Close-up portrait. It is a man in general's uniform.* MRS. BERTHOLT *watches* HAYWOOD *looking up at the painting.*

MRS. BERTHOLT *(quietly).* It's a painting of my husband, as I suppose you've guessed. *(HAYWOOD sits down. She takes a small case from table)* Cigarette? *(pause)*

HAYWOOD *(gently).* Why don't you have one of mine?

MRS. BERTHOLT. Thank you.

HAYWOOD *lights it for her.*

MRS. BERTHOLT *(gently).* Why did you lose the election?

HAYWOOD *(quietly).* I don't know. I was in a long time. I guess they must have gotten tired of me, that's all. *(pause)* A new fellow came along. He promised them more. *(the pain of defeat is still on his face; changing the subject; quietly)* You said you were in the United States. Where?

MRS. BERTHOLT. Ohio mostly.

HAYWOOD *(smiles).* Ohio.

MRS. BERTHOLT. We stayed with some relatives of my husband. On a farm. It was a very happy time for us.

HAYWOOD. Where else did you go?

MRS. BERTHOLT. We took a ride by automobile all over the United States. We were really very impressed.

HAYWOOD *(smiles a little).* What impressed you most?

MRS. BERTHOLT *(speaking as she prepares the coffee).* The space. The wildness of your country. The color. The grandeur of it. Colorado, Wyoming. The Tetons. Have you seen the Teton Mountains in Wyoming?

HAYWOOD. Yes. I have.

MRS. BERTHOLT. I think they are the most beautiful range of mountains I have ever seen. *(pause)* The desert. We camped at a place called Jackson Hole.

HAYWOOD *laughs a little. She laughs.*

HAYWOOD. I think you've seen more of America than I have.

MRS. BERTHOLT *(rises).* We went on a pack trip. It was wonderful. *(pause. Thinking)* We liked the people. They are so outgoing. Uncomplicated. People think it's a pose here. But that's because they don't know Americans. They really are like that.

HAYWOOD *gets up, walks to kitchenette, watching* MRS. BERTHOLT *prepare coffee. She takes small bit of cream in container from ice-box and carefully preserved sugar from cabinet.*

MRS. BERTHOLT. Do you take cream and sugar?

HAYWOOD *(with feeling for her; not wanting to use up her cream and sugar on him).* No thanks.

MRS. BERTHOLT *takes some biscuits with the traditional Nuremberg art designs on them from small tin. She puts them on tray with the cups and coffee.*

HAYWOOD *(with feeling for her).* Things haven't been easy for you, have they?

MRS. BERTHOLT. I'm not used to them being easy. I'm not fragile, Judge Haywood. I'm a daughter of the military. You know what that means, don't you?

HAYWOOD. No. I'm afraid I don't.

MRS. BERTHOLT *takes tray with coffee and cups and biscuits to the table in the center of the living-room.* HAYWOOD *follows her. She moves efficiently.* MRS. BERTHOLT *places coffee and biscuits on table.*

MRS. BERTHOLT. It means that I was taught discipline in a very special way. For instance: *(smiles a little)* When I was a child we used to go for long hikes in the country, but I would never be allowed to run to the lemonade stands with the others. "Control your thirst," I was told. Control hunger. Control emotions. It has served me well.

HAYWOOD. Was your husband like that? Was he part of that heritage too?

MRS. BERTHOLT *looks at* HAYWOOD. *There is a twinge of pain every time the subject of her husband comes up. She smiles a little after a moment.*

MRS. BERTHOLT. He was a soldier. Brought up to do one thing. To fight in the battle and fight well.

*There is a moment.* MRS. BERTHOLT *waits until* HAYWOOD *tries his coffee.* HAYWOOD *tastes it. She watches him.*

MRS. BERTHOLT. Is it all right?

HAYWOOD *(quietly).* Yes. It's fine.

MRS. BERTHOLT. It's ersatz. But I tried to make it strong.

HAYWOOD *(awkwardly).* Fine.

MRS. BERTHOLT. I'm curious. What are your feelings about Ernst Janning?

HAYWOOD *(quietly).* I'm sorry, Mrs. Bertholt. I'm not at liberty to discuss the case at all outside the court.

MRS. BERTHOLT. Yes. Of course. It was just that I knew Ernst Janning a little. We used to attend the same concerts. I remember there was a reception given for Wagner's daughter-in-law. Hitler was there. Janning was there with his wife also. She was very beautiful, very small, very delicate. She is dead now. Hitler seemed quite taken with her. He made advances toward her at the reception. He would do things like that in a burst of emotion. I will never forget the way Janning cut him down. I don't think anybody ever did it quite that way to him. He said, "Chancellor, I do not object so much that you are ill-mannered. I do not object to that so much. I do object that you are such a *bourgeois*." Hitler's face whitened. He just stared at Janning and then walked out.

*There is a moment.*

MRS. BERTHOLT. Are you sure the coffee is all right?

HAYWOOD *nods. She speaks with a rush of feeling.*

MRS. BERTHOLT. Men like Janning and my husband and I. We hated Hitler. I want you to know that. And he hated us. He hated my husband because he was a real war hero and the little corporal couldn't tolerate that. And he hated him because he married into the nobility which was my family. Hitler was in awe of the nobility, but he hated it. (*pause. The human waste comes into her voice*) That's why it was so ironic what happened. You know . . . what happened to my husband?

HAYWOOD. Yes.

MRS. BERTHOLT. What did he know about the crimes they cited him for? (*pause*) He was placed on trial with the other military leaders. He became part of the revenge which the victors always take on the vanquished . . . (*simply, devastatingly*) . . . it was political murder. (*pause. Quietly look at* HAYWOOD) You can see that, can't you?

*Pause. There is a moment.* HAYWOOD *speaks finally. Obviously terribly moved by what she has said but not looking at her.*

HAYWOOD (*finally*). Mrs. Bertholt. I don't know. (*pause*) I don't know what I see. (*pause*) I shouldn't be here right now talking to you. But I want to understand. I want to understand. I have to.

MRS. BERTHOLT *looks at him a moment. The stooped, agonized bulk of man sitting on the couch. She realizes how fully he is involved with his case and how much he really wishes to do what is right.*

*He is giving back to her the memory of the people in America that she had most come to admire. There is a moment.*

MRS. BERTHOLT (*gently*). Would you like some more coffee?

HAYWOOD (*quietly*). Yes. I would.

MRS. BERTHOLT *begins to pour.*

*Interior. Palace of Justice,* COLONEL LAWSON's *Office—Night*

COLONEL LAWSON *is in his shirt-sleeves. Pours coffee on his desk into a paper cup. Some of it spills over violently on to his hand. He swears inarticulately. Then continues to look at affidavits on desk before him.* MAJOR RADNITZ *enters and hands* LAWSON *a memo.*

MAJOR RADNITZ. We found Irene Hoffmann.

COLONEL LAWSON (*looks up at him. Sharply*). Where?

MAJOR RADNITZ (*indicates memo*). Berlin. She got married and changed her name. That's why we had difficulty locating her. (*pause*)

COLONEL LAWSON (*tensely*). When is she coming?

MAJOR RADNITZ. She isn't coming.

COLONEL LAWSON. What do you mean?

MAJOR RADNITZ. She doesn't want to testify. (*pause. Exchange of looks between* COLONEL LAWSON *and* MAJOR RADNITZ) You know what it's like. It's getting harder to get them to testify all the time. (*pause*)

LAWSON *reaches for his coat on the back of the chair.*

COLONEL LAWSON. If I catch the five o'clock, I can make it to Berlin and be back by tomorrow afternoon.

MAJOR RADNITZ. I'm warning you. You can't keep this pace. You haven't had any sleep . . . .

COLONEL LAWSON *rising and starting.*

COLONEL LAWSON. It will be worth it if I can get Hoffmann. Take over in court for me tomorrow morning.

*Goes.* MAJOR RADNITZ *looks after him.*

*Exterior. Establishing Shot, Berlin Ruins—Dawn*

*A military car drives through bombed-out section of Berlin.*

*Exterior. Street, Store Window— Day*

*A sign reading "Photography." A few pitiful, old-fashioned cameras in the window, augmented by displays obviously a few years old. Close-up— doorbell.* COLONEL LAWSON *presses forward and rings it steadily.*

*Interior. Drab, Bare Apartment— Day*

*In the apartment is* IRENE HOFF-MANN. *She is an attractive, although somewhat gaunt woman. It seems impossible that she was ever sixteen. In the apartment with her is her husband,* HUGO WALLNER, *who is a short, dumpy man in his early forties.* COL-ONEL LAWSON *watches them eagerly.* IRENE *has on a thin robe over her nightdress.* HUGO *is wearing the tops of his pyjamas over his trousers. They are deeply disturbed.*

HUGO. She does not have to go. You have no right to order her to go. (*pause*)

COLONEL LAWSON. I am not ordering her to go, Mr. Wallner. I have no authority to order her to go.

HUGO (*sardonically*). You think we get a medal for appearing at these trials. The people do not like them. They do not think Germans should testify against other Germans.

COLONEL LAWSON. I haven't been prosecuting these cases for two years without knowing that.

HUGO. It is easy for you to say go. You will go back to America after the trials. We have to stay here and live with these people.

*Close-up—*COLONEL LAWSON

*There is compassion on his face for* HUGO *and* IRENE. *But there is also determination.*

COLONEL LAWSON. Mr. Wallner— do you think I don't realize what I'm asking—? Do you think I don't believe you are entitled to be left alone—without this horror dumped into your lives all over again?

*Close-up—*HUGO

HUGO (*with emotion*). Then how can you come here, like a Gestapo man in the middle of the night, and . . .

COLONEL LAWSON *bursts out.*

COLONEL LAWSON. Because they must not be allowed to get away with what they did!

HUGO (*quietly*). Do you really think they won't get away with it in the end?

*Full shot*

*A tremendous apprehension coming over* LAWSON. HUGO *turns to* IRENE.

HUGO. I say the hell with them! *(turns to* LAWSON*)* And the hell with you!

*There is a moment. Both of them stand watching* IRENE. *She begins to pace the floor. The fear is on her face. The disbelief that the masters of the Third Reich are really locked up in jail. The fear that Nazism is still not dead.*

IRENE. Emil Hahn will be there?

COLONAL LAWSON. Yes. *(with emphasis)* In the dock.

IRENE. Janning?

COLONEL LAWSON. Yes. *(with emphasis)* In the dock.

LAWSON *stares at her. Before him is what he feels to be the key to his case. The key to something he has worked on for a year or more. And something more. An instrument that may help him to forget the things he saw at Dachau and Belsen when the defendants in the case are justly sentenced.*

IRENE *(quietly to* LAWSON*)* You saw the store downstairs. It is not much, but it is a new start for us. *(pause)* They will come if I go to Nuremberg. They will come and break the windows of the store.

COLONEL LAWSON. I'll place a guard in front of the store—twenty-four hours a day.

IRENE *looks at her husband—at the fear in his face.*

HUGO. You do not have to go, Irene. He has no right to ask you to go.

COLONEL LAWSON *(takes her arm).* Irene. You do have to go. You have to go for a lot of people. A lot of people who can't get on the stand themselves.

HUGO. You do not owe it to anybody. You do not owe it to anybody.

COLONEL LAWSON. Yes. You do. *(significantly)* You owe it to one person at least.

*Close-up—*IRENE'S *face*

*In it is the emotion for the person she knows he is talking about.*

*Close-up—*COLONEL LAWSON

*Watching her intensely.*

*Close-up—*IRENE

*There are tears in her eyes. She looks over at* HUGO.

IRENE *(to* HUGO*).* In the night—every night—we've known somehow it would come to this.

*Interior. Palace of Justice, Courtroom—Day*

DR. GEUTER *is on the stand. He is a quiet, soft-spoken man in his fifties, who gives the impression of quiet intelligence.* MAJOR RADNITZ *has handed him a newspaper.*

*Close-up—Newspaper*

*Headline reads,* DEATH TO THE RACE DEFILER.

DR. GEUTER *lowers the newspaper and looks at* MAJOR RADNITZ *before him.*

MAJOR RADNITZ. Doctor Geuter. Do you recognize this headline?

DR. GEUTER. Yes, Sir.

MAJOR RADNITZ. Would you read it to the Tribunal?

DR. GEUTER *(reads).* "Death to the race defiler."

MAJOR RADNITZ. In what newspaper did it appear?

DR. GEUTER. In Julius Streicher's *Der Stürmer.*

MAJOR RADNITZ. What was it in connection with?

DR. GEUTER. The Feldenstein case.

MAJOR RADNITZ. What was the Feldenstein case?

*Close-up—*ROLFE'S *face*

*Tension and alarm is there.*

ROLFE. Your honor. *(pause)* The defense objects to the introduction of the Feldenstein case.

*Camera pans to the rear of the auditorium where* COLONEL LAWSON *enters with* IRENE HOFFMANN. *He pauses a moment sensing what's happened.*

*Close-up—*ROLFE

*Tension on his face as he sees* IRENE HOFFMAN *with* COLONEL LAWSON.

ROLFE *(continuing).* It is a notorious case. Perhaps the most notorious of the period. It has overtones and appeals to emotion that would perhaps be best not raised.

*Camera pans to rear of auditorium.* COLONEL LAWSON *stands motionless waiting for* HAYWOOD'S *ruling.*

HAYWOOD. There are no issues or overtones that may not be raised in this courtroom. The Tribunal is interested in everything that is relevant. Objection overruled.

*Cut to* LAWSON

COLONEL LAWSON *walks briskly up the aisle. Deposits* IRENE HOFFMANN *gently in a seat in the auditorium. Then continues to the front of the Tribunal. He stops beside* MAJOR RADNITZ. MAJOR RADNITZ *returns to take his seat at the defense table.* COLONEL LAWSON *continues sharply.*

COLONEL LAWSON. What was the Feldenstein case?

DR. GEUTER. The case of a man charged with racial pollution.

COLONEL LAWSON. Will you explain what is meant by racial pollution?

DR. GEUTER. It is the charge referred to in the Nuremberg laws. It says that any non-Aryan having sexual relations with an Aryan may be punished by death.

COLONEL LAWSON. When did you first become acquainted with the Feldenstein case?

DR. GEUTER. The police contacted me in September. They said that Lehmann Feldenstein was being held and had asked for me to represent him as counsel.

COLONEL LAWSON. Had you known Mr. Feldenstein before?

DR. GEUTER. Yes. Very well.

COLONEL LAWSON. What position did he hold in the community?

DR. GEUTER. He was a well-known merchant and one of the heads of the Jewish Congregation in Nuremberg.

COLONEL LAWSON. Did you go to see Mr. Feldenstein?

DR. GEUTER. Yes.

COLONEL LAWSON. What was the nature of the charge against him?

DR. GEUTER. He was accused of having intimate relations with a sixteen-year-old girl, Irene Hoffmann.

COLONEL LAWSON. What did Mr. Feldenstein say to you about the case?

DR. GEUTER. He said it was false. He said he had known the girl and her family a long time and had visited her since they died. But there had never been anything of the kind charged between them.

COLONEL LAWSON. Will you tell the Tribunal what happened then?

DR. GEUTER. Mrs. Feldenstein was indicted before the special court at Nuremberg.

COLONAL LAWSON. Where was the special court?

DR. GEUTER. It was here. In this building. In this very courtroom.

COLONEL LAWSON. What were the circumstances surrounding the trial?

DR. GEUTER. It was used as a show-place for National Socialism. It was the time of the September celebrations. The Nuremberg Rallies. The courtroom was packed. *(indicates rear of auditorium with a nod of the head)* There were people standing back there. *(indicates)* Julius Streicher was sitting in one of those front seats with the members of the S.A. all around him.

COLONEL LAWSON. What were your expectations for the trial in this climate? *(pause)*

DR. GEUTER. I expected the worst when I saw Emil Hahn was the public prosecutor. *(looks toward dock)*

*Close-up—*HAHN

*He stares steadily back at* DR. GEUTER.

DR. GEUTER *(continuing)*. He was a fanatic. His trials were always marked by his brutality. *(there is a pause)* But I still had some hope for the outcome because sitting in the judge's bench was Ernst Janning.

*Looks over at* JANNING.

*Close-up—*JANNING

*Staring ahead as though seeing nothing.*

DR. GEUTER. His reputation was known all over Germany. He was known to have devoted his life to justice and the concept of justice.

*Close-up—*JANNING

*Close-up—*HAYWOOD
*Looking at* JANNING.

COLONEL LAWSON. Thank you.

HAYWOOD *(looking toward* ROLFE*)*. Any questions?

ROLFE. No questions.

HAYWOOD. The witness is excused.

DR. GEUTER *rises and exits through the door*.

COLONEL LAWSON. The prosecution calls to the stand Mrs. Irene Hoffmann Wallner.

*Interior. Palace of Justice, Courtroom—Day*

IRENE HOFFMANN *enters through door and crosses to the witness stand.* CAPTAIN BYERS *rises and crosses to her.*

CAPTAIN BYERS. Will you raise your right hand and repeat after me the following oath? I swear by God the Almighty and Omniscient that I will speak the pure truth and will withhold and add nothing.

IRENE *repeats the oath.* CAPTAIN BYERS *returns to his seat, and* IRENE *sits down on the stand.* COLONEL LAWSON *starts his questioning.*

COLONEL LAWSON. Will you please state your name to the Tribunal?

IRENE. Mrs. Irene Hoffmann Wallner.

COLONEL LAWSON. Mrs. Wallner, did you know Lehmann Feldenstein?

IRENE. Yes.

COLONEL LAWSON. When did you first meet him?

IRENE. It was in 1925 or 1926. I am not sure exactly.

COLONEL LAWSON. How old was he at this time?

IRENE. He must have been in his fifties.

COLONEL LAWSON. How old was he at the time of the arrest?

IRENE. He was sixty-five.

COLONAL LAWSON. What was the nature of your relationship?

IRENE. We were friends.

COLONAL LAWSON. Did you continue to see him after your parents died?

IRENE. Yes.

COLONEL LAWSON. Why?

IRENE *(with some emotion. There is a dignity and independence in her emphasis on the word "friends").* We were friends. He owned the building I lived in. His business took him there quite often.

COLONEL LAWSON. What did you say to the police when they questioned you about having intimate relations with him?

IRENE. I told them it was a lie.

COLONEL LAWSON. Could you tell me who the Public Prosecutor was? *(pause)*

IRENE *(staring straight ahead).* It was Emil Hahn.

COLONEL LAWSON. Did the Public Prosecutor question you? *(pause)*

IRENE *(looks toward* EMIL HAHN *in dock).* Yes.

COLONEL LAWSON. What did he say to you?

*Close-up—*IRENE'S *Face*

*As she looks toward* EMIL HAHN *at the dock. In it is still the fear. There is also the fascination for this monster being in the dock. This man who spoke so solemnly and so piously about his own brand of righteousness.*

*Close-up—The Dock—*EMIL HAHN

*He stares at* IRENE *steadily.*

IRENE *(mixed fear, fascination and hatred).* He took me into a separate room where we were alone. He told me that it was no use repeating my story because no one would believe it. There had been race defilement and the only pardon for this was in killing the violator.

*All eyes turn to* HAHN. *He does not flinch from those eyes.*

IRENE *(continuing).* He said that if I protected Mr. Feldenstein, I would be held under arrest for perjury.

COLONEL LAWSON. What did you reply to him?

IRENE. I told him what I had said again and again. *(with emotion)* I told them I could not say anything else. I could not lie about someone who had been so kind to me. *(pause)*

COLONEL LAWSON. Were you held under arrest?

IRENE. Yes. *(pause)*

COLONEL LAWSON. What was the manner in which Emil Hahn conducted the prosecution? *(pause)*

IRENE *(reliving that day in her face).* He mocked everything Mr. Feldenstein tried to say in his defense. He used every opportunity to hold him up to ridicule.

COLONAL LAWSON. What was the reaction of the audience?

IRENE. They . . . laughed again and again. *(looks at the front row as though she can still see the mocking spectators)*

COLONEL LAWSON. How long did the trial last?

IRENE. Two days.

COLONEL LAWSON. Was the verdict passed at the end of the second day?

IRENE. Yes.

COLONEL LAWSON. What was the verdict?

IRENE. Guilty.

COLONEL LAWSON. What was the sentence?

IRENE. Mr. Feldenstein was sentenced to be executed. I was sentenced to be imprisoned for two years for perjury. *(pause)*

COLONEL LAWSON *(with emphasis).* Who was the presiding judge? *(pause)*

IRENE. Ernst Janning.

COLONEL LAWSON. Were the sentences carried out?

IRENE. Yes.

COLONEL LAWSON. That's all.

*Turns. Starts back to prosecution table. As he does, his eyes go in-*

*advertently to* ROLFE *in the dock. Their eyes meet.*

*Close-up—*ROLFE

*It is a moment before* ROLFE *rises. He speaks quietly.*

ROLFE. Your Honor. I would like to request that the witness be kept available. We will present further evidence on the Feldenstein case when it comes to the time for the defense to present its case.

HAYWOOD. The witness will hold herself so available.

IRENE *rises and exits through door.* COLONEL LAWSON *turns toward the bench.*

*Close-up—*COLONEL LAWSON

*The apprehension rises in* COLONEL LAWSON *but he continues.*

COLONEL LAWSON. Your Honor. I offer in evidence a decree signed by Adolf Hitler directing that all persons accused or suspected of disloyalty or resistance of any sort might be arrested secretly with no notice to friends, relatives, without any trial whatsoever and put into concentration camps. *(submits documents to* MAJOR RADNITZ. *He hands it to* CAPTAIN BYERS *who hands it to* HAYWOOD*)* I also offer a group of orders issued under that decree, each one signed by one of the defendants by which hundreds of persons were arrested and placed in concentration camps.

COLONEL LAWSON *gives documents to* CAPTAIN BYERS. BYERS *takes them from him and gives them to* HAYWOOD *at bench.*

COLONEL LAWSON. The evidence clearly shows that the defendants conspired to place the last protection of German law beyond the reach of political opponents and religious minor-

ities and that the defendants furnished legal justification for robbery and murder and that they collaborated in the illegal transportation of Germans and foreigners.

*There is a moment before* LAWSON *continues. He speaks quietly. As he speaks, a screen is set up in the Tribunal by two sergeants-at-arms.*

COLONEL LAWSON *(continuing).* Your Honors. The defendants on trial here today did not personally administer the concentration camps. They never had to beat victims or pull the levers that released the gas in the chambers. But as the documents we have introduced into this case have shown, these defendants fashioned and executed laws and rendered judgments which sent millions of victims to their destinations. *(pause; looks toward prosecution table)*

MAJOR RADNITZ *rises and comes forward.*

MAJOR RADNITZ. I would like to request that Colonel Lawson is sworn in as a witness. *(pause)*

MAJOR RADNITZ *and* COLONEL LAWSON *look toward* HAYWOOD.

*Close-up—*HAYWOOD

HAYWOOD *(nods).* Request is granted.

COLONEL LAWSON *goes to the stand.* CAPTAIN BYERS *swears him in.*

CAPTAIN BYERS. Will you raise your right hand and repeat after me the following oath? I swear by God the Almighty and Omniscient that I will speak the pure truth and will withhold and add nothing.

COLONEL LAWSON *repeats the oath.* MAJOR RADNITZ *steps forward and stands before* COLONEL LAWSON *on the stand.*

MAJOR RADNITZ. Were you active in the United States Army in 1945 near the closing of the war?

COLONEL LAWSON. Yes. I was.

MAJOR RADNITZ. Were you in command of troops liberating concentration camps?

COLONEL LAWSON. Yes.

MAJOR RADNITZ. Were you in Dachau and Belsen?

COLONEL LAWSON. Yes. I was.

MAJOR RADNITZ. Were you present when the films we are about to see were taken?

COLONEL LAWSON. Yes. I was.

*The Tribunal is darkened. The projector flashes its light across the screen.* COLONEL LAWSON *sitting on the stand relates his story. As he does so, we see the genesis of* COLONEL LAWSON'S *emotions about the Germans. Although he speaks quietly, we know how deeply he is feeling. His hatred explodes in our face.*

*Screen*

*On the screen is a map of Germany. It is dotted with all the places in which concentration camps existed. The dots become so large that they practically smother the map.*

*Interior. Courtroom—Day*

COLONEL LAWSON. The map shows the number of location of concentration camps under the Third Reich. *(pause; as he watches the events that he is to talk about march across the screen)*

COLONEL LAWSON *(continuing).* The Buchenwald concentration camp was founded in 1937. The inmates of the camp numbered about eighty thousand. There was a motto at Buchenwald: "Break the body. Break the spirit. Break the heart." The ovens of Buchenwald. The evidence of last-minute efforts to dispose of bodies.

*Close-up—*HAYWOOD'S *Face*

COLONEL LAWSON *(continuing).* The stoves were manufactured by a well-known company which also specialized in baking ovens. The name of the firm is clearly inscribed.

*Close-ups—Faces of People in the Tribunal Watching Films*

*They are divided into different groups. There are the ones who refuse to see what their eyes tell them. There are the ones who stare incredulously that this nightmare really happened. The lapse of a few years' time makes it seem all the more incredible.*

*Interior. Courtroom—Day*

COLONEL LAWSON. An exhibition of by-products of Buchenwald was displayed for local townspeople by an Allied officer. A lampshade made of human skin—made at the request of the wife of one of the operators of the camp. Skin being used for paintings—many having an obscene nature. The heads of two Polish laborers, shrunken to one-fifth their normal size. A human pelvis used as an ashtray is displayed.

*Close-up—*HAYWOOD

*The horror on his face. The astounding revelation of what human beings can do to one another.*

*Interior. Courtroom—Day*

COLONEL LAWSON *(continuing).* Children who had been tattooed to mark them for eventual extermination.

*Interior. Courtroom—Day—Close-up—The Bench—*HAYWOOD

*Reacting to the children.*

*Close-up—Faces in the Courtroom*

*Some of them not believing their eyes. Some of them appalled. Some of them weeping sentimentally. Some of these are the same ones who used to weep sentimentally at Hitler's speeches. They are the same ones who weep in audiences at* The Diary of Anne Frank. *This to them is a drama ordained by the gods without responsibility on their part. It is simply the march of history in which they play no part. They weep today and would not raise a finger to do anything different if the same events were to take place tomorrow.*

*Interior. Courtroom—Day*

COLONEL LAWSON *(continuing)*. The bodies of those who had come in box-cars without food and without air and who had not survived the journey to Dachau. Hundreds of inmates were used as human guinea-pigs for atrocious medical experiments.

COLONEL LAWSON'S VOICE. A witness at one of the executions at Dachau gave the following description: "Inmates were made to leave their clothing on a rack. The inmates were made to believe they were going to take baths. The doors were locked. Tins of Cyclon B were released through the specially constructed apertures."

*Interior. Courtroom—Day—The Dock*

*Reactions of the defendants.* WERNER LAMMPE. *Tears in his eyes. Staring ahead disbelieving. Staring ahead as though someone were playing a gigantic hoax on him.* EMIL HAHN. *Looking down. Shading his eyes, refusing to look at the picture.* FRIEDRICH HOFFSTETTER. *Looking ahead as though confused about something.*

*Close-up—*HAYWOOD

*He looks over to* JANNING. JANNING'S *face seems unmoved.*

*Screen—Actual Signal Corps Army Films*

*Corpses. Acres of corpses. Corpses as far as the eye can see.*

*Interior. Courtroom—Day*

COLONEL LAWSON. This is what was filmed when British troops liberated Belsen concentration camp. Women guards at Belsen were forced to bury some of the dead inmates. For sanitary reasons, a British bulldozer was forced to bury the bodies as quickly as possible.

*Screen—Actual Signal Corps Army Films*

*We see British soldier, handkerchief to his nose, trying to prevent himself from becoming overcome by the stench, operate bulldozer. The gigantic mouth of the bulldozer picks up its human cargo.*

COLONEL LAWSON'S VOICE. Who were the bodies? Members of every occupied country of Europe. Two-thirds of the Jews of Europe exterminated. More than six million according to reports from the Nazis' own figures.

*We see the face of a woman among the bodies—a child—an expression that is all too identifiable.*

*Interior. Courtroom—Day*

COLONEL LAWSON'S *face. He speaks quietly.*

COLONEL LAWSON *(quietly)*. But the real figure—no one knows.

*Close-up—The Bench—*HAYWOOD

*Close-up—The Dock—*JANNING

*The screen sends its shadows across his face.*

*Interior. Palace of Justice, Prisoners' Dining-Room—Night*

*A long wooden table at which* HAHN, HOFFSTETTER, LAMMPE *and* JANNING *sit. They are waited on by* N.C.O.s *in uniform. There are* OTHER MEN *at the table. None of the defendants speak.* HAHN *speaks finally. His voice choked with rage.*

HAHN. How dare they show us those things? How dare they? We're not executioners. We're judges.

*He looks around the table angrily.*

LAMMPE *(finally).* You do not think it was like that, do you? There were executions, but it was nothing like that. Nothing at all.

*Looks about the table as though for support.* HAHN *looks at him as though he were an old fool. Where has he been for the last years?* HOFFSTETTER *cannot look the old man in the face.* JANNING *stares at him. There is not a word forthcoming.* LAMMPE *looks farther down the table at a very ordinary-looking, small, bald* MAN *eating at the table. He is breaking bread and eating some of it.* LAMMPE *talks to him.*

LAMMPE. Pohl. Pohl. You ran those concentration camps. You and Eichmann. *(laughs a little)* They say we killed millions of people. Millions of people. *(laughs a little)* How could it be possible? *(pause)* Tell them. How could it be possible? *(pause)*

POHL *looks at* LAMMPE *a moment. He speaks finally.*

POHL. It's possible.

*There is a moment.*

LAMMPE. How?

POHL *breaks another piece of bread. Puts it into his mouth.*

POHL. You mean technically?

*Close-up—*LAMMPE

*Staring at him.*

POHL *(continuing).* It all depends on your facilities. *(pause. Takes another piece of bread into his mouth)* Say you have two chambers which will accommodate two thousand people apiece. *(pause)* Figure it out. It's possible to get rid of ten thousand in half an hour.

HAHN, HOFFSTETTER *and* JANNING *look at him silently.*

POHL *(continuing).* You don't even need guards to do it. *(pause)* You can tell them they are going to take showers and then instead of the water, you turn on the gas. *(pause)* It's not the killing that is the problem. It's disposing of the bodies. That's the problem.

SERGEANT *brings food over to the table in his mess kit. There is a moment. No one touches their food for a moment. Even* HAHN *cannot bring himself to eat.*

*Close-up—*JANNING

*He stares into empty space.*

*Interior. Beer Hall—Night*

HAYWOOD *sits at table waiting. He looks over at bandstand.*

*Bandstand*

*Tenor sings with small oom-pah-pah band in a sentimental Richard Tauber manner.*

*Close-up—*HAYWOOD

*Watching them. The impact of the concentration camp scenes is still on his face.* MRS. BERTHOLT *enters. She comes to table.* HAYWOOD *rises.*

MRS. BERTHOLT. I'm sorry I'm late.
HAYWOOD. That's all right. *(helps her to her seat)*

MRS. BERTHOLT. I was doing some work for the rebuilding committee.

*She looks at folders in her hands.*

MRS. BERTHOLT *(continuing).* I brought down these folders for you. We can decide what you should see next. *(shows him folders)* You must see the Albrecht Dürer house. And the museum. *(looks at him)* When do you think you could make it? *(pause)*

HAYWOOD *(quietly).* Oh. Any time.

*Close-up—*MRS. BERTHOLT

*Sensing his preoccupation. Knowing the reason why.*

*Close-up—*HAYWOOD

*Not wanting to communicate his mood.* WAITER *comes over.*

WAITER. Would you like to order now?

MRS. BERTHOLT. What would you like? Can I help you with the menu? *(pause)*

HAYWOOD *(quietly).* I don't think I'll have anything.

MRS. BERTHOLT *(looking at* HAYWOOD, *then, to* WAITER) Just a glass of Moselle, please.

HAYWOOD *(absently).* All right. Moselle.

WAITER *goes.* MRS. BERTHOLT *stares at* HAYWOOD *a moment. Pause.*

MRS. BERTHOLT. What's the matter? *(pause)*

HAYWOOD. I'm just not hungry. That's all.

HAYWOOD *picks up folders in his hands. Looks at them a moment.*

HAYWOOD *(quietly).* You know. These last few days have meant a lot to me. *(pause)*

MRS. BERTHOLT *(quietly).* How? *(pause)*

HAYWOOD *smiles a little.*

HAYWOOD. Well, I don't think you realize what a provincial man I am. I've been abroad exactly once before. When I was a doughboy in World War I. I used to pass places like this and wonder what they were really like.

*There is gratitude in his voice. There is also wonder.*

MRS. BERTHOLT. They've meant a lot to me too.

HAYWOOD. How?

MRS. BERTHOLT *stares steadily at* HAYWOOD.

MRS BERTHOLT *(with warmth).* They've given back to me the feelings of the Americans I had. The feeling I had when I went to your country.

*There is a moment. The two of them listen a minute to the rich voice of the German tenor on the stand. He is singing an over-lush Viennese kind of song. The two of them smile a little at the over-lush sentiment of the song.*

HAYWOOD *(quietly).* You know. It's too bad this isn't fiction and we aren't characters in a magazine story. *(pause)*

MRS. BERTHOLT *smiles a little.*

MRS. BERTHOLT. Why?

HAYWOOD. Well. If this were fiction, it would be the kind of place, wouldn't it, where two people like us, the rapidly aging judge—

MRS. BERTHOLT *(gently).* No. No—

HAYWOOD *(firmly).* Yes. Yes. The rapidly ageing judge . . . and the beautiful widow transcend their differences and go travel in a place that is not by land and not by sea.

*Close-up—*MRS. BERTHOLT

*Her eyes saying it is not impossible.* WAITER *brings glasses of wine.*

HAYWOOD *(to* WAITER). Thank you.

WAITER *leaves*. MRS. BERTHOLT *lifts her glass and sips the wine*. HAYWOOD *doesn't touch his*.

*Close-up*—MRS. BERTHOLT

*Sensing his feelings.*

*Close-up*—HAYWOOD

*Averting his eyes from hers.* MRS. BERTHOLT *speaks finally.*

MRS. BERTHOLT. I saw Mr. Perkins today. He told me they showed those pictures in the courtroom.

*There is a moment.* MRS. BERTHOLT *looks over at the bandstand. They are now playing a drinking song.*

MRS. BERTHOLT *(continuing; quietly, bitterly)*. Colonel Lawson and his pictures. He drags them out on any pretext, doesn't he? *(quietly)* Colonel Lawson's private chamber of horrors.

HAYWOOD *watches her. Wondering about her in spite of himself.*

*Close-up*—MRS. BERTHOLT

*Catching the look. Taking him up on it.*

MRS. BERTHOLT. Well. Is that the way you think we are? Do you think we were aware of those things? Do you think we wanted to murder women and children? Do you believe that? Do you?

*There is a moment.*

HAYWOOD. Mrs. Bertholt. I don't know what to believe.

*There is a moment.* MRS. BERTHOLT *looks at him incredulously.*

MRS. BERTHOLT. Dan. My God. We're sitting here drinking. You don't know much about me but we have experienced a few things together. How can you think that we knew?

HAYWOOD *(quietly; gently but with a searching voice and with irony)*. As far as I can find out, no one in this country knew.

*Close-up*—MRS. BERTHOLT

*Staring at him with horror.*

*Close-up*—HAYWOOD

*Then* HAYWOOD *speaks finally.*

HAYWOOD. Margarete. Your husband was one of the heads of the Army—

MRS. BERTHOLT *almost screams out.*

MRS. BERTHOLT. He didn't know! I tell you he didn't know! *(pause)* It was Himmler. It was Goebbels. The S.S. knew what was happening. We didn't know.

*There is a moment. She looks at him. Speaks finally. She finds her voice with difficulty.*

MRS. BERTHOLT. Listen. Listen to me. There are things that happened on both sides. My husband was a military man all his life. He was entitled to a soldier's death. He asked for that. I tried to get that for him. Just that. That he should die with some honor. I went from official to official. I asked for that. I begged for that. Just that he be permitted the dignity of a firing squad. You know what happened. He was hanged with the others.

*There is a moment of terror in her face as she thinks about it. She is shivering inwardly. Shivering at the thought of the death of her husband. Shivering at the thought of the way he died. The music on the bandstand becomes more strident. The men at the next table are beginning to bang their mugs in time to the music.*

MRS. BERTHOLT. *Her voice reaching out to* HAYWOOD.

MRS. BERTHOLT. After that I knew what it meant to hate. I never left the house. I never left my room. I drank. I hated with every fiber of my being. I hated every American I had ever known. Dan. One can't live with hate! I've learned that.

*Puts a hand on his. The hand is quivering with emotion.*

*Close-up*—HAYWOOD

*It is obvious he is terribly moved by what she is saying.*

*Close-up*—MRS. BERTHOLT

MRS. BERTHOLT. Dan. Dan. We have to forget! We have to forget if we are to go on living!

*Close-up*—HAYWOOD

*Looking at her, wondering. Feeling perhaps she is right after all. Perhaps it is best to forget after all. The oom-pah-pah music and the banging of the mugs continue. They rise in sound.*

*Interior. Palace of Justice, Courtroom—Day*

ROLFE *stands before the Tribunal. He speaks quietly. But we can sense the emotion underneath. His body is quivering with it.*

ROLFE. Your Honor. *(pause)* Yesterday the Tribunal witnessed some films. They were shocking films. Devastating films. *(quietly)* As a German I am ashamed that such things could take place in my country. There can never be a justification for them. Not in generations. Not in centuries. *(pause. His feelings coming to the fore)* But I do think it was terribly unfair to show these films—in this case, at this time, against these defendants! . . . *(turns to look at* COLONEL LAWSON*)* And I cannot protest too strongly against such tactics!

*Close-up*—COLONEL LAWSON

*He is smiling at* ROLFE *a little.*

ROLFE *(continuing)*. What is the prosecution trying to prove? Is it trying to prove that the German people as a whole were responsible for these events? Or that they were even aware of them? The secrecy of the operation, the geographical location of the camps. The breakdown of communications in the last days of the war when the exterminations rose into the millions show only too clearly that he is not stating the truth. The truth is that these brutalities were brought about by the few extremists. The criminals. Very few Germans knew what was going on. None of us knew what was happening in the places shown in these films. None of us. *(there is a moment in which he is able to control his feelings)* The most ironic part of it is that the prosecution showed the films against these defendants. Men who stayed in power for one reason only—to prevent worse things from happening. Who is the braver man, the man who escapes in times of peril or the man who stays at his post at the risk of his own personal safety? *(there is a moment)* The defense will present witnesses and letters and documents from religious and political refugees all over the world telling how Ernst Janning saved them from execution. The defense will show the many times Ernst Janning was able to effect mitigation of sentences when, without his influence, the result would have been much worse. We will present affidavits from legal authorities and famed jurists the world over. We will begin now.

*Interior. Palace of Justice, Courtroom—Day*

MRS. MARIA KOFFKA *is on the stand. She gives the impression of an upper middle-class woman with dignity.*

ROLFE. Would you state your name, please?

MRS. KOFFKA. My name is Maria Koffka.

ROLFE. Do you know the defendant, Janning?

MRS. KOFFKA. Yes, Sir. I have known him since 1929.

*She looks at* JANNING *in the dock. There is warmth in her voice as she does.*

ROLFE. Under what circumstances?

MRS. KOFFKA. He was a friend of my husband, Hans Koffka.

ROLFE. Is your husband still living?

MRS. KOFFKA. No. He is not.

ROLFE. What position did your husband hold, Mrs. Koffka?

MRS. KOFFKA. He was a judge in the Ministry of Justice until 1936.

ROLFE. What happened then?

MRS. KOFFKA. He was taken to a concentration camp.

ROLFE. For what reason?

MRS. KOFFKA. For political reasons.

ROLFE. What was the relationship between your husband and the defendant, Janning?

MRS. KOFFKA. It was a very friendly relationship. It was only because of Herr Janning's understanding that my husband was able to hold his position in office as long as he did.

ROLFE *(sharply)*. Was Janning aware of your husband's political views?

MRS. KOFFKA. He was very fully aware of the fact that my husband was very much opposed to the Nazis and that he emphasized this at every opportunity.

ROLFE. Were there discussions held in your house when Ernst Janning was present?

MRS. KOFFKA. Yes. There were.

ROLFE. What was the nature of these conversations?

MRS. KOFFKA. The nature of them was that a great part of the judges who were members of the Ministry of Justice were against Hitler, but thought it their duty to remain in office to prevent worse things from happening.

*Interior. Palace of Justice, Courtroom—Day*

DR. ALEXANDER COHN *is on the stand. He is an imposing man in his seventies, with a shock of white hair.*

ROLFE. What is your name?

DR. COHN. Dr. Alexander Cohn.

ROLFE. What is your profession?

DR. COHN. I am a physician.

ROLFE *(sharply)*. Were you Ernst Janning's personal physician?

DR. COHN. Yes.

ROLFE *(rapidly)*. From what years?

DR. COHN. From 1919 until the present time.

ROLFE *(sharply)*. You are still his physician?

DR. COHN. Yes. I am.

ROLFE *(sharply)*. May I ask your religion, Dr. Cohn?

DR. COHN. I am non-Aryan according to the Nuremberg laws. I am of the Jewish religion.

*Interior. Palace of Justice, Courtroom—Day*

HANS EBERSBERG *is on the stand. He wears a pince-nez. His manner is correct. Punctilious. His resemblance to one of the defendants,* HOFFSTETTER, *is striking.*

ROLFE *(impatiently)*. Would you state your name for the Tribunal?

*As the witnesses continue to parade before him,* ROLFE *seems to grow more and more impatient, almost abrupt with them. He makes his points for his client rapidly, almost scathingly, as though to underline in this manner what he seems to consider the unjust and seemingly to him, preposterous claims of the prosecution.*

EBERSBERG. My name is Hans Ebersberg.

ROLFE. What is your profession?

EBERSBERG. I am an attorney in the Ministry of Justice.

ROLFE. Did you serve under the defendant, Janning?

EBERSBERG. Yes, Sir.

ROLFE. What is your impression of the defendant?

*There is a moment before* EBERSBERG *replies.*

EBERSBERG. I received my first impression of Janning in connection with the events of 9 November 1938.

ROLFE. What were these events?

EBERSBERG. The outrage against Jews and Jewish property.

ROLFE *(impatiently)*. What was the reaction of Ernst Janning to these events?

*There is a moment.*

EBERSBERG. He very strongly condemned it. He firmly stated this again and again.

ROLFE. What was your general impression of the defendant Janning? What was his attitude toward his work?

EBERSBERG. His entire activity was inspired by the endeavor to preserve justice and the concept of justice.

ROLFE *reads to the Tribunal from the last of the affidavits swearing to* JANNING'S *character. The pile of affidavits is so high now that it reaches to* ROLFE'S *shoulders on the table near to where he stands.*

ROLFE *(reading)*. "I obtained a deep impression of him as a stout supporter of the first-rate, impartial and politically independent judiciary, as well as an excellent scholar of law. In both respects he enjoyed the esteem of the judges of the old school. He was a man with an incorruptible sense of law and justice."

ROLFE *puts the final affidavit down, then looks up at* HAYWOOD.

ROLFE. I ask you to accept this document into evidence as Exhibit 40.

ROLFE *hands the document to* BYERS *who places it before* HAYWOOD.

HAYWOOD. The Exhibit is received in evidence.

ROLFE. These are the witnesses we have to present for Ernst Janning. *(indicates with sweep of hand the affidavits on table near desk)* Now . . . what does the prosecution have to offer against this? The prosecution has in fact presented only one piece of evidence against Ernst Janning. A notorious case as the defense has stated. A case which never should have been reopened. A case which the defense is obliged to review now. The defense calls Mrs. Elsa Lindnow.

*Interior. Palace of Justice, Courtroom—Day*

MRS. ELSA LINDNOW *is on the stand. She is a woman in her early forties. She watches* ROLFE *carefully as he asks questions of her.*

ROLFE. Mrs. Lindnow. What is your occupation?

MRS. LINDNOW. I am a cleaning woman.

ROLFE. Where are you employed?

MRS. LINDNOW. 345 Grossplatz.

ROLFE. Mrs. Lindnow. Did you know Lehmann Feldenstein?

MRS. LINDNOW. Yes. I knew him.

ROLFE. In what capacity?

MRS. LINDNOW. He was my employer in 1935.

ROLFE (*indicates her in courtroom*). Do you know the witness, Irene Hoffmann?

MRS. LINDNOW. Yes.

ROLFE. In what capacity?

MRS. LINDNOW. She was a tenant in the building.

ROLFE. Did you ever see Miss Hoffmann and Mr. Feldenstein together?

MRS. LINDNOW. Yes.

ROLFE. How did this happen?

MRS. LINDNOW. Mr. Feldenstein came to see Miss Hoffmann at her apartment.

ROLFE. Often?

MRS. LINDNOW. Quite often.

ROLFE. Mrs. Lindnow. Were there any occasions in which you noticed anything unusual?

MRS. LINDNOW. Yes, I saw Miss Hoffmann kissing Mr. Feldenstein in the door of her apartment.

ROLFE. Was there any other occasion in which you noticed anything unusual?

MRS. LINDNOW. Yes. There was one.

ROLFE. What was it?

MRS. LINDNOW. I came into Miss Hoffmann's apartment. I wanted to clean up. I thought it was empty. (*pause*) I saw Miss Hoffmann sitting on Mr. Feldenstein's lap.

*Interior. Palace of Justice, Courtroom—Day*

IRENE HOFFMANN *is on the stand.*

ROLFE. Miss Hoffmann. Did you come here voluntarily? Did you report voluntarily to speak as a witness?

IRENE (*rattled and uncertain of the question*). Yes.

ROLFE. Is it not true that Colonel Lawson asked you to come here? (*pause*) Is it not true that it was very disagreeable for you to come here? (*pause*)

IRENE (*with dignity and anger at ROLFE*). It is always disagreeable to live over that time. (*pause*)

ROLFE (*smiling a little*). That would be in agreement with the information I have that you yourself did not want to come, Miss Hoffmann. The Nuremberg laws were stated on September 15th. Where were you at that time?

IRENE. In Nuremberg.

ROLFE. So you were aware that physical relationship with Jews was against the law?

IRENE. Yes.

ROLFE. Do you know that in Nuremberg, and Nuremberg in particular, not only a physical relationship with Jews was viewed with disdain, but every social contact?

IRENE. Yes.

ROLFE. Were you aware that it might have some danger for you personally?

IRENE. Yes. I was aware of it.

ROLFE *starts to speak.* IRENE *continues speaking.*

IRENE (*continuing*). But how could a friendship be discarded from one day to the next because of—

ROLFE (*interrupts politely. There is even some sensitivity in his voice as he does so*). That is another question. I did not ask you that question, Miss Hoffmann. (*pause*) Were you aware of it? (*pause*)

IRENE. Yes. I was aware.

ROLFE. And yet you still continued to see each other?

IRENE. Yes.

*There is a moment.* ROLFE *smiles a little as though acceding. Bows a little.*

ROLFE. Do you remember it was brought out at the trial that Mr. Feldenstein bought you things? Candy and cigarettes?

IRENE. Yes.

ROLFE. Remember that he sometimes bought you flowers?

IRENE. Yes. *(with emotion)* He bought me things but it was because he was kind. He was the kindest man I ever knew. *(pause)*

ROLFE. Miss Hoffmann, do you know the witness, Mrs. Elsa Lindnow?

IRENE. Yes. I know her.

ROLFE. Was she a cleaning woman in the apartment you lived in?

IRENE. Yes.

ROLFE. Did Mr. Feldenstein come to see you in your apartment? *(pause)*

IRENE. Yes. He came to see me.

ROLFE. How many times?

IRENE. I don't remember.

ROLFE. Several times? *(pause)*

IRENE. Yes. *(pause)*

ROLFE. Many times? *(pause)*

IRENE. Many times. *(pause)*

ROLFE. Did you kiss him? *(pause)*

IRENE. Yes. I kissed him. *(pause)*

ROLFE. Was there more than one kiss? *(pause)*

IRENE. Yes. *(with emotion)* But not in the way you are making it sound! He was like a father to me. He was more than my father—

ROLFE. Did you sit on his lap?

COLONEL LAWSON *(on his feet)*. Objection, Your Honor. Counsel is persecuting the witness in the pretext of gaining testimony.

ROLFE *looks at* HAYWOOD, *heatedly demanding his rights.*

*The Bench*

HAYWOOD *recoils from the ferocity of* ROLFE'S *cross-examination and its implications. He looks over to* NORRIS *and* IVES.

NORRIS *(quietly)*. Overruled.
IVES *(quietly)*. Overruled.

HAYWOOD *(not quite looking at participants)*. Objection overruled.

COLONEL LAWSON. I cannot accept this ruling, Your Honor.

HAYWOOD *looks at him quietly.*

HAYWOOD. I think you'll have to accept it.

COLONEL LAWSON. The defense is being permitted to re-enact what was a travesty of justice in the first place!

HAYWOOD. Colonel Lawson, the Tribunal makes the rulings in this case, not the prosecution. *(then to* ROLFE) You may continue.

COLONEL LAWSON *remains standing on his feet in anger.*

ROLFE *(heatedly)*. Did you sit on his lap? *(pause)*

IRENE. Yes! But there was nothing wrong or ugly about it—

ROLFE. Did you sit on his lap?

IRENE *(with tears in her eyes)*. Yes. *(pause)*

ROLFE. You sat on his lap. *(pause)* What else did you do?

COLONEL LAWSON *(on his feet)*. Your Honor—

ROLFE. What else do you admit to?

IRENE *(crying out)*. Stop it! Stop it!

ROLFE *(insistent)*. What else?

*The Dock*

JANNING *is standing. He speaks almost inaudibly*

JANNING *(almost inaudible)*. Again—?

*Full Shot*

ROLFE, *not seeing him, continues.*

ROLFE. What else?

JANNING. Are you going to do this again?

*There is a gasp from the audience. Then a roar.* ROLFE *turns as though stunned, unable to believe his ears.*

*Close-up*—ROLFE

*Close-up*—COLONEL LAWSON

*Not believing his eyes.*

*Close-up*—HAYWOOD

*Close-up*

*Exchange of looks between* ROLFE *and* JANNING.

ROLFE (*finds a voice somehow*). Your Honor. The stress the defendant has been under is so great that he is not aware of . . .
JANNING. I am aware. I am aware.

*A roar again.*

COLONEL LAWSON (*in a hoarse voice*). Your Honor. I believe the defendant wishes to make a statement.
ROLFE (*simultaneously*). Your Honor. I believe the defense has a right to request—

*The confusion and the roar in the courtroom rises.*

HAYWOOD (*bangs gavel. Firmly*). Order— (*then raising his voice firmly*) Order!

*M.P. rises in readiness to quell any demonstration. There is a moment.* HAYWOOD *turns to* JANNING.

HAYWOOD. Does the defendant wish to make a statement? (*pause*)
JANNING. Yes. I wish to make a statement.
ROLFE (*rapidly*). Your Honor. I believe the defense has the right to request a recess so that I may speak with my client.
COLONEL LAWSON. Your Honor. The defendant has the right to make his statement now!

*There is a moment.* HAYWOOD'S *eyes go from* ROLFE *to* LAWSON *to* JANNING. *He speaks finally.*

HAYWOOD. Tribunal will recess until ten-thirty tomorrow morning.

*Explosion of noise and speculation in the courtroom.*

*Palace of Justice, Prison Waiting-Room—Night*

ROLFE *and* JANNING *sit facing each other over a small wooden table. The shadow of the* GUARD *is seen walking back and forth not far from them. It is obvious they have been talking for some time.*

ROLFE. What are you doing? What do you think you are trying to do? (*then with emotion*) They've had Göring, Frank, Streicher. It's enough!

JANNING *does not respond.* ROLFE *keeps trying. With emotion.*

ROLFE (*continuing*). Do you think I enjoyed being defense counsel during this trial? Do you? There were things I had to do in that courtroom that made me cringe! Why did I do them? Because I want to leave the German people something. I want to leave them a shred of dignity. I want to call a halt to these proceedings! If we allow them to discredit every German like you, we lose forever the right to rule ourselves forever! (*with emotion rising*) We have to look at the future. We can't look back. (*quietly. Indicating* GUARD) Do you want the Americans to stay here forever? Do you want that? (*trying to reach* JANNING) I could show you a picture of Hiroshima and Nagasaki. Thousands and thousands of burnt bodies! Women and children! (*indicates* GUARD *with a thrust of his thumb*) Is that their superior morality? Where do you think they take us? Do you think they know? Do you think they have any concept of our problems? (JANNING *does not respond*) What can I say to you? What can I say to you to make you see?

*The face of the once-eminent jurist stares at him from across the wire netting. A face which understands all and more than* ROLFE *is saying. A face that can now evaluate him for the opportunist and rationalizer that he is. A face that can hate him completely at last.*

JANNING. There is nothing you can say.

*Interior. Grand Hotel, Lobby—Day*

GENERAL MERRIN *stands surrounded by international journalists,* PERKINS *among them. On the periphery of the crowd are* SENATOR BURKETTE, HAYWOOD *and* IVES. *A radio is stating the news on the loudspeaker.*

ANNOUNCER. The crisis reached a head this afternoon when all rail travel between Western Zones and Berlin was stopped. The blockade by land is now complete. There is no sign, however, that the Americans will withdraw under pressure from Berlin. In a message to the Secretary of the Army, this afternoon . . .

PERKINS. What do you think we're going to do, General? Do you think we'll withdraw?

GENERAL MERRIN. We can't withdraw. If we withdraw under pressure, our prestige all over the world is threatened. The Communists will move in on every front.

ENGLISH JOURNALIST. What about these trials, General? How do you feel about them now?

GENERAL MERRIN *(carefully).* We're committed to the trials. But I think it's only realistic to expect now that they should be accelerated as much as possible.

*Close-up-*HAYWOOD

*Close-up—*GENERAL MERRIN

*There is a conflict in their faces. Camera moves to* SENATOR BURKETTE, HAYWOOD *and* IVES *on the periphery of the group.*

SENATOR BURKETTE. How about a drink?

IVES. Good idea.

SENATOR BURKETTE, HAYWOOD *and* IVES *make their way toward section of table at which drinks are being served. As they go across the room, we get a smattering of the voices of the people on the staff of the Nuremberg trials. There is an overtone of panic and hysteria in their voices. A* SERVANT *passes* HAYWOOD *and* SENATOR BURKETTE, *carrying a tray of strudel.*

SENATOR BURKETTE. Try one of these, Dan. They're wonderful here.

HAYWOOD *takes one absently.*

SENATOR BURKETTE. Scotch, please.

IVES. Scotch.

HAYWOOD. Nothing, thank you.

*They sit at a table, taking their drinks.*

SENATOR BURKETTE *(quietly).* I've just come back from Berlin, as you know. *(pause, quietly)* I don't think this is going to be it. A lot of people do, but I don't. But it is going to be a fight for survival. Maybe the next ten years. Maybe the next twenty. *(pause. Significantly)* Germany is the key to that survival. Any high-school student in geography can tell you that. *(pauses a moment as though a bit apprehensive of saying what he has to say)*

HAYWOOD *(crisply).* What are you trying to say, Senator?

SENATOR BURKETTE. What I'm trying to say is this. *(pause)* While no one's trying to influence your decision, it's important that you understand this because it's a fact of life. Let's face it, gentlemen. The writing is on the wall. We're going to need all the help we can get here. We're going to need the support of the German people.

WAITER *passes them again. Speaks with heavy accent.*

WAITER. Some more strudel, gentlemen?

*Interior. Palace of Justice, Courtroom—Day*

JANNING *is on the stand.* HAYWOOD *is looking over at him. The courtroom is in silence. Electric silence.*

HAYWOOD. Ernst Janning. Do you wish to make a statement? *(pause)*
JANNING. I do.
HAYWOOD. Proceed.

*There is a moment.* JANNING'S *eyes seem to go to every face in the courtroom.* JANNING *is a junker, and to understand this, is to understand how difficult it is for him to speak to the Tribunal. It means the casting off of his reserve. It means the opening up of a wound that it has been his profession not to tamper with these last ten years. He speaks finally. The* NEWSMEN *take down every word.*

JANNING. I wish to testify about the Feldenstein case because it was the most significant trial of the period. *(pause)* It is important not only for the Tribunal to understand it, but the German people. *(pause)* But to understand it, one must understand the period in which it happened.

*He tries to bring the period into words. This is not easy.*

JANNING *(continuing).* There was a fever over the land. A fever of disgrace, of indignity, of hunger. We had a democracy, yes, but it was torn by elements within. There was, above all, fear. Fear of today, fear of tomorrow, fear of our neighbours, fear of ourselves. *(pause)*

*The Bench—Close-up—*HAYWOOD

*He understands. The last few days since the Berlin crisis have brought fear home to him.*

*Close-up—*JANNING

JANNING. Only when you understand that can you understand what Hitler meant to us. Because he said to us: Lift your heads! Be proud to be German! There are devils among us! Communists, Liberals, Jews, Gypsies—Once the devils will be destroyed, your miseries will be destroyed!

*Pause.* JANNING *smiles sardonically.*

JANNING *(continuing).* It was the old, old story of the sacrificial lamb. *(pause)*

*He seems to look inside himself. The words are hard to come.*

JANNING *(continuing).* What about those of us who knew better? We who knew the words were lies and worse than lies? Why did we sit silent? Why did we participate? *(pause)* Because we loved our country!

*The Bench—Close-up—*HAYWOOD

*The revelation is a bombshell to him which is self-explanatory. The last meeting he had had with* SENATOR BURKETTE *and* IVES *has made it self-explanatory.*

*Full Shot*

JANNING. What difference does it make if a few political extremists lose their rights? What difference does it make if a few racial minorities lose their rights? It is only a passing phase. It is only a stage we are going through. It will be discarded sooner or later. Hitler himself will be discarded sooner or later. "The country is in danger." We will "march out of the shadows." "We will go forward."

*He looks toward people in Press section.*

JANNING *(continuing)*. And history tells how well we succeeded, Your Honor! *(looks at* HAYWOOD*)* We succeeded beyond our wildest dreams. The very elements of hate and power about Hitler that mesmerized Germany, mesmerized the world! *(remembering with sardonic bitterness)* We found ourselves with sudden powerful allies. Things that had been denied us as a democracy—were open to us now. The world said, go ahead, take it! Take Sudetenland, take the Rhineland—re-militarize it—take all of Austria, take it! *(pause)* We marched forward. The danger passed. *(pause; simply)* And then one day we looked around and found we were in an even more terrible danger. The rites began in this courtroom, swept over our land like a raging, roaring disease! What was going to be a passing phase had become a way of life.

*There is a moment. He speaks quietly.*

JANNING *(continuing)*. Your Honor, I was content to sit silent during this trial. *(dryly)* I was content to tend my roses. I was even content to let counsel try to save my name. *(pause; looks over at* ROLFE*)* Until I realized that in order to save it, he would have to raise the specter again. *(pause; as he looks over at* ROLFE*)* You have seen him do it. He has done it in this courtroom. He has suggested that the Third Reich worked for the benefit of people. He has suggested that we ster-

ilized men for the welfare of the country. *(dryly)* He has suggested that perhaps the old Jew did sleep with the sixteen-year-old girl after all. *(pauses; sardonically)* Once more it is being done out of love of the country. *(looks over at* ROLFE*)*

*Close-up—*ROLFE

*Close-up—*JANNING

*Pause. His eyes seem to reach out to every German in the audience.*

JANNING *(continuing)*. It is not easy to tell the truth.

*Looks out into audience.*

*Full Shot*

JANNING *(continuing; with emotion)*. But if there is to be any salvation for Germany those of us who know our guilt must admit it no matter the cost in pain and humiliation. *(pause)* I had reached my verdict on the Feldenstein case before I ever came into the courtroom. I would have found him guilty whatever the evidence. It was not a trial at all. It was a sacrificial ritual in which Feldenstein the Jew, was the helpless victim—

*There is a bombshell of noise.* ROLFE *is on his feet. He is making this one last attempt to reach* JANNING.

ROLFE. Your Honor, I must interrupt. The defendant is not aware of what he is saying—he is not aware that—

JANNING. I am aware. I am aware. *(turns to* HAYWOOD*)* My defense counsel would have you believe that we were not aware of concentration camps. *(pause; cries out)* Not aware? *(pause)* Where were we? Where were we when Hitler began shrieking his hate in the Reichstag? Where were we when our neighbors were being dragged out in the middle of the night to Dachau? Where were we when every village in Germany had a railroad terminal where cattle-cars were filled with children who were being carried off to their extermination? Where were we when they cried out into the night to us? Were we deaf, dumb and blind?

ROLFE *(again on his feet)*. Your Honor, I must—

JANNING. My counsel says we were not aware of the extermination of millions. He would give you the excuse we were only aware of the extermination of the hundreds. Does that make us any the less guilty? *(pause; looks around the room; scathingly)* Maybe we didn't know the details. But if we didn't know, it was because we didn't want to know.

ROLFE *stands motionless.* JANNING *has flung his final rationalization back in his teeth.* ROLFE *is powerless to answer it, although he refuses to accept it emotionally. But* HAHN *rises to his feet.*

HAHN. Traitor! Traitor!

*The Bench*

HAYWOOD. Order! Order! There will be order! *(losing his New England temper)* Put that man in his seat and keep him there!

HAYWOOD *gestures to a husky, colored soldier who stands close to* HAHN, *his truncheon ready.*

*Full Shot*

JANNING *(looking at* HAHN *steadily)*. I am going to tell them the truth. I am going to tell the truth if the whole world conspires against it. I am going to tell them the truth about their Ministry of Justice. *(looks at men in dock)* Werner Lammpe.

*The Dock—Close-up—*LAMMPE

JANNING'S VOICE. Werner Lammpe. An old man who cries into his Bible now. An old man who profited by the property expropriation of every man he sent to the concentration camp.

*Full Shot*

JANNING. Friedrich Hoffstetter, the good German who knew how to take orders. Who sent men before him to be steriized like so many digits.

*The Dock—Close-up—*HOFFSTETTER

*Full Shot*

*The excitement in the courtroom is rising.*

JANNING. Emil Hahn—

EMIL HAHN'S *defense attorney rises to his feet and shouts.*

DEFENSE ATTORNEY. Your Honor—!

JANNING *(continuing)*. The decayed, corrupt bigot, obsessed by the devil within himself.

*The Dock—Close-up—*HAHN

*Close-up—*JANNING

JANNING *(finally)*. And Ernst Janning, worse than any of them because he knew what they were and went along with them.

*There is a moment. There is shouting in the courtroom but* JANNING *does not hear it. He continues.*

JANNING *(continuing)*. Ernst Janning who made his life . . . excrement because he walked with them.

*The noise in the courtroom mounts and grows into the thundering, overwhelming crescendo of sound. But* ERNST JANNING *does not hear it. He is spent now. Spent now with the release and with the shame. He sits there shivering inwardly at the sight of himself that he has presented to the courtroom. The roar continues.* JANNING *gets up finally. He goes to his seat.*

*Close-up*—HAYWOOD

*Close-up*—GENERAL MERRIN

*Sitting in audience. He looks over at* COLONEL LAWSON.

*Close-up*—COLONEL LAWSON

*There is a moment.* ROLFE *rises finally from defense table. All eyes in the courtroom are on him. He walks slowly to the stand. He carries, as though by habit, his portfolio with him. He stares at the judges a moment, thinking. He opens the portfolio. He looks down at all the carefully arranged affidavits, arguments, etc. Then he closes them. Then begins to speak quietly.*

ROLFE. Your Honors, my duty is to defend Ernst Janning. And yet Ernst Janning has said he is guilty.

*He pauses. Turns to look over at* ERNST JANNING *in the dock.*

ROLFE *(continuing).* There is no doubt he feels his guilt.

*The Dock—Close-up*—JANNING

*He is steadily looking at* ROLFE.

*Full Shot—Courtroom*

ROLFE. He made a terrible mistake in going along with the Nazi movement, hoping it would be good for his country. But . . .

*He finds within himself the strength for what he feels he must say.*

ROLFE *(continuing).* If he is to be found guilty, there are others who also went along who must also be found guilty. Herr Janning said we succeeded beyond our wildest dreams. Why did we succeed? *(bends forward)* What about the rest of the world, Your Honors? *(smiles scathingly)* Did they not know the intentions of the Third Reich? Did they not hear the words of Hitler broadcast all over the world? Did they not read his intentions in *Mein Kampf,* published in every corner of the world? *(pause; bends forward)* Where is the responsibility of the Soviet Union who in 1939 signed a pact with Hitler and enabled him to make war? Are we now to find Russia guilty? *(pause)* Where is the responsibility of the Vatican who signed the Concordat Pact in 1933 with Hitler, giving him his first tremendous prestige? Are we now to find the Vatican guilty? *(bends forward)* Where is the responsibility of the world leader, Winston Churchill, who said in an open letter to the London *Times* in 1938—1938, Your Honors! "Were England to suffer a national disaster, I should pray to God to send a man of the strength of mind and will of an Adolf Hitler." Are we now to find Winston Churchill guilty? *(bends forward; smiles a little)* Where is the responsibility of those American industrialists who helped Hitler to rebuild his arms and profited by that rebuilding? Are we to find the American industrialists guilty? *(pause; smiles a little)* No, Your Honor. Germany alone is not guilty. The whole world is as responsible for Hitler as Germany. It is an easy thing to condemn one man in the dock. It is easy to condemn the German people—to speak of the "basic flaw" in the German character that allowed Hitler to rise to power—and at the same time comfortably ignore the "basic flaw" of character that made the Russians sign pacts with him, Winston Churchill praise him, American industrialists profit by him!

*There is a moment.* ROLFE *stands with dignity before the Tribunal.*

ROLFE *(continuing).* Ernst Janning says he is guilty. If he is, Ernst Janning's guilt is the world's guilt. No more and no less.

*He collects his papers from stand and goes back to defense table. Camera goes to faces of German people in the audience. There is no applause but we see the applause in their eyes. There are tears of emotion in some of their eyes. There is no need for them to rationalize any further.* ROLFE *has done it all for them.*

*Close-up—* GENERAL MERRIN

*Watching* COLONEL LAWSON *tensely.* COLONEL LAWSON *looks over at* GENERAL MERRIN. *They exchange a meaningful glance.*

*Interior. Palace of Justice,* GENERAL MERRIN'S *Office*

*It is a large office. Much larger than* COLONEL LAWSON'S. *There are pictures of Eisenhower and Truman on the wall and of* GENERAL MERRIN'S *graduating class at West Point. There is also a map on the wall designating divisions of Germany with colored pins.* GENERAL MERRIN *is busy on the phone.* COLONEL LAWSON *stands before him watching him.*

GENERAL MERRIN *(into phone).* What do you mean they won't let you have it! You can comandeer them! We want every plane that can fly in the air!

*He hangs up. Looks at* COLONEL LAWSON

GENERAL MERRIN *(continuing).* Tad, just a minute.

*Phone rings. He picks it up.*

GENERAL MERRIN *(continuing).* Merrin. *(pause)* I know there are some of them that don't know the territory. *(pause)* I know some of them have never been to Berlin.

*Pause. With some exasperation that the man on the other side of the phone has not known enough to take the initiative. . . .*

GENERAL MERRIN *(continuing).* Major, we have to give the Military Governor every help we can give him. We have to get seven hundred tons in the air a day. Seven hundred tons!

*He hangs up. Looks at* COLONEL LAWSON. *Shakes his head a little.*

GENERAL MERRIN *(continuing).* This is some operation. Did you ever think we'd be flying coal and tomatoes in these crates? *(looks at* COLONEL LAWSON; *crisply)* Tad, what are you going to do in court tomorrow? *(pause)*

COLONAL LAWSON *(looks at him a moment).* You know damn' well what I'm going to do.

GENERAL MERRIN *rises from his desk. Comes from behind it. Smiles ruefully at* COLONEL LAWSON.

GENERAL MERRIN. I know what you want to do. You'd like to recommend they put them behind bars and throw away the key. *(pause)* Me too. *(pause)* You know what's going on here now?

COLONEL LAWSON *looks at* GENERAL MERRIN *steadily.*

COLONEL LAWSON. I know what's going on.

GENERAL MERRIN. Tad, you're an Army man. You know what we're up against. The others may not, but you do.

*He goes to map of Germany. Glares at it.*

GENERAL MERRIN *(continuing).* I'll tell you the truth. I don't know what's going to happen if they fire on one of those planes. I don't know what's going to happen. But I do know this. *(indicates map)* If Berlin goes, Germany goes. If Germany goes, Europe goes. *(pause)* That's the way things stand, boy. That's the way they stand.

COLONEL LAWSON. I'm going to go the limit. And not you. And not the Pentagon. And not God on his throne . . .

GENERAL MERRIN, *his face pale, bursts into a speech.*

GENERAL MERRIN *(interrupting).* Who do you think you're talking to? Who the hell do you think you're talking to?

*He comes close to* COLONEL LAWSON.

GENERAL MERRIN *(continuing).* Listen, Buster! When you were marching into Dachau with those troops, I was there too! You think I'll ever forget it? For God's sakes, I can smell the stench of those gas ovens. It's still in my clothes! *(pause)* You're not the only one who still dreams about the things he saw there. But I'm charged with something else . . . the protection of our country . . . and so are you.

*Close-up*—COLONEL LAWSON

*Still staring at* GENERAL MERRIN *steadily.*

*Close-up*—GENERAL MERRIN

*Speaks quietly to* COLONEL LAWSON *with sympathy and understanding.*

GENERAL MERRIN. Look. I'm not your commanding officer. I can't influence your decision and I don't want to. You have an oath of office to uphold. *(pause)* But I want to give this to you and I want to give it to you

straight! *(with deadly precision)* We need the help of the German people. *(bitterly)* And you don't get the support of the German people by sentencing their leaders to stiff prison sentences.

*Close-up*—COLONEL LAWSON

*It is obvious that* GENERAL MERRIN'S *words have rocked* COLONEL LAWSON *and rocked him hard.*

*Close-up*—GENERAL MERRIN

GENERAL MERRIN. All right. *(pause)* I've said it. It's your decision. *(pause)* I don't envy you.

*Close-up*—COLONEL LAWSON

*The conflict within him raging.* GENERAL MERRIN *watches him a moment. His understanding and feeling for* COLONEL LAWSON'S *dilemma coming to the fore. He speaks again, more quietly this time. Almost gently.*

GENERAL MERRIN *(continuing).* Tad, the thing to do is survive, isn't it? Survive as best we can, but survive.

*Close-up*—COLONEL LAWSON

*Close-up*—GENERAL MERRIN

*Close-up*—COLONEL LAWSON

*He is staring at* GENERAL MERRIN *coldly.* COLONEL LAWSON *turns and starts. Stops at door without looking at* GENERAL MERRIN.

COLONEL LAWSON *(bitterly).* Just for laughs, Matt. What was the war all about? *(scathingly)* What was it all about?

COLONEL LAWSON *goes.*

*Interior. Palace of Justice, Courtroom—Day*

*Close-up large pile of documents on the stand beside* COLONEL LAWSON *as he stands before Tribunal. He is coming to the last ones now and is reading from one of them.*

*Close-up*—COLONEL LAWSON

COLONEL LAWSON (*reading from document in flat voice*). "—instructions were requested that executions of N.N. defendants, whose number in the future would be 'very large', should be by guillotine or by shooting. Exhibit 312, defendant Emil Hahn prepared, signed and circulated reports summarizing N.N. cases receiving the death penalty at the following special courts on 1 September 1942: Kiel—262 defendants from Norway; Essen—863 defendants from Belgium and France; Cologne—331 defendants from France." (*puts last document on table; pause*)

COLONEL LAWSON *looks at Tribunal.*

*Close-up*—GENERAL MERRIN

*Wondering what* LAWSON *is going to say.*

*Close-up*—HAYWOOD

*Close-up*—ROLFE

*Close-up*—COLONEL LAWSON

*Reads from paper he has prepared.*

COLONEL LAWSON (*continuing in a flat voice*). Your Honors. During the three years that have passed since the end of the war in Europe, mankind has not crossed over into Jordan. Small but terrible wars rage in Greece and Palestine. And the chorus of international voices is discordant. In our country, the fear of war has revived and we are constrained to look once more to our defenses. There is talk of "cold war" and, meanwhile, men and women die in real wars and the echoes of persecutions and atrocities will not be stilled. These events cannot help but color what happens in this courtroom. But somewhere in the midst of these events, the responsibility for the crimes we have brought forward during this case must be placed in true perspective. This is the decision that faces Your Honors. It is the dilemma of our times. It is a dilemma that rests with your conscience. That is all, Your Honors.

COLONEL LAWSON *goes back to prosecution table.*

*Close-up*—HAYWOOD

*Shocked and surprised at the equivocation in* COLONEL LAWSON'S *speech.*

*Close-up*—LAWSON

*He cannot quite meet* HAYWOOD'S *eyes. Finally, he turns and looks over at* RADNITZ *beside him as though for some iota of comfort.*

*Close-up*—HAYWOOD

HAYWOOD (*speaks finally*). The defendants may make their final statements. Emil Hahn.

*The Dock—Close-up*—HAHN

HAHN (*quietly*). Your Honors, I do not evade the responsibility for my actions. (*pause; head erect*) On the contrary. I stand by them before the entire world.

*He looks at the judges on the bench and* HAYWOOD *in particular, challengingly.*

HAHN (*continuing*). I will not follow the policy of others. I will not say of our policy today that it was wrong when I say yesterday it was right. (*quietly; with conviction*) Germany was fighting for its life! Certain measures were needed to protect it from its enemies. *(quietly; with conviction)* I cannot say that I am sorry we applied those measures.

*Close-up*—COLONEL LAWSON

*The anger and outrage building within him. Feeling helpless and impotent.*

HAHN *(with emotion).* We were a bulwark against Bolshevism! We were a pillar of Western culture!

*There is bite and satisfaction in his voice.*

HAHN *(continuing).* A bulwark and a pillar the West may yet wish to retain.

*He sits down.*

*Close-up*—HAYWOOD

HAYWOOD. The defendant Friedrich Hoffstetter may address the Tribunal.

HOFFSTETTER *rises. The security and justification that the German people feel is present in the courtroom. Even the attitude of* HOFFSTETTER *has changed since the news of the Berlin crisis. He speaks with more authority than we have ever seen him. He looks over at his* WIFE *and* SON *in the audience.*

*Close-up*—MRS. HOFFSTETTER *and* SON *in the Audience*

*The Dock—Close-up*—HOFFSTETTER

HOFFSTETTER *speaks with an air of dignity, feeling now he represents the German people against the invaders.*

HOFFSTETTER. I have served my country throughout my life and in whatever position I was assigned to, in faithfulness, with a pure heart and without malice.

*Close-up*—HOFFSTETTER'S ELDEST SON *in Audience*

*Looking at his father with admiration.*

*The Dock—Close-up*—HOFFSTETTER

HOFFSTETTER. I followed the concept I believed to be the highest in my profession. The concept that says: "To sacrifice one's own sense of justice to the authoritative legal order. To ask only what the law is and not if it is also unjust." As a judge, I could do no other.

*He looks at the bench unflinching.*

HOFFSTETTER *(continuing).* I believe Your Honors will find me and millions of Germans like me who believed they were doing their duty to their country to be not guilty.

*Pause. He sits down.*

*Full Shot*

HAYWOOD. The defendant Werner Lammpe may address the Tribunal.

*Microphone is placed in front of* LAMMPE.

*The Dock—Close-up*—LAMMPE

*He rises slowly. He looks about him. There is a moment before he starts to speak.*

LAMMPE. Your Honors . . . *(pause)* Your Honors.

*There is an instant. He would speak but he cannot bring himself to speak. The words which* JANNING *used which he knew to be true and the effect of the concentration-camp films have rendered him helpless to speak. He looks about confused, retreating from reality completely. He has to be helped back down to his seat.*

HAYWOOD. The defendant Ernst Janning may address the Tribunal. *(pause)*

JANNING *rises slowly, with dignity.*

*Close-up*—JANNING

JANNING. I have nothing to add to what I have already said.

*Close-up*—HAYWOOD

*There is a moment.*

HAYWOOD. The testimony has been received in the case. Final arguments have been heard. There remains only the task of the Tribunal to render its decision. The record is closed. Tribunal will recess until further notification.

*He bangs gavel, rises, starts out.* NORRIS *and* IVES *follow.*

*Interior. Palace of Justice, Chambers—Close-up*—HAYWOOD—*Day*

IVES *and* NORRIS *sitting around table.* IVES *is concluding summing up the evidence before him.* HAYWOOD *is farther down the table looking at something else before him. We do not see what it is immediately.*

IVES. This is the last of the papers on the "Night and Fog" decrees. Do you have anything more on that, Norris?

NORRIS. No. That's all.

IVES *(picks up some other papers).* Now I've collected some precedents here that bear on the basis of the case. The conflict between allegiance to international laws and the laws of one's country. . . .

*He looks over at* HAYWOOD *impatiently.*

IVES *(continuing).* Dan. We have a mountain of stuff to go over here.

NORRIS. What are you looking at, Dan?

*There is a moment.* HAYWOOD *speaks finally.*

HAYWOOD. I was just looking at the pictures attached to some of these warrants for arrest.

IVES. What pictures?

HAYWOOD *puts them on the desk one by one.*

HAYWOOD. This is a picture of Peterson before they operated on him . . . .

*Close-up*—*Photo*

*Pictures of Petersen. It hits the screen with impact. Petersen ten years ago. The young baker's helper. Just having been fingerprinted, he stares into the camera confused and frightened.*

HAYWOOD. Here's a picture of Irene Hoffmann. She really was sixteen once.

*He puts in on desk.*

*Close-up*—*Photo*

IRENE HOFFMANN *staring into the camera. It is obvious she is past crying. Tears have been replaced with terror. Wondering where there is justice in the world.*

HAYWOOD. Mr. Feldenstein.

*Close-up*—*Photo*

LEHMANN FELDENSTEIN—*a small man with rimless glasses, in his late sixties. There is fear in his face, but there is dignity, too.*

HAYWOOD. Here's a situation of a boy. He must have been no more than fourteen. Executed for saying things against the Third Reich.

*He reads down below at the bottom of the warrant.*

HAYWOOD *(continuing).* "Authorized by the jurisdiction of Judge Friedrich Hoffstetter."

*Close-up*—*Photo*

*A good-looking fourteen-year-old boy staring into the camera with terror. Just apprehended.* IVES *looks at* HAYWOOD *with impatience. Wondering why he has placed the photos on the table.*

IVES. Now, pertaining to the basis of the case, here is a passage from the opening address of the French Chief Prosecutor before the International Military Tribunal: "It is obvious that in the state organized along modern lines, responsibility is confined to those who act directly for the state since they alone are in a position to judge the legitimacy of the given orders. They alone can and should be prosecuted."

*While* IVES *is speaking,* HAYWOOD *gets up and walks to the window and looks out.* IVES *continues.*

IVES *(continuing).* Another one from Professor Jahrreisa's Legal Aspects—"Trial of the Major War Criminals"—"If a judge is not even entitled to examine the law as to its constitutionality, so it can be conceded even less that he may refuse to apply a law because according to his opinion it does not stand up to ethics and justice."

*As* IVES *continues speaking,* HAYWOOD *looks out of window.*

*Courtyard—*HAYWOOD'S *Point of View*

*We see* JANNING *sitting alone on a bench in the yard.*

*Exterior. Courtyard—Close-up—* JANNING*—Day*

*Interior. Chambers—Close-up—* HAYWOOD*—Day*

*His face is filled with compassion for* JANNING *as he sits there. His di-* *lemma. The courage that it took to get up in the courtroom and state the truth.*

IVES *puts papers aside. Looks up at the other two men.* IVES *continues speaking.*

IVES *(continuing).* Now on the basis of these, I can't see where we can interpret that the prosecution has put forth a really clear-cut case against the defense pertaining to the charges in the indictment.

NORRIS. What about Janning's confession?

IVES. Regardless of the acts committed, I don't see how we can interpret it that the defendants were really responsible for crimes against humanity. *(pause)*

*Close-up—*NORRIS

*Uncertain.* NORRIS *looks toward window at* HAYWOOD.

NORRIS. What do you think, Dan?

IVES *(exploding and pressing* NORRIS*).* We've been going over these documents for two days, If it isn't clear by now—*(turns to* HAYWOOD *at window in frustration)* Look at these precedents and opinions. Look at them if you're interested at all!

HAYWOOD *speaks finally.*

HAYWOOD. I'm interested, Curtiss! *(pause)*

*He turns from window.*

HAYWOOD *(continuing; quietly).* You were speaking of crimes against humanity. You were saying these men were not responsible for them. *(pause)* I'd like you to explain it to me. *(pause)*

*Close-up—*IVES

IVES. I've just been explaining it. *(pause)*

HAYWOOD (*looking at him*). Maybe. But all I've heard was legalistic double talk. And rationalizations. (*pause; continues quietly*) Curtiss, when I first became judge, I knew there were certain people in the town I wasn't supposed to touch. I knew if I wanted to remain judge this was so. (*quietly*) But how do you expect me to look the other way at six million murders?

*There is a moment.*

NORRIS. I'm sure he doesn't mean that, Dan. There is after all—
IVES. I'm not asking you to look the other way at them! (*then bursts out*) I'm asking you what good it's going to do to pursue this policy!

*Close-up—*HAYWOOD

*Seeing the rationalization before him. The corruption before him not too different from the corruption he has been hearing about on the judge's bench. Corruption that is all the more terrible because it is not recognized as corruption.* HAYWOOD *walks slowly to the table. Speaks quietly to* IVES.

HAYWOOD. Curtiss, you were saying they weren't responsible. (*pause; quietly*) You're going to have to explain it to me. You're going to have to explain it very carefully.

*Close-up—*IVES'S *face*

*Realizing that by his voice and his face* HAYWOOD *has thrown down the gauntlet to him.*

*Close-up—*HAYWOOD

*Interior. Palace of Justice, Courtroom—Day*

*The court sits expectantly.* HAYWOOD *enters, followed by* NORRIS *and* IVES.

CAPTAIN BYERS. The Tribunal is in session. God save the United States of America and this Honorable Tribunal.

HAYWOOD *and the others are seated.* HAYWOOD *looks about the courtroom a moment before speaking.*

HAYWOOD. The trial conducted before this Tribunal began over eight months ago. The record of evidence is over 10,000 pages long and the final arguments of counsel have been concluded. Simple murders and atrocities do not constitute the gravamen of the charges in the indictment. Rather, the charge is that of conscious participation in a nation-wide government-organized system of cruelty and injustice in violation of legal and moral principles common to all civilized nations. (*pause; then vigorously*) The Tribunal has carefully reviewed the record and found therein abundant competent evidence to support, beyond a reasonable doubt, the charges brought against these defendants.

*Pause. There is a sensation in the courtroom.*

*Close-up—*COLONEL LAWSON

*In surprise.*

*Close-up—*JANNING

*Close-up—*MRS. BERTHOLT *in the rear of the audience*

*Full Shot*

HAYWOOD. Herr Rolfe, in his skilful defense has asserted that there are others who must share the ultimate responsibility for what happened here in Germany. There is truth in this. (*pause*) The real complaining party at the bar in this courtroom is civilization. (*pause*) In all our countries, it is still a struggling and imperfect thing. This Tribunal does not believe that the

United States or any other country has been blameless of the conditions which made the German people vulnerable to the blandishments and temptations of the rise of Nazism. But this Tribunal does say that the men in the dock are responsible for their acts. Men who sat in black robes in judgment on other men. Men who took part in the enactment of laws and decrees the purpose of which was the extermination of human beings. Men who, in executive positions, actively participated in the enforcement of those laws, illegal even under German law. The principle of criminal law of every civilized society has this in common. Any person who sways another to commit murder, any person who furnishes the lethal weapon for the purpose of this crime, any person who is an accessory to this crime is guilty. *(pause)* Herr Rolfe further asserts that the defendant Janning was an extraordinary jurist who was acting in what he thought to be the best interests of this country. *(pause)* There is truth in this also.

*The Dock—Close-up—*JANNING

HAYWOOD. Janning, to be sure, is a tragic figure. We believe he loathed the evil he did.

*The Bench—Close-up—*HAYWOOD

HAYWOOD. But compassion for the present torture of his soul must not beget forgetfulness of the torture and death of millions by the government of which he was a part.

*Close-up—*MRS. BERTHOLT

*Close-up—*HAYWOOD

*Pause. He continues without looking at* MRS. BERTHOLT.

HAYWOOD. Janning's record and his fate illuminate the most shattering truth that has emerged from this trial. If he and the other defendants were all degraded perverts—if all the leaders of the Third Reich were sadistic monsters and maniacs—these events would have no more moral significance than an earthquate or other natural catastrophes.

*The Dock—Close-up—*JANNING

HAYWOOD. But this trial has shown that under the stress of a national crisis, ordinary men—even able and extraordinary men—can delude themselves into the commission of crimes and atrocities so vast and heinous that they beggar the imagination.

JANNING *winces, unable to take in the significance of all that* HAYWOOD *is saying.*

*The Bench—Close-up—*HAYWOOD

HAYWOOD *(continuing; quietly with feeling).* No one who has sat through this trial can ever forget them. The sterilization of men because of their political beliefs. . . . A mockery made out of friendship and faith. . . . The murder of children. . . .*(quietly)* How easily it can happen. *(looks up)* There are those in our own country today, too, who speak of the protection of the country. Of survival.

*Pause. Looks about courtroom.*

*Close-up—*COLONEL LAWSON

*Close-up—*HAYWOOD

HAYWOOD. The answer to that is: *Survival as what?* A country isn't a rock . . . and it isn't an extension of one's self . . . it's what it stands for, when standing for something is the most difficult. Before the people of the world—let it now be noted in our decision here that this is what we stand for: Justice, Truth . . . and the value of a single human being.

*There is a moment.*

HAYWOOD *(continuing).* The Marshal will produce before the Tribunal the defendant Hahn.

HAHN *rises in dock.*

HAYWOOD *(continuing).* Emil Hahn, the Tribunal finds you guilty and sentences you to life imprisonment.

*Close-up—*HAHN

HAHN *(shrieks out).* Today you sentence me! Tomorrow the Bolsheviks sentence you!

*The noise in the courtroom has reached a crescendo.* HAYWOOD *continues as though he is not aware of the noise in the courtroom . . . or of the words of* HAHN.

HAYWOOD. The Marshal will produce the defendant Hoffstetter.

HOFFSTETTER *rises in dock.*

HAYWOOD *(continuing).* Friedrich Hoffstetter, the Tribunal finds you guilty and sentences you to life imprisonment.

*Close-up—*HOFFSTETTER

*There is a stir in the audience again. There is an outcry in the audience. There is a cry from* HOFFSTETTER'S WIFE *as though she were crying out at the injustice of it.* HOFFSTETTER *sits down slowly.* HAYWOOD *continues.*

HAYWOOD. The Marshal will produce the defendant Lammpe.

LAMMPE *rises slowly.*

HAYWOOD *(continuing).* Werner Lammpe. The Tribunal finds you guilty and sentences you to life imprisonment.

*Close-up—*LAMMPE

*He stands a moment looking around bewilderedly. Realizing that this sentence will incarcerate him for the rest of his natural life. He has to be helped back down into his chair.*

HAYWOOD. The Marshal will produce the defendant Janning.

*There is a moment. It is the first time that* HAYWOOD *pauses in the reading of his sentencing.*

*Close-up—*HAYWOOD

*Close-up-*JANNING

*Close-up—*HAYWOOD

HAYWOOD. The Tribunal finds you guilty . . . and sentences you to life imprisonment.

*Close-up—*MRS. BERTHOLT

*Face diffused. Unable to accept the implication and meaning of* HAYWOOD'S *judgment. Tears in her eyes.*

*Close-up—*JANNING

*There is a moment.* HAYWOOD *stares at* JANNING *with a justification of his sentences. As though he were glad that he had the courage in himself to find the sentences that must be found. Then in looking into the eyes of a man he cannot help but relate to, he lowers his eyes at the human waste.*

*Prosecution Table—*COLONEL LAWSON

MAJOR RADNITZ *still sits stunned.*

GENERAL MERRIN *(finally).* He doesn't understand. He just doesn't understand.

*There is a moment.* GENERAL MERRIN *gets up and goes.* COLONEL LAWSON *still sits watching* HAYWOOD.

*Close-up—*HAYWOOD

*Close-up—*LAWSON

COLONEL LAWSON (*to* MAJOR RADNITZ, *quietly*). He understands all right.

*Close-up*—HAYWOOD

*Close-up*—LAWSON

*Watching him.*

COLONEL LAWSON (*quietly; feeling for him*). Mr. Justice Haywood, Republican from Maine, is one hell of a guy.

IVES (*vigorously; outrage in his voice*). I wish to point out strongly my dissenting vote from the decision of this Tribunal as stated by Justice Haywood in which Justice Norris concurred. The issue of the actions of the defendants who believed they were acting in the best interests of their country is an issue that cannot be decided in a courtroom alone. It can only be decided objectively in years to come in the true perspective of history. . . .

*Interior.* HAYWOOD'S *Quarters, Study—Day*

HAYWOOD *is dialing on phone. He waits for answer.* HALBESTADT *enters with a large package of books, followed by* CAPTAIN BYERS.

HALBESTADT. Where shall I put these, Your Honor?

BYERS. We'll put those in the trunk, Mr. Halbestadt.

MRS. HALBESTADT *enters, with cake wrapped in paper. Hands it to* HAYWOOD

MRS. HALBESTADT. Here's something for you to have on the plane.

HAYWOOD (*looks at her a moment. Smiles a little*). Mrs. Halbestadt. If I take all the food you've given me, we won't have room to pack anything else.

MRS. HALBESTADT. But it's strudel, Judge! The way you like it.

HAYWOOD (*smiles gently*). Thank you, Mrs. Halbestadt.

MRS. HALBESTADT *goes.*

HAYWOOD (*to* BYERS). Give my regards to Miss Scheffler.

BYERS. That's one you owe me.

HAYWOOD. What do you mean?

BYERS (*dryly*). Americans aren't very popular in Germany this morning. I'll take care of things at the airport. See you there no later than an hour.

HAYWOOD. Thanks.

CAPTAIN BYERS *goes.* HAYWOOD *dials the number again. There is no answer. He hangs up slowly.*

*Interior.* MRS. BERTHOLT'S *Apartment—Day*

MRS. BERTHOLT *sits in the semi-darkness of her apartment. Her husband's painting is prominently behind her.*

*Close-up*—MRS. BERTHOLT'S *Face*

*Unable to face the truth. The things that* HAYWOOD *has said in the courtroom. She pours herself another drink from the decanter. The tears are in her eyes. We know that she is going to retreat inside herself again. Even further from reality this time. One day she will retreat so far that she will never be able to find it again. Camera lingers on* MRS. BERTHOLT'S *face.*

*Interior.* HAYWOOD'S *Quarters, Study—Day*

HAYWOOD *hangs up slowly. He is suddenly aware of someone standing in the entrance to the study. It is* ROLFE. *He enters, slowly.*

ROLFE (*pleasantly; but there is an undercurrent underneath*). Good afternoon, Your Honor.

HAYWOOD *(quietly).* Good afternoon.

ROLFE. I came here at the request of my client, Ernst Janning. He wishes to see you.

HAYWOOD. I'm just leaving for the airport.

ROLFE. He said it would mean a great deal to him.

*Close-up—*HAYWOOD

*He nods, then walks to chair where his overcoat is lying.*

*Interior. Car—Day*

HAYWOOD *and* ROLFE *sit in the back seat.*

*Exterior. Karolinenstrasse—From* HAYWOOD's *Point of View*

*The people on the street are much different now from when we have first seen them. They are dressed better now. Their clothes now match—the jackets and trousers. They have a brisker pace. Even more assurance. Even more purpose. We pass shopfronts. They are now filled with merchandise as though overnight.*

*Interior. Car—Day*

ROLFE *looks at* HAYWOOD. *There is a moment before he speaks. He cannot help speaking.*

ROLFE. Things are changing already under the currency reform. *(gestures to the wall around the old square of Nuremberg)*

*We see the wall from the point of view of the car.*

ROLFE. The new wall is almost finished.

*Interior. Car—Day*

ROLFE. The stores are beginning to get butter in even. *(pause.* HAYWOOD *doesn't answer)* Did you hear about the verdict in the I.G. Farben case,

Judge? (HAYWOOD *does not answer)* Most of them were acquitted. The others received light sentences. The verdict came in today. *(pause)*

HAYWOOD *(quietly).* No. I had not heard.

ROLFE *(stares at* HAYWOOD a moment; *smiles a little).* I will make you a wager.

HAYWOOD *looks at* ROLFE *wearily. He manages a smile in response.*

HAYWOOD. I don't make wagers.

ROLFE *(smiling politely).* A gentleman's wager. In five years, the men you sentenced to life imprisonment will be free.

*There is a moment.* HAYWOOD *stares ahead of him. He speaks finally.*

HAYWOOD. Herr Rolfe. I have admired your work in the courtroom for many months. (ROLFE *nods politely, accepting the compliment)* You are a brilliant attorney. You will undoubtedly go very far. (ROLFE *nods again)* You are particularly brilliant in your use of logic. *(pause; dryly)* Therefore, I have no doubt that what you suggest may well happen. *(dryly)* It is logical in view of the times in which we live. *(then looks at* ROLFE *for a moment before he continues)*

*The car has stopped.*

HAYWOOD. But to be logical is not to be right. And nothing on God's earth could ever make it right. *(gets out of car and closes door with a slam)*

*Close-up—*ROLFE's *face*

*He is a little stunned.* HAYWOOD *has stopped him for a moment, making him think. But only for a moment. It is not long until the old rationalizations come into his face. He is indeed the symbol of the New Germany.*

*Interior. Palace of Justice, Prison Cell—Door—Black*

*The door swings open.* GUARD *is standing there. Behind him silhouetted against the fading light through the bars is* JANNING. *His face is tense. He stands waiting, anxious.*

GUARD. Someone to see you.

*We follow the shoulders of a man going into the cell. The man is* HAYWOOD. *There is a moment. The two men stand staring at one another.* GUARD *goes.*

HAYWOOD *(speaks finally)*. Herr Janning.
JANNING. Judge Haywood.

*Pause. Gestures with a touch of awkwardness at their meeting here in this barren cell.*

JANNING *(continuing)*. Please. Sit down.

*There is a moment.* HAYWOOD *remains standing.*

HAYWOOD. You wanted to see me.
JANNING. Yes. *(pause)* There is something I want to give you. A record. A record of my cases. The cases I remember.

*Pause. Goes to table. Picks up thick notebook with papers in it.*

JANNING *(continuing)*. I want to give it to someone I can trust. *(pause)* Someone I feel I got to know during the trial.

*Pause. Picks it up. Hands it to* HAYWOOD.

HAYWOOD. Thank you. I'll take good care of them. *(pause)*

JANNING *smiles self-deprecatingly.*

JANNING. It won't do any good. *(pause)* But it is a record of what can happen. *(pause)*

*The two men look at each other awkwardly.*

JANNING *(continuing; finally)*. I know the pressures that must have been brought on you. *(pause)* Your verdict will not be a popular one. You will be criticized greatly. *(pause)* Nuremberg will not be a pleasant word for Germans for years to come. *(pause; quietly with emotion)* But if it means anything to you, you have the respect at least of one man you convicted. By all that is right in this world, your verdict was a just one. *(pause; with emotion)*

HAYWOOD *(quietly)*. Thank you. *(pause)* What you said in court—it needed to be said.

*He starts to go.* JANNING *stops him with a word.*

JANNING. Judge Haywood.

HAYWOOD *stops.* JANNING *speaks with difficulty not knowing himself what he is going to say until the words are out.*

JANNING *(continuing; pause)*. The real reason I asked you to come. I want to know. I want to hear from a man like you. A man who has heard what happened. I want to hear—not that he forgives—but that he understands.

HAYWOOD *looks at* JANNING, *feeling for him from the bottom of his heart. Feeling impotent, wanting to say something to this man. But he can't. Understand, Haywood says to himself. I understand the pressures you were under. In these months I have been here I understand that. But how can I understand the deaths of millions of men, women and children in gas ovens, Herr Janning? How can I understand that? How can I tell you I understand it?* JANNING *looks at*

HAYWOOD, *sensitive to what he must be feeling.*

*Close-up*—JANNING

JANNING *(speaks finally; it seems almost as though he was reading* HAYWOOD'S *mind).* I did not know it would come to that. You must believe it. You must believe it.

*Close-up*—HAYWOOD

*Stands staring at the man before him.*

HAYWOOD *(almost without thinking; says the words finally as though he were speaking to a child).* Herr Janning. It came to that the first time you sentenced a man to death you knew to be innocent.

*Close-up*—JANNING

*Stunned. The impact on him is enormous. He watches* HAYWOOD *go.*

*Close-up*—HAYWOOD

*Exterior. Nuremberg Prison—Day*

*The huge iron gate clangs behind* HAYWOOD *as he walks out of Nuremberg prison. Before him is the city itself. We see the people of Nuremberg. People without a past in their faces. The signs of rebuilding everywhere.* HAYWOOD *gets into car. The car drives off. Camera remains on Nuremberg. Over the scene the final words emblazon themselves on the screen one by one.*

On 14 July 1949, judgment was rendered in the last of the second of the Nuremberg trials. Of ninety-nine sentenced to prison terms, not one is still serving his sentence.

*Fade Out*

# THE LION IN WINTER

## *Screenplay by James Goldman*

| | |
|---|---|
| KING HENRY II | Peter O'Toole |
| QUEEN ELEANOR OF AQUITAINE | Katharine Hepburn |
| PRINCESS ALAIS | Jane Merrow |
| PRINCE GEOFFREY | John Castle |
| KING PHILIP OF FRANCE | Timothy Dalton |
| PRINCE RICHARD | |
| THE LIONHEARTED | Anthony Hopkins |
| WILLIAM MARSHAL | Nigel Stock |
| PRINCE JOHN | Nigel Terry |

Directed by Anthony Harvey
Produced by Martin Poll
Executive Producer: Joseph E. Levine
Music Composed by John Barry
Cinematographer: Douglas Slocombe
Set Director: Peter James
Film Editor: John Bloom

In the screenplay of *The Lion in Winter,* which the author adapted from his own stage play, James Goldman has given us a fascinating historic study of a warped, power-driven family headed by King Henry II, a double-dealing, brilliant monarch. This is the same Henry who dealt off his best friend, Becket, to assassins in earlier years. (The movie *Becket* won an Oscar for Best Screenplay for writer Ed Anhalt.)

Character studies of royal families whose members vie with one another for power have been seen mostly in historical contexts on the stage and screen, going back to Shakespeare and beyond. But they also fascinate writers and audiences in the more mundane family world. For example, Henry and his family bear more than a slight resemblance to that "sweet" family in Lillian Hellman's play *The Little Foxes,* and television's "Dynasty" owes more than a little to this sustaining fascination with family autocrats and those who seek to wrest power from them. In a sense this is the history of family at its worst. Wherever there is something of value to fight about, there is where you find your Henrys, your Richard IIIs, and so on. And the power struggles and relationships fraught with drama continue to be a source of inspiration and fascination for major writers.

James Goldman's dialogue is exemplary in *The Lion in Winter*. It's exciting, witty, driven. It pulsates with power itself. The screenplay's dramatic structure

341

is equally fine, never letting up, piling surprise upon surprise, holding us captive until we cross the finish line with the winner.

James Goldman was born in Chicago, Illinois, on June 30, 1927. He graduated from the University of Chicago and was a postgraduate in musicology at Columbia University (1950–52). He is married and now resides in New York.

His play *They Might Be Giants* was produced in London in 1961, and *The Lion in Winter* was produced as a play in New York in 1966. In 1968 Mr. Goldman adapted it to film and won not only an Oscar for Best Screenplay (based on material from another medium), but also the Writers Guild of America Award for screenwriters. Among Mr. Goldman's other credits for screenplays are *Nicholas and Alexandra* (1971) and *Robin and Marion* (1976). His musical credits include the book for *Follies* (1971), and notable among his novels is *Waldorf* (1965).

# A WORD ABOUT CASTLES

*The Lion in Winter* was a special and peculiar sort of history play. To make its style and intention clear on film, the look of the castle where it occurs and the sense of castle life need to be earthily realistic and, at the same time, strikingly different from what we're used to seeing in King Arthur movies.

Almost nothing is known about the castle at Chinon as it was in Henry's time; and little enough is known about twelfth-century castles in general. One thing is clear, however, and important for our purposes: namely, that such castles looked nothing like what we expect.

The stone fortresses that remain today were only the shell of castles as they were lived in. Most of the shelter for most of the staff, all of the workshops—the armories, forges, stables and so on—were made of wood. A castle courtyard was a crowded, teeming, dirty place with much more wood than stone to greet the eye.

A major castle, as Chinon was, was like a miniature town. Everything necessary to the life of the establishment existed inside the walls. Poultry, livestock, looms and tailors, mills for grinding grain, vast storerooms, water wells, boot makers, gardens—everything vital to life under siege was somehow packed in.

At special times, like the Christmas Court during which the film occurs, the congestion was even worse than usual. All guests, the visiting nobles and clergymen, traveled with trains of varying size. So, in addition to the usual crowding, we find hundreds of soldiers and servants living out doors, jammed together in tents, huddling for warmth around dozens of fires.

Living conditions, even for royalty, were crude and rough. The castle rooms were spartan: a bed, a few chairs, chests for storage, clothes hung in the open on racks. Floors were covered with straw, which was swept away and replaced only occasionally. Interiors at high noon on a clear day were always dark, illumination coming from extremely smoky torches and candles. In winter, wind whistled through the open slit windows and the place was freezing cold.

A lot of the habits of the time seem oddly contradictory. In spite of the cold, everyone from the king to his vassal slept naked. In the midst of the general crudeness, nobles wore the most exquisite fabrics—cloths of gold and silver, delicate brocades. Clothing was generally dirty and even at a Christmas Court, nothing looked clean. Tables were set with fine linen, and napkins of a king were used; yet most of the eating was done with fingers. Sanitary conditions were appalling. For some reason, castles, in addition to their human tenants, were populated by hundreds of dogs.

All these things—the grime and dirt and cold, the coarseness and crudity of life in general—are vital to the look of the film. On the whole, there are few specific references to these elements in the screenplay. Rather than clutter up the goings on with data, it seemed better to suggest them here and let the castle that the story moves in be imagined.

*[James Goldman]*

THE CHARACTERS

HENRY II, *King of England; age 50*

ELEANOR OF AQUITAINE, *his wife; age 61*

RICHARD THE LIONHEARTED, *their oldest boy; age 26*

GEOFFREY, *their middle boy; age 25*

JOHN, *their youngest boy; age 16*

ALAIS CAPET, *a French princess; age 23*

PHILIP CAPET, *the King of France; age 18*

WILLIAM MARSHAL, *a noted soldier and friend of the family; age about 35*

THE TIME: *Christmas, 1183*

THE PLACE: *Henry's castle at Chinon, France*

*(Blue sky. A few light clouds. A bird flies past. We follow it, then suddenly veer down and see* HENRY PLANTAGENET *close up: His eyes are bright, his teeth bared in a grin of fierce excitement. He is poised for dueling, sword in hand.)*

*(*HENRY *is 50, an age at which, in his time, men were either old or dead. Not* HENRY. *Very nearly all he ever was, he is enjoying that final rush of physical and mental vigor that comes to some men not before the end but just before the start of the decline.)*

*(The story starts as* HENRY *barks out:)*

HENRY. Come on. Come for me.

*(He brings his sword down and the duel begins. His opponent, whom we see from behind, charges at him, raining blow after blow.* HENRY *parries only, never striking back, always retreating.)*

*(They fight across the field. Suddenly,* HENRY, *moving backwards, trips and falls. With a cry, his opponent charges at him. Effortlessly,* HENRY *strikes his first blow. The opponent's sword flies from his hand as he sprawls flat on the ground.* HENRY

*bounds to his feet, moves to his fallen opponent, looks down, and we see—*

JOHN, *his son of 16, who, in 18 years, was to become the worst king in English history. Still pudgy with baby fat, he has a round open face that is enchanting when he smiles. He is frightened now and shaken up.* HENRY *glares down, sword in hand. Then, with a quick, gruff smile, he reaches down and yanks* JOHN *to his feet.)*

HENRY. You're gaining on it, Johnny.

JOHN. Am I, Father? Am I really?

HENRY. Off you go, now. Run along and practice.

*(*JOHN *picks up his sword, starts across the field toward a knight, his dueling master, who stands waiting.* HENRY, *a look of affection on his face as he looks after* JOHN, *turns and starts across the field toward the little tent. He waves. We can just make out a figure by the tent. It waves back.)*

*(We see* JOHN *and the knight.* JOHN *casts a look in* HENRY'S *direction. There is no love lost. He turns back and dueling practice begins.)*

*(In a tent, food for a royal picnic is handsomely arranged. The figure we saw is a girl.* HENRY *lies, his head on her lap.)*

*(We see the girl, close up.* ALAIS CAPET *is 23 and exquisitely beautiful. She is like a fine porcelain figure— fragile, delicate, pure, the only person in this story easy to break. She is happily and desperately in love with* HENRY; *it's all over her as she looks down at him.)*

ALAIS *(Singing softly in her native tongue; bright and gay).* Allons gai, gai, gai, bergère; allons gai. Allons gai, soyez legère, suivez moi.

*(*HENRY'S *gaze is out across the field.)*

HENRY. He'll make a good king. He'll be ready.

*(For a moment we see* JOHN *and the knight:* JOHN *flailing away, stumbles and staggers about.)*

That's it, that's the way, lad.

ALAIS. Have you found religion, Henry? Will you look down from the clouds and see who's sitting on your throne?

HENRY *(He sits up, takes a chicken leg from a platter, starts devouring it).* I've got to know before I die. There is a legend of a king called Lear, with whom I have a lot in common. Both of us have kingdoms and three children we adore and both of us are old. But there it stops. He cut his kingdom into bits. I can't do that. I've built an empire: all of England, half of France. I am the greatest power in a thousand years and after me comes John.

ALAIS. I'm going to lose you, Henry, aren't I?

HENRY. Alais, in my time, I've known contessas, milkmaids, courtesans and novices, whores, gypsies, jades and little boys, but nowhere in God's western world have I found anyone to love but you.

ALAIS. And Rosamund.

HENRY. She's dead.

ALAIS. And Eleanor.

HENRY. The new Medusa, my good wife.

ALAIS. How is your queen?

HENRY. Decaying, I suppose. No, don't be jealous of the gorgon; she is not among the things I love. How many husbands do you know who lock their wives away? I haven't kept the great bitch in the keep for ten years out of passionate attachment.

*(He sees something across the field.)*

Ah, there's Captain Marshal.

*(He rises, beckons, calls.)*

William.

*(Across the field on horseback, riding past them toward* HENRY, *is* WILLIAM MARSHAL.)*

*(He is 35 and looks like the distinguished soldier he is. A rugged face but honest, open and friendly. He was totally devoted to* HENRY *and his children and through all their wars and conflicts somehow manged always to be loyal to all of them.)*

*(*HENRY *smiles as* MARSHAL *stands before him, bowing.)*

HENRY. We will be holding Christmas Court at Chinon. We have asked the King of France to join us. I want Richard there. And Geoffrey. Find my boys and tell them so. And then go fetch the Queen from Salisbury Tower.

MARSHAL. If the Queen refuses?

HENRY. Eleanor? She wouldn't miss this for the world.

*(*MARSHAL *nods, moves toward his horse. The horse whinnies.)*

I'm afraid it's going to be a family Christmas.

ALAIS. I'm afraid, too.

HENRY. What of?

ALAIS. Just afraid.

*(He looks at her with enormous tenderness, takes her in his arms. They hold each other.)*

*(*HENRY *looks out across the field. Anxiety crosses his face.)*

*(We see* JOHN, *sweating, red-faced, flailing away.)*

*(The sound grows sharply and a knight in full armor fills the screen. He is on horse, facing another armored knight. They lower lances, then they charge, meeting with tremendous impact. One of them is hurled violently to the ground.)*

*(We are in the lists, watching a contest. It is not the set we're used to seeing—grandstands, canopies, banners. At this time, the lists consisted of the broad, shallow, muddy trench that lay between the inner and outer walls of a castle. It is primitive and crude, not glamorous. The audience either stands or sits on straw spread on the mud. There are one or two crude benches for the most important nobles present.)*

*(The victorious knight, himself a large man, leaps from his horse, throws off his visor and we get our first look at* RICHARD LIONHEART.*)*

*(*RICHARD, *at 26, looks like his legend: handsome, impressive, fierce, powerful. He loves the blood and violence of war. He is caught up in this passion when we see him and his face is frightening.)*

*(He moves to the fallen knight, who lies stunned, sprawled in the mud. He draws his sword. He is going to kill the man.)*

*(The audience is appalled but afraid to speak. Behind them,* MARSHAL *strides down toward the lists.)*

*(*RICHARD *stands sword poised. His face is frightening.)*

MARSHAL *(Calling out).* Richard!

*(*RICHARD *hesitates, turns.)*

*(*MARSHAL *walking into the lists toward him. In ordinary, conversational tones:)*

Hello, Richard.

*(Suddenly, we're on a rocky seacoast: sand, sky, cliffs, everything looks metal-gray. A large body of footsoldiers is marching along the shore.)*

*(Out of nowhere, a mass of knights on horse come charging up the sand. They attack the footsoldiers, throwing them into frightened confusion.)*

*(Watching it all from the top of the cliff is* GEOFFREY PLANTAGENET, *Count of Brittany,* GEOFFREY *is 25, lithe, attractive, quick of speech and movement. His was the best brain of a brainy family and his face shines with intelligence. Dressed for the palace, not the field, he raises his hand in a signal.)*

*(The footsoldiers, in rout now, are running up the beach when, from behind a rise, more knights on horse come charging, cutting off all possible escape.)*

*(It is all neatly planned and deftly executed. The slaughter at the water's edge is terrible. The pleasure that we see on* GEOFFREY'S *face is not at the death below but at a maneuver nicely done.)*

*(*MARSHAL *appears behind him. He speaks quietly.)*

MARSHAL. Geoffrey.

GEOFFREY *(Turning to Marshal).* Father wants to see me.

*(*MARSHAL *nods.)*

Where and when?

*(Dark, rolling late autumnal countryside. A castle on a hilltop in the distance.* MARSHAL *rides past us toward the castle.)*

*(Then we're in a large, cold, relatively barren castle room. A few chairs, wooden chests, a bed, a few wall tapestries, straw on the floor. The camera takes in the room. Two maids-in-waiting sit huddled by the fire, doing needlework. Perched on a high stool by the room's one slit of a window sits* ELEANOR OF AQUITAINE. *She is 61 and looks nothing like it. She is a truly handsome woman of great temperament, authority and presence. She has been a queen of international importance for 46 years and you know it. Finally, she is that most unusual thing: a genuinely femi-*

nine woman thoroughly capable of holding her own in a man's world.)

(She has been painting an exquisite miniature on ivory. She still holds the brush but is motionless now, listening to the unbolting of the door. Her face shows nothing.)

MARSHAL. Your majesty.

ELEANOR. There is to be a Christmas Court.

MARSHAL *(Voice over)*. Yes, madam.

ELEANOR. Where?

(Nothing but her face. The look is enigmatic but the excitement is unmistakable.)

MARSHAL. At Chinon.

(We see the castle in the dim gray light of predawn. It is winter now. Mist rises. In the castle yard, no sign of life. Silence. A dog walks by.)

(Then, veering up, we see the rising sun. Its first rays strike the top of the bell tower. The bell starts to swing. Its clapper comes crashing down.)

(A large bowl of water. Ice has formed across the top. Two hands come smashing through the ice.)

(We're in HENRY'S bedroom. Bare, spartan, cold; no elegance at all. HENRY, half-dressed, stands before the bowl of water. ALAIS, blankets clutched around her, sits on the bed. She speaks.)

ALAIS. Henry, what if, just for once, I didn't do as I was told?

HENRY *(Splashing water on his face)*. It's going to be a jungle of a day. If I start growling now, I'll never last.

(ALAIS, on the bed, robe over her shoulders, is starting to dress.)

ALAIS. You'll last. You're like the rocks at Stonehenge. Nothing knocks you down.

HENRY *(Drying his face with a towel)*. In these rooms, Alais, on this Christmas, I have all the enemies I need.

ALAIS. You have more than you think.

HENRY. Are you one? Has my willow turned to poison oak?

ALAIS. If I decided to be trouble, Henry, how much trouble could I be?

HENRY. Not much.

(HENRY and ALAIS, dressed now, are moving down a corridor. They pass an occasional servant, who stops and bows. We follow them as HENRY strides briskly along, ALAIS half-running to keep up.)

ALAIS. I could give away your plans.

HENRY. You don't know what they are.

ALAIS. I know you want to disinherit Richard.

HENRY. So does Eleanor. She knows young Henry's dead. The Young King died in summer and I haven't named an heir. She knows I want John on the throne and I know she wants Richard. We are very frank about it.

(HENRY and ALAIS are at a table eating breakfast. They eat, as was the custom, with spoons and fingers from a common bowl that sits on the table between them.)

ALAIS. Henry, I can't be your mistress if I'm married to your son.

HENRY. Why can't you? Johnny wouldn't mind.

ALAIS. I do not like your Johnny.

HENRY. He's a good boy.

ALAIS. He's got pimples and he smells of compost.

HENRY. He's just sixteen; he can't help the pimples.

ALAIS. He could have a bath.

(HENRY is striding briskly down a corridor, ALAIS hurrying after him.

*The corridor is more crowded now. There are knights and high clergymen who, as* HENRY *passes, stop and bow.* HENRY *ignores it all, striding on until he reaches a niche in the corridor. He stops abruptly, turns on* ALAIS.)

HENRY. It isn't such a dreadful thing to be a queen of England. Not all eyes will weep for you.

ALAIS. Will yours?

HENRY. I don't know. Very likely.

ALAIS. All I want is not to lose you. Can't you hide me? Can't I simply disappear?

HENRY. You know you can't. Your little brother Philip's King of France now and he wants your wedding or your dowry back. I only took you for your dowry. You were seven; two big knees and two big eyes and that's all. How was I to know?

*(We pull back as* HENRY *moves to kiss her lightly. There is a sound of running down the corridor. It's* JOHN. *He slows down as he sees his father and fiancée kissing. He doesn't like it. Sensing someone,* HENRY *turns, takes* JOHN *in.)*

What's wrong, lad?

JOHN *(Producing a smile)*. Nothing.

*(With a skip and a wave,* JOHN *resumes running down the corridor. We follow him as he turns a corner, reaches a great high door, tugs it open, slips through and starts racing down a broad exterior flight of steps into the castle yard. Calling, waving, excited and happy:)*

Geoff! Geoff!

*(We see the yard.* GEOFFREY, *on horseback, is riding toward us. He waves back. The yard is a mob scene, crammed with soldiers, servants, peasants, tents, outdoor kitchens, livestock, poultry, horses, the lot. The*

soldiers are lined up for morning chow.)

*(*JOHN *threads his way through it all, reaching* GEOFFREY *as he dismounts.)*

GEOFFREY *(As they hug each other roughly)*. Johnny.

JOHN *(A large bundle hangs from* GEOFFREY's *saddle. Pointing to it)*. Is that for me?

*(*GEOFFREY *nods.)*

I love Christmas.

*(An enormous Christmas tree, close up, is being raised to standing position.)*

*(*HENRY *nods at the tree in brisk approval.* ALAIS *stands near him, wanting to speak but hesitant. We are in the parlor, a fairly spacious place which functioned as a kind of family room. There are the usual tapestries, some furniture, a desk and, scattered about, piles of holly boughs.)*

*(*HENRY *turns to leave the room.* ALAIS *stops him, saying:)*

ALAIS. What difference does my dowry make? Let Philip have it back. It isn't much.

HENRY. I can't. The Vexin is a little county but it's vital to me.

ALAIS. And I'm not.

HENRY. It's been my luck to fall in love with landed women. When I married Eleanor, I thought: "You lucky man. The richest woman in the world. She owns the Aquitaine, the greatest province on the Continent—and beautiful as well." She was, you know.

ALAIS. And you adored her.

HENRY. Memory fails. There may have been an era when I did.

*(He arranges a loose lock of her hair.)*

Let's have one strand askew; nothing in life has any business being perfect.

If I say you and I are done, we're done. If I say marry John, it's John. I'll have you by me and I'll use you as I like.

(JOHN *and* GEOFFREY, *in the courtyard, turn at a great clatter of horse's hooves behind them. They stop and turn.*)

(RICHARD *arrives in the yard at full gallop. He reins in with great bravado and leaps from his horse.*)

(GEOFFREY *starts toward* RICHARD *with a friendly wave of greeting.* JOHN, *glaring sullenly at* RICHARD, *hangs back, then follows* GEOFFREY.)

(*We see* RICHARD, JOHN *and* GEOFFREY *crossing the courtyard toward the stables,* RICHARD *leads his horse.*)

GEOFFREY. Ah, Christmas; warm and rosy time. The hot wine steams, the Yule log roars and we're the fat that's in the fire. She'll be here soon, you know.

JOHN. Who?

RICHARD. Mother.

GEOFFREY. Does she still want you to be king?

RICHARD. We are not as friendly as we were.

JOHN. If I'm supposed to make a fuss and kiss her hairy cheek, I won't.

RICHARD. What you kiss, little prince, is up to you.

JOHN. I'm Father's favorite; that's what counts.

RICHARD (*Stopping, looking down at* JOHN, *with quiet, total conviction*). You hardly know me, Johnny, so I beg you to believe my reputation. I'm a constant soldier and a sometime poet and I will be king.

JOHN. Just you remember: Father loves me best.

(HENRY *is seated at a desk, busily going through state papers.* ALAIS *hovers about.*)

ALAIS. Why John? John doesn't care for you at all.

HENRY. We love each other deeply.

ALAIS. None of them has any love for you.

HENRY. Because we fight? Tell me they all three want the crown, I'll tell you it's a feeble prince that doesn't. They may snap at me and plot and that makes them the kind of sons I want. I've snapped and plotted all my life. There is no other way to be a king, alive and fifty all at once.

ALAIS. I'm going to fight for you.

HENRY. Oh, fine.

(*We're on the walk that runs along the top of the castle wall.* HENRY *is pacing impatiently, repeatedly looking out in expectation toward the River Vienne, which runs quite near, below them. Suddenly, excitedly, he points.*)

Look.

(*A boat rounds a bend in the river near the castle.*)

(ELEANOR *is enthroned on the deck of the boat.* MARSHAL *stands near her.* ELEANOR'S *guard, on duty, stands stiffly in the background.* ELEANOR'S *two maids-in-waiting stand near him.*)

(HENRY *hurries down stone castle steps. His face is lit with a sense of eagerness and anticipation that have nothing to do with affection.*)

(*The boat is near the dock now.* ELEANOR'S *face is alive with suppressed excitement. She pats her hair, finds it in order, anxiously tugs at her cloak.*)

(HENRY *strides through the turmoil of the castle yard. Far behind him,* ALAIS *hurries after.*)

(*We move back and forth between* HENRY *and* ELEANOR. *She edges forward, eager, on her throne. He stomps through the bracken and the*

*muck along the river banks. Sailors
throw ropes. The boat glides firmly
home through the mud. The Oarsmen
raise their oars in salute as, rising,
she strides down the boat to land and*
HENRY.)

HENRY. How was your crossing?
Did the Channel part for you?
ELEANOR. It went flat when I told it
to. I didn't think to ask for more. How
dear of you to let me out of jail.
HENRY. It's only for the holidays.
ELEANOR. Like school. You keep
me young.

*(They turn, start up the dock
toward the castle. She sees* ALAIS.)

Here's gentle Alais.

*(*ALAIS *starts to curtsy.)*

No, no; greet me as you used to.

*(She takes* ALAIS *into her arms,
holding her lightly.)*

Fragile I am not; affection is a pressure I can bear.

*(As she releases* ALAIS, *she looks
up toward the castle.* JOHN, RICHARD
*and* GEOFFREY *are standing there, by
the main gate.)*

Oh, but I do have handsome children.

*(She busses* JOHN *on the cheek. We
pull back and see that they are in the
parlor.)*

John—you're so clean and neat. Henry takes good care of you.

*(She moves to* RICHARD, *kisses him
lightly.)*

And Richard. Don't look sullen, dear.
It makes your eyes go small and piggy
and your chin look weak. Is Philip
here?
GEOFFREY. Not yet.
ELEANOR. Let's hope he's grown up
like his father—simon pure and simon

simple. Good, good Louis; if I'd managed sons for him instead of all those
little girls, I'd still be stuck with being
Queen of France and we should not
have known each other. Such, my angels, is the role of sex in history.

*(Great flourishes on horns and
trumpets are heard from the castle
yard.)*

That will be Philip.

*(She turns and starts toward the
door.)*
*(We pick her up crossing a hallway
by some stairs, her boys strung out
behind her. She slows, pauses, looks
around expectantly.)*

Where's Henry?
RICHARD. Upstairs with the family
whore.
ELEANOR. That is a mean and taw-
dry way to talk about your fiancée.
JOHN. My fiancée.
ELEANOR. Whosoever fiancée, I
brought her up and she is dear to me
and gentle.
RICHARD. He still plans to make
John king.
ELEANOR. Of course he does. My,
what a greedy little trinity you are:
king, king, king. Two of you must
learn to live with disappointment.

*(*HENRY *strides toward them.)*

HENRY. Ah, but which two?
ELEANOR. Let's deny them all and
live forever.
HENRY. Tusk to tusk through all
eternity.

*(Two servants approach bearing a
crown and a great formal cloak.
Briskly, to his boys, as he shrugs into
the cloak and claps the crown on:)*

The King of France and I will shortly
have a tactile conversation, like two
surgeons looking for a lump. We'll

state positions and I'll make the first of many offers. He'll refuse it, naturally, I'll make a better one and so on through the holidays until I win. For the duration of this joyous ritual, you will give, to your father, your support.

*(With which he wheels toward the door. The two servants throw it open and* HENRY, *the others following, strides forward into the courtyard.)*

*(We see a very grand and formal state occasion. Nobles and clergymen stand in formal ranks along the broad descending steps. All the common folk have lined up, as common folk always do, along the edges of a broad aisle, soldiers, at attention, line the aisle.)*

*(Down the aisle marches a gorgeous, stately retinue of knights and soldiers. At their head is* PHILIP, *King of France.* PHILIP CAPET *is 18 years old and absolutely gorgeous. He is tall, well proportioned and handsome without being at all pretty. His manner is open, direct, simple and strikingly authoritative. He has been King of France for three years and has learned a lot.)*

HENRY *(As they greet each other)*. My lord.
PHILIP. Your grace.
HENRY. Welcome to Chinon.

*(More horns and trumpets as* HENRY *turns.)*

*(The door of the parlor, seen from inside the room. The door flies open and* HENRY *bursts in,* ELEANOR *and* PHILIP *just behind him. There is a general change of manner, from formal to informal, as* RICHARD, GEOFFREY, JOHN *and* ALAIS *follow into the room.)*

*(*HENRY *takes off his formal robe, feeling more comfortable.)*

Well, that's better.

ELEANOR. *(To* PHILIP*)*. I was told you were impressive for a boy of seventeen. I'm Eleanor, who might have been your mother. All the others here you know.
PHILIP *(Bowing)*. Queen Eleanor.
HENRY *(Informal, settling himself comfortably in a chair)*. I gather you're disturbed about your sister and her dowry.
PHILIP *(Standing before him, stiff and formal)*. Sixteen years ago, you made a treaty with us. It is time its terms were executed.

*(The scene, through most of the following exchange between* PHILIP *and* HENRY, *is a domestic one,* ALAIS *passes among them with a tray of drinks and hors d'oeuvres.* ELEANOR *settles comfortably, takes some needlework from a bag and works at it.* JOHN *busies himself decking the hall with boughs of holly.* GEOFFREY, *finding the hors d'oeuvres delicious, settles by a table that holds an assortment of them. Only* RICHARD *fails to relax. He stands apart from all of them, suspicious and hostile.)*

HENRY. I should think so.
PHILIP. Our position comes to this: that you either hold the marriage or return the Vexin. Alais marries Richard or we'll have the country back at once.
HENRY. That's clear, concise and well presented. My position is—well, frankly, Philip, it's a tangle.

*(As he rises and moves to* RICHARD, *all affability.)*

Two years ago, the Queen and I, for reasons passing understanding, gave the Aquitaine to Richard. That makes Richard very powerful. How can I give him Alais, too? The man she marries has you for an ally.
PHILIP. It's their wedding or the

Vexin back. Those are the terms you made with Louis.

HENRY (*Moving to* PHILIP. *Just the two of them now*). True but academic, lad. The Vexin's mine.

PHILIP. By what authority?

HENRY. It's got my troops all over it: that makes it mine. Now hear me, boy—

PHILIP. I am a king: I'm no man's boy.

HENRY. A king? Because you put your ass on purple cushions?

PHILIP. Sir.

(*He turns on his heel, starts for the door.*)

(HENRY *and* ELEANOR *exchange amused glances.*)

HENRY. Philip, you haven't got the feel of this at all. Use all your voices. When I bellow, bellow back.

PHILIP. I'll mark that down.

HENRY (*Moving close to* PHILIP). This, too. We are the world in small. A nation is a human thing. It does what we do, for our reasons. Surely, if we're civilized, it must be possible to put the knives away. We can make peace. We have it in our hands.

PHILIP. I've tutors of my own. Will that be all?

HENRY. Oh, think. You came here for a reason. Don't you want to ask me if I've got an offer?

PHILIP. Have you got an offer?

HENRY. Not yet—but I'll think of one.

(PHILIP *is half out the door.*)

Oh, by the way . . .

(PHILIP *turns,* HENRY *smiles agreeably.*)

You're better at this than I thought you'd be.

(PHILIP *smiles agreeably back.*)

PHILIP. I wasn't sure you'd noticed.

(PHILIP *goes.* HENRY *turns, taking in his family.*)

(*We see* JOHN *with holly,* ELEANOR *with her needle,* GEOFFREY *licking his fingers,* ALAIS *serving more wine and* RICHARD *glowering.*)

(HENRY *makes a friendly, expansive gesture.*)

HENRY. Well—what shall we hang? The holly or each other?

RICHARD (*Moving into the picture*). Would you say, Father, that I have the makings of a king?

HENRY. A splendid king.

RICHARD. Would you expect me, Father, to give up without a fight?

HENRY. Of course you'll fight. I raised you to.

RICHARD. I don't care what you offer Philip. I don't care what plans you make. I'll have the Aquitaine and Alais and the crown. I won't give up one to get the other. I won't trade off Alais or the Aquitaine to this—

(*He gestures toward* JOHN.)

—this walking postule.

(*We see* JOHN's *outrage.*)

No, your loving son will not.

(*As he turns to go,* JOHN *rushes up to* HENRY.)

JOHN. Did you hear what he called me?

ELEANOR. Clearly, dear. Now run along. It's nearly dinnertime.

JOHN. I only do what Father tells me.

HENRY. Go and eat.

JOHN. Did I say something wrong? I'm always saying something wrong.

HENRY. Don't pout.

JOHN (*Pouting*). I'm not.

HENRY (*Giving him a slap on the butt*). And stand up straight. How often do I have to tell you?

(JOHN *scurries toward the door.*)

(HENRY, *the exasperated parent, sighs.*)

(ELEANOR *gazes with amusement at* HENRY.)

ELEANOR. And that's to be the king.

GEOFFREY. And I'm to be his chancellor. Has he told you? John will rule the country while I run it. That's to say, he gets to spend the taxes that I get to raise.

ELEANOR. How nice for you.

GEOFFREY. It's not as nice as being king.

HENRY. We've made you Duke of Brittany. Is that so little?

GEOFFREY. No one ever thinks of crowns and mentions Geoff. Why is that?

HENRY. Isn't being chancellor power enough?

GEOFFREY. It isn't power that I feel deprived of; it's the mention that I miss. There's no affection for me here. You wouldn't think I'd want that, would you?

(*He is going as he says this.* ELEANOR *bleakly watches him go.*)

ELEANOR. Henry, I have a confession.

HENRY. Yes?

ELEANOR. I don't much like our children.

(*Rising, moving toward* ALAIS.)

Only you. The child I raised but didn't bear.

ALAIS. You never cared for me.

ELEANOR. I did and do. Believe me, Henry's bed is Henry's province. He can people it with sheep for all I care. Which, on occasion, he has done.

(*The subject of Rosamund is clearly a raw nerve.*)

HENRY. Still that? When Rosamund's been dead for seven years.

ELEANOR. Two months and eighteen days. I never liked her much.

HENRY. You count the days?

ELEANOR. I made the numbers up. He found Miss Clifford in the mists of Wales and brought her home for closer observation. Liking what he saw, he scrutinized her many years. He loved her deeply and she him. And yet, my dear, when Henry had to choose between his lady and my lands . . .

ALAIS. There is no sport in hurting me. It is so easy.

ELEANOR. After all the years of love and care, do you think I could bring myself to hurt you?

ALAIS. Eleanor, with both hands tied behind you.

(*We see* HENRY, *as* ALAIS *turns and goes. His concern for her is clearly on his face.*)

HENRY. She is lovely, isn't she.

ELEANOR. Yes, very.

HENRY (*Joining her*). If I'd chosen, who could I have picked to love to gall you more?

ELEANOR (*Smiling up at him*). There's no one.

(*She settles by the Christmas tree.* HENRY *joins her. He fiddles with a Christmas ornament, then hangs it as they talk.*)

HENRY. Time hasn't done a thing but wrinkle you.

ELEANOR. It hasn't even done that. I have borne six girls, five boys and thirty-one connubial years of you. How am I possible?

HENRY. There are moments when I miss you.

ELEANOR. Many?

HENRY. Do you doubt it?

ELEANOR. (*Reaching out and tousling his hair*). That's my wooly sheep dog. So wee Johnny gets the crown.

HENRY. I've heard it rumored but I don't believe it.

ELEANOR. Losing Alais will be hard, for you do love her.

HENRY. It's an old man's last attachment; nothing more. How hard do you find living in your castle?

ELEANOR. It was difficult in the beginning but that's past. I find I've seen the world enough.

HENRY. I'll never let you loose. You led too many civil wars against me.

ELEANOR. And I damn near won the last one. Still, as long as I get trotted out for Christmas Courts and state occasions now and then, for I do like to see you, it's enough. I'm famished. Let's go in to dinner.

HENRY (*Extending his arm*). Arm in arm.

ELEANOR. And hand in hand.

(*She takes his arm. They start out of the room.*)

You're still a marvel of a man.

HENRY. And you're my lady.

(*He opens the door, moves into the corridor. She follows. We go with them down the hallway. It is dimly lit by smoky wall torches. The corridor is empty except for occasional, quietly prowling dogs.*)

It's an odd thing, Eleanor. I've fought and bargained all these years as if the only thing I lived for was what happened after I was dead. I've something else to live for now. I've blundered on to peace.

ELELANOR (*Wry amusement on her face*). On Christmas Eve.

HENRY. Since Louis died, while Philip grew, I've had no France to fight. And in that lull, I've found how good it is to write a law or make a tax more fair or sit in judgment to decide which peasant gets a cow. There is, I tell you, nothing more important in the world. And now the French boy's big enough and I am sick of war.

ELEANOR. Do you still need the Vexin, Henry?

HENRY. It's as crucial as it ever was. My troops there are a day away from Paris, just a march of twenty miles, I must keep it.

ELEANOR. Henry, dear, if Alais doesn't marry Richard, I will see you lose the Vexin.

(*They stop outside a large double door.*)

HENRY. Well, I thought you'd never say it.

ELEANOR. I can do it.

HENRY. You can try.

(*A servant appears, moves to the door.*)

We've got a pack of barons we should look the loving couple for.

ELEANOR (*Smiling a terrible smile at him*). Can you read love in that?

HENRY. And permanent affection.

(*The door is opened. They start forward into—*

*The castle's Great Hall. It is an enormous, high-ceilinged, stone-walled room. Long trestle tables run the length of it, Nobles and clergymen sit on benches at the tables. Court musicians and entertainers are poised on a platform at one side. Servants stand formally at serving tables piled high with food. The royal table is at the far end of the hall on a platform,* PHILIP, RICHARD, GEOFFREY, JOHN *and* ALAIS *are there.*)

(*The hall is heated by a huge fire that blazes on the stone floor in the center of the room. Some of the smoke rises to escape from a hole in the ceiling. Torches are everywhere. The smoke is terrible. There is much howling from a multitude of dogs.*)

(*As* HENRY *and* ELEANOR *move into the hall, the orchestra plays a fanfare and everybody rises.*)

ELEANOR (*As she and* HENRY *make their stately way down the long hall to their table, nodding to his noble, smiling at that one).* My Richard is the next king, not your John. I know you, Henry. I know every twist and bend you've got and I'll be waiting round each corner for you.

HENRY. Do you truly care who's king?

ELEANOR. I care because you care so much.

HENRY. Don't fight me, Eleanor.

ELEANOR. What would you have me do? Give out, give up, give in?

HENRY. Give me a little peace.

ELEANOR. A little? Why so modest? How about eternal peace? Now there's a thought.

HENRY. If you oppose me, I will strike you any way I can.

*(They have reached their table. Their eyes are locked;* HENRY'S *cold with warning,* ELEANOR'S *bright with defiance.)*

*(The pose breaks and they sit. Servants appear by each of them with bowls of water and towels. They start to wash their hands. Then:)*

ELEANOR *(She leans toward* HEN-RY. *They are close enough to kiss).* Henry?

HENRY. Madam?

ELEANOR. Did you ever love me?

HENRY. No.

ELEANOR. Good. That will make this pleasanter.

*(She sits back, wipes her hands. We draw away from her, taking in more and more of the hall until we see all of it—the bustle and smoke, the howling and shouting, the music and caroling.)*

*(We see a Christmas present, wrapped up, tied and tagged.* ELEANOR *is carrying it to a table piled with presents in a corner of her bedroom. As she puts it down, a door behind her opens and* RICHARD *appears. Aware he's there, she studiously inspects the writing on a tag. He waits, then moves toward her saying:)*

RICHARD. All right. I've come. I'm here. What was it you wanted?

ELEANOR. Just to talk. We haven't been alone, the two of us in—how long is it, lamb? Two years? You look fit. War agrees with you. I keep informed. I follow all your slaughters from a distance. Do sit down.

RICHARD. Is this an audience, a good-night hug with kisses or an ambush?

ELEANOR. Let us hope it's a reunion. Must you look so stern? I sent for you to say I want your love again, but I can't say it to a face like that.

RICHARD. My love, of all things. What would you want it for?

ELEANOR. Why, for itself. What other purpose could I have?

RICHARD. You'll tell me when you're ready to.

ELEANOR. I scheme a lot; I know. I plot and plan. That's how a queen in prison spends her time. But there is more to me than that. Can't I say I love a son and be believed?

RICHARD. If I were you, I'd try another tack. I have no dammed-up flood of passion for you. There's no chance I'll overflow.

ELEANOR. You are a dull boy. Dull as plainsong: la, la, la, forever on one note. I gave the Church up out of boredom. I can do as much for you.

RICHARD. You'll never give me up—not while I hold the Aquitaine.

ELEANOR. You think I'm motivated by a love of real estate.

RICHARD. I think you want it back. You're so deceitful you can't ask for water when you're thirsty. We could tangle spiders in the webs you weave.

ELEANOR. If I'm so devious, why don't you go? Don't stand there quivering in limbo. Love me, little lamb, or leave me.

RICHARD *(Not moving)*. Leave you, Madam? With pure joy.

ELEANOR. Departure is a simple act. You put the left foot down and then the right.

*(JOHN runs into the room, excited in high spirits. GEOFFREY follows him.)*

JOHN. Mother—

ELEANOR. Hush, dear. Mother's fighting.

JOHN. Father's finished working out the treaty terms.

ELEANOR *(Getting to her feet)*. How nice. Where is your father?

*(He is outside in a corner of the courtyard, busy distributing Christmas largesse to the deserving poor. ALAIS is with him. A servant follows them along, pulling a cart filled with roast geese, pastries and such.)*

*(They are in front of a row of wooden hovels that line the high stone castle wall. Gardeners, poultry keepers, smiths and armorers live in these huts. We see them receiving gifts with bows and smiles.)*

*(It is late afternoon and cold. The shadows are sharp and clear. Activity in the yard, when we see it, is slight. Soldiers and peasants are settling down by tiny fires, eating and drinking. From across the yard comes the sound of carolers.)*

ELEANOR *(Voice over)*. There you are.

*(HENRY and ALAIS turn.)*

*(ELEANOR, wearing a heavy robe, is crossing the yard toward them. RICHARD, JOHN and GEOFFREY come along behind her.)*

Well—have you put the terms to Philip?

HENRY. Not yet, but we're shortly granting him an audience. I hope you'll all attend.

ELEANOR. Are we to know the terms or would you rather tease us?

HENRY *(He stops handing out food, moves away from the huts and people toward an area where livestock are kept)*. Not at all. The terms are these.

RICHARD. What are you giving up to Philip? What of mine?

JOHN. Whatever you've got goes to me.

GEOFFREY. And what's the nothing Geoffrey gets?

HENRY. For God's sake, boys, you can't all three be king.

RICHARD. All three of us can try.

HENRY. That's pointless now. I want you to succeed me, Richard. Alais and the crown: I give you both.

RICHARD. I've got no sense of humor. If I did, I'd laugh.

HENRY. I mean to do it.

JOHN. What about me? I'm your favorite, I'm the one you love.

HENRY. John, I can't help myself.

*(He takes JOHN, moves him next to RICHARD. JOHN scowls up, RICHARD glowers down.)*

HENRY. Could you keep anything I gave you? Could you beat him on the field?

JOHN *(Scurrying to his father)*. You could.

HENRY. But John, I won't be there. I'm losing, too. All of my dreams for you are lost.

JOHN. You've led me on.

HENRY. I never meant to.

JOHN *(The tears start to come)*. You're a failure as a father, you know that?

HENRY. I'm sorry, John.

JOHN *(He sinks down to the frozen ground, a sorry little heap. Pigs peer at him curiously from the enclosure just behind him).* Not yet you're not. But I'll do something terrible and you'll be sorry then.

ELEANOR. Did you rehearse all this or are you improvising?

HENRY. Good God, woman, face the facts.

ELEANOR. Which ones? We've got so many.

HENRY. Power is the only fact. How can I keep him from the crown? He'd only take it if I didn't give it to him.

RICHARD. No—you'd make me fight to get it. I know you; you'd never give me anything.

HENRY. True; and I haven't. You get Alais and you get the kingdom but I get the one thing I want most. If you're king, England stays intact. I get that. It's all yours now—the girl, the crown, the whole black bloody business. Isn't that enough?

*(HENRY turns and storms away across the courtyard. The caroling resumes.)*

*(The little group stands by the pigsty, watching HENRY go. No one moves until—)*

ALAIS. I don't know who's to be congratulated. Not me, certainly.

*(She looks at them, eyes bright with anger.)*

Kings, Queen, knights everywhere you look and I'm the only pawn. I haven't got a thing to lose. That makes me dangerous.

*(At the brink of tears, she turns and runs away from them—not after HENRY, but in another direction.)*

ELEANOR. Poor child.

JOHN *(Suffering at the pigsty).* Poor John—who says "Poor John"? Don't everybody sob at once. My God, if I went up in flames, there's not a living soul who'd pee on me to put the fire out.

RICHARD. Let's strike a flint and see.

JOHN *(Softly, from the heart, the absolute truth).* You're everything a little brother dreams of, you know that? I used to dream about you all the time.

ELEANOR *(Arms open).* Oh, Johnny . . .

JOHN *(Fighting back the tears).* I'll show you, Eleanor, I haven't lost yet.

*(He starts to move off with dignity but can't keep it up. Bursting into tears, he breaks into a run.)*

*(ELEANOR, RICHARD and GEOFFREY start moving thoughtfully across the yard, past squatting figures, small groups of soldiers drinking. Dogs bark. The wind blows.)*

GEOFFREY. Well, Mummy, if you want me, here I am.

ELEANOR. John's lost a chancellor, has he?

GEOFFREY. And you've gained one.

ELEANOR. It is a bitter thing your mummy has to say.

GEOFFREY. She doesn't trust me.

*(They stop by a stone well in the yard. GEOFFREY perches on it. RICHARD, always wary, stands apart. In the distance, carolers appear, singing something jolly.)*

ELEANOR. You must know Henry isn't through with John. He'll keep the Vexin 'til the moon goes blue from cold, and as for Richard's wedding day, we'll see the Second Coming first; the needlework alone can last for years.

GEOFFREY. I know. You know I know, I know you know I know, we know that Henry knows and Henry knows we know it. We're a knowledgeable family. Will Richard take me for his chancellor or won't he?

ELEANOR. Why are you dropping John?

GEOFFREY. Because you're going to win.

ELEANOR. I haven't yet.

GEOFFREY. You will, with me to help you. I can handle John. He'll swallow anything I tell him and I'll take him by the hand and walk him into the trap you set.

ELEANOR. You're good, you're first class, Geoff. You'd sell John out to me or me to John or—you can tell me—have you found some way of selling everyone to everybody?

GEOFFREY. Not yet, Mummy, but I'm working on it. I don't care who's king, but you and Henry do. I want to watch the two of you go picknicking on one another.

ELEANOR. You've a gift for hating.

GEOFFREY. You're the expert; you should know.

ELEANOR. Dear Lord, you've loved me all these years.

GEOFFREY. Well, God forgive me, I've upset the Queen. Madam, may you rot.

ELEANOR. We need you. Help us.

GEOFFREY. What? And miss the fun of selling you?

ELEANOR. Be Richard's chancellor.

GEOFFREY. Rot.

*(He strides away.)*

ELEANOR *(Close up, watching him go. A spasm of regret and loss crosses her face).* Oh, Geoffrey.

*(Bleakly as she starts walking again, across the yard toward a low stone wall.)*

Well, that's how deals are made. We've got him if we want him. He will sell us all, you know, but only if he thinks we think he won't. Why did I have to have such clever children?

*(They reach the wall, stopping before a small wooden door. She opens the door, moves through and we see—*

*A small, cloistered herb garden. It is a perfectly beautiful place; small formal beds of rich, black frozen earth, delicate arches and columns along the walls, graceful stone benches. Distant hills rise high and stark beyond the far wall. On the hills are little scattered houses, small farms, neat fields. Occasionally scraps of caroling come floating to us. It is a setting of great gentleness and peace.)*

*(ELEANOR settles on a bench, looks up at her son.)*

ELEANOR. What's the matter, Richard?

RICHARD. Nothing.

ELEANOR. It's a heavy thing, your nothing. When I write or send for you or speak or reach, your nothings come. Like stones.

RICHARD. Don't play a scene with me.

ELEANOR. I wouldn't if I could. I'm simpler than I used to be. I had, at one time, many appetites. I wanted poetry and power and the young men who create them both. I even wanted Henry, too, in those days. Now, I've only one desire left: to see you king.

RICHARD. The only thing you want to see is Father's vitals on a bed of lettuce. You don't care who wins as long as Henry loses. You'd do anything. You are Medea to the teeth but this is one son you won't use for vengeance on your husband.

ELEANOR. How my captivity has changed you. Henry meant to hurt me and he's hacked you up instead.

*(She touches his cheek with her hand. She raises the hand, looks at it.)*

Men coveted this talon once. Henry was eighteen when we met and I was

Queen of France. He came down from the north to Paris, with a mind like Aristotle's and a form like mortal sin. We shattered the Commandments on the spot. I spent three months annulling Louis, and in spring, in May, not far from here, we married. Young Count Henry and his Countess. But in three years' time, I was his Queen and he was King of England. Done at twenty-one. Five years your junior, General.

RICHARD *(He moves away from her).* I can count.

ELEANOR. No doubt the picture of your parents being fond does not hang in your gallery, but we were fond. There was no Thomas Becket then, or Rosamund. No rivals—only me. And then Young Henry came and you and all the other blossoms in my garden.

*(Looking straight at him. We see them both.)*

Yes, if I'd been sterile, darling, I'd be happier today.

RICHARD. Is that designed to hurt me?

ELEANOR. What a waste. I've fought with Henry over who comes next, whose dawn it is and which son gets the sunset and we'll never live to see it. Look at you. I loved you more than Henry and it's cost me everything.

RICHARD. What do you want?

ELEANOR. I want us back the way we were.

RICHARD. That's not it.

ELEANOR. All right, then. I want the Aquitaine.

RICHARD. Now that's the mother I remember.

ELEANOR. We can win. I can get you Alais. I can make the marriage happen—but I've got to have the Aquitaine to do it. I must have it back.

RICHARD. It's mine. I'll never give it up.

ELEANOR. I'll write my will. "To Richard, everything." Would you believe me then?

*(She starts to go.)*

Where's paper?

RICHARD. Paper burns.

*(He turns to go.)*

ELEANOR. I love you.

RICHARD. You love nothing. You are incomplete. The human parts of you are missing. You're as dead as you are deadly.

ELEANOR. Don't leave me.

RICHARD. You were lovely once. I've seen the pictures.

ELEANOR. Oh, don't you remember how you loved me?

RICHARD. Vaguely.

ELEANOR. We were always hand in hand.

*(She thrusts her hand in his.)*

That's how it felt.

RICHARD. As coarse and hot as that.

*(She snatches her hand away and bares her forearm.)*

ELEANOR. This won't burn. I'll scratch a will on this. "To Richard, everything."

*(Suddenly there is a long pin in her hand. She draws it savagely across her forearm. It tears the flesh. We see the blood.)*

RICHARD. Mother.

*(Her arms are open. He comes into them.)*

ELEANOR. Remember how I taught you numbers and the lute and poetry?

RICHARD *(Softly, as they hold each other).* Mother.

ELEANOR. See? You do remember.

*(We draw back from them. We see the garden and the hills beyond. The sun touches the scene with the last warmth of the day and dips behind the hills. We hear a wisp of caroling. The picture holds.)*

I taught you dancing, too, and languages and all the music that I knew and how to love what's beautiful. The sun was warmer then and we were every day together.

*(All at once, sharp, loud and bright, on* HENRY *in close up. He is roaring with laughter. We hear other voices laughing.)*

*(We are in the Great Hall. The dining tables have been removed and the benches rearranged. Seated on them are the nobles and clerics. They are watching a crude pantomime.)*

*(Gesturing toward* WILLIAM MAR-SHAL, *who stands a few paces behind him,* HENRY *says—)*

HENRY. William.

*(*MARSHAL *moves to him.)*

Tell the French King I'll receive him in the parlor.

MARSHAL. Yes, my lord.

HENRY. In half an hour.

*(We see* PHILIP. *He is seated at a table, playing chess.)*

PHILIP. Half an hour. Good.

*(We pull back to see* GEOFFREY *seated at the table with him. They are in a small, quiet chamber by an open fire.* MARSHAL *bows and goes.)*

GEOFFREY *(He makes a move, then says in the most conversational way).* Of course, you know there's not a word of truth to Henry's terms.

PHILIP. If that's a warning, thank you.

GEOFFREY. What if it's an offer?

PHILIP. "What if" is a game for scholars: What if angels sat on pinheads?

GEOFFREY. What if I were king?

PHILIP. It's your game, Geoff. You play it.

*(As* GEOFFREY *leans forward to speak—*

*A grotesque wood-carving fills the screen: an executioner, axe raised, a victim, head on the block. The axe, drops. The severed head falls. Drawing back, we wee* JOHN, *looking with proud approval at the toy.)*

*(He looks up sharply as* GEOFFREY *enters.)*

GEOFFREY. John—

JOHN *(Attention returning to his model).* I made this for Father. All the pieces work. It took me months. I'm not a fool.

GEOFFREY *(Down on one knee next to John).* I know. Now here's my plan.

JOHN. I read three languages. I've studied law—What plan?

GEOFFREY. We've got to make a deal with Philip.

JOHN. Why?

GEOFFREY. Because you're out and Richard's in.

JOHN. What kind of deal?

GEOFFREY. A war. If we three join and fight now, we can finish Richard off.

JOHN. You mean destroy him?

*(*GEOFFREY *nods.)*

And Mother, too?

GEOFFREY. And Mother, too. Well, do we do it? Is it on?

JOHN. I've got to think.

GEOFFREY. You haven't time. We're extra princes now. You know where extra princes go?

JOHN *(Close up as his peril dawns on him).* Down?

*(We go from* JOHN'S *stricken face to—*

PHILIP *seated, as before, at the chess table.)*

PHILIP. Well? Does John want a war or doesn't he?

*(We pull back as* GEOFFREY *steps forward, protecting* JOHN.*)*

GEOFFREY. Do you? If John asks for your soldiers, will he get them?

PHILIP. If John wants a war, he's got one.

GEOFFREY. John, you hear that?

JOHN. I'm still thinking.

GEOFFREY. Let me help. It's either Richard on the throne or you.

JOHN *(To* PHILIP*).* You think we'd win?

PHILIP. I know it.

*(*JOHN *looks at* GEOFFREY, *then back to* PHILIP, *takes a deep breath and resolutely extends his hand. As* GEOFFREY *and* PHILIP *formally reach out for a three-way handshake—*

HENRY *rises from his place in the Great Hall. The pantomime and laughter still go on as he strides briskly off.)*

*(Down a corridor he goes.* ALAIS *is with him now, half-running to keep up, as she jabbers at him, pestering. She is still at it as the door to the Parlor opens and* HENRY *strides in.)*

ALAIS. But Henry—

HENRY I'd appreciate a little quiet confidence. I have enough nits picking at me.

ALAIS. But you've promised me to Richard.

HENRY. Good God, you don't think I meant it?

ALAIS *(Not a bit relieved. If anything, even angrier).* So that whole scene, all you said to John—

HENRY. You think I'd ever give him up? When I've mothered him and fathered him and babied him? He's all I've got. How often do you people have to hear it? Every supper? Should we start the soup with who we love and who we don't?

ALAIS. I think you like it, passing me from hand to hand. What am I to you—a collection plate? Or am I all you've got, like John?

HENRY *(He gets up, starts wandering about the room. The Christmas decorating and tree trimming has been completed. Assorted packages are arranged under the tree. A merry fire burns in the fireplace. It couldn't be more Christmas Eve).* I've got to get the Aquitaine for John.

ALAIS. I talk people and you answer back in provinces.

HENRY. They get mixed up. What's the Aquitaine to Eleanor? It's not a province, it's a way to torture me. That's why she's spent the evening wooing Richard, wheezing on the coals. She'll squeeze it out of him. God, I'd have loved to eavesdrop.

*(Doing a creditable imitation of* ELEANOR.*)*

I taught you prancing, lamb, and lute and flute—

*(*ELEANOR *stands in the doorway, a great pile of Christmas presents in her arms. She can barely see over the top. She laughs delightedly as she weaves into the room.)*

ELEANOR. That's marvelous. It's absolutely me.

*(*HENRY *goes to her, takes some of the packages.)*

I thought as long as I was coming down I'd bring them.

*(They move to the Christmas tree.)*

HENRY. Whatever are you giving me?

ELEANOR. You're such a child. You always ask.

HENRY *(Reading from a package).* "To Henry."

*(He picks it up, weighs it.)*

Heavy.

*(Delighted.)*

It's my headstone. Eleanor, you spoil me.

ELEANOR. I never could deny you anything.

*(She sits at the base of the tree, starts arranging the boxes just so. Across the room,* ALAIS *starts to leave.)*

HENRY. Don't go. It nettles her to see how much I need you.

ALAIS. You need me, Henry, like a tailor needs a tinker's dam.

*(The deep affection he feels for her is clear on* HENRY'S *face.)*

I know that look. He's going to say he loves me.

HENRY. Like my life.

*(She is leaving as* HENRY *joins* ELEANOR *on the floor by the tree.)*

I talk like that to keep her spirits up. Well, how'd you do with Richard? Did you break his heart?

ELEANOR. You think he ought to give me back the Aquitaine?

HENRY. I can't think why he shouldn't. After all, I've promised him the throne.

ELEANOR. The boy keeps wondering if your promises are any good.

HENRY. There's no sense asking if the air's good when there's nothing else to breathe.

ELEANOR. Exactly what I told him.

HENRY. Have you got it? Will he give it back?

*(All lightness and movement stop. The cards are down. They remain locked for a moment. Then—)*

ELEANOR. No Aquitaine for John.

HENRY. I've got to give him something. Isn't some agreement possible?

*(She breaks the pose, rises to her feet. On top of the situation, enjoying herself.)*

ELEANOR. Love, in a world where carpenters get resurrected, anything is possible.

*(*HENRY, *angry, trying to suppress it, rises, dusts himself off. There is, as in all rooms, straw on the floor.)*

HENRY. You bore him, dammit he's your son.

ELEANOR. Oh, heavens yes. Two hundred eighty days I bore him. I recall them all. You'd only just found Rosamund.

HENRY. Why her so damn particularly? I've found other women.

ELEANOR. Countless others.

HENRY. What's your count? Let's have a tally of the bedspreads you've spread out on.

ELEANOR. Thomas Becket's.

HENRY *(Another raw nerve. Furious).* That's a lie!

ELEANOR. I know it.

*(Amused and musing.)*

You still care what I do.

HENRY. *(In an outburst of rage).* I want the Aquitaine for John! I want it and I'll have it!

ELEANOR. Is that menace you're conveying? Is it to be torture? Will you boil me or stretch me, which? Or am I to be perforated?

*(*HENRY *storms to the desk, grabs a pile of papers.)*

HENRY. I have the documents and you will sign.

ELEANOR. How can you force me to? Threats? Sign or I refuse to feed you? Tears? Oh, sign before my heart goes crack. Bribes, offers, deals?

*(They are on opposite sides of the desk, leaning across it toward each other.)*

I'm like the earth, old man; there isn't any way around me.

HENRY. I adore you.

ELEANOR. Save your aching arches. That road's closed.

*(They exchange looks, HENRY breaks it by sitting at his desk, leaning back, very much at ease.)*

HENRY. I've got an offer for you, *ma jolie.*

ELEANOR. A deal, a deal. I give the richest province on the Continent to John for what? You tell me, mastermind. For what?

*(HENRY, close up. Relishing it.)*

HENRY *(Dropping his bomb with quiet precision).* Your freedom.

*(ELEANOR close up. She has just received a terrible blow.)*

ELEANOR. Oh.

*(HENRY moves around the desk to her as he says:)*

HENRY. Once Johnny has the Aquitaine, you're free. I'll let you out. Think: on the loose in London, winters in Provence, impromptu trips to visit Richard anywhere he's killing people. All that for a signature.

ELEANOR. You're good.

*(She backs away as he nears her, stopping with her back to a charming crèche lit by flickering candles.)*

HENRY. I thought it might appeal to you. You always fancied traveling.

ELEANOR. Yes, I did. I even made poor Louis take me on Crusade.

How's that for blasphemy? I dressed my maids as Amazons and rode bare-breasted halfway to Damascus. Louis had a seizure and I damn near died of windburn but the troops were dazzled. Henry, I'm against the wall.

*(There is no pleasure on HENRY'S face.)*

To be a prisoner, to be bricked in when you've known the world—I'll never know how I've survived. These ten years, Henry, have been unimaginable. And now you offer me the only thing I want if I give up the only thing I treasure.

*(HENRY, sensing victory, picks the papers up.)*

HENRY. Sign them and we'll break the happy news. The Queen is free, John gets the Aquitaine and Richard marries Alais.

*(We look from face to face. Will she give in or won't she?)*

ELEANOR. Yes. Let's have it done. I'll sign.

*(Delight floods HENRY'S face. He bends over the desk, fiddling with the papers as ELEANOR moves to the desk chair and sits.)*

On one condition.

HENRY. Name it.

ELEANOR. Have the wedding now.

*(HENRY is absolutely flummoxed.)*

HENRY. What's that?

ELEANOR. Why, I surprised you. Surely it's not sudden. They've been marching down the aisle for sixteen years and that's a long walk. John can be the best man—that's a laugh—and you can give the bride away. I want to watch you do it.

HENRY. Alais—I can live without her.

ELEANOR. And I thought you loved her.

HENRY. So I do.

ELEANOR. Thank God. You frightened me: I was afraid this wouldn't hurt.

HENRY. You fill me full of fear and pity: what a tragedy you are.

ELEANOR. I wonder, do you ever wonder if I slept with Geoffrey?

HENRY. With my father?

ELEANOR. It's not true but one hears rumors. Don't you ever wonder?

*(The tension spirals. One of them is going to explode.)*

HENRY. Is it rich, despising me? Is it rewarding?

ELEANOR. No—it's terrible.

HENRY. Then stop it!

ELEANOR. How? It's what I live for!

HENRY *(Exploding, hurling it at her)*. Rosamund, I loved you!

*(ELEANOR's reaction is triumph. He is ready to strike her. Instead, he storms toward the door, roaring:)*

I'll show you! By Christ, I will! I'll do it!

*(He throws open the door, bellows into the hallway:)*

Where's a priest? Somebody dig me up a priest!

*(Servants are standing formally in the hallway. WILLIAM MARSHAL is among them. He hurries forward to HENRY.)*

You. Bring me a bishop.

*(ELEANOR appears in the doorway behind HENRY. She addresses MARSHAL.)*

ELEANOR. Get old Durham. He's just down the hall.

*(As MARSHAL bows, turns to go.)*

Ask him to meet us in the chapel.

HENRY *(Roaring)*. John! Richard! Geoffrey!

*(He storms off down the hall. ELEANOR follows serenely after. Servants scatter, running off to find the boys.)*

*(We see servants running. Then brief shots of JOHN, PHILIP, GEOFFREY, RICHARD and ALAIS as each turns sharply, startled. Then—*

*The BISHOP OF DURHAM in his bed. A SERVANT, trying to be both reverential and quick about it, is shaking him awake. The BISHOP is full of food and wine and years; he knows something important is up and, as he tries focusing on what it is, we—*

*Glimpse JOHN, RICHARD, GEOFFREY, PHILIP and ALAIS as they race along, tearing upstairs, downstaris, through halls and corridors.)*

*(In the central hallway, HENRY is pacing, fidgeting and fuming. ELEANOR, calm and composed, stands watching him. HENRY turns abruptly as one by one, RICHARD, JOHN, GEOFFREY, PHILIP and ALAIS come hurrying into the hall through various doors. JOHN reaches HENRY first. As he pulls up in front of his father, breathless, skidding to a stop:)*

JOHN. What's wrong? What's happened?

ELEANOR. Richard's getting married.

*(The camera moves across all faces as they absorb the startling news.)*

JOHN. Now? He's getting married now?

ELEANOR. I never cease to marvel at the quickness of your mind.

JOHN. You can't hurt me, you bag of bile, no matter what you say.

*(Moving to HENRY, supplicating.)*

But you can. Father, why?

HENRY. Because I say so.

(MARSHAL *slips in through the large door.*)

MARSHAL. My lord, the bishop's waiting in the chapel.

(HENRY *dismisses him with a brusque gesture.*)

HENRY. Good. Let's get this over with.

(*He strides forward, throws open a door that gives onto a corridor. He storms off.* ELEANOR *moves to* ALAIS *as they all hurry after him.*)

ELEANOR. You'll make a lovely bride. I wonder if I'll cry.
ALAIS. You sound as if you think it's going to happen.
ELEANOR. And I do.
ALAIS. He's only plotting. Can't you tell when Henry's plotting?
ELEANOR. Not this time.
ALAIS. He'll never give me up.
HENRY. You think I won't?
ALAIS. Because you told me so.
HENRY. You're not my Helen. I won't fight a war to save a face. We're done.
ALAISE. I don't believe you.
HENRY. Wait ten minutes.

(*They go rushing through the Great Hall. It is quiet.* ALAIS'S *words are jumbled by panic.*)

ALAIS. You don't want me, Richard. Honestly, you don't. We're not right for each other. Our marriage wouldn't work. We're not in love, we'd never be happy. . . .

(*All at once we're at the Chapel.* HENRY *drags* ALAIS *up the stairs, throws open the doors. He pulls her in. The others hurry after. Once inside, they form a straight line, shoulder to shoulder, across the back of the* Chapel. Through this, ALAIS carries on.)

Not yet, Oh, please not yet.

(As HENRY *all but drags her back toward her place.*)

I won't do it. I won't say the words, not one of them.

(*The procession stands at the foot of the aisle, behind the last pew. The chapel is an exquisite, intimate place. Candles burn, shedding soft, warm light. The* BISHOP OF DURHAM *stands waiting on the altar.* HENRY, *settling* ALAIS *into position, casts an embarrassed-father look toward* DURHAM.)
(DURHAM *smiles back with paternal understanding.*)
(ALAIS, *making one last stab, says:*)

Henry, please. It makes no sense. Why give me up? What do you get? What are you gaining?
HENRY (*With vast innocence as, rather like a bridal consultant, he checks over the bridal party*). Why, the Aquitaine, of course.

(*We take in their faces.* JOHN'S *puzzlement,* GEOFFREY'S *amusement,* ELEANOR'S *dismay,* RICHARD'S *dawning rage,* RICHARD *moves to* HENRY.)

RICHARD. What's that again?
HENRY. Your mother gets her freedom and I get the Aquitaine.

(*To* ELEANOR.)

That is the proposition, isn't it? You did agree.
RICHARD. Of course she did. I knew, I knew it. It was all pretense. And I believed you. I believed it all.
ELEANOR. I meant it all.
RICHARD. No wedding. There will be no wedding.

(HENRY *throws* DURHAM *a look of excruciating parental embarrassment as he draws* RICHARD *aside and whispers.)*

HENRY. But, my boy. Look—Durham's waiting.

*(*DURHAM *is beginning to look a bit puzzled by it all.)*
*(*RICHARD'S *face is set and stony.)*

You've simply got to marry her. It isn't much to ask. For my sake, Richard.

RICHARD. Never.

HENRY *(So embarrassed and upset)*. But I've promised Philip. Think of my position.

RICHARD. Damn the wedding and to hell with your position.

HENRY. You don't dare defy me.

RICHARD. Don't I?

*(*HENRY *throws a glance of badly rattled desperation in* DURHAM'S *direction, then beckons* PHILIP *forward.)*

HENRY. You're the King of France, for goodness sake. Speak up. Do something.

*(*RICHARD *strides forward as* PHILIP *approaches.)*

RICHARD. Make a threat, why don't you? Scare me.

PHILIP. Dunce.

RICHARD. Am I?

PHILIP. He never meant to have the wedding.

HENRY. Come again?

PHILIP. You're good at rage. I like the way you play it.

HENRY. Boy, don't ever call a king a liar to his face.

PHILIP. I'm not a boy—to you or anybody.

HENRY. Boy, you came here asking for a wedding or the Vexin back. By God, you don't get either one. It's no to both.

PHILIP. You have a pact with France.

HENRY. Then damn the document and damn the French. She never marries, not while I'm alive.

PHILIP. Your life and never are two different times.

HENRY. Not on my clock, boy.

*(*PHILIP, *stiff with anger, turns and strides out of the chapel.* ALAIS, *weak with relief, leans against the door frame.* HENRY *is just turning to her when—)*

RICHARD. Listen to the lion. Flash a yellow tooth and frighten me.

HENRY. Don't spoil it, Richard. Take it like a good sport.

RICHARD. How's your bad leg and your back and all the rest of it? You're getting old. One day you'll have me once too often.

HENRY. When? I'm fifty now. My God, boy, I'm the oldest man I know. I've got a decade on the Pope. What's it to be? The broadsword when I'm eighty-five?

RICHARD. I'm not a second son. Not now. Your Henry's in the vault, you know.

HENRY. I know. I've seen him there.

RICHARD. I'll have the crown.

HENRY. You'll have what daddy gives you.

RICHARD. I am next in line.

HENRY. To nothing.

RICHARD. Then we'll have the broadswords now.

HENRY. This minute?

RICHARD. On the battlefield.

HENRY. So we're at war.

RICHARD. Yes, we're at war. I have two thousand men at Poitiers.

HENRY. Can they hear you? Call and see who comes. You are as close to Poitiers as you're going to get.

RICHARD. You don't dare hold me prisoner.

HENRY. Until we've all agreed that John comes next, I can and will.

(RICHARD *starts to stalk away.*)

You are a king's son so I treat you with respect. You have the freedom of the castle.

RICHARD (*With great bravura as he goes*). The castle doesn't stand that holds me. Post your guards.

(ELEANOR, ALAIS, HENRY, GEOF-
FREY *and* JOHN *stand watching him go. Cut to—*
JOHN, *close up, as the miracle dawns.*)

JOHN. My God, I'm king again. Fantastic. It's a miracle.

(*He turns to* GEOFFREY.)

Are you happy for me, Geoff?

GEOFFREY. I'm happy for us both.

(GEOFFREY *throws a loving arm around* JOHN's *shoulders as they start out past* ELEANOR. *We stay with* ELEANOR.)

ELEANOR. I came close, didn't I?

(*She turns to* ALAIS, *who stands near her.*)

I almost had my freedom and I almost had you for my son. I should have liked it, being free.

(*She turns to* HENRY. *Cut to him. Seated comfortably in a pew, he gives an apologetic shrug and sigh to* DURHAM.)
(*Cut to* DURHAM *who, both bewildered and pleased to be dismissed, starts to leave the altar.*)
(*Cut back to* ELEANOR.)

You played it nicely. You were good.

HENRY (*Stretches out, luxuriating, loving it*). I really was. I fooled you,

didn't I. God, but I do love being king.

ELEANOR. Well, Henry, liege and lord, what happens now?

(*Cut to* HENRY *as he rises, moves toward her.*)

HENRY. I've no idea. I know I'm winning and I know I'll win, but what the next move is . . . You're not scared?

ELEANOR. No.

HENRY. I think you are.

ALAIS. (*Moving into the picture*). I was. You mustn't play with feelings, Henry. Not with mine.

HENRY (*Cupping her face in his hands*). It wasn't possible to lose you. I must hold you dearer than I thought.

(*He looks up, toward* ELEANOR.)

You've got your enigmatic face on. What's your mood, I wonder.

ELEANOR. Pure delight. I'm locked up with my sons: what mother doesn't dream of that?

(*She starts toward the door, then stops and turns.*)

One thing.

HENRY. Yes?

ELEANOR. May I watch you kiss her?

(*We see the three of them.* ELEANOR *is in the background, framed in the doorway.*)

HENRY. Can't you ever stop?

ELEANOR. I watch you every night. I conjure it before I sleep.

HENRY. Leave it at that.

ELEANOR. My curiosity is intellectual. I want to see how accurate I am.

(HENRY *opens his arms to* ALAIS.)

HENRY. Forget the dragon in the doorway: come.

*(ALAIS moves into his arms.)*

Believe I love you, for I do. Believe I'm yours forever, for I am. Believe in my contentment and the joy you give me and believe—

*(HENRY, close up as he breaks, turns toward ELEANOR.)*

You want more?

*(ELEANOR'S eyes burn at him. He stares back, then turns to ALAIS.)*

I'm an old man in an empty place. Be with me.

*(She raises her lips to his. They kiss tenderly at first, then passionately. The camera moves across their faces, ELEANOR always in the background. The sound of caroling grows louder as we begin moving closer to ELEANOR'S face. She watches and she watches.)*

*(We move past her, out into the courtyard. Little fires burn in the midnight darkness. Everything is still. Here and there, a huddled figure edges closer to the flames. Though there is quiet now, there is no peace. Slowly, we move across the yard. High in a tower, pale light flickers out from one small window.)*

*(ELEANOR. She is seated at a table in her room, alone. She has been putting on jewelry for quite some time. Rings, bracelets, necklaces; she is covered with the stuff. Her face looks ravaged. As she puts the necklace on, she says:)*

ELEANOR. How beautiful you make me. What might Solomon have sung had he seen this.

*(There is a mirror on the table. She starts to pick it up, then stops.)*

I can't. I'd turn to salt.

*(Mask slipping for a moment.)*

I've lost again. I'm done for now.

*(Finding the mask again.)*

Well, there'll be other Christmasses.

*(She takes an extremely elaborate necklace from the chest. Addressing it.)*

I'd hang you from the nipples but you'd shock the children.

*(She puts it on. For a moment, her pain shows clearly.)*

They kissed sweetly, didn't they?

*(Hardening again as she leans over the jewel chest.)*

I'll have him next time. I can wait. Ah—there you are:

*(Cut to the crown in the chest. Voice over.)*

my comfort and my company.

*(Her hands appear. She picks the crown up.)*

We're locked in for another year: four seasons more. Oh, what a desolation, what a life's work.

*(GEOFFREY appears in the doorway some distance behind her. She turns, smiling brightly as she puts the crown on. She already wears a small coronet and the effect of two crowns on at once is a little mad.)*

Is it too much? Be sure to squint as you approach. You may be blinded by my beauty.

GEOFFREY. Merry Christmas.

ELEANOR. Is that why you're here—to tell me that?

GEOFFREY. I thought you might be lonely.

*(ELEANOR removes the crown, holds it out to him.)*

ELEANOR. Here, Chancellor. Try it on for size.

GEOFFREY. It's puzzling. I remember my third birthday. Not just pictures of the garden or the gifts, but who did what to whom and how it felt. My memory stretches back that far and never once can I remember anything from you or Father warmer than indifference. Why is that?

ELEANOR. I don't know.

GEOFFREY. That was not an easy question for me and I don't deserve an easy answer.

ELEANOR. There are times I think we loved none of our children.

GEOFFREY. Still too easy, don't you think?

*(He is by the table, looking down at her. They are close.)*

ELEANOR. I'm weary and you want a simple answer and I haven't one.

*(She reaches up, gently touches his cheek.)*

I am so sick of all of you.

*(JOHN pops jauntily into the room.)*

JOHN. I thought I'd come and gloat a little.

*(ELEANOR starts removing jewelry.)*

ELEANOR. Mother's tired. Come stick pins tomorrow morning. I'll be more responsive then.

JOHN. It's no fun goading anyone tonight.

*(RICHARD storms into the room.)*

RICHARD. The bastard's boxed us up.

*(ELEANOR, utterly unconcerned, goes on removing jewels.)*

ELEANOR. What's that, dear?

*(RICHARD strides over to her.)*

RICHARD. We're his prisoners, if that interests you.

ELEANOR. Why should it? I'm his prisoner anyway.

RICHARD. It was—correct me if I'm wrong—but it was my impression that you wanted Henry's throne for me.

ELEANOR. We've lost it this time, Richard. We can't win.

RICHARD. You think I'm finished, do you?

ELEANOR. So I do. I've suffered more defeats than you have teeth. I know one when it happens to me. Take your wormwood like a good boy. Swallow it and go to bed.

RICHARD. I will be king.

ELEANOR. And so you will. But not this year. Oh, leave it, Richard. Let it go for now.

RICHARD. I can't.

*(JOHN is across the room.)*

JOHN. It's not so hard. Try saying after me: "John wins, I lose."

*(RICHARD starts across the room to JOHN.)*

RICHARD. What if John died?

*(JOHN registers instant panic.)*

JOHN. You wouldn't dare.

RICHARD. Why on earth wouldn't I?

*(RICHARD's hand moves to his dagger. JOHN races across the room to the protection of his mother.)*

JOHN. A knife. He's got a knife.

ELEANOR. Of course, he has a knife. He always has a knife. We all have knives. It is eleven eighty-three and we're barbarians.

*(Her eyes rake across her children.)*

How clear we make it. Oh, my piglets, we're the origins of war. Not history's forces nor the times nor justice nor the lack of it nor causes nor religions nor ideas nor kinds of government nor any other thing. We are the killers; we breed war. We carry it, like syphilis, inside. Dead bodies rot in field and stream because the living ones are rotten.

*(We see them all as she draws them close together.)*

For the love of God, can't we love one another just a little? That's how peace begins. We have so much to love each other for. We have such possibilities, my children. We could change the world.

*(They want to be loved. She wants to love them. As she starts to reach out for* RICHARD, GEOFFREY *says:)*

GEOFFREY. And while we hugged each other, what would Philip do?
JOHN *(In total dismay).* Oh, good God, Philip. We're supposed to start a war. If Father finds out, I'll be ruined.

*(*JOHN *starts for the door.* GEOFFREY *joins him.)*

GEOFFREY. Steady, John; don't panic.
JOHN. Some adviser you are.

*(*JOHN *hurries from the room as* GEOFFREY *says:)*

GEOFFREY. Don't do anything without me. Let me handle it.
ELEANOR *(She is alive again).* He's made a pact with Philip.

*(To* GEOFFREY *as he joins them.)*

You advised John into making war. That peerless boy! He's disinherited himself. When Henry finds out, when I tell him what John's done—I need a little time. Can you keep John away from Philip 'til I say so?
GEOFFREY. Anything you say.

*(He kisses her hand and bounds from the room as she turns to* RICHARD.*)*

ELEANOR. I want you out of here before this breaks. And that needs Philip. Go to him. Be desperate, promise anything: the Vexin, Brittany. Then once you're free and John is out of favor, we'll make further plans.
RICHARD. You talk to Philip. You're the diplomat; you see him.
ELEANOR. You're a friend. You know him; I don't.

*(*RICHARD *looks at her expressionlessly, then starts to the door.)*

And Richard.

*(He stops in the doorway.)*

Promise anything.

*(We see* RICHARD *close up. He either loves his mum or loathes her. This is loathing. As he turns and goes—*
*We move to* ELEANOR *alone in the center of the room. As she turns round full circle:)*

I haven't lost. It isn't over. Oh, I've got the old man this time. The damn fool thinks he loves John. He believes it. That's where the knife goes in.

*(Close up, all triumph gone.)*

Knives, knives . . . it was fine thought, wasn't it? Oh, Henry, we have done a big thing badly.

*(She starts to look for something. We follow her gaze about the room.)*

Where's that mirror? I am Eleanor and I can look at anything.

*(The camera finds the mirror. Her hand appears, picks the mirror up. We see her reflection, wavy and distorted in the primitive glass.)*

My, what a lovely girl.

*(The camera moves from the reflection to her face.)*

How could her king have left her?

*(We hold on her face. Then, suddenly, we see—*

*A door. A hand appears, taps lightly on it and we hear:)*

GEOFFREY *(Whispering)*. Philip?

(PHILIP, *preparing for bed, stands in shirtsleeves in his bedroom. The room is more luxuriously furnished than the others in the castle,* PHILIP *having brought his own refinements with him. There is a canopy bed. Wine glasses and decanter sit on a table.)*

(PHILIP *turns sharply as we see him. He moves to the door, opens it.* GEOFFREY *slips in, closes it behind him. He is keyed high; quiet, tense, excited.)*

It's working out. By morning I can be the chosen son. The crown can come to me. Are you still with me?

(PHILIP *nods.)*

We'll have to fight them all. They'll band together once this happens. Have I got your word?

PHILIP. Do I have yours? All England's land in France if I support you?

(GEOFFREY *nods.* PHILIP *looks at him speculatively.)*

GEOFFREY. Are we allies, then?

PHILIP *(Warmly taking his hand).* We were born to be.

GEOFFREY. I should say something solemn but I haven't time.

*(Halfway to the door.)*

I'm off to Father with the news that John's a traitor. After that—

(JOHN, *livid, charges out from behind a tapestry.)*

JOHN. You stink, you know that? You're a stinker and you stink.

(GEOFFREY *doesn't bat an eye.)*

GEOFFREY. Come along. We're finished here.

*(Looking wildly about the room.)*

JOHN. I'll kill you. Where's a dagger?

*(He can't find anything. Then, seeing a lethal-looking, massive candlestick, he grabs it, raises it high over his head and charges at* GEOFFREY.)

(GEOFFREY *crouches slightly as* JOHN *comes tearing at him. At the last moment,* GEOFFREY *sidesteps gracefully, tripping* JOHN *as he hurtles by.)*

(JOHN *sprawls out painfully on the floor.* GEOFFREY *glares at him, anger and derision on his face.)*

GEOFFREY. Dumb. If you're a prince, there's hope for every ape in Africa.

*(He goes to one knee beside* JOHN *as* JOHN *sits up.)*

I had you saved. I wasn't on my way to Father but he was. He would have gone to Henry and betrayed you. Look: it's in his face.

(JOHN *looks up.)*

JOHN *(Convinced and dismayed).* It's true. I don't know who my friends are.

*(There is a tapping at the door.* PHILIP *and* GEOFFREY *exchange a quick glance.)*

(RICHARD *is in the corridor. He darts a look one way, then the other. Satisfied he's still alone, he raps again and whispers:)*

RICHARD. Philip.

(GEOFFREY *bounds to his feet and indicating the tapestry where* JOHN *was hidden, asks:)*

GEOFFREY. May we?

PHILIP. That's what tapestries are for.

(PHILIP *starts toward the door.* GEOFFREY *tugs* JOHN *to his feet, bustles him toward the tapestry.*)

JOHN. I've ruined everything. I'll never learn.

(JOHN *and* GEOFFREY *duck behind the tapestry.*)

(*We see* PHILIP *standing by the door.*)

PHILIP. Is someone there? I heard my name.

(*He opens the door.* RICHARD *stands in the doorway.*)

RICHARD. I called it.
PHILIP. Richard. Hello, Richard.
RICHARD. You're halfway to bed. I'll wait for morning.
PHILIP. Come in.

(*He moves into the room. We stay with* RICHARD *in the doorway.*)

RICHARD. Mother sent me.
PHILIP. Come in anyway.

(*He picks up the decanter, pours.* RICHARD *moves into the picture.*)

Our alchemists have stumbled on the art of boiling burgundy. It turns to steam and when it cools, we call it "brandywine."
RICHARD. I'm Henry's prisoner.

(PHILIP *smiles.*)

You find that charming?
PHILIP. No.
RICHARD. Then why the charming smile?
PHILIP. I thought, I can't think why, of when you were in Paris last. Can it be two whole years ago?
RICHARD. It can. I need an army, Philip.

(PHILIP *hands him a glass.*)

PHILIP. It will take the cold away.
RICHARD. I must have soldiers.

(PHILIP *strolls away, moving casually about the room.*)

PHILIP. Have I aged? Do I seem older to you? They've been two fierce years. I've studied and I've trained to be a king.
RICHARD. I'll have your answer—yes or no.

(PHILIP *spins sharply toward* RICHARD.)

PHILIP. You'll have it when I give it.

(*Charming again, he moves across the room to* RICHARD.)

You see? I've changed. I'm not the boy you taught to hunt two years ago. Remember? Racing after boar, you flying first, me scrambling after, all day into dusk—

(RICHARD *turns abruptly away from him, starts to go.*)

Don't go.
RICHARD. I must know: Will you help me?

(PHILIP *sits in one of the chairs by the table.*)

PHILIP. Sit and we'll discuss it.

(RICHARD *moves to the other chair and sits stiffly.*)

You never write.
RICHARD. To anyone.
PHILIP. Why should I make you King of England? Aren't I better off with John or Geoffrey? Why have you to fight when I could have the cretin or the fiend?

(*Behind the tapesty,* JOHN *is indignant,* GEOFFREY *amused.*)

RICHARD. Would we fight?
PHILIP. We're fighting now. Good night.

*(He starts to rise, the interview terminated.)*

RICHARD. You're still a boy.

PHILIP. In some ways. Which way did you have in mind?

RICHARD. You haven't asked how much your help is worth.

PHILIP. You'll tell me.

RICHARD. You can have the Vexin back.

PHILIP. And what else?

RICHARD. All of Brittany.

*(Behind the tapestry,* GEOFFREY *is angry now and* JOHN *amused.)*

PHILIP. That's Geoffrey's.

RICHARD. Does that matter?

PHILIP. Possibly to Geoffrey. And what else?

RICHARD. That's all your help is worth.

PHILIP. And in return, what do you want from me?

RICHARD. Two thousand soldiers.

PHILIP. And what else?

RICHARD. Five hundred knights on horse.

PHILIP. And what else?

RICHARD. Arms and siege equipment.

PHILIP. And what else?

RICHARD. I never wrote because I thought you'd never answer.

*(*PHILIP *is expressionless.)*

You got married.

PHILIP. Does that make a difference?

RICHARD. Doesn't it?

PHILIP. I've spent two years on every street in hell.

RICHARD. That's odd. I didn't see you there.

*(*PHILIP *rises, eyes on* RICHARD. *Then* RICHARD *stands. Slowly,* PHILIP *extends his hand.* RICHARD *takes it.* PHILIP *turns and, in measured step,* starts moving toward the bed. RICHARD, *still holding his hand, follows.)*

*(The interior of the bed.* PHILIP'S *hand comes through the curtains, draws them back. We see them through the opening.)*

You haven't said you loved me.

PHILIP. When the time comes.

*(There is a tapping at the door.* PHILIP *and* RICHARD *paralyzed, exchange startled glances.)*

*(*HENRY *is in the corridor. He glances about. Then raps again and whispers:)*

HENRY. Philip.

*(At the bed,* RICHARD *is in great confusion.* PHILIP *is thinking hard.)*

*(Behind the tapestry,* JOHN, *frightened, turns to* GEOFFREY. GEOFFREY, *alive with excitement, puts a finger on* JOHN'S *lips.)*

*(*PHILIP *puts a finger to* RICHARD'S *lips, helps him into the bed.* PHILIP *draws the curtains shut, moves to the door and opens it.)*

HENRY. Philip, lad. It's not too late at night?

PHILIP. I'd hoped you'd come.

HENRY. *(We see the room from* HENRY'S *point of view as he enters).* Good; we can't leave negotiations where they are.

*(Turning to* PHILIP, *who moves to the table and pours from the decanter.)*

I keep looking for your father in you.

PHILIP. He's not there.

*(We see them both as* HENRY *settles in* RICHARD'S *chair.)*

HENRY. I miss him. Has Richard or the Queen been here to see you?

PHILIP. Does it matter? If they haven't yet, they will.

HENRY. I want to reach a settlement. I left you with too little earlier.

(PHILIP *hands* HENRY *a glass, sits in the other chair.*)

PHILIP. Yes; nothing is too little.

HENRY. I'm sorry you're not fonder of me, lad. Your father always said, "Be fond of stronger men."

PHILIP. No wonder he loved everyone.

HENRY. I've come to you to offer peace.

PHILIP. Piss on your peace.

HENRY. Your father would have wept.

PHILIP. My father was a weeper.

HENRY. Fight me and you'll lose.

PHILIP. I can't lose, Henry. I have time. Just look at you. Great heavy arms. Each year they get a little heavier. The sand goes pit-pat in the glass. I'm in no hurry, Henry. I've got time.

(HENRY *rises, angry.*)

HENRY. Suppose I hurry things along? What if I say that England is at war with France?

(PHILIP *calmly looks up at* HENRY.)

PHILIP. Then France surrenders. I don't have to fight to win. Take all you want—this county, that one. You won't keep it long.

HENRY (*Scornful*). What kind of courage have you got?

PHILIP. (*Cool and unperturbed*). The tidal kind: it comes and goes.

(HENRY *breaks out into a delighted smile and sits again. We see them both.*)

HENRY. By God, I'd love to turn you loose on Eleanor.

(*The decanter in his hand.*)

More Brandywine?

PHILIP. You recognize it?

HENRY. (*Filling his glass*). They were boiling it in Ireland before the snakes left.

(*Sitting back, settling in his chair.*)

Well—things look a little bleak for Henry, don't they? You'll say yes to Richard when he comes; arms, soldiers, anything he asks for.

PHILIP. I'd be foolish not to.

HENRY. And withdraw it all before the battle ever started.

PHILIP. Wouldn't you, in my place?

HENRY. Why fight Henry when his sons will do it for you?

PHILIP. Yes, exactly.

HENRY. You've got promise, lad. That's first-class thinking.

PHILIP. Thank you, sir.

(HENRY *raises his glass and drinks.*)

(RICHARD, *in the bed, looks angry and betrayed.*)

(*We see behind the tapestry, more anger and betrayal.*)

(HENRY *wipes his lips and puts his glass down.*)

HENRY. Good night.

(HENRY *rises.* PHILIP *looks up, uncertain for the first time.*)

PHILIP. Good night? You're going?

(HENRY *nods benignly.*)

But we haven't settled anything.

HENRY. We open Christmas packages at noon. 'Til then.

(HENRY *starts to go.* PHILIP *rises.*)

PHILIP. You can't be finished with me.

HENRY. But I am. And it's been very satisfactory.

PHILIP. What's so satisfactory?

HENRY. Winning is. I did just win. Surely you noticed.

PHILIP. Not a thing. You haven't won a damn thing.

*(We see them both as* HENRY *moves slowly to* PHILIP, *saying:)*

HENRY. I found out the way your mind works and the kind of man you are. I know your plans and expectations. You have burbled every bit of strategy you've got. I know exactly what you will do and exactly what you won't. And I've told you exactly nothing. To these aged eyes, boy, that's what winning looks like. *Dormez bien.*

*(With which he turns and, as we follow him, moves toward the door.)*

PHILIP. You—

*(*HENRY *stops and turns.)*

You made my father nothing. You were always better. You bullied him, you bellied with his wife, you beat him down in every war, you twisted every treaty, you played mock-the-monk and then you made him love you for it.

*(He begins stalking toward* HEN-RY.*)*

I was there. His last words went to you.

HENRY. He was a loving man and you learned nothing of it.

PHILIP. I learned how much fathers live in sons. A king like you has policy prepared on everything. What's the official line on sodomy? How stands the crown on boys who do with boys?

*(We see* RICHARD *in the bed, disbelief, shock on his face. It can't be happening.*

*(*HENRY *moves away from* PHILIP.*)*

HENRY. Richard finds his way into so many legends. Let's hear yours and see how it compares.

*(As* PHILIP *speaks, he follows* HENRY, *pressing him.)*

PHILIP. He found me first when I was fifteen. We were hunting. It was nearly dark. My horse fell. I was thrown. I woke to Richard touching me. He asked me if I loved him—"Philip, do you love me?"—and I told him yes.

*(*RICHARD *in the bed. He is wracked with pain and rage. It is excruciating.*

*(*PHILIP *bears down harder.)*

You know why I told him yes? So one day I could tell you all about it. You cannot imagine what that "yes" cost. Or perhaps you can. Imagine snuggling to a chancred whore and, bending back your lips in something like a smile, saying: "Yes, I love you and I find you beautiful." I don't know how I did it.

*(*RICHARD *leaps through the curtains.)*

RICHARD. No—it wasn't like that!
PHILIP *(Cold and cutting)*. But it was.
RICHARD. You loved me.
PHILIP. Never.

*(*RICHARD *turns to* HENRY.*)*

RICHARD. Get out. Please! I don't want you here.
HENRY. It's no great joy to be here.
RICHARD. So the royal corkscrew finds me twisted, does he?
HENRY. I'll go tell your mother: she'll be pleased.

*(He starts to go.* RICHARD *follows him.)*

RICHARD. She knows. She sent me.
HENRY *(Turning on* RICHARD. *They stand face to face)*. How completely hers you are.
RICHARD. You've had four sons. Who do you claim? Not Henry. Not my buried brother. Not that monument to muck, that epic idiot. Why him? Why always him and never me?

HENRY. He was the oldest—he came first.

RICHARD. Christ, Henry, is that all?

HENRY. You went with Eleanor.

RICHARD. You never called for me. You never said my name. I would have walked or crawled. I'd have done anything.

(HENRY *turns away, unable to face it.*)

HENRY. It's not my fault. I won't be blamed.

RICHARD. I only wanted you.

HENRY. No—it's my crown. You want my kingdom.

RICHARD. Keep your kingdom.

(HENRY *wheels toward* RICHARD.)

HENRY. That I will!

RICHARD. I hope it kills you!

HENRY. Thank God I have another son. Thank God for John.

(GEOFFREY *steps out from behind the tapestry.*)

GEOFFREY. Who shall we thank for Geoffrey?

(*Moving to* HENRY.)

You don't think much of me.

HENRY. Much? I don't think of you at all.

GEOFFREY. Nurse used to say I had your hands. I might have had more of you. Try seeing me. I haven't Richard's military skill but he was here betraying you, not I. I haven't John's I don't know what—God knows what you can see in John—and he's betrayed you, too.

(JOHN, *red with rage, peeps through a slit in the tapestry.*)

HENRY. You think I'd ever make you king?

GEOFFREY. You'll make me king because I'm all you've got.

(*Pointing at* RICHARD.)

I was to be his chancellor. Ask him why.

HENRY (*Starting to leave the room*). I've heard enough.

GEOFFREY. For moving John to treason.

HENRY. I don't doubt he offered, I don't doubt you tried and I don't doubt John loves me.

(GEOFFREY *steps to the tapestry.*)

GEOFFREY. Like a glutton loves his lunch.

(*He pulls the tapestry back, revealing* JOHN. JOHN *glares at* GEOFFREY *with pure loathing.*)

JOHN. You turd.

HENRY. Well, John?

JOHN. It isn't what you think.

HENRY. What do I think?

JOHN. What Geoffrey said. I wouldn't plot against you, ever.

HENRY. I know; you're a good boy.

(JOHN, *encouraged, moves toward* HENRY. *Just* JOHN *and* HENRY *now.*)

JOHN. Can I go now, please? It's late. I ought to be in bed.

(HENRY *grabs* JOHN *by the shoulders, shakes him.*)

HENRY. Couldn't you wait? Couldn't you trust me? It was all yours. Couldn't you believe that?

JOHN. Will you listen to the grief?

HENRY. Who do you think I built this kingdom for?

(JOHN, *in a rage, shakes himself loose.*)

JOHN. Me? Daddy did it all for me? When can I have it, Daddy? Not until we bury you?

HENRY. You're just like them. And after all I've given you.

JOHN. I got it. I know what you gave.

HENRY. I loved you.

JOHN. You're a cold and bloody bastard, you are, and you don't love anything.

(HENRY *is stunned, blank with shock.*)

GEOFFREY. I'm it, I'm all that's left. Here, Father; here I am.

(*We move toward* HENRY, *closer and closer to his unseeing eyes.*)

HENRY. My life, when it is written, will read better than it lived. Henry Fitz-Empress, first Plantagenet, a king at twenty-one, the ablest soldier of an able time. He led men well, he cared for justice when he could and ruled, for thirty years, a state as great as Charlemagne's. He married out of love a woman out of legend. Not in Rome or Alexandria or Camelot has there been such a queen. She bore him many children—but no sons. King Henry had no sons.

(*Cut to* JOHN, RICHARD *and* GEOFFREY *side by side. Then back to* HENRY.)

He had three whiskered things but he disowned them. You're not mine. We're not connected. I deny you. None of you will get my crown. I leave you nothing and I wish you plague. May all your children breech and die.

(*He turns, moves to the doorway, stops and looks back.*)

My boys are gone.

(HENRY *starts unsteadily down the corridor.*)

I've lost my boys.

(*He stops, glares up toward the Deity.*)

You dare to damn me, do You? Well, I damn You back.

(*Like a Biblical figure, shaking his fist at the sky.*)

God damn You.

(*Moving blindly down the corridor again.*)

My boys are gone. I've lost my boys. Oh, Jesus, all my boys.

(*We follow him as, stunned and stumbling, he moves painfully through his quiet, darkened castle. He pauses in the Parlor doorway, not seeing the Christmas tree and presents and the embers in the fireplace. We see him in the doorway of his bedroom, uncertain where he is.*)

(ALAIS, *still in bed, starts at the sight of him. Alarmed, she starts to rise. He turns and leaves. She follows to the bedroom door, looks after him, love and concern for her man mingled on her face.*)

(*We see him all alone, high on the ramparts of his castle. The night is clear and bitter cold. He looks down at the river bank.* ELEANOR'S *barge, empty and dark, is there.*)

(*We see him lying down on icy stones. He doesn't feel the cold. He looks up unblinking at the sky. The picture fades.*)

(*We come up slowly on a tiny bed of gently glowing coals, very close up. As we see them, we hear:*)

ALAIS (*Singing*).
The Christmas wine is in the pot,
The Christmas coals are red.
I'll spend my day the lover's way,
Unwrapping all my gifts in bed.

(*As she sings, we pull slowly back. The coals are in a small copper brazier. On the brazier, we see a small pot.* ALAIS's *hands appear. One holds a tiny spice jar; the other takes a pinch of spice and drops it in the pot.*)

(*We continue back as we see* ALAIS *sitting on the floor by the brazier.*

*Then we see* HENRY'S *bedroom beyond her and, at the last,* ELEANOR *standing in the doorway. She looks absolutely desolate.)*

The Christmas Mass is over now,
      The Christmas—

*(She stops singing as she senses someone. She turns.)*
*(We see her pull herself together. As if nothing in the world were wrong, she moves into the room saying:)*

ELEANOR. No one else is caroling tonight: it might as well be Lent. When I was little, Christmas was a time of great confusion for me. The Holy Land had two kings, God and Uncle Raymond, and I never knew whose birthday we were celebrating.

*(Reaching* ALAIS, *she looks fondly down at her.)*

ALAIS. Henry isn't here.
ELEANOR. Good; we can talk behind his back.
ALAIS. What happened?
ELEANOR. Don't you know?

*(*ALAIS *shakes her head,* ELEANOR *sits on the floor by her.)*

There was a scene with beds and tapestries and many things got said.

*(She leans forward over the pot on the brazier.)*

Spiced wine. I'd forgotten Henry liked it. May I stay?
ALAIS *(She rises, puts the spice pot on a table).* It's your room just as much as mine: we're both in residence.
ELEANOR. Packed in, like the poor, three to a bed.
ALAIS. Did you love Henry—ever?
ELEANOR. Ever? Back before the flood?
ALAIS. As long ago as Rosamund.
ELEANOR. Ah, that's prehistory, lamb; there are no written records or survivors.
ALAIS. There are pictures. She was prettier than you.
ELEANOR. Oh, much. Her eyes in certain light were violet and all her teeth were even. That's a rare fair feature, even teeth. She smiled to excess but she chewed with real distinction.
ALAIS. And you hate her even now.
ELEANOR. No . . . but I did. He put her in my place, you see, and that was very hard. Like you, she headed Henry's table: that's my chair.
ALAIS. And so you had her poisoned.
ELEANOR. No, I never poisoned Rosamund. Oh, I prayed for her to drop and sang a little when she did. . . . Why aren't you happy? Henry's keeping you. You must be cleverer than I am.
ALAIS. I've tried feeling pity for you but it keeps on turning into something else.
ELEANOR. Why pity?
ALAIS. You love Henry but you love his kingdom, too. You look at him and you see cities, acreage, coastline, taxes. All I see is Henry. Leave him to me, can't you?
ELEANOR. But I left him years ago.
ALAIS. And I thought I could move you. Were you always like this? Years ago, when I was young and worshiped you, is this what you were like?
ELEANOR. Most likely. Child, I'm finished and I've come to give him anything he asks for.
ALAIS. Do you know what I should like for Christmas? I should like to see you suffer.
ELEANOR *(The suffering clear on her face).* Alais, just for you.

*(*ALAIS *understands and all the love and tenderness she used to feel for*

ELEANOR *come flooding back. With a small cry, she throws herself into* ELEANOR'S *arms.* ELEANOR *holds her, rocks her, like a child, gently back and forth.*)

ALAIS. *Maman, ô Maman.*
ELEANOR. *Alors, ma petite.*
ALAIS. *J'ai peur, Maman.*

(*Still rocking,* ELEANOR *starts to hum* ALAIS'S *little song. Then something catches her eye. She stops humming, turns.*)

(HENRY *stands in the doorway. He sees them but he doesn't really take them in. His manner is brisk, keyed high, with a kind of mad energy.*)

HENRY. The sky is pocked with stars. What eyes the wise men must have had to spot a new one in so many.

(ALAIS *rises and moves to the wine pot on the brazier.*)

ELEANOR. You look cold.
ALAIS. I've mulled some wine.

(HENRY *moves into the room.*)

HENRY. I wonder, were there fewer stars then? I don't know. I fancy there's a mystery in it.

(ALAIS *moves into the picture with a goblet of wine.*)

What's this?
ALAIS. Warm wine.
HENRY. Why, so it is.

(*He takes the wine, touches her cheek.*)

You are as beautiful as I remembered.

(*Sending her toward the door.*)

Off to bed. My widow wants to see me.

(ALAIS *moves closer to him.*)
ALAIS. Let me stay.
HENRY. I won't be long.

ALAIS. She came to find out what your plans are.
HENRY. I know that.
ALAIS. She wants you back.
HENRY. Go to your room.

(ALAIS *turns slowly and goes.* HENRY *moves to his chair by the fireplace and sits.*)

So you want me back.
ELEANOR (*Settling in a chair on the other side of the fireplace*). She thinks I do. She thinks the need for loving never stops.
HENRY. She's got a point. I marvel at you. After all these years, still like a democratic drawbridge, going down for everybody.
ELEANOR. At my age, there's not much traffic any more.

(*He raises his goblet in a toast.*)

HENRY. To your interminable health.

(*He drinks.*)

Well, wife, what's on your mind?
ELEANOR. Oh Henry, we have made a mess of it.
HENRY. Yes, haven't we? You look like doomsday.
ELEANOR. Late nights do that to me. Am I puffy?
HENRY. Possibly. It's hard to tell.
ELEANOR. I've just seen Richard.

(*We see them both, flanking the fireplace. The logs burn low and warm.*)

HENRY. Splendid boy.
ELEANOR. He says you fought.
HENRY. We always do.
ELEANOR. It's his impression that you plan to disinherit them.
HENRY. I fancy I'll relent. Don't you?
ELEANOR. I don't much care.

(HENRY *turns sharply to face her.*)

In fact I wonder, Henry, if I care for anything. I wonder if I'm hungry out of habit and if all my lusts, like passions in a poem, aren't really recollections.

HENRY. I could listen to you lie for hours. So your lust is rusty. Gorgeous.

ELEANOR. Henry, I'm so tired.

(HENRY *rises, starts moving toward her.*)

HENRY. Sleep, then. Sleep and dream of me with *croûtons. Henri à la mode.*

(*As he reaches her, she rises with a surge of energy.*)

ELEANOR. Henry, stop it.

HENRY. Eleanor, I haven't started.

ELEANOR. What is it you want? You want my name on paper, I'll sign anything. You want the Aquitaine for John? It's John's. It's his, it's yours, it's anybody's.

HENRY. In exchange for what?

ELEANOR. For nothing, for a little quiet, for an end to this, for God's sake, sail me back to England, lock me up and lose the key and let me be alone.

(HENRY *nods appreciatively. Then, raising his hands, he starts to applaud.*)

(*The applause grows louder and louder.*)

You have my oath. I give my word.

(*The applause grows thunderous, then cuts off abruptly. Bone weary, nodding,* ELEANOR *sinks into a chair.*)

Oh, well. Well, well.

(HENRY *circles her like a dog that's trapped its prey.*)

HENRY. Would you like a pillow? Footstool? How about a shawl? Your oaths are all profanities. Your word's

a curse. Your name on paper is a waste of pulp.

(*She is not reacting. He bends toward her, bellowing:*)

I'm vilifying you, for God's sake! Pay attention!

(*She looks up, only half seeing.*)

ELEANOR. How, from where we started, did we ever reach this Christmas?

HENRY. Step by step.

ELEANOR. What happens to me now?

(*We follow* HENRY *as he moves away from her.*)

HENRY. That's lively curiosity from such a dead cat. If you want to know my plans, just ask me.

ELEANOR. Conquer China, sack the Vatican or take the veil. I'm not among the ones who give a damn. Just let me sign my lands to John and go to bed.

(HENRY *stretches out luxuriously in his chair.*)

HENRY. No, you're too kind. I can't accept.

(ELEANOR *moves to the chair, glares down at him.*)

ELEANOR. Come on, man. I'll sign the thing in blood or spit or bright blue ink. Let's have it done.

HENRY. Let's not. No, I don't think I want your signature on anything.

ELEANOR. You don't?

HENRY. Dear God, the pleasure I still get from goading you.

ELEANOR. You don't want John to have my provinces?

HENRY. Bull's eye.

(*She bends down over him.*)

ELEANOR. I can't bear you when you're smug.

*(HENRY grins up at her, reveling in it.)*

HENRY. I know, I know.

*(She straightens up, draws slightly back.)*

ELEANOR. You don't want Richard and you don't want John.

HENRY. You've grasped it.

ELEANOR. All right, let me have it. Level me. What do you want?

HENRY *(Savoring each syllable)*. A new wife.

*(ELEANOR, close up. She is utterly dismayed.)*

ELEANOR. Oh,

*(She sits slowly on the floor by his chair.)*

So I'm to be annulled. Well, will the Pope annul me, do you think?

HENRY. The Pontif owes me one Pontificate. I think he will.

ELEANOR. Out Eleanor, in Alais. Why?

HENRY. A new wife, wife, will bear me sons.

*(ELEANOR rises, glaring down at him.)*

ELEANOR. That is the single thing of which I should have thought you had enough.

*(He rises. They stand face to face.)*

HENRY. I want a son.

ELEANOR. Whatever for? Why, we could populate a country town with country girls who've borne you sons. How many is it? Help me count the bastards.

HENRY. All my sons are bastards.

ELEANOR. You really mean to do it.

HENRY. Lady love, with all my heart.

*(HENRY turns away from her, moves energetically to a narrow slit of a window, stands with his back to her, looking out.)*

ELEANOR. Your sons are part of you.

HENRY. Like warts and goiters; and I'm having them removed.

ELEANOR. We made them. They're our boys.

HENRY. I know—and good God, look at them. Young Henry: vain, deceitful, weak and cowardly. The only patriotic thing he ever did was die.

ELEANOR. I thought you loved him most.

HENRY. I did.

*(He turns to face her.)*

And Geoffrey—there's a masterpiece. He isn't flesh: he's a device; he's wheels and gears.

ELEANOR. Every family has one.

HENRY. But not four. Then Johnny. Was his latest reason your idea?

*(She shakes her head.)*

I have caught him lying and I've said he's young. I've seen him cheating and I've thought he's just a boy. I've watched him steal and whore and whip his servants and he's not a child. He is the man we've made him.

ELEANOR. Don't share John with me. He's your accomplishment.

HENRY. And Richard's yours. How could you send him off to deal with Philip?

ELEANOR. I was tired. I was busy. They were friends.

HENRY. Eleanor, he was the best. And from the cradle on you cradled him. I never had a chance.

ELEANOR. You never wanted one.

HENRY. How do you know? You took him. Separation from your husband you could bear. But not your boy.

ELEANOR. Whatever I have done, you made me do.

HENRY. You threw me out of bed for Richard.

ELEANOR. Not until you threw me out for Rosamund.

HENRY. It's not that simple. I won't have it be that simple.

ELEANOR. I adored you.

HENRY. Never.

ELEANOR. I still do.

(*Cut to* HENRY, *close up.*)

HENRY. Of all the lies, that one is the most terrible.

(*Cut to* ELEANOR, *close up.*)

ELEANOR. I know: that's why I saved it up for now.

(*Their eyes lock, blazing. Neither moves. Then, suddenly, they throw themselves into each other's arms. They hold tight, wanting shelter from the storm they've made.*)

Oh, Henry, we have mangled everything we've touched.

HENRY. Deny us what you will, we have done that.

(*He pulls away from her, looks gently down into her face.*)

Do you remember when we met?

ELEANOR (*Looking radiantly up at him*). Down to the hour and the color of your stockings.

HENRY. I could hardly see you for the sunlight.

(*She settles on the floor. He goes down close beside her.*)

ELEANOR. It was raining but no matter.

HENRY. There was very little talk as I recall it.

ELEANOR. Very little.

HENRY. I had never seen such beauty and I walked right up and touched it. God, where did I find the gall to do that?

(*She bends tenderly toward him.*)

ELEANOR. In my eyes.

HENRY. I loved you.

(*They kiss, then gently part, each lost in reverie.*)

ELEANOR. No annulment.

HENRY. What?

ELEANOR. There will be no annulment.

HENRY. Will there not?

ELEANOR. No, I'm afraid you'll have to do without.

HENRY (*Anger just bottled in*). Well—it was just a whim.

ELEANOR. I'm so relieved. I didn't want to lose you.

HENRY. Out of curiosity, as intellectual to intellectual, how in the name of bleeding Jesus can you lose me? Do you ever see me? Am I ever with you? Ever near you? Am I ever anywhere but somewhere else?

(ELEANOR, *close up, delighted.* HENRY'S *rage mounts.*)

Do we write? Do I send messages? Do dinghies bearing gifts float up the Thames to you? Are you remembered?

ELEANOR. You are.

HENRY. You're no part of me. We do not touch at any point. How can you lose me?

ELEANOR. Can't you feel the chains?

HENRY. You know enough to know I can't be stopped.

ELEANOR. But I don't have to stop you. I have only to delay you. Every enemy you have has friends in Rome. We'll cost you time.

HENRY (*Rising, backing away from her*). What is this? I'm not moldering; my paint's not peeling off. I'm good for years.

ELEANOR (*On her feet, pursuing him*). How many years? Suppose I hold you back for one? I can—it's possible. Suppose your first son dies?

Ours did—it's possible. Suppose you're daughtered next? We were—that, too, is possible. How old is daddy then? What kind of spindly, ricket-ridden, milky, semiwitted, wizened, dim-eyed, gammy-handed, limpy line of things will you beget?

HENRY. It's sweet of you to care.

ELEANOR. And when you die, which is regrettable but necessary, what will happen to frail Alais and her pruney prince? You can't think Richard's going to wait for your grotesque to grow.

HENRY. You wouldn't let him do a thing like that?

ELEANOR. Let him? I'd push him through the nursery door.

HENRY. You're not that cruel.

ELEANOR. Don't fret. We'll wait until you're dead to do it.

(HENRY *moves to her, into the picture.*)

HENRY. Eleanor, what do you want?

ELEANOR *(Beating down on him with great intensity).* Just what you want: a king for a son. You can make more. I can't. You think I want to disappear? One son is all I've got and you can blot him out and call me cruel. For these ten years you've lived with everything I've lost and loved another woman through it all. And I'm cruel. I could peel you like a pear and God himself would call it justice.

HENRY. I will die sometime soon. One day I'll duck too slow and at Westminster they'll sing out "Long Live the King" for someone else. I beg you, let it be a son of mine.

ELEANOR. I am not moved to tears.

HENRY *(Desperate).* I have no sons.

ELEANOR. You have too many sons. You don't need more.

(He glares at her. She glares back. There is a strong sense of stalemate. *Just as we think there is nothing either can do,* HENRY *breaks into a broad and terrible smile.*)

HENRY. Well, wish me luck. I'm off.

(*He turns, strides toward the door.*)

ELEANOR. To Rome?

HENRY *(Not pausing, moving out of the room into the corridor).* That's where they keep the Pope.

(*She follows him into the corridor.*)

ELEANOR. You don't dare go.

(HENRY *stops and turns to face her.*)

HENRY. Say that again at noon, you'll say it to my horse's ass. Lamb, I'll be rid of you by Easter. You can count your reign in days.

ELEANOR. You go to Rome, we'll rise against you.

HENRY. Who will?

ELEANOR. Richard, Geoffrey, John and Eleanor of Aquitaine.

HENRY. The day those stout hearts band together is the day that pigs get wings.

ELEANOR. There'll be pork in the treetops come the morning. Don't you see? You've given them a common cause: new sons. You leave the country and you've lost it.

HENRY. All of you at once.

ELEANOR. And Philip, too. He'd join us.

HENRY. Yes, he would.

ELEANOR. Now how's your trip to Rome?

(HENRY *seems cornered, beaten.*)

Oh, I've got you, got you, got you.

HENRY. Should I take a thousand men-at-arms or is that showy?

ELEANOR. Bluff away. I love it.

(*He starts moving forward toward her. She begins retreating. We keep with them as they edge their way back into the bedroom.)*

HENRY. Ah, poor thing. How can I break the news? You've just miscalculated.

ELEANOR. Have I? How?

HENRY. You should have lied to me. You should have promised to be good while I was gone. I would have let your three boys loose. They could have fought me then.

ELEANOR. You wouldn't keep your sons locked up here?

HENRY. Why the devil wouldn't I?

ELEANOR *(Desperate)*. You don't dare.

HENRY *(Unstoppable victorious)*. Why not? What's to stop me? Let them sit in Chinon for a while.

*(We see them both.)*

ELEANOR. I forbid it!

*(Cut to HENRY.)*

HENRY. She forbids it!

*(He storms toward the door.)*

ELEANOR. Did your father sleep with me or didn't he?

*(HENRY stops. Color drains from his face. It is a thought he cannot bear. He turns toward her.)*

HENRY. No doubt you're going to tell me that he did.

ELEANOR. Would it upset you?

HENRY *(Stalking toward ELEANOR)*. What about the thousand men? I say be gaudy and to hell with it.

ELEANOR *(Retreating, she finds herself against his bed)*. Don't leave me, Henry. I'm at rock bottom. I'll do anything to keep you.

HENRY. I think you think you mean it.

*(We see them both, their faces close together. She is kneeling on the bed.)*

ELEANOR. Ask for something.

HENRY. Eleanor, we're past it; years past.

ELEANOR. Test me. Name an act.

HENRY. There isn't one.

ELEANOR. About my fornication with your father—

HENRY. Yes, there is. You can expire.

ELEANOR. You first, old man. I only hope I'm there to watch. You're so afraid of dying. You're so scared of it.

HENRY. Poor Eleanor; if only she had lied.

ELEANOR *(She sits on the bed, starts to stretch out)*. She did. She said she never loved your father.

HENRY. I can always count on you.

ELEANOR. I never touched you without thinking "Geoffrey, Geoffrey."

*(She lies back moving sensuously. He crouches over her.)*

HENRY. When you hurt me, I'll cry out.

ELEANOR. I've put more horns on you than Louis ever wore.

HENRY. Am I supposed to care?

ELEANOR. I'll kill you if you leave me.

HENRY. You can try.

*(She leans up, close to him.)*

ELEANOR. I loved your father's body. He was beautiful.

HENRY *(Retreating from the impact of it, sitting on the edge of the bed, turning away from her)*. It never happened.

ELEANOR. I can see his body now. Shall I describe it?

HENRY. Eleanor, I hope you die.

*(She rises to her knees on the bed, seeming to tower over him.)*

ELEANOR. His arms were rough, with scars here—

HENRY. Stop it!

ELEANOR. I can feel his arms. I feel them.

HENRY *(Crying out).* Aahhh!

ELEANOR. What's that? Have I hurt you?

*(He rises like a stricken animal, stumbles blindly against a table, falls, keeps on moving, wriggling, crawling toward the door. She is on her feet, looming over him in terrible triumph. He drags himself somehow to his feet and staggers through the door. She rushes toward the doorway.)*

ELEANOR *(Hurling it after him).* We did it! You were in the next room when he did it!

*(She reaches the door frame, leans against it for support, sinks to the floor, her face a picture of total desolation.)*

Well, what family doesn't have its ups and downs?

*(Eyes moving aimlessly about.)*

It's cold. I can't feel anything. Not anything at all. We couldn't go back, could we, Henry?

*(We fade slowly on her desolate and anguished face. The moment we reach black—*
*A great hand slapping down with tremendous impact on the buttocks of a body asleep in bed. There is a howl of surprised pain as the body bolts upright and we pull back to reveal—*
HENRY, *a flaming torch in hand, looming over* WILLIAM MARSHAL, *who is wide awake, naked to the waist in bed.* HENRY *is bursting with energy, his eyes bright.)*

*(*HENRY, *torch in hand, strides down a crude stone barracks room. Sleeping soldiers in uniforms lie on the floor.* MARSHAL *follows* HENRY *along.)*

HENRY *(More a bellow than a word).* Hey—hey—hey.

*(General stirring as soldiers wake up.)*

When the King is off his ass, nobody sleeps.

*(A squad of soldiers,* MARSHAL *in command, strides down a corridor. They halt beside a door.)*

*(Interior of the room,* JOHN *and sad-faced servant girl are in bed, covered up, naked.* JOHN *is asleep, his head on her breast. She is awake, pathetic eyes staring sadly at nothing.)*

*(In the corridor,* MARSHAL *gestures an order. Two soldiers break ranks, move to the door.* MARSHAL *gestures again and the squad moves down the corridor.)*

*(Servant girl sees something, gasps in fear as rough hands appear in the picture. The hands hurl back the blankets.* JOHN'S *eyes fly open. His scream of terror is cut off as a hand covers his mouth.)*

*(*GEOFFREY *lies in bed, awake. Cool and clear as always, he is busy thinking. He hears a sound. Only his eyes move. None of the panic that he feels shows in his face.)*

*(A thick door opens.* MARSHAL, *in the corridor, stands in the doorway. Cautiously, he enters. We follow his gaze as he takes in* RICHARD'S *room. It is empty. Tense, he advances. We see* RICHARD *crouched behind the door in back of him.)*

*(*RICHARD *makes his move, lunging for the open door. Soldiers block his way. He turns back.* MARSHAL'S *sword is leveled at his throat.)*

*(A dungeon-like place. Vague shapes and shadows.* JOHN, GEOFFREY *and* RICHARD *are hurled into view. A great door clanks closed. A candle burns. The boys pick themselves up.*

*We follow them in candlelight as, crouching and tense, they start exploring the mysterious and vast cellars of the castle.)*

*(*HENRY, *with his torch, strides into the vast kitchen of the castle.* MAR-SHAL *follows after him. Fires glow in fireplaces. Vassals lie asleep on the floor amidst carcasses of beef and poultry and the day's debris.* HENRY *strides among them, kicking them awake.)*

*(We see* HENRY, *striding through the poultry yard outside, kicking chickens, ducks and geese awake. The chicken keeper, half asleep, stands listening to orders from* MARSHAL. *There is much honking and squawking.)*

*(We see* HENRY, *close up, bending over coals at the Smith's forge. His energy seems manic; sweat pours off his face. He is looking at a glowing piece of metal, part of a suit of armor. The armorer brings his hammer crashing down.)*

*(*HENRY *and* MARSHAL *stride across the courtyard. All about him, shadowy figures are stirring. Men are pushing a heavy wagon. Horses neigh. Still with his torch, he pauses, looks up at a tower. A light comes from* ELEANOR'S *window.)*

HENRY. Tell her to pack. She's leaving when it's light out.

*(*MARSHAL *nods and strides off. As* HENRY *plunges back into the melee of the yard, we see—*

ELEANOR *in her bedroom, dressed for travel. Before her, on the table, is the jewel chest. Behind her, in the background, her two maids-in-waiting are busy packing clothes.)*

*(*ELEANOR *is tense with concentration. There must be some move that she can make, some gambit . . . Her fingers drum nervously on the table.)*

*(Back in the yard, we get the sense that* HENRY *is everywhere. We see him pushing, heaving, lifting, swearing. Soldiers march past, servants race about us, horses whinny as they strain at wagons, dogs howl.)*

*(*ELEANOR'S *room again. Still at her table, fingers drumming, she looks up. Her guard appears. She looks at him more closely. Then, eyes bright, she comes to a decision.)*

*(Outside,* HENRY *pauses in the melee of the yard. Close up, he looks a little mad. His eyes are red, his face smudged. He seems to vibrate with nervous energy. He tears a great chunk from a loaf of bread and, devouring it, makes for his castle.)*

*(Lunging down a corridor he goes. He grabs a door, hurls it thunderously open and strides into a room.* ALAIS, *dressed as we saw her last, lies curled up, sound asleep. She jumps as the door bangs, wide awake.)*

ALAIS. Henry? What's wrong?

HENRY. We're packing up and moving out.

ALAIS. Is there a war? What's happened?

*(He throws his arms around her in a great bear hug.)*

Henry, what's the matter?

HENRY. Nothing, for a change. Would you believe it?

ALAIS. Where've you been all night?

HENRY. Out making us an entourage.

ALAIS. What for?

HENRY. We're off to Rome to see the Pope.

ALAIS. He's excommunicated you again.

HENRY. He's going to set me free. I'm having Eleanor annulled. The nation will be shocked to learn our marriage wasn't consummated.

ALAIS. Oh, be serious.

HENRY. I am. It seems that you and I are getting married. By the Pope himself.

ALAIS. You mean it?

HENRY. Shall I kneel?

ALAIS. It's not another trick?

HENRY. The bridal party's drilling on the cobblestones.

ALAIS. She still loves you, Henry.

HENRY. So she says.

ALAIS. She'll find a way to stop us.

HENRY. How? She won't be here. We're launching her for Salisbury Tower when the winds change. She'll be barging down the River Vienne by lunchtime.

ALAIS. If she doesn't stop us, Richard will.

HENRY. Not any more. I've corked him up. He's in the cellar with his brothers and the wine. The royal boys are aging with the royal port. You haven't said yes. Would you like a formal declaration?

*(He goes to one knee, turning his profile to us.)*

There—my finest angle; it's on all the coins. Sad Alais, will you marry me?

*(She looks down at him lovingly.)*

Be my Queen.

*(She goes down to him, melts in his arms. He kisses her cheecks, her hands, her neck.)*

We'll love each other and you'll give me sons. Let's have five—we'll do Eleanor one better. Why, I'll even call the first one Louis, if you like. Louis le Premier: how's that for a King of England?

*(They start to laugh. They try to kiss but both of them are laughing. Gradually, as HENRY roars on, her laughter subsides, then stops, all joy fading from her face.)*

ALAIS. Henry—you can't ever let them out.

HENRY *(Laughter subsiding).* You've lost me. Let who out?

ALAIS. Your sons. You've put them in the dungeon and you've got to keep them there forever.

HENRY. Do I now?

ALAIS. If they're free when you die, it's the dungeon or the nunnery for me. I don't care which—a cell's a cell—but, Henry, what about the child.

HENRY *(Anger beginning, he gets to his feet).* Don't bother me about the child. The damn thing isn't born yet.

*(Furious, he wheels about and starts to go.)*

ALAIS. Henry?

*(Near the door, he stops. She moves to him.)*

Are you going down?

*(He nods.)*

To let them out or keep them in?

HENRY. Could you say to a child of yours, "You've seen the sunlight for the last time"?

ALAIS. Can you do it, Henry?

HENRY. I shall have to, shan't I?

*(ALAIS watches him go, both elated and aghast at what she has accomplished. She hesitates, then runs out of the room after him.)*

*(HENRY comes bounding down the broad stone steps to the courtyard. ALAIS appears at the top of the steps, hesitates again, then hurries after him.)*

*(We watch them moving through the yard. The troup of actors wanders blearily into the picture. We lose HENRY and ALAIS as, for a moment, we follow the actors along, leaving them as we pick up ELEANOR in a corner of the yard. She carries the*

*jewel chest. Her guard follows along behind.)*

*(ELEANOR goes down a flight of stone steps, moving from daylight into gloom. Her guard follows.)*

*(ELEANOR moves down a dark, twisting corridor. She reaches another flight of steps, starts down. Her guard follows.)*

*(The wine-cellar door. The soldier stands by it in the recess, alert. We pull back, taking in the curve of the corridor. ELEANOR rounds the curve, stops and draws back.)*

*(She turns to her guard. He is very close to her now. She nods. They exchange a look of understanding. The guard draws a short, blunt, heavy dagger and starts stealthily forward.)*

*(We see them all: ELEANOR tensely watching; her guard edging forward, pressed along the curving wall; the soldier in the recess, unaware but listening.)*

*(ELEANOR's guard stops just before the recess. He crouches, ready to leap. Both he and the soldier wear armor from the waist up. The guard raises his dagger. His armor squeaks.)*

*(The soldier spins at the sound. The guard leaps. His knife flashes down, glancing harmlessly on the soldier's armor. They face each other in the confines of the recess. There is no room. They feint, armor making the moves heavy and slow. The soldier lunges. His dagger slides and scrapes along the guard's armor, searching for a point of entry. The only sounds are natural ones: grunts, heavy breathing, the clank and rattle of armor, the squeal of dagger points on steel. It's all so clumsy. Every move is graceless. Nothing works. The walls keep getting in the way. They wheeze and stumble. It is ludicrous—and it is this that gives the fight its special horrors.)*

*(ELEANOR's guard is thrown clear of the recess. He lunges back. They fall, rolling and clanking about in the shadowed niche. Slow-moving arms and thrashing legs. We pull back to include ELEANOR. She wills herself to watch. There is a strangled cry. One pair of legs goes into spasm. She goes on watching as her guard rises, keys to the door in hand.)*

*(Deep in the wine cellar, we find JOHN, RICHARD and GEOFFREY. JOHN lies sprawled out, asleep. RICHARD, apparently placid, lies staring at nothing. GEOFFREY sits, tense, his face a picture of concentration. The tiny candle on the floor is guttering out. Echoing down long corridors comes the distant rattle of chains and bolts on the cellar door. JOHN wakes with a start. The others stiffen.)*
*(They exchange looks as the sound of the closing door reverberates and dies, RICHARD is the first to rise.)*

RICHARD. He's here.

*(The others get to their feet. There is nothing to say. RICHARD starts into a low, dark, twisting corridor. The others follow. It is very dark. The corridor curves and curves. We follow as they twist along. Softly, really to himself, RICHARD mutters.)*

He'll get no satisfaction out of me. He isn't going to see me beg.

GEOFFREY. Why, you chivalric fool—as if the way one fell down mattered.

RICHARD. When the fall is all there is, it matters.

*(They go around a corner. Far ahead of them, we make out an area of brighter light.)*

*(RICHARD, the others just behind him, moves into brighter light. He registers surprise.)*

*(ELEANOR is standing in the center of the large room near the cellar*

*door. Several candles flicker on the walls. She carries the jewel chest.)*

ELEANOR. My barge is leaving any minute and I've come to say goodbye.

GEOFFREY. Does Henry know you're here?

ELEANOR. I've brought you each a little something.

GEOFFREY. What's he planning?

RICHARD. Is he going to keep us here?

ELEANOR *(Moving toward a crude wooden table).* I picked them out especially.

RICHARD. For God's sake, Mother—

*(She slams the chest down on the table. It makes a heavy, meancing, metallic clatter.)*

*(*RICHARD *looks at* ELEANOR.*)*

*(At once he's at the chest, throwing it open. We see a clutter of blunt, heavy, brutal-looking daggers.)*

*(*RICHARD *turns toward* ELEANOR.*)*

RICHARD. How heavy is the outside guard?

ELEANOR. That's taken care of.

RICHARD. What about the courtyard and the gates?

ELEANOR. They're putting Henry's train together and it's chaos. You can walk right out.

RICHARD *(Moving to* JOHN *and* GEOFFREY).* We'll go to Poitiers. He'll expect that but we'll meet him with an army when he comes. Keep close to me and, when you run, run hard.

GEOFFREY. Why run at all? I think we ought to stay.

JOHN. Stay here?

GEOFFREY. 'Til Henry comes.

*(He turns toward* ELEANOR. *Cut to her. Voice over.)*

He will come, won't he—

*(Turning back to his brothers.)*

—and he'll come alone. I count three knives to one.

RICHARD. You think we could?

JOHN. I'd only do it wrong. You kill him and I'll watch.

GEOFFREY. The three of us together. We must all three do it.

*(*ELEANOR *moves angrily to them.)*

ELEANOR. You don't think I'm going to let this happen?

GEOFFREY. If you tell, there'll be a rash of executions and you don't want that. No, you don't want to lose a one of us: not even me.

ELEANOR. You're clever but I wonder if you're right.

GEOFFREY. You warn him, it's the end of us: you warn him not and it's the end of him. It's that clear.

ELEANOR *(She turns to* RICHARD).* Take the knives and run.

RICHARD. No. Geoffrey's right; we'll stay.

ELEANOR. You, too? Oh, Richard.

RICHARD *(Striding to the knives).* Spare me that. You brought these things.

*(He picks one up, holds it out toward her.)*

You want him dead, you do it.

*(Cut to* ELEANOR, *close up. Spitting it at him.)*

ELEANOR. You unnatural animal.

*(*RICHARD *starts moving slowly toward* ELEANOR. *When he gets close to her, she starts edging away, back toward the dank stone walls. he follows, pressing her.)*

RICHARD. Unnatural, Mummy? You tell me, what's Nature's way? If poisoned mushrooms grow and babies come with crooked backs, if goiters thrive and dogs go mad and wives kill husbands, what's unnatural? Here stands your lamb. Come cover him with kisses. He's all yours.

ELEANOR. No, you're not mine. I'm not responsible.

RICHARD. Where do you think I learned this from? Who do you think I studied under? How old was I when you fought with Henry first?

ELEANOR. Young . . . I don't know.

RICHARD. How many battles did I watch?

ELEANOR. But those were battles, not a knife behind a door.

RICHARD. I never heard a corpse ask how it got so cold. What were you thinking when you fought with him?

*(She is against the wall now, pressed to the damp stones. He keeps moving in until their faces are inches apart.)*

ELEANOR. Of you.

RICHARD. Of your unnatural animal?

ELEANOR. I did it all for you.

RICHARD. You wanted Father dead.

ELEANOR. No, never that.

RICHARD. You tried to kill him, didn't you?

ELEANOR. Yes!

RICHARD. Why?! What did you want?!

ELEANOR. I wanted Henry back.

*(It is an answer he cannot bear. He turns away, moving out of the picture.)*

RICHARD. You lie.

ELEANOR. I wanted Henry.

*(She looks about, eyes on her children.)*

*(The sound of chains and bolts being drawn is heard. ELEANOR stiffens, tense.)*

*(The boys freeze.)*

*(We're at the door as ELEANOR's guard opens it. We see HENRY's head only—his face ashen, his eyes un-* *blinking, fixed straight ahead—as he passes through the door. ALAIS, holding a lighted taper, follows.)*

*(The boys hear the door close. GEOFFREY, the first to recover, looks at RICHARD, RICHARD looks back, ready to do the deed if GEOFFREY is. Then, suddenly, JOHN is running, racing to the chest. He slams the lid down just as—*

HENRY *moves into view. He carries a load of large candles in his arms. ALAIS, holding a lighted taper, follows him. He pauses, peers about and then announces:)*

HENRY. It wants light.

*(He begins moving about the area, placing candles in empty candlesticks. ALAIS follows, lighting them with her taper. He doesn't seem to see his sons as he passes by them. They, however, are on wires, at the brink, not quite sure how or when to make their move.)*

What we do in dungeons needs the shades of day. I stole the candles from the chapel. No one minded. Jesus won't begrudge them and the Chaplain works for me.

*(He stops by ELEANOR.)*

ELEANOR. You look dreadful.

HENRY. So do you.

ELEANOR. I underslept a little.

HENRY *(We pull back, including them all, as HENRY deposits his last candle and steps back to survey the effect)*. We can all rest in a little while. That's better. Bright and clear, just like the morning.

*(His eyes traveling from son to son, meaning it.)*

Fine-looking boys.

RICHARD *(Striding angrily into the picture)*. What do you want from us? You must be mad. Why did you have to come here? Damn you, why'd you come?

HENRY. You were the best

*(Indicating* ELEANOR.*)*

I told her so.

*(To* JOHN.*)*

You—you, I loved.

RICHARD. You're going to lock us up.

*(*HENRY *neither nods nor shakes his head.)*

You've got to. You can't ever let me out. You know you can't. I'll never stop.

HENRY. I can't stop either.

*(*RICHARD *and* HENRY *stand, eyes locked.* RICHARD *turns sharply away, looks toward—*GEOFFREY, *close up. He is white with tension. Will he do it? Won't he?)*

*(As for* JOHN, *he's terrified.)*

*(*RICHARD *flies across the room toward the chest.)*

*(*HENRY *draws his dagger.)*

*(*RICHARD *throws the chest open and grabs a dagger. He looks at—*

GEOFFREY. *He hasn't moved. Nor is he going to.)*

*(*JOHN *is ready to cry.)*

*(*HENRY *strides toward* RICHARD *and chest.)*

Brave boys. That's what I've got.

*(At the chest, he picks up a dagger and tosses it to* GEOFFREY. *And another which he tosses to* JOHN.*)*

*(The boys are spread out in a semicircle. They have daggers in hand but none of them moves.)*

*(*HENRY *crouches, ready for them all, wanting them all to come at him.)*

Come on. What is it? Come for me!

*(*ALAIS, *stiff with fear, stands pressed against a wall.* ELEANOR, *her face a mask, only her eyes alive, registers no change as—*

HENRY *starts slowly moving across the room toward* RICHARD. *He stops near him, crouching, his dagger held low, close, lethal.* RICHARD *makes no move.)*

What's wrong? You're Richard, aren't you?

RICHARD. But you're Henry.

JOHN *(Near tears)*. Daddy? Take me back? Please? Can't we try again?

HENRY *(Trying to take in the idea)*. Again?

JOHN. We always have before.

HENRY. Oh, yes . . . we always have.

*(With a cry of joy,* JOHN *drops his dagger and starts running across the room to his father, arms outstretched. He skids to a stop and crumples to the floor as* HENRY, *with a terrible animal sound, starts for him with his dagger.)*

*(*HENRY, *his face dreadful, goes to one knee, crouching over his son, ready to shove the dagger into* JOHN'S *vitals. The man is absolutely going to do the deed.)*

ELEANOR *(Sharp and commanding)*. Go on.

*(*HENRY *turns to look at her as she moves into the picture.)*

Execute them. They're assassins, aren't they? This was treason, wasn't it? You gave them life—you take it.

*(They exchange a long look. Then* HENRY'S *eyes leave her and travel to his sons.)*

*(They are hardly breathing, save for* JOHN, *who is whimpering on the floor.)*

*(*HENRY'S *eyes return to* ELEANOR.*)*

HENRY. Who's to say it's monstrous? I'm the king. I call it just.

(HENRY *turns from her and, alone now, draws his great sword and strikes a ritualistic, formal pose. His face shines with sweat and his eyes are mad.*)

Therefore, I, Henry, by the grace of God, King of the English, Lord of Scotland, Ireland and Wales,

(*We see the whole room.* JOHN *makes little animal sounds of fear.* GEOFFREY *believes he's done for but is still trying to think of a way out.* RICHARD *is ready to die with dignity and style.*)

Count of Anjou, Brittany, Poitou and Normandy, Maine, Gascony and Aquitaine, do sentence you to death.

(*Then to* HENRY *close up, still in his pose.*)

Done this Christmas Day at Chinon in God's year eleven eight-three.

(*As he lowers his sword, we cut back to see them all. In a formal, measured way,* HENRY *moves across the damp stone floor to* RICHARD. *It seems a long walk.*)

(*Cut to* HENRY *and* RICHARD, *close, as* HENRY *comes to a stop before him.* RICHARD, *eyes unswervingly on his father, stands motionless.* HENRY *slowly raises his sword—higher, higher—With a howling cry,* HENRY *brings the sword whistling down, flat edge against* RICHARD'S *shoulder. It makes a stinging slap-crack of a sound.*)

(RICHARD *staggers slightly, masking the pain as best he can, staring steadily at his father.* HENRY'S *face is bewildered, as if he has lost contact for a moment, not knowing where he is or what he's doing. The moment hangs suspended as the camera moves to the other faces.* JOHN *still whimpers, unable to grasp what has hap-*

*pened.* GEOFFREY, *eyes bright with anticipation, is still waiting for the violence.* ELEANOR'S *face tells us nothing at all.* ALAIS'S *fear changes suddenly to concern as, with a little grasp, she steps forward, then stops herself. She is looking at—*
HENRY *as, spent and shattered, he sinks slowly to the floor. He sits there seeing nothing.*)

Surely that's not what I intended. Children . . . children are . . . they're all we have.

(*Unable to look at his sons, he waves them from the room.*)

Go on. I'm done, I'm done, I'm finished with you. You and I are finished. Never come again.

(*We draw back to take in the sons.* GEOFFREY *is the first to understand. He gives a short, sharp nod and starts into the shadows toward the cellar door.* JOHN *scurries after him.* RICHARD *hesitates—as if he had something to say but can't—then follows them out the door.*)

ELEANOR. You spare the rod, you'll spoil those boys.
HENRY (*Huddled on the floor*). I couldn't do it, Eleanor.
ELEANOR. Nobody thought you could.
ALAIS (*Moving tenderly to* HENRY). Come rest.
HENRY. I want no women in my life.
ALAIS. You're tired.
HENRY. I could have conquered Europe, all of it, but I had women in my life.

(*To* ALAIS *gruffly.*)

Get out. Go on. Go.

(ALAIS *moves toward the door, out of the picture as* HENRY, *like a great cat, moves to* ELEANOR.)

I should have killed you years ago.

ELEANOR. There's no one peeking. Do it now.

HENRY. You put me here. You made me do mad things. You've bled me.

ELEANOR. Shoulder it yourself. Don't put it on my back. You've done what you have done and no one but yourself has made you do it. Pick it up and carry it. I can. My losses are my work.

HENRY. What losses? I've been cheated, not you. I'm the one with nothing.

ELEANOR. Lost your life's work, have you? Provinces are nothing. Land is dirt. I've lost you and I can't ever have you back again. You haven't suffered. I could take defeats like yours and laugh. I've done it. If you're broken, it's because you're brittle. You are all that I have ever loved. Christ, you don't know what nothing is.

*(A shudder passes through her, like a stab of physical pain.)*

I want to die.

*(HENRY's initial doubt is followed by terrible dismay.)*

HENRY. You don't.

*(She is doubled up by the intensity of it, scarcely able to stand.)*

ELEANOR. I want to die.

HENRY. I'll hold you.

*(She shakes her head, edges away.)*

It might help.

ELEANOR *(Lacking the strength to stand, sinking to the floor)*. I want to die.

HENRY *(Going to one knee beside her)*. Let me do something, damn you. This is terrible.

ELEANOR. Henry, I want to die.

HENRY. You will, you know. Wait long enough and it'll happen.

ELEANOR *(Surprised by a smile she didn't expect)*. So it will.

*(He takes her hand.)*

HENRY. We're in the cellar and you're going back to prison and my life is wasted and we've lost each other and you're smiling.

ELEANOR. It's the way I register despair. There's everything in life but hope.

HENRY. We have each other and, for all I know, that's what hope is.

ELEANOR. We're jungle creatures, Henry, and the dark is all around us. See them?

*(Her eyes range the room.)*

In the corners, you can see the eyes.

HENRY. And they can see ours.

*(HENRY rises to his feet, a picture of enormous strength and majesty.)*

I'm a match for anything. Aren't you?

*(ELEANOR looks up at him with the most profound affection.)*

ELEANOR. I should have been a great fool not to love you.

*(HENRY nods in brisk agreement, bends down, helps her up. They start toward the cellar door.)*
*(We see the prow of ELEANOR's barge. Pulling back, we see HENRY and ELEANOR moving energetically through the mud along the river bank. With surprised delight, ELEANOR is saying:)*

ELEANOR. You'll let me out for Easter?

HENRY. Come the Resurrection, you can strike me down again.

ELEANOR *(Alive again, ready for anything)*. Perhaps I'll do it next time.

HENRY. And perhaps you won't.

ELEANOR. It must be late and I don't want to miss the tide.

*(She sweeps past him, out onto the boat. Lines are cast off, the oarsmen dip their oars. The boat begins to ease out into the river.)*

*(On the bank, eyes never for a moment leaving her,* HENRY *leans forward, shouting)*

HENRY. You know, I hope we never die.

ELEANOR. I hope so, too.

HENRY. You think there's any chance of it?

*(He starts to laugh. She joins him. The music rises and the boat glides toward the center of the sweeping river. We see his laughing face, then hers, eyes never wavering.)*

*(He throws his arms out in a gesture of animal vitality. The boat moves on. But to the end we can see* ELEANOR, *unmoving, eyes on* HENRY, *standing on the shore, arms open to the world.)*

# TERMS OF ENDEARMENT

*Screenplay by James L. Brooks*
*Adapted from the Novel by Larry McMurtry*

| | |
|---|---|
| AURORA GREENWAY | Shirley MacLaine |
| EMMA HORTON | Debra Winger |
| GARRETT BREEDLOVE | Jack Nicholson |
| VERNON DAHLART | Danny DeVito |
| FLAP HORTON | Jeff Daniels |
| SAM BURNS | John Lithgow |
| PATSY CLARK | Lisa Hart Carroll |

Produced and Directed by James L. Brooks
Cinematographer: Andrzej Bartkowiak
Film Editor: Richard Marks
Production Designer: Polly Platt
Costume Designer: Kristi Zea
Music Composed by Michael Gore

In 1983 *Terms of Endearment* won James L. Brooks three Academy Awards—for Best Screenplay (adapted from the novel of the same name by Larry McMurtry), Best Director, and Best Picture. The screenplay is notable for its skill in transferring a rich, very human story from the narrative form to the cinema.

Virtually the first work that Mr. Brooks put together for theatrical film and marking his debut as producer, writer, and director, *Terms of Endearment* is also quite notable for its success both creatively and commercially. We do not usually accord newcomers' works so quickly to the pages of *Best American Screenplays,* because their work is not yet voluminous enough to judge as a body of writing. Be that as it may, we are happy to have *Terms of Endearment* in this anthology, particularly because it is a fine example of adapting a novel to the screen. At first glance, it is easy to make the judgment that adapting a screenplay from a novel is no big deal, since the characters, the plot, and even the tone of the story are already drawn. Mr. McMurtry is a novelist of the highest skill, and he gave Mr. Brooks much to work with. Mr. Brooks did not have to start from scratch as Mr. McMurtry did.

For those of you who are particularly interested in a career as a screenwriter, let me urge you to read Mr. McMurtry's novel first. Then read this screenplay and observe how Mr. Brooks focused, honed, and brought into dramatic life this most potent relationship between Aurora, the mother, and Emma, her daughter, and how they met the challenges that life—and death—had to offer.

In particular, take note of Mr. Brook's outstanding creativity in fashioning the memorable character of Garrett Breedlove, the astronaut, a minor character in the novel, which enables Aurora to achieve a richer dimension than that achieved by Mr. McMurtry—no mean feat, especially as it was done without sacrificing the novelist's conception and realization of her, or his story, in my opinion.

Mr. Brooks was born on May 9, 1940, in Brooklyn, New York. He attended New York University and went to work as a copyboy for CBS News and was soon promoted to a newswriter. In 1966 David Wolper brought him to Hollywood as a documentary writer. In 1970 he became co-creator, co-executive producer, and writer for the "Mary Tyler Moore Show," then went on to do the same for "Rhoda," "Lou Grant," and "Taxi" through the remainder of the seventies. His first feature film was *Starting Over*, which he wrote and produced in 1979. In 1987 he wrote, produced, and directed *Broadcast News*.

*Open on:*

*A black screen, at the lower left hand corner of which shines a small clown's face. It is barely noticeable as we begin titles.*

*The music is bright but not so full that we don't discern with ever-increasing awareness the off-screen voices of a man and a woman,* AURORA *and* RUDYARD GREENWAY.

AURORA *(O.S.).* Let me go, just for a minute.

RUDYARD *(O.S.).* Honey, you been looking at that baby so much, you're gonna stare her right into a coma.

AURORA *(O.S.).* Oh, stop exaggerating!

RUDYARD *(O.S.).* Honey, it's not good for ya to be checkin' on the baby every five minutes, and imaginin' one terrible thing or another.

*The door at screen right opens and we now can recognize from the light flowing in from the hall that we are in a baby's room—the clown's face a small night light. The infant is in a hand-worked, excellent and therefore memorable crib.* AURORA'S *back is to the camera—her rear end a large one, perhaps tempting to some—and her back-lit outline is round and cushy. And now she turns toward the room and is facing the camera, still illuminated from behind—the mother's form we may all remember framed in the doorways of our rooms as we lay helpless and needing.* AURORA *stands still for a beat and then says her first on-screen words.*

AURORA. I know. I know.

RUDYARD *(O.S.).* Here it starts, here we go.

AURORA. Rudyard . . . Rudyard, she's not breathing.

RUDYARD *(O.S.).* Honey, she's sleepin'. The baby's sleepin'.

AURORA. No. Rudyard, it's crib death.

RUDYARD *(O.S.).* It's sleep. She's asleep, honey!

*She pads quietly to her infant daughter's bed and coos softly.*

AURORA. Maybe.

RUDYARD *(O.S.).* Come on.

AURORA *(to* BABY EMMA*).* Emma.

*The infant lies still.* AURORA *leans over . . . then hikes herself up by placing her foot on the mattress so she fully leans over the bars—gracelessly to place her ear almost atop the infant's chest. She had heard something, but doubt still lingers. Very deliberately,* AURORA *pinches the infant, who instantly begins wailing.*

AURORA *(to* BABY EMMA*).* Oh, good.

AURORA *(to herself).* There . . . that's better.

*She moves swiftly from the room and exits without a thought of pacifying the crying baby. As she closes the door:*

*Cut to:*

*Ext.* AURORA'S *House—Eight Years Later—Day*

*A dark two-door car arrives. From the driver's seat steps a* MAN *of forty in a dark blue suit and cowboy boots. He was* RUDYARD'S *employer. He holds a hand out to assist* ROSIE DUNLOP, AURORA'S *maid for years and, though she doesn't know it, the last white maid in Houston. She refuses the hand and he concentrates on the next one out, folding the front seat for* EMMA GREENWAY, *misshapen for a child of eight—her legs too short, her hands too thick, that sort of thing—hair, unusually stringy, is even worse after the sweaty and emotional fu-*

*neral; a black ribbon hangs lifeless in her tresses. She, too, refuses help and indicates that the man should instead help the next occupant. That's* AURORA, *who emerges in black, one hand held by the* MAN, *the other by the maid. The first thing she does on emerging from the car is to remove her shoes. She has her arm around her young daughter as she moves barefoot across the lawn.*

AURORA *(to* MAN*).* No, thank you.

AURORA *is totally composed. The* MAN *stands there granite strong, West Texas' best.*

AURORA *(cont'd) (to* MAN*).* Thanks. *(to* EMMA*)* Emma!

MAN *(to* AURORA*; overlap).* Glad to help. Ah, he was one of the most dependable men that ever worked for us.

EMMA *(to* MAN*).* I know, thank you very much.

MAN *(to* AURORA*).* He was a good man. *(O.S. to* EMMA*)* Hey, I'm real sorry about your daddy. Take care of your Mommy.

EMMA *shifts uncomfortably as her mother looks at her, wanting the man's words to register. She absently removes the ribbon from her hair.*

Int. AURORA'S *Bedroom—Night*

*This room is more a symbol of compromise than a couple's private lair. A single headboard, two twin beds, barely separated, with separate bedding.* AURORA *is vigorously brushing her teeth in the background. There is a great deal of energy about her since she has an emotional obstacle to overcome. Like someone running to the take-off mark in the broadjump, she now marches into the room from the bathroom to get into the one bed which is turned down. She can't do it—it's as if she hits an invisible wall.*

*She makes a sudden detour and sits on the window seat, eyes the two beds, and then walks quickly out of the room.*

Int. AURORA'S *House—Stairwell*

*As she marches down and enters her daughter's room. She goes directly to the child, turns on the lights. An original movie soundtrack of "The Wizard of Oz" is in evidence along with a picture of her father.*

AURORA. Emma. Emma wake up. Please, wake up.

EMMA. What's wrong?

AURORA. I was tense. I was tense, and I was wondering how you were feeling. Would you like to sleep in my bed?

EMMA. No, thank you. Would you like to sleep in my bed again?

AURORA. Yes.

*As* EMMA *makes room and* AURORA *slides in next to her, griping about the number of stuffed animals, she glances at her daughter's limp, stringy tresses.*

AURORA. What will we ever do with your hair?

*She turns out the lights.*

Ext. AURORA'S *Block—Mid-Summer (Eight Years Later)—Day*

EMMA, *sixteen-years old, her hopeless hair unaided by the style of the day, is the kind of high school girl whose near dumpiness seems only a minor hindrance because she so totally accepts it.*

PATSY *(O.S.).* Hey, Emma.

EMMA. Patsy, hurry up, you're gonna miss him!

PATSY CLARK. PATSY *is a bright, blonde Bayou Club beauty. She is athletic, warm and sensitive. Seemingly perfect in every way, with even the good grace to have a bit of a tortured soul.*

*They are sitting on the lawn in their party dresses, protected from the grass by* EMMA'S *white cardigan, which they are sharing.* PATSY *is sitting in a lady-like manner.* EMMA *is unaware that her dress is slightly above her knees, almost exposing her white underwear. They are gawking at some moving men carrying exotic furniture into the house immediately next door. Seeing the moving men looking at* EMMA'S *underpants,* PATSY *jerks* EMMA'S *dress down.*

EMMA. That's what they were lookin' at. *(laughs)*

ROSIE *exits from the side door of the house, having finished her day's work. She is carrying left-over food in a Tupperware container and wearing a rumpled, stained white maid's uniform that shows the effects of having worked eight hours in a hundred-degrees-plus weather.*

ROSIE *(to* EMMA*)*. Good night, honey.

EMMA. Where's Mama?

ROSIE *(matter-of-fact)*. She's out back with that old fart who's trying to get into her pants.

EMMA. Thanks. Aren't you going to wait and see if the astronaut shows up?

ROSIE. Oh, they have one on every block in Houston. Come on, I gotta get my bus.

*She starts off.* EMMA *goes after her and kisses her good night.*

EMMA. Okay. Say hi to Royce for me.

ROSIE. Okay. *(kiss)*

EMMA. Okay.

ROSIE. Love ya. Astronauts.

EMMA *(to* PATSY*)*. So?

PATSY. We better get goin'.

EMMA. Oh, I'm gonna go say good bye to my mother. You wanna go with?

PATSY. No, I don't think I'm up to it today.

EMMA. Sure would be nice to have a mother somebody liked.

*Ext.* AURORA'S *Backyard—Day*

AURORA, *nearing forty, is sadly slouched in a shaded settee, fiddling with a discarded bouquet. Next to her, sitting erectly, is* EDWARD JOHNSON, *fiftyish, wearing Bermuda shorts and a golf hat. As we meet him, he is making a bold move. He puts his hand deliberately on top of* AURORA'S *thigh. She sits up and looks at him. He looks at her hopefully. She points at his hand. He withers and removes it.*

EDWARD. Why don't you face up to the fact that you have certain biological needs?

AURORA *(absently)*. Because I don't.

EMMA *(O.S.)*. I'm going now.

AURORA *(to* EDWARD*)*. Excuse me.

AURORA *goes to* EMMA *and immediately sets to work pulling and tugging* EMMA'S *dress, suddenly distinctly more alive. She annoys her daughter all the more because she is improving her appearance.*

AURORA *spits on her hand to plaster down some stray hairs.*

AURORA *(to* EMMA, *stifles laugh)*. Can you believe it, he wants to . . . take me to Tahiti?

EMMA *(laughs)*. I don't know why you treat these men like this. They have feelings, too. Ouch!

AURORA. You always make so much of things.

EMMA. Ow!

AURORA. Has the astronaut moved in yet?

EMMA. Who?

AURORA. Who? Is Patsy teaching you coy lessons? Breedlove, Garrett. Next door.

AURORA *makes her final adjustment on her daughter—not only shoving her bra straps so they are not in evidence, but tugging each one to hoist her daughter's breasts higher.*

AURORA *(cont'd)*. Has he moved in? Pull your socks up!

EMMA. All right! Come say good bye to Patsy for me.

AURORA. Eleven o'clock. You be home by eleven o'clock. No later than eleven o'clock.

EMMA. Say good bye to Patsy.

AURORA. Good bye, Patsy.

EMMA. Thank you.

PATSY *(O.S.)*. Goodbye, Missus Greenway!

EMMA *kisses her mother good night, then runs toward the driveway to meet* PATSY.

*Ext.* AURORA'S *House—Night*

*We see* AURORA *pacing through her bedroom window.*

*Int.* EMMA'S *Room—Night*

PATSY *and* EMMA *are in jeans, the stuffed animals still in evidence. Ethel Merman's "Anything Goes" is playing as* EMMA *ties together a stack of original cast albums, some blues, some jazz vocals.* EMMA'S *a mark for a good lyric.* PATSY *is rubbing a Marlboro back and forth between her fingers, the tobacco running out into an ashtray. She now begins to stuff the empty cigarette with marijuana. The wedding gown and maid of honor's dress hang prominently in the background.*

EMMA *(O.S.) (in unison with album)*. "In this day and age, anything goes / The times have changed /

And we've often rewound the clock / Since the Puritans got a shock / When they landed on Plymouth Rock / If today, any rock they should try to stem / Instead of landing on Plymouth Rock / Plymouth Rock would land on them."

*Int.* AURORA'S *Room—Night*

*She sits at her window seat eating from a box of chocolates. She is troubled. She sighs, rises and starts downstairs.*

*Int.* EMMA'S *Room—Night*

*The girls are smoking their revised Marlboro. Mary Martin is singing "Cockeyed Optimist" from "South Pacific."*

PATSY. I feel really kind of foolish gettin' stoned to hear Mary Martin.

EMMA. See Patsy, this is Mary Martin, this is not Mary Martin, um, this is Ethel Merman!

PATSY. This is the last time we're gonna be like this.

EMMA. Oh, I just plain refuse to get into that kind of thinking, Patsy. I mean, we're gonna be best friends. Our babies are gonna be best friends. And we're all gonna grow up and be best friends.

*As they hug there is a knock on the door.*

AURORA *(O.S.)*. Emma?

*Instantly the two girls part and grab four aerosol cans and spray the room, a can in each hand.*

EMMA *(to* PATSY*)*. Oh, God! *(to* AURORA*)*. Just a minute, Mom!

AURORA *(O.S.)*. Open the door!

EMMA. Ah. . . .

AURORA *(O.S.)*. Emma?!

EMMA. Yes?

AURORA *(O.S.)*. Would you open the door, please?

EMMA. Ah, just a minute, Mom.

AURORA (*O.S.*). What do you mean? Emma! I need to talk to you!

EMMA. All right! All right! I'm gettin' married, what the hell.

*She opens the door. The marijuana cigarette in her mouth.* PATSY *is hysterical in the background.*

PATSY. Damn!

AURORA (*O.S.*) (*to* EMMA). Would you meet me in my room?

*We hear her walk away.* EMMA *is curious and a bit apprehensive.*

EMMA (*to* AURORA). Yes. (*to* PATSY) Whadda ya think she wants?

PATSY. I don't know, maybe . . . she's gonna tell ya how to have sex.

EMMA. She's gonna what? (*laughs*) No, she only knows how to avoid it. Okay, move.

PATSY. I can't believe you said that.

EMMA. I didn't mean it. I didn't mean it, I swear.

*She kisses* PATSY.

*Int.* AURORA's *Room—Night*

AURORA *sitting under her favorite painting—a small Renoir of two handsome women wearing hats and gowns. She looks grim.*

AURORA (*O.S.*). What have you been doing, Emma?

EMMA. Nothing. What is it, Mama? I really would like to get some sleep, you know, so I could look halfway decent for tomorrow. Go on, what is it?

AURORA. You wouldn't want me to be silent about something that's for your own good, even if it might hurt a little, would you?

EMMA. Yes, ma'am, I certainly . . . would.

*She dashes out, closing the door behind her. We hear her laughing, giddy—high on life, Texas weed and her own wit.* AURORA *is thrown by the totally unexpected behavior. She starts after* EMMA *who reappears, still having a great time.*

Okay, come on. Come on. Come on.

AURORA *can't say what she has to in this atmosphere. Sulky and beleaguered, she retreats to the comfort of her window seat. It looks out on her garden; it is soft and well-cushioned and safe.* EMMA *moves to join her.* AURORA *looks at her, examining her daughter's face, liking the eyes, the round cheeks, distressed with the limp hair.*

AURORA. I've been in here all night. I've been trying to decide what . . . what wedding gift to get you. I thought of that Renoir, that my mother gave me.

EMMA *waits her out.*

But I couldn't reach a conclusion. And then I came to grips with the reason why I couldn't think of a wedding gift . . . for you.

EMMA. Oh, Mama, it's all right. I need dishes of any kind, Corning Ware, rotisserie . . . the car . . . a house.

AURORA. Emma, I'm totally convinced if you marry Flap Horton tomorrow . . . it will be a mistake of such gigantic proportions it will ruin your life and make wretched your destiny.

EMMA *reacts.*

EMMA. Why are you doin' this to me?

AURORA. You are not special enough to overcome a bad marriage. Emma . . . use your brains. Flap is limited. He hasn't got any imagination. Even at this age all he wants is . . . a secure teaching job.

EMMA. No, Mother, anybody can do this to anybody. God, hurting people is so easy. I'm marrying Flap

Horton tomorrow. I thank God for Flap, for getting me outta here. And I think if this is your attitude, you shouldn't bother showing up at my wedding.

AURORA. Hum. That's . . . that's right. No, I think you're right. The, the hypocrisy was bothering me, too.

EMMA. My own mother's not coming to my wedding.

EMMA *exits in disbelief.*

*Ext.* FLAP *and* EMMA'S *Home—Day*

*This is a garage apartment.* EMMA *sits at the top of the stairs with her new husband, still half dressed in the clothes they were married in, a bit drunk from champagne, with their belongings inside awaiting the setting up of housekeeping if energy ever strikes. The air is extraordinarily sensual.* FLAP *is twenty-three and looks like a nice guy. The phone begins ringing.*

EMMA. Listen to her, she's goin' crazy. I'm gonna give her till noon tomorrow. That's about all she could take.

FLAP *(as if to a simpleton).* Emma, your mother boycotted your wedding. She hates your husband and she only holds you in medium esteem.

EMMA. "Medium esteem"—that is so cute. That is so cute.

*She gives him a little kiss, and hand-in-hand they walk across their threshold.*

*Int.* FLAP *and* EMMA'S *Home—Day*

*Books are stacked in piles, most of them paperbacks. As they move past the stacks:*

EMMA. Oh, wouldn't it have been strange if one of us married a person who didn't read, I mean, God, there's millions of interestin' people out there

who just never pick up a book. Flap, I feel so totally good about us. I hope I get pregnant tonight.

FLAP. That would be nice. Emma, um . . . I love the way you look. You were j— . . . you're so nice. You're my sweet-ass gal.

EMMA. Oh. *(sighs)*

FLAP *embraces her in good-natured sexuality and moves her toward the mattress lying on the floor without a box spring. We are waist high on* EMMA *as her husband lifts her bridal gown. As it covers her head and* EMMA *disappears in a white cloud, the telephone continues to ring.*

Here comes the bride. How do you do that?

FLAP. Eh, well. . . .

EMMA. Wait, Flap, where'd you learn how to do that?

FLAP. Quit moving.

EMMA. Flap.

*Int.* EMMA'S *Apartment—Morning*

EMMA *and* FLAP *have just finished making love again.* EMMA'S *wedding dress is carefully laid over some boxes of books.* FLAP'S *tuxedo is on another pile of books. The phone is ringing—the ringing is ignored by the newlyweds.*

FLAP. That is the strangest music to make love to.

EMMA. I know.

*He smiles and reaches next to him for a paperback book.* FLAP *makes a sour face.* EMMA *decides to answer. She leans across* FLAP. *The phone is on its eighteenth ring.*

EMMA. I'm not ready to forgive you. I'm happy—leave me alone. I don't want to talk now.

*She starts to hang up, then reconsiders.*

Oh, did you see the tablecloth Rosie made me? Oh, it's beautiful . . . No, not yet . . . I thought omelettes . . . No, I'll do them sort of Tex-Mex. I don't feel like talking now . . . No, I mean it. That was the worst thing you ever did to me . . . Well, I think you owe my husband an apology . . . Well, until you do tell it to my husband, I'm not going to listen to any of your gossip . . . He's right here, hold on.

FLAP *gestures he wants no part of the phone.* EMMA *mimes that he must do this. He shakes his head.*

FLAP. No.
EMMA. Yes.
FLAP. No.
EMMA. Yes.
FLAP. No. No!
EMMA. Yes!

*Finally she wins the debate,* FLAP *taking the phone.* EMMA'S *concentration on his end of the conversation is extraordinary.*

FLAP. Hello, Mrs. Greenway . . . No, ma'am, I'm not enjoying your predicament.
EMMA *(shouting toward phone).* Mama, you be nice! I swear!
FLAP *(overriding her).* As a matter of fact, I don't need or desire an apology. All I want is for you to understand and appreciate my position, to respect our marriage and to maybe wait another fifteen minutes before you call in the morning . . . Yes, I guess I've said my piece . . . Okay. I'll put her on.

EMMA *gives him a big kiss, takes the phone.*

EMMA. He's so great! I told you! I'll talk to you later, all right?

*She hangs up.*

*Int.* AURORA'S *Bedroom—Window Seat—Day*

*As* AURORA *hangs up the phone, she hears the noise of vulgar male "walla" from outside. She looks out the window.*

*Int./Ext. Street—*GARRETT'S *House—Day—*AURORA'S *POV*

*An all-night party breaking up. A motley group of spent revelers saying goodbye to* GARRETT *at the door. He accepts their embraces while holding a waste basket full of empty liquor bottles in the other hand. Now he restrains one girl, bidding her to stay; she nods acquiescence. She waits for him while he happily goes around to the side of the house—the driveway adjoining* AURORA'S*—and removes the lid from one of his main garbage cans to empty his container into it. He misses. The bottles crash. He looks at the mess, then does some twinkle-toe through broken glass, running back to the girl. She laughs.*

*Int.* AURORA'S *Bedroom*

*As she looks at him with disgust, then pulls shut the Venetian blinds.*

*Int.* EMMA'S *Apartment—Several Months Later—Dusk*

*It's furnished now—hand-crafted bookcases, bed, etc.* EMMA *enters from the bathroom.*

EMMA *(to* FLAP*).* I bought you somethin'.
FLAP. What?

*She hands him a box. He opens the cover and finds a tie.*

FLAP. A tie. Emma. You didn't buy this tie for me. You were worried about how I was gonna look to your mother. Now, I wish you would stop being such a quisling where she is concerned.

EMMA *is hurt as she looks at him.*

EMMA. Why is it every time I get happy you turn perverse?

FLAP. Buying this tie made you happy?

EMMA. Yes. Yes! I wish you would understand this, 'cause you really don't. I mean, it made me very happy buying this tie! I went to two or three places before I finally found the right place. And then describing your jacket to the salesman. And knowing how perfect it would match with what you were wearing. Which, by the way, it certainly does. I mean, it was fun! It was goddamn Mardi Gras, and you're just too dumb to understand that kind of happiness.

FLAP. I'm sorry, I'm just, I'm being terrible. It's, it's going to your mother's. It makes me a little irrational.

*Int.* AURORA'S *House—Night*

AURORA *during the last tense moments before she serves dinner.*

FLAP *(to* AURORA*).* Can I help?

AURORA. Yes! Thank you Flap. Would you take this candle in to Emma, I need another one.

FLAP. In the kitchen?

AURORA. Yes.

FLAP. That looks great.

FLAP *reaches in and dips a cracker into the beautiful pate* AURORA *has just set out. She reacts.*

*We see* ROSIE *and* PATSY *in the background and* VERNON DAHLART, *a short Texan in a suede jacket and expensive boots.* EDWARD *approaches* AURORA.

EDWARD. Who is that short gentleman?

AURORA. Not that it's any of your business, but . . . let's leave it at that.

EDWARD *approaches* VERNON.

EDWARD *(to* VERNON*).* What are you lookin' at? She isn't there anymore.

VERNON. She'll be back.

EDWARD. I'm Edward Johnson, Aurora's friend.

VERNON. I'm Vernon Dahlart. God, isn't she something? I'm tongue-tied around her. You, too?

EDWARD. How long have you known Aurora?

VERNON. I met her two weeks ago at church. First time I saw her, my knees buckled. You might say she's God's gift to Vernon Dahlart.

EDWARD. Then you like her?

VERNON. Oh, no, does it show?

*Int. Dining Room—Night*

*They are all seated and halfway through the meal.*

EDWARD. Good food.

AURORA. I used to serve this when I lived in Boston. You haven't said a word, Vernon.

VERNON. Is that right? I feel like I haven't stopped talking since I came in. I guess it's because I've been thinking about you so much.

AURORA. Vernon, can I give you a suggestion on how to handle me?

VERNON. Yes, ma'am.

AURORA. Don't worship me until I've earned it.

VERNON. Thank you ma'am, I appreciate any advice that you give me.

AURORA. And don't talk with your mouth full, Vernon.

*He pretends to take the food from his mouth and hold it in his hand.* AURORA *cringes.* VERNON *opens his hand to reveal it is empty.*

VERNON. I wouldn't do that. Really.

EMMA *laughs.*

VERNON. I just did it to make you laugh.

AURORA. Put your hand down. *(to EMMA)*. What's wrong with you?

EMMA. I got some good news.

AURORA. What's that?

EMMA. I'm unofficially pregnant. Well, we haven't gotten the tests back yet, but you know me. I'm never late.

AURORA. Well! No, I don't, ah, understand.

EMMA. Um . . . if you're not happy for me I'm gonna get so mad . . . if you're not happy.

*The truth comes out of AURORA in a shriek, which jolts the diners.*

AURORA *(to EMMA)*. Why should I, why should I be happy about being a grandmother?!!!

*Several beats of silence. Then:*

FLAP *(to AURORA)*. Does this mean you won't be knitting the baby any booties?

PATSY *stifles a laugh.*

AURORA. Flap . . . every time you get more than two drinks in you, you confront me! *(with a cry in her voice)* And I won't have it. I won't have it, not in this house!

*Sound of hit.*

Excuse me.

AURORA *rises and stalks out.*

*Ext.* AURORA'S *House—Night*

AURORA *walks the lawn barefooted under the stars. This moment staggers her. She moves into a darker area so that we can just see her, but we hear her sighing, collecting herself. Suddenly she is illuminated by headlights as a long Lincoln pulls into the bordering driveway.*

*Angle on car as it stops. We see* GARRETT *in the passenger seat sitting beside two beautiful and beautifully-dressed* YOUNG WOMEN. *They're almost as young as the girls we've seen him with earlier, but there is a great difference. They are privileged, upper strata young women. The world owes them a living and it has shown every intention of paying up.*

DORIS. Do you need some help?

GARRETT *(a drunken slur)*. No, ah, I'll be fine just as s-soon as I stretch my legs.

*He opens the car door and falls flat on his face. He laughs.* DORIS *leans out the window. She has obviously had her hands full with him for a good part of the evening.*

DORIS. Oh, God. Mister Breedlove . . . you're bleeding.

GARRETT. Yeah. It's okay. Come on in.

DORIS. No.

GARRETT. What're you afraid of, Doris?

AURORA *has almost forgotten herself and her problems to take a few steps closer where she stands, taking everything in.*

DORIS. Afraid?

GARRETT. Well, then, Doris, why not come in?

DORIS. Because you're much older than the boys I date, because you're drunk, because when I went there tonight to see a United States astronaut give a lecture, I didn't expect him to prowl after us all night long. I didn't expect some silly flirt who has to keep his jacket open because his belly's getting to big. I expected a hero.

GARRETT *(indignantly)*. Okay, Doris, don't come in. I don't want you in my house. *(hopefully addressing other girl)* Lee Anne, would you like to come in?

LEE ANNE. You'd better tend to that cut.

*The car moves off.*

*Int.* AURORA'S *Laundry Room—Three Years Later—Day*

EMMA, *five months pregnant, is doing her laundry.* AURORA *is looking out the window at her grandson.* TOMMY, *now a toddler, is moving after* ROSIE, *who darts away from him.*

EMMA (*to* TOMMY). Tommy, show me your belly. Come on. Come on!

AURORA (*to* EMMA). How can you let him run around dressed like that?

EMMA. He's adorable. Look at him. Uh-oh. (*mimicks* TOMMY, *laughing*) Uh-oh. Get it, Tommy. Uh-oh.

*The phone rings, jolting* AURORA *from her reverie.* EMMA *picks it up.*

AURORA (*to* EMMA). That's Vernon, I'm sure, so tell him that I'm . . . ah . . .

EMMA. Out?

AURORA (*to* EMMA). No. Tell him I'm resting.

EMMA. Hello . . . Hi, Flap! . . . Where?! . . . No, tell me now! I wanna know now! . . . Oh, Flap, you did not expect I'd be happy. Let's be honest with each other before . . . we start pretending . . . Um, look, Mom's starin' at me right now, so, ah, can I talk about it later to ya? . . . Yeah. All right. 'Bye.

*She hangs up. The phone is barely on the cradle, then:*

AURORA. How long are you going to keep this a secret?

EMMA. The only school that's accepted Flap as an associate professor is in Des Moines.

AURORA *has a dark moment, then mutters to herself.*

AURORA. He can't even do the simple things—like fail locally.

EMMA *is briefly pissed at her mother.*

EMMA. It's gonna be fine, Mama. It's Des Moines.

*Ext.* EMMA'S *Apartment—Day*

*An open trailer filled with their furniture is attached to the rear of the Horton's Nash Rambler.* PATSY'S *car and* AURORA'S *Chrysler are in evidence.*

FLAP (*to* TOMMY). Say, bye-bye house.

TOMMY. Bye-bye house.

AURORA (*to* EMMA). Be careful comin' down these steps. I don't want ya to break your leg.

FLAP, *holding* TOMMY *in his arms, leads the family down the stairs, all helping to carry boxes and luggage, for the leave-taking.* EMMA, *carrying hand luggage and very pregnant, follows* FLAP, *as do* PATSY, ROSIE *and* AURORA. PATSY, EMMA *and* ROSIE *fall into each other's arms, hugging and kissing as* AURORA *stands near by.*

PATSY. Okay, come here. (*soft moan*)

ROSIE. Stay sweet, honey.

AURORA. Rosie. Ah, that's enough, Rosie, they have to get started.

EMMA (*to* ROSIE). You tell Mama to drive you home when you work late. Have some fun, Rosie. (*to* AURORA) Don't act so brave. I know you're gonna go crazy without me to nag.

AURORA. Well, I'm glad someone's able to be in a joking mood.

*As* EMMA *and* AURORA *move to car, we see* PATSY *go to* FLAP, *who is standing near the front of car. They embrace.* PATSY *breaks away.*

PATSY. You be good to her, or else we're gonna get you! I mean it!

AURORA. 'Bye, Flap. Have a good drive.

FLAP *kisses* AURORA *on the cheek.*

EMMA *(to* TOMMY*).* Okay, fingers and toes in. Take Mama's purse.

EMMA *and* AURORA *move to rear car door, embrace.* EMMA *breaks away as* AURORA *continues to hug her.*

EMMA. Oh . . . that's the first time I stopped hugging first. I like that.
AURORA. Get yourself a decent maternity dress.
EMMA *(whispers).* Had to get one in, didn't ya?

AURORA, *still standing at rear of car, calls to* PATSY *near front of car.*

AURORA. Will you tell her, Patsy? She keeps thinking it's me when I say those things.

AURORA *turns to* TOMMY. *He stares at her. They are not close.*

Tom . . . are you going to be good to your mother and take care of her?

*She pats his head absently.*

TOMMY. 'Bye, Missus Greenway.
AURORA *(to* TOMMY*).* Good bye.

ROSIE, *at rear of car, starts to cry and slowly move away.* PATSY *turns to* EMMA, *who is now in the front seat of the car.*

PATSY. Write as soon as you get there so I know your address and all. Okay?
EMMA. You shape up, Patsy.
TOMMY *(to others).* Oops! Dropped my gum.
AURORA *(to* TOMMY*).* Well, we'll get it later.
EMMA *(to* TOMMY*).* Oh, we'll get ya another piece, sweetheart.

AURORA *kisses* EMMA.

AURORA. The phone bill is gonna be enormous, you know that?
EMMA *(to* AURORA, *with a cry in her voice).* I'll miss you, Mama.

AURORA *stifles a sob.*

FLAP. Can we go now?
EMMA. Yeah. Pull away slow.

*The squeal of tires.* FLAP, *in the driver's seat, pulls out fast and we see all waving goodbyes.* AURORA *and* PATSY *are left standing together with just the length of the car separating them.* PATSY *starts to move toward* AURORA. AURORA, *seeing this, quickly turns away from* PATSY *and moves off. This leaves* PATSY *alone as we move in to CU on* PATSY, *staring off at the receding car.*

EMMA'S *POV*

*Her mother,* PATSY *and* ROSIE *disappearing from sight.*

*Int.* FLAP'S *Car—Day*

EMMA *looking for the right radio station.* FLAP *driving.*

FLAP. Honey.

*She looks at him.*

I think it's going to be good for us to be away from your—our—families.

EMMA *nods, edges closer to him.*

TOMMY. I miss Houston.
EMMA. You don't know how lucky you are. Everybody wants to go to Des Moines. People come from all over the world to get one look at Des Moines before they die. Some people think it's the best city in Iowa.

FLAP *grins at her.*

TOMMY. I know you're teasing. Texas is the best.

EMMA *gets on her knees and begins to fix up a bed for* TOMMY *in the back seat. As she does so . . .*

EMMA. Stop worrying. We're going to see terrific new things.

*As she turns back, her eye is caught and her spirit jolted by something out the window.*

EMMA'S POV

*A sign lit by a billboard lamp. It reads,* YOU ARE NOW LEAVING TEXAS.

*Ext.* AURORA'S *House—Day*

AURORA *upset—barefoot, walking her backyard, working the garden. We hear a man running, whooping, then the splash of water, then swimming, then a man emerging from a pool.* AURORA *does not approve.*

AURORA *(yelling for quiet).* Would you please . . . if you will, hold it down over there?

GARRETT *(O.S).* Sorry, I can't . . . hear you.

AURORA. Hold it down! Have some respect for other people's feelings!

GARRETT *(O.S.).* Come over a little closer! Hey, you in the bush, I can't hear ya!

GARRETT, *toweling himself, naked to the waist, at least from what we can see, comes to the fence separating the property.*

I'm sorry, but I just took a sauna, and it's real hard not to yell when ya hit that cold water.

*She nods and continues puttering, unnerved by his near presence.*

You're not going to ignore me when I speak directly to you?

AURORA. I'm not ignoring you. What am I supposed to say? Okay. I suppose it is hard not to yell when you hit that cold water.

*He grins, muses whether to confess something to her. She has turned away.*

GARRETT. Hey, ah, come here.

AURORA *(turning).* Come here?

*She almost looks straight at him but is unable to and busies herself again.*

GARRETT. What is your name—Aurora?

AURORA. Yes.

GARRETT. You want a shock?

AURORA. No, not especially. What?

GARRETT. Well . . . we're gonna have this, ah . . . dinner, NASA dinner, at the White House. And, you know, some cosmonauts and all of us and, ah . . . I didn't know who I could take. 'Cause all the people that I flew with, well, their wives are givin' me "bitch bites" all up and down my back if I showed up with one of my regular girls. I didn't know anybody old enough, so I thought, well, I'll, I'll ask my next door neighbor.

*She looks at him with astonishment.*

*(easily)* Well, then . . . well, anyway, they cancelled the dinner. But I was really thinkin' about askin' ya out, seriously. Ain't that a shocker? Huh?

AURORA. Yes. Imagine you having a date with someone where it wasn't necessarily a felony.

GARRETT. What would you have said if I asked ya? Seriously.

AURORA—*just a bit unnerved—thinks for a beat, then:*

AURORA. I would have said I'd like to see the White House.

GARRETT. So you would have gone.

*She starts in.*

What the hell? You want to have dinner out sometime?

AURORA *(too fast).* No, thank you.

GARRETT. What about lunch? Ladies like you have lunch a lot, don't you?

*She turns, suspecting she's being teased, ready to be angry.* AURORA *walks to her shoes and picks them up. She wiggles her toes in the grass, looks at the attractive, grinning man.*

AURORA. You know, there's something about your manner . . . it's like you . . . you're . . . you're trying to toy with me.

GARRETT. That's right, Aurora. I'm playing with you.

*She crosses to him, then stops a few feet away.*

AURORA. No, this is the element. This is exactly . . .

GARRETT *(cutting her off).* Do you wanna play, Aurora? Wanna go to lunch? *(softly)* Wanna have lunch?

AURORA. Well, if you want to have lunch with me in some restaurant so we could improve the atmosphere in this neighborhood, I wouldn't exactly say no.

GARRETT *gestures to her.*

GARRETT. Come here. We're too far apart to talk.

*She moves closer to the fence, trying to seem amused and patronizing when she actually feels terrified and 16 years old.*

GARRETT. Now, Aurora, since you've agreed . . . *(pause)* Why don't we just forget about the rest of it. I mean, I know how ya feel, and all, there were countdowns when I had my doubts. But I said to myself, you agreed to do it, you're strapped in, and you're in the hands of something bigger and more powerful than yourself. So, ah, why not just lay back and enjoy the ride?

AURORA. I am not going. There is something wrong with you.

*She half-runs to the house.* GARRETT *chuckles.*

GARRETT. Oh, God, I'm such a shit . . .

*Ext.* HORTON *House—Des Moines —Six* A.M.

*We are looking through bug-splattered glass—the windshield of the* HORTON'S *car, the bug bodies so prominent that they lend irony to* EMMA'S *first comment on her new home.*

FLAP. Wait a minute, wait a minute, that must be it right over there.

EMMA. Where? There? Oh, God! Oh Flap, it's great. Is that it really? Oh, it's great. Isn't that sweet?!

TOMMY. Oh, that was a bump.

EMMA. Yeah.

TOMMY. What is that?

EMMA. Shall we go see the house? You stay here, I'll come around and get you.

*Ext.* HORTON *House—Day*

*The house is simple, close-set on either side to very similar homes.* FLAP *begins toting the many boxes inside while* EMMA *struggles to manage* TOMMY'S *absolutely dead weight out of the rear seat of their two-door car.*

FLAP *(to* TOMMY, *overlap).* Let's go see.

EMMA *(to* TOMMY*).* Stay right there.

FLAP *unhooks* TOMMY'S *seat belt.*

FLAP *(to* TOMMY*).* Let me get this off. Come on, let's get it off.

*Finally, she gets him on her shoulder and moves on wobbly legs toward the front door of her new home while her husband carries in two stacks of books. There is in her a growing excitement. This far away from her mother, there comes a vague feeling of extra power, a kind of maturity.*

EMMA. Come on! Whoa! Come on.

FLAP *exits rear door.* EMMA *lifts* TOMMY *out of car.*

EMMA (*cont'd*). Come on. Oh!

TOMMY *trips*.

EMMA (*cont'd*). Come on, sweetheart. Did you hurt yourself?
TOMMY. Nope. Not yet!
EMMA. Do you like it? Do you like it?

EMMA *and* TOMMY *open door to house as* FLAP *follows them up the steps*.

EMMA (*cont'd*). Oh, it's great. Flap, it's great.

FLAP *takes hold of the door, pauses, and then enters house*.

*Dissolve to:*

*Int.* HORTON *House—Several Hours Later—Day*

EMMA'S *happy as she and* FLAP *get into spoon-style sleeping position. Even though the shade is down, the sun is up and the room is fairly well illuminated.*

EMMA. Well, leave the mattress down here. We can sleep here. Oh, I'm really tired.

FLAP *lays his knee on her swollen belly. She reacts.*

EMMA (*cont'd*). Ow, ow.

FLAP *moves his leg*.

FLAP. Oh.

EMMA *sighs*.

FLAP. You ever made love in Iowa?
EMMA. Oh, you know what's great? Tommy's room is clear on the other side of the hall, so we can get as noisy as we want.
FLAP. Oh, good, honey, you get to make your little, high-pitched squeak. (*imitates* EMMA) Oh, oh, oh.
EMMA. Stop it!

*Sound of hand on mouth.*

EMMA (*cont'd*). What about you? What about you? (*imitates* FLAP) Here I come! Here I come again. Yes! Yes! Yes!
FLAP (*sexy, soft*). Oh, God, here I come again. Yes—yes—yes.
EMMA. Oh, God, you just made me wet. How can you do that with your voice, just like that?

*They kiss.*

EMMA (*cont'd*). You just make your voice like that. Oh, God, if Tommy can't hear us, we can't hear Tommy.

*She gets out of bed. He scowls at her.*

FLAP. He's fine, Mother.
EMMA. Oh, don't get pissy, I'll be right back.

*On* EMMA

*As she moves through the house made maze-like by cartons and boxes. She stops at* TOMMY'S *door, then deliberately catches herself and stops herself from entering. As she walks back to her own room and husband:*

*Dissolve to:*

*Int.* HORTON *House—Six Months Later—February, 1974—Morning*

*Some furniture has been purchased, the place homey. It's notably different from Houston; as* FLAP *has moved from poor student to poorer teacher, his furnishings have kept pace. We are looking at* TOMMY *who is taking on the sophistication of an aging toddler (about 3 ½ years old). We hear* FLAP AND EMMA'S *conversation from their bedroom, as does* TOMMY, *who is not especially interested. They are talking in loud whispers.*

FLAP (*O.S.*). I have eight or nine papers left to grade—this isn't love, it's selfishness.

EMMA *(O.S)*. It's been almost a week since we've been together. We've never gone a whole week, Flap.

*Int.* HORTON's *Bedroom—Morning*

EMMA *in bed, pulling on her dressed husband's arm. Even though they have conflicting priorities at this moment, this is more fun than argument. The reason they're whispering is apparent in the background, where we see* EMMA'S *old crib holding her baby,* TEDDY, *about 5 months old.*

FLAP. Sure, we've gone a week.

EMMA. No, only in the real pregnant months. And you're always getting home so late, Flap. Forget it. Just do me a favor. Don't make me feel silly and I won't make you feel guilty, all right?

FLAP. Fair enough. I have to hurry.

*Int.* HORTON's *Outer Room— Morning*

FLAP *gives his son a kiss on the way out.*

FLAP. Be a good boy.

TOMMY *watches his father leave, then watches his mother enter from the bedroom. She is blowing her nose, having just cried a little bit.* TOMMY *is about to speak, then hears the noise of his father returning.* FLAP *takes* EMMA *by the hand.*

FLAP. Emma!

EMMA *(gleefully)*. I absolutely love that you came back! You're saving our lives. Do you know, you're saving our lives by doing this. I love that you came back, Flap. I love it! *(to* TOMMY*)* Tommy, breakfast will be ready for . . . in a minute. You just wait right there.

FLAP. Let's hurry. I gotta grade those papers.

EMMA. Oh, gosh, I just can't believe it!

FLAP. I'll just give everybody a "B."

*The bedroom door closes behind them.* TOMMY *walks to the door and outside.*

*Ext.* HORTON's *House—Day*

*As* TOMMY *sits on the steps we hear the faint sound of a woman's squeak.*

*Int.* AURORA's *Bedroom—Morning—5 Years Later—Winter 1978–79*

AURORA *enters bearing a tray— coffee, fresh rolls and small chocolate cakes. She sets the tray down near her window seat, plumps a pillow, gets in position and picks up the phone.*

*Int.* HORTON *House—Day*

*It is quite early.* EMMA *(now four months pregnant with* MELANIE*) is looking out her front window. The alarm clock goes off in the bedroom. Almost simultaneously, the phone starts to ring.*

*Only one side of the bed looks slept in. She picks up the phone so that it stops ringing, and then before saying anything puts it down, turns off the alarm clock, then returns to the phone.*

EMMA *(into phone, anxiously)*. Hello . . . Oh, hi, Mother. Could we talk later? I've got the boys to get off . . . It's not a good time for me to be on the phone.

*Int.* AURORA's *Bedroom—Day*

AURORA. Don't be so inconsiderate.

*There's a splash. She looks and can see next door where* GARRETT *is doing energetic laps. She closes the window to shut out the sound.*

AURORA *(cont'd)*. I'm all set for a good talk with you. You have almost an hour to get the boys off. What's wrong?

EMMA. Nothing.

AURORA. You stop right here, tell me what it is.

EMMA *(drawing breath)*. Okay, Mother, I need some money. I need you to loan me some money. I really and truly need it, so will you?

*A beat.*

EMMA *(cont'd)*. Don't you be quiet. You know how hard that was for me to ask. Say no if you want—just don't be quiet.

AURORA *(tenderly compassionate)*. I'm sorry, sweetheart. I was just thinking.

EMMA *(softening)*. Thinking what?

AURORA. How much I hate to part with money.

EMMA. I wouldn't ask if . . . well, don't yell, but I really think I may be pregnant again.

AURORA. Oh, no. And I suppose you're going to go ahead and have it.

EMMA. Yes, of course. What's happening to you, anyway?

AURORA. Oh, don't act like it's so terrible, Emma. I keep hearing about bright young women who are having simple abortions and getting wonderful jobs. You can go right next door to Colorado and have it!

EMMA. I don't know why I tell you anything. I seem to like you less and less, Mama.

AURORA. That's because I'm the only person who tells you the truth.

TOMMY *enters.*

EMMA *(to TOMMY)*. Go get dressed!

AURORA. How is your life going to get better if you keep having children with that man? How? What miracle is going to come along to rescue you?

EMMA. Leave me alone. *(then, mad)* I need money. Why not just give me my painting to sell?

AURORA. No! I won't do that. That's your security. I'm not going to let you use it for rent.

*We hear the sound of the front door closing.*

EMMA *(beaten)*. Let's not do this. All right? I'll talk to you later.

AURORA. All right. If the money really would mean that . . .

EMMA. No! No. Don't give me the money. It would make you crazy.

AURORA *(realistically)*. Yes, it would.

EMMA. We'll talk later. Call me tonight if you want . . . All right? Goodbye . . .

*Int.* HORTON *House—Boy's Room— Day*

TOMMY, *almost 9;* TEDDY, *5 ½.*

TEDDY. Daddy just got home.

TOMMY. Hey, no kidding? Is it tough being a genius?

TEDDY. Boy.

*Int.* EMMA'S *Room—Day*

*She hangs up as* FLAP *enters— unshaven. She walks to him, studies him. He is scared. She sniffs at his fear.*

FLAP. Great news, I know what my thesis topic is, I have it all figured out. What's wrong?

EMMA. Where've you been all night, Flap?

FLAP. I'm sorry, Ems. I fell asleep on that big sofa at the library again. I don't know what's wrong with me.

FLAP *walks to her, pats her belly, trying to avoid her gaze.*

EMMA *(low)*. I'm on to you.

FLAP. I'm not doing anything.

EMMA. Oh, yes, you are!

FLAP. . . . Please, I hate it when you get this unhappy, okay? We go through this stage . . . every time.

EMMA. No. No. Don't change the subject.

FLAP. What's the subject?

EMMA *(ominous)*. That I'm on to you.

*They look at each other.*

EMMA *(cont'd)*. You wouldn't try to look so innocent unless you were guilty.

FLAP. You have to take my word for it. You have no other choice.

*He starts to walk away. She blocks his path.*

EMMA. No. No, no. No.

FLAP. Jeeze!

EMMA. No, no, no, no.

EMMA *forces* FLAP *onto the couch. She lands on his lap.*

FLAP. Emma, you . . . you always get a little paranoid in your first few months. Okay? Just . . .

EMMA *(quietly)*. If you are doing something and you're trying to make me feel like I'm crazy because I am bearing our child, then you may have just sunk to a point so low you may never recover. You may have just panicked, Flap, and trying to save yourself, you have thrown out your character and principles. The only way you can possibly redeem yourself and be the man God intended you to be is to take the responsibility and admit anything that you may have been doing tonight. If you don't do that now—right now—you are a lost man, a shell, a bag of shit dust. You've gotta tell me. For us, honey.

FLAP *is uncertain.* EMMA'S *gaze is unwavering, then the phone rings.* FLAP *grabs it.*

FLAP. Oh, hi—Aurora. How are you? . . . Yes, she's right here. It was nice hearing your voice again.

*He hands her the phone and exits.* EMMA *looks after him.*

*Ext.* HORTON *House—6 Months Later—Spring, 1979*

TOMMY *is 9,* TEDDY *is 6,* MELANIE *is 1 month.* TOMMY *and* TEDDY *are sitting in front of the house and hearing the off-stage argument their parents are having.* BABY MELANIE *can be seen through the front window.*

FLAP *(O.S.)*. I don't know why you don't get a job if you're so worried about money.

EMMA *(O.S.)*. What am I going to do with the baby?

FLAP *(O.S.)*. It's supposed to be a great day when you get tenure.

EMMA *(O.S.)*. Oh, Flap, we don't have enough money to pay the bills now. All tenure means is we won't have enough money forever.

*They continue to fight.* TOMMY *begins to walk off.*

TEDDY. Mommy said to wait right here.

TOMMY. You stay if you want.

TEDDY *is torn, reluctant to disobey his mother, but unable to resist scurrying after his brother. They move down the block.*

FLAP *(O.S.)*. Then I don't see why you can't ask your mother for money.

EMMA *(O.S.) (cuts him off)*. Oh! When it's convenient for you, I should ask my mother!

*In the b.g. the* BABY *is crying.*

FLAP *(O.S.)*. Go ahead, call her! Why should this day be any different?! Get on the phone, Emma! Get on the phone!

EMMA *(O.S.)*. Why don't you call?!

FLAP *(O.S.)*. Yeah, I'm gonna call Aurora, right?! Get on the phone! Get on the phone!

*The boys are both upset,* TEDDY *seeking camaraderie,* TOMMY *withdrawn.*

*On* EMMA

*Coming out of the house in the distance, distraught, looks up and down, spots her kids and comes marching toward them.* TEDDY *sees her and runs toward her, hugging her hard. She hugs him back. She is thirty years old and obviously distraught. She comforts* TEDDY *and eyes* TOMMY, *who has refused to budge.*

EMMA. What are you guys doin' huh? I told you to wait out in front of the house. Answer me, Tommy!

TOMMY. I didn't want people to think we lived there.

EMMA. What?!

TOMMY. I said, "I didn't want people to think we lived there!"

TEDDY *(to* TOMMY, *whispering)*. Cut it out. Cut it out.

EMMA *is more angered than guilty by the remark.*

EMMA *(to* TOMMY*)*. Okay, you're allowed to say one mean thing to me a year. That'll do till you're ten.

TOMMY. You're driving Daddy away!

EMMA. Okay, Tommy, stand up and follow me, and don't make me hit you on the street. I said hurry. Come on!

*They walk to the car.*

*Int. Supermarket—Checkout Stand —Day*

*As the checker rings up the sale, a few people waiting in line behind the*

HORTONS. *The* CHECKOUT GIRL *rings up the total.*

GIRL. Forty-four dollars.

EMMA *digs in her purse, stalls for a time while digging for additional money.*

EMMA *(to* CASHIER*)*. Twenty. Thirty. Let's see, that's thirty-eight, forty.

TOMMY *(to* EMMA*)*. You don't have enough money!

EMMA *(to* CASHIER*)*. I don't have any checks. Ah, I guess I'll have to put some things back.

*The* GIRL *rolls her eyes.* EMMA *surveys what she's bought. As she does, the* GIRL *addresses her colleagues at the next counter.*

GIRL *(loudly)*. Could I have the register key? She doesn't have enough money.

TOMMY *stands a few steps off.* TEDDY *clings to her. He suspects he's supposed to be mortified.*

EMMA *(to her boys)*. There's nothing wrong with this. I just took the wrong purse.

*She hands back the "TV Guide." The* GIRL *deducts twenty-five cents.*

GIRL. Forty-three dollars and seventy-five cents.

EMMA *feels at her hair, gives back the conditioner.*

Forty-one dollars and thirty-five cents.

EMMA *examines the remainder. She needs the meat and produce. She gives back a package of miniature candy bars.*

TOMMY. You promised I could get something.

EMMA. I'm not giving back real food.

TOMMY. Give her this.

*He indicates a box of Midol.*

EMMA. No way.

EMMA *hands back the candy bars. She has just taken candy from her baby.*

GIRL. Forty dollars and thirty-five cents.

TOMMY *(squawking).* Mom!

EMMA *quickly takes a single bar from the rack and hands one to* TOMMY.

GIRL. Forty dollars and forty-five cents.

*She looks at* TEDDY *who does not complain.* EMMA *takes another candy bar from the rack and gives it to* TEDDY.

Forty dollars and fifty cents. Hey, we're going in the wrong direction.

EMMA *(to* GIRL). Why do you have to be so goddamn nasty? I mean, it's not gonna help anything. We're both people, you know.

GIRL *(somewhat muted).* Forty dollars and seventy-five cents.

TEDDY *offers his mother his candy bar.*

TEDDY. I don't need it.

EMMA *looks up. She is deeply touched by her son's action. There's something wrong with you if you don't want to hug her just now.*

MAN'S VOICE. Mrs. Horton.

SAM BURNS, *a man in his early 50's, stands there, a bottle of ginger ale sticking out of the paper bag he carries under his arm. He has a great desire to rescue* EMMA *from embarrassment. It's not the sort of thing he does well.*

SAM. I'm Sam Burns from the bank. *(jogging her memory)* I turned you down on the second on your house?

EMMA. Of course. I remember who you are.

SAM. Ah, look, could I help make up the difference here?

EMMA. Thanks, I'd appreciate it. I'll pay you back tomorrow.

*He starts to hand the* GIRL *some money.*

SAM *(to* GIRL). You're a very rude young woman. I know Douglas from the Rotary and I can't believe he'd want you treating customers so badly.

GIRL. I don't think I was treating her badly.

SAM. Then you must be from New York.

*She hands him his change.*

*Ext. Supermarket—Day*

*as the four of them walk toward the car.* TEDDY *pushes the grocery cart forward off the curb toward the station wagon.*

EMMA. Be careful, Teddy!

TEDDY. What?

EMMA. Be careful!

*As* TEDDY *looks over his shoulder, he pushes the cart forward and into the side of the car.*

EMMA *(cont'd) (to* SAM). Where's your car?

SAM. Right here.

EMMA. It was lookin' like the worst time I've ever had. I didn't know I could get cheered up so fast. I'm grateful.

SAM. No problem.

*They smile, eyes meet. They shy from the contact, then resume it. Two people who never flirt are discovering what they've been missing.*

TOMMY. Come on, Mom.

TOMMY *reaches and takes hold of* EMMA'S *arm and tugs on it.*

EMMA. Wait over by the car a second, honey.

TOMMY. Come on!

EMMA. Wait over by the car, honey.

TOMMY. No! Come on!

EMMA. Wait over by the car, honey!

TOMMY. But I . . .

EMMA *(shouts, cutting him off).* Wait over by the car, honey!! Over by the car!!

TOMMY. But . . .

EMMA. Now!! Now!! Now!!

*Throughout this confrontation* TEDDY *has been trying to get* TOMMY *moving, and now he finally does.* SAM *smiles after them.*

SAM. Nice boys. You're great with them, too. Really.

EMMA. I think all three of us are going through a stage . . . *(a beat, then)* Hey. Thanks again.

SAM. No thanks required. I've had a lovely time.

EMMA. Me, too.

*They seem to have just had a retroactive date. There is enormous reluctance to draw apart before confirming the contact.*

EMMA *(cont'd).* I'll get the money back to you.

SAM. Don't bother yourself. You could just drop it in the mail.

EMMA. To the bank?

SAM. Sure. You could even use a check-by-mail envelope . . . *(a daring moment)* . . . or you could come in. Whichever.

EMMA. Maybe I'll just come in sometime.

SAM. Well, that would be fine.

EMMA *shakes* SAM'S *hand, turns and walks away.* SAM *looks after her.*

SAM *(cont'd).* Oh, hey, can I help you with that?

EMMA. No. Thanks, I'm used to this.

*Int.* AURORA'S *Dining Room— Night*

*Gathered around the table, a birthday cake in the center, are* AURORA, VERNON, *and* EDWARD, *the banker who wanted to take* AURORA *to Tahiti, and a new face, the newly widowed* DR. DOUGLAS RATCHER, *a family physician—he delivered* TOMMY. ED-WARD *is finishing reading a poem he wrote especially for the evening while* AURORA *busies herself licking the icing from some of the burnt-out candles.*

EDWARD. "And so another birthday for a gal named Aurora Greenway / Even though fifty, she still takes my breath away / Mere mortals just gaze as she lights up their sky / A heavenly object—a siren's cry."

*The poem has come from his heart. He looks at her.*

You're the best . . . Happy Birthday.

*He kisses her.*

AURORA. Thank you, Edward. Thank you. (to VERNON) Do you want one, Vernon? Would you like a kiss?

AURORA *puts her hand under* VER-NON'S *chin, leans in and kisses him.*

DR. RATCHER. You're not lying about your age, are you?

AURORA. Of course not!

DR. RATCHER. I thought you were fifty-two. Ah, she's really fifty-two. Come on, Aurora, how do you expect to fool the family doctor?

*She stares at him.*

VERNON *(to* RATCHER*).* It seems to me she said her age.

AURORA. Thank you, Vernon, thank you.

RATCHER. My point is, the number doesn't matter, but the effort to conceal it does.

AURORA. Rosie, why does he keep talking about it?

ROSIE. Doctor Ratcher . . .

RATCHER. Dammit! I'm trying to do some good here. Now, the way to adjust to old age . . .

AURORA *is on her feet. She flees toward the kitchen.*

RATCHER *goes after her.* ROSIE *grabs* RATCHER *in a bear hug from behind.*

ROSIE. Ah, Doctor . . . I think you're a might confused because of being recently widowed and all.

*Ext.* AURORA'S *House—Night*

*In her stocking feet she walks her lawn. In the background we can see her guests gathered at the window staring at her.*

AURORA'S *POV*

*The three male faces in the window—*VERNON, *the idiot* DOCTOR, *the pathetic* EDWARD*—slim pickings.*

VERNON. You okay? Hum? Aurora? Aurora? *(to* EDWARD *and* RATCHER*)* Let's give her some privacy.

*On* AURORA

*as she looks across at the astronaut's house. Through the side window we get a glimpse of his moving from view, apparently cooking. Now with sudden and extraordinary purpose, she runs across the lawn to his door where she rings the bell. She waits, then nervously backs up several steps.*

GARRETT *(O.S.).* Yeah? The door's open. Just a minute.

*She backs up some more so that she stands her ground strangely in the shadows a good ten feet away when* GARRETT *opens the door. He's in his fifties now. His face and body show it. His blessing is that he's blissfully unaware of that fact. He is wearing one of those short, velour bathrobes with nothing on underneath.*

*On* GARRETT

*At first he doesn't see her, then does.*

AURORA. Well, hello.

GARRETT. Hi.

AURORA. I was curious if you still wanted to take me to lunch.

GARRETT. I wasn't aware that we . . . I don't know what you . . .

AURORA. A few years back you invited me to lunch.

GARRETT. A few years back, and . . .

AURORA. That's right, and I wondered if the invitation still exists? Would you like to? Have lunch? Not dinner, remember, it was lunch!

GARRETT *pauses. She stares daggers from the dark. He then takes the easiest out.*

GARRETT. Why not?

AURORA. Good. *(pause)* When?

GARRETT. Ah, tomorrow.

AURORA. Tomorrow! All right. All right.

*She walks back to her house,* GARRETT *looking after her.*

GARRETT. Good.

AURORA. Twelve-thirty?

GARRETT. Twelve.

AURORA. Good.

*Ext.* GARRETT'S *Driveway—Day*

*As* GARRETT *opens the door of his Corvette and* AURORA *slides in with some difficulty. The top is down.* GARRETT *gets in, puts on his seat belt, glances at her as she pats at herself.*

GARRETT. If you mind the open air, I can . . . ah, get the top.

AURORA. No, don't worry. Grown women are prepared for life's little emergencies.

*She removes a scarf matching her outfit. As she ties it in place, they pull out.*

*Ext. Houston—Memorial Drive—Day*

*An eight-track playing loudly to override the force of wind in the open car.* GARRETT *is relaxed. He shouts over the wind to her.*

GARRETT. Us going out together. Not bad.

AURORA *is trying to be inconspicuous as she holds onto her scarf. She turns to give him a tight returning smile. The scarf flies off and her carefully-created hair whips wildly in the air.*

AURORA. Do you think . . . do you think you could possibly put the top up?

GARRETT. The top's home in my garage.

*She takes this in. The camera shows the huge, expansive sweep of road yet still ahead of them as her scarf blows away.*

*Int. Restaurant—Day.*

*Through the glass doors we see* GARRETT'S *car as it stops at curb.* AURORA *with the hair of a wild lady.*

VALET *(to* AURORA*).* Hello there, how are you?

GARRETT. How are ya, Ali?

VALET. Hello, how are you?

GARRETT. It's nice to see you.

*Int. Restaurant—Ladies' Room—Day*

AURORA *is using every muscle in her arm to brush the knots out of her hair.*

*Int. Restaurant—Day*

*As* AURORA *slips into her chair across from* GARRETT, *not looking at him.*

AURORA. Well, I'm starving. No hidden meaning in that remark.

GARRETT. Well, ah, would you like an oyster?

AURORA. No. Thank you.

*Four younger women are seated at a nearby table.* GARRETT *glances over.*

GARRETT *(speaking with food in his mouth).* It's good.

AURORA. Well, I think that is extremely rude. Noticing other women when you're with me.

GARRETT. I think we're going to have to get drunk.

AURORA. I don't get drunk and I don't care for escorts who do.

GARRETT. No, you got me into this, and you're just gonna have to trust me about this, this one thing. You need a lot of drinks.

AURORA. To break the ice?

GARRETT. To kill the bug you have up your ass.

*She starts to take offense but he is grinning at her, perhaps giving her some test.*

WAITER. May I get you something?

AURORA. Ah, yes, I think I will have some bourbon. Preferably Wild Turkey.

GARRETT *(impressed).* Aurora.

AURORA. Yes?

GARRETT. You're not fun by any chance?

AURORA. I don't really think we should think about that right now. Impatient boys sometimes miss dessert.

*Int.* EMMA's *Old Station Wagon—Des Moines—Day*

*as it moves into a parking place at a shopping center in Des Moines. She gives herself a quick once-over in the cracked rearview mirror. This is interrupted by the horn beep from the next car. An incredibly brief beep, like a man coughing ever so slightly to let someone know he's there.* EMMA *looks over.*

EMMA'S *POV*

SAM BURNS *getting out of his car trying not to show the strain of being more nervous than he's been in . . . ever. His grin is too wide. He is shrugging with his face, a sort of helpless gesture of raising his eyebrows and ears. He's a lucky man, for he is approaching one of the few women around who would find his machinations endearing.*

SAM. We both got here the same time.

EMMA. Hi, Sam. How are you? Nice to see you.

SAM. It's always so nice to see you. I can hardly believe it.

EMMA *(touched)*. You, too.

*In an attempt to seal this romantic juncture,* SAM BURNS *looks away and pats her on the back. They move toward the restaurant.*

*Int. Coffee Shoppe—Des Moines Outskirts—Day*

*The lights are brighter than the restaurant we just left. This place is not designed for leisurely dining or a midday rendezvous. It is fast-order functional, kids with ketchup on their faces, but there is a knotty pine bar in the back which is where we find* SAM

*and* EMMA. *They are holding hands in the shy manner of decent people preparing for mortal sin.* SAM *is being overwhelmed by both his good fortune and inner guilt. He's between a rock and a soft place.*

SAM. You know, the thing I didn't expect was that there would be moments where I forget to be scared someone will see us together.

EMMA. Sam, you don't have to be so scared. Contemplating sin is all we've done. It doesn't mean anything.

SAM. I'm glad that you've been contemplating it, too. I didn't know that.

EMMA. During all these lunches—all this hand holding.

SAM. Emma, I'm not going back to the bank this afternoon. I have to go out and inspect a new home. It's pretty far out and it's empty.

*A silence.*

EMMA. I have to pick up the kids at five.

SAM. Oh—okay. I understand. Don't give it a thought. *(then)* Emma, I haven't made love to a woman for almost three years.

EMMA. How come?

SAM *(embarrassed)*. My wife has a disc problem in her back and she can't take having . . . any weight on her.

EMMA *(puzzled)*. Sam, I hope you don't mind my asking this. Well, have you ever thought of her getting on top?

SAM. Oh, she wouldn't do that.

EMMA. She might surprise you.

SAM. I don't think so. That would be so unlike her.

EMMA. Did you ask?

SAM *(ruefully)*. About six hundred times.

EMMA *laughs out loud.*

*Ext. Iowa Highway—Day*

*As* SAM BURNS' *Fairlane moves along between rows of corn fields. It is being routinely passed by other cars. A tractor slows them down.*

EMMA. What are you thinkin'?

SAM. Tell me, do you prefer Texas to Iowa?

EMMA. Oh, come on, Sam, what were you really thinkin'?

SAM. No, really! That's what I was really thinkin' when you just asked me that.

*Int. Sam's Car—Day*

EMMA. I don't know. There seems to be an absence of wildness, you know? Even in the people.

SAM. Well, we're farmers, and we talk poor because the farmer aspect of things is, don't let anybody know you have anything. And . . . don't call attention to yourself. My wife says . . . well, I guess we shouldn't talk about Dotty.

*Ext. Houston Highway—Day*

*As* GARRETT'S *convertible at about thirty mph sways along the waterside roadway connecting Galveston and Houston. Large ships in the background.* GARRETT *is sitting atop the driver's seat steering with his feet.* AURORA, *reluctantly playing his accomplice, one of her feet on the gas pedal, an awkward reach from her side of the car. She must shout to make herself heard over the wind.*

GARRETT *(shouts).* Wind in the hair! Lead in the pencil! Feet controlling the universe! Breedlove at the helm! Just keep pumpin' that throttle. Keep givin' it that gas. I see the Gulf of Mexico below me!

AURORA. I'm not enjoying this.

GARRETT. Give it a chance.

AURORA. I'm stopping.

GARRETT *(sings).* "Fly me to the moon . . ." What?

*She puts on the brake. He falls over the windshield, flipping onto the hood of the car, then bouncing off to the side onto the beach and into the water.* AURORA *runs toward him, a bit panicked. They stand there in the surf.*

AURORA. How are you?

*He moves. There are some bruises. She is bending over him.*

It's not my fault, but I'm sorry.

GARRETT. If you wanted to get me on my back, you just had to ask.

*He grabs her and pulls her down. Kissing her, she begins to come close to relaxing in the embrace, then* GARRETT *sticks his hand inside her blouse and into her bra. She pulls quickly away, but his hand is stuck there at an awkward angle.*

Ow!

AURORA. Ouch!

GARRETT. Ow, my hand.

AURORA. Get it, get it outta there!

GARRETT. I can't.

AURORA. Get it out!

GARRETT. I swear, I swear I can't.

AURORA. Get it out!

GARRETT. I can't get it out, I swear to God. Oh, please.

AURORA. We were having such a good time and you had to go do this. Get it outta there.

GARRETT. Oh, please! Please, anything. Bend down. Bend down.

*She bends over and he extracts his hand. The wrist is severely sprained.*

AURORA. Why did you have to get drunk?

GARRETT. I'm not drunk anymore. The pain sobered me up. Let's go.

*He starts back toward the car, rubbing his wrist. He keeps walking.* AURORA, *vulnerable, realizing if she doesn't hurry, he'll actually leave her alone, hurries to catch up. It is striking to see her, for the first time, tagging after a man.*

*Ext. House—Long Shot—Day*

*As* EMMA *gets out of her side of the car and moves up the walk, then waits.* SAM *finally getting out from behind the steering wheel and walking toward her.*

SAM. Emma, this might be a terrible thing to ask, but are you thinking about your husband at all?

EMMA. Oh, I was a little.

SAM. Look, we can go back right now.

EMMA. No, Sam. Stop it. Look, I want to do this. I'm glad that I don't know whether or not Flap's been with someone else. I'd hate to think that I was doing this just to get even.

*Ext.* AURORA'S *and* GARRETT'S *Houses—Day*

GARRETT'S *car skids to a stop, hitting a car parked in front of* GARRETT'S *driveway.*

GARRETT. Oh, just fucking great. Fine! Great! *(shouting to neighborhood)* You're parked in my driveway! You're breaking the law!

*As* GARRETT, *still pissed, walks her to her door.*

AURORA. Would you like to come in?

GARRETT. I'd rather stick needles in my eyes.

AURORA. Everything would have been fine, you know if you hadn't gotten drunk.

*He looks at her, contemptuously.*

I mean, I was . . . I . . . I just didn't want you to think I was like one of your other girls.

GARRETT. Not much danger in that

unless you curtsy on my face real soon.

AURORA. Garrett! What is it that makes you so insistent on shocking and insulting me? I mean, I really hate that way of talking. You must know that. Why do you do it?

*She has a point. He considers it.*

GARRETT. I tell you, Aurora, I don't know what it is about you, but you bring out the devil in me.

*Dissolve to:*

*Int.* HORTON *House—Bathroom— Night*

EMMA *stands holding phone with receiver braced between her shoulder and ear.*

EMMA. Where are you?

SAM *(O.S.).* I'm in the laundry room, so nobody could hear me.

EMMA. Yes, but Sam, I can't hear you either.

*Int. Laundry Room—Night*

SAM BURNS *stands with washer-dryer working.*

*Intercut Phone conversation*

SAM. Oh . . . Wait a minute, we're getting a quieter cycle.

*The spin cycle stops and now he lowers his voice.*

Can you hear me now? Good. Is it bad to call?

EMMA. No, no, I am definitely in the market for a little sweet talk.

TEDDY *starts knocking on the bathroom door.*

TEDDY *(O.S.).* Mom, I have to go. Really.

EMMA. Just a second.

*She opens the door.* TEDDY *enters and starts to pee while looking over at this mother.*

EMMA (to TEDDY). Ssh. Ssh.

*He looks confused as to how to make pissing quieter. Then, seeing she means it, he aims for the side of the bowl. From the muted sound, we know he has succeeded.*

EMMA (into phone). What were you saying?

SAM. Just how absolutely good I feel. And even though I'm scared— and we've committed adultery—no matter what happens, I'm just so grateful to God or the devil for letting me feel this way again.

EMMA. I'm so glad you told me.

TEDDY *reaches to flush.* EMMA *gestures him away, fearful the noise of the flush will break the mood.*

EMMA (to TEDDY). Don't flush!

TEDDY. But you told me always to . . .

EMMA. No! Not this time.

SAM. Listen, Emma, is everything okay? (softly) Can you talk?

EMMA. No, it's all right.

*Sound of door.*

TEDDY. Can I hold Melanie?

EMMA (to TEDDY). Yes! Yes.

*She moves him out.* EMMA *picks up the phone again.*

SAM. Honey, is everything okay?

EMMA. What?

SAM. Is everything okay?

EMMA. Everything's fine. Oh, yeah! Everything's fine.

SAM. Emma . . .

OPERATOR (thru phone). I have an emergency phone call from Missus Aurora Greenway in Houston, Texas . . . for Missus Emma Horton.

SAM. Oh, no.

EMMA. Oh, no, she always does that when the line's busy, it's fine.

OPERATOR (thru phone). Will you release?

SAM. Oh, of course, Operator, ah, it's all right, we were just talking.

EMMA. I'll talk to ya later, Sam. 'Bye.

*She hangs up and the phone rings immediately.*

EMMA. Hi. How'd it go?

*Int.* AURORA's *Bedroom—Night*

*She is wearing a bathrobe and eating a chocolate eclair.*

AURORA. The astronaut's impossible. An arrogant, self-centered, and, yes, somewhat entertaining man— who has realized his ambition and is at last forever a spoiled child.

EMMA (pleased). Talk about your match made in heaven.

AURORA. You'd think so, wouldn't you? But I really think he's just not going to have any more to do with me.

EMMA. Aw, why?

AURORA. I don't want to go into it.

EMMA. Is it because you won't go to bed with him?

AURORA. On a first date, Emma!

EMMA. Well, it's hardly a first date, Mom . . . He's been living ten feet away from you for fifteen years. I mean, why don't you at least talk about the real reason?

AURORA. I don't—I don't know what you mean.

EMMA. Because it's been about that long since you've done it.

AURORA. Shut up! I mean it! Shut up!

EMMA. Oh, come on. It's just me.

AURORA. No!

EMMA. Call him!

AURORA. No, no! I'm hanging up.

EMMA. No, no. I'm sorry! Okay, I'm sorry . . .

AURORA. I'm hanging up!

EMMA. Call him, now!

AURORA *replaces receiver in cradle.*

EMMA *(cont'd).* So long.

AURORA *stands there in the middle of the room. She walks to her window and opens it.*

*Her POV*

*Over the fence, she can see* GARRETT *doing laps in his pool.*

AURORA *taking a bite of her eclair and then throwing it into a wastebasket. She is experiencing the first gnawing stages of an anxiety threatening to escape and ravage her after decades of quiet. She crosses to a dresser and searches for a particular nightgown, finds it. She sits, nightgown on her lap, and goes through the phone book. She writes down a number which she finds. All the while, through the open window, we hear* GARRETT *doing his laps. She takes off one earring and tosses her head a bit to get the receiver just right before dialing. The phone rings until eventually we hear the sound of laps stop. We hear the muffled voice of* GARRETT *at the other end saying, "Hello."*

AURORA. Hello, Garrett.
GARRETT *(V.O).* Yes?
AURORA. Well, I was just sitting here realizing . . . realizing that I'd never shown you my Renoir.
GARRETT. What are you talking about?
AURORA. I'm inviting you to come over and look at my Renoir.
GARRETT. You're inviting me to bed.
AURORA. Yes, it happens to be in my bedroom.
GARRETT. Is the Renoir under the covers? *(laughs)*
AURORA. Don't cackle, Garrett. Do you wanna see it?

GARRETT. Do I wanna come to your bedroom? Let me think, ah.
AURORA. Do you?
GARRETT. Just—j-just give me a minute. It's a tough one. Um. I ca— I don't . . . Yeah, okay. I — I guess so. Sure, why not. *(small laugh)*
AURORA. All right, I'll see you in a bit. Now, if I don't answer the bell, that means the back door is open.
GARRETT. The back door is open.

*She hangs up, holds herself briefly. The excitement is so great that it's unwelcome. She stands and crosses to the bathroom, more frightened than she expected.*

*We remain in the bedroom area where we hear the rustle of satin and then the doorbell ring.*

AURORA *(O.S.).* Oh, my God, he ran it!

*She rushed from the bathroom dressed in her nightgown and carrying a largish mirror which she sets up near the door* GARRETT *will soon enter. Now she turns off the light, moves quickly back to the doorway of the bathroom and poses, backlighted, in the doorway trying to make out her own image. The nightgown is simple and sexy. Then we hear* GARRETT *on the stairs. She rushes across the room, takes the mirror back inside the bathroom. There is a knock on the bedroom door.* AURORA *enters wearing a bathrobe over her nightgown.*

AURORA. Garrett?
GARRETT *(O.S.).* Hi.

*She opens the door. He is wearing wet swimming trunks.*

I was doing laps when you called. Lucky for us, I only did eight.

*He grins at her. She turns her back on him and looks up at her painting as he approaches from behind. He puts his hands on her shoulders.*

AURORA. This is it. This is the Renoir.

GARRETT. I like it. I like the painting. I like everything in here. *(into her ear)* Relax, baby, it's gonna be great.

*She wheels on him, sputtering in indignation, feeling genuinely and deeply reduced and insulted.*

AURORA. Now, just who do you think you're talking to like this? Don't you realize I'm a grandmother!

*And with that, she takes his face and gives him a stunning, open-mouthed, expert kiss. They break. He's staggered.*

It's not flattering if you look too surprised. I'll just be a minute.

*Her self-image buoyed by her own actions, she moves toward the bathroom pausing to scoop up a perfume atomizer from her dresser.* GARRETT *waits, a hand reaches around to turn off the light and then we see* AURORA *as she posed earlier, backlighted and intriguing.*

GARRETT. I like the lights on.
AURORA. Then go home and turn them on. Oh, I'm sorry.

*He accepts her conditions and stands waiting in the shadows. She moves toward the bed. In the darkness, we can see him stepping out of his elasticized swim trunks, hopping a bit as he fails to release the second leg smoothly while* AURORA *turns back the covers and slips inside. He joins her under the covers.*

*Int.* EMMA'S *Bedroom—Night*

EMMA *and* FLAP *are asleep, her arms over his chest.* TOMMY *and* TEDDY *enter.* TEDDY *begins to move toward his mother's side of the bed to wake her.* TOMMY *restrains him and leads the way to* FLAP. *In the b.g. now that the door is open, we hear a fierce, barking cough.*

TOMMY. Dad? Dad? Come on. Wake up.

*He awakens, terrified, making noises of fear for a second so that the boys, alarmed, back off.* EMMA *remains asleep.*

FLAP. What? What?
TEDDY. Melanie's sick.
FLAP. What?
TEDDY. Melanie's sick.

FLAP *listens for a second, then jostles* EMMA *vigorously.*

FLAP. The baby's sick.
EMMA. The baby's sick.

EMMA *is sleepily but nonetheless quickly on the move. In the instant before she's awake she has already covered a good deal of floor space and mumbled some comforting words. Now, awake, she turns the lights on at the door, turns to* FLAP, *sitting in bed.*

EMMA. You coming?
TEDDY. See, Mom, see? See, whadda ya think is wrong?
EMMA. I have to look first.
TOMMY. Come on, Dad.

FLAP *gets out of bed.*

*Int. Dining Room—Night*

*Which has been turned into a nursery. As* EMMA *turns the lights on and hears* MELANIE'S *seal-like cough and notes the baby's limbs are going.*

EMMA. I need a thermometer.

FLAP, *standing in the doorway, starts to think about where the thermometer might be.* TEDDY *dashes to a drawer, tearing at things inside. He brings the thermometer.* TOMMY, *an old hand, gives her a nearby bottle of Vaseline.*

*(to* TEDDY*)* Thank you. You can go to bed. She's gonna be all right. She is, go on.

TEDDY. I can't sleep, so why can't I stay up?

EMMA. Just go to bed, I'll be there soon.

FLAP *(to* BOYS*)*. It's bad enough we're making this a drama. It's not going to qualify as high drama.

EMMA *(to* MELANIE, *soft and soothing)*. It's okay. *(to* TOMMY*)* Thanks. *(to* FLAP*)* I'm sure it's the croup. Remember, Tommy had it twice.

FLAP *shakes his head "no."*

Guess you were in the library.

FLAP. Oh.

*Int. Bathroom—Night*

EMMA *sitting on the toilet seat,* MELANIE *in her lap, gorgeous even in sickness.* FLAP *turns on the hot water full blast as the steam begins to gather.*

EMMA. God, that's the worse sound in the world.

FLAP. How long do you keep her in here?

EMMA. Why, are you goin' back to bed?

FLAP. I just asked how long.

EMMA. Well, I don't know! Until her throat clears, or I lose twenty pounds. Which ever comes first. I don't know! I don't know! About twenty minutes I guess.

FLAP *leans against the sink.*

FLAP. I've been offered a job.

EMMA. Why didn't you say something?

FLAP. I wanted to think about it. It's head of the English department at Kearney State College for about the same money.

EMMA. Oh, where is that?

FLAP. Nebraska.

EMMA. I really don't want to move from here. You know? I love the school, pediatricians.

FLAP. Head of the department.

EMMA. Well, we'll talk about it, all right? I like it here, Flap. Head of the department . . . that's, that's great.

*Int.* EMMA's *Kitchen—Morning*

*The boys going off to school.* EMMA *hasn't slept all night, there are kettles boiling on the stove to provide some mist for* MELANIE, *whose cough sounds better.* EMMA *picks up the phone.*

TOMMY. Good-bye, Mom.

EMMA. 'Bye.

TOMMY. Hey, come on, Teddy.

EMMA. Hey, don't kiss the baby! She may still be sick. *(calls after boys)* Have a good day at school.

EMMA *dials the phone.*

EMMA *(into phone)*. Oh, you don't know the night I had. Melanie decided to get the croup, and of course it happened at three A.M. So I don't think I've even gotten any sleep yet. Anyway, I don't know if he's kidding—Flap told me that he's takin' us to some college in Nebraska. And, I'm not sure, but . . . I think Sam is becoming someone that I—I need in a strange way, and . . .

*Int.* AURORA's *Bedroom—Morning*

AURORA *(whispering)*. I'm lying here next to the astronaut.

*Angle on* GARRETT

*His face turned toward us and away from* AURORA. *His eyes click on at the mention of his occupation. While in Des Moines,* EMMA *forgets her own life on hearing this awesome news.*

EMMA. Are you really?

AURORA. Um-hmmm.

EMMA *(boldly)*. How was it?

AURORA. I'll speak to you later.

EMMA. Okay, I'll let you go. So long. I feel so good for you. You call me as soon as you can? Okay? Okay?

EMMA *hangs up, her spirits buoyed. She checks out her baby daughter, sees that she's looking better, says some words of encouragement. She turns off the kettles, wipes away some perspiration and resumes her own day.*

*Ext. Houston Neighborhood—Day*

AURORA *and* GARRETT *walking.*

GARRETT. I just wanna make this clear, you know. I see, I see . . . other women.

AURORA. I didn't exactly think we were engaged.

GARRETT. Okay. Okay.

AURORA. Your ego, really!

GARRETT. Okay! Let's stay in tonight.

AURORA. Boy, you're saving a fortune on me.

GARRETT. I'll cook. It's been three weeks and ya haven't even seen my house.

AURORA. My best instincts had me avoiding it.

*Int.* GARRETT'S *Kitchen*

*Steak, fries and a bottle of wine.* AURORA *aglow, the living room filled with astronaut memorabilia—pictures, a piece of rock, a NASA flag, a model of a missile.* AURORA *now stares at a moon globe with raised surfaces denoting the craters of the moon.*

GARRETT. What are you thinkin'?

AURORA. Oh . . . I'll tell you what. I think this is really sad. That you feel that you need all this stuff to impress girls with.

GARRETT. Need it!

AURORA. Uh-hum.

GARRETT. Sometimes it isn't enough. But I don't think there's anything wrong with using all your assets.

AURORA. Ah, except, you see, I think that it turns your profession into a "sex trap"!

GARRETT. Ah, come on, everybody uses whatever they have. I earned it! There's a hundred and six astronauts in the whole fuckin' world, I'm one of 'em! It's as much a part of me as anything else.

AURORA. I'm sorry, I didn't . . . I didn't mean to trip on such a deeply felt principle.

*A silent beat. He is a bit perturbed at himself for letting her get under his skin.*

*Int.* GARRETT'S *Bedroom—Night*

*He is in* AURORA'S *arms, the moonlight filtering through the window.* GARRETT, *for now anyway, feels understood, challenged, loved. He is talking about himself in the manner of a hungry man having his first meal in months. She is, as he will later comment, a girl you can really talk to.*

GARRETT. You know what bothers me? None of us ever got together, in one room, locked all the doors and compared notes on the experience. I think there was a rule that we had to pretend that it wasn't the fun that it was.

AURORA *giggles softly.*

And the way you do sense the speed. I remember looking out the window of the spacecraft . . . I sound like somebody with a big belly tellin' their stories about Korea. Anyway, at this one point, I'm lookin' out the window, see. I can see a piece of the space-craft, and it's whistling along the ground. It doesn't make a sound. The only sound you hear, the only noise in the entire world . . . is your heart beating. *(softly imitates heart beat)*

AURORA *laughs softly.*

It's indescribable, or anyway, I can't think of a better way of sayin' it, but that was it. That was my moment, the one that doesn't go away! You know what I mean?

AURORA. Yes. Hey . . . *(whispers)* this is my moment.

*He shifts uncomfortably.*

No. Don't get nervous.

*He laughs.*

*Int.* EMMA'S *House—Day*

*Empty. She goes from room to room, then exits.*

EMMA. Flap! Anybody!

*Ext. University of Des Moines—Day*

EMMA *is walking and searching near the English building of* FLAP'S *college. She stops.*

FLAP, *his back to her and us, but we recognize the winter jacket. He is talking with what appears to be intimacy to a tall, attractive woman in her late 20's, a colleague. They are under a street light. The girl has her hand up to* FLAP'S *face. They are clearly lovers. Her name is* JANICE.

EMMA

*Her suspicions confirmed. The truth jolts her and turns her mean. She advances on the couple with the stealth of Indians and wronged, plump women.*

EMMA'S *POV*

*Now she is close enough to make out murmured voices.*

JANICE. You don't think it's fun because we're having fun. Love can be fun! Would you stop making faces!

FLAP *chuckles.*

That's wonderful.

FLAP. I think . . . what we have here is a typical gradeschool girl crush.

JANICE. Would you please, please, please, stop telling me that this is just a crush?

FLAP. Janice, the whole fun of getting involved with someone who is unavailable and a little bit older . . . is that sometimes you get to hear what's really goin' on.

JANICE. Flap, you are such a . . .

EMMA *leans forward from a few feet away and shouts in a wild rush.*

EMMA. . . . Incredible asshole!

*She turns away. He reacts.*

FLAP *(to* JANICE*).* Excuse me.

*On* FLAP

*As he turns and begins to run after his outraged wife and we see for the first time that he has their beautiful baby in a pouch over his chest. The baby is making it enormously difficult for* FLAP *to catch up with* EMMA *because he has to keep his hand on* MELANIE *to keep her from bouncing around too much. Though not long—this is our chase scene.*

FLAP. Emma—Emma! Goddamn it, you're going to ruin us.

*On* EMMA

*Fleeing but listening.*

You're a spectacle, Emma.

*On* FLAP *and* MELANIE

FLAP, *a bit over the edge with guilt, shame and fear.* MELANIE *is having the best time she has ever had in her life.*

*On* EMMA

*As she rounds a corner, breathing hard, she sneaks a little look back at her husband and child. She slows, looks again, stops and faces* FLAP.

EMMA. Stop jiggling her. She's going to throw up!

FLAP *slows to a walk, catches his breath.* EMMA *walks quickly and ignores* FLAP *while checking out the baby strapped to his body.*

FLAP. Your timing was great. You caught us before we did anything.

EMMA *looks at him briefly and contemptuously. He has insulted her intelligence.*

EMMA. Give me the baby!

*She starts yanking at the pouch straps.*

*(difficulty with straps)* I'm taking the car. I'm taking the kids and going to Houston.

FLAP. You don't know what I did! You just, you don't know. Just like I don't know what you do on your— your little—your afternoon drives. Take the . . .

EMMA *rolls her eyes as if having heard the most preposterous sentence she has ever suffered.*

EMMA. You ought to be happy that I'm goin' off. If I stayed here, I'd make life hell for you. Don't . . . follow me!

*With that she walks off and* FLAP *wisely lets her go.*

*Int.* AURORA'S *House—Early Evening*

ROSIE *dashes out the side door.* EMMA *begins beeping the horn.* GARRET'S *door opens. By the time she comes into the driveway,* ROSIE *is right alongside the car looking at* MELANIE.

ROSIE. It's them! The kids!

*On* AURORA

*Pausing in the driveway separating her house from* GARRETT'S. AURORA *is flushed, excited, trying to contain it.*

AURORA. Garrett! Come on, baby. You're gonna meet Emma and then . . .
GARRETT *(overlap)*. Oh, no, no, no, you don't need outsiders now.
AURORA. You're no outsider.
GARRETT. Ah, I'll see them later.

EMMA *is out of the car several feet away.*

AURORA *(to* GARRETT). Please come. *(to* EMMA) Emma! Em! This is Garrett.
EMMA. Oh!
AURORA. The one!
EMMA. A pleasure to meet you. I've heard so much about you!

GARRETT *waves. He would like not to be here.*

GARRETT *(uncomfortably)*. Your mother's been looking forward to this. *(to* AURORA) Go ahead.
AURORA. Anything wrong?
GARRETT. No. *(to* EMMA) Must be nice to be home, huh?
EMMA. Oh, it's great! It's great!
AURORA *(to* GARRETT). I'll be over later. They're probably tired, anyway, and want to get to sleep early. *(suggestively)* And I'd like to get to bed early.

TEDDY. Grandma! Grandma! Grandma!

AURORA *shushes* TEDDY *while maintaining a tight smile. She senses* GARRETT'S *discomfort, but this is not time to deal with it.*

AURORA. See you later.

*She starts towards her family.* ROSIE *is just finishing her first round of emotional embraces. She is on* TEDDY *and in the process of making a discovery which delights her and she announces to the world.*

ROSIE. This one likes to squeeze.

AURORA *goes to* TOMMY. *She kisses him and* TEDDY *and they have a none-too-good embrace.*

AURORA. That's it, Teddy likes to Squeeze! Tommy likes a squeeze. You both get a squeeze, and a — *(makes a funny sound)*

*The boys laugh.*

AURORA *(to* EMMA*)*. The baby. Where is the baby?

EMMA *takes her mother over to the passenger's side of the station wagon where* MELANIE *is still strapped in her car-seat.*

AURORA. Oh, there's my baby. Look at the baby! Ooooh.

EMMA. I keep thinkin' she looks a little like you.

AURORA. A little like? It's like looking in the mirror!

EMMA. She loved the ride. She hardly cried at all.

AURORA. Bring in the suitcases.

AURORA *walks toward the house, carrying the* BABY, *leaving* EMMA.

EMMA. Mom?!

AURORA. Well, I talk to you every day.

*Int.* EMMA'S *Old Bedroom—Night*

*Where a roll-away has been added to* EMMA'S *old bed.* TOMMY *and* TEDDY *are in bed,* AURORA *and* EMMA *alternating tucking and kissing. They turn the light out and then stand together framed in the doorway saying their goodnights.*

*Int.* AURORA'S *Bedroom—Night*

*The two women in flannel nightgowns, sharing the window seat having Wild Turkey and soda.*

EMMA. Mother, you look great.

AURORA. Emma, you look terrible. You know, nobody wants a girl that's washed out and tired looking all the time, Emma.

EMMA. I just drove about a thousand miles. Besides, all the men love me the way I am, Mother.

AURORA. Well, ya know, it's just like you, that when you finally take one small step away from Flap, it's with a—it's with a married, unavailable, older Iowan.

EMMA *(whispers)*. Tell me about the astronaut.

AURORA *snickers.*

Really?! Oh, really?!

AURORA. Yes. He has a name, though.

EMMA. You really like him.

AURORA. Well, it's just so—it's so strange, that relatively—*relatively* late in life . . . I found that sex is so, so, so, sooo, so fan-fucking-tastic!! Anyway, that's what he calls it. Oh, Emma, I'm a moth to a flame. This affair is gonna kill me.

EMMA. No. Maybe not. Why do you say that? Come on, Mama.

AURORA *(a cry in her voice)*. I never thought I'd start to need him.

EMMA. Oh.

*Ext.* PATSY'S *House—Back Yard—Day*

*Top River Oaks stuff, this house. The back yard is lush and deep. It has a swimming pool with a 12-foot slide and decking and a rather substantial treehouse.* PATSY, *some seven years older than when we last saw her, is sitting next to* EMMA *in a cushy chaise lounge, holding and marveling over* MELANIE *while, in the b.g.,* TOMMY *and* TEDDY *are having a terrific time swimming with* PATSY'S *daughter,* MEG, *who is just between the two boys in size and age.* TOMMY *is notably more animated and joyous than we've seen him.* PATSY *is still a knock-out, though not a natural one.* EMMA *watches with pleasure as her blonde friend cuddles her blonde daughter.*

TOMMY *(to* MEG*).* You're so lucky, you have a pool.

EMMA *(to* PATSY*).* Okay.

PATSY *(to* EMMA*).* Okay.

EMMA. Let's talk about Los Angeles. Do you miss it?

PATSY. Well, it was so interesting dating Jews after the divorce. They're so lively.

EMMA. Really . . .

PATSY. Yeah. Well, in Los Angeles, they were, like, so anxious to make you feel they understood your secret thoughts better than anybody . . .

*O.S., a phone rings.*

PATSY'S MOTHER *(O.S.).* Patsy!

PATSY *(to* EMMA*).* And I was just glad I had some.

PATSY'S MOTHER *(O.S.).* Honey, there's a phone call.

PATSY'S MOTHER *hands* PATSY *a cordless phone.*

PATSY. Hello. Oh, hi, Flap, how are you? . . . I'm fine. . . . Oh, I guess I look older like, everyone else.

EMMA *(to* FLAP*).* She does not.

PATSY. Flap, you sound the same, and I'm not sure that's such a good thing . . . Yeah, she's right here . . . No, we have not. We have other things to talk about besides you. *(raspberries)*

*She hands the phone to* EMMA.

EMMA. Hello . . . I'm fine. What's up? . . . Feeling contrite. You don't seem to understand, Flap. I saw you together . . . What?! You know, Flap, I can't believe you're doin' this to us! *(a cry in her voice)* Well, I think you're spiteful, and I don't know when in the hell that happened. *(loudly)* No! Goodbye. I—I'll . . . Goodbye.

*She hangs up.*

Flap accepted the job at Kearney, Nebraska. I gotta go back, we're gonna move in a week.

PATSY. Emma, I don't know why you don't leave him.

EMMA. Honestly, I don't know either . . . *(as she gathers her things)* He's cute.

*Ext.* EMMA'S *House—Des Moines*

*As her car pulls up, the kids run to see their father.* FLAP *emerges from inside and embraces the boys, moves over to greet* MELANIE, *all the while avoiding contact with* EMMA.

FLAP *(conciliatory to* EMMA*).* Hey. I've been packing for us all week.

FLAP *kisses* MELANIE, *who reacts with delight.*

EMMA. She sure remembers her daddy.

FLAP. So, you going to stay mad?

EMMA *(ironically).* I thought being uprooted with my children without my consent is at least worth a pout, don't you?

*She walks towards the house, loaded down.*

*(to boys)* Come on.

FLAP. Head of the department.

EMMA. I know. I know.

FLAP. Here.

*Ext.* AURORA'S *House—Garden Area—Evening*

GARRETT *(calls out)*. Aurora!

AURORA *(O.S.)*. Garrett! I'm back here. *(to* GARRETT*)* Well, hello, stranger. What's it been, about two days?

GARRETT. Your family still around?

AURORA. No, they left. What?

GARRETT. You probably know what I'm gonna say.

AURORA. Oh, maybe not. I hope not.

GARRETT. Well, you're some kind of woman, but I'm the wrong kind of man. And it doesn't look like my shot at being the right kind is as good as I was hoping for.

AURORA. Are you intentionally sounding like an idiot to make this easier for me?

GARRETT. Well . . .

*Several beats, she looks at him, he shifts, embarrassed. Some code insists that he can't leave until she dismisses him.*

AURORA *(continuing low)*. You don't even know how much you're gonna miss me.

GARRETT. I don't wanna blow smoke up your ass.

AURORA. Oh? What a relief.

GARRETT. It's just I'm starting to feel . . . an obligation here. It makes it rough, especially living next door. I'm starting to think I gotta . . . watch what I'm doing . . .

AURORA *(cutting him off)*. Blah, blah, blah, blah, blah, blah, blah . . . *(mouths word)* Blah.

GARRETT. I—I am going to miss you. And I do feel bad.

AURORA. You're lucky. I feel humiliated.

*She is nakedly pained and angry as she looks at him. It's unsettling and there is a trace of real anguish in* GARRETT *as he awkwardly exits. We hold on* AURORA *for a beat then:*

*Ext. Kearney State College—Day*

*A campus which would consider "functional" a compliment. A* KEARNEY STATE COLLEGE *sign is in the right foreground.* EMMA *is walking with* MELANIE, *now aged two, in a stroller and wearing her best dress. They turn into one of the older buildings, the English Department.*

*Int. English Department—Day*

*A perfect older, white-haired elderly* SECRETARY *is seated behind a desk.* JANICE *is talking to her. The elderly* SECRETARY *is genuinely delighted to see the new arrivals.*

JANICE *(to* SECRETARY*)*. When you finish this, I need this kind of type, or something close to it.

SECRETARY. All right. *(then)* Hello, Emma.

EMMA. Hi.

SECRETARY. Hi, baby.

MELANIE *responds.*

EMMA. She wanted her daddy to see her dressed up before we went to . . .

JANICE *starts gathering her things. She rises and walks past* EMMA, *exiting.* EMMA *looks after her.*

. . . the doctor.

SECRETARY. He'll be here any minute.

JANICE *(to* SECRETARY*)*. I'll talk to you later.

SECRETARY *(softly)*. Okay.

EMMA *(to* SECRETARY*)*. Excuse me.

EMMA *breaks out after* JANICE, *pushing* MELANIE'S *stroller.*

*Int. Long Hallway—Day*

*It is heavily trafficked with students and faculty.* EMMA, *pushing* MELANIE *in her stroller, walks quickly down the hallway passing students along the way.*

EMMA *(to* JANICE*)*. Miss!
MELANIE *(mimics* EMMA*)*. Miss!
EMMA *(louder)*. Miss!!!
MELANIE *(mimics* EMMA*)*. Miss!

EMMA, *pushing* MELANIE *in the stroller, follows* JANICE *through a doorway.*

*Ext. Building—Kearney State Campus—Day*

EMMA *struggles with* MELANIE'S *stroller on the stairs.* JANICE *walks across lawn.*

EMMA *(shouts).* Don't make me run after you, I have a toddler here!

JANICE *turns. She's the same young woman* EMMA *caught* FLAP *with in Des Moines.* EMMA *looks at her, now certain who she is.*

Are you the reason that we came to Nebraska?
JANICE. I think Flap should talk to you. We discussed that. I don't want to say anything until he does, except that I don't think there's an emotion you're having that I couldn't validate.
EMMA. Tell you what, if you see Flap, you tell him that his wife and his baby went to the doctor's to get flu shots, all right? Why don't you do that?

*Int.* DR. BUDGE'S *Office—Day*

DR. BUDGE *is an overweight version of a Norman Rockwell G.P. He is giving* MELANIE *a shot.*

DR. BUDGE. Just hold still. That's a girl. Ooo!
MELANIE *(overlaps).* Oow!
EMMA. Okay?

MELANIE *starts to cry.* EMMA *lifts* MELANIE *up and sets her down on a chair as* DR. BUDGE *stands near the table.*

EMMA. There. If it makes you feel any better, Mommy's going to get a shot, too. *(to* DR. BUDGE*).* Can I give her one of the pops?
DR. BUDGE. Sure. Here.

DR. BUDGE *hands* EMMA *a lollipop.* EMMA *takes it and gives it to* MELANIE. MELANIE *calms and smiles.* EMMA *sits on examining table. The* DOCTOR *swabs her arm and then begins moving it.*

EMMA *(to* DR. BUDGE*).* Oh. *(to* MELANIE*)* There ya go. *(to* DR. BUDGE*).* Are they gonna tell me in the other room if my husband calls?

*The* DOCTOR *begins feeling around in* EMMA'S *armpit.*

DR. BUDGE. You have a lump in your armpit. How long has it been there?

MELANIE *is kicking the cabinet and she sits in b.g.* EMMA *looks over her shoulder at her.*

EMMA. I don't know. *(to* MELANIE*)* Melanie . . . stop kickin' the cabinet!
DR. BUDGE. There's two of them. They're not very big, though. I have to be out of town next week, and I hate to make it wait that long. It should come out and be looked at.
EMMA. Come out? Should I be scared?
DR. BUDGE. All it means if you're scared is that you'll be that much happier when it turns out to be nothing.
MELANIE. Dr. Budge! Mom should get a pop, too, for her shot.

DR. BUDGE *(chuckles)*. All right. *(to* EMMA*)*. Here, Mom.

EMMA *(to* MELANIE*)*. Thanks, Mel.

*Int.* AURORA's *Living Room—Day*

AURORA *is sitting at the table alone, the light is on.*

AURORA *(into phone)*. Well, I know what it is. You don't know how to keep yourself up, so you're sweat glands have clogged up. It's a cyst.

*Ext. Phone Booth—Day*

EMMA *is in the booth with* MELANIE.

EMMA. So, I shouldn't worry, right?

AURORA. It's a cyst! It's right where your oil glands are, and they're clogged up! You never did know how to eat right.

*Int.* AURORA's *House—Day*

AURORA *is seated, holding receiver to her ear.*

AURORA. And you've never learned how to wash.

EMMA. You're right! You're right!

*Ext. Phone Booth—Day*

EMMA *is holding receiver to her ear as she plays with* MELANIE.

EMMA. Thanks! Talk to Melanie. *(whispers to* MELANIE*)* Say "hi".

MELANIE. Hi.

*Int. Aurora's House—Day*

AURORA. Hello, how are you? I sent you a blouse.

EMMA *(V.O.)*. Say, goodbye.

MELANIE. 'Bye.

AURORA. Are you ha—oh. Say, say good, say goodbye to your mother.

*She hangs up . . . she is clearly fearful.*

*Int.* HORTON *House—Night*

FLAP *is standing there, taking in the news.*

EMMA. What's her name.

FLAP. Janice. What did the doctor say?

EMMA. I told you, Flap, the scariest thing about it is that he wants to do it so fast. Janice, with her little folder under her arm . . .

EMMA *stands and mimics* JANICE.

"I can't say anything until he does. We've discussed it, Flap and I." I mean, really, Flap! Validate my feelings! Your taste!

FLAP. But that, that thing the doctor said about, about feeling good when it turns out to be nothing.

EMMA *(overlapping)*. No, no, no forget about it! I'm not gonna make you feel better, I'm too mad! *(shouts to family)* Dinner!

*Int. Hospital Room—Nebraska—Night*

EMMA *is lying there, playing with her hair, watching at "The Waltons".* DR. BUDGE *enters. He sits on the bed. For the merest beat* EMMA *avoids dealing with him, then looks his way.*

DR. BUDGE *(sighs)*. Dear, you have a malignancy.

EMMA *(in unison)*. Malignancy. Say it again.

DR. BUDGE. Malignancy.

*Int.* AURORA's *Kitchen—Day*

AURORA, *stricken, hangs up the phone.* ROSIE *is busy nearby.*

AURORA. Rosie! Rosie, our girl is in trouble. She had a cyst, a kind of a cyst and it turned out to be malignant. And they're gonna take her to a hospital in Lincoln, Nebraska.

ROSIE. Oh.

*The two women embrace.* ROSIE *does with ease something she has never done before: She kisses* AURORA *on the cheek.*

### Int. Lincoln General Hospital— Doctor's Office—Day

PATSY *sits alongside* AURORA. PATSY *is wearing a fur coat and looks dazzling. This is a new doctor,* DR. MAISE. *He is too calm. He also cannot seem to control his eyes from clicking over to* PATSY *occasionally.* AURORA *does not miss this aspect of the interview.*

DR. MAISE. We'll release her in a few days. We do more and more on an out-patient basis. We shouldn't need to take her back here at all unless the illness escalates.

AURORA. But you're not telling me anything.

DR. MAISE. What are you confused about?

AURORA. How is she?

DR. MAISE. I always tell people to hope for the best and prepare for the worst.

AURORA *(dumbfounded).* And they let you get away with that.

DR. MAISE. Look, ah . . . you're wrong to take the attitude that everything is so desperate, and serious now. And it won't do your daughter any good to get those signals, either.

### Int. Hospital Room—Day

EMMA *is reading the kids' letters and enjoying herself.* AURORA *and* PATSY *enter with broadly fixed smiles on their faces.*

EMMA. What's wrong now?

PATSY *and* AURORA *smile with some sincerity at their transparency.*

AURORA *(sitting on bed).* I just get so frustrated with the doctor. But it all boils down to you're getting out of here tomorrow and you won't have to stay here again.

EMMA. Unless the illness spreads. I really don't feel sick.

PATSY. Hey, Emma, I want you to come to New York for a visit. My treat!

EMMA. Oh, great! I mean, we'll have to see. Oh, you guys have to see this letter, it's from the kids. Teddy says he can't sleep but Melanie slept fine. Tommy says that he really doesn't think that there's anything to be concerned about.

PATSY. Hey! I mean it! You have some time before you have to see the doctor again. Come see New York for a few days!

AURORA. I don't think it's a bad idea. Have a vacation by yourself. Rosie and I are here with the kids. Take advantage of your freedom.

PATSY. I know you wanna go.

EMMA *(draws deep breath).* This isn't like when they take those kids to Disneyland, you know, right before the end.

PATSY. Oh, stop!

PATSY *slaps* EMMA'S *leg.*

EMMA. Ow!

PATSY. Oh, I'm sorry.

EMMA. Patsy, I'm kiddin'.

PATSY. Okay. Okay. *(nervous laugh)*

### Int. Hospital Room—Next Day

EMMA *is sitting on the edge of the bed as* FLAP *packs her things into a box.*

FLAP. Do you feel funny about leaving the kids?

EMMA. I'm not leaving them! I'm entrusting them to their father.

FLAP. Oh, I thought as long as your Mother and Rosie are in town, that, you know . . .

EMMA *(cutting him off).* Not them, you!

### Ext. 59th Street Bridge—Night

*Int. Limousine—Night*

PATSY *is sitting in the back seat with* EMMA, *who looks strange in this setting.*

PATSY. Emma. Emma, look, look!

*Their POV*

*New York City lit up.*

*On* EMMA

EMMA *(delighted).* I can't believe I'm here!

PATSY'S HUSBAND. Isn't it beautiful?

*Int. River Cafe—Day*

PATSY *and* EMMA *and three other* WOMEN *in their late 20's or early 30's are being seated at a large round table. The East River traffic just a few feet away, the Brooklyn Bridge overhead, the city beyond, a piano player at work on the atmosphere.*

*There isn't a Welsh coal miner who wouldn't instantly guess which of the five women was the rube.* EMMA *is out of her element, but there is enough inner security to make her only vaguely uncomfortable amid these well-groomed seemingly-sure-of-themselves contemporaries.*

PATSY *(making introductions).* Emma, this is Lizbeth.
EMMA. Hi, Elizabeth.
LIZBETH. Hi, it's Lizbeth.
EMMA. Isn't that what I said?
LIZBETH. You said Elizabeth with an "E." It's Lizbeth.
EMMA. Two names—Liz Beth?
LIZBETH. No, one name—Lizbeth. Never mind.
PATSY. And this is Jane.
EMMA. Thank heavens.

*She gets a nice little laugh.*

*Later*

*There is a good deal of intelligent, though nonetheless chirpy, chatter. The women are just finishing examining two photographs of* EMMA'S *kids.*

EMMA. There, that's Melanie. That's Teddy, he's the younger one, and Tommy's the older one.
LIZBETH. The little girl, she's incredible.
PATSY. Yeah, and don't think she doesn't know it.
EMMA. Oh, Patsy's got a real thing goin' with her. I mean, the boys, too. It's . . .
VICTORIA. Are you going to wait until she's in school before you go back to work?
EMMA. Oh, I never really worked.

*There's a half-beat of silent shocked reaction.*

JANE *(firmly and democratically).* Well, that's okay.
EMMA. Thanks.

*The* WAITER *gives coffee to all and sets an incredibly gooey dessert down in front of* EMMA.

(TO WAITER) Oh, great!

EMMA *starts to eat her dessert and then feels all eyes on her. She stops a spoonful of the stuff and sees her diet-conscious table mates looking on ravenously.*

*Ext. River Cafe Parking Lot—Day*

*Breezy, right on the water.* PATSY *is talking to her three New York friends as they wait for taxis. The mood seems different. Two of the women are genuinely aghast, and then the conversation stops.*

*On* EMMA

*The three women are staring at her as she approaches.*

EMMA. What's wrong?
LIZBETH. Nothing.

*A cab approaches. Suddenly, the women are pressing too hard to seem natural.*

VICTORIA *(shaking hands).* It was a great honor meeting you, Emma. I hope you have a wonderful time here.

JANE. I think those beautiful children are lucky to have you for a mommy.

PATSY. Go ahead, you girls take the first one. We're not in a hurry.

LIZBETH *(to* EMMA*).* You sure?

EMMA. Yeah, it's fine.

VICTORIA *(mouthing word).* Hope.

JANE. Bye bye, Patsy.

EMMA *is a bit down.* PATSY *is embarrassed. The cab pulls away.*

EMMA. You told 'em, didn't you?

PATSY. Yeah, you don't mind, do ya?

EMMA. Of course not.

EMMA *walks to the water's edge and starts to cry. This young Texas woman, this midlander, standing on an alien coast smack in front of one of the world's sophisticated cities, feeling sorry for herself for the first time.*

PATSY *(calling after* EMMA*).* They're jerks, they don't know anything!

PATSY *walks quickly after* EMMA.

EMMA *(sighs).* Why did those women have to act like that?

PATSY. Emma, talk to me!

EMMA. It's not you, Patsy. I don't care. I mean, I don't mind them knowing. *(getting mad)* In less than two hours, two of them told me that they had had abortions. Three of them told me they were divorced. One of them hasn't talked to her mother in four years! And that one that has her "little Natalie" in boarding school because ah, ah, she has to travel for her

job. I mean, hell, Patsy, that's all . . . oh, the one with the yeast disease that thought she had vaginal herpes. If that's fit conversation for lunch, what's so godawful terrible about my little tumors?

PATSY. Yeah, of course, but what do you want me to do? I . . .

EMMA. I want ya to tell 'em it ain't so tragic! People do get better. Tell them it's okay to talk about the cancer!

*Int.* PATSY's *Living Room—Night*

*A few couples, well-dressed, are casually seated around* PATSY's *living room.* MEG, PATSY'S DAUGHTER, *is kissing her mother and father goodnight.* PATSY'S *husband,* JACK, *is a good looking, well-connected, young partner at Solomon Brothers. They are drinking and eating little chili canapes that* PATSY'S *made. One of the women fills a silence.*

WOMAN *(bright and conversational).* Patsy tells us you have cancer.

PATSY *laughs so suddenly she spits out her little chili dog. It virtually flies across the room.* EMMA *breaks up laughing with her.*

WOMAN. We should really talk later. I'm a nutritionist and my husband's with Ticketron.

EMMA *(laughing).* Thanks, Patsy.

EMMA *nods and exits to terrace.*

*Ext.* PATSY's *Terrace—Night*

*An attractive 5 foot 5 inch, intense man,* PHIL, *who's often told he looks like Richard Dreyfuss, is standing close to* EMMA *smoking a joint.*

PHIL. Want a hit—maybe to help with the nausea?

EMMA. No. I think that's only if you're having chemotherapy.

PHIL. Were you feeling anything tonight?

EMMA. Sick, you mean?

PHIL. No. Between us.

EMMA. Not really. But I liked that you sit forward in your chair like you're very interested in what people are saying but it's really so your feet will touch the floor. It's sweet.

PHIL. I wouldn't be bringing up the cancer, but Patsy said it was okay.

EMMA. It is okay.

PHIL. I work for her husband. My older brother had cancer and now he's fine.

EMMA. What kind did he have?

PHIL. Skin cancer.

*Before she can say anything:*

PHIL *(defensively)*. I know. That's the best kind. *(a beat)* I'd really like to take you out sometime.

EMMA. I'm sorry. I have to go back very soon and Patsy has a lot planned—Broadway shows and things—and I'm married and have three kids—and there is the cancer.

PHIL. Yeah, I figured it was a long shot.

*They stand there for a beat.*

EMMA. Excuse me.

*She walks inside.* PATSY *is standing with her husband.*

PATSY. You don't feel like meeting somebody right now who had a mastectomy, do you?

EMMA *(polite)*. Maybe in a bit.

*Int.* AURORA'S *House—Day*

AURORA *has phone to her ear.*

FLAP. Hello.

AURORA. Hello, Flap?

FLAP. Yes?

AURORA. Have you heard anything?

*Ext.* FLAP *and* EMMA'S *Backyard—Day*

FLAP *is barbecuing hamburgers and hotdogs. He holds the receiver braced between his ear and shoulder.*

FLAP. Ah, no, Em, Emma hasn't called you, then, either?

AURORA *(V.O)*. No. How are the children?

FLAP. Oh, I wish I were so carefree.

*Int.* AURORA'S *House—Day*

AURORA. Yes, well, they don't have anything to feel ashamed about.

*Ext.* FLAP *and* EMMA'S *Backyard—Day*

FLAP. You know something, Aurora? You always seem to lose your manners around me.

*Int.* AURORA'S *House—Day*

AURORA. Stop it, Flap. Let me know if you hear. And if you talk to Emma, don't sound as frightened . . .

*Ext.* EMMA *and* FLAP'S *Backyard—Day*

AURORA *(V.O)* . . . as you do now.

FLAP *(loudly)*. I don't sound f-frightened.

FLAP *puts down the receiver.* TOMMY *looks at his father.*

*Int.* PATSY'S *House—Night*

EMMA *(V.O.)*. Hi, Mother.

*Int.* EMMA'S *Room—Night*

EMMA *is lying on the bed holding the phone to her ear.*

Look, they're havin' this party for me, so I can't talk for very long, but I think I'm comin' home a few days early . . . Not really.

*Int. Lincoln Memorial Hospital—* EMMA'S *Room—Day*

AURORA, *dressed colorfully, is supervising two workmen who are hanging* AURORA's *Renoir and Klee. She squeezes her armpit occasionally.* EMMA *is in bed, genuinely cheered by the additions.*

AURORA. It's about time they gave us this room!

EMMA. God, Mother, I can't believe you did this. It's great.

AURORA. Sure. *(to workmen)* Careful there! These are worth more than you'll ever make in your lifetime.

*Oblivious to the looks the men cast at her,* AURORA *steps up to paintings and adjusts them.*

EMMA *(to workmen)*. I grew up with it my whole life, you can take it for a couple of minutes.

AURORA *(to workmen)*. That's fine. Thank you so much.

EMMA. Thank you. *(to AURORA)* Hum! Oh, they're wonderful!

AURORA. They look good next to each other.

*Int. Hospital Waiting Room—Day*

AURORA *sits on the floor with* TEDDY *and* MELANIE. TOMMY *is seated in a chair.* AURORA *points to puzzle pieces on the floor.*

AURORA. Help me with this, Melanie. Gorgeous isn't everything. This one. This one. Two more.

AURORA *kisses* TEDDY.

*Int.* EMMA's *Hospital Room—Day*

DR. BUDGE *stands at* EMMA's *bed looking down at his chart. He shuts the file.*

DR. BUDGE. The response to the drugs we tried isn't what we hoped. But there are investigatory drugs, which we are willing to utilize. However, if you become incapaci-

tated, or it becomes unreasonable for you to handle your affairs for a block of time . . . *(draws breath)* . . . it might be wise to make some decisions now. Any questions?

EMMA *(tearfully)*. No. I know what you're saying. Um, I have to figure out what to do with my kids. *(now she sobs)*

*Int. Hospital Hallway—Nurses' Station—Night*

AURORA *is at the nurses' station. There is a large clock prominent in the background which reads seven minutes past ten.* AURORA *is extraordinarily agitated, hyper, manic. A* NURSE *is seated at a counter holding a receiver to her ear as she writes with the other hand.* AURORA *leans on counter looking at* NURSE.

AURORA. Excuse me, it is after ten. Give my daughter the pain shot . . . please.

NURSE. Missus Greenway, I was going to.

AURORA. Oh, good, go ahead.

NURSE. In just a few minutes.

AURORA *(loudly)*. Please, it's after ten! It's after ten. I don't see why she has to have this pain!

NURSE #2. Ma'am, it's not my patient.

AURORA *(shouting)*. It's time for her shot! You understand, do something! All she has to do is hold on until ten! And it's past ten! She's in pain! My daughter's in pain! Give her the shot! You understand?!

NURSE #3. Are you going to behave?

AURORA *(screaming)*. Give my daughter the shot!!

*The* NURSE *looks wide-eyed.* AURORA *did not anticipate her outburst. The* NURSE *scurries toward* EMMA's *room.* AURORA *is breathing heavily.*

AURORA (*to nurses, quietly*). Thank you very much. Thank you.

*Int. Hotel Lobby—Day*

*A* WOMAN *stands in front of counter as* AURORA *enters and walks to desk* CLERK *with glasses. The* CLERK *hands key to* AURORA. *The* WOMAN *is talking to a bearded* CLERK.

WOMAN. Is there any mail for me?
AURORA (*to* CLERK *with glasses*). Can I have two-two-two, please?

*The* CLERK *hands* AURORA *her key. She turns and walks away.*

*Int. Pleasure Dome—Day*

AURORA *stands watching* TOMMY *and* TEDDY *swim in the indoor pool. They are having a fine time.* PATSY *and* ROSIE *sit in the b.g.* PATSY *is holding* MELANIE. *TEDDY hops out of the pool and, giggling, pretends he's going to push* AURORA *in.* TOMMY *calls to his brother from the pool.*

TOMMY. Let's get her.
TEDDY. Pushin' Grandma in the pool.
TOMMY. Come on, let's get her.

TEDDY *climbs out of the pool and advances ominously on* AURORA. *She fixes him with a look.*

AURORA. Don't you dare. I mean it!
TOMMY (*to* TEDDY). Come on.

TOMMY *touches* TEDDY'S *arm and they exit.* PATSY *is holding* MELANIE *on her lap.* ROSIE *sits on the far side of the table, and we see* VERN *in the b.g.*

PATSY (*to* MELANIE). Say hi, Granny.
MELANIE. Hi, Granny.
GARRETT (*O.S.*). Aurora.

AURORA *looks up.* GARRETT *is standing at the top of the stairs.* AU-RORA *starts up the stairs and* GARRETT *down the stairs. They meet on the steps and embrace, then stand looking at each other. She is trying very hard, with noteworthy success, not to cry.*

AURORA. Well . . . now who would have expected you to be a nice guy?

GARRETT *chuckles, sighs. He takes her hand as they sit on the steps.*

AURORA (*repeating*). Who?
GARRETT. It's good to see ya.

GARRETT *removes his sunglasses.* AURORA *puts her hand on his chest.*

AURORA. Whoa!

AURORA *puts her hand to her face as* GARRETT *puts his arm around her shoulders.*

*Ext. Lincoln Airport—Day*

*Where* AURORA *sees* GARRETT *off. They embrace and, as part of the embrace, he grabs a handful of her rear end.*

GARRETT. Take care of yourself, huh? I'll call ya. I'm real glad I came.
AURORA. Your coming meant a lot to Em. It meant a lot to me, Garrett. I'll be at the hospital all the time. I'll call you. No, if I do that and there's someone there I'll hear that funny sound in your voice. I don't care, who cares, I don't care. I'm glad you came. I love you.

*They hug again.* AURORA *mimics* GARRETT *and grabs a handful of his behind. She starts away from him, stops.*

(*calling*) Garrett. Garrett, come here.

*He stops, she walks up to him.*

I was curious. Do you have any reaction at all to my telling you I love you?

GARRETT. I was just inches from a clean getaway.

AURORA. You're stuck, so face it.

GARRETT *(sighs)*. Well, I, I don't know what else to say, except my stock answer.

AURORA. Which is?

GARRETT. I love you too, kid.

GARRETT *smiles and reaches for* AURORA. *He takes her face in his hands and kisses her. He turns and walks into the terminal.* AURORA *stands watching the glass doors slide together after him.*

AURORA. Goodbye.

*Int.* EMMA'S *Hospital Room—Day*

AURORA *and* EMMA *each in their own thoughts. A trace of a smile on* AURORA'S *face. Now* AURORA *looks at her daughter.*

AURORA. I took him to the airport, and we were standing there . . . and we were standing there in front of the door hugging and kissing and saying goodbye. And you know what?

EMMA. What?

AURORA. I got up the nerve to tell him I loved him. You know what his reaction was?

EMMA. I don't give a shit, Mom, I'm sick. Not everything has to do with you. I got a lot to figure out.

AURORA. I just don't want to fight any more.

EMMA. What do you mean? When do we fight?

AURORA. When do we fight? You amaze me! I always think of us as fighting.

EMMA. That's just from your end. That's 'cause you're never satisfied with me.

*Int. Hospital Cafeteria—Day*

FLAP, *with a huge tray of food and two books under his arm, is just about to set himself down at an empty table for respite. He sits and props up a book, savoring fifteen minutes of ease and peace, but then he looks up.*

FLAP'S POV

*His mother-in-law. She is looking at him.*

*On* FLAP

*as reluctantly and dutifully he folds his book, hefts his tray, and walks to* AURORA'S *table.* FLAP *is wearing the distinctive tie that* EMMA *bought for him with* AURORA'S *money years ago.*

FLAP. Have you seen her yet today?

AURORA. Yes, I've been with her most of last night and today.

FLAP. I haven't, ah . . . really talked to the kids yet. I'm not sure how much they realize, but . . . *(clears throat)* . . . they know something bad is happening.

AURORA. Flap, Patsy wants to raise Melanie. And maybe the boys. I think they should be with me, don't you?

FLAP. W-what can you be thinking about?

AURORA. Raising three children, working full time and chasing women requires a lot more energy than you have. You know, one of the nicest qualities about you has always been that you recognized your weaknesses. Don't lose the quality now when you need it the most.

FLAP. You have no right, nor any invitation, to discuss where or how my children live.

FLAP *picks up his books and leaves* AURORA *seated at the table alone.*

*Int.* EMMA'S *Hospital Room—Day*

EMMA *is sitting in a chair.* FLAP *stands near window.*

EMMA. Well, from what the doctor says, it's time that we have the talk now.

FLAP *looks at her, then away. Some quality he doesn't have may be expected of him. Then he turns back and holds her gaze.*

FLAP. Do you know how much I hate the idea of losing you?

EMMA *(whispers).* Yes.

FLAP. Well, no . . . *(small laugh)* . . . nobody seems to know, except you. I'd, well . . .

EMMA. What?

FLAP *(small laugh).* I'm just, I'm thinking about my identity, and not having one anymore. I mean, who am I if I'm not the man who's failing Emma?

EMMA. You didn't fail me, Flap.

FLAP. No? Well, I don't want to talk about this. I feel like I'm sucking after forgiveness—which I probably am.

EMMA. You weren't any more terrible than I was.

FLAP *(small laugh).* Oh, except for the cheating.

EMMA. You're right, let's not do this. Look, we had problems, it was never over whether we loved each other . . . Oh, God, the tie! Oh, God, the mess it must have been for you to find it.

*He grins. There is a strange but uncommonly easy intimacy between them. As they relax, this visit begins to have some of the elements of a good time.*

FLAP. The house still isn't in one piece. It was in the last box I looked in.

EMMA *laughs.*

FLAP. God, you're so easy to please. I don't know why I couldn't do more of it.

EMMA. I'm so glad we're talking! I just am! It just means so much to me that we can still feel like this so much.

FLAP *(amazed at her).* I swear. I don't know.

*She grabs one of his ears and holds it affectionately.*

EMMA. Listen, I'm getting tired. Just tell me, hon, do you really want to raise them?

*He looks down, thinks, then at her.*

FLAP. I never thought I was the sort of man who'd give up his kids.

EMMA. It's a lot of hard work. As hard as you think it is, you'd end up wishing it were that easy.

*He thinks.*

FLAP. Where do you want them?

EMMA. I don't want them to end up with Janice.

FLAP *(hesitantly).* Ya know, she's not so bad.

EMMA. I really don't think they should be with you, honey.

FLAP *(draws breath).* Well . . . to tell ya the honest truth . . . I'd probably screw it up. I'll really miss them. But maybe we should let Patsy take them, because it would be very easy for me to work research summers in New York.

EMMA. No. *(soft laugh)* Patsy really only wants Melanie. Mother should have them.

FLAP *sighs.*

FLAP *(ruefully).* I guess they should be with your mother. I probably have that coming.

EMMA. Flap, will you bring the boys by tomorrow? I got that one waiting for me, I gotta do it.

FLAP *(barely audible).* Yeah, okay.

*Int.* EMMA's *Hospital Room—The Next Day*

PATSY *is putting some makeup on* EMMA, *getting her spruced up for her boys.*

EMMA. Come on, Patsy, I gotta get ready. Patsy! The makeup . . .

PATSY. Is it terrible of me to say that I just can't stand for your mother to get her hands on that little girl? I'd just love to raise that little girl.

EMMA. I'd let you. But Teddy can't spare her.

PATSY *pauses. She always adored the way* EMMA *thinks. She is heavy-hearted but is working against the emotion, trying to supply energy to her friend's hospital room.*

EMMA. I can't stall anymore. All right, you go out there and send the boys in.

PATSY. Well, do I ever get to say something, ever?

EMMA. No.

PATSY *laughs.*

EMMA *(laughs).* We don't have to do that, right? Come here.

*They kiss. Tears come.* PATSY *dries them, does some patch work with the makeup. Then she patches herself.*

EMMA. You'll be fine. You will.

PATSY *(faltering).* It's just this . . . you're my touchstone, Emma.

EMMA. The boys!

PATSY *exits.* EMMA *sits there alone, preparing to tackle the final task she has set for herself: Her farewell to her children. At this moment she is thinking hard, concentrating on how she will deal with this. She is at work. We hear the door open; she looks toward it.*

EMMA. Hi. Come on.

TOMMY *and* TEDDY *enter their mother's room.* TOMMY *steeling himself, his younger brother already in tears. He moves quickly to his mother and buries his head in the covers.* TOMMY *is enormously uncomfortable*

*and rigid.* TEDDY *is a bit out of control because, suddenly, here with his mother, he feels comfortable enough to say what he's been thinking since she was hospitalized.*

TEDDY. I love you. I miss you. God, I want you to come home!

*On* TOMMY

*as he hesitates for half a beat, then walks to the bed.* EMMA *touches his face.*

EMMA. Close the door. God, you both look so gigantic to me. I guess I look pretty bad to you, huh?

TEDDY *is so shocked by her appearance he can't answer, just looks embarrassed.* TOMMY *shows a small measure of grace.*

TOMMY. Not so bad.

*On* EMMA

*Strangely she feels deep appreciation for* TOMMY'S *words.*

EMMA. You both have beautiful eyes. And your hair is too long. *(a cry in her voice)* I mean, I don't care how long it gets in the back, but keep your bangs cut, okay? It's too long.

TOMMY. It's a matter of opinion.

EMMA. Just keep it shorter, all right?

TOMMY. Are you getting well?

EMMA. Uh-huh.

TEDDY'S *eyes dart, as if looking for escape.*

I'm sorry about this, but I can't help it. And I can't talk to you for too long, or I'll get real upset. I want you to make a lot of friends. And I want you to be real nice to the girls, cause they're gonna be real important to you, I swear.

TOMMY. We're not afraid of girls. What makes you think that?

EMMA. Well, you may be later on.

TOMMY. I doubt it.

TEDDY (*sobbing, to* TOMMY). Why don't you shut up?! (*shouts*) Shut up!

TOMMY (*half-heartedly*). You shut up.

EMMA (*to* TEDDY). Teddy, give me a kiss.

*They kiss on the lips.* TEDDY *kisses her a few extra times and so does she. She does the last extra kiss in a way which makes him smile. She gestures to* TOMMY, *who kisses her cheek quickly. He is tortured and somehow being stiff, and foul is simpler for him right now.*

EMMA. Tommy, you be sweet. Be sweet. And stop tryin' to pretend like you hate me. I mean, it's silly.

TOMMY (*strained*). I like you.

EMMA. Okay, then will you listen especially close?

TOMMY. What?

EMMA. You'll listen real hard?

TOMMY. I said, what?!

EMMA. I know you like me. I know it! For the last year or two you've been pretending like you hate me. (*draws breath*) I love you very much. I love you as much as I love anybody . . . as much as I love myself. In a few years, when I haven't been around to be on your tail about something, or irritating you, you're gonna . . . (*draws breath*) . . . remember. You'll remember that time that I bought you the baseball glove when you thought we were too broke. Or when . . . I read you those stories, or when I let you goof off instead of mowing the lawn, lots of things like that. And you're gonna realize that you love me. And maybe you're gonna feel badly, because you never told me, but don't! I know that you love me. So don't ever do that to yourself, all right?

TOMMY *pauses, his brother looking at him with hope and urging that he say, "I love you." He doesn't.*

TOMMY. Okay.

EMMA. Okay?

TOMMY. I said okay.

EMMA. Okay, you two should run along. Take care.

EMMA (*to* TOMMY). Gimme me a kiss.

*He does. The boys begin to exit. She looks after them.*

I was so scared. I think it went really well, don't you?

TEDDY *pauses holding the door open. He nods his head, too fearful and overwhelmed to dare a word.*

EMMA. Yeah.

*Ext. Hospital—Day*

*Moving Shot—Close on* TOMMY

*as he moves along, glancing back occasionally.*

*Ext. Hospital Grounds—Day*

AURORA *is making conversation to soothe* TEDDY, *who keeps lapsing unexpectedly into tears or sniffling.* TOMMY *lags behind, pausing, looking back at the hospital, then catching up.*

AURORA. Tommy, if you need to talk, your dad will listen. He's a very smart man, you know. All you have to do is go up to him and say, "Dad, I'm confused, I need to have a talk." You know, I met this boy, back in River Oaks where I live, and he was tellin' me that the Cub Scouts in Houston are the best ever.

TOMMY. We were never scouts. Our mother was too lazy to check it out.

AURORA'S *hand hits him so hard that he's knocked down and several feet away from the blow.* MELANIE *giggles nervously.* TOMMY *starts to scamper away.* AURORA *goes after him. He almost runs for it. She has him by the arm.*

TOMMY. No! Stop! Come on, stop it! No!
AURORA. Listen to me. It's okay!

TOMMY *struggles to get free and starts to raise his hand to slap* AURORA—*she slaps his face again.*

Hey! *(she slaps him)* Stop it! I'm sorry, but I can't have you criticizing your mother around me.

AURORA *hugs* TOMMY *to her.*

*Int.* EMMA'S *Hospital Room—Night*

*One light on.* FLAP *dozing in a chair.* AURORA *seated across the room, looking at* EMMA, *who is on even more life support systems, and now* EMMA *looks back at her. Her mother smiles at her with a quiet and mystic reassurance—their final communication.* EMMA *turns;* AURORA *looks out the window. The door opens, a* NURSE *enters. She checks* EMMA.

*This is the same* NURSE *who had the run-in with* AURORA. *She's a bit reluctant to approach her. She touches* FLAP, *who awakens.*

NURSE. Mr. Horton. She's gone.

FLAP *gets to his feet. He looks at* AURORA, *who rises.*

AURORA. Oh, God, I'm so stupid. I'm so stupid, somehow I thought when she finally went . . . that it would be a relief. Oh, my sweet little darling . . .

FLAP *reaches forward and touches* AURORA'S *back—* AURORA *rises and* FLAP *hugs her. She cries in her son-in-law's arms.*

AURORA. There's nothing harder, is there?

*Ext.* AURORA'S *House and Garden—Day*

GARRETT, VERNON, EDWARD *the banker, the* DOCTOR, TOMMY, TEDDY, MELANIE, ROSIE, FLAP, PATSY, *her* HUSBAND, MEG *and* CECIE HORTON. *The casual, unconstructed conversation of our characters as they eat, drink and talk about* EMMA, *and inevitably talk about her mother as well.*

TOMMY *is standing alone off to the side, taking in his mother's wake.* FLAP, *moves to him.*

FLAP. Why are ya standing over here?
TOMMY. I don't know.
FLAP. Well, you wanna come over and sit with me? Everything's going to be all right, Tommy.
TOMMY. Sure.

TOMMY *stands his ground.* FLAP, *beaten, agonized, walks off.*

*On* FLAP *and* PATSY

TEDDY *playing nearby the father who has given them up. Seeking some ease, finds himself shell-shocked—as he begins to cry.*

*Full Shot—The Wake*

GARRETT *appears at the entrance of the gazebo in the b.g., holding* MELANIE'S *hand. They're talking.*

GARRETT. Ah, there's fantastic dance schools in Houston.
MELANIE. Tap?
GARRETT. Tap. Ballet. Aerobics. Anything you want. Come over here and see your dad.

*On* AURORA *as she is joined by* PATSY. *They look at* GARRETT.

AURORA *(to* PATSY*)*. He really knows the pretty girls.

GARRETT *(to* MELANIE*)*. We'll talk about this a little later.

AURORA *(to* PATSY*)*. She's too old for him, actually.

GARRETT *(to* MELANIE*)*. Oh, you're eating a wet bunny? There, you go on over to Daddy and eat it. *(to* VERNON*)* Hey, Vern.

VERNON *(to* GARRETT*)*. How ya doin', Garrett?

GARRETT *crosses to the driveway where* TOMMY *is standing. They stand for a beat.*

GARRETT. I hear you're a swimmer.

TOMMY. Yeah.

GARRETT. Me, too.

TOMMY. But you're an astronaut, right?

GARRETT. Yep. I'm an astronaut *and* a swimmer. Pretty good lookin' suit there.

AURORA *has* MELANIE *at her side and works with more patience than* we've *seen to get the child to move immediately next to her.*

AURORA. A little closer. A little closer. A little closer.

*On* GARRETT *as he pats* TOMMY *on the shoulder.*

GARRETT. Wanna see my pool?

TOMMY. Well, ah, I don't know if the time is right, ya know.

GARRETT. Oh, I think it is. Come on. I'll show you the internationally infamous Breedlove crawl.

GARRETT *puts an arm on* TOMMY'S *shoulder and guides him down the driveway.* MELANIE *babbles.*

It's a little stroke I picked up out in space.

*On* AURORA *and* MELANIE

AURORA *watching* GARRETT *shepherd* TOMMY. MELANIE *giggles a bit as her grandmother smiles at her and we . . .*

*Fade out.*

# JULIA

## *Screenplay by Alvin Sargent*

| | |
|---|---|
| LILLIAN | Jane Fonda |
| JULIA | Vanessa Redgrave |
| HAMMETT | Jason Robards |
| MR. JOHANN | Maximilian Schell |
| ALAN | Hal Holbrook |
| DOTTIE | Rosemary Murphy |
| ANNE MARIE | Meryl Streep |

Directed by Fred Zinnemann
Produced by Richard Roth
Cinematographer: Douglas Slocombe
Film Editor: Walter Murch
Set Designers: Pierre Charron and Tessa Davies
Music by Georges Delerue
Production Design: Gene Callahan, Willy Holt, and Carmen
Dillon

*Julia,* by Alvin Sargent, is based on Lillian Hellman's alleged recollection of a friend, which was published in her book *Pentimento*.

It is not within the province of this anthology to get involved in the controversy that still exists over whether Miss Hellman's account of Julia is fact or fiction, and further, whether much or most of her highly politicized and polarized life as a writer and espouser of causes as she recalls it are lies or distortions of the truth.

Suffice it to say there are grounds for this controversy, and if our readers wish to learn more concerning this fascinating dispute, I would recommend they read the latest biography of her life, *Lillian Hellman: Her Legend and Her Legacy,* by Carl Rollyson (published by St. Martin's Press, 1988). For our purposes here, we will be concerned only with the screenplay of *Julia* and its contribution to a very fine motion picture.

Mr. Sargent won an Academy Award for Best Screenplay (adapted from another medium) for *Julia* in 1977. His scripts are noted for their lucid intelligence and vivid, skillful characterizations of women, well evidenced in *Paper Moon* (1973), *The Sterile Cuckoo* (1969), and, of course, this screenplay, a story of a deep and enduring friendship between two women.

Particularly admirable is Mr. Sargent's method in adapting Miss Hellman's recollections of her friend into the screenplay, which serves this fine film so well. He achieves much through his most skillful use of flashbacks in time and his fleshing out of certain details, such as Miss Hellman's trip through Nazi-controlled Berlin from Paris in 1937, which is laden with suspense. This journey, in a real sense, is the climax of the story. As Miss Hellman discovers in herself the courage to make that journey despite her numbing fears that she might be caught and punished by the Nazis while helping Julia, we also make that discovery with her. Also well drawn and portrayed is the depth of the friendship and bond between Miss Hellman and her most courageous friend, Julia, which concludes so painfully and tragically in Julia's death and the disappearance of her child.

One further note of interest, particularly for would-be screenwriters. Although the first scene between Pratt and Lillian Hellman, as written by Mr. Sargent, was shot, Fred Zinnemann, the director, chose not to include it in the final print. Mr. Sargent feels this scene would have been of value. In his opinion, it would have clarified and held together "the otherwise confusing, disjointed structure of the screenplay's early scenes," which was its intention.

I understand fully Mr. Sargent's interpretation and feelings about this scene being omitted. However, I also understand Fred Zinnemann's decision to leave it out as well. In this early scene Pratt and Miss Hellman are discussing people we have not yet met nor know nothing about. I think that Mr. Zinnemann felt that Lillian's negative attitude toward these people would come out more dramatically and meaningfully in a natural way as the story unfolded and we would come to know why she felt this way about Julia's mother and grandparents as they acted and reacted to each other. It is true we are somewhat at sea as to where we are as an audience in the early scenes. But I personally did not find that confusing in a negative sense. Nor detrimental to the screenplay or to the film itself.

This illustrates well a valid difference of opinion between a skilled, intelligent writer and an equally skilled and intelligent director. Happily, in this case it seems to have been a small difference, judging by the results of this fine collaboration. In any case, you be the final judge.

Born in Upper Darby, Pennsylvania, on April 12, 1927, Mr. Sargent currently resides in Santa Monica, California. Besides winning an Academy Award for *Julia,* he also won an award for his screenplay of *Ordinary People* (1980), which makes him one of a handful of writers who have won two Oscars. He perhaps should have been awarded one for *Dominick and Eugene* (1988), which was unfortunately passed over in other categories as well.

*Fade in*

*Long shot a woman* (LILLIAN) *(1962)—day*

She is sitting in a rowboat on very quiet water, a shadowy silhouette in the morning mist. Reeds in foreground.

LILLIAN *is past middle-age. She is wearing an old, wide-brimmed straw hat, a man's loose shirt, dark pants, glasses. She is fishing, deep in thought. Finally:*

LILLIAN'S VOICE *(O.S.).* Old paint on canvas as it ages sometimes becomes transparent. When that happens, it is possible, in some pictures, to see the original lines; a tree will show through a woman's dress, a child makes way for a dog, a boat is no longer on an open sea. That is called pentimento because the painter 'repented,' changed his mind.

*Dissolve*

*Close up* LILLIAN'S *eyes*

*as they look into the past.*

LILLIAN'S VOICE *(O.S.).* The paint has aged now and I want to see what was there for me once, what is there for me now.

*Dissolve*

*Long shot a passenger train (1937)—night*

*moving through the French countryside towards the German border.*

*Angle up at one of the compartment windows, showing a diffused view of three figures (women). A prismatic, multicoloured distortion.*

*Final shot train*

*as it roars frighteningly close. Under the sound of the train we can* barely make out the first few, distorted bars of "You're the Top" played by a small, stringed orchestra.

*Cut to*

*Ext. expansive lawn on Long Island Sound summer (1952)—day*

*A garden party at a large estate.*

*Very tight shot a plump young man*

*Overdressed for boating, Captain's cap. Blue blazer. White ducks. Full rosy cheeks. A highball in one hand. A small sandwich, dripping, in the other. He is looking at something O.S.*

*Camera pans to show a somewhat younger* LILLIAN *away from the heart of the party, standing at a stone wall which surrounds the estate. She holds a drink. The plump young man decides to move in her direction.*

*Angle on* LILLIAN

*at the stone wall. She drinks, looks out at the boats in the water. She looks back at the party. She is bored.*

*The plump young man moves into frame.*

PRATT. Hello, I'm Arthur Pratt. I'm a great admirer of yours, I hope you don't mind my saying so.

LILLIAN *(a polite smile).* That's very nice of you. Thank you very much.

*She takes a sip of her drink.*

PRATT. My father was Arthur Pratt, Senior.

LILLIAN *looks up. Stunned.*

Actually your name came up once when we were talking, I guess it was about one of your plays, and I remember him telling me you wrote him a letter about . . .

*She continues to stare at him.*

Wasn't it Julia?

LILLIAN *(softly; controlled).* Yes.

PRATT *(a proud smile).* Well . . . some small world. I'm Julia's third cousin.

LILLIAN *(quietly).* Are you.

PRATT. Being a great admirer of yours . . . it's really rather satisfying to be linked with you in some way.

*An uncomfortable pause. Then:*

LILLIAN. Where is your father?

PRATT. My father died.

LILLIAN. Your father never answered my letter.

PRATT. He died two years ago. I'm surprised you didn't read about it, large piece in The Times.

LILLIAN. He was supposed to contact me *before* he died.

PRATT. Pardon me?

LILLIAN. You heard me.

PRATT *(pause—nervous laughter—self-conscious).* I'm not a lawyer, I'm not in the firm. I'm a banker.

LILLIAN. I don't care what you are.

PRATT. Pardon me?

LILLIAN. What ever happened to Julia's family?

PRATT. Did I upset you? I didn't mean to say . . .

LILLIAN. What ever happened to Julia's mother, is she dead? Is her mother dead?

PRATT *(carefully).* I think she lives in Argentina or Brazil. Really, if I said *anything* to annoy you, I'm . . .

LILLIAN. You said very much to annoy me. What about her grandparents? They must be dead. Are they dead?

PRATT *(waits; then quietly).* Yes, ma'am. They're dead.

*Long pause.*

LILLIAN *(quietly).* Good . . .

*(stares at him)*

Every one of them was a bastard.

PRATT. Actually, you're talking about my cousins. I really don't understand . . .

LILLIAN *(sharply).* I don't care who I'm talking about, did they ever find the baby?

PRATT. I'm afraid there's been a misunderstanding.

LILLIAN. There is nothing of the kind. Did they ever find the baby?

PRATT. What baby?

LILLIAN. You know damned well what baby. The one they didn't want to find.

PRATT. I'm really sorry, but I don't know what you're talking about.

LILLIAN. Don't you?

*Silence. She looks at him another moment, then softly, controlling her rage:*

LILLIAN. I don't believe you.

*She waits a few more beats, then moves quickly away. The young man remains frozen at the wall.*

*Angle favouring* LILLIAN

*as she nearly collides with a woman who is carrying two highball glasses. She overhears conversation as she moves on.*

1ST VOICE *(O.S.).* Eisenhower can have it if he wants it. And frankly I think he wants it.

2ND VOICE *(O.S.).* I don't think he wants it, and I don't think he would know what to do with it if he had it.

*Cut to*

*Ext. a beach house—day*

*Secluded. Its own beach. High grass along the dunes. Near the house is a small vegetable garden.*

LILLIAN'S VOICE *(O.S.).* Dash?

*Int. beach house—day*

LILLIAN *enters. Dressed as she was.*

LILLIAN *(shouting).* Dash!

*Camera pans with her as she moves through the hallway into the living room, continually moving.*

LILLIAN *(bellowing).* Hammett!

*New angle favouring* HAMMETT

*He's in his early fifties. He is standing in a doorway. Cool. Calm. He holds a cloth and a part of a shotgun which has been broken down.*

LILLIAN *(seeing him).* You're never here.

HAMMETT. Mr. Sanderson wants you to call him about repairing the shutters.

LILLIAN. I don't give a goddamn about the shutters.

HAMMETT. He can come Tuesday morning.

LILLIAN. I didn't want to go to that party. I told you I didn't want to go alone!

HAMMETT *watches her.*

LILLIAN *(mimicking* ARTHUR PRATT JNR.*).* 'I'm Julia's third cousin,' said the silly damn fool.

*She is staring at some bookshelves.* HAMMETT *goes to a table with whisky on it. Pours a drink. He brings it to* LILLIAN. *He picks up his own drink on the bookshelf, already half gone.* LILLIAN *lowers her head, almost cries. Doesn't.*

HAMMETT *(gently).* The baby's dead, Lilly.

LILLIAN *takes a stiff drink. She moves to a table. Finds a cigarette. Lights it. Then she turns to* HAMMETT.

LILLIAN. If I had tried harder to find her . . .

HAMMETT. You tried, Lilly. Get done with it.

LILLIAN. I can't get done with it. I can't get done with things the way you do! I'm not as strong as you are.

*He doesn't speak. He waits. He knows her. Finally,* LILLIAN *moves into another room.*

LILLIAN *(mimicking the young man).* 'I don't know what you're talking about' . . . said the skinny third cousin with his goddamned nautical hat.

*Int.* LILLIAN'S *workroom*

*A typewriter set up in a corner. More books. More than we saw in the living room. Her work on a table. She looks at it. Scratch pads everywhere. Notes and newspaper articles and pictures and postcards tacked to a bulletin board. On one wall is a large map of the world. She goes to her table, slumps in a chair, lays her head on her arms. We begin to hear the sound of a train.*

*Shot a train leaving Paris (1937)— night the steam filling the screen.*

LILLIAN'S VOICE *(as in Sc. 1).* I think I have always known about my memory.

*Shot the train through countryside racing from Paris. We hear its whistle.*

LILLIAN'S VOICE *(continuing).* I know when the truth is distorted by some drama or fantasy.

*Shot a hatbox on a seat in train compartment*

*Words on the box:* MADAME PAULINE.

LILLIAN'S VOICE *(continuing).* But I trust absolutely what I remember about . . .

*Cut to*

*Int. Grandparents' dinning room (1920)—night. Close shot* JULIA *(young)*

LILLIAN'S VOICE *(continuing).* . . . Julia.

*Int.* JULIA'S *grandparents' house dining room (1920)—night*

*Favour* JULIA'S *grandmother at one end of a long, narrow dining table. At the other end of the table we can see* JULIA'S *grandfather. They are formally dressed. Between them on either side of the table are the young* LILLIAN *and* JULIA. *We are in the dining room of a Fifth Avenue mansion. Endless chic-shabby rooms, walls covered with pictures, tables covered with objects of unknown value. Walls covered with garnet-coloured velvet.*

*Sherbet has just been served between courses. A butler (*RAINES*) is prominent. No one speaks. They eat.* LILLIAN *looks to* JULIA *to check the proper spoon.*

*Various shots*

*The* GRANDPARENTS. *Old. Proper. Lifeless. It is all terribly dreary. The faint tinkling of glass and silver. The* OLD WOMAN *sees the* OLD MAN *looking at his plate. She casually snaps her fingers.* RAINES *approaches. She indicates the* GRANDFATHER'S *plate.* RAINES *nods and begins to cut the meat on the dish into small pieces as the* OLD MAN *watches.*

*Angle favouring* JULIA

*very serious, clearly unhappy, wanting the dinner to be over.*

*Angle favouring* LILLIAN

*aware of it all. She looks toward the* GRANDMOTHER. *Camera pans to a shot of the* GRANDMOTHER'S *hand: the ancient fingers with an exquisite heirloom ring, a finely jewelled bracelet.*

*Full shot*

*as the dinner continues in silence. The* GRANDFATHER *eats. The* GRANDMOTHER *drinks whisky from a small crystal goblet. The* GRANDFATHER *begins to doze.*

*Another angle—dining room*

*Camera pans room to show its valuable and depressing clutter. It passes the* GRANDFATHER, *the* BUTLER, *the* TWO YOUNG GIRLS, *and finally the camera stops at the* GRANDMOTHER *who nods, oh so slightly, to* JULIA. JULIA *rises.* LILLIAN, *too.* JULIA *moves to her* GRANDMOTHER. *Curtsies.*

JULIA *(resentful . . . barely audible).* Happy New Year, Grandmother.

*She moves to her* GRANDFATHER, *kisses his brow.*

JULIA. Happy New Year, Grandfather.

LILLIAN *is not certain what to do. She nods at the two old people as* JULIA *starts out of the room indicating for her to follow.*

LILLIAN *(moving, whispering).* Why did we have sherbet in the middle of the meal?

JULIA *(with contempt).* It clears the palate between the fish and the meat.

*As they are about to leave the room, they pass a table with framed photographs on it. One stands out. A Cecil Beaton kind of thing: a most beautiful woman at a costume ball, in a silver harlequin suit, wearing a silver top hat, and silver eye mask. Her body in a straight line as it leans against the wall with one arm extended, her white-gloved hand being kissed by a gigolo in dinner clothes who is kneeling at her feet as she stares down at the top of his head.*

LILLIAN *(as they move—whispering)*. Who's that?
JULIA. It's my mother.
LILLIAN. My God!

LILLIAN's *eyes linger on the photograph as she and* JULIA *exit.*

JULIA *(as they exit)*. She just got married again.

*Int. foyer*

LILLIAN *and* JULIA *approach the ornate staircase. They move up the wide carpeted steps.*

LILLIAN. Where does your mother live?
JULIA. In Scotland. My mother owns a very fancy castle.
LILLIAN. Have you been there?
JULIA. Once.
LILLIAN. What's it like?
JULIA. Full of fancy people with fancy titles.
LILLIAN. Who were they?
JULIA. I don't remember. They didn't interest me. They're all very rich and famous. They just said hello to me and I don't remember.

*They continue up the steps.*

*Cut to*

*Int.* JULIA's *room angle on phonograph*

*as a hand puts the arm on the record. We hear an English woman's voice (Maggie Teyte) singing in amorous French, a popular song of the period.*

*Another angle* JULIA *and* LILLIAN

*They are dancing separately, then they come together and dance in the middle of the room. After a moment:*

LILLIAN. Happy New Year, Julia.

JULIA. Happy New Year.

*Int. darkened room (New Year's Eve)*

LILLIAN *and* JULIA *(both teens) lie on the floor. They've been drinking wine. Smoking cigarettes. They speak in whispers.*

JULIA *(inventing it)*. I am . . . Paris.
LILLIAN. I am Paris . . . and . . . I am a string of beads. *(Pause)*
JULIA. I am Paris . . . and I am a string of beads on a hot dancer.
LILLIAN *(laughs; thinks; then)*. I am Paris and I am a string of beads on a hot dancer . . . and outside it's Renoir and Cezanne . . .
JULIA *(thinks; then a great grin)*. I am Paris and I am a string of beads on a hot dancer . . . and outside it's Renoir and Rembrandt . . . and inside it is *hard and hot!*
LILLIAN. Oh, Jesus, Julia!
JULIA. I don't care, I don't care!

*They squeal, drink wine, giggle, still flat on the floor.*

*Suddenly we hear bells from outside. It is midnight. They both listen for a long time and then:*

LILLIAN. Happy New Year, Julia.
JULIA. Happy New Year.

*They stare up at the ceiling as the bells continue. Camera studies them as they listen and think of their lives that lie ahead.*

*Cut to*

*Int. Beach House (1934)—day*

LILLIAN *(now about 30) sits at a table. She wears her bathrobe and little white socks. We can see a calendar hanging on the wall with a picture of FDR on it. A typewriter on the table. She is working hard. The work clearly not coming easily. In frustra-*

*tion, she stands up, kicks a waste basket.*

*Ext. beach angle on a younger* HAMMETT—*dusk*

*as he moves up beach towards the house.* HAMMETT *pulls a gunnysack behind him.*

*Angle on* LILLIAN *at door (through screen)*

*She has a drink in her hand.*

LILLIAN. It's not working again, Hammett. It's falling apart again.

*Wider angle* LILLIAN *and* HAMMETT

*He is dumping the gunnysack outside the door into a pail. Clams. He looks up at her.*

HAMMETT. Put on your sweater. Pick some corn. Bring some whisky. I'll build a fire, we'll have some dinner . . . Don't forget the smokes.

*He turns and starts away.*

LILLIAN *(shouts)*. I'm not here to take orders. I only want advice.

*Pause, then she pushes open the door, still shouting.*

LILLIAN. You're not a general, Hammett. *(pause, then louder)* And I ain't the troops!

*Ext. beach (1934)—night*

*They have eaten. There's light from the house in b.g. and something left of the beach fire.* HAMMETT, *with a drink in hand, sits on the sand in a tacky wooden armchair. He looks out at the dark water.* LILLIAN *lies on her side, they are both pleasantly drunk. Finally:*

HAMMETT. If you really can't write, maybe you should go find a job.

*She mumbles something unintelligible.*

HAMMETT. You could be a waitress, or what about a fireman . . . you could be the chief. *(considers it)* Not a bad idea, maybe some little town . . . get yourself li'l fire station . . . I'll be the mayor.

LILLIAN. Why the hell should you be the mayor?

HAMMETT. Somebody has to appoint you if you're going to be the chief.

LILLIAN. I'm in trouble with my goddamn play and you don't care. Just because you've stopped writing . . .

*Silence. She is sorry she said it.* HAMMETT *drinks more.* LILLIAN *stares at him. Finally, she gets to her knees. She lights another cigarette. She turns away and starts to move up the beach into the darkness. Silence. Finally it is too dark to see her.*

HAMMETT. Tell you what I'll do, Lilly. I'll send you on a trip to Paris.

LILLIAN'S VOICE *(O.S.) (from the darkness)*. I don't want to go to Paris.

HAMMETT. Why not, I hear it's a swell town. You could finish your play there, have a little fun, visit your friend Julia.

LILLIAN. You know damn well Julia's not in Paris.

HAMMETT. Well, wherever she is. Go to Spain. There may be a civil war in Spain. You could help somebody win it. You're scrappy.

LILLIAN'S VOICE *(O.S.)*. I'm not scrappy! Don't call me scrappy. You make me sound like the neighbourhood bulldog and don't tell me I'm brave again.

HAMMETT *(sarcastic)*. You are brave, Lilly, and you are noble, and you *are* the neighbourhood bulldog except you have some cockeyed dream about being a cocker spaniel.

LILLIAN'S VOICE *(O.S.) (shouting)*. I *am* a cocker spaniel and I'm in trouble and you won't listen to me. *(exasperated)* I can't work here.

HAMMETT. Then don't work here, don't work any place, it's not as if you've written anything before. Nobody'll miss you. It's the perfect time to change jobs.

LILLIAN'S VOICE *(O.S.) (louder).* You're the one who talked me into being a writer. You're the damned one who said stick with it, you have talent, kid! You soft soaped me with all that crap and look where I am now.

HAMMETT *(standing up).* You want to cry about it, stand alone on the rocks, don't do it around me. If you can't write your play here then go someplace else! Give it up! Open a drugstore! Be a coal miner! Be a six day bike rider! *Anything,* but don't snivel over it.

HAMMETT *picks up the bottle of whisky, begins to kick sand over the fire. He puts it out. We cannot see him now and all we can see are the lights from the little house. In a few moments we hear a screen door slam and after that the lights in the house go out and there is nothing but blackness.*

*Silence. Finally, after a few moments:*

LILLIAN'S VOICE *(O.S.).* Hammett?

*Hold for a long time. Waiting for some sign of her. There is none.*

LILLIAN'S VOICE *(O.S.).* Hammett, I'm lost!

*Hold. She still doesn't appear.*

*Int. beach house—night*

*It is black. We hear the screen door fly open. Then it slams closed.*

LILLIAN'S VOICE *(O.S.) (young).* But what about Paris? What about Rome? And Cairo? What about Michelangelo?

*Ext. road to summer lodge (1922)—day*

*P.O.V. over the hood of tan Rolls Royce towards an imposing gate which is slowly opened.*

*Int. Limousine tight on* JULIA—*day*

*When the camera pulls back we see she is seated in the jump seat of the Rolls and we get a glimpse of* LILLIAN *at her side. The* GRANDPARENTS *are in rear seats.* GRANDMOTHER *drinking from a silver flask.* JULIA *looks disturbed and* LILLIAN *is aware of it.*

*Ext. summer lodge (1922)—day*

*The limousine approaches the fortress-like lodge.* THREE SERVANTS *(two men and a woman) are waiting at the front of the wooden steps as the car stops. One man opens the door.*

JULIA *is out by herself. She moves quickly away from the car followed by* LILLIAN. *Camera stays on the* OLD PEOPLE *who leave the car as their luggage is taken in by the* CHAUFFEUR *and the* MAN. *The* WOMAN *takes the* GRANDMOTHER'S *arm.*

*Angle on* LILLIAN *and* JULIA

JULIA *walking towards the water. The fortress-like lodge in b.g.* LILLIAN *catching up. Now they walk together.*

LILLIAN *looking out at the lake.* JULIA *walking straight ahead. Very tense.* LILLIAN *looks at her. They walk in silence. Then:*

LILLIAN. Please tell me what's the matter.

JULIA. I don't want to be here. Not with them. I hate them.

*They walk along the lake,* JULIA *slightly ahead of* LILLIAN.

*Tight shot* LILLIAN

*Looking at* JULIA.

*Angle past them*

*at the water.*

JULIA. They wouldn't see.

LILLIAN. What wouldn't they see?

JULIA. If something smelled bad. We had to move away to some other place.

LILLIAN. I don't know what you mean. What would smell bad?

JULIA. Streets, houses . . . the people.

LILLIAN *(a beat, then)*. What about Paris? What about Rome? And Cairo? What about Michelangelo?

JULIA *(sharp)*. You aren't listening!

LILLIAN. I *am* listening!

*Extreme long shot boat landing—day*

LILLIAN *and* JULIA *in bathing suits sitting with their feet in the water. Camera moves slowly towards them as we hear:*

JULIA. They took me to see Cairo. They told me how beautiful Cairo would be, but it wasn't beautiful. I remember saying to my grandfather, 'Look at those people, they're hungry, they're sick, why don't we do something?' And he said, 'Don't look at them.' I said, 'But they're sick,' and he said, 'I didn't make them sick.' *(pause—camera closer—her anger grows)* Where my mother lives the servants live under the ground. Seventeen people in three rooms. No windows. One bathroom. *(pause—we are in tight now)* It's wrong. They can't do that. *(she turns slowly and looks towards the house)* It's wrong.

*A moment of silence and then suddenly* JULIA *dives into the water.* LILLIAN *is up and dives in after her. We watch them swim off.*

*Cut to*

*Int. beach house* LILLIAN'S *workroom (1934)—night*

LILLIAN *at the window. She looks out. She turns, looks at the work on her table, then she goes out of the room.*

*Int. stairway—night*

LILLIAN *moves slowly up the stairs.*

LILLIAN'S VOICE *(O.S. age 18)*. Goodbye, goodbye! How many times do I have to say it? Goodbye!

*Int. bedroom—night*

LILLIAN *enters. She moves to the bed, sits on it, looks at* HAMMETT *who is asleep. She lies down. She looks up at the ceiling.*

LILLIAN. Maybe I *could* do better work someplace else . . . Dash? . . .

HAMMETT. . . . What?

LILLIAN. If I were to go to Paris and work . . . Are you awake? *(he grunts)* If I went away would you start writing again? *(pause)* Do I keep you from writing?

HAMMETT. No, sleeping, you keep me from sleeping, Lillian.

*Silence. She turns to him. It is clear from the moment that she loves him. Without even opening his eyes, he reaches out and gently rubs her leg. In tight shot,* LILLIAN *looks back up at the ceiling.*

JULIA'S VOICE. I heard from Oxford . . . from Medical School. *(pause)* I was accepted.

LILLIAN'S VOICE. When will you go?

JULIA'S VOICE. The end of the summer.

LILLIAN'S VOICE. But that's next, the end of summer.

*Cut to*

*Int.* JULIA'S *bedroom—night*

*Close-up fire in a small fireplace. Camera pans up to close shot introducing the* GROWN JULIA. *She is resting on one elbow, dreaming into the fire.*

LILLIAN'S VOICE *(O.S.).* I cannot say now that I knew or had ever used the words gentle or delicate or strong, but I did think that night that it was the most beautiful face I had ever seen.

*We begin to hear a ship's orchestra playing "Over the Waves" and the growing sounds of celebrant voices.*

LILLIAN'S VOICE *(O.S.).* Goodbye, goodbye! How many times do I have to say it? Goodbye!

*Quick cut to*

*Ext. main deck the S.S. Majestic very tight shot* JULIA *(older) (1923)—day*

JULIA. We'll write.

*Another angle favouring* JULIA *and* LILLIAN

*on deck. The ship's orchestra plays "Over the Waves." Confetti floats through the air. The main deck filled with departing passengers and their friends. Bon Voyage parties in full swing. A going-ashore gong is sounding.*

LILLIAN. I've already written you . . . it's in the mail.

VOICE *(over loudspeaker).* All ashore that's going ashore!

LILLIAN. Oh, my God, look who's travelling with you.

JULIA. Who?

LILLIAN. Anne Marie.

JULIA. Where?

LILLIAN. There. She's got her brother, Sammy, with her.

*Another angle*

ANNE MARIE *with her brother* SAMMY *at her side. They hold champagne glasses.* SAMMY *is 25, a tall, gangly, bitchy man with a moustache. He smiles with an inappropriate affectation.* ANNE MARIE *is 18. She has a passive quality that hides her anger.*

ANNE MARIE. Julia! Lillian! Are we all crossing? I don't believe it!

LILLIAN. Julia's crossing. Hello, Sammy.

SAMMY *(hangs on them).* Hello, my beauties. Control yourselves, Jack Dempsey's on board.

*He looks to see who else is.*

ANNE MARIE. And the *Dolly* Sisters with 97 pieces of luggage.

SAMMY. Lillian, you shouldn't stay home. It's a woman's world now, you can be morally independent, if you know what I mean.

LILLIAN. I'll try that, Sammy.

SAMMY. After all, the Paris mademoiselles are wearing French flags for underwear.

VOICE *(over loudspeaker).* All ashore that's going ashore!

ANNE MARIE. My God, I have people to see. Julia, we'll see each other later. We'll have fun. You're looking slim, Lillian.

ANNE MARIE *throws* LILLIAN *a kiss.*

SAMMY. It's true, Lillian, you look very svelte . . .

ANNE MARIE *and* SAMMY *move off.*

LILLIAN *(to* JULIA). You poor thing.

JULIA. Don't worry. I'll avoid them. You'd better go.

LILLIAN. When do we see each other again? It'll be too long.

JULIA. Think of it this way, when we do, we'll have everything to talk about.

VOICE *(over loudspeaker).* All ashore that's going ashore. All ashore.

*They embrace. We hear the ship's whistle.*

LILLIAN. Oh, Jesus, I don't want to cry, please write me . . . Goodbye, take care . . .

JULIA. And you take care, and practise left from right, watch your smoking, don't give up on Albert Wakeman, I think he's ready to make a move.

LILLIAN. I don't care about Albert Wakeman, promise you'll write me.

JULIA. You know I'll write you. *(hugs her)* Work hard. Take chances. Be very bold.

*We hear the ship's whistle.*

You hear me, *very, very* bold.

LILLIAN. You're going to be a remarkable doctor . . .

JULIA. My boat's leaving, Lilly. Get off my boat.

LILLIAN *(moving away reluctantly).* Goodbye.

JULIA. Goodbye.

*Ext. gangplank*

*as* LILLIAN *stands on it, looking for a last glimpse of* JULIA *waving. She moves on down the gangplank.*

LILLIAN. Goodbye. Goodbye.

*Very tight on* LILLIAN

LILLIAN *(suddenly angry; trying not to cry).* Goodbye, goodbye. How many times do I have to say it. Goodbye.

*P.O.V.* JULIA

*In the crowd, her arm held up straight, strong and steady. The band strikes up "Auld Lang Syne."*

*Back to* LILLIAN

*waving at* JULIA. *The air filled with confetti. "Auld Lang Syne" continues. The ship's whistle cuts through the air.*

LILLIAN'S VOICE *(O.S.).* It was in our nineteenth year that she went away. I wasn't to see her again for a very long time . . . until I went to visit her at Oxford.

*Ext. A formal lawn at Oxford long shot* JULIA *(1925)—day*

*walking across the lawn toward camera. As she approaches we hear:*

LILLIAN'S VOICE *(O.S.).* There are women who reach a perfect time of life, when the face will never again be as good, the body never as graceful or as powerful. It had happened that year to Julia, but she was no more conscious of it than of having been a beautiful child.

JULIA *is close now. And* LILLIAN *moves into frame to greet her.* JULIA *does have that power and grace, but her clothes are loose, carelessly chosen . . .*

*They embrace*

*Cut to*

*Int/Ext. The colleges at Oxford (various shots)*

LILLIAN *and* JULIA *moving through. They speak with quick enthusiasm. Dialogue overlapping. One scene dissolving into another.*

LILLIAN. You have a lot of friends?

JULIA. Not many.

LILLIAN. Get to the theatre?

JULIA. There's not enough time.

LILLIAN. But we always went to the theatre.

JULIA. When you write your play I'll go again, how's your writing?

LILLIAN. I'm still at the publishing house. I wish I could write full time.

JULIA. You will.

LILLIAN. Do you have a beau?

JULIA. No, do you?

LILLIAN. I'm not sure. I think maybe I've met someone. You?

JULIA *(shakes her head)*. I did but it didn't work out.

*Cut to*

*Ext. St. John's College—Oxford*

*Panning shot. Beautiful ancient architecture.*

LILLIAN'S VOICE. My God, it's so old, everything you want to know is right here.

*Cut to*

*Another area—Oxford*

LILLIAN. What are you reading now?

JULIA. Everything. Webb, Huxley, Engels, even Einstein.

LILLIAN. Can you understand Einstein?

*A* STUDENT *passes, smiles at* JULIA.

STUDENT. Hello, Julia.

JULIA *(continuing on)*. Hello.

*Moving shot* JULIA *and* LILLIAN *pass through gateway to the Radcliffe Square day*

LILLIAN. Will you come home next Summer?

JULIA. No, I'm going to Vienna, and I'm going to finish my medical studies and then I'm going to try to study with Professor Freud.

LILLIAN. Can you do that, I mean I know you can do that, but, Jesus . . .

JULIA. I think I can, there's a good chance, I think he'll accept me. Lilly, you have to visit Vienna once . . . then you'll know what to write about. People are coming alive there, working people who never had a chance before, they've built their own part of the city, in Floridsdorf. They have their own orchestra, their newspaper's the best in Vienna, Lilly, finally, there's some real hope in this world.

*Angle favouring* LILLIAN

*Her look shows her respect. As we begin to hear soft, Viennese, band music in b.g.*

JULIA. Do you understand?

LILLIAN *(uncertain)*. Yes, of course.

*Shot crossing the meadow behind Christ Church*

LILLIAN *and* JULIA *walk across the meadow as camera pulls slowly away from them. As it does we hear:*

LILLIAN'S VOICE *(O.S.)*. But I didn't understand. Not fully. Who of us did? She wrote me from time to time. She had gone to live in the Floridsdorf District of Vienna. And as the years went on, she wrote of Mussolini and Adolf Hitler and of radicals and Jews and of the holocaust that was on the way. She wrote angry things of the armed political groups in Austria. The threat of the Nazis, the criminal guilt of the English and French in pretending there was no danger in Fascism . . . She couldn't understand why the world refused to see what was coming.

*Camera is far from them now and they are very small, distant images.*

*Int. beach house bedroom (1934)—night*

LILLIAN *and* HAMMETT *in bed.*

LILLIAN. Maybe I *could* do better work someplace else . . . Dash?

HAMMETT. What?

LILLIAN. I'll take you up on your offer.

HAMMETT. What's that, Lilly?

LILLIAN. . . . Paris.

*Ext. Paris street establishing shot (1934)—night*

*It is a calm, romantic Parisian scene. The lights flicker against the Paris architecture and all seems serene. Django's hot guitar is playing against this.*

*Ext. Hotel Jacob Paris—night*

*A small, inexpensive hotel. Django's guitar continues.*

*Int. hotel corridor angle on* LILLIAN *at telephone—night*

LILLIAN *(into phone)*. Hello? Allo? Danke . . . danke . . . *Julia? It's Lillian* . . . Hello? Is it you? It doesn't sound like you. I don't believe it, it's been so long. I called you, didn't you get my message? I've been trying to reach you for weeks . . . I'm fine, I'm in Paris, when can I see you? I'll be here for a few more weeks. I'm finishing my play, didn't you receive my letter? About my play? Why are we talking so fast . . . Are you okay? What's difficult . . . Hello . . . Are you there? . . . I'm at the Hotel Jacob, but I can come to Vienna . . . Why not? . . . How about halfway, I'll meet you halfway . . . Hotel Jacob, yes, you have no idea how good it feels to hear your voice. I won't leave till I hear from you . . . Are you all right . . . Hello? . . . *(jiggles phone)* Hello! Hello! Hello!

*It is all so sudden. Over. She holds the phone. She lowers it into the cradle. She is afraid . . . senses something. Not sure what.*

*Cut to*

*Int.* LILLIAN'S *room angle on* LIL-LIAN

*at the typewriter, working. Suddenly there is the sound of police whistles and the clanging of the police wagon in b.g.*

*Angle at* LILLIAN'S *window*

*as she moves to look out.*

*P.O.V. shot*

*The street's now filled with people running, police and gendarmes pursuing them. Some people drop placards and torches as they run, others stop to throw stones at the pursuing police. Sound of shouts and screams in the distance.*

*Back to* LILLIAN

*looking out window frightened but curious. Begin a quiet musical pulse.*

*Cut to*

*Ext. Paris street—night*

LILLIAN *moving along sidewalk, cautiously, looking ahead. We can hear gunshots and the wild shouts of demonstrators. A fight has developed a short distance from hotel (police, workers, soldiers, students). We can see flames of burning cars. An ambulance moving towards riot passes* LIL-LIAN.

*Close* LILLIAN

*She stops and watches from a distance, then turns back towards hotel.*

*Cut to*

*Int. hotel corridor angle on* LILLIAN *at wall phone*

LILLIAN *(into phone)*. Hammett? Are you still there? . . . Something terrible has begun here . . . Hello? I can't hear you . . . Hammett? HAM-METT?

*Cut to*

*Int. hotel room angle on* LILLIAN—*night*

*She is writing a letter.*

LILLIAN'S VOICE *(O.S.)*. Dear Hammett. I try to concentrate on my play. But I feel sick. And there's no reason for my nausea other than fright.

*Cut to*

*Ext. Paris streets—night*

*Damp cobblestones. Dark-clothed men moving through barely lighted alleyways coming from everywhere, carrying clubs and steel pipes.*

LILLIAN'S VOICE *(O.S.)*. There's something ugly here. Something deep and very ugly.

*The number of dark figures has increased alarmingly in these past few seconds.*

*Cut to*

*Long shot volksgarten*

*Fascist troops on parade.*

LILLIAN'S VOICE *(continuing—more anxious)*. And it's not only in Paris, Hammett!

*Cut to*

*Long shot Fascist poster sinister*

*Camera moves rapidly into C.U. of three helmeted figures.*

*Cut to*

*Ext. buildings Floridsdorf District Vienna (1934)—night*

*Sounds of gunfire. Smoke pours from burning buildings. Fires rage.*

LILLIAN'S VOICE. Hammett! Something awful is happening.

*Cut to*

*Int. Paris hotel room—night*

*Close shot LILLIAN looking off, uncertain of something, sensing something.*

LILLIAN *(barely audible)*. Julia?

*Cut to*

*Int. university staircase—day*

*Feet of STUDENTS running up flight of marble stairs leading to top floor of great Renaissance staircase. Angry distorted cruel faces. Weapons in the air: clubs, metal pipes etc. STUDENTS run to top of staircase where others are awaiting them.*

*Int. door of lecture hall and corridor at top of staircase—day*

*Shooting over the backs of the mob. We are aware that the door of the Lecture Hall is forcibly pushed open. Most of the STUDENTS rush into Lecture Hall and presently emerge triumphantly pushing a small group of resisting, terrified students ahead of them. There is fighting, screaming and the sound of blows. Books are thrown from students' arms and thrown down stairwell. Swinging fists, bloodied faces, falling bodies. Three or four GIRL STUDENTS are among those who have been hauled out of the Lecture Hall. All of them make themselves as scarce as possible, with the exception of one girl— JULIA—who seems to be protecting one student. She is engulfed and disappears in the mob.*

*Cut to*

*Ext. Vienna street—night*

*Workers, police, students, soldiers with steel helmets, in fierce combat. The uniforms are Austrian.*

*Big explosion!*

*Cut to*

*Int. LILLIAN'S hotel room, Paris (1934)—dusk tight shot*

*Silence. Newspaper on dresser showing the headline:*

AUSTRIAN ARMY BOMBARDS
WORKERS' BUILDING IN
FLORIDSDORF DISTRICT

FIRES RAGE. 200 DIE IN VIENNA.

*Camera pulls back to show* LILLIAN *moving out of the bathroom with a pair of wet stockings and some undergarments. She drapes them over a chair near the radiator. She is tired, extremely anxious. She sits in the chair at the desk as the camera pans the room, establishing a sense of disorder: clothing, food, whisky, newspapers, filled ashtrays, etc. We should feel she is desperately fighting to control panic.*

*Int.* LILLIAN'S *hotel room, Paris (1934)—night*

LILLIAN *in bed unable to sleep.*

*Int. corridor angle on a* WOMAN *(manager)—night*

*in nightclothes. She knocks on* LIL-LIAN'S *door.*

WOMAN. Mademoiselle. Telephone. Mademoiselle. They call from Vienna.

*Int. corridor angle on* LILLIAN—*night*

*talking on wall phone. A* WOMAN *watches, listens from up the hall.*

LILLIAN *(into phone—frantic).* Yes . . . What happened? . . . Is she all right? How serious is it? . . . Of course I'll come, tell her I'm coming. Where do I go . . . yes? . . . Yes, I'll come! . . . Just a moment, who am I talking to? . . . Hello?

*Int. a taxicab (moving) angle on* LILLIAN *(1934)—dusk*

*Looking lost, dazed.*

*Ext. Vienna street taxi (1934)— dusk*

*driving down the street.*

*Int. the taxi angle on* LILLIAN—*dusk*

*looking out anxiously.*

*Her P.O.V. dusk*

*Policemen and soldiers patrol the dark streets.*

*Back to* LILLIAN

*Her anxiety.*

*Ext. hospital Vienna—dusk*

*A mean part of town.* LILLIAN *gets out of taxi; has trouble making change. Finally, not caring, giving the* DRIVER *more than enough. She is aware the area is ringed with* POLICE-MEN *and* MEN *in other uniforms, wearing steel helmets.*

*Int. hospital corridor—night*

*as* LILLIAN *enters. She is close to camera. Great apprehension.*

*Shot* LILLIAN *moving through hospital corridor night*

*It is a place that appears to be uncared for. Very old. Overworked personnel.* LILLIAN *is being led by a* PREGNANT WOMAN *in a grey dress.*

*Angle on entrance to hospital ward—night*

LILLIAN *moving to it. Stops. Looks in.*

LILLIAN'S *P.O.V. the ward—night*

*About thirty* PATIENTS. *The beds close together. Emergency cots. The room, bleak, distressing. Mops, medicine tables, wash pails are all about.* THREE UNIFORMED MEN *are standing about in the room.*

*Shot the* PREGNANT WOMAN—*night*

*Indicates for* LILLIAN *to follow. They move through the ward. Only a few of the* PERSONNEL *are in hospital uniforms. Other* WORKERS *in civilian clothes. Finally, the* PREGNANT WOMAN *indicates a bed at the end of the ward. We see a body heavily*

*wrapped in bandages. The right side
of a "face" is also bandaged. The
bandages are carried around the head
and onto most of the right side, leaving only the left eye and mouth exposed. The right arm lies outside the
bed cover. The right leg rests on an
unseen platform.*

*Tight on* LILLIAN—*night*

*Her reaction as she moves slowly
toward the bed.*

*Shot* LILLIAN *and* JULIA *(18 years
old) (1923)—day*

*Favour* JULIA *as they embrace on
the deck of a ship. Great smiles, hugs.
Bon Voyage, tears, confetti!*

YOUNG BOY'S VOICE *(O.S.).* Ihre
Freundin, Fraulein.

*Back to hospital favour* JULIA—
*night*

*as a* YOUNG BOY *(8 years old) in
short pants, oversized shirt, overdue
haircut, brings* LILLIAN *a stool to sit
on. Then the* BOY *slowly turns* JULIA'S
*bandaged head for her.*

YOUNG BOY *(to* JULIA*).* Ihre Freundin, Fraulein.

JULIA'S *left eye opens.*

YOUNG BOY *(indicating* LILLIAN*).*
Ihre Freundin. *(taps* JULIA'S *hand)*
Ihre Freundin.

JULIA'S *eye looks towards* LILLIAN.
*Neither it, nor the hand, move as* JU-
LIA *and* LILLIAN *stare at one another.
The* BOY *backs off and picks up a pail
of water, moves across the ward,
stands with the pail in b.g., looking
towards* JULIA *and* LILLIAN, *who do
not speak.*

*Camera moves to favour* LILLIAN,
*who starts to say something but then
doesn't.*

*A moment more as* JULIA'S *eye
stares at* LILLIAN. *Then the head turns
again and the eye looks across the
room, the free hand comes up
and slowly points at a* NURSE *to whom
the young* BOY *is speaking. The* NURSE
*looks toward* JULIA *and moves to the
bed. She turns* JULIA'S *head to the
other side and puts her hand in a
more comfortable position. Then she
indicates for* LILLIAN *to leave.*

NURSE *(in Viennese) (to* LILLIAN*).*
Please go now.

LILLIAN *nods and gets up. She turns
to go, looking back once, twice, a
third time at* JULIA. *Camera with her
as she moves slowly through the
ward. She passes the other patients.
She is close to the pain. It disturbs
her. Frightens her.*

*Int. hospital corridor—night*

LILLIAN *moves out of the ward. The
young* BOY *waiting for her. He moves
to her. Stops her.*

YOUNG BOY *(in Viennese) (quickly).*
Fraulein. Hotel Imperial. There is a
reservation for you at the Hotel Imperial, reservation.

LILLIAN *studies him a moment, then
nods and turns and moves down the
hallway. She suddenly begins to move
very fast.*

*Faster. The screen becomes a blur
as* LILLIAN *turns a corner, and walks
even more swiftly down another corridor.*

*Int. Hotel Imperial Dining Room
(1934)—night*

*A Viennese orchestra plays a bub-
bly rendition of "You're the Top."*

*Int. hotel lobby angle on* LILLIAN—
*night*

*as she moves to the desk. The* BELL-MAN *carries her well-worn suitcase. The* DESK CLERK *watches her approach. We hear music in b.g.*

DESK CLERK *(quick, efficient, overly polite).* So good to have you with us, Fraulein.

LILLIAN. Who made this reservation?

DESK CLERK. Ah yes, Herr Von Fritsch, Fraulein Hellman. He wants me to tell you that everything is arranged and you will be comfortable and well.

*He hits the bell on the counter.*

LILLIAN. Is Herr Von Fritsch in the hotel?

DESK CLERK. No, Fraulein, he is not.

LILLIAN. Do you know where I can reach this Herr Von Fritsch?

DESK CLERK. I do not know, Fraulein. He came and he went very quickly. *(to* BELLMAN*)* Dreinhundertundsechs . . .

*The* BELLMAN *takes the key from the* CLERK.

BELLMAN. *Dreihundertundsechs (to Lillian)* Bitte Schon, Bitte Sehr.

*He marches off with her bag.* LILLIAN *hesitates, then follows through this elegant lobby.*

*Int. hotel dining room—night*

*The string orchestra continuing to play "You're the Top." Hold on them.*

*Cut to*

*Int. hospital corridor—day (morning)*

LILLIAN *about to enter the ward.* NURSE NO. 2 *moves to her. She speaks in broken English.*

NURSE. She is resting from the operation. You will please come tomorrow.

*She turns to go.*

LILLIAN. What operation?

*But the* NURSE *is moving away.* LILLIAN *moves after her.*

LILLIAN. What operation?
NURSE. She is resting.
LILLIAN. I want to know what you're talking about.
NURSE *(continuing to move).* Come tomorrow, please.
LILLIAN. Isn't there someone who speaks English? What's wrong? What operation?

LILLIAN *hesitates then turns and moves towards the ward. But the* NURSE *too has turned and calls sharply.*

NURSE. Come back tomorrow!
LILLIAN. No! I will not come back tomorrow. I will wait right here.

*The* NURSE *has gone.* LILLIAN *remains in the corridor. Looks toward entrance to ward, then takes out a cigarette and moves to stand against the wall of the corridor. Lights her cigarette. Turns and looks out window.*

*Her P.O.V. angling past her day*

*We see an area surrounded by* UNI-FORMED MEN. *She stares a few moments, then sits on wooden bench.*

*Dissolve*

*Int. hospital corridor—dusk*

LILLIAN *still on bench, still smoking, she's weary, smashes out her cigarette in the ashtray, already filled with her other cigarette butts. Then she turns and looks out of the window again. A* NURSE *walks by and into the* ward. LILLIAN *keeps her eye on where the* NURSE *entered.*

*Dissolve*

*Int. corridor* LILLIAN *dozing on wooden bench—night*

*She awakens as the door of the ward opens. A* NURSE *appears and beckons to* LILLIAN. *She gets up and moves quickly toward the* NURSE *and into the ward.*

*Int. hospital ward—night*

LILLIAN *moving slowly toward* JULIA'S *bed. The* YOUNG BOY *brings* LILLIAN *a stool, just as he did before.*

*Closer shot* LILLIAN *and* JULIA— *night*

*The little* BOY *carefully turns* JULIA'S *head to* LILLIAN. JULIA'S *right leg is no longer on the platform. She looks at* LILLIAN *with the one exposed eye. Then she raises her arm and touches* LILLIAN'S *hand.* LILLIAN *stares at* JULIA'S *hand, then* JULIA *takes her hand away and points to her mouth, indicating she cannot talk.* LILLIAN *nods.* JULIA *raises her hand toward the window, points outside. She makes a pushing movement with her hand.* LILLIAN *tries to understand.* JULIA'S *one eye stares at* LILLIAN. LILLIAN *leans in closer.*

LILLIAN. I don't know what you mean.

*Silence.* JULIA'S *eye continues to look toward* LILLIAN. *Then the eye closes. It remains closed.* LILLIAN *looks at the bandaged head.*

JULIA'S VOICE (O.S.—age 16). Come to my room says the blackmailer and you may have possession of the film.

*Tight on* LILLIAN—*night*

*looking at* JULIA O.S.

LILLIAN'S VOICE (O.S.—age 16). Does she go?

LILLIAN *continues to look at* JULIA. *Then she seems sleepy. Still on the stool, she leans back against the wall and looks down.*

*Cut to*

*Ext. Ketch sailing off a Massachusetts shore (1921)—day*

LILLIAN *and* JULIA *(age 16) on deck. They have to shout to be heard. Again we hear Django's guitar strumming "Hot Lips"—but slow, romantic.*

JULIA. She and her lover arrange to meet on a lonely country road where he takes her in his arms and kisses her passionately.

LILLIAN. Good.

JULIA. Her husband is Richard Arlington, the Colonel of the Twenty-Fourth Cavalry commanding Fort Wallace, but even so, she needs to be kissed.

LILLIAN. I like it.

JULIA. But someone is there, hiding in the trees. Someone who wants her madly. And he takes a photo of the illicit kiss.

LILLIAN. What happens?

JULIA. Come to my room says the blackmailer, and you may have possession of the film.

LILLIAN. Does she go?

JULIA. At 2 A.M. And when she gets to his room, the blackmailer is dead, murdered in his own bed. The photo of the illicit kiss still in his hand.

LILLIAN. What does she do?

JULIA. She takes the photo and runs from the room, but she's caught on the way down the stairs. The police arrive and she's arrested and charged with murder.

LILLIAN. There must be a trial.

JULIA. Oh, yes. A long one. And she's convicted. Guilty.

LILLIAN. And the real killer never tries to save her?

JULIA. Never! And her husband, Richard Arlington, disowns her.

LILLIAN. What about her lover?

JULIA. He joins a monastery.

LILLIAN. What happens to her?

*Quick cut to*

*Hospital ward angle on* LILLIAN— *night*

*A* NURSE *shakes her awake.* LILLIAN *is startled.*

LILLIAN *(quick).* What!

*She looks at the bed. Empty.*

LILLIAN. Where is she?

NURSE. Treatment.

LILLIAN *(standing).* Is something wrong?

NURSE *(sharp).* No. Treatment.

*The* NURSE *moves away.* LILLIAN *looks around the ward.*

*Ext. hospital—night*

UNIFORMED MEN *in b.g.* LILLIAN *has just left hospital and is moving along the sidewalk. She looks around at every shadow. Moves quickly.*

*Ext. hospital new angle—night*

*Favour the* LITTLE BOY *from the hospital.*

YOUNG BOY. Fraulein?

*She turns. He hands her a note.*

*Wider angle*

LILLIAN *looks at the* BOY.

LILLIAN. Who gave you this . . . ?

*The* BOY *stares at her, hesitates as if to answer, then bows and suddenly runs and disappears in the shadows.*

*Tight on* LILLIAN

LILLIAN *watches him go then stands alone against the side of the building. She reads the note.*

JULIA'S VOICE *(O.S.) (short of breath, hurried).* "Go back to Paris fast. Leave your address at the Hotel. They will take me now to another place. Something else is needed. Love, Julia."

LILLIAN *looks up, frightened. Everything seems too quiet now.*

LILLIAN'S VOICE *(O.S.).* I returned to Paris and waited to hear from Julia, but no word came.

*We begin to hear a typewriter.*

*Cut to*

*Int. Paris hotel room—day*

*Angle on* LILLIAN *typing, trying to work, but she's nervous, her thoughts elsewhere. Her work papers scattered about.*

*Cut to*

*Another angle* LILLIAN—*night*

*On her bed. She can't sleep. Suddenly, she gets up, puts on a robe and moves out of the room.*

*Int. Hotel corridor wall phone* LIL-LIAN—*night*

*on the phone.*

LILLIAN *(into phone).* What do you mean? . . . What? . . . Please speak clearly . . . I can't understand you.

*A* WOMAN *passes through the corridor.*

LILLIAN. Un moment . . . A moment . . . a moment . . . *(quickly to* WOMAN*)* Do you speak German? . . . Parlez Deutsch . . .

WOMAN *(shaking her head).* Non.

LILLIAN *(back to phone)*. Allo? . . . Hello, hello . . . Un moment.

*She turns and looks around. An* OLD MAN *(Middle-European) is entering his room.*

LILLIAN. Monsieur? Parlez Deutsch? *(into phone)* Wait, please . . . Warten, bitte . . . *(to* OLD MAN*)* Parlez Deutsch?

*The* OLD MAN *smiles, extends his arm.*

OLD MAN *(very alive)*. Oui . . .

*Cut to*

*Another angle the* OLD MAN *on the phone—night*

LILLIAN *is at his side.*

LILLIAN. They *have* to have her name, tell them I was there, I saw her.

OLD MAN *(to* LILLIAN*)*. They say she was never there, Madame. *(into phone in German)* Look again, please. She was there . . . *(listens, then to* LILLIAN*)* No, Madame, she was never in that hospital.

LILLIAN. But I saw her there. They have to know where she went.

OLD MAN. Madame, they do not even know the name.

LILLIAN *takes the receiver.*

LILLIAN *(into phone)*. Hello . . . hello . . . *(jiggles phone)* Hello!

*She hangs up. Looks at the* OLD MAN. *He takes out a packet of cigarettes. Offers her one. He smiles at her. She takes a cigarette. The* OLD MAN *lights it. As he does, we hear typing again.*

*Cut to*

*Int. Beach house (1935)—day*

LILLIAN *at the typewriter in her bathrobe and white socks. A heavy sweater under her bathrobe.* HAM-METT *is not there now.* LILLIAN *is exhausted, but eager. She continues to work. She rewords something. She reads it. She retypes it. She lights a new cigarette. She gets up, paces the room. She moves to her desk. She picks up a page. Reads it. She's disturbed. She sits down, scratches something out. Puts a new piece of paper in the typewriter. Begins to work, then stops. She stares out of the window.*

LILLIAN *(calling)*. It's going to snow, Hammett . . . *(pause)* Hammett? . . .

*No answer. She looks towards the door. Then she moves back to the typewriter.*

*Another angle—night*

LILLIAN *is sitting in a chair in her bathrobe, eating a sandwich, a bottle of beer next to her. She seems optimistic. She puts the half-finished sandwich on the table, refills her glass with beer, moves with the beer to the typewriter and starts to work again. Camera begins to pan the room to show its disarray. The feeling is that she's been through some great war and as we hear the typewriter in the b.g., we should get the feeling that she's into the last, winning battle.*

*As camera moves in on the page in the typewriter and as* LILLIAN *hits the keys, we see the words "The End" appear.*

*Close on* LILLIAN

*She stares at the page then she types the words "The End" again, and then again . . . and again.*

*Int. beach house close on* LILLIAN*—day*

*in her heavy sweater lying on a couch, her eyes closed, knees pulled up. Pan to window through which we see* HAMMETT *bundled up, sitting outside on the porch reading a script.*

*Angle on* LILLIAN

*She opens her eyes, sits up, waits a moment, then stands and moves to where she can see* HAMMETT *through the window. She looks for a cigarette, finds one, lights it.*

*Ext. beach house—day*

HAMMETT, *as he continues to read. Finally, he closes the script, and he just sits there. We can only see the back of his head.*

*Ext. beach house—day*

LILLIAN *moves out, carefully closing the door so it won't bang. She moves along the side of the house and approaches* HAMMETT, *staring at him, knowing that he is aware of her. She waits another moment, then sits in a chair. She waits. Finally, he turns to her. Then gently:*

HAMMETT. You wanted to be a serious writer. That's what I liked, that's what we worked for. I don't know what's happened, but tear that up. *(pause)* It's not that it's bad, it's just not good enough, not for you.

*Hold on* LILLIAN

*She closes her eyes. Silence.*

*Int.* LILLIAN'S *workroom (1935)—night*

*Big close up typewriter keys as they strike hard and fast. The screen filled with cigarette smoke.*

LILLIAN'S VOICE. Shit!

*Wider angle*

LILLIAN *typing. Coffee cups nearby. She is in her bathrobe again. She stops for a moment, closes her eyes, lowers her head on to the typewriter.*

*A moment passes, then she suddenly sits up and starts to type again.*

*Camera pulls back until we are looking at her through the window.*

*Finally, her figure is small and alone. Her aloneness is absolute as the camera gets further away. Finally it stops. Holds.*

*Angle on* LILLIAN

*walking angrily along shoreline towards camera. The boat, on shore, and* HAMMETT *in b.g. She exits. Hold on* HAMMETT *in distance. He is sitting against the boat.*

*New shot another area of beach*

LILLIAN *sitting against a tree. Waiting. Closes her eyes. Opens them. Takes out her cigarettes. Puts one in her mouth but she's out of matches.*

*Her P.O.V.*

HAMMETT *moving toward her, the script in his hand. He stops next to her.* LILLIAN *is asleep now. He squats down, reaches out, touches her hair. He smiles as she wakes. Then, finally:*

HAMMETT. It's the best play anybody's written in a long time.

LILLIAN *is hesitant, begins to smile but doesn't quite. We begin to hear distant voices: "Author," "Author," "Author," "Author."*

LILLIAN. Are you sure?
HAMMETT. I'm positive.

*Long pause.*

LILLIAN. But are you sure?

*He remains where he is and strokes her hair. Her smile changes to a look of worry. The distant voices O.S. continue.*

*Long shot*

LILLIAN *and* HAMMETT *walking down the beach. Distant voices: "Au-*

thor," "Author," "Author," "Author."

*Cut to*

*Ext. Sardi's restaurant—night*

*The press is there. Opening night theatregoers are there. It's all so dazzling.* LILLIAN *enters and is escorted to her table. As they pass the tables, people begin to stand and applaud her. We hear "bravos" and a few pretentious "bravas."* LILLIAN *seems nervous.*

*Close on* LILLIAN

*as she moves forward.*

*Her P.O.V.*

*The glitter of the people, the crystal, the whole room. Then over these sounds we begin to hear:*

YOUNG BOY'S VOICE *(O.S.) (from Vienna Hospital).* Ihre Freundin . . . Ihre Freundin . . .

*For a moment, Sardi's*

*Dissolves into*

*Int. entrance to hospital in Vienna (1934)—night*

*Back to Sardi's restaurant*

LILLIAN *moving through the restaurant, the applause in the b.g.*

*Full shot all*

*People standing, applauding, reaching to congratulate* LILLIAN.

*Angle on* ANNE MARIE TRAVERS

*moving to* LILLIAN, *giving her a hug.*

ANNE MARIE. Lillian, it was beautiful. You're going to be famous. This is my husband, I made him come down to see it.

*She tries to introduce a* MAN *to* LILLIAN, *but they are separated by other* people *as* LILLIAN *moves deeper into the restaurant. She looks O.S., reacts with enormous relief.*

*Her P.O.V.*

*Her table featuring* DOTTIE *and* ALAN *(good friends) waiting to greet her.*

*Closer shot* LILLIAN'S *table*

*as* DOTTIE *and* ALAN *move to her. A highly emotional three-way embrace.*

LILLIAN. Just give me a drink and don't leave me!

*Some people move into frame to congratulate her.*

*Int. Sardi's new area*

*It is later.* LILLIAN *at her table. People moving in and out to congratulate her, staying a moment or two, then moving off. But* ANNE MARIE *has invaded* LILLIAN *and is kneeling at her side and is carrying on a conversation, despite interruptions by* LILLIAN'S *well-wishers.*

ANNE MARIE. I knew Picasso was on the boat. And I was sure he was the figure I saw going to the deck. And there in the moonlight who do you think I was facing at the rail?

LILLIAN *(her attention elsewhere).* I don't know, Anne Marie, who?

ANNE MARIE. Mitzi Dinsmore, can you imagine? And I thought she was Picasso. She's built like that. Can you believe it? In the dark it was difficult to tell if she was a woman. You know the type. *(a beat)* By the way, I tried to see Julia in Vienna, but she wouldn't see me, can you imagine? I hear she's leading a strange life, pretending not to be rich. She's doing something called Anti-Fascist work, and not only is she in great danger, but she throws her money away on whatever she's doing. Imagine, deciding to live like a pauper in some rundown part of the city. What do you think? I think it's insane. Do you ever hear from her?

LILLIAN. Yes.

ANNE MARIE. Didn't she drop out of medical school?

LILLIAN. Yes.

ANNE MARIE. Sammy tried to kill himself again. I wish he would stop doing that.

LILLIAN *(getting up)*. He will one day, Anne Marie.

ANNE MARIE *laughs a little uncertainly . . . Then her finger comes slowly to her tooth. She looks at LILLIAN, a slight smile.*

ANNE MARIE. I am so happy for you, and you look so slim, and now you're famous, too, Lilly. And to think you nearly became an architect.

LILLIAN. Excuse me. *(to a WAITER)* Where's the Ladies' Room?

*Int. phone booth at the restaurant*

LILLIAN *is very drunk now, talks louder than necessary into the phone.*

LILLIAN. Hammett? I hope I woke you from a sound sleep, do you want to hear the good news, they think I'm wonderful. I'm the toast of the town. Everybody came and you . . . you had to go to Hollywood . . . I'm celebrating, everybody's here but you . . . Of course I'm drunk, I've been drunk for two days, how the hell do you think I got through the night? . . . Who's there with you? Some Hollywood floozie? . . . No, I will not send you the reviews . . . the second act was fine, you were right about everything, you know that. When are you coming home? . . . Hammett, are you listening to me? No I don't want to talk in the morning, I might not be famous in the morning, I'll be alone in the morning, Hammett, and I don't want to be alone in the morning, I don't care how famous I am tonight.

*Pull back from the booth*

*showing* LILLIAN *continuing to talk animatedly to* HAMMETT. *But we can't hear her over the restaurant sounds. The lights in Sardi's are bright. The crystal glitters and there is an air of high celebration. It is all dazzling, unreal. The picture begins to go out of focus until all we can see is glitter. We hear applause again.*

*Begin overlap dissolve*

LILLIAN'S VOICE *(O.S.)*. Dear Julia. I sent you a copy of my play. Did you ever get it? It opened on Broadway, just as we always pretended it would. They liked it. I only wish you had been there. Maybe I wouldn't have had to get drunk. I haven't heard from you in such a long time.

*End overlap dissolve to*

*Ext. beach house angle on rural mailbox (1936)—day*

LILLIAN *has removed a large pile of mail from the box, is moving toward the house, looking through the letters. She opens one envelope, takes something from it, then raises it in the air as she continues toward the house.*

LILLIAN *(calling)*. More royalties, Hammett!

*Ext. the water high angle long shot*

HAMMETT *rowing away from the shore.*

LILLIAN'S VOICE *(O.S.)*. I could buy a sable coat, couldn't I?

HAMMETT'S VOICE *(O.S.)*. If that's what you want.

LILLIAN'S VOICE *(O.S.) (defensive)*. I have a right to a sable coat! *(beat)* Maybe I ought to give my money to Roosevelt.

HAMMETT *gives her a look.*

HAMMETT'S VOICE. You could do that too.

LILLIAN'S VOICE. Ickes says Roosevelt was psychoanalyzed by God. Maybe if I could be analyzed by God, maybe I'd buy myself a sable coat.

*New shot the fishing boat*

*They sit and fish. Finally:*

LILLIAN. I'd look swell in a sable coat.

*Ext. campsite—night*

LILLIAN *wrapped in a blanket. She wears a knitted cap pulled down over her eyes. Both she and* HAMMETT *are watching a fish frying. We all watch the fish frying. Then, finally:*

LILLIAN *(quietly).* Hammett . . .

HAMMETT *(eyes on the fish).* Mmmmm?

LILLIAN *(the confession).* I like being famous.

*He looks up at her then back down at the fish.*

*Ext. campsite another angle—night*

LILLIAN *(continuing).* You know what happens when I buy the groceries now? I'm famous. I buy mayonnaise, Hammett, and I'm famous. I've been invited to Yale and Vassar. I get mail from people in Idaho, I don't even know where Idaho is!

HAMMETT *looks at her.*

LILLIAN *(continuing).* You aren't listening to me.

HAMMETT. I am listening to you, Lilly.

LILLIAN. I don't want you to think I only care about sable coats.

*He reaches out. Touches her gently.*

HAMMETT. I know that . . .

LILLIAN. You know about fame, Dash, it never seems to bother you, this is such a dopey conversation.

HAMMETT. It's only fame, Lilly, it's just a paint job. You want a sable coat, buy one. Just make sure you know it's nothing but a sable coat and doesn't have anything to do with writing.

LILLIAN. You'll never find anyone who'll fish better than I do.

HAMMETT. Never. Not as long as I live.

ANNE MARIE'S VOICE *(O.S. 1937).* . . . And now you've been invited to Moscow . . . What is it, some sort of political thing?

*Dissolve*

*Int. small New York hotel cocktail lounge (1937)—day*

LILLIAN *and* ANNE MARIE TRAVERS *at a table.* LILLIAN *staring into her glass, bored.*

ANNE MARIE. Did you know about the McPhee boy . . . the little one? He was killed in Spain. Imagine having your brother die a Communist. Actually, I can't stand up for any of them. I'm sorry he lost his life, but I wonder why they rush over there.

LILLIAN *looks at her watch.*

ANNE MARIE *(continuing).* Well, I'm glad you had time to see me. Lillian, you look so very slim.

LILLIAN. Thank you, Anne Marie.

ANNE MARIE *(her finger comes to her tooth).* I'm sorry your second play failed.

LILLIAN. Thank you.

ANNE MARIE. But you know I loved your first play.

LILLIAN. Thank you, Anne Marie.

ANNE MARIE. . . . And now you've been invited to Moscow . . . What is it, some sort of political thing?

LILLIAN *(looks at watch again).* Not exactly. It's only a theatre festival, Anne Marie.

ANNE MARIE. But still! Imagine! Russia! My God! Of all places!

*Cut to*

*Int. tent—night*

HAMMETT *and* LILLIAN *together in a sleeping bag.* LILLIAN *stares at the stars through an opening in the tent.*

LILLIAN. Why won't you come to Russia with me?

HAMMETT. I don't want to go to Russia.

LILLIAN. Why? Don't you want to see the Russian theatre?

HAMMETT. I don't give a damn about Russian theatre.

LILLIAN. Maybe I'll go with somebody else. Somebody who'll take me as I am. *(suddenly she explodes)* Goddamn it, why should I be afraid to go to Moscow without you.

HAMMETT. Same reason you're afraid to go to Jersey City.

*Ext. tent high angle—night*

*Angle down through trees.*

LILLIAN'S VOICE. Come on, Hammett. Come with me to Russia.

*We hold outside the tent and we begin to hear a ship's orchestra playing "When My Dreamboat Comes Home."*

LILLIAN'S VOICE. Hammett?

*Hold a moment as the music continues. Builds.*

*Ext. ocean liner angle on ship's band (1937)—night*

*playing a jazzed up version of "When My Dreamboat Comes Home."*

*Long shot the ocean liner "The Normandie" midnight sailing*

*about to depart. We can see* LILLIAN *on deck next to* DOTTIE *and* ALAN. *The noise is tremendous. Screams and horns combining with the ship's band, tons of confetti.*

*Ext. ship's deck* DOTTIE, ALAN, LILLIAN

*They all hold champagne glasses.* DOTTIE'S *a little drunk.*

LILLIAN. Where is he *now*, he keeps moving.

ALAN. By the post.

LILLIAN. Does he see us?

DOTTIE. He's looking straight at us.

LILLIAN. He's not waving. He just stands there.

ALAN *(exuberantly).* Let him stand there if he wants to. We're going to Paris, Lillian!

*He sees that their champagne glasses are empty.*

ALAN. Where's the Steward?

*He takes their glasses, moves off to look for* DRINK STEWARD, *smiling at a* WOMAN *as he goes.*

DOTTIE *(looking after* ALAN). He's looking for celebrities. You think he'll be sleeping with everything in sight while I'm seasick?

LILLIAN. Odds are.

DOTTIE. Oh, well, why shouldn't he. Why the hell shouldn't all of us?

LILLIAN *(looking at* HAMMETT). He's waving. Look! He's waving!

DOTTIE. My God! He's lifting his hat.

LILLIAN *smiles as the band plays "Goodnight Sweetheart."*

*Tight on* HAMMETT

*His hat held up at the side of his head.*

*Tight shot* LILLIAN

*looking down at* HAMMETT. *The screaming, the tooting, the confetti. The ship's whistle and "Goodnight Sweetheart" and we cannot hear* LIL-LIAN *as her lips form:* "HAMMETT!"

*Cut to*

*Int.* LILLIAN'S *elegant Paris hotel room (1937)*

LILLIAN *is on the phone. At one side of the room is her trunk. She is just finishing dressing.*

LILLIAN *(into phone).* Well, will you see her? . . . Does she live there or doesn't she? Will you give Julia a message, please . . . A message . . . Does anyone there speak better English? . . . Sprechen better English? . . . No! I want somebody *better* than you . . . All right, all right . . . Tell her Lillian . . . Lillian . . . Tell Julia Lilly's in Paris, Hotel Meurice. *(we hear someone knocking at the door)* Tell her Lilly will be in Paris for two weeks and then I'm going to Moscow . . . Hello . . . Tell her I can stop in Vienna and see her . . .

*The knocking continues and gets louder. We begin to hear* ALAN'S VOICE *calling* "Lillian."

LILLIAN *(continuing).* Do you ver-stehen . . . understand? . . . Are you sure you verstehen? . . . Hello? . . . I'm losing you, is someone on the line . . . Yes, yes . . . Tell her! Tell her!

*She hangs up as the knocking con-tinues. By now, she has moved with the phone to the door. She opens it and we see* ALAN *and* DOTTIE *in dinner clothes.*

*Another angle* LILLIAN'S *room*

LILLIAN. Jesus Christ, why don't you just break it down.

ALAN. It's twenty after eight, we're due at the Murphys' for cocktails at eight-thirty. Who were you talking to? *(moving to* LILLIAN*)* You missed a button.

LILLIAN *(pulling away from him).* Dottie . . . button this damn thing.

ALAN. We'll be half an hour late and we're supposed to have supper at the Rothschilds'.

LILLIAN. Will you tell him to settle down, for God's sake.

DOTTIE. He's afraid he'll miss Hemingway.

ALAN. Who were you talking to on the phone?

LILLIAN. Hemingway?

ALAN. He's coming up from Spain.

*He sees invitations on* LILLIAN'S *dresser.*

ALAN *(continuing).* You have an in-vitation to Louise de Vilmorin's. Dot-tie, did we get an invitation to Louise de Vilmorin's?

LILLIAN *(as* DOTTIE *buttons her).* Tell him to get out of my things.

DOTTIE. Get out of her things, Alan.

LILLIAN *(moving out).* Hemingway?

ALAN *(as he pushes them out).* Hemingway, and Cocteau and his red necktie, and the creme de la creme.

DOTTIE *(as he exits).* Way down deep, he's very superficial.

*They all leave as the music goes up and the door closes.*

*Cut to*

*Montage* LILLIAN, DOTTIE *and* ALAN *day and night*

*in and around Paris. At an elegant Russian Night Club, an official State Function, another Night Club with frenetic Cuban Band Music and final-ly at Dawn, staggering out of Harry's Bar.* LILLIAN *does not enjoy herself as much as her companions.*

## PARIS MONTAGE SCENE 171

*1. Insert Electric Sign "Scheherezade."*

*2. Int. Scheherezade*
Elegant Russian night club in full swing. LILLIAN *and party at table. Balalaika Band in f.g.* WAITERS *in Cossack uniforms serve flaming skewered meat. Russian music.*

*3. Int. ornate staircase*
LILLIAN *and party walking up steps which are flanked by Garde Republicaine at attention, sabres drawn. They are welcomed at top of steps by very dignified official.*

*4. Insert Posters:*
*Josephine Baker*
*Maurice Chevalier*
*(Dolly Sisters)*

*5. Electric Sign "Boeuf sur le toit" Night*

*6. Int. night club night*
Cuban Band, frenetic music, people dancing, LILLIAN *and friends drinking.*

*7. Possibly Harry's Bar*
LILLIAN *and friends, fairly stoned, staggering slightly as they exit.*

*Int. Paris hotel lobby—morning (8 A.M.)*

LILLIAN, DOTTIE *and* ALAN *move in. They are past being drunk now. It's hangover time.* ALAN *is in his tuxedo,* DOTTIE *in an evening gown.* LILLIAN *in her fur coat and a short evening dress. They move toward the elevator. They stand in front of it, waiting for the car to appear.*

*Closer shot—all*

LILLIAN *(exhausted).* Go ahead up. I'll check and see if I have any messages.

*She turns and walks back toward the desk.*

LILLIAN *(to Clerk).* Hellman, six vingt et un.

*The* CLERK *looks in her letter box, turns back to her.*

CLERK. Nothing, Madame.

*She turns away from the desk. As she does, a man,* MR. JOHANN, *gets up from a bench and moves toward her. He is dressed in an ill-fitting suit, and is carrying a rather well-used briefcase. There is a distinct old world charm about him. He represents something beautiful that is being destroyed. He speaks with a German accent.*

JOHANN. Madame Hellman?
LILLIAN. Yes . . .
JOHANN. I have come to talk to you about the tickets and your travel plans.
LILLIAN. What?
JOHANN. Miss Julia has asked me to see you. I have the travel folders.
LILLIAN. Oh . . .

*Angle on* DOTTIE *and* ALAN

*at the elevator. It has arrived and they are getting in.* ALAN *is looking toward* LILLIAN *and the* MAN. *He watches carefully as the door closes.*

*Back to* LILLIAN *and* JOHANN

LILLIAN. What's the trouble? Something wrong with Julia?
JOHANN. Do you think I could have an egg, hot milk and a roll? I cannot pay for it, however.
LILLIAN. Of course.

*She looks at him for a moment, still rather disorganized. She looks down at her fur and evening dress and then toward the hotel dining room where breakfast is being served.*

JOHANN. Thank you.

*He starts toward the dining room.*
LILLIAN *moves with him, taking off
her jewelery, putting it in her handbag.*

*Int. dining room*

*They have entered, and the* MAITRE
D' *is taking them toward a table. He
eyes* LILLIAN'S *attire with some disdain.*

*Cut to*

*Int. dining room*

LILLIAN *and* MR. JOHANN *are seated
at the dining table. Tight on* LILLIAN
*opening a note.* MR. JOHANN *is eating
a full breakfast.* LILLIAN *has half a
glass of tomato juice before her. She
starts to read the note.*

JULIA'S VOICE *(O.S.)*. This is my
friend, Johann. He will tell you what I
need. But I tell you . . . don't push
yourself. If you can't you can't, no
dishonour. Love, Julia.

LILLIAN *puts down the note, looks
up, confused.* MR. JOHANN *is eating
his egg and roll. Though he is
obviously hungry he tries to control
the appearance of being hungry. He
smiles as if remembering something
from long ago. He looks up at* LIL-
LIAN. *Takes the note from her, folds it
and puts it back in his pocket.*

LILLIAN. Is something wrong with
Julia?

JOHANN *has finished his meal without answering the question.*

JOHANN. I am sorry I could not pay
for myself, but someday perhaps.

LILLIAN. Yes, I am sure some day.
JOHANN. I thank you for the fine
breakfast. Could we walk now in the
Tuileries?

LILLIAN *nods.* JOHANN *looks
around, then with his napkin he wipes
his dampened brow. He shows for the
first time a sign of nervousness. He
smiles again.* LILLIAN, *still not understanding, tries to smile back.*

*Ext. the gardens of the Tuileries
long shot*

LILLIAN *and* JOHANN *moving along
a path.* LILLIAN *feeling self-conscious
in her evening clothes.*

*Closer shot* LILLIAN *and* JOHANN

*as they approach a bench. We
should get the distinct feeling that*
JOHANN *is watching to see if they've
been followed. At the bench, he takes
out his handkerchief and mops his
brow again. Then he lays the handkerchief on the bench for* LILLIAN *to
sit on. She sits. He sits next to her.*

JOHANN. I cannot take long, there is
much to do. So if I am not cordial,
you will understand.

LILLIAN. Yes, of course, you're
very cordial, I think you're *very* cordial.

JOHANN. You are going to Moscow
by way of Vienna.

LILLIAN. Yes.

JOHANN. We would like to change
your travel plans. We would like you
to travel by way of Berlin.

LILLIAN. Why?

JOHANN. You would have to leave
immediately. You would need a German visa. You would stay a short time
in Berlin and change trains there to
Moscow.

LILLIAN *(taking out a cigarette)*.
You aren't being clear.

JOHANN *reacts to some people moving up the path toward their bench.*
LILLIAN *takes out a cigarette. The
people have now passed. She puts the
cigarette away.*

JOHANN. We would like you to carry for us $50,000. We think you will be without trouble, but we do not guarantee that. The money is Julia's money. With it we can bribe out many already in prison. And many who soon *will* be.

*A* BUSINESS MAN *with a briefcase walks briskly by.* JOHANN *is silent for a moment, then continues:*

JOHANN. We are a small group who work against Hitler. We are of no common belief or religion. The people who will meet you for the money, if your consent is given, were small publishers. We have Catholic, Communist, many beliefs. Do you understand?

LILLIAN. Yes.

LILLIAN *lights her cigarette.* JOHANN *watches her, aware of her nervousness. Her anxiety is growing.*

JOHANN. Julia said I must remind you for her, that you are afraid of being afraid, and so will do what sometimes you cannot do. That could be dangerous to you, and to us. Please do not try to be heroic.

LILLIAN *(sharp).* I assure you I would never try to be heroic.

LILLIAN *puffs hard on the cigarette. She stares at* JOHANN.

LILLIAN. Could we go and have a drink, please?

JOHANN. I am sorry time is too short. I am aware you are ill at ease and not prepared for this meeting. I must repeat we think all will go well, but much could go wrong. We realize that you are not the best person for this mission because you are Jewish. But unfortunately there is no one else we can ask. Julia says I must tell you that, but you should know this: if anything should happen, if the Nazis

should arrest you, Julia will use the American Ambassador through her Uncle John.

LILLIAN *(fast and sharp).* She despised her Uncle John!

JOHANN. I am to tell you that Uncle John is now Governor. Julia knows he could be of value to us. I am to tell you also Julia's mother has another divorce and is now dependent too on Julia.

LILLIAN. What about her grandparents?

JOHANN. I do not know of the grandparents.

*Silence.* LILLIAN *takes out another cigarette.* JOHANN *watches her light up again. She looks at him as she waves out her match.*

JOHANN. Will you help us?

LILLIAN *(nervously).* I need a few hours . . . just to think it through.

JOHANN. It is best not to be too prepared for matters of this kind.

LILLIAN. I know that.

JOHANN. You must not think too hard.

LILLIAN *(fast . . . defensive).* I only want to think it over for a while, Julia would want it that way.

*Silence. Finally:*

JOHANN. There is a six-thirty train to Berlin this evening from the Gare du Nord. Number five gate. I will be there. If you agree to carry the money, you will say hello to me. If you have decided it is not right for you—

LILLIAN *(testy).* I have not decided that. I only need time to think it over.

JOHANN. . . . . If you decide it is not right for you, then pass me by. Otherwise, you will simply say "hello" to me. And I will tell you then what is necessary.

LILLIAN. "Hello"! All I say is "hello"?

JOHANN. Just "hello."

LILLIAN. Where will you be?

JOHANN. Do not be concerned. I will find you.

*She puffs more on her cigarette. Then:*

JOHANN. Please, Madame. If you cannot do it, do not do it.

LILLIAN. Please stop saying that!

*After a few moments,* JOHANN *looks up at the sky. He stretches. And when he's through, he puts on a great grin. He looks at* LILLIAN *and rises.*

JOHANN *(a full voice)*. Thank you for the tour. *(takes her hand, bows)* It was a wonderful morning.

*He kisses* LILLIAN'S *hand.*

*Ext.* LILLIAN'S *hotel*

*Angle up to show* ALAN *and* DOT-TIE'S *window. We can see* ALAN *standing by the curtains with a glass. He is looking down toward the gardens.*

*His P.O.V. long shot*

*showing* JOHANN *standing at the bench in front of* LILLIAN. *He turns and moves away, stopping once to smell a flower.*

*Angle favouring* LILLIAN

*She remains on the bench alone and afraid. She's no longer self-conscious about her dress. Finally, she gets up. She moves a few feet away then stops, turns and goes back and picks up the handkerchief that* JOHANN *had put down. She looks toward where he went.*

*Her P.O.V.*

JOHANN *is no longer in view.*

*Back to* LILLIAN

*with the handkerchief. She doesn't quite know what to do with it. She looks at a litter can, considers throwing it in there, but doesn't. She rolls it up and holds it in her hand. Then she takes out another cigarette, lights it, and with the cigarette, she moves through the park, smoking, thinking.*

*Another angle* LILLIAN

*walking on the path.*

JULIA *(O.S.—young girl)*. Lilly, you don't have to come this way. Go down under. Wade across.

*Cut to*

*Ext. a trail in the Adirondack Mountains—day*

*Angle on a fallen tree which serves as access from one side of a relatively deep ravine to the other. Water rushes down the ravine.* JULIA *and* LILLIAN *(children) have approached the tree. They study the pros and cons,* LILLIAN *with some trepidation. Finally,* JULIA *moves with great alacrity across the fallen tree.* LILLIAN *remains on the edge of the ravine behind her. She is contemplating the depths. Quite clearly her fear is increasing.*

*Angle on* JULIA

*on the tree trunk as she reaches the other side. She looks back toward* LIL-LIAN.

*Her P.O.V.* LILLIAN

*Standing frozen in the distance.*

*Full shot*

*We wait a moment for* LILLIAN *to decide. Finally she makes her move. Carefully, she puts one foot on the log.*

JULIA *(calling out)*. Lilly, you don't have to come this way . . . go down under. Wade across.

LILLIAN *looks toward* JULIA, *then she makes a quick decision; steps out onto the log and starts to walk across. When she's less than halfway over, she stands frozen. For a moment she nearly loses her balance.*

*Close shot* LILLIAN

*She looks toward* JULIA.

*Her P.O.V.* JULIA

*on the other side, waiting. Looking strong and able.*

*Med. shot* LILLIAN

*She's perspiring as she looks down at the water beneath her, then looks up again, and once more steps forward.*

*Full shot*

*as* LILLIAN *continues on slowly. She moves closer to the other side. Finally, she is only a few yards from making it. She freezes again. We can feel the panic coming on her. She is about to lose her balance and starts to get down to her knees, but she slips off the log. As she does, she throws her arms around it and holds on for dear life. She is hanging beneath the log.*

JULIA. Pull yourself up!
LILLIAN. I can't!
JULIA. Hold tight—just hold tight.

JULIA *moves out on the log to* LILLIAN; *she gets down on her knees, then straddles it and grabs hold of one of* LILLIAN'S *wrists.* JULIA *starts to pull her up, but the weight is too much, and she is nearly pulled off. She grabs* LILLIAN'S *other wrist and working together, but not without moments of suspense, they finally get* LILLIAN *up over the log on her stomach.*

JULIA. Now straddle it! . . . You're not listening to me! *Straddle it!*

*Carefully* LILLIAN *straddles the trunk and* JULIA, *holding onto one of her hands, moves carefully backwards toward safety, as* LILLIAN *slides in her straddled position after her.*

*Closer shot* LILLIAN *and* JULIA

*as they lie on their sides, exhausted.*

LILLIAN. I'm sorry.
JULIA. It's all right.

*She looks at* LILLIAN *like a good teacher, smiles.*

JULIA. You'll do it next time.

*Cut to*

*Ext. the Tuileries angle on* LILLIAN

*walking on the path. The gardens are breathtaking, but* LILLIAN *is oblivious to everything around her, even a line of schoolchildren who nearly bump into her as they move with their teacher along the path.*

*Cut to*

*Ext. Paris sidewalk angle on* LILLIAN

*moving into the* PEOPLE *who are on their way to work now. She is totally involved in herself. She crosses the street, nearly getting hit by more than one automobile.*

*Int. French restaurant—day*

*A small cafe.* LILLIAN *at a little table. Coffee is brought to her. She drinks it.*

*Ext. Paris street angle on* LILLIAN—*day*

*walking.*

*Int. German Consulate—day*

*A long, narrow room, beige. Only a picture of Adolf Hitler in the center of the otherwise bare wall. A long, narrow empty table.* LILLIAN *at the end of it, sitting stiffly. A young* GERMAN WOMAN *sits across from* LILLIAN. *She holds* LILLIAN'S *passport, and speaks quietly.*

GERMAN WOMAN. Why do you change your plans?

LILLIAN. It's an impulse. I thought it would be pleasant to see Berlin, but I thought I could stay longer than a few hours.

GERMAN WOMAN. You are going to Moscow, so regulations permit only that you will have a transit visa.

LILLIAN. Why is that?

*The* WOMAN *ignores the question, writes on a form, stamps* LILLIAN'S *passport, closes it, and slides it neatly in front of* LILLIAN.

GERMAN WOMAN *(dismissing her).* There you are.

*Cut to*

*Int. Paris hotel lobby angle on main desk—dusk*

LILLIAN *stands there. She is overdressed to compensate for her insecurity. She carries a large, overstuffed handbag and a small suitcase. The* CLERK *is handing* LILLIAN *an envelope.*

CLERK. Your train tickets, Madame.

LILLIAN. Thank you. Where's my trunk?

CLERK. It is on the way to the station, Madame.

LILLIAN. Did Mr. and Mrs. Campbell get my note?

CLERK. Yes, Madame.

LILLIAN *nods and turns and starts toward the main entrance. A bellboy moves ahead of her with her suitcase. She is exhausted, extremely tense, and in her hurry she bumps into a* woman leading a dog and gets entangled for a moment in the leash before reaching the door.

*When she's at the door, we see* ALAN *and* DOTTIE *coming out of the elevator wearing evening clothes.* ALAN *looking quickly through the lobby.* LILLIAN *sees him, moves hurriedly outside.* ALAN *sees her and points her out to* DOTTIE, *and they move toward the door.*

*Ext. hotel—dusk*

*A taxi is waiting. The* BELLBOY *gives the suitcase to the* DOORMAN *who is opening the car door for* LILLIAN, *as* ALAN *and* DOTTIE *move outside.* ALAN *has taken a piece of notepaper from his pocket. He moves to* LILLIAN *who is half-in, half-out of the car.*

ALAN. You think you can be invisible? *(takes note out of pocket)* What's this mean, you're leaving us, you'll find us again after Moscow?

LILLIAN. I'm in a hurry, I can't explain now.

DOTTIE. Lilly, what's wrong?

LILLIAN. Nothing is wrong. I've changed my plans. I've had enough partying and I want to leave.

ALAN. It's not like you to be so mysterious, Lillian.

LILLIAN. I have to go. I'm late.

ALAN. We'll see you to the station, whatever this is about.

LILLIAN. No! I don't need you! I'll write you, I'll phone you from Moscow.

ALAN *is pushing* DOTTIE *into the car.*

DOTTIE. Alan, why are you doing this?

ALAN. Because our friend Lilly's gone berserk.

*He stuffs himself into the taxi and pulls the door closed behind him.*

LILLIAN'S VOICE (*from inside the taxi*). Goddamn it, Alan, you drive me nuts!

DOTTIE'S VOICE. Christ, dear, you'd be psychotic if he didn't.

LILLIAN'S VOICE. I insist you don't come.

*Taxi drives off.*

*Cut to*

*Ext. Gare du Nord—dusk*

*The car pulling to a stop.* LILLIAN, ALAN *and* DOTTIE *get out.* ALAN *taking charge. He has* LILLIAN'S *suitcase.* LILLIAN *pays the* TAXI DRIVER.

ALAN (*to* LILLIAN). What gate? Where's your ticket?

LILLIAN *takes her ticket from her purse.* ALAN *grabs it, looks at it.*

LILLIAN. It's gate Five, six-thirty. You don't have to come in with me. Thank you both. (*she takes her suitcase from* ALAN) I'm already late. Now let me do it alone or I'll miss my train.

DOTTIE. My God, Lilly, will you relax.

ALAN. Let's go, let's go, we'll be late.

LILLIAN (*grabs her ticket from* ALAN). Give me back my ticket.

*They move into the station.*

*Int. Gare du Nord—night*

*The station is full. They are moving through,* LILLIAN *carrying her suitcase, looking around for* MR. JOHANN.

*New angle approaching gate 5—night*

LILLIAN *looking around.* ALAN *looks up at the schedule board, a clock says 6:25. A loudspeaker calls the departure of the train to Berlin.*

ALAN. By way of Berlin. Why are you going by way of Berlin?

DOTTIE. I thought you wanted to see your friend Julia in Vienna?

LILLIAN (*looking nervously around*). I never heard from her. Listen, say goodbye to me here.

LILLIAN *reacts to O.S.*

ALAN. It's all too mysterious for me. You haven't even had a day's sleep.

LILLIAN'S *P.O.V.—night*

MR. JOHANN *moving her way on the platform toward the gate separating the platform from the station.*

*Back to* LILLIAN—*night*

*watching* JOHANN. *He walks through the gate.* ALAN *looks up the platform, following* LILLIAN'S *eyes.*

ALAN (*as he looks at* JOHANN). At any rate, don't accept anything but the light grey caviar.

DOTTIE. Which is your car, Lillian?

ALAN. Isn't that the man I saw you with in the Tuileries yesterday?

LILLIAN *shoots* ALAN *a look, is about to say something to him as* MR. JOHANN *moves past them toward the station exit.* LILLIAN *watches* MR. JOHANN.

ALAN. Is he a friend of yours or something?

*Wider angle—night*

*as suddenly* LILLIAN *runs after* MR. JOHANN.

LILLIAN. Mr. Johann. Please, Mr. Johann.

LILLIAN *loses her head and screams.*

LILLIAN. Please don't go away! *Please!*

MR. JOHANN *turns to look at her.*

*Close shot* LILLIAN *and* MR. JOHANN—*night*

*She stops, a few yards from him. He stands still for what seems a long time. Then he walks slowly toward* LILLIAN.

LILLIAN. I only wanted to say hello. Hello to you, Mr. Johann. Hello!

JOHANN *(a polite nod)*. Hello, Madame.

ALAN *has edged closer to him, and is now behind him, within hearing distance. The P.A. system is calling out departures in the b.g.* DOTTIE *moves closer.*

LILLIAN *(quickly, her words jumbled)*. This is Mr. Campbell and, uh, that's Miss Parker, uh, and Mr. Campbell says he saw us yesterday in the Gardens, and now he will ask me who you are and say that he didn't know we knew each other so well that you would come all this way to say goodbye to me . . .

JOHANN *(calm)*. I wish I could say that this was true, but I have come to seek for my nephew, who is en route to Poland. He is not in his coach. He is late as is his habit. His name is W. Franz, car four, second class, and if I do not find him I would be most grateful if you would say to him I came.

*He lifts his hat.*

LILLIAN. His name was what?

JOHANN. W. Franz, second class, car four. I am most glad, Madame, we had this chance to say hello.

LILLIAN. Oh, yes. Indeed. Hello. Hello. Hello, Mr. Johann. Hello!

JOHANN *smiles at her, then turns and moves away through the crowd.* ALAN *moves next to* LILLIAN.

ALAN. What funny talk. You're talking like a foreigner.

LILLIAN *(sharp)*. Sorry. Sorry not to speak as well as you do in Virginia.

*The train is ready. The steam is hissing and swirling up on the platform. People scurrying to board.*

LILLIAN. Have to go. Goodbye.

*They all embrace quickly, awkwardly, as* LILLIAN *runs to board.*

LILLIAN *(to herself)*. Franz, car four, second class.

*Angle favouring* LILLIAN—*night*

*at the steps of the car. The* CONDUCTOR *is there. The steam is up around* LILLIAN. *She trips on the step and falls to her knee. Her purse tips over and some of its contents fall back out onto the platform. She scrapes them up and then she is quickly back onto the steps, and the* CONDUCTOR *helps her into the car, but she is limping a bit.*

*Angle favouring* ALAN *and* DOTTIE—*night*

*watching* LILLIAN *in the car as the train starts off.* LILLIAN *turns once for a brief look at them, along with a sick smile and then she's gone as if swallowed up by something she can't understand.*

*Int. train 1st coach corridor/ platform—night*

LILLIAN *moves between the cars, limping. She moves past a* LARGE, HEAVYSET YOUNG WOMAN. *On the connecting platform before she reaches the next coach is a* YOUNG MAN, *holding a valise and some packages.* LILLIAN, *with her own suitcase and purse, moves past him, but before she gets through:*

YOUNG MAN. Madame Hellman?

LILLIAN *turns.*

I am W. Franz, nephew, car four, second class. This is my birthday present from Miss Julia.

*He hands* LILLIAN *a box of candy and a hatbox marked:* MADAME PAULINE. *Then he turns and moves off in the direction from which* LILLIAN *just came.* LILLIAN *is left alone with the hatbox, the candy, her purse and her valise. She's not sure what to do for a moment. She's extremely anxious. She finally turns and continues into the next coach.*

*Int. 2nd coach corridor—night*

LILLIAN *moving through the car, checking her ticket envelope and looking at the compartment numbers. She can't find hers. The train is getting up steam and slowly moving from the station.* LILLIAN *makes her way through the narrow passageway. She sees a* FAT, DARK-COATED MAN *coming her way. They will have trouble passing one another. When they meet, it's a close, comic fit, but they make it. She continues on. Further down the corridor a* CONDUCTOR *approaches her.* LILLIAN *gets her ticket in front of him. He looks at it. Points the other way.*

CONDUCTOR *(in French).* You have come the wrong way, Madame.

*He passes her and she turns and starts back again, looking around as she does.*

*Close shot the hatbox 2nd coach corridor—night*

*The name "Madame Pauline" is prominent as it flops up and down, moving with* LILLIAN *along the train passage.*

*Int. train platform—night*

LILLIAN *moves through. She stops for some air. Then continues. She is still limping.*

*Int. 1st coach corridor—night*

*We see the* FAT MAN *coming back now.* LILLIAN *approaches him. They*

*come together. Try to pass one another. This time it is more difficult. The* MAN *starts to cough. It grows worse. It is a serious coughing fit. In order for them to pass, the* MAN *takes the hatbox, holds it over his head, continuing to cough.* LILLIAN *keeping her eye on the box. The* MAN *moves on, coughing as he disappears into the next car.*

*Angle on* LILLIAN *corridor 1st coach—night*

*Finally she finds her compartment. She opens the door, looks in.*

*Int. compartment night* LILLIAN'S *P.O.V.*

*On one of the benches sits a* SMALL GIRL, *very thin, carrying a cane, a book on her lap. She is in her late twenties.*

*Int. compartment—night*

LILLIAN *enters. She smiles politely and the* YOUNG WOMAN *nods.* LILLIAN *sits down, putting her packages next to her. She looks at the* WOMAN *who only glances at her, then looks out the window.* LILLIAN *is extremely nervous. She looks down at her knee. The stocking is torn and the knee bruised.*

LILLIAN *now looks toward the hatbox and sees a note has been pasted to it. She stares at it a moment, then looks to see if the* WOMAN *is watching. She is not. Then she peels the note from the box, opens the envelope, her hands trembling. She lowers her hands so that they rest on her purse. She starts to read the note, but stops as the door opens. The* LARGE WOMAN LILLIAN *passed earlier on the train enters. She is wearing a heavy coat, tightly wrapped. She seems out of breath. Carries a small valise. She looks at* LILLIAN *and the other* WOMAN, *then sits next to the latter.*

*She catches her breath, organizes herself, and finally stares out the window.* LILLIAN *waits a moment, then returns to the note.*

*Insert note*

*As we read it, we hear:*

JULIA'S VOICE *(O.S.).* Open this box and wear the hat. When you reach the border, leave the candy box on the seat. There is no thanks for what you will do for them. No thanks from me either. But there *is* the love I have for you . . . Julia.

*Back to* LILLIAN

*as she holds the note. She looks at the women. She looks at the hatbox and the candy box while the women continue to look out the window.* LILLIAN *moves about in her seat. Finally she puts the note in her purse and stands up. The* TWO WOMEN *look at her. She smiles, nervously. Then she picks up the hatbox and the candy box and starts out.*

THIN GIRL *(with thick German accent).* This is compartment F. Do you not want F?

LILLIAN. F. Yes. I'm just going to the washroom. I . . .

*They stare at her. She can't decide what to do. Finally:*

LILLIAN. Oh . . . well . . . perhaps I won't go to the washroom.

*She half laughs then puts the packages down again and sits. Nervously.*

*Ext. long shot train in France—night*

*Train moves across the countryside.*

*Angle through window—night*

*at* LILLIAN *looking out. The* TWO OTHER WOMEN *looking out.* LILLIAN

*turning to look at them. She looks at the door, then back out window.*

*Tight shot* LILLIAN *through window—night*

*She pulls her palm across her forehead, then she smiles politely and looks back out the window, just past camera. The she takes out a cigarette. Lights it.*

*Ext. long shot the engine—night*

*straight at camera.*

*Int. compartment—night*

*The* THIN GIRL *still has a book on her lap. Untouched.* LILLIAN *stares at her cane. A carved fox head on the handle. The* LARGE GIRL *is now reading a newspaper, Frankfurter Zeitung.*

LILLIAN *looks at the compartment door window. A* WOMAN *with sharp features, wearing a green hat passes by. She looks in the glass for a moment. Something about her frightens* LILLIAN. *Then she's gone.* LILLIAN *relights her cigarette. Everything seems to frighten her now.*

*Ext. train—night*

*It approaches a tunnel.*

*Int. compartment—night*

*Suddenly the train is in the tunnel and the sound is thunderous. We remain in the tunnel for what seems a long time. Always there is* LILLIAN'S *tension . . .*

*Still in the tunnel the sound remains thunderous but then it's suddenly over as the train leaves the tunnel.* LILLIAN *is terrified. She looks at the* TWO WOMEN. *The* HEAVY GIRL *is looking at her paper. The* THIN GIRL *stares at* LILLIAN *a brief moment, then back out the window.*

LILLIAN *looks at the hatbox, the candy box. She looks at her purse. She takes the note out again. Reads it. Puts it back in. Wipes her brow again. The train whistles.*

*Suddenly, noisily, the door opens.* LILLIAN *turns quickly. The* CONDUCTOR *is there.*

CONDUCTOR *(in French)*. First call for dinner.

LILLIAN *gets up quickly, too quickly, then she looks at the* TWO WOMEN. *Then she looks at the hatbox and the candy. Then she sits back down. She smiles at them.*

LILLIAN. I guess I'm not hungry. *(in French)* I am not hungry.

*The* WOMEN *stare at her. The* THIN GIRL *looks at* LILLIAN'S *sealskin coat. Studies it.*

THIN GIRL. Nice coat.
LILLIAN. I beg your pardon.
THIN GIRL. Coat. Is nice.
LILLIAN. Yes, yes, nice. My coat . . . Thank you.
THIN GIRL. Warm. What fur it is?
LILLIAN. It's sealskin. Yes, it's warm.
THIN GIRL *(looks at hatbox)*. Your hat is also fur?
LILLIAN. I don't know, I . . . the hat, yes . . . oh, yes, the hat.

*She sits paralyzed a moment. Then she takes the hatbox, opens it. Takes out the hat, a high, fluffy hat of grey fox, as both* WOMEN *murmur their admiration. Finally:*

HEAVY GIRL *(German accent)*. Nice with coat? . . . You would put on?

LILLIAN *hesitates. She looks at the hat, then stands up and prepares to put it on. As she does, she reacts to something she feels in the hat's lining.*

*Large close up*

LILLIAN'S *fingers feeling the lining inside the hat. Something is in it.*

*Back to compartment—night*

LILLIAN *continues to put on the hat. Once on, she looks at herself in the mirror between the two compartment doors. Then she turns to the* TWO GIRLS. *They smile and nod their heads.*

GIRLS. Ahh . . . Yes . . . is nice . . .

LILLIAN *sits back down.*

HEAVY GIRL. Is pretty.
LILLIAN. Thank you . . .

*They continue to watch her.*

LILLIAN. I think I'll keep it on.

*They smile at her. Then the* THIN GIRL *looks at her watch. Looks outside. Suddenly, the* HEAVY GIRL *stands. She towers over* LILLIAN *and the* THIN GIRL.

HEAVY GIRL *(to* THIN GIRL *in German)*. I will go to the dining car now. I would have some dinner now. You would have some dinner with me?
THIN GIRL *(in German)*. Thank you, no.
HEAVY GIRL *(to* LILLIAN *in English)*. I eat now. You would like dinner?
LILLIAN. Dinner! Yes! I would, but I don't know when we cross the border and I . . .

*She stops herself.*

THIN GIRL. The border . . . we do not stop for the border until morning. There's much time now.
HEAVY GIRL. You would come and eat, then?
THIN GIRL *(to* LILLIAN*)*. Do not worry of your things, I stay here, I eat here.
*(shows her a small box with her dinner in it)* Is too much money to pay for food on train.

HEAVY GIRL. I would not pay, too, but I must take medicine. My doctor tells me I must take hot food with it, and a glass of wine. You would have a glass of wine with me? You would talk with me of America?

LILLIAN *considers, then picks up her coat and drops it over the candy box. The* THIN GIRL *watches the move, then looks out the window.*

LILLIAN *and the* HEAVY GIRL *leave the compartment,* LILLIAN *looking back towards her seat, as she goes. She wears her fur hat.*

*Int. 1st coach corridor—night*

LILLIAN *and the* HEAVY GIRL *moving through the car.* LILLIAN *puts her hand up to hold her hat on. It is clear* LILLIAN *doesn't feel well.*

*Int. dining car—night*

LILLIAN *and the* HEAVY GIRL *finding a table. The car is half-full. A* WAITER *moves to them with menus, then moves on.* LILLIAN *looks as if she's fighting the feeling of nausea. She looks at the menu, then looks up and sees the* FAT MAN *and the* WOMAN IN THE GREEN HAT *sitting silently side by side at a table.*

HEAVY GIRL *(in French).* I think the Bisque, and a half bottle of table wine. *(to Lillian)* I think it is the best, the Bisque.

LILLIAN *(feeling ill).* Bisque, yes.

HEAVY GIRL. You see, I must have the hot . . . For the lungs. I study in Paris. And I get ill, you see. I am at the University and I am not good, my health. I was at concert . . . one night . . . I cannot breathe of a sudden. You see?

LILLIAN *(getting up).* I wonder . . . if you wouldn't mind . . . pardon me . . . Je malade . . .

*She turns and starts away from the* HEAVY GIRL *who watches her carefully.* LILLIAN *knocking over a glass of water on a table as she rushes for the end of the car.*

*She holds the hat on her head as she leaves the car.*

*Int. 1st coach corridor—night*

LILLIAN *moving fast, passing a* COUPLE *on their way to the dining car. She holds her hat on. Feels dizzy. She sees the washroom. Turns the knob to enter, but it's occupied. Suddenly the door between the cars opens and* TWO MEN *enter and move toward her. She presses against the washroom door as they approach her. To her, their look is menacing. But they pass her and as they do, the door to the washroom opens behind her. She turns quickly. A rather well-dressed* MIDDLE-AGED WOMAN *moves out as* LILLIAN *moves in, pulling the door closed behind her.*

*Int. washroom—night*

*She sits on the toilet lid, leans forward. She's breathing very hard. Then she raises her head and catches a glimpse of herself in the mirror. The hat looks preposterous.*

*Int. compartment—night*

*as* LILLIAN *enters. She's shaken. The* THIN GIRL *eating from her box, reading her book. She looks up questioningly.* LILLIAN *looks at her, then at her seat, at the coat draped over the candy box.*

THIN GIRL. Is wrong? Something?

LILLIAN. No . . . I was just . . . I wasn't hungry . . .

THIN GIRL. Ahhhhh . . .

LILLIAN *lifts her coat, sees the candy box is still there. She puts the coat back, then she sits, rubs her sore* knee. *Takes off the hat, puts it next to her.*

THIN GIRL. Here is food . . . if you become of a hunger.

LILLIAN. Thank you, but no . . . thank you . . .

*The* THIN GIRL *reads and eats.*

*Tight on* LILLIAN—*night*

*She looks through the compartment door window into the corridor.*

*Shot the train*—*night*

*racing across the countryside. The whistle blows.*

*Int. train compartment*—*night*

*The* THIN GIRL *sleeps.* LILLIAN, *with the hat still on, stares out the window. The door swings open.* HEAVY GIRL *is there. The* THIN GIRL *awakens.*

HEAVY GIRL. You are better now?

LILLIAN. I'll be all right, thank you. Yes. Better. I'm sorry.

HEAVY GIRL (*to* THIN GIRL, *in German*). She was sick.

THIN GIRL (*in German*). I know.

*Then silence. The* HEAVY GIRL *sits.*

*They look out the window. The* THIN GIRL *closes her eyes again.*

*Angle on* LILLIAN—*night*

LILLIAN *looks straight ahead, her body bobbing back and forth with the movement of the train, her panic growing as the train gets closer to Border. Then she looks toward the window.*

*Tight shot* LILLIAN'S *reflection*

*through the train window. Sound of train continuing. Superimposed over* LILLIAN'S *reflection, we see* LILLIAN *and* JULIA *(17 years old) running across a field in the Adirondacks.* JULIA *moving gracefully.* LILLIAN, *be-*

hind her, fighting to keep up. JULIA *doesn't slow down or even look back.* LILLIAN *falls once, gets up, laughing. Continues after* JULIA, *still laughing and impressed by* JULIA'S *stamina.*

*Ext. a stream*

LILLIAN *and* JULIA *ankle-deep in the water, squatting.*

*Close shot*

JULIA *reaching into the water, her hands quickly catching a fish.*

*Angle on* LILLIAN

*as she watches in awe.*

*Ext. Adirondacks (1922)*—*night*

JULIA *and* LILLIAN *under blankets by a campfire.* JULIA *reciting poetry.*

JULIA. "Whenas in Silks my Julia goes, Then, then, methinks, how sweetly flows, The liquefaction of her clothes. Next, when I cast mine eyes, and see That brave vibration each way free, O, how that glittering taketh me." (*looks up, smiles*) That's his tribute to me.

*Silence.* LILLIAN *looks at* JULIA.

LILLIAN (*softly*). Julia?

JULIA *looks up.*

LILLIAN (*barely audible*). I love you, Julia.

JULIA *waits a moment, then slowly reaches to* LILLIAN. *She takes* LILLIAN'S *hand and brings it to touch her own face. Then she reaches her other hand to* LILLIAN *and as she touches her cheek she moves closer to her and they lie side by side.* JULIA'S *face against* LILLIAN'S. *We can see* LILLIAN'S *eyes. Hold.*

*Cut to*

*Int. the train compartment*—*dawn*

LILLIAN *is dozing. The* THIN GIRL *reaches to tap* LILLIAN *on the knee.* LILLIAN *looks up quickly.*

THIN GIRL. We will be in Germany. It comes now the border.

LILLIAN *looks outside into the morning light. She is beginning to grow warm, anxious again.*

*Ext. France the train—dawn*

*Angle on the train moving slowly past camera. We hear the screeching sound of the train's brakes as train continues to slow. We see the three women looking out the window.*

*Ext. train station German border—dawn*

*as the train moves in. There are* CUSTOMS MEN, POLICE, MEN *with swastika armbands. The train is nearly at a stop, the doors are being opened.* POLICE *and* CUSTOMS MEN *moving onto the train. We can see signs with arrows pointing to customs.*

*Int. 1st coach corridor—dawn*

*People moving through the passageway to get out.*

*Int. compartment—dawn*

LILLIAN *looks through the compartment door window now extremely frightened. People moving through the car. The* TWO GIRLS *get up.*

THIN GIRL *(to* LILLIAN*).* We must go out now to the check gate. It is necessary for your passport.
LILLIAN. Yes. I will. I have a temporary visa.
HEAVY GIRL. You will need your coat and hat, it is of a windiness.
LILLIAN. Thank you. Yes, of course.

*In her growing panic and utter confusion she picks up the candy box.*

THIN GIRL *(suddenly very sharp).* You will have need of your coat. Your hat is nice on your head.

*A momentary pause, and* LILLIAN *puts the candy box down on the seat. Then she puts her coat around her shoulders, picks up the hat and puts it on her head. The* HEAVY GIRL *moves out of the compartment.* LILLIAN *hesitates for a moment, looks at the candy box on the seat, then follows the* HEAVY GIRL. *The* THIN GIRL *moves behind her.*

*Ext. station platform—dawn*

LILLIAN *moving off the train steps. The* TWO GIRLS *are in a line by the check gate.* LILLIAN *moves towards them. They are separated from her by a few people. The* THIN GIRL *drops her purse, moves to pick it up and as she does so, she gets in line directly behind* LILLIAN. LILLIAN *senses the move. Questions it.*

LILLIAN *is next in line now.*

THIN GIRL *(to* LILLIAN*).* If you have a temporary travel visa, it could take more minutes than others. It is nothing. Do not worry.

LILLIAN *stares at the* GIRL.

BORDER POLICE OFFICER. Nachste!

LILLIAN *waits a moment, then steps to the table. She hands her passport to the* OFFICER. *He looks through it. Looks at her to check the picture. Looks back at the passport. Then up at her again.*

*The* THIN GIRL *watches carefully. The* HEAVY GIRL *is already through and watches from the side as she lights a cigarette. We see the* WOMAN IN THE GREEN HAT *talking to a* POLICE OFFICER.

BORDER POLICE OFFICER. Temporary visa . . .

LILLIAN. Yes.

BORDER POLICE OFFICER. Hellman . . . *(pause, looks at her, looks at her hat)* Why do you go to Berlin?

LILLIAN. Friends. See some friends and . . . to see it, I've never seen Berlin.

BORDER POLICE OFFICER. Not business?

LILLIAN. Not business, no.

BORDER POLICE OFFICER. You cannot see much in a day of Berlin.

LILLIAN. I can only stay a short while. I have to be in Moscow.

BORDER POLICE OFFICER. What is your occupation?

LILLIAN. I'm a writer.

BORDER POLICE OFFICER. Ahhh, writer.

LILLIAN. Yes.

BORDER POLICE OFFICER. So you would write of Berlin?

LILLIAN. Oh, no, I wouldn't.

BORDER POLICE OFFICER. Perhaps your impressions, you would write.

LILLIAN. My impressions. Yes, I *will* write of my impressions.

*The* BORDER POLICE OFFICER *looks up, looks at her hat again, then into her eyes, then he stamps her passport.*

BORDER POLICE OFFICER. All right. Thank you very much. *(call out)* Nachste!

LILLIAN *moves out of line. The* THIN GIRL *steps up to the* BORDER POLICE OFFICER. *She smiles, suddenly charming.* LILLIAN *starts back to the train.*

*Angle on* LILLIAN *at steps to car—dawn*

*She looks around. She sees the* FAT MAN *and* ANOTHER MAN *looking at her. She hesitates, then re-enters the train.*

*Int. train 1st coach corridor—dawn*

LILLIAN *among passengers returning to their compartments. We see the* CUSTOMS MEN *in the compartment next to* LILLIAN'S *inspecting luggage.*

*Int. compartment—dawn*

*The door opens.* LILLIAN *enters. The* HEAVY GIRL *is sitting down, her ear to the wall, listening to the two* CUSTOMS MEN *talking good-naturedly to people in the adjoining compartment.* LILLIAN *sits down. After she does, the* THIN GIRL *moves in quickly.*

THIN GIRL *(to* HEAVY GIRL*).* They take great time with the luggage.

HEAVY GIRL. I know.

*The* CUSTOMS MEN *are moving toward their compartment. The* THIN GIRL *sits down and as she does she reaches for the candy box on* LILLIAN'S *seat. She quickly unties the ribbon and opens the box.*

LILLIAN. What are you doing?

THIN GIRL *(firm).* Thank you, I am hungry for a chocolate, most kind.

LILLIAN *(sharp).* Please don't open that. I'm carrying that for a friend, it's a gift.

*The* CUSTOMS MEN *open the door. They move in. The* THIN GIRL *is chewing on candy, the box open on her lap.*

1ST CUSTOMS MAN *(in German).* Heitler . . . customs, open your bags!

*The* CUSTOMS MEN *take down the luggage. One of them goes through it.* LILLIAN'S *suitcase takes longer. They are very careful with each piece and very thorough. The* CUSTOMS MAN *opens the hatbox, he looks into the hatbox. Then he looks at the hat on* LILLIAN'S *head. The* THIN GIRL *offers him a piece of chocolate. The* CUSTOMS MAN *looks at the candy but shakes his head. Not interested.*

*Everything has been neatly replaced. The men salute perfunctorily.*

*They close the door.* LILLIAN *and the* TWO GIRLS *sit quietly for a few moments. The* THIN GIRL *puts the top on the candy box and slowly, carefully reties the bow with the ribbon.* LILLIAN *simply watches her. The* THIN GIRL *puts the box back on the seat next to* LILLIAN. *No one speaks.*

*We hear the train whistle. The steam comes up over the windows. The sounds of men's deep voices outside calling commands and the train jerks and begins to move again. Finally, the train moves out of the station.*

*The* TWO GIRLS *look out the window and then the* HEAVY GIRL *turns and stares at* LILLIAN. LILLIAN *returns the look. Then the* HEAVY GIRL *and the* THIN GIRL *exchange a look, then they look back out the window again.* LILLIAN *looks at them both, waits, then lights a cigarette. The* HEAVY GIRL *starts to cough. Leans forward, the cough is strong.* LILLIAN *puts out her cigarette. The train picks up speed.*

*Ext. the train—day*

*moving through Germany. We can hear the* HEAVY GIRL'S *coughing.*

*Angle through window—day*

*at* LILLIAN *looking out past camera.*

*Ext. long shot train—day*

*moving through Germany. A sense of Germany's pastoral countryside.*

*Int. train 1st coach corridor—day*

CONDUCTOR *moving through cars.*

CONDUCTOR *(in German).* Berlin. Half hour.

*Int. compartment—day*

*The* CONDUCTOR *opens the door and looks in.*

CONDUCTOR *(in German).* Berlin. Half hour.

*He exits.* LILLIAN *looks at the girls. They sit straight. There is their tension now. More so than ever before.* LILLIAN *sits straight, too. She is ready. More ready than before. But still very tense. She lights another cigarette.*

*Ext. Berlin train station—day*

*Much activity. Sombre. Steam fills the screen. Large clock reads 4:45.*

*Angle on the engine as it passes camera*

*The brakes applied. The screeching.*

*Angle on* LILLIAN—*day*

*Through the window. The screeching in b.g. She looks around. Looking for someone.*

*Her P.O.V. The station personnel day*

POLICE. *Nazi uniforms.*

*Tight on* LILLIAN—*day*

*Again the anxiety. She turns. Pull back to show the* TWO GIRLS *standing up. Waiting for her. She gets her things together. The candy box under her arm.*

*Ext. train platform—day*

*The people awaiting departures. The train stopped now. The doors open and the other* PASSENGERS *move out.*

*Int. train 1st coach corridor—day*

LILLIAN *moving behind the* HEAVY GIRL *and the* THIN GIRL. *It is very close in there.* LILLIAN, *claustrophobic.*

*Ext. platform—day*

*People moving towards the station gate. People kissing and shaking hands all along the way.* LILLIAN *and the* TWO GIRLS *come out of the train. Move down to the platform. They move along the platform towards the gate.*

*Tight on* LILLIAN—*day*

*She moves forward, carrying the hatbox, the candy box, her purse and her suitcase. Her coat and hat on. Flanked by the* TWO GIRLS. *We hear someone calling:*

WOMAN'S VOICE *(O.S.).* Lillian! Lillian!

LILLIAN *looks.*

*Angle on a* MAN *and* WOMAN—*day*

*Both about fifty. They are moving toward* LILLIAN. *The* WOMAN *holding out her arms and exclaiming as she approaches* LILLIAN.

WOMAN. Lillian, how good it is to see you. How naughty of you not to stay more than a few hours, but even that will give us time for a nice visit.
THIN GIRL *(quickly to* LILLIAN*).* Give her the candy box!
LILLIAN. I'm so glad to see you again.

*They embrace.*
I've brought you a small gift . . . gifts . . .

*But the candy box has already been taken from her, and* LILLIAN *is being moved by* THE MAN.

*New shot* LILLIAN *and* THE MAN—*day*

LILLIAN *looking around as she and the* MAN *walk through the crowd toward the gate.*

LILLIAN'S *P.O.V. The* TWO GIRLS *and* THE WOMAN—*day*

*all moving away, quickly, in different directions. The* WOMAN *with the candy box beneath her arm.*

*Angle on* LILLIAN *and* THE MAN—*day*

*as they move. With a slight movement of his head, the* MAN *indicates the side entrance.*

MAN. Go through that gate. It will lead to the side entrance. When you get outside you are to look directly across the street. You will see a restaurant called Albert's. You will cross the street and go into that restaurant. *(louder)* Good luck. Enjoy yourself. Pleasant to see you again.

*The* MAN *moves off, leaving* LILLIAN *alone. For a moment she looks toward the* MAN *moving away. Then she turns and looks at the gate. Then she looks back at the* MAN. *Then with growing anxiety she just stands there and waits a moment and catches a deep breath. She starts for the gate. Camera moves with her and follows her to the gate, through it, to the side entrance of the station.*

*Ext. street at side entrance of station—dusk*

*She looks across the street as she was directed.*

LILLIAN'S *P.O.V. across the street—dusk*

*We can see an electric sign reading* ALBERT'S.

*Back to* LILLIAN—*dusk*

*She moves slowly, anxiously across the street. Finally, at the other side, in front of Albert's, she looks into the window, but it is not possible to see anyone inside. She moves to a revolving door. A group of people are coming out. She has to wait to catch a slot in the door. She does and she pushes the door in. It is difficult with the hatbox and her small suitcase.*

*Int. Albert's restaurant—night*

LILLIAN *appearing out of the revolving door. She stops. She looks around. Suddenly, she reacts to something o.s.*

*Her P.O.V.—*JULIA*—night*

*sitting at a table at the rear of the restaurant. She is looking at* LILLIAN. *Leaning against the wall behind her chair are two crutches. A drink is on the table. Cigarettes.*

*Angle favouring* LILLIAN*—night*

*Frozen. She only looks.*

*Angle favouring* JULIA*—night*

*She smiles. She raises one hand.* LILLIAN *slowly moves toward* JULIA.

*Closer angle—*LILLIAN *and* JULIA*— night*

LILLIAN *closer to her now. For the first time she sees the crutches.* JULIA *takes her hand.* LILLIAN'S *eyes begin to tear. They do not speak.* LILLIAN *looks again at the crutches, then she sits next to* JULIA. JULIA *continues to hold her hand.* LILLIAN *can't speak. Then finally:*

JULIA. Fine, fine.

LILLIAN *studies her, looks at the crutches.*

JULIA. I've ordered caviar. We'll celebrate. Albert had to send for it, it won't be long. Look at you. Oh, just look at you!

LILLIAN *(whispers).* Tell me what to say to you.

JULIA. It's all right. Nothing will happen now, everything's fine now.

LILLIAN. I want to say something.

JULIA. I know.

LILLIAN. How long do we have?

JULIA. Not long.

LILLIAN. You still look like nobody else. *(pause)* Why do you have the crutches?

*Pause.*

JULIA *(quickly).* I have a false leg!

LILLIAN. What?

JULIA. I have a false leg!

LILLIAN. No! I don't want to hear that. Don't tell me that!

JULIA *(sharp).* No tears, Lilly.

LILLIAN. I'm sorry.

JULIA. It's done. It's what it is.

LILLIAN. When?

JULIA. You know when. You were there. In Vienna.

LILLIAN. I don't want to hear about it, please, just let me look at you.

JULIA. You have to hear about it, you have to hear about everything. *(taking* LILLIAN'S *hand)* Your fingers are cold, here . . .

*She begins to rub* LILLIAN'S *hands.*

LILLIAN. They took the candy box. A man and a woman.

JULIA. That's right. Everything's fine and what I want you to do now is take off your hat, the way you would if it—Lilly, listen to me, you aren't listening.

LILLIAN. I'm listening, I am.

JULIA. Take off your hat, as if it were too hot in here. Comb your hair. Put your hat on the seat between us. Do as I tell you . . . Make conversation . . . It has to be this way.

LILLIAN *looks around the room. Then she looks at* JULIA. *She takes off the hat.*

JULIA *(calmly).* Who were you with in Paris? Good friends?

LILLIAN. Yes. Good friends. But they don't know anything about this.

*She puts the hat on the seat between them.*

JULIA. Get your comb.

LILLIAN. Comb . . .

*She reaches for her purse. Opens it. Looks for the comb. The purse is full.*

LILLIAN. I still carry too much.

JULIA *(looking in purse).* There it is, take it out and use it.

LILLIAN *takes out the comb. Starts to comb her hair back.*

JULIA. Keep talking to me. I read your play. Don't look down. Look at me. Be natural. You look so very well.

*During this* JULIA *has pulled the hat into her open coat. Then she'll proceed to pin it deep inside the lining.*

LILLIAN. Did you like it? My play?

JULIA. I'm proud of you. It was wonderful.

LILLIAN. But my second play failed.

JULIA. I know. I heard. Are you writing your third?

LILLIAN. I'm writing it.

JULIA. Now, I'm going to the toilet. You come with me. If the waiter tries to help me up, wave him away.

JULIA *reaches for her crutches.* LILLIAN *goes to help her.*

JULIA. I'm all right, I can do it. If I had more time to practice, I wouldn't need the crutches. But this leg doesn't fit properly. Come along. Act gay. Can you act gay?

LILLIAN *tries to laugh.*

LILLIAN. No, I can't act gay.

*They start on, toward the washroom. We can see a man,* ALBERT, *bring caviar, wine to their table.*

JULIA. What's your new play about?

LILLIAN. I don't know. I'm not sure yet. Shall I come with you?

JULIA *(in German) (re caviar—to* ALBERT). Thank you very much, Albert.

*They reach the washroom door.*

LILLIAN. Shall I come in with you?

JULIA. No, the toilet door will lock. If anybody tries to open it, then knock very hard and call to me. But I don't think that will happen.

JULIA *opens the toilet door. Moves in. As the door closes, her crutch is at a wrong angle. It gets caught. She pulls irritably at the crutch. There's some humiliation in the gesture. The door closes.* LILLIAN *waits outside the door. Some* PEOPLE *are moving in to be seated. One of them is the* FAT MAN *we saw on the train. He is alone. He moves to a small table against the wall and takes a newspaper from his side pocket.*

LILLIAN *looks toward their table. The wine and caviar have been placed on it. She looks back toward the* FAT MAN *at his table. She looks at other faces. They all "seem" to be looking at her.*

*The door to the toilet opens.* JULIA *moves out. She smiles at* LILLIAN. *She starts slowly back toward their table. As they go:*

JULIA. The German public toilets are always clean. Much cleaner than ours. Particularly under the new regime. *(under her breath)* The bastards. The murderers.

*New shot*

*as they sit.* JULIA *nearly losing her balance. But managing.* LILLIAN *next to her. The* WAITER *comes to pour the wine.* JULIA *smiles, acts "gay."*

JULIA *(in German) (to* WAITER*).* Aren't we fancy people. Maybe you'll start stocking caviar from here on.

WAITER *(in German).* We don't want to serve caviar, we'll all have to be too polite.

*They laugh and the* WAITER *moves away.* JULIA *slips the hat from under her coat, back onto the seat.*

JULIA. Nothing will happen now. We're all right now. I want you to know this. You've been better than a good friend to me. You've done something important . . . It's my money you brought in. We can save five hundred people, maybe. If we bargain right, maybe a thousand.

LILLIAN. Jews?

JULIA. About half are Jews. Political people. Socialists, Communists, plain old Catholic dissenters. Jews aren't the only people who suffer here. But that's enough of that. We can only do today what we can do today. And today you did it for us.

*She drinks some wine.* LILLIAN *drinks too.*

Do you need something stronger?

LILLIAN. No.

JULIA. We have to talk fast now. There isn't much time.

LILLIAN. How much?

*Some people move by.*

JULIA. A few minutes. *(louder, to be heard)* You must have some pictures for me. Do you have a picture of Hammett?

LILLIAN. Yes, yes, I do. *(opens her purse, wallet)* One. I have one picture.

JULIA. Show me!

LILLIAN. I wrote you about him. Did you get that letter? Do you get my letters?

JULIA. Some *(looks at snapshot— speaks loud)* Ahh, this is Hammett! Is he the one we dreamed of? I like the face. Tell me what he is?

LILLIAN. He's remarkable, and difficult, and it isn't simple together. I can't describe him. He's an extraordinary kind of American man, I want you to meet him.

JULIA. I want to.

LILLIAN. When?

JULIA. Soon.

LILLIAN. How soon?

JULIA. I'll be coming to New York.

LILLIAN. When?

JULIA. A few months. My leg is clumsy. I need a better one. *(laughs)* My God, Lilly, are we having this conversation?

LILLIAN. Just come back, I don't care about the conversation.

JULIA. There's something else. I'll need you to do something else for me.

LILLIAN. You know I will . . . What?

JULIA *waits. Then, quickly:*

JULIA. I have a baby.

*Pause.* LILLIAN *is stunned.* JULIA *doesn't speak. She smiles, touches* LILLIAN's *face.* LILLIAN *trying not to cry, lighting a cigarette, fumbling with it. Finally:*

JULIA. She's fat and she's handsome and she's very healthy. She's not even one yet. Can you imagine not even being one yet?

LILLIAN. Yes . . .

JULIA. And I don't even mind that she looks like my mother.

LILLIAN. Where is she?

JULIA. She's across the border in Alsace in a town near Strasbourg. She lives with good people. The man is a baker. Remember we used to want to live in a bakery? I can see her whenever I can cross over. But she shouldn't be in Europe. It ain't for babies these days.

LILLIAN. When can I see her? What's her name?

JULIA (*pause*). Lilly.

LILLIAN *is obviously very moved, she does not speak. Close to tears.*

JULIA. When I come to New York for my leg, I'll bring her with me. I want to leave her with you. You're the only one there I can trust.

LILLIAN. I'll take care of her. You know that.

JULIA. I won't stay away long. I can't last much longer in Europe. The crutches make me too noticeable. There'll be plenty of money. You won't have to worry about anything.

LILLIAN. I don't care about that. You know that doesn't matter.

JULIA. And you don't have to worry about her father, he doesn't want anything to do with her. Or with me. A medical student I knew. I don't know why I did it. But I know I wanted to. Maybe a person finally needs their own blood to be more courageous. And, oh God, but we need such courage now. All of us.

*They are quiet another moment. Then:*

LILLIAN (*quiet rage*). What is it? Why is it like this?

JULIA (*studies* LILLIAN *a moment*). Are you as angry a woman as you were a child?

LILLIAN. I try not to be. It isn't easy.

JULIA. I like your anger. Don't let people talk you out of it.

JULIA *reacts to O.S.*

JULIA. The man who will take care of you has just come into the street.

LILLIAN. But we haven't talked. We've had no time. I need more time.

JULIA. Now I want you to stand up.

Take the hat . . . Listen to me. Put the hat back on, and then say goodbye to me and then go. Walk across the street.

LILLIAN *has become visibly upset.*

The man will see that you get on the train safely. Someone else will stay with you 'til Warsaw tomorrow morning. He's in Car A, Second Class, compartment thirteen. Zweite Klasse. Say it!

LILLIAN. Zweite Klasse.

JULIA. Compartment 13. Abteilung Dreizehn. Say it!

LILLIAN. Abteilung Dreizehn. I don't want to leave you. I want to stay with you longer.

JULIA. No. Something could still go wrong. We aren't sure who anyone is anymore.

LILLIAN. I'll have room for Lilly. I'll try to make it wonderful.

JULIA. I know you will. Put the hat on . . . Lillian, put the hat on!

LILLIAN *waits for a beat, then puts on the hat. As she does:*

Write to me from Moscow to American Express in Paris. Someone picks up for me every few weeks. (*takes* LILLIAN'S *hand and raises it to her lips*) Oh, yes . . . Oh, yes, my beloved friend.

*She kisses* LILLIAN'S *hand. Another pause. Then* JULIA *brings her hands down.*

JULIA. Leave! . . . (*sharp*) Leave!

LILLIAN *gets up quickly as if powered by something outside of herself.*

*Wider angle—night*

LILLIAN *turns and moves to door. When she gets there she stops, turns, looks back at* JULIA, *who is holding her glass of wine.* LILLIAN *seems to take a small step toward her,* JULIA *quickly shakes her head, looks at an-*

*other part of the room.* LILLIAN *turns and moves out through the revolving door.*

*Ext. the street outside Albert's— night*

LILLIAN *alone. Her purse, the hatbox. Her small bag. She looks up and down the street. Then she looks across the street at the station entrance. She crosses. Much traffic. In her confusion she has to dodge a few cars. Is stranded a moment in the middle. Suddenly a* MAN *is at her side. He takes her arm. She looks at him and they continue to the station.*

*Int. train station Berlin—night*

*Angle on* LILLIAN *and the* MAN *walking on the platform alongside the train. They pass Car B, reach Car A.*

MAN *(German accent—very alive).* Take care of yourself. My best to everybody.

LILLIAN. Yes. Thank you. My best to you.

*He nods and turns and goes.* LILLIAN *boards. Then she turns on an impulse and calls out:*

LILLIAN. My very best to you.

*He looks back, smiles, raises his hand and moves away.*

*Angle on* LILLIAN—*night*

*She turns and moves into the train.*

*Int. train—night*

LILLIAN *moving through the car. She passes compartment 13. She looks in. We can see a* YOUNG MAN *sitting at the window, a paper in his lap. He is blowing his nose. He doesn't look at* LILLIAN. LILLIAN *continues on. When she's gone, the* MAN *looks toward the door.*

*New shot* LILLIAN—*night*

*in the passageway. A* CONDUCTOR *appears as she finds her compartment.*

CONDUCTOR. Fraulein Hellman?
LILLIAN. Yes?
CONDUCTOR. You will be asleep when the border is crossed to Poland. Put here your luggage for the Customs. I will not wake you.
LILLIAN. Yes, fine, I will.
CONDUCTOR. You have a trunk?
LILLIAN. In the baggage compartment, yes. A green trunk.
CONDUCTOR. I would need the key.
LILLIAN. Yes, yes, of course. *(searches her purse)* Here you are.
CONDUCTOR. Thank you.

*He moves off. Knocks on the next compartment door.* LILLIAN *looks after him a moment, then goes in.*

*The train—night*

*as it travels across Germany.*

*Int.* LILLIAN'S *compartment—night*

LILLIAN *in her berth. Eyes open. We hear the wheels on the track.* LILLIAN *turns and looks at the hat sitting on a narrow shelf.*

*Tight on* LILLIAN *in the berth— night*

JULIA'S VOICE *(O.S.).* The bastards. The murderers.
SAMMY'S VOICE *(O.S.).* She's turned into a wild socialist, giving away all her money.

*Silence.* LILLIAN *turns on her side. Remembers. We hear the tinkle of a piano.*

*Int. Small's Paradise—Harlem—* SAMMY *and* LILLIAN *(1930)—night*

*A Harlem speakeasy.* SAMMY *with a great number of drinks in him.* LILLIAN *sitting politely across from him. She is sloshed. He sits sprawled, his arms fly about as he speaks. Jazz combo in b.g.*

SAMMY. I was with Anne Marie in Vienna. I was really in Elba most of the time, I'm doing a book on Napoleon. I tried to kill myself in Elba.

LILLIAN. You've been doing that for years, Sammy, I don't think you should continue with Napoleon. Why don't you try the Wright Brothers, or try one of them, try Orville.

SAMMY *(leaning in)*. What about marriage?

LILLIAN. What about it?

SAMMY. Still a virgin? Why don't you marry my brother Eliot?

LILLIAN. Sammy, I have to go now.

SAMMY. You're afraid of me, you still think I want to get in your bloomers, God, Lilly, if you married Eliot I'd be your brother-in-law and Anne Marie would be your sister-in-law.

LILLIAN. Sammy, it's too late for horror stories. You drink too much.

SAMMY. You're always so tough on Anne Marie. What did she ever do to you? She's really warm and passionate. Ask me, I know. By the way, she saw your old friend, Julia.

LILLIAN. Where?

SAMMY. In Vienna. She's turned into a wild socialist, giving away all her money.

LILLIAN. You tell Anne Marie I don't want to hear attacks on Julia's beliefs or Julia's life. Not from your sister and not from you. *(starts to get up)* Goodbye, Sammy.

SAMMY *(takes her hand)*. Aw, come on, Lillian, Anne Marie doesn't hold ill thoughts. You understand about relationships, why Anne Marie and I were a battleground all our lives and here's something you don't know: On my graduation day my little sister cried like an infant. She took my arm and kissed me and gave me a tender

touch and within minutes, within *minutes,* Lillian . . . it was done. What I wanted to do for years. She had the same ideas I had. All tucked up inside her someplace. And to this day, of all the girls I ever had, my sister was the best. She was thrilling, Lillian. And did I ever suspect what she had in mind? Not for a minute. *(smiles)* Don't look at me like that, she was sixteen. She's very complicated. Come on now you're so slick, so unruffled. You have no right to put up your nose. Your life's no closed book. No one is scott free, you know. After all, the whole world knows about you and Julia.

LILLIAN. What does the whole world know, Sammy?

SAMMY. Ohhh . . .

LILLIAN. What does the world know?

SAMMY. Ohhhh, don't be that way. *(smells the centerpiece rose)* I'm a sophisticated man. If anybody understands the sex urge of the adolescent girl it's me. Do you know that in Paris the women are wearing watches around their legs. Little garters with timepieces in them.

*As he speaks,* LILLIAN *stands up, leans across the table and with lightning speed slaps his face, his chair falls over and she pushes the table over on top of him.*

*Int. train compartment—angle on* LILLIAN—*morning*

*asleep in her berth. The train is pulling into a station. A knock on the door. She sits up. Looks past the drawn shade. It is morning. The knock again on her compartment door. She gets out of the berth. Opens the door, looks out. The* YOUNG MAN *who was in compartment 13 and sat at her table is there.*

YOUNG MAN (*English accent, bright and rosy*). Good morning! Just to say goodbye to you, and have a happy trip. *(very, very softly)* Your trunk was removed by the Germans. Last night. They kept it. They must be suspicious. But you're in no danger. You're across the border. You're in Warsaw now. Do not return from Moscow through Germany. Travel another way. *(his bright voice again)* My best regards to your family. Take care of yourself. Wrap up well. Not to worry. Bye-bye, now!

*Int. train compartment—day*

YOUNG MAN *moving briskly away from camera.*

*Ext. long shot—Poland—day*

*The train moving across countryside. Outside we can see Polish farmers at work.*

*Int. compartment—day*

LILLIAN *is sitting by the window. Deep in thought. We begin to hear Shakespeare's Hamlet spoke in Russian.*

HAMLET'S VOICE (*O.S.—In Russian*). I'll be with you straight, go a little before. How all occasions do inform against me, and spur my dull revenge!
What is a man, if his chief good and market of his time be but to sleep and feed?

*Int. theatre—Moscow—night*

*Side angle from wings.* HAMLET *in f.g. Heavy proscenium arch. A segment of the* RUSSIAN AUDIENCE *in stalls suggesting the theatre is packed.* LILLIAN *is in a box with her* OFFICIAL PARTY.

HAMLET (*in Russian*). . . . A beast, no more. Sure he that made us with such large discourse looking before and after, gave us not that capability and godlike reason to bust in us unused.

*Int. theatre—close shot* LILLIAN—*night*

*Her eyelids heavy. She is bored, she stifles a yawn.*

HAMLET (*in Russian*). . . . Now whether it be bestial oblivion, or some craven scruple of thinking too precisely on th' event . . .

*We begin to hear other sounds over Hamlet's speech. Heavy footsteps. Boots. Running up steps, across wooden floors. The sound of a door being pushed open violently. Suddenly* LILLIAN *comes wide awake. She looks over her shoulder as if someone had called her.*

*Int. dark room—night*

*We see* GREY FIGURES. *Converging.* MEN *entering a room. Grappling. Shots fired. A knife exposed, it slashes down hard. One* FIGURE *stumbling, other* FIGURES *move in on it, the* FIGURE, *limping, tries to move away. But the knife cuts cruelly into flesh again, and the* FIGURE *falls and other* FIGURES *move around it and fight off the* MURDERERS.

*(Over all this begins a deep, sombre, musical note)*

*Int. theatre night*

*Angle on the audience, standing. Applauding. Sombre note continues.*

*Int. theatre—night*

*Angle on* HAMLET *and the* TROUPE *on stage. Applauding. Sombre note continues.*

*Int. hotel corridor—night*

LILLIAN *says goodbye to a group of friends. Gets her key from a* WOMAN FLOOR SUPERVISOR. *She moves toward* her door. LILLIAN *opens her door. Looks in. Turns on the light. She reacts. Sombre note stops.*

*Her P.O.V.*

*Her trunk is in her room.*

*Int. hotel room*—LILLIAN

*looking at the trunk. She closes the door. Then she moves to the trunk. The key has been attached. She is about to open it when she reacts to something O.S.*

*Angle at the door*

*There is a message, a cablegram.* LILLIAN *moves to it. Picks it up. Starts to open it. But then she stops. The dark, musical note resumes in b.g. It grows gradually louder, fuller. She looks apprehensively at the envelope. She starts to open the envelope again.*

*Int.* LILLIAN'S *room— night*

*Dark. We can barely see where we are. Camera moves past an open cablegram and comes to* LILLIAN *sitting in a chair on the far side of the room. As camera moves toward her we hear:*

MAN'S VOICE *(O.S.)*. Julia has been killed. Please advise Moore's Funeral Home Whitechapel Road, London what disposition. My sorrow for you . . .

*We are moving in close on* LILLIAN. *She has been drinking. She looks off.*

MAN'S VOICE *(O.S.)*. My sorrow for all of us. Signed John Watson.

*Camera stops. Holds on* LILLIAN.

JULIA'S VOICE *(O.S.) (young girl)*. I see a gun.

LILLIAN'S VOICE *(O.S.) (young girl)*. I see a gun. A handsome soldier is going to shoot it.

*Dissolve to*

*Ext. Adirondacks (1922)—day*

*A relatively steep hillside, open, free of trees. Long shot* JULIA *and* LILLIAN *(as young girls) walking towards the top of the hill. They are silhouetted against the skyline.*

JULIA. I see a gun and a handsome soldier is going to shoot it but it won't shoot.

LILLIAN. I see a gun and a handsome soldier is going to shoot it but it won't shoot and the brave, handsome soldier says, "I need another gun!"

JULIA. I see a gun and a handsome soldier is going to shoot it but it won't shoot and the soldier says, "I need another gun", and someone shouts back . . . "Sorry, soldier . . . that's the last gun."

*Pause. They continue up the hill. Then:*

JULIA *(a great, wonderful cry)*. That's the last gun!

LILLIAN *(laughing)*. Yeah. Oh, yeah.

*They move off . . . laughing . . . into the wind, and as they move away the camera pans up into a blinding sun.*

*Int.* LILLIAN'S *room—Moscow*

LILLIAN *in the dark.*

*Angle on her trunk*

LILLIAN *is in b.g. in chair. After a moment she begins to rise. Slowly. She moves toward camera and the trunk. She kneels in front of it. Takes the key and opens the lid. Her reaction to:*

*Close on trunk*

*The lining is in shreds. Everything has been torn apart. Drawers broken. Linings of clothing pulled apart. It has been ravaged.*

*Angle on* LILLIAN

LILLIAN *(her face slowly twists into pain).* Ohhhh!

*Int. funeral parlour—London—day*

*We are in a small, stuffy, salmon-coloured room.* LILLIAN *and the* UNDERTAKER.

UNDERTAKER. There was a rather deep slash on her face. It was difficult to remove. However, I did meet with some success. Although I wasn't half so clever on the rest of her. Of course, if you wish to look at . . .

LILLIAN *(sharp).* No! I don't wish to look. Of *course* I don't!

UNDERTAKER. Oh, beg pardon, Mum!

*He waits a moment then quickly brings an envelope from his drawer. Hands it to* LILLIAN.

UNDERTAKER. This here note was left for you.

LILLIAN *takes it. Opens it. Starts to read. We hear a man's voice. The same one we heard reading the cablegram in Moscow.*

MAN'S VOICE *(O.S.).* It is your right to know that the Nazis found her in Frankfurt.

*Cut to*

*Int. a long dark corridor*

LILLIAN *moves through. Camera holds as she moves away. The* UNDERTAKER *is moving slightly ahead of her.*

MAN'S VOICE *(O.S.) (continuing).* She was in the apartment of a colleague. We got her to London in the hope of saving her. None of us knows what disposition her family wishes to make. We could not reach the grandparents or the mother. I am sorry that I cannot be there to help you. It is better that we take our sorrow for this wonderful woman into action and perhaps revenge. Yours, John Watson, who speaks here for many others.

*The* UNDERTAKER *stops far up the corridor and indicates a doorway to* LILLIAN. *She turns and looks into the room. Moves in.*

*Int. funeral parlour—slumber room*

LILLIAN *moves in from the corridor. Pull back to show an open casket.*

*Another angle*

LILLIAN *moves a few feet from the casket. Fearful of looking in at first. Then slowly she approaches it. She stops when she is over it. She looks down at it. Then she slowly leans over the face. She is about to kiss the cold cheek, but instead stops and brings her hand to the face and touches it gently with her fingertips.*

*Tight shot—*LILLIAN'S *face*

*Tight shot—*LILLIAN'S *eyes*

*They stare as if they can't close. They stare . . . and then they shut.*

*Int.* UNDERTAKER'S *office*

LILLIAN *and* UNDERTAKER.

LILLIAN. Where will I find John Watson?

UNDERTAKER. I don't know a John Watson, Mum.

LILLIAN. You gave me a note. He wrote me a note.

UNDERTAKER. I picked up the note when I collected the body, Mum.

LILLIAN. And where did you collect the body?

UNDERTAKER. The house of a Dr. Chester Lowe, Thirty Downshire Hill.

*Ext. London street*

LILLIAN *at a London town house. The number "30" on the door. An older* WOMAN *opens the door.*

WOMAN. Yes?

LILLIAN. Dr. Chester Lowe?

WOMAN. There's no Dr. Chester Lowe here.

LILLIAN. But this is thirty Downshire Hill.

WOMAN. There's no Dr. Lowe, I'm sorry.

LILLIAN. Perhaps John Watson, then?

WOMAN. I'm sorry, you have the wrong address.

LILLIAN. I'm a friend of Julia's.

WOMAN *(a slight hesitation).* I'm sorry!

LILLIAN. I don't believe you.

WOMAN. Excuse me!

LILLIAN. The undertaker gave me this address.

WOMAN. You have the wrong address.

LILLIAN *(pushing the door).* I'm not even sure what I'm looking for, only I need to know something more. I can't put it all together. Look, I have a letter here from John Watson. See it's addressed to me. You can trust me!

*The door slams shut.*

LILLIAN *(calling out).* I'm Julia's friend!

*Ext. int. small bakery (Strasbourg)*

*Camera shooting from outside into a modest display in bakery window. Inside is* LILLIAN, distraught, dishevelled, *concluding unheard discussion with the baker who shakes his head, shrugs and escorts her to door. Outside he says:*

BAKER *(not overly polite).* Madame, it's impossible . . . Alsace is not a village, it is a big province.

LILLIAN *walks away.*

*Ext. C.U. cobble stones*

*Travelling shot on* LILLIAN's *feet as she struggles along.*

*Ext. L.S. street in Strasbourg (near cathedral)*

*Bus moving across screen, disclosing view of busy street and* LILLIAN *approaching. Pull back to show that we are inside another bakery, the shop window in f.g.* LILLIAN *looks in.*

*Int. bakery*

*POV the* BAKER, *having sold long loaves of bread to two women who are just leaving.*

*Int. bakery*

LILLIAN *enters. The* BAKER *turns to her, appraising her unusual appearance.*

LILLIAN. Do you speak English?

BAKER. Oui, a little.

LILLIAN. I would like to ask you a question.

BAKER. Yes.

LILLIAN. I'm from America.

BAKER. Ah . . .

LILLIAN. Do you know any Americans?

BAKER. Americans? *(he stops, looks at her questioningly—then protective).* No, I know no Americans. What is it you want, Madame?

*Pause.*

LILLIAN *(impulsively).* I'm a friend of one you might know, I'm looking for her baby.

*The* BAKER'S WIFE *has appeared.* LILLIAN *looks at her.*

BAKER. I am very busy now. If you don't want bread, I cannot help you.

LILLIAN *(to* BAKER'S WIFE*).* I am a friend of Julia's, Madame.

*The* WIFE *looks at the* BAKER.

LILLIAN *(continuing)*. Do you know that Julia is dead?

*The* WIFE *looks at* LILLIAN.

WIFE *(French)*. Who is she? What does she want?

BAKER *(French)*. Just sit quietly, it will be all right.

WIFE *(French)*. What does she want?

LILLIAN. Would you know about a baby named Lilly?

BAKER. There is no baby here. There is no baby. *(moves to curtain, pulls it back)* Look.

LILLIAN *moves to the curtain. Looks past it.*

LILLIAN'S *POV through curtain*

*We see a modest kitchen. A small bedroom. There is no sign of a baby.*

*Close shot* BAKER

BAKER *(with compassion)*. There is no baby. I'm sorry.

LILLIAN *finally accepts this. She feels powerless. We begin to hear the distant strains of a band playing "East Side, West Side."*

*Ext. New York Harbour (1937)— day*

*Angle on Ocean Liner (the "De Grasse") docked. We hear the ship's band playing "East Side, West Side" as we favour a casket being lowered to the dock. We continue to hear the music in the b.g.*

*Int. customs area*

LILLIAN *with* CUSTOMS MAN *who is going through her luggage.* HAMMETT *is waiting for her on the other side of a picket fence.*

*Int. a dark place (sudden silence)*

*Silence.* LILLIAN *wearing the Madame Pauline hat. She is stone still, then turns and looks confused.*

LILLIAN. Hello!

*Angle on* LILLIAN—*Gare du nord, Paris*

*She is running through the station wearing the hat.*

LILLIAN *(frightened)*. Mr. Johann. Hello! Hello! *(a beat, then:)* Hellooooo!

*Int. beach house—bedroom—night*

LILLIAN *sitting up quickly from a nightmare. Perspiring,* HAMMETT *is next to her. She turns and looks at him.*

HAMMETT *(gently)*. Go back to sleep, Lilly.

*Hold a moment. She nods. Lies back down. Stares at ceiling.* HAMMETT *moves closer. Holds her.*

LILLIAN'S VOICE *(O.S.)*. I have Julia's ashes. Tell me what to do with them. Their grand-daughter had a baby. Don't they care about it?

*Cut to*

*Int.* JULIA'S GRANDPARENTS' *house —entry hall—day*

*Close shot* MAID *peering through a crack in the open door.*

MAID. I'm sorry. They're not at home.

LILLIAN. I don't believe that.

LILLIAN *moves into camera pushing past the* MAID *into the house.*

MAID. Please, Ma'am, you'll have to wait outside.

LILLIAN. No! I will *not* wait outside!

*The* BUTLER (RAINES) *appears. (We met him twenty years ago.)*

RAINES. What's the trouble, Anna?
LILLIAN. Do you remember me? I used to come with Julia on weekends.

We were children, remember her friend, Lillian?

RAINES. I'm afraid I don't.

LILLIAN. Of course you do.

MAID. She won't leave, Mr. Raines.

RAINES. Please to step outside, Madame.

LILLIAN. I will not please to step anywhere until I speak to Julia's grandparents. I know you remember me.

RAINES. They are on a cruise, Madame, they will not be returning for eight weeks.

LILLIAN. I don't believe you!

RAINES. I will take the information, Madame, and see that they . . .

LILLIAN. Julia's been murdered, it is not to be referred to as "information." I have Julia's ashes. Tell me what to do with them.

RAINES. If you don't leave, Madame, I will have to call the police.

LILLIAN (*calls upstairs*). What about her mother? Maybe her mother cares about her daughter's baby and her daughter's ashes.

RAINES. Telephone the police, Anna.

ANNA *moves away quickly.* LILLIAN *stares at* RAINES.

LILLIAN (*to* RAINES). You took care of her, I remember you, you cared about her, you held her, she's the only one who treated you like a human being.

*Ext. long shot—train—day*

*It is crossing the European countryside.*

*Int. compartment of train—day*

LILLIAN *sits, eyes straight ahead. Next to her is a* MAN *looking out the window. We cannot see his face.*

*Tight shot—*LILLIAN*—day*

*continuing to look straight ahead. Suddenly, the* MAN'S *arm moves behind* LILLIAN. LILLIAN *turns and looks toward the* MAN.

*Her P.O.V.—Adolf Hitler (stocking mask)*

*moving to embrace her. To kiss her on the mouth.*

*Full shot—day*

LILLIAN *tries to scream. He keeps coming at her, she twists away, runs out of the compartment.*

*Int. train corridor—day*

LILLIAN *running away from camera. We hear the sound of a baby crying.*

*Int. train platform—day*

*Angle on* LILLIAN *away from camera. Close shot* LILLIAN *as she opens the door between cars.*

*Her P.O.V.—day*

*The* GERMAN WOMAN *we saw in the German Consulate in Paris holding a* BABY. LILLIAN *reaches desperately for the* BABY.

*She struggles to take it. The* BABY *screaming.* LILLIAN *pulls at the* BABY *and her own desperate and terrified screams merge with the baby's as shot goes out of focus.*

*Int. beach house—bedroom—night*

LILLIAN *and* HAMMETT *in bed. They both stare at the ceiling.* LILLIAN *smoking. Then, suddenly, she gets out of bed, sits on the side, then stands up . . . moves to the window, looks out. Camera follows her into bathroom. She stands up against the sink. She begins to get tears in her eyes. Quickly, she turns and splashes water on her face, tries to dry off the tears along with the water but the tears continue. Angrily, she throws her cigarette into the toilet. She flushes it, turns the water in the sink back on. Waits a few moments, and, finally, when she can't contain the tears any longer, she begins to sob against the tile wall.* HAMMETT *moves into frame. He leans against the door, watches her. Then gently:*

HAMMETT. They never wanted to find the baby.

LILLIAN *(crying, without looking up)*. But *I* did.

HAMMETT. You tried.

LILLIAN. I didn't try hard enough.

HAMMETT. You hired detectives, you had lawyers. You did what you could.

LILLIAN. I don't know.

HAMMETT. They never wanted to find the baby. They wanted Julia's money and they got it.

LILLIAN. The bastards.

HAMMETT. So now let it be.

LILLIAN. But maybe she's alive someplace.

HAMMETT. The baby is dead, Lilly.

LILLIAN *(getting very upset)*. I won't believe that, you don't know that!

HAMMETT. Get done with it, now.

LILLIAN. Don't tell me to get done with it! I can't get done with it, ever.

HAMMETT. Lillian! The baby is dead! Julia was and isn't, that's all.

LILLIAN. And when you die will you want me to feel that way about you?

HAMMETT. Oh, I'll outlive you. But then maybe not, you're stubborn.

*Quick dissolve to*

*Ext. rowboat*—LILLIAN *(as in SC. 1) (1962)—day*

*As she waits for a fish to bite:*

LILLIAN'S VOICE *(O.S.)*. Hammett didn't outlive me and I've gone on for a good many years since. Sometimes fine—not always. But he was right. I am stubborn. I haven't forgotten either of them.

*Hold a beat, then camera pans down to a C.U. of the line being gently tugged by a fish. We watch it for a moment and then from O.S. we hear:*

*Ext. ketch (off Massachusetts Shore as in Sc. 113) (1921) long shot—day*

*The small figures of* LILLIAN *and* JULIA *on deck. Screaming to be heard.*

LILLIAN. There must be a trial.

JULIA. Oh, yes. A long one. And she's convicted.

LILLIAN. Guilty?

JULIA. Guilty!

*Close shot the ketch* LILLIAN *and* JULIA

LILLIAN. And the real killer never tries to save her?

JULIA. Never! And her husband, Richard Arlington, disowns her.

LILLIAN. What about her lover?

JULIA. He joins a monastery.

LILLIAN. What happens to her?

JULIA. She's hung by the neck until she's dead.

LILLIAN. No kidding.

JULIA. But *before* she dies . . . she raises her head high . . . and she speaks these immortal words: "It was worth it. The kiss was WONDERFUL."

*They scream with delight.*

JULIA. It's a risky business, love.

LILLIAN. But it's WONDERFUL.

*They laugh wildly.*

*Long shot the ketch*

*cutting through the water. Sailing away from camera.*

THE END

# HOLY MATRIMONY

*Screenplay by Nunnally Johnson*
*Adapted from the Novel by Arnold Bennett*

| | |
|---|---|
| PRIAM FARLL | Monty Woolley |
| ALICE CHALLICE | Gracie Fields |
| MR. OXFORD | Laird Cregar |
| HENRY LEEK | Eric Blore |
| MRS. LEEK | Una O'Connor |

Produced by Nunnally Johnson for Twentieth Century-Fox
Directed by John Stahl
Cinematographer: Lucien Ballard
Music: Cyril Mockridge

Witty and charming and civilized, the screenplay of *Holy Matrimony* was nominated for an Academy Award in 1943, the year that *Casablanca* walked away with so many Oscars. *Holy Matrimony* represents Mr. Johnson's work at its best—lucid, intelligent, and beautifully fashioned.

Mr. Johnson works with such clarity and economy that it is a pleasure to watch his plots unfold. In just the first fifteen pages of script we have the whole situation of Mr. Farll's deception—his taking the identity and place of his dead butler—beautifully rendered and set into motion with a delightful momentum that never falters as it spins out toward its entertaining conclusion.

Born in Columbus, Georgia, in 1897, Mr. Johnson had a successful career in Hollywood as a screenwriter, producer, and director until he died in 1977. He began his career as a reporter for the Brooklyn *Eagle,* following that with several other stints, on *P.M.* and the New York *Herald Tribune.* Writing short stories successfully for the *Saturday Evening Post,* Mr. Johnson was called to Hollywood in 1932 and began writing for the screen the following year. His scripts include *The Grapes of Wrath* (1940); *The House of Rothschild* (1934); *Jesse James* (1939); *The Three Faces of Eve* (1957), for which he was also producer and director; *The World of Henry Orient* (1964); and *The Dirty Dozen* (1967).

*Fade in*

*Stock Shot of London—Day*

*The more lifeless this shot is, the better for us, for over it is a title:*

LONDON IN 1905

*Dissolve to:*

*Ext. Oxford Galleries—Day*

*An imposing edifice, an art gallery, with the name and the character clearly discernible. Camera moves in as*

*Dissolve to:*

*Office*

*In the period of 1905,* MR. OXFORD, *suave, elegant, and oily, is seated in a spring-chair in front of his roll-top desk, rocking back and forth gently. In his hands is a square white envelope which he handles with great respect. The door opens and a young woman* SECRETARY *enters, possibly the first white-collar girl in London.*

SECRETARY. You sent for me, Mr. Oxford?

OXFORD. Take a letter, please.

*She seats herself in a straight chair, notebook and pencil ready on a crossed knee.*

OXFORD. To Mr. Priam Farll.

*He stops. His rocking ceases. His cold eye rests disapprovingly on the brazen display of about three-quarters of an inch of ankle. Catching her breath, she sees her unconscious wantonness and lowers her dress so that it covers the instep.* MR. OXFORD *continues.*

OXFORD. Dear Mr. Farll colon As you well know comma, it is one of the regrets of my life that I have never had the privilege of meeting you in person comma although the Oxford Galleries have had the honor of representing you here for some ten years full stop I appreciate your shyness comma I sympathize deeply with you in your dread of the celebrity which you have gained as the most distinguished of English painters comma and I would not dream of intruding on your desire for privacy if it were not that extraordinary circumstances would seem to demand your presence in London at the earliest possible moment comma as you will note from the enclosed communication from Buckingham Palace full stop.

SECRETARY *(timidly)*. Would you mind repeating that, sir?

OXFORD. You mean the last sentence?

SECRETARY. No, sir, the whole thing. I didn't get any of it.

*Dissolve to:*

*Montage—Letter*

*Occupying much of the screen, the envelope is stamped and addressed to* PRIAM FARLL, ESQ. *The address itself should be indecipherable. Superimposed on the letter are:*

(1) English railway train.

*Dissolve to:*
(2) Ocean liner.

*Dissolve to:*
(3) Black native paddling dugout canoe up river.

*Dissolve to:*
(4) Black native driving primitive ox-cart along dirt road.
(5) Black native runner racing through jungle.

*Dissolve to:*

*Veranda—Day*

*Seated at an easel on the veranda of a lodge in the tropics,* PRIAM FARLL *(Monty Woolley) is at work with brush and palette as* HENRY LEEK *(Eric Blore), his valet, a shifty-looking fellow, comes out of the door and lays the letter on a low table cluttered with tubes, brushes, etc., which stands at the side of the easel. After a glance at it,* FARLL *continues to paint as* LEEK *starts back into the house.*

FARLL. I take it as a matter of course that you've already read this.

LEEK *(blandly).* Yes, sir.

FARLL *(working).* Against a bright light?

LEEK. No, sir. The envelope was too thick. I was compelled to steam it open over the tea kettle.

FARLL. Why on earth do you bother? *(looking at him)* Don't you find my letters dreadfully dull?

LEEK. Frightfully so, sir.

FARLL *(back at work).* They bore me—except, of course, those containing checks.

LEEK. My position is somewhat different from yours, sir. You relish this isolation. I am by nature a very sociable, even gregarious character. This existence in the suburbs of civilization, with only yourself and a few anteaters for company, is one that I have never quite been able to accept wholeheartedly. Your correspondence, as dreary as it is, provides at least a momentary relief from the broad wretchedness of my doom.

FARLL. Oh, come now, Leek. Are you sure you've given it a fair chance?

LEEK. Twenty-five years, sir, next Tuesday afternoon at twenty-seven minutes past three.

FARLL *(startled by the figure).* Not really! I had no idea!

LEEK *(gloomily).* Asia, Africa, Australia—even America.

FARLL *(sitting back).* Twenty-five years. . . . Twenty-five years of peace and solitude. . . . And yet, Leek, under certain conditions I shouldn't mind seeing London again.

LEEK *(softly).* That's fortunate, sir.

FARLL *(dreamily).* If I were a complete nobody . . . like you . . . or if all the art lovers of England could be exterminated overnight . . . *(sighing, he resumes work)* The reward of success, Leek, is an acquaintanceship with ten thousand pests and the privilege of ten million useless, empty, agonizing conversations. That may all be very well for an insurance salesman or a dentist, but for a man who wears his nerves on the outside of his body, like a fishnet . . .

LEEK. As it happens, sir, the decision has already been made for you.

FARLL *(intent on work).* What?

LEEK. The letter, sir. It says you're to come back to London immediately.

FARLL *(wearily).* Who says it this time?

LEEK. The King, sir.

FARLL *(working on).* No, Leek, my boy, I'm afraid that's not for us—that world of teas and parties and women who paint designs on commodes. That's the world we have renounced—*(he stops, startled)* Who did you say?

LEEK. The King, sir. Enclosed in Mr. Oxford's letter is a communication from Buckingham Palace. You're to be knighted.

FARLL *(in horror).* No! . . . That's impossible! . . . I couldn't FACE such a thing! . . .

LEEK *(after a pause).* Which shall I lay out for the trip, sir—your bags or your knickerbockers?

*With a groan of misery,* FARLL *buries his face in his hands as . . .*

*Fade out.*

*Fade in.*

*Stock Shot of London—Day*

*Scored with as much nerve-wracked discord and dissonance as possible, over it is superimposed an enormous shot of* FARLL'S *face, his eyes roving wildly, his breath coming in desperate gasps, as—*

*Dissolve to:*

*Ext.* FARLL'S *London House—Day*

*It is a residence of some substantiality, but deserted looking, with windows blank with shutters or curtains. Its number is 91. A cab (check for type) stops at the curb. It is loaded with luggage.* FARLL, *arrayed in a travelling cape-coat, etc., gets out and surveys the house gloomily for a moment and then turns to help* LEEK *out.*

FARLL. All right, all right, easy does it.

LEEK *(faintly).* I'm terribly sorry, sir.

FARLL. No apologies necessary—can't be helped.

LEEK *falls into a spasm of croupy coughs, leaning on* FARLL, *as the* CABBY *gets the luggage to the sidewalk.*

CABBY. Two and six, guv'nor.

FARLL *(paying him).* Do you mind bringing these bags in, please.

CABBY. Right, guv'nor.

FARLL. All right, now.

*This to* LEEK *as he supports him up the steps, for* LEEK *is clearly very ill. He can hardly stand.* FARLL *props him against the door post as he gets out his keys and unlocks the door. The door opens with some difficulty. Its hinges are rusty and screechy. And dust sifts from the top of the door as the movement disturbs it.*

FARLL. Steady.

*As they enter, the* CABBY *following with the bags . . .*

*Entrance Hall*

*The light from the door shows that it is a shambles of dust and disintegrating furniture, most of it covered with cloths that have rotted into rags. The* CABBY, *setting the bags down, gapes at it in astonishment.* LEEK *steadies himself against a chair as* FARLL *goes to a window and tries to throw the great drapes open, at which the whole paraphernalia of the draperies crashes to the floor in a cloud of dust.* FARLL *regards it moodily.*

FARLL. Should have left somebody in charge, I suppose.

*As he moves into . . .*

*Parlor*

*This room is larger and more of it. Every step raises a little cloud of dust. The decor visible is heavy Victorian, but dust cloths cover the enormous pieces of furniture.* FARLL *stands in the center of the room regarding it without pleasure.* LEEK *appears at the door, holding the jamb, and gives a sickly look around.*

FARLL *(finally).* Well, I can't say I've ever been very homesick for it.

LEEK. Would you be good enough to call a doctor, sir?

FARLL *(helping him).* Of course. Just sit here and I'll fetch one myself.

LEEK. The cab driver would . . .

FARLL. Nonsense. I'll be back in a moment.

*He exits.* LEEK *slumps in the chair, coughing weakly, croupily, as . . .*

*Dissolve to:*

*Name Plate—Day*

*It reads:* DOCTOR CASWELL. *Camera pulls back enough to show a door and* FARLL, *still attired as before, ringing the bell. The door opens and a housekeeper appears.*

HOUSEKEEPER. Yes?

FARLL. May I see the doctor?

HOUSEKEEPER. Dr. Caswell's not in now but I expect him back shortly. Will you come in?

FARLL. Thank you, no, but when he comes in will you ask him to drop over to Selwood Terrace, No. 91—Farll's.

HOUSEKEEPER. Farll's?

FARLL. That's right. It's rather serious—*(anxiously)*—if you don't mind.

HOUSEKEEPER *(staring)*. Not at all. I'll tell him.

FARLL. Thank you.

*As he moves away and the housekeeper closes the door . . .*

*Dissolve to:*

*Stock Shot—Big Ben—Night*

*It is striking twelve midnight as . . .*

*Ext.* FARLL'S *House*

*The street is deserted, with its gaslights and dark windows, as a doctor's buggy clop-clops into scene and stops. The* DOCTOR *gets out, ascends to the front door, and rings the bell.*

*Front Door*

*After rather a long wait . . .*

FARLL'S VOICE. Who is it?

DOCTOR. This Farll's?

FARLL'S VOICE. Yes.

DOCTOR. This is Dr. Caswell.

FARLL'S VOICE. Are you alone?

DOCTOR. Of course.

*Then the door opens and* FARLL, *disheveled looking in an old dressing gown, steps aside for the* DOCTOR *to enter. Until he is provoked near the end of the sequence, he is as shy and timid as a man can be, hesitant of manner and miserable in his contact with this stranger.*

FARLL. I'm sorry. Come in, please.

*Entrance Hall*

*It is just as before, nothing having been done about it during the afternoon, but the* DOCTOR *pays little attention to it as he shucks out of his coat.*

DOCTOR. Sorry I couldn't get here earlier.

FARLL. Not at all, I'm sure.

DOCTOR. How is he?

FARLL. He's quiet now. I've got him in bed.

DOCTOR. Well, we'll have a look. Which way?

FARLL. Upstairs, if you don't mind.

*Camera takes them up the stairs, the* DOCTOR *leading, as . . .*

DOCTOR. What seems to be the trouble?

FARLL. I don't know. We only returned to England yesterday—and it was chilly on the ship, you know, after the tropics.

DOCTOR. Temperature?

FARLL. I expect so. First I knew anything was wrong, he simply collapsed on the boat train from Plymouth. *(on upper landing)* Here, please.

*He opens a door and stands nervously back as the* DOCTOR *enters. He follows him into the room as . . .*

*Bedroom*

*It is a dark and dismal room cluttered with Edwardian furniture, some still draped, and everything dusty. There are innumerable heavily framed pictures on the walls. The bed is monstrous, obviously a master's bed, while the rest of the stuff is half valuable museum items and half third-hand junk. One tall candle at the head of the bed lights the room and the face of* LEEK *on the pillow, his breathing sharp and shallow.*

FARLL *(gently).* Here we are, my boy. Here's the doctor.

DOCTOR *(bending over* LEEK*).* Wellwellwellnow, let's seeeeeee.

*The* DOCTOR, *after examining the sick man, while* FARLL *watches worriedly, straightens up with his bag, silently indicates that* FARLL *follow him, and goes out of the door again,* FARLL *following.*

*Upper Landing*

*The* DOCTOR *closes the door softly.*

DOCTOR. He's quite bad off. It's pneumonia.

FARLL. Oh, poor chap!

DOCTOR *(encouragingly).* But we'll see what we can do. Any women up?

FARLL. There's no women here— only ourselves.

DOCTOR *(opening his bag).* Then if you'll tell me where the kitchen is . . .

*He has taken out a small flask and is pouring brandy into an eyecup.*

FARLL. It's below, second door to the right.

DOCTOR. This is brandy. Get him to sip it. I'll be back up in half a moment.

*He hurries down the stairs as* FARLL *carries the brandy back into the . . .*

*Bedroom*

*Going to the bed,* FARLL *sits on the side and lifts* LEEK's *head, pillow and all, very gently, to give him the brandy.*

FARLL. All right, my boy. Everything well in hand now.

LEEK *(weakly).* I hope so, sir, but I doubt it.

FARLL. Nonsense. This chap's a perfect wizard. He'll have you up and about in a day. Sip this.

LEEK *(after sipping).* Awkward time, sir, isn't it?—the very eve, you might say, of the court ceremony.

*Upon being reminded of this ordeal,* FARLL *takes a swallow of the brandy himself.*

FARLL. I'll probably need about a quart of this. Excuse me.

*He gives* LEEK *another sip. After taking it . . .*

LEEK. I'm afraid, sir, I have a confession or two to make.

FARLL. Don't be a fool. Never make a confession until you actually feel rigor mortis setting in. You might recover.

LEEK. That's it, sir. This time I'm done for. I know it.

FARLL *(firmly).* Nevertheless, I don't want to hear it. I haven't the slightest doubt you're a first-rate scoundrel at heart. If you don't mind my saying so, you're such a shady-looking character. But I daresay this is no time to discuss your morals.

LEEK. I suppose not, sir.

FARLL. You're going to get well and I have no intention of facing a future in which you loathe me because once, in a moment of melodrama, you confessed to me that you had kissed the milliner's daughter.

LEEK. Yes, sir.

FARLL. I'm convinced that if you put your mind to it we can be out of here and off for Patagonia tomorrow night.

LEEK *(weakly).* You do make life sound so attractive, sir.

DOCTOR *(entering with kettle)*. Get some blankets—quickly.

*But* FARLL, *nervous and disturbed, lingers anxiously in the background as the* DOCTOR *sets the kettle on the hob, opens his bag, and fumbles among its contents.*

FARLL. He *will* get well, won't he? *(desperately)* I *need* him, you know.

DOCTOR *(angrily)*. Will you stop asking idiotic questions and do what I tell you!

FARLL *(after a gasp)*. Why, yes, of course, certainly.

*He hurries out of the room. The* DOCTOR *stares after him in exasperation and then gets a thermometer from the bag and goes to* LEEK'S *side.*

DOCTOR *(drawing up a chair)*. Now now now now now . . .

*As he puts the thermometer in* LEEK'S *mouth and takes out his watch to take his pulse . . .*

*Closeup—*DOCTOR

*He is looking down at his patient. His lips tighten. As he studies* LEEK, *he shakes his head slowly.* LEEK *is a doomed man and the* DOCTOR *knows it.*

*Dissolve to:*

*Parlor—Day*

*The great window-drapes have been pulled aside for light. Seated in a large chair, his hands clinched,* FARLL *looks crushed, bowed, older under the blow he has sustained. The* DOCTOR *sits at a table writing out what might be his report on the matter. He too looks tired and worn after a night of effort. There is an air of depression over the scene.*

FARLL *(finally)*. Will there be an autopsy?

DOCTOR *(writing)*. No need. I can give a certificate—acute double pneumonia. Sometimes happens like that, although I've rarely seen one so rapid.

FARLL. What I'll do without him I simply don't know. We've been together so long—he's done so much for me—already I feel lost . . . alone . . . absolutely defenseless.

DOCTOR. There was no pain. He simply fell asleep.

FARLL. Thank God for that.

DOCTOR *(still writing)*. Where will Mr. Farll's relatives be found?

*Close Shot—*FARLL

*For a moment he seems to be lost in thought, until presently the phrasing of the question penetrates his consciousness. Then he looks up slowly at the* DOCTOR *off-screen.*

FARLL. What did you say?

DOCTOR

DOCTOR *(looking up)*. His relatives. They'll have to be notified.

FARLL

FARLL *(at length)*. Mr. Farll's relatives?

DOCTOR

DOCTOR *(impatiently)*. Yes, Mr. Farll's relatives. Hadn't he any?

*Full Shot*

FARLL *considers the question thoughtfully. The chance does not often come to a man, unsought and unexpected, to doff an unsatisfactory identity. It is an immediate decision to be made, and a dangerous one. As rapidly as he can he examines the possibilities in his mind. Then he proceeds carefully, warily, cautiously.*

FARLL (*slowly*). Only a distant cousin, I believe. Duncan Farll, a solicitor. They hadn't seen each other since they were boys.

DOCTOR. Have you his address?

FARLL. Temple Inn . . . sir.

DOCTOR (*looking up*). I take it, of course, that you were his valet.

FARLL (*after a long pause*). Yes, sir.

DOCTOR (*writing again*). What was Mr. Farll's first name?

FARLL. Priam.

DOCTOR (*writing*). P-r-i-a-m— (*starting*) Priam Farll? You mean that's *the* Priam Farll?—the painter?—who was to be knighted tomorrow?

FARLL. It was today, sir.

DOCTOR (*after a whistle of amazement*). Well, by Jove! My wife won't be *half* thrilled by *this!* She's *passionately* fond of art and all that rot.

FARLL (*stiffening*). Is she indeed!

DOCTOR (*gazing up regretfully*). Pity I couldn't have pulled him through. I might have persuaded him to come to one of her teas. (*chuckling*) They would have had a high old time together, those two—guzzing away over that muck.

FARLL. I can well imagine, sir.

DOCTOR (*preparing to go*). A bit dotty, wasn't he?

FARLL. Dotty?

DOCTOR (*tapping his head*). Cracked—a bit?

FARLL. On the contrary, sir, Priam Farll was universally regarded as one of the soundest men of this or any other generation.

DOCTOR. But didn't I read somewhere that he ran away from England years ago to marry a Fiji witch?

FARLL (*trying to control his indignation*). It is far more likely, sir, that he ran away from England years ago to escape your wife!

DOCTOR (*startled*). Great Scot, did *he* know *her!*

FARLL. I speak, of course, sir, in hyperbole.

DOCTOR. Oh! (*dazed*) Naturally . . . naturally . . .

*Bewildered by* FARLL'S *sudden air of savagery, the* DOCTOR *clears his throat once or twice and then goes out, casting a nervous glance back over his shoulder as he goes.* FARLL *follows slowly.*

*Entrance Hall*

*The* DOCTOR, *hurrying on his wraps, watches nervously as* FARLL *follows him into the hall.*

DOCTOR. No hard feelings, I hope?

FARLL. None, sir.

DOCTOR. I'll attend to the formalities—certificate—registrar, et cetera.

FARLL. Thank you.

DOCTOR. Well . . .

*His hand on the doorknob, he notices a letter thrust under the door and picks it up. Handing it to* FARLL, *he smiles ingratiatingly.*

FARLL. Thank you again.

DOCTOR (*at a loss*). Well—er— good day—eh?

FARLL. Good day, sir.

*The* DOCTOR *exits with relief, and* FARLL, *after glaring after him a moment, glances at the letter.*

*Insert—Letter*

*in* FARLL'S *hand. In a woman's handwriting on the envelope:*

HENRY LEEK, ESQ.,
91 SELWOOD TERRACE,
LONDON, S.W.

FARLL

*He starts to thrust the envelope in the pocket of the dressing gown and then stops. After all, he remembers, he is* HENRY LEEK *now. Curiously, he studies the envelope on both sides, and then he opens it. First he draws out a letter. As he begins to read it . . .*

*Insert—Open Letter*

*in* FARLL'S *hands. It is likewise in a woman's handwriting.*

> 33 Werter Road
> Putney
>
> Dear Mr. Leek: I think the photograph of you is most gentlemanly, so I enclose one of mine. I am glad your gentleman has decided to come back from abroad, and I shall be pleased to meet you as you suggest. How about outside the Empire Music Hall Saturday evening? In case the photo is too flattering—ha ha—shall wear red roses in my hat.
>
> Yours sincerely,
>
> Alice Challice
>
> P.S. I am a widow of ten years standing. Over.

FARLL

*Enthralled by this intrigue, he turns the page over, as—*

*Insert—Reverse of Letter*
P.S. There are always a lot of dark spots in the Empire. I have no doubt you will behave as a gentleman should. Excuse me. I merely mention it in case.

> A.C.

FARLL

*Looking in the envelope, he takes out a photograph.*

*Insert—Photograph*

*in* FARLL'S *hand. It is of a pleasant-looking woman, forty-odd, comfortable and agreeable looking, obviously an eminently respectable person.*

FARLL

*Sighing, he shakes his head as he tears up the letter and the photograph.*

FARLL *(turning to go upstairs)*. Oh, Leek . . . you rogue. How many poor women . . .

*As he moves off . . .*

*Dissolve to:*

*Montage*

*Of London newspaper headlines fanned out like spokes.*

SUDDEN DEATH OF PRIAM FARLL
ENGLAND'S GREATEST PAINTER PASSES
DEATH ON DAY OF KNIGHTHOOD

*Dissolve to:*

*Insert—Newspaper Story*

*Part of story . . .*

> Abnormally shy, Farll fled London 25 years ago because, he said, his celebrity was torture to him. Since then he lived the life of an eccentric genius in lands and among people who knew nothing of him. With them he was happy . . .

*Dissolve to:*

*Ext. House—Day*

*A mourning symbol of heavy black crepe hangs beside the door to explain the occasion. One fine carriage is just driving away as another stops in front of the house. There are callers on foot, too. Mostly men, they are the distinguished people who might be expected to call to pay their last respects to a great man, all of them in formal habit, their manner grave, properly funereal, with polite bows and murmured words. Some are emerging, others are entering.*

*Entrance Hall*

*The door remains open, so constant is the movement of visitors in and out. Greeting the callers is* DUNCAN FARLL *(Franklin Pangborn). His manner is properly mortician.*

DUNCAN. I'm Mr. Farll's cousin. How do you do. To the left, please. How do you do, Sir Basil. To the left, please.

FARLL *has appeared at his side, in the drab habit of a valet of the period, and waits respectfully for an opportunity to speak.*

FARLL *(quietly)*. This is very painful for me, sir. If you don't mind . . .
DUNCAN *(sharply)*. It's painful for me *too!* But I don't desert *my* post, do I? Please return . . . *(to a newcomer)* How do you do, Lord Haven, etc.

FARLL *moves back toward the parlor as . . .*

*Parlor*

*This room as well as the entrance hall have been cleaned up for the occasion. The parlor is crowded. Just under the camera is the casket past which the callers move, slowly, politely, glancing down at the features which none of them has ever seen in life. It is behind the casket that* FARLL *takes his post, resentfully, as* OXFORD, *after looking into the casket, pronounces his judgment solemnly.*

OXFORD. Just as I would have imagined him—with all the nobility of his work in those majestic features.

*Astonished at this tribute to* LEEK'S *looks,* FARLL *stares at* OXFORD, *whom of course he doesn't know, and then looks again into the casket at* LEEK'S *features as . . .*

TWO CRITICS

*They stand quietly together behind* FARLL'S *back, close enough for him to hear.*

1ST CRITIC. No, no, dear boy, not *the* great painter of this generation— not by a long shot!
2ND CRITIC. But Carlton, he hadn't a weakness!

*Reverse Angle*

*To show* FARLL'S *face and the* TWO CRITICS *talking behind him.*

1ST CRITIC. Nooo?

FARLL *looks fearful.*

2ND CRITIC. What do you mean?

*The* 1ST CRITIC *leans to the* 2ND CRITIC'S *ear with cautious air of an old gossip about to impart a particularly juicy bit of dirt, whereupon* FARLL *leans definitely back, cocking an ear.*

1ST CRITIC *(insinuatingly)*. What about his purples?
2ND CRITIC *(shocked)*. You don't care for his purples?
1ST CRITIC *(shaking his head slowly)*. Very, very weak, if you ask me.

*Wounded by the reflection on his purples,* FARLL'S *head bows unhappily. But it lifts at the* 2ND CRITIC'S *next words.*

2ND CRITIC. I'm afraid I beg to disagree.
1ST CRITIC *(stiffly)*. That of course is your privilege.
2ND CRITIC *(boldly)*. I will go further. In my opinion, Farll was never

stronger than with purple! He was a *master* of purple!

1ST CRITIC (*angrily*). That's pure *rot!*

2ND CRITIC (*angrily*). Rot!

FARLL (*turning humbly to the* 2ND CRITIC). Thank you, sir—thank you very much indeed.

*As they stare at him . . .*

*Another Angle*

DUNCAN FARLL, *showing excitement, stands in the doorway to the entrance hall, a hand upraised for attention.*

DUNCAN. Gentlemen! . . . His Majesty!

*There is a murmur of surprise and pleasure from the assemblage as . . .*

*Close Shot—*FARLL

*He swallows out of pure worry and distress at this new honor and glances unhappily toward* LEEK'S *remains as . . .*

*Ext. House*

*A closed carriage stops and an* EQUERRY *gets out followed by* KING EDWARD VII. *The gentlemen about the sidewalk and steps to the house remove their hats and make an informal lane as the* KING *acknowledges their bows and ascends to the door. As he enters . . .*

*Entrance Hall*

*The callers here form another lane with proper deference to the Imperial visitor.*

EQUERRY. Your Majesty, may I present Mr. Duncan Farll, Mr. Priam Farll's cousin.

KING. Please accept my deepest sympathy, Mr. Farll.

DUNCAN. Thank you, Your Majesty.

*Guided by the* EQUERRY, *the* KING *moves down the hall and as he enters the parlor . . .*

*Parlor*

*Royal respect from all greets him as he enters and crosses to the casket behind which* FARLL *stands watching the* KING'S *approach solemnly. The* KING *looks down into the casket.*

KING (*to the* EQUERRY). He'll be buried in the abbey, of course?

FARLL (*involuntarily*). The Abbey!

*The* KING *lifts his eyes at this unexpected exclamation.*

FARLL (*a whisper*). Forgive me, Your Majesty.

KING. Don't you think he deserves it?

FARLL (*after a pause*). Of course, Your Majesty.

*His eyes remain down as the* KING, *after a curious look at him, turns with his* EQUERRY *and departs.*

*Close Shot—*FARLL

*A buzz of restrained excitement marks the* KING'S *exit and then* FARLL *takes another anguished look into the casket.*

FARLL (*a whisper*). Leek in the Abbey! Heaven help us all!

*He closes his eyes and groans as . . .*

*Dissolve to:*

*Entrance Hall—Night*

*It is that evening. The crowd has gone. One of* DUNCAN FARLL'S CLERKS *precedes* FARLL *down the stairs.* FARLL *is dressed in* LEEK'S *clothes to leave and carries two bags. Waiting in the hall is* DUNCAN FARLL.

DUNCAN. Did you go through those?

CLERK. Yes, sir. Nothing but his own stuff.

DUNCAN. Very good. (*taking out banknotes*) Now in lieu of notice I am giving you a month's wages.

*The* CLERK *has gone into the parlor.* FARLL, *laboring under great agitation, sets his bags down.*

FARLL. It's no use. I can't go through with it.

DUNCAN. In addition, the will provides that the estate pay you two pounds a week for life, an extremely handsome allowance. If you will leave your address at my office . . .

FARLL. Duncan, don't you really recognize me?

DUNCAN. I *beg* your pardon!

FARLL (*suffering*). It's all very difficult—very stupid—but the truth is that I'm not Leek. I'm—I'm Priam.

DUNCAN (*automatically*). That's impossible. Priam's dead.

FARLL. No. It's *Leek* that's dead. That's Leek in there. (*desperately*) Don't you understand? You're burying the wrong man!

DUNCAN (*bewildered*). But he's *dead!* We've *got* to bury him! Can't just leave him out, you know!

FARLL. But not in the Abbey! He's a very decent fellow and all that—but *I'm* the one to be buried in the Abbey! Not him—*me!*

DUNCAN (*beginning to retreat*). Why, now, n-no need for excitement old boy!

FARLL. I confess it's not an easy situation to explain . . .

DUNCAN. N-n-nonsense! Most natural thing on earth—man wants to be buried in Westminster Abbey, b-b-but after all, it'd be b-b-better if you d-d-died first, don't you think?

FARLL (*earnestly*). You see, when Leek died, the doctor thought it was *I* who was dead . . .

DUNCAN. W-w-will you excuse m-me, just a s-s-second, p-please!

*He nips into the parlor as . . .*

*Parlor*

*The* CLERK, *working on a paper, looks up in surprise as the trembling* DUNCAN *darts to his side.*

DUNCAN. We've got to get a policeman—quickly! This man—he's unhinged!

CLERK (*starting up*). What do you mean?

DUNCAN. Don't ask questions! Just get down to the corner and get the p-p-policeman!

*Another Angle*

FARLL *is looking in the door, bug-eyed.*

FARLL. Policeman!

DUNCAN (*terrified*). It's quite all right now! Just be calm! (*to the* CLERK) Quickly—please! (*as the* CLERK *passes* FARLL) Don't you touch him—don't you dare!

FARLL. Why, you ruddy fool . . .

DUNCAN. Run, Herber, run! (*to* FARLL) I'll sell my life dearly, I w-warn you!

*Baffled and enraged,* FARLL *turns as . . .*

*Entrance Hall*

*Grabbing up his bags, he hurries out.* DUNCAN *peers out of the parlor cautiously, finds him gone, and follows shouting . . .*

DUNCAN. Police! Police!

*Ext. House*

*At the sound of* DUNCAN'S *cries,* FARLL *begins to run down the street. On the steps* . . .

DUNCAN. Police!

*Hansom Cab*

*Down the street* FARLL *comes panting with his bags and throws them into the cab.*

FARLL *(gasping)*. Quickly, let's go!
DUNCAN'S VOICE. Help! Police!

*The cab pulls away as* . . .

*Int. Cab*

DUNCAN'S *cries can still be heard as the* CABBY *opens the door in the top of the cab and looks down.*

CABBY. Excuse me, sir, but where did you want to go?
FARLL. Anywhere, it doesn't matter!
VOICES *(behind)*. Stop! Stop!
CABBY. Would you mind repeating that, sir? I'm a little hard of hearing.
FARLL. Thank heaven for that!
CABBY *(promptly)*. Very good, sir. Thank you, sir.

*The lid slaps down and the hoofbeats pick up speed.* FARLL *sits panting and miserable as* . . .

*Dissolve to:*

*Stock Shot—Westminster Abbey—Day*

*Superimposed is a newsboy and newspaper bill:*

PRIAM FARLL IN ABBEY
HIGHEST HONOR FOR PAINTER
IMPRESSIVE CEREMONIES

*Dissolve to:*

*Series of Stock Shots—Day*

*Of the pageantry of crowds, soldiers in ceremonial uniforms, carriages, etc., along route to the Abbey (library shots) building up the overpowering importance of an Abbey interment.*

*Facade of Abbey*

*A tremendous crowd throngs in front as distinguished guests in formal mourning alight to enter.*

*Two* MEN *in Crowd*

*Packed in, tiptoeing to see* . . .

MAN *(to friend)*. A better attendance than Lord Tennyson's, if you arsk me.

*Wall*

*Nervous, timid, agitated by the impossibility of the whole situation,* FARLL *stands back against the wall of a nearby building watching the spectacle. A* CONSTABLE *passes* . . .

CONSTABLE. All right now, no loitering.

FARLL *draws a deep breath and moves off* . . .

*Crowd*

*There is a police cordon about the entrance to the Abbey.* FARLL *shoulders through the crowd and attempts to pass.*

CONSTABLE. Have you a card?
FARLL. No, but I—I was a member of Mr. Farll's household.
CONSTABLE. Sorry. You can't pass without a card. Stand back, please.

FARLL *looks wistfully past the* CONSTABLE *and then turns away as* . . .

*Side of Abbey*

*Such a set and situation must be checked for approximate accuracy, but pending that, it is an ancient wall, of the same character of the Abbey construction, and presumably a small door set flush with the street and side-*

*walk leads into one of the Abbey group of edifices. Parked carriages line the curb and people hurry toward the Abbey. But from the Abbey, against the current, walks the crestfallen* FARLL, *unhappy at his inability to get into his own funeral. Once or twice he glances back regretfully and then he notices the small door. He stops. For a moment he studies it thoughtfully. Then he glances left and right to determine that there is no official in sight. The coast being apparently clear, he goes boldly to the door, tries it, and rather to his astonishment it opens. After another quick glance about, he enters, closing the door behind him, as . . .*

### Corridor

*It is almost pitch dark as* FARLL *moves slowly along a low-arched corridor, like a tunnel, medieval in character. And now the sound of organ music can be heard from the service.*

*Dissolve to:*

### Winding Stairs

*An iron circular staircase which* FARLL, *still nervous but determined, ascends as the music becomes louder. As he disappears upward . . .*

### Hole in Floor

*This is a square opening in the floor of the organ loft and now the music is in full force as up through this hole arises the head and shoulders of* FARLL, *alert and cautious. As he looks off . . .*

### Reverse Angle

*What* FARLL *sees is the organ loft (from the description in the novel but must be checked) atop the "screen," actually a wide wall across the nave of the church, the top being spacious*

*enough for the organ console, several chairs, a table, etc. At the far end the organist is still softly playing Chopin's Funeral Dirge. Two other young men, lay employees of the Abbey, are occupied with a paper on the table as* FARLL, *unnoticed, ascends the steps to emerge from the hole in the floor and moves to the parapet overlooking the nave, where he is hidden from the young men by a column or buttress. As he looks down into the church . . .*

### Nave of Church

*Angling down, perhaps with some kind of telescopic lens, if that might heighten the illusion, to show (from* FARLL'S *angle) the solemn throng gathered, all standing, to form an aisle down the middle of the nave. Diplomatic uniforms, full dress, all of the proper panoply of a state funeral dignify the occasion as . . .*

### Close Shot—FARLL

*His mouth is open as he stares. Just then the organ music swells, a hidden choir lifts its voices in the "Order for the Burial of the Dead."*

### Organist

*The organ is set athwart the "screen" so that the organist can peer over the parapet to keep track of the progress of the ceremony.*

### Nave

*All eyes are on the end of the nave as first appears a tall cross borne by a beadle. Following him is a stately procession of ecclesiastics in pairs.*

### Royal Box

*The term is used for lack of a better. In the Movie-tone Newsreel of the Coronation, such a reservation for royalty in the Abbey is shown, a kind of loge or box, and in it now are* KING

EDWARD VII *and a retinue of majestic looking ladies and gentlemen.*

*Close Shot*—FARLL

*He is looking off at the royalty. Then, dazed with the staggering wonder of it all, he looks down again into the nave as . . .*

*Nave*

*Following the ecclesiastics comes the scarlet-robed choristers singing in time to the beat of a robed leader who walks backward in front of them. Then comes the coffin covered with a purple pall on which is a single cross of white flowers.*

*Close Shot*—FARLL

*Overcome with emotion, tears appear in his eyes and his face begins to take on the contortions of a man nearing an outburst of sobs.*

*Nave*

*The coffin moves slowly followed by the pallbearers, gentlemen of the highest dignity: a duke, the president of the Royal Academy, ancient magnificos, and* DUNCAN FARLL.

FARLL

*A dry rasping sob breaks from his lips.*

*Organ*

*The organist and the two young men start and look off. The sound of the sob is repeated, and louder. As they look at each other in bewilderment and then toward the other end of the loft . . .*

FARLL

*He is now completely unmanned, and his uncontrollable sobs mingle with the choir and organ music like a strong new note. It is then that the first head appears around a column.*

1ST MAN. Hushshshshshsh!

FARLL. I—

*He breaks down again, pointing helplessly down at the ceremony.*

1ST MAN. *Shut Up!*

*Shaken as he is,* FARLL *manages to achieve silence.*

2ND MAN *(appearing)*. Who are you, what are you doing here?

FARLL. I—

*Again his moans rise as the two men try to stem his emotions with desperate gestures.*

ORGANIST

*Yelling over his music . . .*

ORGANIST. Get him out of here!

FARLL *and* MEN

1ST MAN *(grabbing* FARLL*)*. Come on! Come on!

FARLL. I can't . . .

*Dazed and irresponsible, he seizes the nearest projection and hangs on as the* 2ND MAN *joins the pull.* FARLL'S *unhappiness mounts as . . .*

ORGANIST

*Playing louder, more desperately, to drown out the racket and moans from* FARLL.

FARLL *and* MEN

1ST MAN *(hoarsely)*. Come on, I tell you!

*With which, he gives a yank that tears* FARLL *loose so suddenly that they all stumble back over a chair. The chair goes down,* FARLL *grabs at something else, and . . .*

*Nave*

*A number of people are glancing with shocked disapproval in the direction of the organ loft.*

*Dissolve to:*

*Side of Abbey*

*The door is opened and the two young men literally wrestle* FARLL *out to the sidewalk.*

1ST MAN. There!

FARLL *(mumbling)*. I want my hat. Where's my hat?

*Stupidly, muddled by it all, he tries to go back in the door, and the two men resist grimly.*

MEN. No you don't! No you don't!

*Another Angle*

*To show a young* POLICEMAN *strolling up. People begin to watch.*

POLICEMAN. Now, now! What's all this?

FARLL *(doggedly)*. I'm simply trying to get my hat.

1ST MAN. 'is 'at 'e says! 'E's up in the organ loft 'owling like an 'ound right in the middle of the service! 'Ow 'e got there nobody knows.

POLICEMAN. 'Owling in the Abbey, eh? What about that, my man?

FARLL. I'm very sorry . . .

2ND MAN. He's drunk, if you arsk me.

FARLL. Nobody arsked you!

POLICEMAN. All right, then, let's have a smell of your breath.

FARLL. I am not drunk and I haven't the slightest intention in the world of permitting you to smell my breath.

POLICEMAN. R!

FARLL. If you will allow me to explain . . .

*At this point a police* SERGEANT *has entered the picture.*

SERGEANT. What's all this?

POLICEMAN. 'Owling like an 'ound in the organ loft, sir. Drunk and disorderly in the Abbey during service.

FARLL. I am not drunk, I tell you.

SERGEANT. What's your name?

FARLL *(catching his breath)*. My name?

SERGEANT. You 'ave one, 'aven't you?

FARLL. No. *(with some dignity)* At least, none that I care to give at the moment.

SERGEANT *(taking his arm)*. All right, then, let's go along quietly.

FARLL *(desperately)*. But I've broken no law . . .

POLICEMAN *(taking other arm)*. In that case, no 'arm'll come to you. Just be easy!

*Forcing him along firmly, the* SERGEANT *and the* POLICEMAN *steer* FARLL *through the gathering crowd as. . . .*

*Further Down the Sidewalk*

*Flanked by the policemen,* FARLL *submits in resignation and disgust.*

FARLL. All right, all right, there's no need to pull. I'm coming quietly. *(after a sigh)* I suppose it's no more than I deserve.

ALICE CHALLICE

*Dressing in her best, she is looking off with interest. To describe* ALICE CHALLICE *is to describe a remarkable woman. Between 40 and 50, she fears no man or circumstance and no man could ever see any reason to fear her. She is unruffled, infinitely understanding, sympathetic, patient, tolerant, amiable and as strong as Gibraltar. Few things would disturb her, fewer would shock her. In all human events she has the warm and patient detachment of a comfortable middle-aged goddess. Men to her are sometimes children but always masters. They simply must be handled gently. With this she has a quiet soothing charm and disposition that conquer without effort. She gets what she wants without even trying. Things and people are won to her. She smiles as she recognizes* FARLL.

*Full Shot*

*She does not move from the middle of the sidewalk as* FARLL *and the law approach. She smiles as she would greet a friend under any other circumstances and she speaks evenly and with a calm assurance.*

ALICE. Good morning, Mr. Leek.

SERGEANT. Pardon me, Madam . . .

ALICE *(immovable)*. Is the service over?

SERGEANT. Stand aside, please. This man . . .

ALICE *(gently)*. I am speaking to Mr. Leek—if you don't mind.

*The* POLICE *have made a slight move to by-pass her but* ALICE *has shifted easily to circumvent that. Meanwhile* FARLL *is staring at her in bewilderment. The face is vaguely familiar but he has long since completely forgotten the letter and photograph.*

POLICEMAN. This man is drunk and disorderly . . .

ALICE. How silly! Mr. Leek doesn't drink. *(looking at* FARLL *sympathetically)* He was simply overcome, I expect—and no wonder, with such a loss.

FARLL *(gratefully)*. Thank you, madam.

SERGEANT *(warily)*. And what loss is that, if I may ask?

ALICE. My goodness, don't tell me you don't know who he is!

SERGEANT. Who is he?

ALICE. Mr. Farll's *valet*. For twenty-five years—with Mr. Farll literally depending on him for every thought and wish. *(FARLL is staring)* For twenty-five years Mr. Farll never made a move, never a decision, never had a thought without first talking it over with Mr. Leek.

SERGEANT. But he had no ticket!

ALICE. Then more shame on them—after the best years of his life—giving every satisfaction—and what is his reward? No ticket!

SERGEANT *(to* FARLL*)*. But why didn't you tell us, sir?

FARLL *(mumbling)*. I'm very sorry . . .

ALICE *(after studying* FARLL *thoughtfully)*. Mr. Leek is a very shy man.

*Closeup*—FARLL

*Startled by this insight, he is staring harder at* ALICE.

ALICE'S VOICE. He is not accustomed to policemen.

*Full Shot*

SERGEANT. I should hope not. *(to* FARLL*)* Sorry, sir. No harm meant. Would you like us to take you back to the organ loft?

FARLL *(hastily)*. No, no—thank you. If you don't mind now . . .

SERGEANT. Quite all right, sir. You go right along with the lady.

ALICE *(taking* FARLL'S *arm)* Thank you, sergeant.

SERGEANT. Not at all, mum.

*Dazed,* FARLL *walks away with* ALICE'S *arm in his. The* SERGEANT *gazes paternally after them. Then he turns to the* POLICEMAN, *and such has been the contagiousness of* ALICE'S *gentleness that he is clearly affected by it.*

SERGEANT *(gently)*. You should be more careful, officer.

POLICEMAN *(even more gently)*. Yes, indeed, sir, and you may be sure that next time I will be.

*Truck Shot*—FARLL *and* ALICE

*They walk arm in arm down the sidewalk. Warily* FARLL *looks down at her, wracking his brain to recall who this is.*

ALICE. First we'll get you a hat.

*As* FARLL *looks again . . .*

*Dissolve to:*

*Int. Hat Store—Day*

*A few minutes later, in a small hat store a stiffish* CLERK *smirks automatically as* FARLL *and* ALICE *enter. Watching* FARLL *thoughtfully,* ALICE *remains in the background as* FARLL *braces himself to cope with a purchase. Never has he been so nervous and so shy as now, with her looking on.*

CLERK. Good day, sir.

FARLL. I'd like a hat, a bowler.

CLERK. Very good, sir. What size?

FARLL. Seven and a half.

CLERK. Very good, sir.

*He disappears into the back of the store.* FARLL *looks around helplessly at* ALICE. *Smiling gently, encouragingly, she comes to him and begins to adjust his tie and collar, which have become disarranged in the morning's misadventure.*

ALICE. Now, now . . .

*She stops, peering into the opening of his shirt in the vicinity of his neck.*

FARLL *(uncomfortably)*. May I ask . . .

ALICE. *Two* moles! That's very lucky, you know.

FARLL. Is it?

ALICE. Didn't you ever notice them?

FARLL *(stiffly)*. Of course. As a small boy, my view was not impeded by a beard.

*At that moment the* CLERK *appears with a bowler.* ALICE *steps modestly back.*

CLERK. Here you are, sir.

FARLL *puts it on. It is much too small for him. He studies it solemnly in a glass.*

FARLL. Doesn't it seem rather small to you?

CLERK *(the smile disappearing)*. You said seven and a half, sir.

FARLL. But—er . . .

CLERK. All seven and a halfs, sir, are the same size, sir. Of course if you don't know your own size . . .

FARLL *(hastily)*. Not at all! Perfectly all right! *(reaching for money)* That's my size all right, seven and a half.

CLERK. In that case . . .

*He stops as* ALICE *lifts the hat from* FARLL'S *head and hands it back to the* CLERK.

ALICE *(smiling amiably)*. Mr. Leek doesn't like this size, he doesn't like this style, he doesn't like this color, he doesn't like this hat. Now will you get out some others, please?

*As* FARLL *and the* CLERK *both stare at her soft firmness . . .*

*Dissolve to:*

*Table in Restaurant—Day*

*A few minutes later, it is a table for two in a very small but elegant restaurant. Off-screen a string ensemble is playing. A* CAPTAIN *of waiters stands over the table as* FARLL *and* ALICE *study their menus. The* CAPTAIN *is looking at* ALICE, *who is shaking her head and tchk-tchking in disapproval of the prices.* FARLL *looks up. Their eyes meet.* ALICE *smiles.*

ALICE. French, isn't it?

FARLL. Yes—or . . .

ALICE (*to the* CAPTAIN). What is that?

CAPTAIN (*after looking where her finger rests*). That is the name of the selection that the orchestra is playing, madame.

ALICE (*unruffled*). Well . . . not much nourishment in that. (*to* FARLL) Will you order for me—anything at all.

FARLL. Er—des hors d'oeuvres— waiter!

*But the* CAPTAIN, *a harassed and unaccountable man, is gone.*

ALICE (*encouragingly*). He'll be back.

FARLL (*miserable*). I suppose so.

ALICE (*a stage whisper*). I saw those prices.

FARLL. Er—did you?

ALICE. Are you sure you can afford it?

FARLL. Oh, yes, certainly.

ALICE (*the intimacy of a wife*). Did they give you your month?

FARLL. My month?

ALICE. You were entitled to it, you know, no matter *what* happened.

FARLL. Oh, yes. I was provided for in the will.

ALICE. It doesn't matter. I simply don't want you to be extravagant for *my* sake. There's no call for it. I'm just as I am—just as you see me now—and no amount of foolish spending would affect me one way or the other. (*smiling*) You understand, don't you?

FARLL (*dazed*). Oh, yes . . . of course.

*Pleased, she gives him a warm wink, the wink of a friend appreciating that they are in accord on a certain matter. With no understanding whatever,* FARLL *returns the wink. Then . . .*

FARLL. Would you be good enough now to tell me how you recognized me?

ALICE. Oh, you're *very* like your photograph.

FARLL. Am I?

ALICE. I knew you at once. (*getting picture from handbag*) By the beard, of course—and also your shyness.

*He gazes at her for a moment and then looks at the photograph.*

*Insert—Photograph*

*In* FARLL'S *hand, a photograph taken on the veranda of the tropical lodge of* FARLL *and* LEEK, *and* ALICE'S *mistake is easily understandable, for* FARLL (*on the left*) *is shrinking away from the camera with his habitual shyness while* LEEK (*on the right*) *has assumed a bold and dominating pose and look. Written under it in* LEEK'S *handwriting is, "I and my gentleman. Expectantly, Henry."*

ALICE'S VOICE. It's very good, don't you think?

*Two Shot*

FARLL *hands it back to her and she studies it for a moment before returning it to her handbag.*

ALICE (*simply*). I love it.

*The* CAPTAIN *appears to set a small vase of flowers on the table, and still hurried and preoccupied as . . .*

FARLL. Waiter!

*Heedless, the* CAPTAIN *is almost out of the scene before he is aware that a firm hand is holding his coat-tail. Astonished, he stares at* ALICE.

ALICE *(reproachfully).* Mr. Leek is *speaking* to you.

*From her the* CAPTAIN *turns to* FARLL, *who is just about as awestruck as he is.*

CAPTAIN. Yes, sir?

ALICE. If I do anything to embarrass you, pardon me, please. *(gazing about with interest)* I've never eaten in a restaurant before.

*As* FARLL *and the* CAPTAIN *regard her with awe and wonder . . .*

*Dissolve to:*

*Close Shot—Bus Sign—Day*

*It is a couple of hours later. Camera is on the placard on the front of a London bus, emphasizing Putney. Then the camera moves up to a two-shot of* ALICE *and* FARLL *in or on top of the bus.*

ALICE *(without heat).* Such prices are scandalous. When you think that in Putney a good housekeeper can keep everything going on ten shillings a head a week . . . *(she shrugs)*

FARLL. I don't believe I've ever been in Putney before.

ALICE. And for such food! Sole, they said! That was no more sole than this glove's sole. And if it had been cooked a minute, it had been cooked an hour, and waiting.

FARLL. Really? I thought it was quite good.

ALICE. For anyone who hasn't been used to good cooking—*(sympathetically)*—perhaps. *(then studying him)* You haven't told me yet, but I fancy you've never been married—have you.

FARLL. No, I haven't.

ALICE. You've always lived like that, just traveling about with no home—and nobody to look after you properly?

FARLL. One gets accustomed to it.

ALICE. Yes, I can understand that.

FARLL. No responsibilities.

ALICE. I can understand that too—but I do feel so sorry for you—all these years.

*There is no coquetry, no guile in her face, only sympathy as she sits placidly facing front.*

FARLL *(helplessly).* Putney, eh?

*Dissolve to:*

*Close Shot—Name Sign—Day*

*The name of this Putney home is on a sign on the gatepost:* PARADISE VIL-LA. *Camera pulls back as* ALICE *leads* FARLL *up the short path to the front door of a neat trim little house with a small yard of flowers in front.* FARLL *is watching the competent, comfortable woman with fascination; she does everything with such neatness and dispatch, with such a natural quiet and efficiency. Approaching the door and taking the key from her bag . . .*

ALICE. It won't take a moment. The tea things are all ready . . .

FARLL *(entering).* Thank you.

*Hall*

*Taking his coat, lifting it from his shoulders, she brushes the sleeves before hanging it up.* FARLL *is looking around at a hall which is neither good taste nor bad, but simple and neat and as clean as a hound's tooth.*

ALICE. It's not Buckingham Palace, but it's been quite large enough for myself alone—and I daresay . . .

*She does not finish what she daresay, but leads the way into the sitting room, flicking a bit of dust from here and there as she goes.*

*Living Room*

*This is the pleasantest and most comfortable sitting room in Putney. Conspicuously over the mantel is a motto:* "HOME IS WHERE THE HEART IS." ALICE *is already poking up the fire on the hearth as* FARLL *enters and stands watching her.*

ALICE *(rising)*. Sit down, won't you? *(fixing the most comfortable chair minutely)* This one. I think you'll find it comfortable. Have you your pipe? Would you like to smoke?

FARLL. You don't mind?

ALICE. Mind! Dear me, no. How else could a man be happy without his pipe and tobacco. *(as he takes out his pipe)* Now if you'll just sit and relax, I'll have the tea up in a jiffy!

*Only now does she take off her hat as she exits into the kitchen.* FARLL *looks all around, taking everything in. He draws a deep sigh of relief.*

FARLL. It's—it's very—peaceful.

*Dissolve to:*

*Living Room—Another Angle—Dusk*

*It is perhaps an hour later. The scene is one of domestic peace and contentment.* ALICE *sits on one side of the fire with her knitting or crocheting, now using glasses. The remains of a tea are on a small table.* FARLL, *for probably the first time in his life, is 120% happy. All restraint is gone, all stiffness so customary in him, and he sits back in the comfortable chair, puffing on his pipe and speaking with a forthrightness and authority which*

he never expected to use again after the death of LEEK.

FARLL *(expansively)*. The truth of the matter is that Priam Farll was not a happy man.

ALICE *(sympathetically)*. I suppose not, poor creature.

FARLL. All he wanted, actually, was to paint and to be left alone. But that didn't seem to be possible in London, which he really loved very deeply. For instance, Priam Farll— *(after a pause)*—God rest his great, tormented soul—would never have been allowed to enjoy such a day as this. *(she silently fills his cup)* A painter, my dear Alice, is essentially a simple fellow—a workman—and should live as such, enjoying the frugal wages, the course comforts, and the humble pleasures of the honest craftsman. *(regretfully)* Priam Farll would have loved this.

ALICE. Well . . . it all just goes to show.

FARLL. And what does it all just go to show, my dear?

ALICE *(resting her knitting)*. They all said if I wrote to a matrimonial bureau I'd be cheated.

FARLL *(sitting up)*. I beg your pardon!

ALICE *(thoughtfully)*. But I'm like you. If you want to get married, it's no use pretending you don't. There's no shame in wanting to get married. It's sensible and it's normal. *(he is staring at her in bewilderment)* And in such a case a matrimonial bureau is a good, useful thing. *You* thought so evidently, and so do I. And I'm sure —*(smiling at him pleasantly)*—if anything comes of this, I'll pay the fee with the greatest pleasure. *(after a pause)* What about you?

*Once again* PRIAM FARLL *is called on for a quick decision, one to have an important bearing on his whole life, and presently, with a sigh of contentment and a glance about the room and at her, he comes through again. He smiles shyly.*

FARLL. With the greatest of pleasure.

*They smile at each other for a moment and then* ALICE *resumes her knitting and* FARLL *lies back and takes a long draw on his cigar as . . .*

*Dissolve to:*

*Insert—Night*

*Close shot of newspaper bill:*

> DISTINGUISHED
> PAINTER
> LAID TO REST

*Fade out.*

*Timed properly, the fade out and fade in is scored with a bright playing of Mendelssohn's "Wedding March."*

*Fade in.*

*Full Shot—House—Day*

*The "Wedding March" dies away. This is now the home of* MR. AND MRS. HENRY LEEK. *Superimposed is a title:*

> PARADISE IN 1906

*The title fades out and the front door opens and* FARLL *appears. As he stands for a moment admiring the day and pulling on his gloves . . .*

*Closer Shot*

ALICE *in a house dress appears with the morning paper which she is folding for him to carry conveniently under his arm.*

ALICE. Forgetting your paper!
FARLL. Thank you, dear.
ALICE (*adjusting his tie*). Where d'you think you'll stroll today?

FARLL. I don't know. Perhaps down by the river.
ALICE. Will you be passing the fishmonger's?
FARLL. That's a good idea. What about a bit of cod?
ALICE. See what's nice.
FARLL (*leaving*). Cod might go very well tonight.
ALICE. Whatever you wish.

*As he approaches the sidewalk, the* POSTMAN *appears.*

FARLL. Morning, Hubert.
HUBERT. Morning, Mr. Leek. No, this is for Mrs. Leek.
ALICE. Well! (*waving after* FARLL) Watch the crossings, Henry!
HUBERT (*grinning*). Not half bad, eh?
ALICE (*jovially*). Not half!

*Glancing idly at the envelope, she reenters the house as . . .*

*Dissolve to:*

*Ext.* FISHMONGER'S—*Day*

*A few minutes later* FARLL *is examining an array of dead fish laid out on a marble slab. The* FISHMONGER *is watching helpfully. Indicating his choice . . .*

FARLL. That's a magnificent looking animal.
FISHMONGER. The best, sir. Shall I save a piece out of the middle for Mrs. Leek?
FARLL. Do that. She'll be along presently.
FISHMONGER. Very good, sir.

*As* FARLL *moves off, a man contented with himself and the world . . .*

*Dissolve to:*

*Int. Tobacconist's Shop—Day*

*A few minutes later. It is small, dusty, comfortable.* AYLMER, *the tobacconist, is behind the counter. A lounger stands down the counter. As* FARLL *enters . . .*

FARLL. Morning, Aylmer.

AYLMER. Morning, Mr. Leek.

FARLL *(jovially).* An ounce of the usual, if you please—and my impedimenta, if it's not too much trouble.

AYLMER *(reaching under counter).* Impedimenta, eh?

*He comes up with a batch of sketchpads and a number of heavy pencils in a tight rubber band.*

FARLL. Ah! Thank you!

AYLMER *(to the* LOUNGER*).* Mr. Leek draws—but he doesn't want the Missus to know anything about it. So he always leaves his things here.

LOUNGER *(hoarsely).* That's right. Tell 'em nothing.

FARLL *(uncomfortably).* That's not it exactly. It's simply that—er—certain explanations, you know . . .

LOUNGER *(flatly).* Tell 'em nothing. That's my motto.

AYLMER *(weighing out the tobacco).* Oh, well, there's no 'arm in a bit of drawing—as long as it's 'eld under control. *(confidentially)* You want to know where the danger comes in, Mr. Leek?

FARLL *(puzzled).* Danger in drawing?

AYLMER *(nodding firmly).* The danger comes in this way. A man starts to drawr. First 'e drawrs a tree or an ocean or something else dead. Then he gets *past* dead stuff and so what does he drawr? He drawrs a dog or a cat or an 'orse. But that's not the end. The next thing you know he wants to drawr a *woman!*

LOUNGER. Ah!

AYLMER. First with 'er clothes on! And *then! (with a shrug)* You can see the position that that puts Missus Leek in.

FARLL *(slowly).* I see. Well—er—thank you very much.

AYLMER *(as* FARLL *leaves)* Just be on your guard, that's all, sir.

*Dissolve to:*

*Street Scene—Day*

*A few minutes later. On the edge of the sidewalk an organ grinder is providing the music for five or six children, eleven or twelve years old, to dance. In the b.g.* FARLL *is leaning against a building or post, sketching rapidly.*

*Dissolve to:*

*Kitchen—Day*

*It is that afternoon.* ALICE *is about the kitchen, snatches of song on her lips as she prepares to bake bread. Then there is a heavy knock at the front door, a very heavy knock which makes* ALICE *look up in astonishment at such fierceness. Wiping her hands on her apron, she starts out as. . . .*

*Ext. Front Door*

*Standing at the door in funereal black, the blackest black that money could buy, is a frail middle-aged spectacled woman,* MRS. LEEK, *who is doing all in her power to look tragic. Disposed about the yard, so that they cannot be seen immediately by whoever answers the door, are two pale, thin ascetic-looking young men, and twins,* HARRY *and* MATTHEW LEEK, *and a third son, older and more muscular,* JOHN. ALICE *opens the door.*

ALICE. Yes?

MRS. LEEK. Is this Mr. Henry Leek's?

ALICE. Yes?

MATTHEW *(leaping out).* Hold it, mother!

*Followed by his two brothers, also leaping from ambush,* MATTHEW *dashes forward and puts a firm hand on the door, to* ALICE'S *amazement but not fear.*

ALICE. What on earth!

MATTHEW *(triumphantly).* Not going to keep *us* out! Not likely!

HARRY *(ushering her).* Right in, mother—now!

*With much bustling of the mother, the three sons push in past* ALICE, *who stares at them in bewilderment.*

*Hall*

MATTHEW. Where is he?

ALICE *(bridling).* Never mind where he is! Who are you and what do you mean smashing into this house like that?

HARRY. Who are we, she asks!

ALICE. Yes, and who *are* you?

MRS. LEEK. I'm his wife, ma'am— the rightful Mrs. Henry Leek—and these are our sons—come to see that I get justice.

ALICE *(eyes wide).* Well, indeed!

MATTHEW. Now will you bring him out?

ALICE *(once again mistress of the situation).* Of course—but why don't we all go in and sit down quietly.

MATTHEW. Sit?

ALICE. Certainly. *(moving off)* In the sitting room.

*As she exits, the* LEEK *family exchange puzzled, somewhat suspicious glances.*

JOHN *(deciding for all).* All right, let's sit.

*As they follow* ALICE . . .

*Sitting Room*

ALICE *stands like the perfect hostess as the* LEEKS *trail slowly into the room.*

ALICE. While we're waiting for him—he'll be back soon—don't you think a cup of tea would be cozy?

*Unprepared for such a reception, they all look again at each other warily, and then at* ALICE, *who smiles amiably.*

JOHN *(deciding again).* We'll have tea.

ALICE. Fine!

*As she goes out, the* LEEKS *sit,* MRS. LEEK *in* FARLL'S *chair, the twins side by side on the sofa,* JOHN, *the burly one, in a chair well in the background. They sit gingerly, suspiciously, as . . .*

*Dissolve to:*

*Ext. House—Day*

*A short while later,* FARLL *comes briskly home, newspaper under arm, humming perhaps, as he reaches in his pocket for his front door key. But* ALICE, *smiling serenely, opens the door before he can use it. She puts up her cheek to be kissed.*

FARLL. My dear!

ALICE *(as he enters).* Did you have a nice stroll?

*Hall*

FARLL *(taking off his gloves).* Excellent, excellent! Did you get the fish?

ALICE. Oh, yes, a very nice piece. *(taking his arm)* We have visitors, Henry.

FARLL *(surprised).* Visitors? Us!

ALICE *(leading him).* Old friends— they say.

*Sitting Room*

*From* FARLL'S *angle, to show a tableau of greeting.* MRS. LEEK, *turned to face the door, is still seated but the three male* LEEKS *are standing facing him ominously. Their attitude is so melodramatic that* FARLL *stares at them nonplussed—and this complete failure to start or be frightened or show guilt is not lost on* ALICE *as she studies his reaction. From that moment* ALICE *feels no further apprehensions over the situation. How it came about she doesn't know, hardly cares; it is sufficient that her* HENRY *obviously has no intention of accepting the newcomers to his heart.*

ALICE *(finally)*. Don't you recognize her?

MRS. LEEK *(advancing nearsightedly)*. Henry?

FARLL. I'm afraid you have the advantage, madam.

MRS. LEEK. Thirty years does change a person's appearance.

FARLL *(to* ALICE*)*. What *is* this?

ALICE. You two talk it over while I get another cup.

FARLL *(frightened, as she starts out)*. No, no, you stay here!

ALICE. I'll be right back . . .

FARLL. Never mind that! You stay here with me!

ALICE *(soothingly)*. Of course, dear.

MRS. LEEK. *(who has been studying him closely)*. You've changed, too, Henry.

ALICE. Sit down, everybody.

HARRY *(stiffly)*. I am not so sure that I *care* to sit down with father.

FARLL *(in horror)*. Father!

JOHN *(sitting again)*. Sit.

*Cursing the day he ever met his late valet,* FARLL *gropes unsteadily for a chair and sinks into it. Calm as ever,* ALICE *prepares to toast bread over the fire. The eyes of the others rest angrily, accusingly on the unhappy master of the house.*

ALICE. She says she's your wife, dear—and her sons.

MATTHEW *(glaring)*. *Your* sons, *too,* if you don't mind, sir!

FARLL. Great heavens—*you!* Impossible!

MRS. LEEK. It's the beard, of course . . . and you're heavier. But your eyes—*(to* MATTHEW*)—Your* eyes, my son.

HARRY. Continue, mother.

FARLL *stares at* MRS. LEEK *as if entranced as she turns to* ALICE, *who continues to toast bread.*

MRS. LEEK. And then a year after the marriage came our first-born— John. (JOHN *rises for identification*) Six months later—*(a reproachful look at* FARLL*)*—without so much as kiss-me-foot—he walks out forever— *(dropping her eyes)*—and me again in an interesting condition.

HARRY. Brave, mother, brave!

MRS. LEEK. I had twins—Harry and Matthew. *(they rise in turn)* And after that, no more—*(hastily)*—naturally.

FARLL. I have never laid eyes on this woman before in my life!

HARRY *(springing up)*. How dare you . . .

FARLL *(loudly)*. Never laid eyes on her!

MRS. LEEK. Why he did it I'll never understand, for never a word of sauce did I ever give him back, although he was a cruel man indeed, and knocked me about a bit. For better or worse, he was my husband and I forgave him and still do. Even when he beat me with hand *and* fist. He was the father of my children.

HARRY. Oh, shame, shame, dreadful shame!

FARLL. Never saw the woman before in my whole life!

MATTHEW. Then how do you explain *this,* sir!

*Jumping up, he has pulled a legal-looking paper from his pocket and offered it to* FARLL, *but* ALICE *takes it. As she opens it . . .*

*Insert*

*It is a certificate of marriage of* HENRY LEEK, *valet, and* SARAH FEATHERSTONE, *spinster, at a registry office in Paddington.*

MATTHEW'S VOICE. Let father see it also.

*Full Shot*

ALICE *passes the certificate to* FARLL.

FARLL *(angrily)*. Will you kindly stop referring to me as your *father!* *(after studying the paper)* This means nothing whatever to me.

HARRY *(a born orator)*. Oh, shrug if you will, sir, but you cannot shrug us out of existence!

FARLL *(testily)*. I was not shrugging.

HARRY *(swept on)*. Respect, I suppose, is what you want! And yet how can you hope for our respect?

FARLL. Oh, blast your respect!

HARRY. Did you earn it when you left our poor mother, with the most inhuman cruelty, to fend for herself against the world? Did you earn it when you abandoned your children born and unborn? Did you . . .

ALICE *(handing him the fork)*. Would you mind holding this, please. Mind you don't burn it.

*Cut off in mid-flight,* HARRY *accepts the fork with the piece of bread on it and holds it to be toasted over the fire.*

MATTHEW. I suppose you'll not deny, sir, that your name is Henry Leek.

FARLL *(baring his teeth)*. I deny everything! No matter what you say, I deny it! Is that clear?

ALICE. Do you really recognize my husband?

MRS. LEEK *(earnestly)*. I wouldn't say that I recognize him as he *was*— no more than he recognizes *me*—after thirty years. The last time I saw him he was only twenty-two or three. And clean-shaven at that. But he's the same *sort* of man—and his eyes, *they're* the same.

FARLL *(crossing to her)*. Madame, will you kindly examine my nose. *(his nose in her face)* Presumably you should recognize it. Do you? Go on, look closely. Do you?

MRS. LEEK *(examining it)*. I—I—can't say I remember it so boney.

FARLL. Can a man change his nose?

HARRY. A nose might change with the years.

MATTHEW. All flesh is grass.

FARLL *(at* MATTHEW*)*. The discussion does not concern grass! *(to* ALICE*)* This woman does not recognize my nose!

MRS. LEEK. But you were valet with a gentleman named Mr. Priam Farll, the painter, weren't you?

FARLL. Yes.

MRS. LEEK. That's what my husband was doing, the last time I heard of him.

*This is the crusher. There is nothing* FARLL *can think of to contradict that. Facing the* LEEK *family haughtily . . .*

FARLL *(with dignity)*. To repeat, I not only deny everything that *has* been said—but also everything that *will* be said. And now, with your permission . . .

*Bowing stiffly, he turns to make an exit of dignity, but as he moves toward the hall door,* JOHN *rises from his position near it and plants himself squarely in his path. As he stands glowering at* FARLL, *who studies him uncertainly . . .*

ALICE *(evenly)*. Will you—oh!

*It is very hot tea and* ALICE *has most clumsily spilled it in* MRS. LEEK'S *lap. It is a completely successful diversion.* MRS. LEEK *ululates wierdly, the two curates twitter to her side, and* ALICE *croons with sympathy and apologies.*

ALICE. Oh, how could I be so clumsy! Let me! Henry!

FARLL. Yes?

ALICE *(mopping* MRS. LEEK*)*. Get me a cloth from the kitchen—quick! *(to* MRS. LEEK*)* Oh, now, it's drying nicely!

*Grateful for the opportunity,* FARLL *nips out of the other door,* JOHN *looking after him uncertainly.*

ALICE. Will you forgive me? I couldn't be sorrier!

*Outside there is the heavy slam of a door. The brothers look at each other. But* ALICE *is back to the tea things.*

ALICE. The fire'll dry it in a jiffy. There's another for you, warm and sweet.

MATTHEW *(as she pours)*. Speaking for the family . . .

ALICE. Will you kindly pass this to your mother?

MATTHEW. Certainly.

ALICE. One lump or two, Mr. Harry?

HARRY. Two, thank you.

MATTHEW. On behalf of the family . . .

ALICE *(passing him the cup)*. For your brother.

HARRY. I say, isn't he coming back?

ALICE. Who?

HARRY. Father.

ALICE *(smiling gently)*. Oh, I shouldn't think so. I imagine he's gone for a stroll. He usually does after tea.

HARRY. But that's quite strange—in the very midst of the discussion!

ALICE. He's a rather peculiar man. He has his good points—*(to* MRS. LEEK *intimately)*—as he's not here I can speak candidly—but also he has—other points.

MRS. LEEK. Oh, yes, how true.

ALICE. When you spoke of his cruelty—well, I understand. Far be it from me to say a word against him— he's often very kind to me—but—*(a sigh)*—there's no denying . . .

MRS. LEEK. You mean that he . . . *(*ALICE *nods sadly)* Once he twisted my arm, terribly. One morning he snatched a hot iron out of my hand and . . .

ALICE. Don't please. I know all you can tell me. I know because I've been through . . .

MRS. LEEK *(sobbing)*. He threatened *you* with a hot iron too?

ALICE *(martyred)*. If threatening was only all!

MRS. LEEK. Then he's not changed in all these years!

ALICE. If so, only for the worse. *(to the curates)* And yet nobody, nobody, could be nicer than he is at times.

MRS. LEEK. That's so true. He was always so changeable, so . . . so queer!

ALICE *(remotely)*. Queer . . . strange . . . weird . . . Sometimes I don't think he's quite right in the head. I seldom get up in the morning without thinking, "Well, perhaps today he'll have to be taken off."

MRS. LEEK *(gasping)*. Taken off!

ALICE. To the asylum. *(to the curates)* I'm sorry for you too.

HARRY. What do you mean?

ALICE. You're his sons—it's the

same blood. If I were you I should watch myself very closely.

HARRY (*nervously*). I see.

ALICE (*to* MRS. LEEK). You want him back, of course, because you have first claim on him.

MRS. LEEK (*feebly*). Y-yes, of course.

ALICE. Well, if you can persuade him to go, if you can make him see his duty, you're welcome.

MATTHEW. He wouldn't have to *go*. Mother could come *here*—

ALICE. Oh, but this isn't his house. It's mine. And the furniture. He's got nothing at all, I'm afraid. (*rising distractedly*) Yes, many's the blow he's laid on me in anger, but all the same I pity him, and I shouldn't like to leave him in the lurch. With these three strong young men—(*to* MRS. LEEK)—you should be able to handle him. I'm not sure, for he's as strong as—as those kind of people can be sometimes—and he has such a way of leaping out so sudden like . . .

ALICE *sighs again.* MRS. LEEK *shakes her head like a groggy prizefighter.*

MATTHEW (*angrily*). The fact is he should be prosecuted for bigamy. That's what *ought* to be done.

ALICE. Oh, by *all* means! You're *quite* right! It might be quite expensive—detectives and lawyers and all that sort of thing—and the scandal. Not that *I'd* mind. My reputation wouldn't suffer—not in Putney, where they know me. But you're so right. He *should* be in prison—whatever the expense.

MATTHEW. Oh, but the Crown, the prosecution, would pay for all that.

ALICE. Then there's no reason why he shouldn't be arrested at once—although—(*she hesitates*) You're students, aren't you?

MATTHEW. *Honor* students—at the seminary.

ALICE. Oh, but I don't suppose that would matter particularly to your standing—a father in prison for bigamy—would it?

*At this, the* LEEK *family falls into a moody silence.* ALICE *sighs again, martyred visibly. Finally, clearing his throat,* JOHN *the tough one rises to his feet.*

JOHN. Let's clear out of this.

*The* LEEKS *receive his suggestion with wan smiles of relief. Rising, they look awkwardly at* ALICE, *who sighs again, and then, led by* MRS. LEEK, *trailed by* JOHN, *they shuffle out.* ALICE *stands with head bowed in grief until she hears the door slam outside. Then, humming idly, she sits down and pours herself a cup of tea as . . .*

*Dissolve to:*

*Kitchen—Night*

*It is an hour or so later.* ALICE *is busy about the stove when the back door cracks open slowly, cautiously, and* FARLL'S *nervous eyes peer in. He makes a hissing sound to her, at which she starts and stares at him.*

ALICE. Henry! What on earth!

FARLL (*fearfully*). Are they gone?

ALICE. An hour ago. Come in. Oh, why did you go out without a coat! You'll catch your death!

FARLL (*coming to her*). Alice, I give you my word of honor, I never laid eyes on that woman before in my life.

ALICE. Of course not. (*a peck of a kiss*) And besides—(*back to the stove*)—she's a nagging woman—anybody could see that—and I don't blame you for a second!

FARLL. But darling, I tell you I never saw her before! Don't you believe me?

ALICE *(soothingly)*. Of course, dear. *(heading for the dining room)* Only I hope there won't be any more of them.

*She's gone, but the implication in her words leaves* FARLL *staggered. Stunned by the suggestion, he sits down heavily.*

FARLL. Great Scot! . . . So do I!

*Fade out.*

*Fade in.*

*Ext. House—Night*

*It is cheerfully lighted. Superimposed is a title*

BUT IN 1907

*Dissolve to:*

*Sitting Room—Night*

*It is perhaps some months later.* FARLL, *in his dressing gown, sits in the comfortable chair, pipe in mouth, coffee on the table at his side (they have eaten supper at the round table in the sitting room), reading his paper, a picture of comfort.* ALICE *is clearing the table.*

FARLL. More trouble in Ireland.

ALICE *(going out)*. If you ask my opinion, the Irish are a bit difficult to get along with.

FARLL *(turning a page)*. Ever since I was a small boy, without one hair on my face, I have been reading about more trouble in Ireland.

*Entering, drying her hands on her apron,* ALICE *gets a letter which has been standing on the mantelpiece.*

FARLL. And when I am an old man, broken down with sin and a petrified liver . . .

ALICE. I wish you'd look at this, Henry. *(giving him the letter)* It came this morning, but it's business and of course I can't be bothered with that sort of thing in the morning.

FARLL. Did you put sugar in my coffee?

ALICE. Yes, you forgot to stir it. Let me.

*After looking at the envelope warily, for he had no sense of business whatever, he tears it open.*

FARLL. Cahoon's Brewery Company, eh?

ALICE. That's where I have my money.

*As he reads it . . .*

*Insert—Letter*

*The letterhead is Cahoon's Brewery Company, Ltd., with a proper London address.*

Dear Shareholder:

Owing to a lamentable temperance wave which has been sweeping the country, the Board of Governors of Cahoon's Brewery Company, Ltd., decided at its annual meeting yesterday not to declare its customary dividend on Ordinary Shares.

Respectfully yours,

H. Y. Walker,
Chairman

*Two Shot*

ALICE. What are they up to now?

FARLL. What it means in simple words—*(clearing his throat)*—is that they aren't declaring a dividend this year.

ALICE. No dividend! Oh, but that's quite out of the question! I *have* to have my dividend—and by May, too.

FARLL *(vaguely)*. Well, that's what it says, anyway.

ALICE *(sitting down in dismay)*. Oh, but Henry, this is terrible.

FARLL (irritably). Now how on earth could a brewery have financial trouble? Look at the beer that people drink—buckets of it! I must have put away several hundred thousand gallons of it myself!

ALICE (worriedly). That's what father always said. "Put your faith in an Englishman's thirst," he said; "it is gold in the bank." Everything we had was in brewery shares.

FARLL (hopefully). Well, after all, there's still my two pounds a week.

ALICE. Bless your heart, darling— but I need more than that. It's the payment on the house—and it's due in May. (rising determinedly) But I'm simply not going to worry about it now. I've no patience with worrying. When the time comes . . . (stacking dishes) I said I'd make pastry after supper and I will. See if I don't!

FARLL (vaguely). That's the spirit, old girl!

*She goes out and* FARLL, *relieved to get away from a disturbing subject, goes back at his paper. But only for a moment. Troubled in spite of himself, he lowers it again and ponders. Then he rises, carrying the paper, and goes into the kitchen.*

*Kitchen*

ALICE *is busy about the kitchen table as he enters.*

FARLL. What did you mean about payment on the house?

ALICE. Go on back and read your paper. You don't see *me* worrying, do you?

FARLL. But when did you say it was due?

ALICE. Not for a month yet.

FARLL (relieved). Oh. I was afraid it was soon.

*He shuffles back to the sitting room as . . .*

*Dissolve to:*

*Bedroom*

*Later that evening* ALICE *is already in bed while* FARLL, *dressing gown over his nightshirt, sits staring bleakly into the fire.*

ALICE. Don't you think it's time to shut the windows and come to bed?

FARLL. But about this payment . . .

ALICE. Yes?

FARLL. If we can't meet it, does that mean we'll have to get out of this house?

ALICE. There are other houses, Henry.

FARLL. Not for me! This is the house I like. This is the house I'm happy in. I don't want to change.

ALICE (sleepily). Well . . . it's a month yet. Perhaps something will happen. It usually does.

FARLL (after a pause). There's a way, you know, that I could earn some money.

ALICE (sitting up). If you think I'll consider your taking another situation, you're greatly mistaken, let me tell you right now.

FARLL (puzzled). Situation?

ALICE. I don't want you in service again.

FARLL. No, there's another way— but it involves a certain measure of risk.

ALICE. Nothing crooked, Henry!

FARRL. I was thinking of . . . painting.

ALICE. No, no, darling. You're much too old to be climbing up and down ladders. I'd never have a moment's peace.

FARLL. Not houses. Pictures.

ALICE (after a pause). Come on to bed, dear. You're getting tired.

*She lies back down again. Sighing, he rises and turns off the gaslight.*

ALICE. Don't forget the windows.

*He closes the windows and then crosses to the bed. Sitting on the side, he takes off his slippers.*

FARLL. I don't want to leave this house, Alice. I like it. I don't want to change.

*Dissolve to:*

*Kitchen—Day*

*It is the next morning, a glorious sunny morning, and* ALICE *is humming about the stove as* FARLL *sits moodily stirring his coffee. It was a good breakfast but the depression of the night before still weighs heavily on him.*

FARLL *(finally)*. Alice.

ALICE. More coffee?

FARLL. Not now, thank you. Last night I told you I was thinking of painting again.

ALICE. Now, dear . . .

FARLL. No, let *me* talk, please. There's something I've got to tell you—a certain explanation. Will you sit down? *(she sits)* The truth of the matter is that my name isn't Henry Leek.

ALICE *(calmly)*. Oh, isn't it? . . . But what does it matter? *(smiling)* As long as you haven't committed a murder or anything.

FARLL. My real name is Priam Farll.

ALICE. Farll? *(puzzled)* Wasn't that your gentleman's name?

FARLL. That's what I want to explain. You see, it was my valet who sent you the photograph. His name was Henry Leek. He's dead now.

ALICE. I don't understand.

FARLL *(gently)*. It's really quite simple. It was Leek who fell ill and died. But the doctor made a mistake—and I didn't correct him because—well, there were all sorts of reasons. One, I didn't want to be Priam Farll any more.

*Closeup—*ALICE

*Her face shows what she is thinking, and she is thinking, Oh my God, his poor mind is beginning to slip!*

FARLL'S VOICE *(rather angrily)*. In fact, I was downright sick of being Priam Farll.

*Two Shot*

FARLL. I tell you this so you will understand that when I say I can paint and make a little money I am not being altogether foolish.

ALICE. Then it's this Henry Leek that's buried in Westminster Abbey, instead of you.

FARLL. That is the somewhat quaint fact.

ALICE *(after a while)*. And you've never said a word about this to anybody.

FARLL. Not to anybody who would listen.

*She looks at him soberly, with genuine concern, for a long time before speaking.*

ALICE. You know what?

FARLL. What?

ALICE. You've been worrying too much.

FARLL. Worrying! Of *course* I've been worrying! I've been *happy* in this house!

ALICE. You've been exciting yourself.

FARLL. Great heavens, woman, are you implying . . .

*He refuses to say the implication, but he stares at her indignantly. Leaning forward, she gently takes one of his hands.*

ALICE. Henry love, it was sweet of you to tell me about it—and I quite understand—the whole thing. But you know what I would do if I were you?

FARLL. I am not a looney, if that's what's in your mind!

ALICE. If I were you I would never again mention any of this to anybody. I'd just forget it.

FARLL. But it's the truth!

*She has now begun to remove the remainder of the breakfast dishes.*

ALICE. And above all, you should try to stop worrying.

FARLL. But blast it all, Alice!

*As she puts the dirty dishes in the sink, her back to* FARLL . . .

*Close Shot*—ALICE

*Her eyes are wet with tears.*

FARLL *(on his feet)*. All right, I'll prove it to you!

ALICE *(facing him)*. Henry, I'm not questioning it. All I'm saying is that it doesn't matter.

FARLL *(taking her hand)*. No, I'm going to prove it to you. Come on. *(leading her out)* I'm going to settle this matter right now.

*Sitting Room*

*as he leads her through . . .*

FARLL. I do not intend to go through life being regarded as Foolish Phil the Village Idiot.

*Hall and Staircase*

*Leading her up the stairs . . .*

FARLL. It happens that I have incontrovertible evidence of my true identity.

*Upper Landing*

*Leading her to a door . . .*

FARLL. If you will come into the attic . . .

*Attic*

*A dormer window, open, admits adquate light to show an attic with the usual clutter of odds and ends and an* easel *holding a canvas about three feet wide and two feet high.*

FARLL *(placing her)*. Stand there.

ALICE *(as he arranges the canvas)*. I *thought* I'd been smelling paint.

FARLL *(with a gesture)*. There!

*She looks at it with genuine interest. It is a scene in Putney (after the manner of Walter Sickert) and while it is not radical in its creation, it is impressionistic enough in execution to provide some justification for* ALICE'S *inability to appreciate it.*

ALICE *(presently)*. Did you do that?

FARLL. I did. *(with an affectation of casualness)* How does it strike you?

ALICE. It's beautiful. *(simply)* What is it?

FARLL *(after a pause)*. Study it.

ALICE. Why, that's Putney Bridge, isn't it?

FARLL *(beaming)*. It is.

ALICE *(apologetically)*. On rather a peculiar day, I imagine. But it's very nice, Henry—very nice indeed. *(after a pause)* Quite nice.

FARLL *(as she starts to move closer)*. No, no, no nearer!

ALICE. Well! If you don't *want* me to see it close!

FARLL. But you're at just the right distance.

ALICE *(thoughtfully)*. You know, it's a pity you didn't put an omnibus on the bridge.

FARLL *(grimly)*. There *is* an omnibus on the bridge.

ALICE. Oh.

FARLL *(pointing)*. There.

ALICE. It's stopped, I suppose.

FARLL. Dead still.

ALICE. It's *very* nice, Henry. I suppose you learned from your—*(hastily)* Isn't that the Elk public-house down in the corner?

FARLL. It is.

ALICE. I *thought* I recognized it! And a very good likeness, too.

FARLL. Would it surprise you to know that this canvas is worth at the very least eight hundred pounds?

ALICE (*frankly*). Yes.

FARLL (*with a savage thoughtfulness*). To say *nothing* of the rumpus in Bond Street if it became known that Priam Farll was painting in a Putney attic instead of rotting in Westminster Abbey! *What* a row there'd be!

ALICE (*hands on his shoulders*). Henry darling, don't you realize that you can get *real* pictures—of lakes and even mountains—by *real* artists, for two pounds apiece, at the frame-maker's?

FARLL. *Two* pounds! Dash it, Alice, I've got fifteen *hundred* pounds for things not *nearly* as good as this!

ALICE (*her voice breaking*). Darling, I don't *want* you worrying like this! We'll get the money some way. *Please* don't worry!

FARLL (*earnestly*). Listen, Alice . . .

ALICE (*tears*). But no matter what happens, love, I'll always take care of you—no matter what . . .

*Overcome, she turns away and weeps into her apron. Baffled, he regards her grimly for a moment. Then he takes the canvas from the easel and begins to wrap it loosely in an old newspaper.*

FARLL. Get your hat and coat.

ALICE. I'll never let them take you away . . .

FARLL. Come on. (*grabbing her wrist*) I'm going to prove this thing to you if it's my last act.

*As he practically drags her toward the door . . .*

*Dissolve to:*

*Street—Day*

*It is a few minutes later. Striding along, the painting under his arm,* FARLL *is almost pulling* ALICE *as the camera pans them to enter a small store. The name of the store is* STAWLEY'S *and on the window is indicated that while its principal business is that of stationery, it also does picture-framing, contains a lending-library, and offers painting materials for sale. As* FARLL *leads* ALICE *in . . .*

*Int. Stationer's*

*The walls of* STAWLEY'S *are fairly plastered with framed pictures, the popular engravings and etchings of the period. The shop is small and crowded with the wares announced on the window, and* STAWLEY *himself is a thin, dusty man of sixty-odd. He favors them with a shopkeeper's smile as they enter.*

STAWLEY. Good-day, sir. Good-day, mum.

FARLL. Good-day. I have a painting here. (*unwrapping*) I want you tell me what you think of it.

STAWLEY (*dubiously*). Well, I can hardly claim to be an expert, sir.

FARLL. You're familiar with pictures, aren't you?

STAWLEY. Yes, sir, but—

*He stops, his eyes on the canvas that* FARLL *has set on the counter. Expert or no expert, he has sufficient knowledge of art to recognize something out of the ordinary. His manner shows that, for he studies it from the proper distance with an eye that is properly impressed, and once he turns and gives* FARLL *a long look, all the while murmuring, "Mmmmm! Mmmmmmm!" so cryptically that the bewildered* ALICE *can make little of it. But she too looks at* FARLL *with a new and startled interest, whereupon he responds with a complacent smirk. Meanwhile* STAWLEY *is driving her frantic with little bird-noises of admiration or astonishment at new little discoveries, until finally . . .*

STAWLEY. May I ask—er—where you got it?

FARLL. No.

STAWLEY (*after another long look*). *Awfully* good. Is it a copy?

FARLL. Is it?

STAWLEY. Either a copy or a very good imitation.

FARLL. Would you—er—be good enough to put a price on it?

STAWLEY. Mmmmmm—mmmm—mmm . . . (*finally*) Two pounds?

FARLL. *What!*

STAWLEY (*quickly*). Five?

*Grimly* FARLL *begins to rewrap the canvas, disdaining further discussion.*

STAWLEY. Ten, sir?

ALICE (*goggle-eyed*). Do you mean you'll give *ten pounds* for it?

FARLL. That will be all, thank you!

ALICE. But Henry!

FARLL (*taking her arm*). Come, my love.

STAWLEY. Just a minute, sir!

*He runs out from behind the counter but they are already gone,* FARLL *again pulling the reluctant* ALICE *along. As he goes out . . .*

STAWLEY—*Ext. Shot*

*Standing in the doorway, he calls after them . . .*

STAWLEY. Fifteen, sir?

*Truck Shot*—FARLL *and* ALICE

*Camera trucks back in front of them as* FARLL *strides along, his expression full of pent-up anger and indignation. Behind them in the background* STAWLEY *can be seen still standing in the doorway.*

ALICE. Fifteen *pounds*, Henry! Do you suppose he's *crazy?*

FARLL. Mad as a March—(*glaring at her*) Is it necessary for you to think of *every*one connected with the arts as *crazy!*

*Seething, he pulls her along as . . .*

*Dissolve to:*

*Attic—Night*

*It is that night, late. The scene is in almost complete blackness. The door opens softly and* ALICE *enters with a lamp. She is wearing a dressing gown over her nightdress. Softly she closes the door behind her and then she comes to the easel where the painting of Putney Bridge is again installed. For a moment she looks at it thoughtfully. Then, setting the lamp down, she draws up a chair and sits down squarely in front of the painting, folds her arms, and studies the work of art determinedly, a woman bent on understanding this goddam thing or bust. Then she cocks her head a little to the left, to see if that angle helps, and then to the right.*

*Close Shot*

*Angling slightly down at* ALICE *over the top of the canvas, to show her cover first one eye with a hand and then the other.*

*Another Angle*

*Taking the canvas in her hands, she holds it horizontal and studies it from just over the bottom edge, to see if it looks like anything from that angle. She tries other positions. Then she puts it back on the easel.*

*Close Shot*

*Again angling down over the canvas as she draws a deep breath and shakes her head slowly but firmly. By God, she can't get it! Then her eyes begin to widen as . . .*

*Reverse Angle*

*Over* ALICE'S *shoulder to show the canvas, and on it, fading in, as if in luminous paint . . . L 15.*

*Close Shot*—ALICE

*Spellbound by the vision, she looks around.*

*Pan Shot*

*Leaning carelessly against the wall on the floor are other canvasses, some finished, some unfinished, some in the clear, some overlapped. On each of them in the same luminosity . . . L 15.*

*Close Shot*—ALICE

*Dazed by the whole thing, she swallows nervously.*

ALICE. Bless my soul . . . maybe it's *me!*

*Fade out.*

*Fade in.*

*Ext. Oxford Galleries—Day*

*Superimposed is a title:*

AND SO IN 1908 . . .

*The title fades out and a carriage stops at the curb and* LADY VALE, *a stately grande dame, is assisted to alight (she walks with a stick) by a footman, who aids her into* OXFORD'S *as . . .*

*Office*

*In the same office in which we first met* MR. OXFORD, *he rises from his desk, gleaming with a smile, and goes to the door as it opens to admit* LADY VALE *and the footman.*

OXFORD. How do you do, Lady Vale. I am so pleased to see you looking so well.

LADY VALE *(sitting).* You have another Farll, I believe.

OXFORD *(with a gesture).* It arrived only yesterday.

*The gesture is for the painting framed and setting on an easel in the best position for the lady in the chair to study it to advantage.*

*Close Shot—Painting*

*It is a street scene, of an organ grinder and children dancing, and on one side is a motor-omnibus. On a metal plate on the bottom of the frame is:*

> PRIAM FARLL
> 1849–1905

LADY VALE'S VOICE. A beautiful example.

*Full Shot*

OXFORD. Observe the composition!
LADY VALE. I'll take it.
OXFORD. I congratulate you, my lady.
LADY VALE *(getting out checkbook).* How much?
OXFORD. Would you say that . . . twenty-five hundred pounds was unreasonable?
LADY VALE *(writing).* I would—but I'll pay it.

*As she writes . . .*

*Dissolve to:*

*Close Shot—Painting—Day*

*It is* FARLL'S *painting of Putney Bridge, but now framed handsomely and hung on a wall, and on the bottom of the frame is again the metal plate*—PRIAM FARLL—*1849–1905.*

*Camera pulls back or pans to show that this is the stately drawing room of* LADY VALE. *That she is a prodigious art lover can be observed from the innumerable oil paintings which cover the walls. Even now the* FOOT- MAN *has had to remove one to make place for the new* FARLL *just purchased alongside the one of Putney Bridge. An old painting sits on the floor, face to the wall, while the* FOOTMAN *stands on a stepladder adjusting the new* FARLL *evenly.* LADY VALE *is standing back judging it with her eye. Finally she nods.*

LADY VALE. That's it.

*She hobbles to a delicate, lady's desk and sits heavily at it, engaging herself with accounts and other papers. But the* FOOTMAN, *folding the ladder, remains studying the picture he has just hung, until* LADY VALE *notices this with amusement.*

LADY VALE. You like it?
FOOTMAN. Yes, mum. That's one of the new motor-omnibuses, you know, mum.
LADY VALE *(idly).* Is it?
FOOTMAN. Yes, mum, my darter, the one that married the tram conductor, she rode it the first trip, last winter.
LADY VALE *(hardly noticing).* Did she really?
FOOTMAN *(leaving).* Yes, mum—and a fair treat it was, she said, the way it smelled.

*He is almost out of the room before what he has said registers in* LADY VALE'S *mind. Then, straigtening up . . .*

LADY VALE. The first trip, did you say?
FOOTMAN. Yes, mum, larst New Year's Day. My darter rode it to Putney . . .
LADY VALE *(slowly).* You must be mistaken, surely.
FOOTMAN. Mistaken, mum?

*Puzzled, incredulous, she studies him for a moment, and then rising, she hobbles back to the painting.*

*Close Shot*—LADY VALE

*Angled to show both her face and the street scene in which children are dancing to a hurdy-gurdy near what is unmistakably a motor-omnibus. Turning . . .*

LADY VALE. This *past* New Year's Day?

FOOTMAN

FOOTMAN. January first, mum, 1908.

*Close Shot*—LADY VALE

*She looks again at the painting and then at the metal plate on the bottom of the frame as . . .*

*Dissolve to:*

OXFORD's *Office—Day*

*A day or so later,* OXFORD *sits in his desk chair, a set smile on his face, his ten finger tips tapping together nervously. Facing him with great coolness, great aloofness, stands* LADY VALE'S *solicitor,* MR. PENNINGTON, K.C. *(Alan Mowbray).*

OXFORD. Lady Vale understands, I trust, that I am prepared to return the money—to the last shilling.
PENNINGTON. It is not a question of money. Mr. Oxford. Lady Vale regards herself as the victim of a swindle so outrageous that far greater satisfaction is demanded. In the course of the past year she has paid to you a total of forty-two thousand pounds for twenty-nine paintings represented to her as the work of Priam Farll. Chemical tests of the paint and the canvas now show that these paintings . . .
OXFORD. They *are* the work of Priam Farll, Mr. Pennington. I insist on that.
PENNINGTON *(smirking).* When did Priam Farll die, may I ask, Mr. Oxford?

OXFORD. Priam Farll is not dead.

PENNINGTON *(shrewdly)*. Then why did they bury him?

OXFORD. He is not dead and he's not been buried. *(slowly)* There's been some incredible mistake . . .

PENNINGTON. In that case, of course, you will also be prepared to produce him in court if—*if*, mark you!—you can dig him up! Good day, sir.

OXFORD. Good day.

*As* PENNINGTON *marches out, pleased with what he regards as a rather neat turn of a phrase . . .*

*Close Shot—Oxford*

*The set smile which has remained on his face throughout the conversation dies away slowly into a look of deep concern as . . .*

*Dissolve to:*

*Ext. Stationer's House—Day*

*Dressed very elegantly,* MR. OXFORD *notes the address and name on the window and enters.*

*Int. Stationer's House*

*as* STAWLEY *looks up . . .*

OXFORD. I am afraid, Mr. Stawley, that I must insist upon further information regarding the paintings you've been bringing to me.

*Dissolve to:*

*Back Yard—Day*

*Now that his painting is no longer a secret from* ALICE, FARLL *is at work with palette and easel in the tiny back yard of their home (the scene of a policeman directing traffic) when* ALICE *appears from the house.*

ALICE. Henry.

FARLL *(working)*. Yes?

ALICE. There is a gentleman for you at the front door.

FARLL. What—

*He stops, for the gentleman, possible to guard against any possible refusal to receive him, has followed* ALICE *through the house and now stands in the kitchen door. It is* MR. OXFORD, *very elegantly got up for the call.*

OXFORD *(advancing)*. Have I the pleasure of addressing Mr. Henry Leek?

FARLL *(guardedly)*. Yes?

OXFORD. My card, sir.

FARLL. Darling, may I present Mr. Clive Oxford.

OXFORD. I am honored, Mrs. Leek.

ALICE. Likewise.

OXFORD *(studying the painting)*. A distinguished work, Mr. Leek—truly distinguished.

FARLL. Thank you.

OXFORD. The work of a master.

*At this,* ALICE *looks at the painting with new interest.* FARLL *watches* OXFORD.

OXFORD. Your stature continues to grow with each succeeding work.

FARLL *(surprised)*. Each succeeding work? May I ask . . .

*He stops and his eyes go to* ALICE, *who, suddenly aware that this must be in some way a consequence of whatever clandestine actions she has been up to, picks up a tray of tea things and starts back to the kitchen.* FARLL'S *eyes follow her.*

OXFORD *(as she exits into kitchen)*. I will give you two thousand pounds for it.

*From the kitchen comes the sound of a crashing tray and tea things.*

FARLL *(grimly)*. It is not for sale, thank you.

OXFORD. Three.

FARLL. It is not for sale.

OXFORD. Four.

FARLL. I have told you . . .

OXFORD. Five.

FARLL *(after a long silence)*. This is insanity, of course, but . . . under the circumstances . . . I suppose so.

OXFORD. I don't in the least regard it as insane. *(taking out his checkbook)* May I have . . .

*There is no need for him to continue, for* ALICE *is already coming from the house with pen and ink.*

OXFORD. Thank you. *(as he writes)* Have you by any chance seen the portrait of Ariosto by Titian that they've just bought for the National Gallery, Mr. Leek?

FARLL *(watching* ALICE *return to the house)*. Yes.

OXFORD. What is your opinion of it?

FARLL *(absently)*. Except that it isn't Ariosto, and it certainly isn't by Titian, it's a pretty high-class sort of thing.

OXFORD *(chuckling)*. I rather expected you'd say that. *(giving him the check)* How much more work is there to be done on this?

FARLL. I'll finish it tomorrow, I suppose.

OXFORD *(agreeably)*. There's no hurry, really, so why don't you do me the honor of visiting my gallery now. I have several pictures that I'd very much like you to see.

FARLL *(mumbling)*. I will some day.

OXFORD. Why not now? It might be very much to your advantage . . . Mr. Leek.

*There is a quiet insistence, a somehow ominous note in* OXFORD'S *polite and smiling invitation, that* FARLL *senses without knowing what to do about it. He is desperately trying to persuade himself that* OXFORD *hasn't definitely penetrated his secret, but it's only a weak hope, and he feels helpless and confused and depressed over the development.*

FARLL. All right.

OXFORD *(beaming)*. Splendid.

*As he takes* FARLL'S *arm as they start back to the house . . .*

*Kitchen*

*Angling over the stove to show* ALICE *busy over the stove as the two men pass through behind her.* FARLL *doesn't look at her and she doesn't look at him, and this tiny schism is the only object of the scene.*

OXFORD. I should especially like your opinion on a Priam Farll I picked up recently.

*They go out.* ALICE *begins to hum thoughtfully, busily, as . . .*

*Dissolve to:*

*Picture Gallery—Day*

*It is an hour or so later. This is a small room in the Oxford Gallery where the most precious paintings are hung for the most dignified and effective display. Camera is on another Putney Street scene, with the familiar metal plate at the bottom of the frame. Regarding this painting, their backs to camera, are* FARLL *and* OXFORD, *the latter with coat and hat in hand.*

OXFORD. That, in my humble opinion, is one of the finest Farlls in existence. What do you think?

FARLL. It may be.

OXFORD *(indicating other paintings)*. Vermeer . . . Delacroix . . . Gainesborough . . . What other modern could hold his own in such distinguished company!

FARLL. I don't know, I'm sure.

OXFORD. I've been offered five thousand pounds for it.

FARLL. What did you pay for it?

OXFORD. Twenty pounds. *(taking* FARLL's *arm)* Come into my office and I'll explain to you my rather peculiar difficulty. *(crossing to door)* I shouldn't like to bore you, of course . . .

FARLL. Quite the contrary, I assure you.

OXFORD *chuckles appreciatively as he opens a small door leading into his office as . . .*

OXFORD's *Office*

OXFORD. Sit here.

FARLL. Thank you.

OXFORD. Cigar?

FARLL. Thank you.

OXFORD *lights it for him and* FARLL *sits watching him, angry but helpless.*

OXFORD *(casually).* When did you paint it, Mr. Farll?

FARLL *(after a pause).* You *are* insane!

OXFORD *(smiling).* No, I don't think so. Possibly I should be—with the trouble that faces me—but I'm not.

FARLL. Trouble?

OXFORD. About a year ago a man named Stawley, a frame-maker in Putney, came to me with a picture which I recognized immediately as the work of Priam Farll.

FARLL. Was it signed?

OXFORD. Yes—but not with a name, if that's what you mean. To me, to any connoisseur, Priam Farll could not put a brush on a canvas without signing it indelibly with his genius. So of course I bought it—for twenty pounds.

FARLL *(grimly).* And how much did you get for it?

OXFORD. Under the circumstances I have no objection to telling you. I got two thousand pounds for it.

Altogether, I've bought some thirty-odd Farlls from the man, for which I have received a total of some sixty thousand pounds.

FARLL. Art, I see, is a very profitable business—for the dealer.

OXFORD. In this case it can also be quite profitable for the artist.

FARLL. What do you mean?

OXFORD. Now that I've found him, I shall be delighted to pay him his share—a matter of some thirty thousand pounds, I should say.

FARLL *(slowly).* In other words— you've been caught.

OXFORD. There is an action, yes. Lady Vale, who bought a number of the pictures, has discovered that they were painted since 1905.

FARLL. Splendid! I hope she wins!

OXFORD. This is not a time for facetiousness, Mr. Farll.

FARLL. *Leek,* if you please! Henry Wadsworth Leek!

OXFORD. Mr. Leek—Mr. Farll— whichever you choose to call yourself—you may as well understand now, that I have no intention whatever of standing idly by while the Oxford Galleries are destroyed through some fantastic error in Westminster Abbey. Whoever it was they buried there, it was *not* Priam Farll, for I have this very day seen Priam Farll painting as only Priam Farll could paint . . .

FARLL *(indignantly).* You dare question the Abbey!

OXFORD. I would question the Crown before seeing my business destroyed.

FARLL *(grimly).* And how long, may I ask, have you been under this odd delusion?

OXFORD *(shrugging).* So far as the paintings are concerned, I have *never* been under any delusions. Only, at first, I thought I was buying work done before your alleged death. Then one day about a year ago a bit of fresh paint came off on my thumb.

*He gestures the obviousness of it after that.*

FARLL. Then why didn't you make your inquiries then?

OXFORD *(the weak spot in his position exposed).* I . . . I preferred not to examine a mystery.

FARLL. Or rather, you preferred not to jeopardize those neat profits!

OXFORD *(carefully).* It was not easy to know *what* to do.

FARLL *(grinning).* Mr. Oxford, I can hardly find words to express my warm satisfaction in your misfortune. You have swindled your customer; you have swindled the frame-maker; you have swindled the artist who painted the pictures; and, worst of all, you have swindled the memory of that magnificent genius whose dust lies to-day in Valhalla. *(solemnly)* That last I can *never* forgive you.

OXFORD *(angrily).* You're not going to *deny* that you're Priam Farll!

FARLL *(softly).* To you, no. You're much too clever for me to try that. But if you think for one moment that I'm going to admit it to anyone else—if you think I'm going to sacrifice my peace and happiness simply to save your wretched hide and bankbook, you're mistaken. For, in my opinion, sir, you're a thorough-going, double-dyed, triple-plated rogue and scoundrel, and I wouldn't lift one little finger to save you from frying in perdition for the remainder of eternity. Good day, sir! *(he starts out)*

OXFORD *(angrily).* Mr. Farll!

FARLL *(flaring).* Leek, sir—Leek! Henry Greenleaf *Leek!*

*He slams the door after him, leaving* OXFORD *glaring desperately, as . . .*

*Dissolve to:*

*Sitting Room—Night*

ALICE, *crocheting placidly by the fire, looks up at the sound of the front door opening and closing. She rises as* FARLL *enters and helps him out of his coat. As she puts his coat and hat away,* FARLL *sinks into a chair and stares into the fire. Studying him gravely,* ALICE *draws up a straight chair and sits near him.*

ALICE. I'm very sorry, Priam.

FARLL *(chuckling in spite of himself).* You thought I was daft, didn't you.

ALICE *(gently).* I thought you weren't quite well.

*Reaching out, he takes her hand affectionately.*

ALICE. I shouldn't have done it, I suppose—but there were those pictures—fifteen pounds apiece—and you did nothing with them—just finished them—and threw them in cupboards—never looked at them again.

FARLL. I never thought of it. *(looking at her reproachfully)* I thought you were selling the brewery shares to meet the payments.

ALICE *(smiling gently).* I didn't want you worrying about money.

FARLL *(squeezing her hand).* You're a dear girl.

ALICE. What's going to become of it?

FARLL *(firmly). Nothing!* He's going to be sued and in all probability will go to prison, I hope. But I told him flatly I'd have nothing to do with it. *(angrily)* Do you realize that he was making *ten thousand per cent* profit on my work? Ten thousand per cent! By George, I had no idea percentages *ran* that high!

ALICE *(after studying him thoughtfully).* I should have known. You've

always been so much the gentleman—
so useless.

*Sighing, she rises and goes into the
kitchen.*

FARLL *(seething)*. I wouldn't throw
a pot of tea on him if he were on fire
at my feet.

*Kitchen*

*Shot is on* ALICE. *She is seated,
very erect and thoughtful in a straight
chair, her hands folded, her eyes
filled with grave reflections.*

FARLL *(at the door)*. Alice. *(she
looks)* There's no reason for this to
make any difference, of course.

ALICE. No?

FARLL *(coming in)*. Why should it?

ALICE. I don't know. I'm not sure. I
wish I could be.

FARLL. What do you mean?

ALICE. It's something to wonder
about, you know. As Mrs. Henry
Leek . . . it's been very cozy. The
way I am, the way we've lived, in
Putney, we've been quite happy, I
believe. I can't think of any other
woman who might have suited you
better.

FARLL. There'll be no change, dear.

ALICE. There's bound to be, Henry—or rather Priam, I should say.

FARLL. But I've told you I have no
intention whatever of getting mixed
up in this business.

ALICE *(thoughtfully)*. As Mrs.
Priam Farll . . . the wife of a great
gentleman . . . so great that he could
be buried in Westminster Abbey . . . I
don't know. I don't know *how* I'd be.
But not much, I expect. Like I
couldn't be a duchess, or a bareback
rider. *(after a pause)* I can't feel that
I'd be much use to you anymore.

FARLL. This is the most ridiculous
rot you've ever uttered.

ALICE *(shaking her head)*. I might
be uncomfortable, or too ignorant,
and I couldn't stand that. I'd hate to
lose you, because it's been so nice
together, but it'd do no good if either
of us was unhappy about it. But—
*(rising)*—I'm not going to worry
about it now.

FARLL *(excitedly)*. We could go
away to Borneo, some place like that!

ALICE *(at stove)*. No, Henry. Putney's my home. *(smiling)* Besides,
I'm afraid I'm a bit too old to think of
living in a tree.

FARLL. Very well, we'll stay right
here, in Putney!

ALICE *(looking at him fondly)*. You
do want that, don't you?

FARLL. More than anything else on
earth. This is where I was happy at
last. This is where I want to live and
die. This is my home too now.

ALICE. Well, we'll see. Meanwhile—*(busy)*—there's one thing
we've got to do right away.

FARLL. What's that?

ALICE. We've got to get you a new
suit—for the trial.

FARLL. Trial! *(angrily)* Oh, he'll
never get me in *that* mess! I told him
so—flatly!

ALICE. Oh, but they will, dear.
They can, you know, with what they
call a—a sub-something. I forget its
name, but . . .

*She stops, for* FARLL, *after a gasp
of horror, has run out of the kitchen.
Putting down whatever she has in her
hands, she starts after him as . . .*

*Hall*

FARLL *is locking the door and pulling down the shades as she enters
staring.*

ALICE. What on earth!

FARLL. We're getting out of here!

ALICE. But you can't . . .

FARLL (*pulling her up the stairs*). We'll catch a boat! We'll pack immediately . . .

*As they disappear up the stairs . . .*

*Dissolve to:*

*Ext. House—Night*

*It is an hour or so later. Coming out of the door,* ALICE *and* FARLL *are both dressed for traveling and they have a full complement of luggage for a long trip. As* FARLL *is locking the door . . .*

ALICE. Did you draw the blinds in the bedroom?

FARLL. I don't remember. It doesn't matter . . .

ALICE. I'd better go back and see . .

*His nerves taut,* FARLL *forces her onto the sidewalk.*

FARLL. Upon my soul, Alice, if you don't stop lagging—(*at the sidewalk*) Cab! Cabby! (*waving frantically*) Cabby!

*Down the street*

*A cab approaches at a leisurely trot. As it nears* ALICE *and* FARLL, *he scoops up all the luggage to get in.*

FARLL. Open it.

*Whereupon* ALICE *opens the cab and a neat, precise little* MAN *steps out and looks up at the house.*

MAN. 33?

FARLL (*trying to push by him*). Excuse me, please.

MAN (*peering at him*). Mr. Farll?

FARLL. Yes, yes, what is it?

MAN (*from his pocket*). A subpoena, sir. In re Lady Sybil Vale versus Mr. Clive Oxford, sir. Witness, sir. Thank you, sir. Goodnight, sir. (*stepping back in cab*) Drive on, cabby!

*The cab trots on off, leaving* FARLL *with the subpoena thrust out of his coat-front, where the man stuck it because* FARLL'S *hands were full.*

ALICE (*placidly*). We'll go around to the Bon-Ton the first thing tomorrow morning. There's a brown herringbone in the window that ought to make up into something very nice.

*Dissolve to:*

*Insert—Poster—Day*

*In the greatest letters possible on the screen:*

HORRIBLE
SCANDAL
VALET IN VALHALLA!

*Dissolve to:*

*Close Shot—Tomb in Westminster Abbey*

*Carved in the marble is:*
PRIAM FARLL
1849–1905

*We have just time enough to read it before a frame of rough boards is let down over it, and on the structure is a sign:*

CLOSED
FOR REPAIRS

*Dissolve to:*

*Montage of Headlines*
SHAME!
OUTRAGE!
IMPOSTER!

*Dissolve to:*

*Hallway—Day*

*This is the day of the trial. Two-shot of* ALICE *and* FARLL *just inside the front door, both hatted and coated to leave. Like any wife,* ALICE *is tightening* FARLL'S *tie as the final touch.*

ALICE. Now! You look very nice.

FARLL (*as she opens door*). I feel like . . .

*Ext. House*

*The house is besieged by* PRESSMEN *and photographers and they close in as* ALICE *convoys* FARLL, *cringing with fear and helpless anger, down the steps to the cab waiting at the curb. Twenty or thirty loafers and loungers move nearer to get better sights of* FARLL *and his lady. The* PRESSMEN'S *shouts and questions overlap.*

PRESSMEN. I say, Mr. Farll—Mr. Leek, The Express—Is it true that you killed the valet—This way, Mr. Farll—Mr. Leek, please . . .

*And ad libs as* ALICE, *holding his arm, moves him firmly but surely through the crowd to the cab, always smiling pleasantly. As the cab whips off* . . .

*Dissolve to:*

*Corridor Outside Courtroom—Day*

*This is possibly a half-hour later. We are shooting on the door to the courtroom. The corridor is fairly crowded.* MR. PENNINGTON, *in court wig, etc., stands with* LADY VALE.

PENNINGTON (*looking off*). Here he comes now.

LADY VALE *turns and looks with interest as the miserable* FARLL *and the imperturbable* ALICE *enter to go into the courtroom.*

PENNINGTON. You *are* the fellow, aren't you?

FARLL (*glaring*). Mr. Farll, to you!

LADY VALE (*thoughtfully*). Handsome, isn't he!

*But* FARLL *and* ALICE *have entered the courtroom.*

*Courtroom*

*Shot is on* OXFORD *and his solicitor,* MR. CREPITUDE, *smiling ingratiatingly as* ALICE *and* FARLL *come down the aisle. The courtroom is already well filled.*

CREPITUDE. Good morning, Mr. Farll!

FARLL. But *Leek* to you!

*The smiles disappear from* OXFORD'S *and* CREPITUDE'S *faces as* ALICE *and* FARLL *move past them.*

ALICE *and* FARLL

*As they take their seats together in one of the front rows* . . .

ALICE (*quietly*). Now Henry, you *must* be polite.

FARLL (*loudly*). I hate them all and I haven't the slightest intention in the world of being polite.

*She sighs as* . . .

*Dissolve to:*

*Full Shot—Courtroom—Day*

*There has been a proper lapse of time. The trial is opening. The judge is on his bench, the jury in the box, and* PENNINGTON *is on his feet to outline the case for the plaintiff,* LADY VALE, *who sits near him always, to keep the alignment of forces properly identifiable.*

PENNINGTON. This is a civil action—brought by Lady Vale—to recover the sum of 42,000 pounds—paid by her to Mr. Clive Oxford—for 29 paintings fraudulently represented to her as the work of the late Priam Farll . . .

ALICE *and* FARLL

ALICE *serene,* FARLL *glaring off as* . . .

PENNINGTON'S VOICE. . . .whose remains lie today in the hallowed halls of Westminister Abbey . . .

JURY

PENNINGTON'S VOICE. . . . but the possible consequences involved here are so monstrous that I shudder to contemplate them.

PENNINGTON

*with* LADY VALE *seated close at his side.*

PENNINGTON *(oratorically).* Does an impostor, a valet, a servant, rest today in the sacred precincts of the British Valhalla? *That* is the contention of the defendant! What *they* would have you believe, my lord and gentlemen, is that Priam Farll . . .

OXFORD *and* CREPITUDE

*seated at a counsel table listening.*

PENNINGTON'S VOICE. . . . far from dead, lives today in this very court . . .

JURY

*All heads turn to look off at* FARLL.

PENNINGTON'S VOICE. . . . in the person of a certain mysterious bearded fellow . . .

FARLL

*baring his teeth back at the jury as* . . .

PENNINGTON'S VOICE. . . . whom it will be my pleasure to unmask here as . . .

PENNINGTON

*glaring off at* FARLL.

PENNINGTON. . . . a charlatan, a rogue, a swindler, and a grave-robber!

FARLL

*He half rises, but* ALICE *catches his arm firmly.*

PENNINGTON. But first we'll have the experts on art.

*As he faces the crowd* . . .

*Full Shot*

PENNINGTON. Will the experts for the plaintiff please stand.

*Exactly one-half of the people in the court rise to their feet.*

CREPITUDE *(rising).* With your permission, my lord—*(facing the crowd)* Will the experts for the defendant please stand.

*The plaintiff's army of experts sit down as with mathematical precision the other half of the people in the room stand.*

JUDGE *(puzzled).* Is there anyone in the court who is *not* an expert?

*The other experts sit down simultaneously and* ALICE *rises alone, to stand smiling agreeably as* . . .

*Dissolve to:*

*Witness Box—Day*

*After a lapse of time, the* 2ND CRITIC, *the same introduced in Scene 39, is testifying excitedly.*

2ND CRITIC. The purples alone—the strongest purples known to this generation . . .

*As he glares off* . . .

*Close Shot*—1ST CRITIC

*Seated among the spectators, he snorts with indignation as* . . .

*Witness Box*

2ND CRITIC *(continuing).* . . . prove these works—*(gesturing toward a display of canvases)*—to be from the hand of the master himself—Priam Farll!

*As he glares off again* . . .

*Dissolve to:*

*Another Angle—Witness Box*

*The* 1ST CRITIC *is now in the box, angry and glaring off at you-know-whom.*

1ST CRITIC. These paintings—*(indicating)*—are obviously the work of a clumsy, stupid amateur. As for their so-called purples, they're not even purple!—they're lavender!

2ND CRITIC

*Jumping to his feet angrily . . .*

2ND CRITIC. That's a lie! They are so purple!

*Witness Box*

1ST CRITIC *(shouting)*. They're lavender!

FARLL

*On his feet angrily . . .*

FARLL. They're purple!

*The banging of the judge's gavel, the protests of attorneys, the rising excitement of the spectators and witnesses as . . .*

*Dissolve to:*

*Witness Box—Day*

*After a lapse of time,* DR. CASWELL *stands in the witness box with* PENNINGTON *doing the examination.*

DOCTOR. And then I said to him, 'I take it, of course, that you were Mr. Farll's valet.'

PENNINGTON. And what did he answer to that?

DOCTOR. He said, 'Yes, sir, I was.'

PENNINGTON *(looking off)*. And is this the man to whom you spoke?

FARLL

*He looks back stonily.*

*Witness Box*

DOCTOR. Yes, sir, that's the man.

*Dissolve to:*

ALICE *in Witness Box—Day*

*Another time lapse.* PENNINGTON *is examining.*

PENNINGTON. Now, how did you meet your husband, madam?

ALICE *(pleasantly)*. Through a matrimonial agency.

PENNINGTON. Who first had recourse to this agency?

ALICE. I did.

PENNINGTON. And what was your object?

ALICE *(amused)*. What do people *usually* go to matrimonial agencies for?

PENNINGTON *(sharply)*. You're not here to *ask* the questions, madam—but to *answer* them.

ALICE *(with a good-natured shrug)*. I simply thought you should have known that. *(distinctly)* I went to a matrimonial agency because I wanted a husband. *(amiably)* How's that?

PENNINGTON. Do you think that appealing to a matrimonial agency is quite a nice thing to do?

ALICE *(sharply)*. What do you mean by nice?

PENNINGTON. Womanly, if you prefer.

ALICE *(after a pause)*. And do you think that asking a rude and unnecessary question like that is quite the gentlemanly thing to do?

PENNINGTON *(angrily)*. Madam, I have reminded you . . .

*But the laughter in the courtroom drowns out his protest as . . .*

FARLL

*Beaming, he is applauding with his hands heartily.*

ALICE *in the Box*

PENNINGTON. Under what name did this man write to you?

ALICE. Leek.

PENNINGTON. Under what name did he marry you?

ALICE. Leek.

PENNINGTON. Under what name have you lived with him since that marriage?

ALICE. Leek.

PENNINGTON *(triumphantly)*. Then in your opinion what *is* his name?

ALICE. I can't tell you.

PENNINGTON. You don't know?

ALICE *(amiably)*. Oh, certainly, I know.

PENNINGTON. But you refuse to say?

ALICE. That's it.

PENNINGTON. My lord, will you instruct this witness to answer the question?

JUDGE. May I ask, madam, why you refuse to answer?

ALICE *(after thinking)*. Politeness, I should say.

JUDGE. I'm afraid I don't understand.

ALICE. I feel, my lord, that it would be a bit impudent of me to say who my husband is, when the whole object of this trial is to decide that for me.

*As she smiles agreeably . . .*

*Dissolve to:*

DUNCAN FARLL *in the Box—Day*

*Another lapse of time.* PENNINGTON *still examining for the plaintiff.*

PENNINGTON. Then you definitely recognized the man in the casket, the man who was interred in Westminster Abbey, as your cousin.

DUNCAN. Definitely.

*With a smirking bow to* CREPITUDE, PENNINGTON *sits down and* CREPITUDE *cross-examines.*

CREPITUDE. You were not on especially good terms with your cousin, were you, Mr. Farll?

DUNCAN. We had one slight tiff, yes.

CREPITUDE. How long did it last?

DUNCAN. About forty-five years, I believe.

CREPITUDE. Do you remember the occasion for this little disagreement?

DUNCAN. As rather small boys, we had a fight over a plum-cake.

CREPITUDE *(with heavy rumor)*. And what was the result of this sanguinary encounter, Mr. Farll?

DUNCAN. He loosened one of my teeth.

CREPITUDE. And what did you do to him?

DUNCAN *(to the JUDGE)*. If you will pardon me, my lord—*(modestly)*—I tore off some of his clothes.

CREPITUDE *(skeptically)*. You remember a thing like that after forty-five years?

DUNCAN. I remember it *very* well. I remember . . .

*He stops, closing his lips firmly.*

CREPITUDE. You remember what, Mr. Farll?

DUNCAN. I'm not sure that I care to say it in mixed company.

CREPITUDE. Suppose you whisper it to me.

DUNCAN. Thank you.

*Bending down, he whispers in* CREPITUDE'S *ear.* CREPITUDE *walks over and whispers in* PENNINGTON'S *ear.* PENNINGTON *rises and they both go to the judge and whisper to him. The* JUDGE *looks over at the witness.*

JUDGE. Where *were* the moles?

DUNCAN. Right here. Two of them.

*His eyes drop modestly as he touches his left collar bone . . .*

CREPITUDE. On the left collar bone.

DUNCAN. Approximately.

CREPITUDE *(returning to box)*. Were they close together?

DUNCAN *(measuring with his fingers)*. About so far, as I recall.

CREPITUDE. Now as you remember it, was there anything in any way distinctive about these moles?

DUNCAN. No. Just moles, I should say. Just plain everyday moles.

CREPITUDE. Was either of them hirsute?

DUNCAN. Pardon?

CREPITUDE *(indicating)*. Do you see the gentleman whom the defendant in this case offers as Priam Farll?

DUNCAN *(looking off)*. Yes.

FARLL

*He regards* DUNCAN *(off) without expression.*

CREPITUDE'S VOICE. He is hirsute.

DUNCAN *in Box*

DUNCAN *(puzzled)*. You mean crazy?

CREPITUDE *(angrily)*. No, hairy. Hirsute means hairy. Were these moles hairy?

DUNCAN. Oh, no, these moles were—er—*(rattled)*—oh, quite clean-shaven!

*Dissolve to:*

*Insert—Poster—Night*
THE TRUE FARLL
HAS MOLES
SENSATION IN COURT!

*Dissolve to:*

*Newspaper Head*
FARLL'S MOLES
UNDER SHARP SCRUTINY

*Dissolve to:*

*Corridor Outside Courtroom—Day*

*A mob of excited women are trying to enter the door (or doors) being closed by the attendants. In the jabber of voices is heard . . .*

VOICE. He's taking the stand! I saw him!

FARLL *in Witness Box*

*He is taking the witnesses' oath and kissing the Bible, this business to be checked for accuracy.*

FARLL. I do.

CREPITUDE. Will you give the court your name?

FARLL. Priam Farll.

CREPITUDE. You're sure it's not Henry Leek?

FARLL. Very well, it's Henry Leek.

CREPITUDE. But which *is* it?

FARLL. Either.

CREPITUDE. Well, what are you known as?

FARLL. Both.

CREPITUDE *looks at the* JUDGE, *seeking some judicial assistance in the situation.*

JUDGE. Mr. Leek.

FARLL. Farll is the correct name, my lord.

JUDGE. Very well, Mr. Farll. Aren't you interested in the just and equitable solution of this action?

FARLL. I can't honestly say that I am, my lord.

JUDGE. But you're under oath!

FARLL. I realize that, my lord, and if I so much as hinted that I cared a tuppence what happened to either of these miserable money-changers, I should be guilty of the most outrageous perjury.

ALICE *(rising)*. Henry.

FARLL *(quietly)*. Very well, my dear. *(to* CREPITUDE*)* You may continue if you wish.

*As* ALICE *sits again . . .*

*Dissolve to:*

*Another Angle—Day*

*After a time lapse,* PENNINGTON *is now examining the witness.*

PENNINGTON. Now! *(to* FARLL*)* Mr. Duncan Farll has testified that as a small boy he fought with his cousin Priam. *(ironically)* You would of course remember that.

FARLL. I fought him many times and defeated him on each and every occasion.

PENNINGTON. During one of these battles he observed that Priam Farll had two small moles on his body. *(softly)* Have you any such moles, Mr. Leek?

FARLL *(coldly).* I have.

PENNINGTON *(surprised).* You have!

FARLL. I have.

*There is a rustle of excitement in the court.* OXFORD *and* CREPITUDE *beam. The* JUDGE *is sharply interested.* PENNINGTON *is taken a bit aback but smiles evenly.*

PENNINGTON. Where?

FARLL *(touching his collarbone).* Here.

*Nervous now, because it looks as if he'd got himself into a situation fatal to his case,* PENNINGTON *hesitates.*

CREPITUDE *(from his seat).* Go ahead! Ask him!

PENNINGTON. Er—*(trying sarcasm)*—then of course you will be good enough to show your moles to the court.

FARLL. No, I will not.

PENNINGTON *(startled).* What!

FARLL. I said, no, I will not.

PENNINGTON. You have the moles but you refuse to show them.

FARLL. Precisely.

PENNINGTON *(drawing a breath of relief).* You understand, of course, that the jury will draw its own conclusion on such a statement.

FARLL. Naturally.

CREPITUDE *(rising worriedly).* Perhaps you would prefer to show them just to Mr. Pennington and myself.

FARLL. No, I would not prefer to do that either.

*He sits erect and bland, whereupon* PENNINGTON *and* CREPITUDE *converge simultaneously on the bench and there is a whispering huddle. Meanwhile the courtroom buzzes with excitement and* FARLL *sweeps the room with a look of challenge for any and all. Presently . . .*

JUDGE. Mr. Farll. *(*FARLL *looks)* Don't you think that just the four of us might retire to my private room . . .

FARLL. No, my lord—but thank you.

*The three heads go again into a baffled, whispering huddle.* FARLL *maintains his attitude. Once* PENNINGTON *looks over at him, starts to say something, sees the futility of whatever the idea might have been, and returns to the huddle. Finally . . .*

CREPITUDE. Couldn't you just pull your collar down a bit?

FARLL. Not an inch.

JUDGE. May I ask, Mr. Farll, why you assume this obstinate attitude?

FARLL. Because, my lord, I have testified under oath that my body is afflicted with the moles as described. That, I believe, should be sufficient, since no sane man would claim moles if he didn't have them.

JUDGE. But under the circumstances . . .

FARLL. I'm sorry, my lord, but I believe that I am well within my legal rights in protesting any further effort on the part of this court to compel me to disrobe either in whole or in part.

JUDGE. The court promises you every consideration for your private sensibilities . . .

FARLL. Pardon me, my lord, but it happens in this particular instance that the moles are situated in a relatively decorous precinct of my anatomy. But suppose they were not so favorably located. Would I still be importuned to uncloth myself publicly if the moles were, say . . .

JUDGE *(hastily)*. Excuse me, please! *(loudly)* The court is adjourned until the same hour tomorrow morning!

*Dissolve to:*

*Insert—Newspaper Bill—Night*
"NEVER!"
CRIES FARLL
REFUSING TO BARE
MYSTERY MOLES

*Dissolve to:*

*Law Library—Night*

*The scene is a tableau of musty academic research.* CREPITUDE, OXFORD, *and two or three elderly professorial looking researchers have been burning the midnight oil. A table is the center of the scene, piled high with formidable tomes, and the murky background is shelf upon shelf of other thick law books. Weary and disheveled,* CREPITUDE *closes what must be the hundredth volume he has studied this night.*

CREPITUDE. Well, I'm afraid he's right. Under the common law there is no provision whatever for removing a witness's collar against his will.

*As he slumps gloomily in his chair* . . .

*Dissolve to:*

*Montage of Headlines*

*Dissolving rapidly from one to the other:*

TWO TO ONE, NO MOLES—
LLOYDS OF LONDON
FARLL'S MOLES

DEBATED IN COMMONS
SPECIAL ARTICLE ON MOLES
BY EMINENT MOLE EXPERT
AMERICAN CLAIMS RECORD
ONE HUNDRED AND FIVE MOLES
MOLE FANCIERS STORM
COURT FOR TRIAL CLIMAX

*Dissolve to:*

*Corridor Outside Courtroom—Day*

*It is the next morning. The corridor is packed as* FARLL *and* ALICE *shoulder their way to the door. Cries of* . . .

VOICES. Don't show 'em, guv'nor! Steady, old boy! Keep your collar on, guv'nor! Aw, you got no moles!

*It is a good-natured crowd, as amused as they would be over such a situation, but* FARLL *and* ALICE *are in no mood for good-humor or facetiousness. But as they reach the door one bolder soul reaches forward and gets two fingers in* FARLL'S *collar and pulls, but* FARLL *has taken the precaution of encircling his neck with a good stout linen collar, about as high as collars were made, and there are shouts and laughter as* ALICE *turns sharply and brings her umbrella down with a crash on the bold soul's head. This delights the crowd, most of whom are in* FARLL'S *favor. The bold soul holds his head as* FARLL *and* ALICE *enter the courtroom.*

FARLL *and* ALICE

*They come down the aisle and take their seats. They speak to each other sotto voce.*

FARLL. It's no use, you know.
ALICE. What can they do?
FARLL *(shrugging hopelessly).* They'll call *you* back to the stand and simply ask you if I've got 'em.
ALICE. And if I tell them?
FARLL. The case is over. It's goodbye to Putney, goodbye to peace and

quiet and happiness, goodbye to everything.

ALICE. Goodbye to me?

*Deeply moved,* FARLL *doesn't reply, but looks steadily forward. Smiling,* ALICE *pats his hand comfortingly.*

ALICE. If that's all there is to it, darling, you needn't worry another moment. I know now exactly what to do about it.

*As he looks at her somewhat startled . . .*

PENNINGTON

*A look of smug satisfaction on his face . . .*

PENNINGTON. Will Mrs. Henry Leek step into the witness box?

FARLL *and* ALICE

*Giving him another encouraging little pat,* ALICE *rises.*

ALICE *(amiably to the court in general).* The name is Farll, if you don't mind.

PENNINGTON

PENNINGTON. Not *you,* madame. The *first* Mrs. Leek—if *you* don't mind!

ALICE

*She stops in the aisle at the end of the bench, for* MRS. LEEK, *still in funereal black, comes down the aisle, chin in the air, followed by her three sons.*

*Full Shot*

*Relishing his coup,* PENNINGTON *assists* MRS. LEEK *into the box. The three sons assume a kind of fiercely protective cordon flanking the box.* CREPITUDE *and* OXFORD *look their disturbance. As the oath is administered,* ALICE *sits back down beside* FARLL.

PENNINGTON. Your name, please.

MRS. LEEK. Mrs. Henry Leek.

PENNINGTON. When were you married, Mrs. Leek?

MRS. LEEK *(producing her marriage license).* June 12, 1875.

PENNINGTON *(passing the license to the* JUDGE). And may I ask where your husband is now?

MRS. LEEK *(pointing).* Him.

PENNINGTON. You mean this man with the beard?

MRS. LEEK. He didn't have a beard when I married him. That's something new he's picked up.

PENNINGTON. But are you positive that this is the man?

MRS. LEEK. Oh, yes, that's my Henry all right.

PENNINGTON *(glancing triumphantly around).* Now, Mrs. Leek, will you please tell the court if this man, your husband, the father of these three manly sons, had any bodily disfigurements.

MRS. LEEK. Pardon?

PENNINGTON. Had he any birthmarks?

MRS. LEEK *(shaking her head solemnly).* No, sir.

PENNINGTON. Now think well, Mrs. Leek. Had he any, say, moles?

CREPITUDE *(leaping up).* I submit to your lordship that that is a leading question!

PENNINGTON. The subject has already been admitted, my lord.

CREPITUDE. That has no bearing whatever, my lord. The effort to lead the witness is obvious.

JUDGE. Perhaps you can phrase your question differently, Mr. Pennington.

PENNINGTON *(to the witness).* Did your husband—*(seeking the right words)*—have—any—distinctive . . .

MRS. LEEK. You mean moles?

PENNINGTON *(happily).* Yes, did he have any moles?

MRS. LEEK *(after long thought).* Where?

PENNINGTON. *any*where.

*For a long time* MRS. LEEK, *a conscientious woman, studies the ceiling, thinking deeply, digging down into the recesses of her memory. The court waits. Finally . . .*

MRS. LEEK. No.

PENNINGTON. Not one, is that right?

MRS. LEEK. No, sir, not one. Mr. Leek's skin was as smooth as velvet. I often said to him, Henry, your skin is like . . .

PENNINGTON. That will do, Mrs. Leek. You have answered the question quite satisfactorily.

MRS. LEEK. Is that all?

PENNINGTON. One more question. Have you ever been divorced from this man?

MRS. LEEK. No, sir.

PENNINGTON. Then legally he is still your husband, is that it?

MRS. LEEK. Yes, sir.

PENNINGTON. That's all, Mrs. Leek.

ALICE *(rising).* Just a minute, Mrs. Leek!

MRS. LEEK *stops among her boys, watching suspiciously as* ALICE *approaches the bench.*

FARLL. Alice!

JUDGE. If you have anything to say, Mrs. Farll . . .

CREPITUDE *(quickly).* Step into the witness box, please.

ALICE. Don't go, Mrs. Leek.

MRS. LEEK *and her sons exchange uncertain glances as* ALICE *smiles amiably at them.*

CREPITUDE. You have some additional testimony to give, Mrs. Farll?

ALICE. Yes. *(calling)* Priam. (FARLL *rises uncertainly)* Come here. *(as he hesitates)* Come here, dear.

PENNINGTON *(as* FARLL *comes).* My lord, I protest against such irregular . . .

ALICE *(good-naturedly).* Oh, don't be a stick!

*Stepping out of the box,* ALICE'S *hands go immediately to* FARLL'S *tie, which is an already-tied affair, and pulls it off. As she begins to unbutton his collar . . .*

FARLL. Now wait, Alice!

ALICE. Hold still, dear. *(to the* JUDGE) He's very shy, you know. *(pulling off the collar)* Now if you'll just lift your beard a bit, dear . . . *(turning him)* Can you see, Mrs. Leek? *(indicating the moles)* Smooth as velvet, eh?

MRS. LEEK *(shaken).* Are they . . . are they real?

*Dissolve to:*

*Insert—Newspaper Bill—Night*
HOAX EXPOSED
MYSTERY MOLES REVEAL
FARLL STILL ALIVE
VALET IN ABBEY

*Quick dissolve to:*

*Insert—Newspaper Bill—Day*
VALET COMING
OUT OF ABBEY

*Quick dissolve to:*

*Insert—Newspaper Bill—Night*
VALET OUT
OF ABBEY

*Dissolve to:*

*Veranda of Tropical Lodge—Day*

*Dressed as he was in the first sequence,* FARLL *is seated just about as he was then, and again painting. Now he is humming happily as he dabs the brush here and there, leaning back to contemplate his work. He presently remembers some of the words and sings them. As he does* ALICE'S *voice joins his momentarily in harmony. Then she appears at the door, drying her hands. She is dressed as she might be in Putney.*

ALICE. Luncheon dear.

FARLL. Ah! And not a moment too soon!

ALICE. How's it going?

FARLL *(entering the house)*. Well enough.

*Lingering after him,* ALICE *studies the canvas solemnly. Finally she sighs, shrugs, and turns away. By God, she still can't get it!*

*Living Room*

*This interior may be in the tropics but it is actually Putney. Here are the furniture, the drapes, the rugs and carpets, even to the motto over the fireplace:* "HOME IS WHERE THE HEART IS." *And* FARLL *is seated at the table just as innumerable times before he was in Putney. Lifting a cover from a platter . . .*

FARLL. What have we here?

ALICE *(sitting)*. Kangaroo chops. It was all the hunter had.

FARLL. Splendid, splendid! With a bit of salad they ought to go very well.

*As he begins to serve her plate . . .*

*Fade out.*

THE END

# THE STING

*Screenplay by David S. Ward*

| | |
|---|---|
| HENRY GONDORFF | Paul Newman |
| JOHNNY HOOKER | Robert Redford |
| DOYLE LONNEGAN | Robert Shaw |
| LT. WILLIAM SNYDER | Charles Durning |
| J. J. SINGLETON | Ray Walston |
| BILLIE | Eileen Brennan |

Directed by George Roy Hill
Produced by Tony Bill and Michael and Julia Phillips
Film Editor: William Reynolds
Cinematographer: Robert Surtees
Music by Marvin Hamlisch

David S. Ward's *The Sting,* which won an Academy Award in 1973 for Best Screenplay (based on factual material or material not previously published or produced), is the story of a classic swindle, or "sting," as it is called in American slang. "The Sting" is the culmination of several components: "The Set-up," "The Hook," "The Tale," "The Wire," and "The Shut-out." The whole process is executed deftly in Mr. Ward's script, with its intriguing plot development, its twists, turns, and surprises. It is a palatable dish garnished with Damon Runyonesque characters and seasoned with a little of Ring Lardner.

Interestingly enough, Mr. Ward came upon the world of confidence men—a world with a special lingo and subculture, and its members priding themselves on their skill in fleecing other thieves—when he was doing research on pickpockets for his first feature film, *Steel Yard Blues* (1972).

David S. Ward was born on October 24, 1945, in Providence, Rhode Island. Moving to California in his teens, he graduated from Sunny Hills High School in Fullerton and Pomona College in Claremont, where his major was Political Science. After getting an MFA from UCLA film school in 1970, Mr. Ward had his first screenplay, *Steel Yard Blues,* produced in 1972, followed by *The Sting* in 1973, which won him an Oscar. In 1981 he wrote the screenplay for and directed *Cannery Row,* based on the John Steinbeck novel. In 1988 he wrote the screenplay for *The Milagro Beanfield War,* and wrote and directed *Major League* in 1989.

*Fade in*

*Ext. A Slum Area of Joliet—Day*

It's a bleak, windy morning, the kind that clears the streets of all but the winos (who carry their own heaters), and the point-men for juvenile gangs. We pick up a solitary figure, JOE MOTTOLA, *coming down the street and entering what appears to be an abandoned tenement. He pauses a second to dust his white-winged alligator shoes on the back of his pants legs. Sharply dressed and surrounded by the aura of one who is making money for the first time and broadcasting it on all bands, he seems an incongruity in this part of town.*

We follow him up a flight of rickety stairs to a second floor flat. He knocks on the door, is admitted by a cautious doorman.

*Int. Numbers Spot—Day*

Suddenly we are plunged into a room of chattering, clamoring people. This is a spot for the numbers racket, a place immune from legal interference, where any sucker can bet on a number between 1 and 1000 in the hope of getting the 600 to 1 payoff that goes to those few who guess right. The bettors are queued up in several lines before a long table, where they place their bets and are given receipts in return. Others wait at a cashier's window to pick up previous earnings or to ask for credit.

MOTTOLA *moves through the crowd to a back room where betting slips are being sorted and money counted under the watchful and somewhat impatient gaze of a Supervisor, an older man named* MR. GRANGER. *The Yankee–White Sox game is heard on the radio in the background.*

MOTTOLA, *noticing that his entrance has aroused little interest, saunters over to the* PHONE GIRL *and gives her a little pinch on the cheek. The girls slaps his hand away, obviously having been through this before.*

PHONE GIRL. Beat it, Mottola.

GRANGER *glances up and exchanges a token nod with* MOTTOLA, *who plops down in a folding chair next to the radio. The phone rings.*

PHONE GIRL. 8720 . . . Yes, hold on a second. (*calling over to the Supervisor*) Mr. Granger, Chicago on the line.

GRANGER *is a little apprehensive about talking to Chicago, but takes the phone anyway.*

GRANGER. Yeh?

*Cut to*

*Int.     A     Waterfront     Processing Plant—Chicago—Day*

A flabby, bald man, COMBS, *is on the other end of the line. Visible beyond the door and interior window of his office is a large room, cluttered with tables, typewriters, clerks and adding machines. This room is the clearinghouse for every transaction of the numbers game. All the betting slips and income from the spots are brought in here and processed.*

COMBS. Granger, this is Combs. Why haven't we heard from ya? Everybody else is in.

GRANGER. We had a few problems with the Law this morning. The Mayor promised the Jaycees to get tough on the rackets again, so he shut everybody down for a couple hours to make it look good. Nothing serious, it just put us a little behind for the day.

COMBS. You been making your payoffs, haven't ya?

GRANGER. Hell yes. He does this every year. There's nothing to worry about.

COMBS. Okay, finish your count and get it up here as soon as you can. I don't wanta be here all night.

GRANGER. Believe me, the Man's gonna be real happy. Looks like we cleared over ten grand this week.

COMBS (not impressed). We cleared 22 here.

GRANGER. Well, hell, you got the whole Chicago south side. How do ya expect the eight lousy spots I've got to compete with that?

*Fade in*

*A white on black TITLE appears in the lower left hand corner of the screen:*

SEPTEMBER 15, 1936

*Fade out*

COMBS (*reading off a sheet of paper on his desk*). They did 14 grand in Evanston, 16.5 in Gary, and 20 in Cicero. Looks like you're bringing up the rear, GRANGER.

*Int. Numbers Spot—Day*

GRANGER *burns inside. One of the girls who's been sorting and counting hands him a slip of paper.*

GRANGER. I just got the count. We'll put the take on the 4:15.

COMBS. We'll be waitin'.

COMBS *hangs up, smiling to himself, proud of the way he gave* GRANGER *the needle.*

*Cut to*

*Int. Numbers Spot—Day*

GRANGER *storming over to a safe and jerking open the door.*

GRANGER (*snapping*). Mottola.

MOTTOLA *hustles out of his chair.*

GRANGER (*handing him a bundle of bills*). Take this up to the city on the 4:15. They'll be waitin' for it at the clearing house. And don't stop for no drinks. You can get a cab down the street.

MOTTOLA *takes the money and slips it into his inside coat pocket with all the dramatic flair of the true flunky. No one would ever guess that he was just an overdressed messenger boy.*

*Ext. of the Tenement Again*

MOTTOLA *emerges from a side entrance into a narrow alley. He walks briskly down to the end and turns left into a larger alleyway; this one connecting two streets. The alley is deserted save for one scruffy, slovenly dressed young* STRANGER *coming toward him from the opposite direction. The man carries a battered suitcase and seems to be in a hurry.*

*Suddenly,* MOTTOLA *hears shouting coming from somewhere behind him. He turns around to see a small, weathered looking* THIEF *come racing around the corner and down the alley toward him, frantically pursued by a gray-haired* BLACK MAN. *Limping noticeably, the* BLACK MAN *manages a few cries for help and then stumbles and falls. The* STRANGER *yells at* MOTTOLA *to cover his side of the alley, and then readies himself for the arrival of the* THIEF. MOTTOLA *just stands there, not the least interested in the exercise of justice. Just as the thief is about to run on by, the* STRANGER *throws his suitcase at the little man's legs, sending him sprawling and separating him from the wallet he's been carrying in his left hand.*

*The* STRANGER *makes a dash for the wallet and kicks it back to where* MOT-

TOLA *is standing. Almost by reflex,* MOTTOLA *picks it up. The* THIEF *scrambles to his feet and starts back toward his new-found enemy, brandishing a knife. Both the* STRANGER *and* MOTTOLA *brace themselves for an attack. The* THIEF, *realizing that there are two people to fight, begins to think better of it. He is not a young man, nor particularly strong.*

THIEF (*shaking his fist at the* STRANGER). You goddam nigger-lover. I'll get you for this someday, sucker egg.

MOTTOLA *and the* STRANGER *exchange glances of relief as the* THIEF *flees out onto the street and disappears. The* BLACK MAN, *meanwhile, has struggled to his feet and is staggering toward them. He collapses against the alley wall after a few steps. The* STRANGER *rushes over to him, followed somewhat absently by* MOTTOLA.

BLACK MAN. The wallet. You gotta go after him. He's got all the money.

STRANGER. Don't worry, we got the wallet. What happened? He get ya with the knife?

*The* STRANGER *opens the* BLACK MAN'S *coat to reveal a bloody wound at the top of his leg.*

BLACK MAN (*trying to move*). Give it to me! Please. I gotta know it's all there!

STRANGER. You just sit tight, old man. We're gonna have to get you a doctor. (*starting to leave*) I'll call a cop.

BLACK MAN. No, no cops!

MOTTOLA *has given him his wallet, which the* BLACK MAN *now opens, disclosing a fat bundle of bills tied by a rubber band.* MOTTOLA *and the* STRANGER *are amazed by the amount of money.*

STRANGER (*a little uneasy*). You wanted by the law or somethin'?

BLACK MAN. Naw, it's okay.

STRANGER. You're crazy carryin' that kinda money in this neighborhood. No wonder you got hit.

BLACK MAN (*trying to get to his feet*). Thanks. I'm obliged to ya, but I gotta get goin'. (*his leg gives way under him*)

STRANGER. You ain't goin' nowheres on that leg.

BLACK MAN. I gotta! Look, I run some slots down in West Bend for a mob here. I got a little behind on my payoffs so they figure I been holdin' out on 'em. They gave me to 4:00 to come up with the cash. I don't get it there I'm dead.

STRANGER. It don't look good, gramps, it's ten of now.

BLACK MAN. I got a hundred bucks for you and your friend if you deliver the money for me.

STRANGER (*hesitates*). I dunno. That little mug that got ya is mad enough at me already—what if he's out there waitin' around a corner with some friends.

BLACK MAN. He won't know you're carryin' it. C'mon, you gotta help me out.

STRANGER (*makes up his mind*). Sorry, pal. I'll fix you up, call you a doc, but I ain't gonna walk into a bunch of knives for ya.

BLACK MAN (*desperate to* MOTTOLA). How bout you? I'll give you the whole hundred!

STRANGER. What makes you think you can trust him? He didn't do shit.

MOTTOLA. Hey, butt out, chicken liver. I gave him back his wallet, didn't I? (*to* BLACK MAN) How far is this place?

BLACK MAN. 1811 Mason. Put it in Box 3C. You won't have no trouble. There's five thousand dollars there and here's a hundred for you.

MOTTOLA (*taking the bundle of bills from the* BLACK MAN, *plus the $100 bill*). All right. I'll make your drop for you, old man. And don't worry, you can trust me.

MOTTOLA *puts the bills in his inside coat pocket, right next to the numbers money. The* STRANGER, *who has now finished bandaging, waches him do it.*

STRANGER. If those goons out there decide to search ya, you'll never fool 'em carryin' it there.
BLACK MAN (*suddenly afraid again*). What do we do?
STRANGER. You got a bag or somethin'?
BLACK MAN. No.
STRANGER. How 'bout a handkerchief?
BLACK MAN. Here.

The STRANGER *goes into the right coat pocket and pulls out a wrinkled handkerchief.*

STRANGER. Let me have the money.

MOTTOLA *takes out the* BLACK MAN'S *five grand and hands it to the* STRANGER. *He puts it in the handkerchief.*

STRANGER. You better stick that other in here too, if you wanta keep it.
BLACK MAN (*pleading*). Just hurry, will ya. They think I been holding out on them. My wife got sick and I had to pay the bills. I wasn't holding out —I told them I'd make it up next delivery.

MOTTOLA *pulls out the numbers money and puts it in the handkerchief too. The stranger ties it all up.*

STRANGER (*demonstrating by slipping the bundle down into crotch*). All right. Carry it down in your pants here. (*pulling it back out and tucking it in* MOTTOLA'S *pants*) Ain't no hard guy in the world gonna frisk ya there.
MOTTOLA. Thanks. (*to the* BLACK MAN) So long, partner. Don't worry, everything's gonna be all right.

The BLACK MAN *nods gratefully, but there's still a trace of worry on his face.* MOTTOLA *trots off down the alley and out onto the street, glancing around cautiously for signs of trouble. He walks hurriedly down the sidewalk toward the cab stand in the distance. Suddenly the little man with the knife appears out of a doorway about 15 yards behind him.* MOTTOLA *notices him and quickens his pace, finally breaking into a dead run.*

We *follow him as he dashes headlong down the street, opening a big lead on the guy with the knife. He reaches the taxi zone. He hops in a cab and slams the door.*

*Int. Taxi—Day*

He *jumps in, closes the door, and breathes a sigh of relief.*

CABBIE. Where to?
MOTTOLA. Which way is Mason?
CABBIE. About 20 blocks south.
MOTTOLA. Okay, go north. The Joliet Station—Fast.

MOTTOLA *settles back in his seat and starts to laugh.*

CABBIE. What's so funny.
MOTTOLA. I just made the world's easiest five grand.

He *takes the bundle out from inside his pants in order to gaze upon his new-found fortune. He unties the handkerchief. It's full of toilet paper.* MOTTOLA *looks like he's just been shot.*

*Ext. Alley—Day—The* STRANGER *and* BLACK MAN

*hightailing it down the street, two newly solvent con artists on the lam. It's hard to run they're laughing so hard. The* STRANGER *chucks his suitcase into a trash can, and pulls into an alcove. The older* BLACK MAN *is puffing and out of breath.*

BLACK MAN. Hold on Johnny. Oh man, was that beautiful! Let's see it—

*The* STRANGER *gets out the envelope and starts tearing it open.*

STRANGER. I was sure he was on to us.
BLACK MAN. Naw, you had him all the way. He just. . . .

*He stops as the* STRANGER *pulls the numbers money out of the envelope. They stare at it.*

STRANGER. My God, Luther, we're millionaires.
BLACK MAN. Jesus, what a bundle. Did you know he was that loaded?
STRANGER. Hell no, I just cut into him. I woulda settled for pawning one of them shoes.

*The look at each other in delight. Then the* BLACK MAN *looks over his shoulder.*

BLACK MAN. C'mon, we gotta get out of here! We'll split it tonight. See ya later.

*The two men take off, splitting up this time.*

*Cut to*

*Titles Sequence*

*Done to a driving Chicago blues, the sequence is designed to establish somewhat the milieu of the stranger, known to friends and enemies alike as* HOOKER. *We see the following:*

*Ext. Pawnship—Day—Looking Inside*

HOOKER *is getting a radio and a garish suit out of hock. It's like seeing old friends again. All pantomime.*

*Int.* HOOKER'S *Room—Day*

*A shabby little place he rents above a cigar store. We pick him up in a jerry-built outdoor shower, which he's rigged up on the fire escape. The rinse water drips down through the landing into the grimy alley below.*

HOOKER *(singing).* 'With plenty of money and you-oo-oo. Oh baby, what I wouldn't do-oo-oo. . . .'

*On the Street Again—Night*

*jauntily carrying a magnum of champagne and some flowers, obviously on his way to see someone special.*

*In a Burlesque House*

*Carrying the flowers and champagne,* HOOKER *comes through the stage door and makes his way toward the wings where he brushes by the* FLOOR MANAGER.

MANAGER. Howdy, Hooker, you gettin' married or somethin'?
HOOKER *(irritated).* Get used to it, Ed, I'm gonna look this good from now on.

*He stands in the wings and watches his date for the evening, a 6' stripper named* CRYSTAL *do her routine.*

CRYSTAL *finishes up and comes off the stage.*

CRYSTAL *(tired).* Hi, Hooker, you gettin' married or somethin'? *(going past him)* For God's sake Ed, did you hear that out there? Corio couldn't keep time in a watch factory. How long do I gotta put up with that? *(Ed just walks away)*
HOOKER. You wanna get outa here tonight? Come into a little dough.

CRYSTAL. Can't. I got a 10 o'clock show. I need the five bucks.

HOOKER. I'll spend fifty on ya.

CRYSTAL *looks at him a second and starts to giggle. We're pretty sure she's gonna get outa here tonight.*

*Coming into a Poor Man's Gambling Joint*

*Little more than a converted brick basement, the place contains three shoddy, homemade roulette tables.* HOOKER, *accompanied now by* CRYSTAL, *nods a greeting to the doorman.* CRYSTAL *keeps up a steady stream of conversation.*

CRYSTAL. Ya know, Hooker, I think I need a new band. Hogan don't show up anymore, and Corio's such a lush he can't even keep time. You hear what he was playin' tonight? *(illustrating with appropriate moves)* I do my kick and turn and he comes in with ka chu boom boom instead of ka chu ka chu boom boom. What if some movie agent was there and I'm tryin' to dance to ka chu boom boom, huh? All those years of trainin' down the drain.

HOOKER *goes to a table where there are already several other people laying their bets for the next spin.* HOOKER *knows the wheelman, an old-timer named* JIMMY.

JIMMY *(glad to see him).* Hooker!
HOOKER. How ya doin', Jimmy.
JIMMY *(collecting bets and paying off the winners).* Ain't seen you in months, boy. Thought maybe you took a fall.
HOOKER. Naw, just a little hard times, that's all. It's all over now.
JIMMY. You gonna have a go here? *(pointing to the betting board)* How 'bout a ten spot on the line here. The 4–9 been lookin' good today. Lotsa action on 28th Street down there, too. Pay ya 34-1.

*As* JIMMY *finishes his spiel, he starts the wheel spinning and drops in the ball. Betting is allowed to continue until the ball drops from the outer ring into the center.*

HOOKER *(taking out his wallet).* Three grand on the black.

JIMMY *is stunned. The others at the table, used to dollar bets, look at* HOOKER *like he's some kind of foreign dignitary.*

JIMMY *(worried).* You sure you wanna start off that big? Bet like that could put a real dent in us.
HOOKER. I feel lucky tonight.
JIMMY. Aw, come on, Hooker, why don't you just. . . .
HOOKER. Three grand on the black, Jimmy.

JIMMY *wants to argue some more, but the ball is getting ready to drop into the center. We see* JIMMY *quickly press a hidden lever under the table with his foot. The ball falls and settles into red 27 with a motion that is not quite right. The others at the table fail to notice, but* HOOKER *is not fooled. He stares venomously at* JIMMY, *who knows that* HOOKER *is on to him.*

JIMMY. Sorry, Hooker. *(making an attempt at levity, in order to explain)* Good thing that ball came up red. Guy could get in trouble around here, losin' a bet that big.

JIMMY *reaches for* HOOKER'S *money.* HOOKER *stops him by putting his hand on it.*

HOOKER. Spin it again.

JIMMY *doesn't know what the hell to do. He gives* HOOKER *a little head motion to indicate a large and menacing thug sitting in a corner watching* them. *Suddenly,* HOOKER *understands why* JIMMY *had to cheat him, but it doesn't change his demand.*

HOOKER. Spin it anyway, Jimmy.

JIMMY *is beside himself. If he doesn't spin again,* HOOKER *may expose him. If he does spin, and loses, his management will fire him. He pleads to* HOOKER *with his eyes, but it's no use.* JIMMY *spins the wheel and reluctantly drops in the ball. This time there is no foot on the lever, and it settles into black 15.* HOOKER *stares at the ball a second and then looks up at his terrified friend.*

HOOKER. Don't worry, pal. I knew it was my night.

HOOKER *pushes the money over to* JIMMY *and walks out of the room, nodding to the thug on the way out. He's lost $3,000, but he's still working on a lucky night.*

*Cut to*

*Ext. Gambling Joint—Night*

HOOKER *and* CRYSTAL *out on the street.*

CRYSTAL *(checking her watch).* Well, looks like I can still make the 10 o'clock. Thanks for the big evening, Hooker. The next time you wanna spend 50 bucks on me, mail it.

*She walks off down the street.*

HOOKER *(going into his pocket for more money).* Hey wait a minute. *(he comes up with 30¢)* Aw, the hell with ya.

*Cut to*

*Ext. The Waterfront Processing Plant—Night*

*A late model Ford roars up and screeches to a stop in front of* the plant. *Out bursts a carefully groomed, tight-lipped young man named* GREER, *who hustles into the plant. We follow him through a maze of machinery to the service elevator and up to the third floor where we find ourselves in the clearinghouse room we saw earlier.*

*Int. Plant—Afternoon—Late*

*The working day is over now, and everyone has gone, except for* COMBS, *who sits somberly in his office.*

GREER. They found Mottola. He was drunk in a dive in Joliet. Never got on the train.

COMBS *(aggravated).* I don't wanta hear about his day, Greer. What happened to the money?

GREER. He lost it to a coupla con artists on his way outa the spot.

COMBS. How much?

GREER. Twelve thousand.

COMBS *sits in quiet thought for a second. Finally:*

COMBS. All right. Better get on the phone to New York. See what the big mick wants to do about it. *(pause)* I gotta pretty good idea, though.

*Cut to*

*Int.—An Exclusive New York Gambling Club—Late Afternoon*

*An agitated young man,* FLOYD *weaves his way through the craps and roulette tables, and hustles up a staircase to a second floor room with a drawing of a snarling tiger on the door. Below the tiger, the word "FARO" appears. There is a large man, of thuggish demeanor, guarding the door, but* FLOYD *gives him a small hand signal and walks right by him.*

*Cut to*

*Inside the Faro Room*

*In the center is a beautifully carved wooden table, on which sit a faro board and a dealing box, tended by a stone-faced Dealer, who calls the progress of the game in a continuous monotone. On his right is a bookish little man with an abacus-like device that keeps track of the cards which have already been played. On the opposite side of the table, completely absorbed in the rhythmic appearance of the cards from the dealing box, sits* DOYLE LONNEGAN. *Although his clothes and accessories are those of a wealthy man, there is a coarseness to both his movement and speech which bespeak lower class origins, for which he now has nothing but contempt.*

FLOYD *enters the room and approaches him cautiously, trying hard to make as little noise as possible.*

FLOYD. Doyle, can I see you a minute?

LONNEGAN *(not looking up from the table).* I'm busy, Floyd.

FLOYD. It's important. We had a little trouble in Chicago today. One of our runners got hit for 12 grand. A new man, Mottola.

LONNEGAN. You sure he didn't just pocket it?

FLOYD. No, we checked his story with a tipster. He was cleaned by two grifters on 47th.

LONNEGAN. They workin' for anybody?

FLOYD. I don't know. Could be. We're runnin' that down now.

LONNEGAN. All right, mark this Mottola up a little and put him on a bus. Nothin' fancy, just enough to keep him from coming back. Get some local people to take care of the grifters. *(impassively)* We gotta discourage this kinda thing.

*Cut to*

*Int. An Old Brownstone—Night*

HOOKER, *still in his suit, but looking a little worse for wear, knocks on the door of one of the apartments. A young black woman,* LOUISE, *answers the door, holding a baby.*

HOOKER *(doffing his hat).* Evenin', Louise.

LOUISE *(standing back to appraise him).* Goddamn, Johnny Hooker, if you ain't a sharper in them linens. Wasn't I knew ya so good, I'd swear you had class.

HOOKER *laughs and walks into a big hug from an older black woman,* ALVA. *Beyond her, in the dining alcove, we see the* BLACK MAN *(from here on referred to as* LUTHER COLEMAN), *playing a game of Mah-Jongg with another man whose back is to us. Elsewhere in the room, a 12-year-old boy,* LEROY, *sits in front of a big cabinet radio, listening to a crime-busters serial. Both the radio and the conversation between* LUTHER *and his friend can be heard in the background.* LOUISE *puts the baby to bed.*

OTHER MAN *(putting down a 'bamboo' Mah-Jongg tile).* 5 sticks.

COLEMAN *(not wanting it, so drawing from the pile another tile and discarding it).* North Wind.

OTHER MAN *(snapping it up).* Pung! *(discarding another tile)* 3 cracks.

COLEMAN *(not being able to use that one either, drawing from the pile again and discarding it)* Green dragon.

OTHER MAN *(drawing from pile, reacting with glee).* Another flower! Hot dog, I got all 4! And I get to draw again. How do you like that?

COLEMAN *(he doesn't like it).* Just play the game, will ya Eirie.

ALVA (*embracing him in a bear hug*). Oh Johnny, Luthur said you was somethin' to see today.

HOOKER. I don't know, Alva. I gotta get faster tyin' up that bundle. I'm still givin' 'em too much time to think.

ALVA (*going to the closet and getting her coat and hat*). Aw, boushwah, I played the Switch with slower hands than you got. Course the Up and Down Broadway was my best game. Me and Luther didn't make much on it, but it wasn't so touchy. Them marks used to beat ya up awful bad when they caught ya on the Switch. (*to the boy*) Let's go, Leroy, we'll be late for church.

LEROY (*absorbed in the radio*). Aw c'mon Ma, they're closin' in on McGurn.

ALVA. Who you rootin' for anyway? (*to herself*) Don't seem to be no help for it . . . No matter what we do, the boy turns out good.

LEROY *goes to get his jacket.* LOUISE *is finished putting the baby to bed.*

HOOKER. Since when you been goin' to church at night?

ALVA. Since they started late bingo. I'm gonna call on the Lord for a little cash while he's still payin' off. Luther, you look in on that child from time to time, will ya?

LUTHER *nods that he will.* ALVA, LEROY *and* LOUISE *leave for church.* HOOKER *goes to the dining room table and plops down some money in front of the other man (known as the* EIRIE KID*) who we recognize as the thief who stole* LUTHER'S *wallet.*

HOOKER. Nice goin', Eirie. The guy turned out to be an oil well.

EIRIE *and* HOOKER *share a laugh.* LUTHER *is conspicuously silent.*

HOOKER (*to* EIRIE). Which way did he go?

EIRIE. Due north. He was gonna take it all.

HOOKER. The bastard. He can blow his nose all the way. (*putting a bundle of bills down in front of* LUTHER) Here ya go, Luther. Six gees.

LUTHER *doesn't even look at it.*

COLEMAN. You're late. Where you been?

HOOKER (*flopping into a chair*). I had some appointments.

COLEMAN (*not fooled*). How much did ya lose?

HOOKER (*after a pause*). All of it.

COLEMAN (*pissed*). In one gaddamn night? What are ya sprayin' money around like that for? You coulda been nailed.

HOOKER. I checked the place out. There weren't no dicks in there.

COLEMAN. You're a con man, and you blew it like a pimp. I didn't teach ya to be no pimp.

HOOKER. What's eatin' you? I've blown money before.

COLEMAN. No class grifter woulda done it, that's all.

HOOKER. You think my play is bad?

COLEMAN. I think it's the best. . . .

HOOKER *sinks back, embarrassed that he misread* COLEMAN'S *intentions.*

COLEMAN . . . It's the only reason I ain't quit before now.

HOOKER (*bewildered*). What?

COLEMAN. I'm gettin' too slow for this racket. You hang on too long, you start embarrassin' yourself.

HOOKER. What are you talkin' about? We just took off the biggest score we've ever had.

COLEMAN. It's nothin' compared to what you could be makin' on the Big

Con. You're wastin' your time workin' street marks.

HOOKER. Hey look. You think I'm gonna run out on ya or somethin'? Luther, I owe you everything. If you hadn't taught me con, I wouldn't know nothin'.

COLEMAN (*a little embarrassed*). Aw hell, you sound like some goddam sucker.

HOOKER. But you played the Big Con. You said it was nothin'. A game for flakes and mama's boys.

COLEMAN (*pause*). Hell, I never played no Big Con. I hung around and picked up a few things, but there ain't no rich boys gonna trust a hungry nigger enough to get conned. (*pause, holding up the money*) I been lookin' for this one all my life, Johnny. Now I got a chance to step out at the top.

HOOKER *knows it's no use.*

HOOKER (*after a long silence*). What the hell you gonna do with yourself?

COLEMAN. Aw, I got a brother down in K.C., runs a freight outlet. I can go halfsies with 'em! It ain't too exciting, but it's mostly legal.

HOOKER *just nods.*

COLEMAN. Straighten up, kid. I wouldn't turn ya out if ya weren't ready. (*flipping HOOKER a piece of paper*) There's a guy in Chicago named Henry Gondorff I want you to look up. There ain't a better insideman alive. He'll teach ya everything ya gotta know.

HOOKER. You'll take a cut of what I make, won't ya?

COLEMAN. I'm out, Johnny.

HOOKER. If that's the way you want it.

COLEMAN. That's the way I want it.

*Cut to*

*Ext. A Downtown Section of Joliet—Night*

MOTTOLA, *dapper as ever but roaring drunk and belligerent as hell, stumbles out of a "jump" nightclub, draped all over a young party girl.*

*A doorman offers to assist him to his car, but* MOTTOLA *pushes him away in contempt. The girl, a little wobbly herself, has the presence of mind to signal for a cab. One pulls over immediately and she opens the rear door and helps* MOTTOLA *in. Instead of getting in herself, however, she blows him a little kiss and turns back toward the club.*

MOTTOLA, *not planning on going home empty-handed, reaches out to pull her back when suddenly, out of nowhere, two men wearing gray suits and black fedoras slide in next to him, one on either side. They close their respective doors quickly and signal the cabbie to pull out. Not a word is spoken, but* MOTTOLA *knows he's in big trouble for the second time today.*

*Cut to*

*Ext. A Dimly Lit Street—Night*

*It's late at night now.* HOOKER *and* EIRIE *wander along the street together, not really ready to go home, but with no other ideas either.* HOOKER, *obviously preoccupied, idly strikes a match on a street lamp as he passes and lets it burn out. He does this several times.*

HOOKER. How do you like that Coleman, huh? After five years.

EIRIE. Aw come on, it was the only thing to do. He knew he was holdin' ya back.

HOOKER. We were partners. If it weren't for Luther I'd still be hustlin' pinball down at Gianelli's. I don't need anything more than I got.

EIRIE. You ain't gonna have nothin' if you don't lay off them games of chance. There's a depression on ya know.

HOOKER. There's always a depression on.

EIRIE. If you saved a little, you wouldn't have to grift so much.

HOOKER. I like griftin'.

EIRIE. You could buy yourself some things. Clothes, or a nice car. . . .

HOOKER. I don't look any good in clothes and I don't know how to drive. What else ya got to sell, Eirie?

EIRIE. Forget it.

*They walk on a few more feet, when suddenly a police car pulls up alongside them and two men jump out. The first, a uniformed policeman, grabs* EIRIE *around the neck.*

HOOKER *makes a break for it, but the second figure, a burly detective named* SNYDER *tackles him in the middle of the street, drags him back into the alley and plasters him up against a brick wall. The two have met before.*

HOOKER. Hi there, Snyder. Things a litle slow down at the Bunco Department tonight, eh? Somebody lose the dominoes?

SNYDER. You scored blood money today, Hooker. You need a friend.

HOOKER *(knocking* SNYDER'S *hand away)*. Aw, find yourself a shoplifter to roll.

SNYDER *gives* HOOKER *a swift knee in the thigh and follows it with an elbow across the head.* HOOKER *flies into a row of boxes and garbage cans.*

HOOKER *(getting up slowly)*. You got the wrong guy, pal. I been home with the flu all day. *(rising to a fuller height)* You can stake out my toilet if you want.

*Bang.* SNYDER, *infuriated by* HOOKER'S *irreverance, slams him to the ground again. The policeman is no longer holding* EIRIE *but is almost daring him to make a move.* EIRIE *wants to go to* HOOKER'S *aid, but he knows the policeman will beat him to a pulp.*

SNYDER *(pulling* HOOKER *out of the heap and smashing him against the wall again)*. I'll tell ya what you did, smart boy. You tied into a loaded mark on 47th. You and Coleman played the switch for him and blew him off to a cab on 49th. If he hadn't been a numbers runner for Doyle Lonnegan, it woulda been perfect.

HOOKER *(startled by the information)*. You're crazy. I'm not stupid enough to play for rackets money.

SNYDER. Not intentionally maybe, but that don't make no difference to Lonnegan. He'll swat you like any other fly.

HOOKER. I'll square it with the fixer.

SNYDER. Nobody can buy you a prayer, if I put the finger on ya.

SNYDER *lets go.* HOOKER *sinks back against the wall. He says nothing; he's waiting for the price.*

SNYDER. I figure your end of the score was at least 3 gees. I want 2 no matter what it was.

HOOKER *(lying)*. My end was only one.

SNYDER *(not taking the fake)*. Then you'll have to come up with another grand somewhere.

HOOKER *is beat and he knows it.*

HOOKER. All right.

*He reaches into his coat, pulls out a stack of bills and counts out $2000 to* SNYDER. EIRIE *looks on in* *amazement; he didn't think* HOOKER *had it.*

SNYDER (*pocketing the money and motioning his partner to put his gun away*). You're a smart egg, Hooker. No use dyin' for 2 grand.

SNYDER *and his policeman friend get in their car and start down the street.* HOOKER *and* EIRIE *walk nonchalantly in the other direction.*

EIRIE. I thought you blew all your money.

HOOKER. I did. That stuff I gave him was counterfeit. They'll pinch him the first place he tries to spend it.

SNYDER *and his partner disappear around a corner.* HOOKER *suddenly takes off like a shot.*

*Int. Drugstore—Night*

*He runs into a drugstore and goes to the phone booth. There's already a woman in it.* HOOKER *rips open the door and throws her out. Hurriedly, he begins to dial.*

EIRIE (*standing outside the booth*). What the hell you gonna do when Snyder rushes his finger right to Lonnegan? You're committin' suicide, kid.

HOOKER (*waiting for the ring*). Aw Christ, It doesn't make no difference now. If Snyder knows about it so does everybody else. He never gets anything first . . . Damn, there's no answer at Luther's.

EIRIE. Listen to me, Hooker. Whatever you do, don't go back to your place tonight, don't go anyplace you usually go, ya hear me? Get outa town or somethin', but. . . .

HOOKER, *still getting no answer, slams the phone down and blasts out of the booth.*

*Ext. Street—Night*

EIRIE *chases him frantically, calling him to come back, but he's giving away too many years and there's no stopping* HOOKER *at this point.*

*Cut to*

*Ext.     Street—Night—Shots     of* HOOKER

*pumping down the street.*

*Ext.* LUTHER'S *Brownstone—Night*

HOOKER *races     into* LUTHER'S *brownstone, charges up to the third floor.*

*Int.* LUTHER'S *Brownstone—Night*

HOOKER *runs up through a small group of people on the stairs. He bursts into* LUTHER'S *room, the door of which is already open. The room shows signs of a struggle, a turnedover chair, a broken lamp, but there is no* COLEMAN. HOOKER *goes slowly to the window. He looks down into the courtyard and then suddenly sprints back out the door. As we hear him scrambling down the stairs, the camera dollies to the window and looks out. Over this, the sound of the baby crying.*

*Ext. Courtyard—Night*

*There on the concrete below, face down, is the body of* LUTHER COLEMAN. HOOKER *races out to it and kneels down.*

HOOKER (*shaking the body*). C'mon Luther, get up. You gotta get up, Luther.

*In the distance, sirens are heard. Heads are out of the windows and some people are starting to gather in the courtyard.*

HOOKER. Goddamn you, Luther, will you get up? (*shaking the body*) I'm not waitin' for you, Luther. I'm not waitin' anymore. Get up, you son-of-a-bitch. Goddamn you, Luther, goddamn.

*The sirens are close now, and* HOOKER *tears himself away from* LUTHER *and runs. The others gather to look at the body.*

*Fade out*

*Fade in*

THE SET-UP

*Fade out*

*Fade in*

*Int. The Train Station—Day*

*We open on* HOOKER *sleeping in some remote corner of the station, covered with newspapers for warmth and barely distinguishable from the clutter of junk surrounding him. A station security officer, on his morning sweep, wanders by and delivers a terrific blow to the soles of* HOOKER'S *feet with a nightstick.* HOOKER *jolts awake with a cry of pain, as the officer diffidently moves on toward another sleeping victim.*

*Tired and sore from his night in the station,* HOOKER *struggles to his feet and attempts to take stock of the situation. He tries to smooth the wrinkles out of his suit, but it's futile. A quick check of his wallet finds it as empty as he'd remembered it.*

*Cut to*

*The Station—Gift Shop—Day*

HOOKER *walks in and goes to the toy section. He looks through several small novelties, till he finds what he's looking for—a little tin replica of a policeman's badge. He looks around for station detectives, and seeing none, slips the badge into his pocket.*

*Cut to*

*The Station—Washroom—Day*

HOOKER *rinses out his mouth, towels off his face and slicks his hair back with water. It's a drop in the bucket, but it seems to revitalize him a little.*

*Cut to*

*Station—Hallway—Day*

*We see* HOOKER *removing a sign from a door, but the angle prohibits us from reading it.*

*Int. Station—Day*

*He drops the sign in a waste can and walks out into the crowded passenger lobby. After scanning the area carefully for a minute, he goes up to a conservative young business man, who's busy reading the schedule board.*

HOOKER *(flashing open his wallet to reveal the little tin badge and then closing it again quickly).* Excuse me, sir. Treasury Dept. . . . I'd like to ask you a few questions.

MAN *(flustered).* What for? I haven't done anything.

HOOKER. We don't doubt that, but there's a counterfeiting operation passing bad money in the station. Have you made any purchases here today?

MAN *(reluctantly).* Yes, a ticket to Chicago.

HOOKER. Then I'm afraid we'll have to impound your money until we're sure that it's all good. Can I see your wallet and your ticket, please?

MAN *(handing them over).* But I got a train to make.

HOOKER *(taking out the money and returning the wallet).* It'll only take 20 minutes or so. You can pick it up at the window down the hall.

MAN. But what about all these other people?

HOOKER *(blowing up)*. We'll get 'em. Give us a chance. I'm not the only agent in here, ya know. We go around advertising ourselves, how many counterfeiters do you think we'd catch, huh? *(pointing to his suit)* You think I'm wearin' this rag here 'cause I like it? Christ, everybody thinks life's a holiday or somethin' when you got a badge. *(pouring it on)* I been here since three this morning, Charlie, and I never knew there was so much ugliness in people. You try to help 'em, and they spit on you. I shoulda let ya go and gotten yourself arrested for passin' false notes.

*The* BUSINESSMAN *is totally shamed.*

MAN. I'm sorry, really I am, but my train leaves in ten minutes.

HOOKER. All right. I'll give ya a break. *(pointing to a hall)* Down that hall there, there's an unmarked door on the left. Go on in there and wait at the window. I'll take this . . . *(he holds up the money)* . . . in the back and and run it through right away. We'll have you outta there in a couple minutes.

MAN. Thank you. You don't know how much I appreciate this.

HOOKER *(with a little wave)*. Think nothin' of it.

*The man goes off down the hall, more than grateful to be given a break like this.* HOOKER *heads for the "back." We follow the* MAN *down the hall to the unmarked door. He strides on through to find himself face to face with a wall of busily flushing urinals.*

*Cut to*

*Ext. Station—Day—*HOOKER

*boarding the 8:10 for Chicago*

*Cut to*

*Int. Station—Day*

*The* MAN *wandering up and down the hall, wondering how he could have missed that room.*

*Ext. Chicago Street—Day*

*The street runs alongside an elevated train track. We pick up* HOOKER *coming down the street, eating a hot dog he bought with the money he just earned in the train station.*

*He appears to be looking for an address, referring every now and then to the piece of paper* LUTHER *gave him the night before. Finally he stops in front of an old three-story building which contains a carousel on the bottom two floors and what appear to be apartments on the third floor. He peers inside the big, sliding glass doors and seeing no sign of life, goes around to the side to look for a way in.*

*A 35-year-old woman,* BILLIE, *appears in her bathrobe on the second floor landing and descends the stairs to get the morning paper. She's eating an apple. Although she has just gotten up and looks it, she has the presence of one who is probably quite striking at other hours. The sight of* HOOKER *fazes her not at all.*

HOOKER. Excuse me, I'm looking for a guy named Henry Gondorff. You know him?

BILLIE *(starting back up the stairs)*. No.

HOOKER. Luther Coleman sent me.

BILLIE *stops and comes back down the stairs. It's the first time she's stopped chewing.*

BILLIE *(checking him out)*. You Hooker?

HOOKER. Yeh.

BILLIE. Why didn't you say so. I thought maybe you was a copper or somethin'.

*She goes to a side door and unlocks it.*

BILLIE. It's the room in the back. He wasn't expecting you so soon though.

HOOKER'S *not quite sure what that means, but there's something about* BILLIE *that makes him know that you don't ask.*

*Int. Carousel—Day*

HOOKER *walks past the now motionless carousel to the room in the back and knocks on the door. No answer. He gives the door a little push and it swings open.*

*Int.* GONDORFF'S *Room—Day*

*The room inside is small and cluttered, consisting of a bed, a sink, and a bathroom, all covered by a layer of books, dirty clothes and beer bottles. Draped over a chair, fully dressed, but completely passed out is the one and only* HENRY GONDORFF.

HOOKER *(to himself)*. The great Henry Gondorff.

*Cut to*

*Int. A Shower—Day*

*water blasting out of the fixture. We see* GONDORFF, *still fully clothed, sitting in the bottom of the shower, the spray streaming off his face. An imposing figure, with deep set eyes, he just sits there stoically, looking like a soggy lumberjack.* HOOKER, *sitting on the floor between the toilet and the sink, watches listlessly. Finally—*

GONDORFF. Turn the goddamn thing off, will ya.

HOOKER. You sober?
GODORFF. I can talk, can't I?

HOOKER *makes no move to get up.* GONDORFF *struggles to his knees, turns off the water, and slumps back against the wall. The two men just look past each other a second. Down in the bottom.*

GONDORFF. Glad to meet ya, kid. You're a real horse's ass.
HOOKER. Yeh, Luther said you could teach me something. I already know how to drink.

GONDORFF *wipes his face with his hand. His mood softens a little.*

GONDORFF *(quietly)*. I'm sorry about Luther. He was the best street worker I ever saw.
HOOKER. He had you down as a big-timer. What happened?
GONDORFF. Aw, I conned a Senator from Florida on a stocks deal. A real lop-ear. He thought he was gonna take over General Electric. Some Chantoozie woke him up, though, and he put the feds on me.
HOOKER. You mean you blew it.
GONDORFF *(pause)*. Luther didn't tell me you had a big mouth.
HOOKER. He didn't tell me you was a fuck-up, either. (GONDORFF *looks at him coldly*) You played the Big Con since then.
GONDORFF. No, I lammed it around for a while while things cooled off, Philly, Denver, Baltimore, nuthin' towns.

HOOKER'S *disappointment is obvious.*

GONDORFF. But don't kid yourself, friend. I still know how.

HOOKER *nods, unconvinced.*

GONDORFF *(getting up from the floor and emptying the water out of his pockets).* You gonna stay for breakfast, or do you already know how to eat?

HOOKER *(tired).* I picked something up on the way.

GONDORFF *(sensing something).* Lonnegan after you, too?

HOOKER. I don't know. Haven't seen anybody.

GONDORFF. You never do, kid.

*We go to* HOOKER. *He hadn't thought of that.*

*Ext. A Beautiful Old Colonial Country Club—Long Island—Day*

LONNEGAN, *in plus fours and argyles sits on a bench as other members of his foursome tee off.* FLOYD *comes up to him.*

FLOYD. We just talked to Chicago. They got one of the grifters last night. The nigger.

LONNEGAN. What about the other one?

FLOYD. They're still looking for him.

LONNEGAN. Who does Combs have on it?

FLOYD. He gave it to Reilly and Cole.

LONNEGAN. Hackers.

FLOYD. They staked out the other guy's place last night, but he never showd. They figure maybe he skipped town. You wanna follow 'em up?

LONNEGAN *regards* FLOYD *patiently and then pats the bench beside him.* FLOYD *sits gingerly.*

LONNEGAN. You see the guy in the red sweater over there?

*We cut to one of* LONNEGAN'S *foursome, a short, squat little Irishman in a red sweater. He has a good-time, friendly manner and a winning Irish smile. We like him immediately.*

LONNEGAN. Name's Danny Mc-Coy. Petunias, I called him. We used to work subway entrance to the Brooklyn navy yards, sellin' flowers to the sailors. Danny'd tell 'em where to find a floosy, and I'd pedal 'em the flowers. Danny didn't know any floozies, so he usually gave 'em the address of somebody he was mad at. *(chuckles to himself)* Yeh, Floyd, take a good look at that face, 'cause if he ever finds out we can be beat by one lousy grifter, I'll have to kill him and every other hood who'd like to take over my operation. You understand what I'm sayin'?

FLOYD. Yes sir.

LONNEGAN. Good lad.

LONNEGAN *is called to the tee by one of his foursome. He exchanges a friendly smile with McCoy and belts the ball down the fairway.*

*Cut to*

*Int. The Carousel Again—Day*

GONDORFF, *dried off now and in a new set of clothes, is pulling up the shades of the large facing windows of the carousel building. The morning light pours in, illuminating fully for the first time the ornate merry-go-round and its massive oaken horses.* HOOKER *watches him go about his business.* BILLIE *calls down from the mezzanine which surrounds the carousel.*

BILLIE. You feeling all right this morning, Henry?

GONDORFF. Fine, Billie.

BILLIE. You mind opening the round a little early today? We got some business coming in before hours.

GONDORFF *waves okay.*

GONDORFF *(to* HOOKER). Great little countess, that Billie. Runs a good house up there, too. One of the few left the syndicate doesn't own.

GONDORFF *walks around on the carousel, checking straps, bearings and poles.* HOOKER *follows him.*

HOOKER *(getting impatient).* Gondorff, am I gonna learn some Big Con around here or not?

GONDORFF *(on his back, checking underneath one of the horses).* You didn't act much like you wanted to.

HOOKER. I wanna play for Lonnegan.

GONDORFF *(getting up).* You know anything about him?

HOOKER *(exploding).* Yeh, he croaked Luther. What else do I gotta know?

GONDORFF. Plenty. Does he bet on the fights? Is he a ladies' man? A boozer? Does he play the market? Who does his dirty work? Do you know anything?

HOOKER. He runs the numbers on the South side.

GONDORFF. And a packing company, a chain of Savings & Loans and half the politicians in Chicago and New York. There ain't a fix in the world gonna cool him out if he blows on ya.

HOOKER. I'll take him anyway.

GONDORFF. Why?

HOOKER. 'Cause I don't know enough about killin' to kill him.

*It's the right answer.* GONDORFF *didn't know it himself until now.*

GONDORFF. You can't do it alone, ya know. It takes a mob a guys like you and enough money to make 'em look good.

HOOKER. So I know plenty a guys.

GONDORFF. This isn't like playin' winos on the street. You gotta do more than outrun the guy.

HOOKER *(incensed).* I never played for no winos.

GONDORFF *(going right on, ignoring* HOOKER'S *remark)* You gotta keep his con, even after you spent his money. And no matter how much you take from him, he'll get more.

HOOKER. You're scared of 'em, aren't ya?

GONDORFF. Right down to my socks, pal. We're talkin' about a guy who'd kill a grifter over a chunk a money that wouldn't support him two days.

HOOKER *(giving up).* Then you don't wanta do it.

GONDORFF. I just don't want you comin' back to me halfway through and sayin' it's not enough. 'Cause it's all you're gonna get.

GONDORFF *goes over to start the machinery.*

HOOKER. Can you get a mob together?

GONDORFF. I don't know, this one's kinda risky. I doubt if I can get more than two or three hundred guys.

GONDORFF *switches on the carousel and steps back to admire his handiwork. The carousel makes a grinding sound, does a few lurches, and stops cold.*

*Cut to*

*Music begins and we are into a short:*

*Montage Sequence*

*detailing the arrival of the other three members of* GONDORFF'S *"mob." Throughout,* GONDORFF *wears the fedora hat which is his trademark. We begin with—*

*A tall, good-looking man,* KID TWIST, *making his way through the railway station. Impeccably dressed and carrying a small suitcase, he combs the terrain carefully with his eyes. Finally he catches a glimpse of the thing he's been looking for. It's* GONDORFF, *standing by a newsstand.* GONDORFF *makes a quick snubbing motion on his nose as if flicking off a gnat. This is known among con men as the "office."* TWIST *returns the sign with a barely discernible smile as he walks on by. Con men rarely acknowledge each other openly in public, but it's obvious that these two are glad to see each other.*

*Cut to*

*Int. Barber Shop—Day*

HOOKER *in, having his hair cut and his nails manicured.* GONDORFF *gives instructions to the barber.*

*Cut to*

*Int. Haberdashery—Day*

HOOKER *is modeling a new suit in front of a mirror. He doesn't look too pleased, but* GONDORFF *peels out a bankroll anyway.*

*Cut to*

*Ext. Hotel—Day*

*a pair of white spats stepping off a bus. We follow them into a:*

*Int. Hotel Lobby*

*where we tilt up to reveal* J. J. SINGLETON, *the most flamboyant of the bunch. On his way to the check-in desk, he silently exchanges the "office" with* GONDORFF, *who is sitting on a lounge reading the paper.*

*Cut to*

*Int. Apartment—Day*

HOOKER *being shown into a small apartment room by an old woman. It*

*consists of a bed, a table and a sink.* HOOKER *nods his acceptance to the woman and gives her a bill. He takes another look around the room and decides to go out somewhere, but first he wedges a small piece of paper between the door and the jamb, about an inch off the floor.*

*Cut to*

*Int. A Big Metropolitan Bank—Day*

*We hold on a slight, bespectacled teller,* EDDIE NILES, *in the process of counting a large deposit.* NILES *is all business; if he's ever smiled, no one knows about it. He glances up for a second and sees* GONDORFF *"officing" him from across the bank. Without a word he shoves the money he's been counting back into the hands of a startled customer, abruptly closes up his window, flips his identification tag on the manager's desk and walks out of the bank.*

*Cut to*

*Int. An Upstairs Room of the Carousel Building—Night*

*This room has obviously been relegated to the status of the storage room. It contains the water heater, mops and brooms, old bed springs, etc. In the middle of the room a space has been cleared for a table, around which are seated* HOOKER, GONDORFF, NILES, SINGLETON *and* TWIST. GONDORFF *is in his T-shirt, but still wears his hat.* KID TWIST *is in a suit as usual. The room is illuminated by a single bare bulb hanging from the ceiling.*

NILES (*referring to notes as he reports*). Lonnegan gets most of his income from the numbers, even though he's been puttin' more and more money into his Savings & Loan business.

GONDORFF. You think he's movin' outa the rackets?

NILES. No. He owns most of the stock, and it's traded on the board, but my guess is he's just trying to build himself a respectable image. He came out of the Five Points district, but he's been telling everybody he was born in Forest Hills. He knows the market though. I don't think we can take him on a stocks deal.

GONDORFF. All right, Twist, what do ya got on the numbers?

TWIST. The tipsters say it's run out of a packing house on 14th by a guy named Combs. Lonnegan comes out every three weeks or so to check on it, but stays away from the day-to-day stuff, in case it's raided. *(turning to* HOOKER *and producing two photographs)* These are two of Combs's favorite torpedoes. Riley and Cole. You ever seen 'em?

*We recognize* RILEY *and* COLE *as the two guys who got into* MOTTOLA'S *car.*

HOOKER *(studying the photographs)*. No.

TWIST. They were the guys who hit Luther. They also got the numbers runner you conned. He was found in a quarry with a knife in his eye.

HOOKER's *head comes up from the photographs.*

TWIST *(collecting his papers)*. Lonnegan's had seven or eight people rubbed on his way up. His pattern's been to get close to a racket boss, learn his operation and then move in on it. He's done it to Gorman, O'Donnell, Buchalman, and he took the numbers from Sharkey. All four a these guys are dead. He's vindictive as hell, Henry, and he kills for pride. It doesn't add up that he'd let Hooker get away from him.

GONDORFF *(to* HOOKER*)*. You see anything, you let us know, huh? If they got you on the spot, we'll fold up the con. You'd be too easy to find. You got that?

HOOKER *nods, but we know he hasn't really got that.*

HOOKER. You sure it'll be one of these two?

TWIST. No. They're just the only ones we know of.

BILLIE *has finished gathering the mugs, and leaves the room with them. We follow her down the hall and into the:*

*Receiving Room of Her Brothel*

*Carousel music filters up from the arcade below. The room has a bar along one wall and the rest of the space is taken up by tables and couches. It's a comfortable place, but not opulent. Some of the girls sit patiently on the couches, others play canasta at the tables. Most of the men are at the bar, fortifying themselves for the task at hand.* BILLIE *comes over to the bar.*

BILLIE *(to the bartender)*. Set me up five more beers, will ya Danny.

*As* DANNY *goes to fill the mugs,* BILLIE'S *eyes fix on a man at the end of the bar. We move to reveal* SNYDER, *intently scanning the room, as if he'd lost a dancing partner in the crush. Not finding what he wants, he comes down the bar to* BILLIE.

SNYDER. You the owner here?

BILLIE. That's right.

SNYDER *(flipping out his badge)*. Lieutenant Snyder. Bunco.

BILLIE. Joliet badge, Snyder. Don't cut much up here.

SNYDER *(trying to ignore her remark)*. I'm lookin' for a guy on the lam from a counterfeiting rap. Thought he mighta come in here.

BILLIE. Don't think so. I know everybody in the place and I always bounce the lamsters.

SNYDER. All right if I look around your lobby?

BILLIE. No, but you're welcome to a free beer before you go.

BILLIE *grabs a bottle of beer, pours some in a shot glass and pushes it over to* SNYDER. *He ignores the gesture.*

SNYDER *(with controlled force)*. I don't really need your permission.

*We go to* BILLIE. *She knew that when he came in.*

*Cut to*

*The Storage Room Again*

*The discussion continues.* HOOKER, *a bit out of his depth here, listens and stays silent.*

SINGLETON. I don't know what to do with this guy, Henry. He doesn't drink, he doesn't smoke, he doesn't chase dames, he's a Commander in the Knights of Columbus, and he only goes out to play Faro. Sometimes plays fifteen or twenty hours at a time. Just him against the house.

GONDORFF. Any roulette or craps?

SINGLETON. Won't touch 'em. The croupier at Gilman's says he never plays anthing he can't win.

GONDORFF. What about sports?

SINGLETON. He likes to be seen with fighters sometimes, but he doesn't go to the fights or bet on 'em.

GONDORFF. Jesus. Does he do anything where he's not alone?

SINGLETON. Just poker, and he cheats at that. Pretty good at it, too.

*A little spark of electricity goes around the table. Here's something they can work with.*

GONDORFF. Where does he play?

SINGLETON. The porters say he runs a braced game on the Century Limited when he comes out here from New York. One hundred dollar minimum, straight poker. Lotta high rollers ride that train just to play him.

GONDORFF. Sounds good, J. J. He's slowing down already.

*Cut to*

*The Receiving Room Again*

SNYDER *has completed his inspection of the "lobby" and found nothing.* DANNY, *meanwhile, has set up the five beers on a tray.*

SNYDER. Which way are the rooms?

BILLIE. Who told ya this guy was in here?

SNYDER. Nobody. I just know what kinda women he likes. I'm gonna check all the joyhouses till I find him.

BILLIE. Maybe I could help ya if ya told me his name.

SNYDER. I think I'll keep that to myself. Which way are the rooms?

BILLIE. Right through there. But I wouldn't go in there if I were you. *(picks up the tray)*

SNYDER *(snidely)*. What are ya gonna do, call the cops?

BILLIE. I don't have to. You'll be bustin' in on the Chief of Police just up the hall. *(she exits with the drinks)*

SNYDER *is stopped cold. He calls after her.*

SNYDER. Keep your nose clean, lady. He can't spend all his time here.

*Cut to*

*The Storage Room Again*

BILLIE *comes over to* GONDORFF *and whispers in his ear, while the others talk. His eyes flick momentarily to* HOOKER.

SINGLETON. I think we ought to play him on the Rag. It's the tightest game we got, and it's not all over the papers yet.

TWIST. Lonnegan's a fast egg, J.J. He's not gonna sit still for a standard play.

NILES. So what does that leave us? We can't con the Rag to a banker.

GONDORFF *has nodded to* BILLIE *and rejoins the conversation. She serves the others beer.*

GONDORFF. We'll use the Wire. Never known a poker player who wouldn't like to beat the ponies.

NILES. The Wire is ten years outa date.

GONDORFF. That's why he won't know it.

SINGLETON. I'm not sure I know it.

GONDORFF. Well, it's gonna take two of us workin' the inside. Any objections to Hooker as second man?

*We go around the table. There are none.*

GONDORFF. All right, we'll give Lonnegan the hook on the train and play him here. You think I can get in that poker game, Eddie?

NILES. All you gotta do is show up with some money and look like a fool.

GONDORFF. I also gotta win.

*He looks at* HOOKER. *There is a challenge in their look.* GONDORFF *smiles broadly, then casually, to them all.*

GONDORFF. By the way, any of you guys been passing off green goods lately?

*We go around the table. No reply.*

GONDORFF. Billie, if that Dick comes in again, stall him till I can get a look at him. And let me pay ya for these beers.

BILLIE. What are you talking about? It's on the house.

GONDORFF *(puling out a $5 bill).* Naw, I want ya to have this.

*He hitches up* BILLIE'S *skirt, and puts the bill in her garter.*

GONDORFF. Don't look at it till ya go to bed though or it'll turn to paper.

BILLIE *smiles and leaves the room.*

*Int. Hallway*

*She walks halfway down the hall and stops. She can't wait. Lifting up her skirt, she finds that the five has indeed turned to paper. As she breaks into laughter and continues on down the hall, we:*

*Fade out*

*Fade in*

THE HOOK

*Fade out*

*Fade in*

*Ext. A Sunken Alley—Day*

*Actually little more than a service area between two apartment buildings.* NILES, KID TWIST, *and a middle-aged black man, named* BENNY GARFIELD, *enter the alley with an* OLD MAN *and follow him down a stairwell to a subterranean basement. A faded sign above the door says Stenner's Billiards. We follow them inside to a:*

*Int. A Large Barren Room—Day*

*An office comes off it at one end. Judging from the fluorescent lights overhead and the scattered cue racks which still hang tenuously on the walls, the place, indeed, used to be a pool hall.* NILES *and* GARFIELD *go all the way to the back, while* TWIST *stays near the front with the* OLD MAN.

NILES. Looks all right. It's big enough and off the street.

GARFIELD. I don't know. This is kinda short notice. I'm not sure we can get it all done by Saturday.

NILES. Got to. Gondorff's ridin' the mark in from New York on the Century.

GARFIELD *thinks it over a little. He's taking another look at the place. We go to* TWIST *and the* OLD MAN *by the door.*

TWIST. We'll take it. *(pointing through the door)* You manage the building at the end of the alley?

OLD MAN *(with pride).* For fifteen years.

TWIST. I'll need a room over there that faces this way. How much a week?

OLD MAN. Only rents by the month. Two hundred and fifty for the two of them.

TWIST *(pulling out his wallet).* This is the last time I expect to see you down here.

OLD MAN *(watching the bills being counted into his hand).* Never heard of the place.

*We go back to* NILES *and* GARFIELD.

GARFIELD. Been a while since I stocked a wire store. Not many mobs playing that anymore.

NILES. All we need is the bookie setup for now. We'll worry about the telegraph office later.

GARFIELD. All right, I'll rent ya everything I got in the warehouse for two grand. That'll give ya phones, cages, blackboards, and ticker gear. You supply the guys to move 'em. If you want a counter and bar, that's another grand. I don't know where the hell I'm gonna get 'em though.

NILES. C'mon, you can do better than that. We ain't no heel grifters.

GARFIELD. You want the stuff tomorrow or don't ya? It's gonna take

hours just to clean it up. *(pause)* Besides, Gondorff's still a hot item. Where am I gonna be if he gets hit?

NILES. Just give us what ya can, Benny. We'll send a truck down.

TWIST *has rejoined them by now.*

TWIST *(to* GARFIELD). You wanna work flat rate or percentage?

GARFIELD. Who's the mark?

TWIST. Doyle Lonnegan.

GARFIELD. Flat rate.

*Cut to*

*Int. A New York Train Station— Day*

*We pick up* DOYLE LONNEGAN, *accompanied by two bodyguards and* FLOYD, *making his way through the station. He stops at a cigar counter to buy some cigarettes, and we reveal* GONDORFF *and* HOOKER *sitting on their suitcases on the other side of the room.*

GONDORFF *(eyes fixed on* LONNE-GAN). Guy in the blue pinstripe and grey fedora.

HOOKER *looks and finally spots him in the crowd. We go back to* LONNE-GAN, *as he moves off from the cigar counter, toward his train.* HOOKER *watches him with the intensity of one gazing on a religious object.*

HOOKER. He's not as tough as he thinks.

GONDORFF *(picking up his suit-case).* Neither are we.

*Cut to*

*Ext. Train*

LONNEGAN *and his retainers getting on the train. Two cars down the line, we see* HOOKER *and* GONDORFF *boarding also. On his way in,* GONDORFF *takes the* CONDUCTOR *aside.*

GONDORFF. I hear there's a friendly poker game on this train tonight. You know anything about that?

CONDUCTOR. A little.

GONDORFF. You think you could get me in that game?

CONDUCTOR. I don't know. There's usually a waiting list.

GONDORFF *flashes a $50 bill.*

CONDUCTOR *(loosening up a bit).* That'll get you first alternate, sir.

GONDORFF *pulls out another fifty.*

CONDUCTOR *(taking the money).* I'll see what I can do.

*Cut to*

*Int. A Basement Bar—Early Evening*

KID TWIST *enters and threads his way through the maze of tables to a door at the back of the building. A large bull of a man is stationed there, obviously to discourage those who don't have credentials to enter.* TWIST *is not such a man.*

TWIST *(going right on through).* How ya doin', Lacey.

LACEY *(innocently pleased for one so menacing).* Good to see ya again, Twist.

*Int. Another Room—Early Evening*

*Inside is another room, this one much better lit than the outer one. There are only three tables in here, around which are seated the elite of the Con World.* TWIST *is enthusiastically greeted by* DUKE BOUDREAU, *a large, rotund man whose stylish dress and authoritative manner mark him as a powerful figure in this group.*

BOUDREAU. Twist! When did you get back in town?

TWIST. Coupla days ago. You heard about Coleman, didn't ya.

BOUDREAU. Yeh, some of the boys passed the hat for Alva and the kids. I've never seen 'em so worked up. They don't like bein' gunned.

TWIST. Don't worry, we're gonna send a little callin' card of our own. Gondorff's settin' up a Wire Store on the north side. I need a twenty man boost right away.

BOUDREAU. I got plenty a talent in here tonight. Take your pick.

TWIST. This is a tough one, Dukey. These guys have gotta be the quill.

BOUDREAU *(to one of his assistants).* Get me the sheet, Jake. Let's see who's in town.

*Cut to*

*The Outer Part of the Bar Again*

*A silhouetted figure appears in the entrance doorway. The word "chill" races from table to table and the place falls still. The bartender pushes a button behind the bar and a buzzer goes off in the back room.* BOUDREAU *gets up from his table and opens a small viewing port in the door.*

*The silhouetted figure is now walking slowly past the silent tables. It's* SNYDER *and he's checking out every face in the place.*

BOUDREAU. TWIST, you know this guy?

TWIST *(taking a look through the viewing port).* No. Never saw him before. He's a dick, though.

SNYDER *walks all the way to the back, and then retraces his route. About halfway back, he stops at one of the tables, recognizing a grifter he knows. It's the* EIRIE KID.

EIRIE. Hello, Snyder. What are you doin' up here?

SNYDER. I'm on vacation. You seen your friend lately?

EIRIE. Yeh, he packed it in and enrolled in detective school.

SNYDER, *in no mood for jokes, grabs* EIRIE *by the hair and slams his face into the table.* EIRIE *just stays there; he knows it doesn't pay to assault a detective.* TWIST *is watching all this intently from the viewing port.*

SNYDER. You see him, you tell him he better pay up before I get him.

EIRIE *raises his head slowly, but says nothing. There is a slight trickle of blood from his nose.* SNYDER *turns and walks slowly out of the bar. When he is a safe distance down the street, the chatter and drinking resume.*

*Cut to*

*The Inside Room Again*

TWIST *gives an all clear signal and returns to the table where he and* BOUDREAU *were talking.* BOUDREAU *reads from a list of names.* TWIST *listens with a certain preoccupation. He's still thinking about the little confrontation he just witnessed.*

BOUDREAU. Horse Face Lee, Slim Miller, Suitcase Murphy, and the Big Alabama are in from New Orleans. Crying Jonesy and the Boone Kid from Denver, and Gloomy Gus and Limehouse Chappie from New York. Those and the guys outside should give ya 30 or so to choose from.

TWIST. Good, have 'em down at Stenner's old Pool Hall before 3:00. We're gonna run through the route tonight.

BOUDREAU. Okay, Twist, but you know if this blows up, I can't do ya no good downtown. Gondorff is Federal.

TWIST. Don't worry about it, pal.

*Cut to*

*Ext. Speeding Passenger Train—Night*

*ripping through an open stretch between New York and Chicago.*

*Cut to*

*Int. Train—Night*

SINGLETON *is walking down a passageway and stops at a door and goes in.*

*Int.* GONDORFF'S *Compartment—Night*

GONDORFF *is rapidly shuffling cards to four empty places. He is alone. He looks up as* SINGLETON *enters.*

SINGLETON. You in?

GONDORFF. Yeh, I think so. I gave the kayducer a C-note. You find out the deck?

SINGLETON. He usually plays with a Royal or a Cadenza. *(handing him two sealed decks)* I got you one of each. He likes to cold deck low, 8's or 9's.

GONDORFF. Nice work, J.J.

SINGLETON *slips out as* GONDORFF *unpeels the packs.*

*Int. The Train—Night*

*We pick up* LONNEGAN *coming out of his compartment, flanked by only one bodyguard and* FLOYD. *They start walking single file through the passenger section toward the compartment where the poker game will be held. Suddenly a* DRUNKEN WOMAN *comes staggering around the corner and bumps into him.*

*They grapple a moment and* LONNEGAN *pushes her away in disgust.*

WOMAN *(sloppy drunk)*. Keep your mitts off me, ya big lug. If I'da wanted you handlin' me I woulda asked ya.

LONNEGAN *ignores her and proceeds down the passageway. As the*

woman proceeds in the other direction between passengers, we see it is
BILLIE. *She drops something on a seat
beside a passenger. A hand reaches to
pick it up. It is* LONNEGAN'S *wallet
and it is* HOOKER *who picks it up.*

HOOKER *waits a moment, then
stands and goes in the direction* LON-
NEGAN *has taken. He passes by the
open door to the card room, hesitating only slightly to hear the greetings
exchanged inside before the door is
shut. Then he continues on into the
next car. He turns into* GONDORFF'S
*compartment.*

*Cut to*

*Int.* GONDORFF'S *Compartment—
Night*

GONDORFF *is still practicing. He
looks up as* HOOKER *enters and tosses
him the wallet.*

HOOKER. She got him clean. He
hasn't missed it.

GONDORFF *nods, takes the money
out, counts it.*

GONDORFF. Twenty-five grand.
Looks like he's expecting a big night.

*He takes out his own wallet and
puts the money in it, and tosses the
empty wallet back to* HOOKER, *and
resumes his shuffling and dealing.*
HOOKER *sits back silently and watches
him.*

HOOKER. He's waitin' for you in the
card room.

GONDORFF. Let him wait.

*As he deals, on the second pass he
attempts to cut from the bottom, muffs
it completely and sprays half the deck
on the table.* HOOKER *regards him
steadily as he gathers them back up.*
GONDORFF *finally meets his gaze.*

GONDORFF. You just worry about
your end, kid.

HOOKER. If we ever get to it.

*Cut to*

*Int. The Poker Room—Night*

*A specially outfitted compartment
with a table and chairs in the middle
and leather cushions around the outside for kibitzers.* LONNEGAN *and 3
other players are already there and
seated. They're getting slightly impatient.*

LONNEGAN (*to the* CONDUCTOR).
You sure you checked this guy out?

CONDUCTOR (*nods*). He seemed
pleasant enough and had a lotta
money on him. And quite free with it,
I might add. Two hundred dollar suit,
expensive baggage. I'll vouch for
him.

*Cut to*

GONDORFF'S *Cabin Again.*

GONDORFF *is standing in front of
the mirror dressing. He grabs up a
clean white shirt and rumples it up in
his hands. He then picks up a half-full
bottle of gin.* HOOKER *gives him a dis-
approving look.* GONDORFF *smiles and
pats some on his face.*

GONDORFF. Always drink gin with a
mark, kid. They can't tell when you
cut it.

*He pours part of the bottle down
the sink and starts filling it with
water.*

*Cut to*

*The Poker Room Again*

*Everybody's itchy now.*

LONNEGAN. All right, let's start
without him. Mr. Clemens, give me
the cards.

*The* CONDUCTOR *hands him a sealed deck. As he begins to open it,* GONDORFF *comes into the room, coatless, rumpled, unshaven and looking slightly tipsy. The others at the table, all men of high social or financial standing, are somewhat put off.*

GONDORFF. Sorry I'm late boys. I was takin' a crap.

*This bit of grossness does little to improve his image.*

GONDORFF *(sticking out his hand to no one in particular).* Shaw's the name. Any 'a you boys wanna make a little book in Chicago, I'm the guy to see.

*There are no takers for either the handshake or the bookmaking offer.*

CONDUCTOR *(stepping in to save the situation).* Mr. Shaw is a bookmaker from Chicago. Mr. Shaw, meet Mr. Clayton from Pittsburgh, Mr. Jameson, Chicago, Mr. Lonnegan, New York, and Mr. Lombard, Philadelphia.

GONDORFF. Glad to meecha. *(taking an empty chair)* Guess this is my seat, huh?

CONDUCTOR. Straight poker. 100 dollar minimum, table stakes. Since this is a gentleman's game, we assume you're all good for your debts. How much would you like, Mr. Shaw?

GONDORFF. Five thousand to start with.

*The* CONDUCTOR *makes a note of the figure on a pad, and begins to assemble the proper number of chips.*

LONNEGAN *(shuffling the cards).* Mr. Shaw, we usually require a tie at this table. If you don't have one, we can get ya one.

GONDORFF. Yeh, that'd be real nice of ya, Mr. Lonneman.

LONNEGAN *(coldly).* Lonnegan.

*He begins to deal.*

*Cut to*

*Ext. The Sunken Alley—Night*

*A truck is now parked at the end of the alley, and several workmen are busy unloading it. One group carries a large blackboard; others have boxes of glasses, ash tray stands, furniture, etc. Take several cuts.*

*Cut to*

*Inside the Once-Vacant Pool Hall*

*Now a blaze of activity. We take several cuts of workmen papering the walls, tacking down carpet, putting in new light fixtures, painting signs, all under the supervision of* NILES. *From now on, we will refer to the pool hall as the store.*

*Back in the office,* KID TWIST *is "interviewing" one by one, a group of con men lined up outside the office door. A gray-haired old buzzard,* CURLY JACKSON, *approaches the table which is serving* TWIST *as a desk.* CURLY *is practically in rags and has several days' growth on his face. He wears a little beret which he takes off to address* TWIST.

CURLY. Name's Curly Jackson. I worked for Gad Bryan outa Baltimore.

TWIST. You ever played the Wire, Curly?

CURLY. Used to rope for it long ago. I can shill, mark board, anything you want. I don't run with riffraff and I only drink on weekends. *(affecting an English accent)* Me specialty is an Englishman.

TWIST *is taken with the man, despite his appearance.*

TWIST. All right, Curly, you're in. We got a rack of suits over there. Get yourself a nice tweed one.

CURLY *(exiting).* That's all right. I got all my own stuff.

*Cut to*

*The Card Game Again*

GONDORFF *and* LONNEGAN *have most of the chips.* LONNEGAN *is slightly ahead.* GONDORFF *has made a token attempt to wear the provided tie, having tied it in a knot around his neck, but not having bothered to put it under his collar. He has a shot glass and the bottle next to him, from which he has been drinking heavily. He and* LONNEGAN *are the only ones left in this hand.*

LONNEGAN *(throwing chips in).* Raise 500.

GONDORFF *(likewise).* See ya and raise three.

LONNEGAN *(more chips).* See and raise five.

GONDORFF. Five and call.

LONNEGAN *lays down his hand, a solid two pair.* GONDORFF *turns out three tens.* LONNEGAN *is beat.*

GONDORFF. Tough luck, Lonnihan, but that's what you get for playin' with your head up your ass. Couple more like that and we can all go to bed early, huh boys.

GONDORFF *reaches for his gin bottle, but* LONNEGAN'S *hand is already there, on it.*

LONNEGAN *(like ice).* The name is Lonnegan. Doyle Lonnegan. You're gonna remember that, or you're gonna find yourself another game.

GONDORFF *hesitates, then withdraws his hand from the bottle. He knows he's pushing it.* LONNEGAN *takes the bottle from him and hands it to* FLOYD, *who drops it in a wastecan.*

*Cut to*

*Int. The Store—Night*

*The work is still progressing. We see two workmen installing a ticker tape machine in a secluded area of the store.*

GARFIELD. We bought ya a tap into Moe Anenberg's wire. He's got eyes at every track in the country. You'll get race results, odds, scratches, pole positions, everything; and just as fast as Western Union gets 'em.

NILES. Does J.J. know how to use this thing?

GARFIELD. All he's gotta do is read.

*We go to* KID TWIST, *still conducting interviews in the office. A young, rather sullen man,* BUCK DUFF *steps to the table.*

DUFF. Buck Duff. I was in Maxwell's boost in Troy.

TWIST. You the Duff that didn't come up with his end when Little Jeff was sent up?

DUFF. Wasn't no problem a mine.

TWIST. He was a con man, wasn't he?

DUFF. He was a tear-off rat. He got what he deserved. No sense helpin' pay his bills.

TWIST *(like ice).* Shove off, Duff.

DUFF *stands there a second and then slouches away from the table. He stops however, by the door. The next man up is the* EIRIE KID. TWIST *knows he's seen him somewhere before.*

EIRIE *(nervous as hell).* Name's Joe Eirie.

TWIST *waits for more, but it's not coming.*

TWIST. You played for any particular mobs?

EIRIE. No.

TWIST. You know the Wire at all?

EIRIE. No . . . I never played no Big Con before. But Luther Coleman was a friend a mine. I thought maybe there was something I could do.

TWIST *(pointing to* EIRIE'S *slightly swollen nose).* You get that nose in Duke Boudreau's tonight?

EIRIE *nods a reluctant "yes."*

TWIST. You got moxie, Eirie. Get yourself a suit.

EIRIE *is so happy, he can barely blurt out a thank you.* BUCK DUFF, *enraged that* TWIST *would hire a total amateur, turns in disgust and strides vengefully out of the store.*

*Cut to*

*The Card Game Again*

*The room is dense with smoke now, and the players are feeling the heat.* GONDORFF *has his white shirt open, revealing a stained T-shirt underneath. The bottle next to him is almost empty. He sneezes and wipes his nose with the tie* LONNEGAN *gave him. The chips are now about equally divided between* GONDORFF *and* LONNEGAN. *The others are losing badly.*

GONDORFF. Raise 300.

LONNEGAN. Pass.

JAMESON *(throwing in his last few chips).* Raise 200.

GONDORFF. Two and call.

JAMESON *lays down two pair.* GONDORFF *has a flush.* GONDORFF *rakes in the chips, which now put him ahead of* LONNEGAN.

JAMESON. Well I'm out.

GONDORFF. Don't worry about it pal. They wouldn't a let you in here if you weren't a chump. Lombard over there'll join ya in a couple minutes.

JAMESON. Now see here. . . .

LOMBARD. I've had enough of this game, and more than enough of the company. *(getting up to leave)* Cash me in, Mr. Clemens.

GONDORFF *(indicating* LONNEGAN *and* CLAYTON). Looks like it's just us three, huh?

LONNEGAN *(eyes drilled into* GONDORFF). Yeh, just us three. *(calmly getting to his feet)* Why don't we take a five minute break, Mr. Clayton. Tempers are running a little high.

GONDORFF. Aw c'mon, Lonnegan. I was just startin' to do good.

LONNEGAN, *who is already halfway out the door, ignores it.* FLOYD *follows him out.*

*Cut to*

*Int. Smoking Room*

*We pick up* LONNEGAN *coming down the passageway to enter the smoking room. The smile has vanished.*

LONNEGAN. Stack me a cooler, Floyd.

FLOYD *(trying to settle him down).* C'mon, Doyle, we'll be in the station in a half hour. So you split with him. You still make a nice hunk on the other guys.

LONNEGAN *(an order).* Load me a deck. Set it up for threes and nines. I'll cut it in on his deal.

FLOYD *(taking a deck and beginning to sort it).* What do ya want Clayton to get?

LONNEGAN. Nothin'. He's gotta be outa there early. I'm gonna bust that bookie bastard in one play.

*Cut to*

*Int. The Poker Room Again—Night*

*A pair of hands shuffling. We pull back to reveal that they're* GONDORFF'S. *He passes the deck to* LONNEGAN *to cut.* LONNEGAN *takes the deck and in one lightning motion substitutes a new deck, while making it look like he's cutting the old one. The conductor has finished collecting from* JAMESON *and* LOMBARD, *who remain.* GONDORFF *picks up the deck and begins to deal. As the hand is picked up, we see that* GONDORFF *has four threes,* LONNEGAN *four nines, and everybody else has nothing.*

CLAYTON *(opening the bidding).* Fold.
LONNEGAN. 250.
GONDORFF. Raise 1,000.
LONNEGAN. Raise 500.

GONDORFF *looks at* LONNEGAN *very carefully for a second.* LONNEGAN *meets his stare.*

GONDORFF *(slowly).* Raise 2,000.

*The spectators shift a little. It's the biggest bet of the night.*

LONNEGAN. See and raise 1,000.
GONDORFF *(taking it to him).* Raise 5,000.

LONNEGAN *fingers his remaining chips. He knows he's won, but he wants to bleed it for every bit of suspense.*

LONNEGAN *(going for broke).* See, and raise the rest.

LONNEGAN *pushes in the rest of his chips.* GONDORFF, *who is only required to match* LONNEGAN'S *total, throws in all his too. It's a showdown.*

GONDORFF. Call.

LONNEGAN *puts down his four nines.* GONDORFF *just stares at them a second, lets out a deep sigh and lays*

down four jacks. LONNEGAN *is aghast. This just can't be. He glances at* FLOYD, *who can do nothing but sit there with his mouth open.*

GONDORFF *(raking in the chips).* Well that's all for me tonight, boys, I'm gonna leave ya some cab fare.

*The other players look at each other in disgust.* GONDORFF *starts collecting from the bank.* LONNEGAN *sits in a state of lethal indecision.*

GONDORFF *(to* LONNEGAN*).* You owe me 15 grand, pal.

LONNEGAN, *with a stare that could kill, finally reaches for his wallet. Suddenly the stare goes soft. He tries a few more pockets. No soap.* GONDORFF *finishes collecting from the others.*

LONNEGAN *(getting up to get it).* I guess I left it in my room.
GONDORFF *(blowing up).* What! Don't give me that crap you little weenie. How do I know you ain't gonna take a powder. *(waving his wallet which is full of* LONNEGAN'S *money)* You come to a game like this, you bring your money.

LONNEGAN, *having had all he can take, goes for* GONDORFF, *but is restrained by the* CONDUCTOR.

GONDORFF. All right, buddy. I'm gonna send a boy by your room in five minutes, and you better have that money or it's gonna be all over Chicago that your name ain't worth a dime. You won't be able to get a game of jacks in this town.

GONDORFF *stalks out of the room. We pick him up coming down the passageway to his compartment.*

*Int.* GONDORFF'S *compartment*

*The drunkenness has vanished. We follow him into his cabin, where* HOOKER *is waiting anxiously.*

HOOKER. How'd ya do?

GONDORFF (*modestly*). Well we got some workin' money anyway.

GONDORFF *tosses his winnings on the table. He smiles, but for the first time his hands are shaking.*

GONDORFF. Okay, kid, you're on. But I gotta tell ya, it's a hard act to follow.

*Cut to*

*Int.* LONNEGAN'S *cabin—Night*

LONNEGAN *sits in a chair smoking, eyeing* FLOYD *coldly.* FLOYD *paces in front of him.*

FLOYD. Doyle, I know I give him four threes! He had to switch decks. We can't let him get away with that.

LONNEGAN. What was I supposed to do? Call him for cheating better than me in front of the others?

*There's a knock at the door.* FLOYD *goes and opens it. It's* HOOKER.

HOOKER. My name's Foley. Mr. Shaw sent me.

FLOYD *motions him in without a word.*

LONNEGAN. Your boss is quite a card player, Foley. How does he do it?

HOOKER (*matter-of-factly*). He cheats.

LONNEGAN *looks* HOOKER *over a second. He doesn't like smart asses.*

LONNEGAN. Then I'll just keep my money and we'll have another game.

HOOKER. You don't have any to keep. (*pulling out* LONNEGAN'S *wallet and tossing it on the table*) He hired a dame to take it from ya.

LONNEGAN *just stares at the wallet. Then he looks up at* HOOKER.

HOOKER. Shaw's been planning to beat your game for months. He was just waiting for you to cheat him so he could clip ya.

LONNEGAN *leaps at* HOOKER *in a blind rage, drives a sledge hammer blow into his stomach. Then grabs him by the throat.*

LONNEGAN. Who do you think you're talkin' to, errand boy. Nobody sets me up. (*letting go of* HOOKER *who slips to the floor, turns to* FLOYD) Take him back to the baggage room and put one in his ear. We'll get his friend later and dump 'em both, the first tunnel we hit.

FLOYD. Aw, for Christ sake, there were four witnesses at that table. . . .

LONNEGAN (*viciously*). You wanna get dumped too?

FLOYD. Doyle, we're gonna be in the station in a minute!

HOOKER (*on the floor, barely able to speak*). It's not gonna look too good, killin' a guy you owe money to. There's better ways to take him down.

LONNEGAN. Shut up. Nothin's gonna save your ass.

HOOKER. Shaw'd kill me too, if he knew I was tellin' ya this.

LONNEGAN (*a long pause*). Okay, why the rat?

HOOKER. I'm gonna take over his operation, Lonnegan. (*pause*) I need you to help me break him.

LONNEGAN *is stopped for a second. He looks at* HOOKER *long and hard, as if the intensity of his gaze could separate truth from fiction. Finally he reaches for the wallet and opens it. It's empty.*

LONNEGAN. Where's the money?

HOOKER. Shaw has it. I couldn't very well take it back from him.

*There is a silence—broken suddenly by the noise of the train braking into the station.*

LONNEGAN. C'mon, I'm giving you a lift home.

HOOKER *hesitates*.

HOOKER. I gotta go with Shaw.
LONNEGAN. You'll explain it somehow.
HOOKER. But he's expecting. . . .
LONNEGAN. I'm giving you a lift.
HOOKER. Sure thing.
LONNEGAN. Let's go then.

*Cut to*

*Int.* LONNEGAN'S *Car—Night*

*Driving through the city, the driver and* FLOYD *in front,* HOOKER *and* LONNEGAN *in back. We begin with a twelve block silence, while* LONNEGAN *thinks.* HOOKER *glances out the window from time to time, just to make sure they're really going to his place.*

LONNEGAN. What makes you think you can beat him?
HOOKER. I been plannin' this for two years. I know his organization backwards and forwards. But I need somebody respectable . . . and not completely legit. What I'm gonna do isn't very legal.
LONNEGAN *(insulted)*. I'm a banker, friend. That's legit in this state.
HOOKER. All you gotta do is put down a bet for me at Shaw's place. I'll supply all the money and the information.
LONNEGAN. What about the money you came to collect. Isn't he gonna miss it?
HOOKER. I'll tell him you paid it. I keep all his books. He trusts me. *(pause)* If ya help me out, I'll pay ya back the twenty-five grand he stole outa my own pocket.

LONNEGAN. It's worth that much to ya?
HOOKER. Maybe a couple million.

*We go to* LONNEGAN. *That last phrase has registered. He looks at* HOOKER *with a glint of amused recognition in his eye.*

LONNEGAN. Where you from, Foley?
HOOKER. I was born in Five Points on the east side, but I moved out fast.
LONNEGAN *(chuckling)*. Out and up, eh? Hey, Floyd, I'm gonna have to keep this guy away from you. You're liable to get ideas and throw me out on my can.

LONNEGAN *breaks into deep bellows of laughter.* FLOYD *is totally humiliated. He glares at* HOOKER *with contempt.* HOOKER *flashes him a little smile.*

*Ext.* HOOKER'S *Place*

*The car pulls up in front of* HOOKER'S *place.* LONNEGAN *is still laughing.*

HOOKER *(getting out)*. Klein's Drug Store, 660 Marshall at 12:30, if you're interested.
LONNEGAN. If I'm not there by quarter of, I'm not coming.

HOOKER *nods and walks up the street to his apartment building.* LONNEGAN'S *car speeds away from the curb and his renewed laughter dies in the distance.* HOOKER *breathes a sigh of relief. He's passed his first test—or has he? We follow him up the stairs to his room.*

*Int.* HOOKER'S *Apartment*

*He's just about to unlock the door, when he notices the little piece of paper he left in the door is on the floor. Without the slightest hesitation,*

HOOKER *leaps over the bannister and races back down the stairs. Two gunmen,* RILEY *and* COLE, *burst out of his room and fire at him over the railing, but he's already too far down.* RILEY *and* COLE *give chase.*

*Cut to*

*The Front of the Building*

RILEY *and* COLE *barrel out of the building and onto the sidewalk. There is an empty bus stopped at a light, but they find no sign of* HOOKER. *As the light changes, we cut to the other side of the bus, where we see* HOOKER *crouched on the rear wheel housing, hanging on to a vent. He's a little shaken, but most of all, he's still alive. We hold on him, as the bus moves off.*

GONDORFF *(v.o)*. Everything go all right?

HOOKER *(v.o.) (lying)*. Yeh, it was easy.

*Cut to*

*Int. The Store—Night*

HOOKER *and* GONDORFF *are sitting alone in the back office while the work goes on outside. Their conversation continues.*

GONDORFF. No signs of trouble?

HOOKER. What doya mean?

GONDORFF. You know, somebody tailin' ya. A torpedo or somethin'.

HOOKER. *(wanting to get off the subject)*. No, not a thing.

GONDORFF *has his doubts, but lets them ride.*

*Cut to*

*Other Parts of the Store*

*We concentrate on some of the fine details, i.e.* GARFIELD *explaining how the ticker will read out to* SINGLETON *and* BILLIE; CURLEY JACKSON *showing*

*a younger con man how to mark the odds board properly.*

GONDORFF *(v.o.)*. How 'bout Lonnegan?

HOOKER *(v.o.)*. I gave him the breakdown just like ya told me to.

GONDORFF *(v.o.)*. And?

HOOKER *(v.o.)*. He threatened to kill me.

GONDORFF *(v.o.)*. Hell, they don't do that and you know you're not gettin' through to 'em.

*Continuing: But with Camera Change*

*We concentrate on* NILES, *who's making up the "boodles" or fake bankrolls. He puts a real $100 bill on the bottom, then two inches of cut green paper on top, and then another $100 bill on top of that, so that it looks like he has a whole stack of $100 bills. The bundle is then bound with a sealed label, like those used in banks, that says $10,000. We see that he has already made several of these bundles.*

HOOKER *(v.o.)*. Then he drove me home. He tried to put himself away as legit, so I went right into the pitch.

GONDORFF *(v.o.)*. Did he hold you up on anything?

HOOKER *(v.o.)*. Naw, he just sat there and listened. I don't know if he bought it or not.

*Cut to*

*Int. Store*

TWIST *in the middle of the room giving a route to the* EIRIE KID. *He shows him where to get his drink at the bar, where to sit and finally how to leap up and throw his racing form down in disgust.*

GONDORFF *(v.o.)*. That's all right. Once they start listening, they're in trouble. Just don't give him more than he asks for. If you rattle his imagination a little, he'll come up with all the right answers himself. But all he's gotta do is catch you in one lie and you're dead.

*Cut to*

HOOKER *and* GONDORFF *in the Store Office Again*

*They both look tired.*

HOOKER. You think he'll show?
GONDORFF. Did    he    say    he wouldn't?
HOOKER. No.
GONDORFF *(softly)*. He'll show.

*Fade out*

*Fade in*

THE TALE

*Fade out*

*Fade in*

*We Open on a Wide Shot of the Alley Outside the Store*

*At first it appears to be deserted, but we move to reveal a figure in an upper window of the apartment building which forms one side of the alley. It's* KID TWIST. *His eyes roam the street, for what, we do not yet know.*

*Cut to*

*Int. An Old Drugstore Across from the Alley—Day*

*Probably prosperous at one time, it has since declined, its large fountain and eating area now host to two bums and* HOOKER, *who sits alone in a rear booth near the telephone. Dressed in a tuxedo, he nurses a cup of coffee, and anxiously alternates his glances between the clock and the empty street outside. It's 12:52.*

*Cut to*

*Int. The Store—Day*

*The place is full of people, although we avoid long shot so as not to give away the room as a whole yet. Instead, we concentrate on the tense, waiting faces of some of the more familiar people:*

GONDORFF *and* NILES *in tuxedos behind a barred cashier's area.* GONDORFF *mutilates a piece of gum in his mouth.* NILES *just stares out into space cracking his knuckles.*

GONDORFF. Eddie, cut that out, will ya.

*The boardmarker walking nervously back and forth in front of his odds board, checking every letter and number. He stops to cross a T on one of the horses' names. It was already crossed, but he does it again anyway.*

BILLIE *and* SINGLETON, *in an area hidden from the rest of the room, watching the print-out on the ticker machine. The clicking of the ticker is the only sound we hear in the store.*

CURLY JACKSON *in front of a mirror, pasting a fake Van Dyke on his chin to go with his tweed suit and monocle.*

*A couple of* BILLIE'S *girls adjusting their waitress outfits and primping their hair. Each has a tray full of drinks beside her.*

*The* EIRIE KID *silently retracing his "route" to make sure he has it down.*

*Despite the crowd, there is no talking and little movement, save for the constant swirling of smoke from several cigars and cigarettes. The group is like a theatre company waiting to go on opening night.*

Cut to

The Drugstore Again

*It's 12:56 and* HOOKER *is worried. He looks up to see two large men, obviously racket goons, come in the front door, and take a seat facing him in the next booth. They stare at him impassively, waving the waitress away when she comes to take their order.* HOOKER *knows they're* LONNE-GAN'S *men, but is somewhat unsettled by the fact that* LONNEGAN *is not with them. Suddenly, a voice.*

VOICE. Carver?

HOOKER *turns around to find that* LONNEGAN *is seated in the booth directly behind him. His bodyguard is in the one behind that.*

LONNEGAN. You should always look to the back too, kid.

HOOKER *(sliding out of his booth and into* LONNEGAN'S*).* I was afraid you weren't gonna come. We haven't got much time.

LONNEGAN *(curtly).* Get on with it then.

HOOKER *(pointing to telephone).* Sometime after 1:00 a guy's gonna call here and give you the name of a horse. *(pulling out a wad of bills)* All you do is take this two grand across the street to Shaw's place and bet it on that pony. There's nothin' to it, but don't take too much time. We only have 3 or 4 minutes after you get the call.

LONNEGAN. You're not gonna break him with a $2,000 bet.

HOOKER. This is just a test. The big one comes later. Be careful with that though, it's all I got.

LONNEGAN. And you were gonna pay me back?

HOOKER. I am after this race.

LONNEGAN *says nothing. He's not sure he likes a man who's stupid* enough to bet his last dollar on a horse race.

HOOKER. I gotta get back before Shaw misses me. Good luck.

*Ext. Street*

HOOKER *hustles out across the street and into the alley.*

*Int. Drugstore*

LONNEGAN *watches him through the window and then settles back in his seat to wait for the phone.*

*Outside Store*

*as* HOOKER *descends the stairwell into the store, he gives* KID TWIST *the office.* TWIST *turns away from the window and looks at his watch, 12:58.*

Cut to

*Drugstore*

LONNEGAN *waiting by the phone, idly pinging a knife on the salt shaker. It's 1:40. A man enters the store and walks over to use the phone.*

LONNEGAN. We're waitin' for a call.

*The man looks at* LONNEGAN *a second, and then at his four goons. He decides maybe he'll make the call later.*

Cut to

*Int. Store*

KID TWIST *again.* BILLIE *enters the room with a piece of paper,* KID TWIST *looks at it a second and then picks up the phone and begins to dial.*

*Int. Drugstore*

LONNEGAN *again. He's getting impatient now and lights a cigarette, and then the phone rings. He answers it quickly and we hear:*

TWIST. Bluenote at 6 to 1 on the nose.

*The receiver clicks down at the other end.* LONNEGAN *hangs up and goes out the door, followed by his entourage.*

*Ext. Street*

*We follow him across the street and into the alley, where he signals one of the bodyguards to check the place out.* KID TWIST *pushes a button on his window sill, and a buzzer goes off inside the store. The previously inert figures there spring to life.*

LONNEGAN'S *bodyguard descends the stairwell and knocks at the door, where he is greeted by* HOOKER *in the capacity of host. He looks the place over and motions an okay to* LONNEGAN.

*Int. Store*

*As* LONNEGAN *enters, we see the room for the first time in its entirety. Overnight it has been transformed into a swank private club, with bar, cigarette girls, upholstered furniture and chandeliers.*

SINGLETON. Look at that. He's got four apes with him.
GONDORFF. That's what I like about these guys, J.J.. They always got protection against things we'd never do to 'em.

*Everywhere there is activity. A bank of telephones buzzes incessantly.* SHEET WRITERS *scurry from phone to phone, taking bets of tremendous size from prominent people.*

SHEET WRITER. Yes, Mr. Ruth, 20,000 on Dancing Cloud.

*We reveal that the phones are controlled by a master switch, which one of the recruited con men operates from behind a partition.*

*The boardmarker, wearing headphones suspended from a sliding wire, hurriedly chalks up races and odds on a huge blackboard. From the loudspeakers we hear the words "Last flash." The odds on Bluenote settle down to 8 to 1.*

LONNEGAN *makes his way through the throng toward the betting line. His bodyguards fan out to various positions in the room. The betting crowd itself (known as the "boost") consists of close to twenty people, none of whom, of course are what they're pretending to be. Large amounts of money are changing hands at the betting window. Boodles are in sight everywhere.*

LONNEGAN *slips into the betting line, feeling somewhat estranged from the general merriment around him. There are two men in line ahead of him. The first,* CURLY JACKSON, *slaps down several bundles of cash in front of* NILES, *who's the cashier, and places a $20,000 bet on War Eagle.* GONDORFF *appears at the cashier's window and catches sight of* LONNEGAN.

GONDORFF. Never get enough, huh pal? I'd think you'd get tired of losin', Honnigan.
LONNEGAN (*piercingly*). The name is Lonnegan.
GONDORFF (*to* NILES). Make sure you see cash from this guy, Eddie. He's got the name for bettin' money he don't have.

*The man in front of* LONNEGAN *puts $5,000 on Dancing Cloud. He makes the bet on credit.* LONNEGAN *steps to the window.*

LONNEGAN. Two-thousand on Bluenote.

NILES *(writing out a ticket)*. Is that all?

LONNEGAN *(pissed)*. That's all.

*Bluenote's race is now up on the board. The race caller comes on the loudspeaker.*

CALLER. Ladies and Gentlemen. This is Arnold Rowe, your caller for the second race at Belmont in New York. A mile and ⅛, four year olds and up. And they're off!

*We see that the caller is* SINGLE-TON, *and that he's calling the race from a concealed booth next to the cashier's cage.*

CALLER. Around the first turn it's War Eagle first by a length, Jail Bate second by one and a half, Dancing Cloud third by a half on the outside, followed by Lucky Lady, Mojo, Wits' End and Bluenote.

LONNEGAN *goes to the bar, orders a drink, and settles down at one of the tables. It happens to be the one the* EIRIE KID *is at.* GONDORFF AND NILES *watch it from the cashier's cage.*

GONDORFF *(worried)*. That's not where we want him to sit.

EIRIE *tries to ignore* LONNEGAN *at first, but realizes he better make some conversation.*

EIRIE. C'mon War Eagle. *(to* LON-NEGAN*)* That Dancing Cloud's a hell of a finisher. War Eagle's gonna have to open up a little more on 'em.

LONNEGAN. You know anything about a horse named Bluenote?

EIRIE. Naw, he's never done much. Probably in here just to round out the field. War Eagle's where you wanna have your money.

EIRIE *excuses himself and heads for the bar.*

CALLER. Into the clubhouse turn, it's War Eagle by two lengths, Dancing Cloud has moved up to second by a half, Lucky Lady is third by three followed by Jail Bate, Mojo, Bluenote and Wits' End.

*The heretofore chaotic energy of the parlor is now focused on the race. Several of the patrons begin to yell for their horses.* LONNEGAN *remains seated. He seems bored with it all.* HOOKER *comes over to clear some empty glasses from his table.*

LONNEGAN *(out of the corner of his mouth)*. You really picked a winner, kid.

HOOKER. Give 'em a little time.

CALLER. Into the backstretch it's War Eagle still by a length, Dancing Cloud closing on the inside, is second by two, Lucky Lady is third by one and a half, followed by Bluenote, Jail Bate, Wits' End and Mojo.

LONNEGAN *perks up just a little. Bluenote, at least, has moved up. The rest of the people in the place are really rooting now. Few of them remain seated.*

HOOKER *arrives at the bar, with the glasses he cleared from* LONNEGAN'S *table.* EIRIE *is already there, fortifying himself with a scotch.*

HOOKER. You're doin' great, Eirie. He loves ya.

EIRIE *nods, somewhat unconvinced, and heads back to the table.*

CALLER. Into the far turn, it's Dancing Cloud now by half a length, War Eagle is second by two, Bluenote is third by a half and moving fast on the outside. Lucky Lady is fourth by four lengths, followed by Jail Bate, Wits' End and Mojo.

LONNEGAN *is getting more intent now.*

CALLER. Coming down the stretch, it's Dancing Cloud by one length, War Eagle and Bluenote are neck and neck by two. Now it's Dancing Cloud, Bluenote and War Eagle. *(shouting now)* Dancing Cloud and Bluenote head to head. . . .

*The place is going crazy. Even* SINGLETON *is standing up to get the necessary excitement in his voice.*

CALLER. Dancing Cloud, Bluenote. Dancing Cloud, Bluenote. It's Bluenote by a nose. Dancing Cloud is second by two, War Eagle third by three and a half. Time for a mile and ⅛, 2:01 and ⁶⁄₁₀ seconds.

*Most of the patrons collapse into their chairs like spent lovers.* EIRIE *slams his racing form to the floor. Nobody had Bluenote.*

CURLY *(tearing up his ticket).* Bloody awful. Who in blazes is Bluenote?

LONNEGAN *(to* EIRIE, *very self-satisfied).* War Eagle's where you want to have your money, huh?

EIRIE *doesn't reply. He can't believe Bluenote won.* LONNEGAN *looks to* HOOKER. HOOKER *gives him a wink. For the first time,* LONNEGAN *permits a smile.*

*Cut to*

LONNEGAN *at the Cashier's Window*

NILES *is counting out $16,000 to him (all of which* GONDORFF *won the night before).* GONDORFF *looks somewhat perturbed.* LONNEGAN *picks up the money and tauntingly waves it at him.*

GONDORFF *(getting his name* right *this time).* Don't bother to come back with a piker's bet like that again, Lonnegan. We got a $5,000 minimum here. *(to* HOOKER) Show this bum out.

HOOKER *hesitates a second.*

GONDORFF. Go on, ya goddamn ninny.

GONDORFF *gives* HOOKER *a hard shove in the back with his foot, sending him into a table and sprawling to the floor.*

GONDORFF *(indicating* LONNEGAN'S *bodyguards).* And tell him not to bring his garbage men in here no more. This is a class joint.

HOOKER, *pretending to be humiliated, gets to his feet and escorts* LONNEGAN *to the door.* LONNEGAN *stops, gives* GONDORFF *a derisive smile, and walks out. Once he's gone, the general clatter and hubbub in the room cease, like it had been turned off by a faucet. Most of the boost sit down and relax.* CURLY JACKSON *rips off his Van Dyke. It's been itching him.*

GONDORFF. He's gaffed, kid. He should start coming to you now.

*Cut to*

*Int.* COMBS'S *Office at the Clearinghouse—Day*

COMBS *sits passively on the edge of his desk glancing across the room every now and then at* RILEY, *who is slumped uneasily in a folding chair, looking like a defendant at the Inquisition. Both remain silent, like two men in a waiting room. Suddenly, what they've been waiting for arrives.* LONNEGAN *comes into the office, flanked by his bodyguards. Skipping the usual pleasantries, he walks right over to* RILEY.

LONNEGAN. All right, Riley. What the hell happened?

RILEY *(not looking at him).* We missed him.

LONNEGAN. You weren't hired to miss him.

RILEY. There wasn't any way he coulda known we was in there. We made a clean pick on the lock and didn't leave no footprints in the hall. Somebody musta wised him up.

LONNEGAN. Yeh, and what does Cole say about that?

RILEY. I don't know. He took it hard.

LONNEGAN. All right, get outa here. You're outta work.

RILEY *gets up and drags himself out the door like a whipped dog.*

LONNEGAN. We'll put Salino on it. I need somebody careful.

COMBS. Salino? Why waste our best people on a small-time job like this? It ain't no heavy gee we're after. The guy's a five and dime grifter.

LONNEGAN. Then why isn't he dead?

COMBS. They didn't think he'd be so cagey, that's all. They'll get him next time.

LONNEGAN. Use Salino. It'll take a little longer, but there won't be any holes in it.

COMBS *gives up. The second time's the charm.*

LONNEGAN. And tell Cole I wanta see him when he gets in.

COMBS. He's not comin' in. Not to get bounced off a job anyway.

LONNEGAN. He had his chance and all he did was shoot up a rooming house. Made a lotta noise and woke up a few cops, but didn't hit nothin'.

COMBS *keeps his mouth shut. There's no way to talk to* LONNEGAN *when he's like this.*

LONNEGAN *(cooling a little).* This is Salino's job now, Vince. If Cole wants to muscle in on it, that's his business. But he's breakin' the rules and Salino's not gonna like it.

*Cut to*

*Int.* LONNEGAN's *Hotel—Day*

*The finest the period had to offer. We pick up* HOOKER *coming through the lobby. As he starts up the stairs we:*

*Cut to*

FLOYD *in* LONNEGAN's *hotel room, He hangs up a phone he's been talking on.*

FLOYD *(to* LONNEGAN*).* He's on his way.

HOOKER *knocks at the door and is admitted by a bodyguard.* LONNEGAN, *wearing a silk bathrobe, is seated at a table counting a pile of money. There are two other assistants behind him. They don't look friendly.*

HOOKER. Well, what did I tell ya?

LONNEGAN. You got lucky once. That's not enough.

HOOKER. Lucky, hell. I could do it every day.

LONNEGAN. Why don't ya then?

HOOKER. 'Cause it's better to do it all at once. *(leaning close)* We're puttin' down 400 grand next week. At five to one we make two million. Twenty percent of that is yours if ya stick with us.

LONNEGAN. You got a system, Foley?

HOOKER. No. You can still lose with a system.

LONNEGAN. You're past-posting, aren't ya?

HOOKER. Could be.

LONNEGAN. How?

HOOKER *(pause).* You gonna stay in?

LONNEGAN. Not until I get some answers.

HOOKER *(outflanked).* We got a partner downtown runs the central office of the Western Union. Race results from all over the country come in there and go right across his desk on their way to the bookies. All he does is hold them up a couple minutes until he can call us and get a bet down on the winner. Then he releases the results to the bookies and we clean up on a race that's already been run. It can't miss, unless the Western Union Dicks get onto it.

LONNEGAN *sits back a second, then comes forward again and pushes a pile of bills over to* HOOKER. HOOKER *smiles and begins to count the money.*

LONNEGAN. You got the 400 grand yet?

HOOKER. Not yet, but . . . *(stopping suddenly)* Hey, there's only a grand here.

LONNEGAN. We're gonna place another bet tomorrow.

HOOKER *(getting angry).* What is this? That's my money.

LONNEGAN. You owe me twenty-five grand. Besides, if your setup's as good as you say, you'll get even more.

HOOKER'S *in a jam and he knows it.*

HOOKER *(after a pause).* I gotta talk to my partner first. We can't afford to expose our game too much.

LONNEGAN. Good, I'll talk to him too.

HOOKER. No.

LONNEGAN *(paternally, but still a threat).* You been waitin' a long time for this, Foley. Don't ruin it for yourself. *(after a pause)* We'll pick you up tomorrow at three.

HOOKER *says nothing for a minute.* FLOYD *comes over and presents him with his hat and opens the door.* HOOKER *walks out.*

*Int. An Indoor Telephone Booth—Day*

*one of the old, wooden kind—accordion doors with glass panes in the upper half.* HOOKER *dials rapidly.*

HOOKER. Twist? I told him the tale, but he didn't go for it. He wants to see my partner tomorrow at 3:00.

TWIST. Hell, we'll never get a telegraph store setup by then. Any chance of talking him out of it?

HOOKER. None. I woulda stalled him, but I didn't have many friends in the room.

TWIST. All right, we'll have to play him on the fly. I'll get Eddie lookin' for a place.

HOOKER. Let me know when ya get somethin'.

TWIST. Sure thing, Tootsie.

HOOKER *blows a mock kiss through the phone and hangs up. He turns to leave the booth, when suddenly he sees something that stops him cold. There looking through the glass is the smirking face of* DETECTIVE SNYDER. HOOKER *is immobilized.*

SNYDER *puts his hand inside his coat and slowly draws out his gun. He points it right at* HOOKER'S *face and then violently smashes all the glass in the upper half of the door with the barrel. Fragments of glass spray into the booth, a couple of which imbed themselves in* HOOKER'S *cheek.*

HOOKER *quickly whips open the door, trapping* SNYDER'S *hand in the accordion and jarring loose his gun.* HOOKER *sprints out of the booth as* SNYDER *scrambles for his pistol and gives pursuit.*

*Ext. Alleys and Side Streets—Day—The Two Men*

*We follow the two men up alleys and side streets as they race through the dregs of the city, two panting shadows moving through places that only get light at night. The wind blows drops of blood off* HOOKER'S *cheek as he runs.* SNYDER *still has his gun, but would rather inflict pain than kill him.*

### Condemned Building

HOOKER *makes for a condemned building and scrambles up the stairs, steps giving way under him as he goes.*

### Int. Building

*On the fourth floor, he ducks into a room and quickly locks the door.*

*We pan the room to reveal that the whole back side of the building is gone.* HOOKER *runs toward the ledge and leaps through the air, landing on the fire escape of an adjacent building, some 15 feet away. He kicks in a window and goes off down the hall. We cut back to:*

SNYDER *furiously kicking in the locked door. He finally crashes through, only to find an empty room and a beautiful panorama of the city and its nearest Hooverville.*

### Cut to

### Long Shot—HOOKER

*winding his way through the slum area of town, dashing along back streets, over fences and through vacant lots, making good his escape. From our angle, he looks like a rat in a maze.*

GONDORFF *(v.o.).* Why didn't you tell me about Snyder before?

HOOKER *(v.o.).* I thought I'd lost him.

### Cut to

### Int. GONDORFF'S *Room at the Carousel Building—Day*

HOOKER *sits sullenly at the table.* BILLIE *stands over him putting some*

*ointment on his face to close the cuts.* GONDORFF *looks on. Their discussion continues.*

GONDORFF. Well you found him again and we're gonna have to do somethin' about it. What else haven't ya been tellin' me?

HOOKER. Nothin'. I told ya everything there is.

GONDORFF. Then why'd ya move outa your room?

HOOKER. It was too noisy.

GONDORFF. You can't play your friends like marks, Hooker.

HOOKER *doesn't reply. He knows* GONDORFF'S *on to him.*

GONDORFF. You know how easy it'd be for one of Lonnegan's guys to nail you?

HOOKER. All we need is a couple days, Henry. A couple days and we'll get Lonnegan down and stomp on 'em.

GONDORFF. You just won't learn, will ya. Hell, you come in here, I teach you stuff maybe five guys in this world know, stuff most grifters couldn't do even if they knew it, and all you wanna do is run down a bullet. *(pause)* You're just like all them new jerks. Lotsa nerve and no brains. And ten years from now when me and the others are through and you dumb guys are all dead there won't be one gee left who knows the Big Con was anything more than a way to make a livin'.

HOOKER. A couple days; that's all I'm askin'. I can stay clear that long.

GONDORFF *(trying to be angry and failing).* Christ, they'll probably miss you and hit me.

### Fade out

### Fade in

THE WIRE

*Fade out*

*Fade in*

*Int. A Sleezy Diner—Late After-noon*

*Located across the street from* HOOKER'S *apartment building.* HOOK-ER *sits alone in a booth, with a plate of ham and eggs he's hardly touched.*

*The two cuts on his face have pretty much stopped bleeding. A big fan above the counter area drones away lethargically, its air stream insuffi-cient to either cool the place or drive out the smell of onions and grease.*

*A waitress,* LORETTA, *emerges from the kitchen and ambles slowly over to* HOOKER'S *table. Slim and raven-haired, she manifests an indifference bred from years spent delivering things to people who are rarely grate-ful for what she brings. Only a light scar on her left cheek hints at another side.*

LORETTA. You done?

HOOKER. Yeh, I guess I shoulda had the meat loaf.

LORETTA *(deadpan)*. It isn't any better.

HOOKER. Where's June today?

LORETTA *(figuring up the bill)*. She don't work here no more. I'm fillin' in for a couple days . . . till I can get a train outa here.

HOOKER. Where you goin'?

LORETTA *(putting the check down and walking away)*. I don't know. De-pends what train I get on.

HOOKER *looks for some sign that she's putting him on. He doesn't get it. He takes out some money, drops it on the table and walks out.*

*Cut to*

*Ext. A Western Union Office—Late Afternoon*

*A truck with the words* CLAYTON BROS., CUSTOM PAINTING AND DE-CORATING *stenciled on the side, is parked out front. Two men, wearing overalls and painter's caps, walk into the office carrying paint buckets, brushes and tarpaulins. When they get to the reception counter, we see that they are* TWIST *and* SINGLETON.

TWIST *(to the* RECEPTIONIST*)*. Ex-cuse me. We're here to paint Mr. Har-mon's office.

RECEPTIONIST *(obviously not ex-pecting them)*. Mr. Harmon's office? Hold on just a second.

*She goes to get* MR. HARMON.

*Cut to*

*Ext. The Sleezy Diner—Late After-noon*

HOOKER *is standing on the curb outside the diner, obviously waiting for somebody.* LONNEGAN'S *car pulls up and* HOOKER *hops in the back.*

LONNEGAN. What happened to your face?

HOOKER. Had a little fight with a raggle down on 13th. She got me with her ring.

LONNEGAN. Oughta lay off the skirts. You won't find any of my boys moonin' around that kinda trash.

HOOKER *looks at* FLOYD, *who stares doggedly ahead.*

*Cut to*

*Int. The Western Union Office Again—Late Afternoon*

MR. HARMON *is looking over the authorization papers that* TWIST *and* SINGLETON *have given him. He can't find anything wrong with it.*

HARMON. Brigham signed it all right. I can't understand why he didn't tell me.

SINGLETON. Ah, he's like all them supervisors. They think they're too good for regular people. He says he was in here a while ago and the place was a mess.

HARMON *looks around, hoping it's not true.*

TWIST. We'll try and hurry so we don't keep you out of your office too long.

HARMON. Why can't I work with you in there?

SINGLETON. Look pal, we gotta cover the floor, the furniture, everything, so we don't spill on nothing. Now if you wanta sit in there with a tarp over your head, you're welcome to it.

HARMON. All right, how long will you be?

TWIST. Hour or two at the most. We do good work.

HARMON *is resigned.* TWIST *and* SINGLETON *pick up their gear and march into the office. Once inside, we notice that the office has an exit door which opens to an outside alley.* TWIST *immediately removes his overalls, revealing the suit and tie he's wearing underneath. He takes out a picture of himself, a woman and three small children, and puts it on* HARMON'S *desk, replacing a similar picture of* HARMON'S *family.* SINGLETON, *meanwhile, has spread a few tarps and begins to paint the walls.*

*Cut to*

*Ext. The Western Union Office— Late Afternoon*

LONNEGAN'S *car pulls up and stops across the street.*

HOOKER. We'll go to the side door.

*We follow* HOOKER *and* LONNEGAN *across the street to the side entrance which opens into:*

*Int.* HARMON'S *Office*

HOOKER *knocks and* TWIST, *of course, answers.*

HOOKER. Les, I got Mr. Lonnegan with me. He wants to see you a second.

TWIST *(irritated).* What the hell's the matter with you. We coulda met at a club or somethin'.

HOOKER. I thought it might be good for him to see the setup.

TWIST *(hushed).* Well we can't talk in here. They're having the place painted.

TWIST *walks over to the intercom on his desk. He leaves the door open so that* LONNEGAN *can get a good look at the office,* TWIST'S *picture in it, the painter, etc. . . . .* LONNEGAN'S *not missing any of it.*

TWIST *(talking into the intercom).* Miss Barnes, I'm going home a little early today. Tell anyone that calls that they can reach me here in the morning. Thank you.

*Cut to*

*Int. Front Office*

HARMON'S SECRETARY *at the other end of the intercom.* MR. HARMON *is with her. They look at each other a second and* HARMON *decides he better see what's happening in his office. He opens the door to find it empty except for a pile of painting equipment and one haphazardly painted wall.*

*Cut to*

*Int. A Hotel Bar—Evening*

HOOKER, LONNEGAN *and* TWIST *sit at one of the more secluded tables. They are not eating.*

TWIST. Can't do it. There're telegraph inspectors all over the place.

LONNEGAN. I want to see it one more time.

TWIST. I got 400 grand comin' in from the coast next week. I'm not gonna blow it for a measly 14 gees. No sir, I say when we place our bets.

LONNEGAN. Not if you want me to keep makin' 'em for ya.

TWIST *hesitates.*

LONNEGAN. If it works again tomorrow, I'm gonna finance the whole thing. Half a million dollars worth. We split 60-40.

TWIST. What doya mean? We already got a guy. He's liquidating everything he has for this. And still givin' us half.

LONNEGAN. With 20 per cent off the top for me. Either way you only get 40.

TWIST. What am I supposed to say to him?

LONNEGAN. Tell him to drop dead. With what I know about your operation you should be worryin' about keepin' me happy.

TWIST *(almost pleading now).* But we can't keep goin' into Shaw's place and cleanin' up on longshots. He's bound to get wise.

LONNEGAN (getting up to leave). Then we'll go for short odds this time. You'll just have to give me all three places instead. See ya tomorrow.

TWIST *(feebly).* Yeh, see ya tomorrow.

*On his way out,* LONNEGAN *gives* HOOKER *a little nod, as if to say "That's the way ya gotta handle 'em."* TWIST *and* HOOKER *delay a few seconds and then get up to leave.*

*We frame the shot with a coffee cup large in the foreground. As they go to the door, a black-gloved hand with four fingers enters the frame and puts a nickel down next to the cup.*

*Fade out*

*Fade in*

THE SHUT-OUT

*Fade out*

*Fade in*

*Int. A Downtown Dinette— Morning*

SNYDER *finishes a donut and a cup of coffee, puts down a dime for the lot and exits. We follow him down the street:*

*Ext. Street*

*to a corner newstand, where he stops to buy a morning paper. As he peruses it, he's approached by two large,* CLEAN-CUT MEN *in white skimmers.*

MAN. Are you Lieutenant William Snyder?

SNYDER. I don't know, what's up?

MAN. F.B.I. . . . Special Agent Polk'd like a few words with ya. Ya got a couple minutes?

SNYDER *(completely floored)* Yeh, sure.

*The two men show him to a waiting car.*

*Cut to*

*Int. An Abandoned Warehouse— Day*

SNYDER *stands in the middle of a dusty old machine room, surrounded by four or five Federal Agents. Visible around the room are several folding cots and portable lockers. The agents have obviously been quartered here temporarily. They all wear white skimmers, save for one, a portly man,* SPECIAL AGENT POLK, *who paces the room smoking. There is something long-suffering about him, as if he wondered how he ever got in a service that thought white skimmers were classy.*

SNYDER. What is this? I got work to do.

POLK. Sit down and shut up, will ya. Try not to live up to all my expectations. *(not in the mood to screw around)* We were told you know a hustle artist named Johnny Hooker.

SNYDER *doesn't answer.*

POLK. Do ya know him or don't ya?

SNYDER. Yeh, but I don't know where he is.

POLK. Well we do. He's chummin' around with a Big C named Henry Gondorff. Ring any bells?

SNYDER. Sure. Every bunco man in the country knows Gondorff.

POLK. There's word he's gonna run a con on the North Side here. We got a year-old Florida warrant on him, but it's a thin beef, and he can beat it in court unless we catch him cold. All we want you to do is pick up Hooker for us.

SNYDER. Why don't you pick him up yourself?

POLK. Cause the stoolies are used to street dicks jumpin' him. If word gets around that Feds are in on it too, Gondorff'll fold up the whole thing.

SNYDER. Wouldn't that be too bad. You'd hafta move outa this nice office ya got.

POLK *(enraged).* Don't crack wise to me, flatfoot. I spent a lotta time in dumps like this, eatin' Gondorff's dust while the bunco squad gets rich tippin' him off. But it's not gonna happen this time. We're not even gonna let the police know we're here. If you keep your mouth shut and do a job, there'll be some reward in it for ya. And you better take it, cause I can make ya work for us without it.

SNYDER. What the hell good is Hooker to ya?

POLK. He's gonna set up Gondorff for us.

SYNDER. He'll never do it.

POLK *(self-satisfied).* I think he will.

*Cut to*

*Int. The Drugstore—Day*

LONNEGAN *sits by the phone, watching the clock and sipping a cup of coffee.*

*Cut to*

*Int. The Store—Day*

*Specifically, the small room from which* SINGLETON *does his race broadcasts.* SINGLETON, *himself, is hunched over the ticker machine, reading the print-out.* BILLIE *sits at the microphone table with a pencil and pad, ready to write.*

SINGLETON. Visitation is still up by two at the three-quarters. Single Action second, Fasanella third.

BILLIE. What's the line on Visitation?

SINGLETON *(checking further up on the printout sheet).* 7 to 2. That ain't bad.

BILLIE. He'll probably fall down.

GONDORFF *appears at the doorway.*

GONDORFF. How ya doin'?

SINGLETON *(eyes still glued to the ticker).* Nothin' yet. I got a good one on the lead at Hialeah, but he's fadin'.

BILLIE. Best we had was Cat's Eye in the second at Del Mar, and he was only seven-to-two. Not many longshots comin' in today.

GONDORFF. We don't want big odds on this one, J.J. Take anything at five-to-two or under. And nothin' over four-to-one.

SINGLETON. Okay. Here we go. *(excited)* Billie. You ready?

BILLIE *prepares to write on her pad.*

BILLIE. Yeh, go ahead.

SINGLETON. At the finish, it's Single Action by two, Fasanella second, Visitation third. (*reading up the sheet again*) Line on Single Action . . . five-to-one. Hell with it, that's no good.

BILLIE *crumples up the piece of paper she's been writing on and chucks it in a wastecan.* GONDORFF *leaves the room, as* SINGLETON *turns back to his vigil at the ticker.*

SINGLETON (*a little weary*). Okay, the Fairfield Stakes at Santa Anita. Mile and a quarter for 3 year olds and up.

*Cut to*

*The Floor Area of the Store*

*Everyone is in his place as before. Today, however,* CURLY JACKSON *is playing the part of the aging sport.*

*Well scrubbed and clean shaven, he cuts a dashing figure in his blue blazer and white pants. We go to* GONDORFF *in the cashier's cage. He's talking to* NILES, *who's busy handing out fake bankrolls to members of the boost.*

GONDORFF. He's gonna hit ya with 20 grand, Eddie. How much cash we got?

NILES. Not enough to cover a bet that big.

GONDORFF. Get a coupla extra guys in the line, then, We'll give him the shut-out.

NILES *nods.*

*Cut to*

*Int. The Drugstore—Day*

LONNEGAN *is still waiting. He takes the 20 grand out of his coat pocket and thumbs through it, just to make sure it's all there.*

*Cut to*

*Int. The Store—Day*

SINGLETON *and* BILLIE *at the ticker again.* BILLIE *looks a little sleepy.* SINGLETON *is obviously involved with the progress of a race.*

SINGLETON. Okay, Billie, here we go.

BILLIE *snaps to and prepares to write as* SINGLETON *reads.*

SINGLETON. At the wire it's Wrecking Crew the winner by five, Grand Theft second, Wingless Third (*reading up*) Wrecking Crew was . . . three-to-one. (*ripping the sheet out of the ticker*) That's our boy.

BILLIE *and* SINGLETON *hustle out of the room.*

*Ext. Alley*

*We follow* BILLIE *through the store and across the alley to the building from which* TWIST *keeps his lookout.*

*Cut back to*

*Int. Store*

GONDORFF, *holding the ticker sheet* SINGLETON *has given him, emerges from the office and starts giving instructions to the boost.*

GONDORFF. All right, Furey, your horse is Wingless. Paltrow, the Big Alabama and Phillips'll take Grand Theft. Rodgers and Eirie have Wrecking Crew. Jackson—His Dandy, Cowan—Change of Heart, Fiskin and Chappie—Made to Order. (*pointing to the* EIRIE KID) Eirie, he gets a bang outa seein' you lose, so we oughta use that on 'em. If you play the birds of a feather routine we worked on, it should steam him up pretty good. You think you can handle that?

EIRIE (*a little nervous*). Yeh, sure.

GONDORFF. O.K., you guys in line take your time, and I wanta see lotsa joy on Wrecking Crew.

*Cut to*

*Int.* TWIST'S *Room—Day*

BILLIE *enters and gives* TWIST *the piece of paper she wrote the race results on. He picks up the phone and starts to dial.*

*Cut to*

*Int. Drugstore—Day*

*The phone rings and* LONNEGAN *answers it.*

VOICE. Wrecking Crew at 4-1, Grand Theft to place, Made to Order to show.

LONNEGAN *smiles and hangs up the phone.*

*Cut to*

*Int. Store—Day*

LONNEGAN'S *in line at the betting window. There are four people in front of him this time, and they are moving rather slowly. The "Last Flash" call is heard on the speakers.*

LONNEGAN *(getting impatient).* C'mon, let's hurry up there.

*The man at the head of the line turns around and gives* LONNEGAN *a chilling look, as if he were beneath contempt. He puts down $25,000 on Grand Theft. The next man in line plunges down $30,000 on Wrecking Crew.*

*Just as* LONNEGAN *is about to step to the window,* GONDORFF *gives a quick signal to* SINGLETON. *The speakers come on.*

CALLER. Ladies and Gentlemen, this is Arnold Rowe, your caller for the $100,000 Fairfield Stakes at Hol-lywood Park in Los Angeles. A mile and ⅜ for three year olds and up. And they're off!

LONNEGAN *(counting out his money).* Twenty-thousand on. . . .

NILES. I'm sorry, sir. We can't take bets after the race is started.

*He points to a sign above the window, which says exactly that.* LONNEGAN *grabs up his money in disgust.*

GONDORFF. Don't take it so hard, pal. You probably woulda lost it.

LONNEGAN *wanders over to the bar in a funk.*

CALLER. And around the first turn, it's Wrecking Crew by a half length, Grand Theft second by one, His Dandy is third by one half, followed by Change of Heart, Back Flip, Made to Order and High Ground.

*The assembled patrons are once again thoroughly involved in the race.* EIRIE *comes up to* LONNEGAN *at the bar.*

EIRIE. Who you got?

LONNEGAN *(half-heartedly).* I'm sitting this one out.

EIRIE. I've got wrecking crew. Maybe it'll be my day.

LONNEGAN *nods and wanders away.* HOOKER *comes over to him.*

HOOKER. What happened?

LONNEGAN. I didn't get the bet down in time.

HOOKER *(pissed).* Oh, Jesus.

*Cut to*

*Int. Store Office*

GONDORFF *and* NILES, *back in the office.*

NILES *(looking out at the floor).* Looks like he's sulking.

GONDORFF. If we're lucky, this'll bring him back stronger than ever.

*Cut to*

*The Floor*

CALLER. Coming for home, it's Wrecking Crew by six lengths, Made to Order is second by two and a half, High Ground is third by a length and Grand Theft is coming fast on the rail. It's Wrecking Crew, Made to Order and Grand Theft. Wrecking Crew wins it by five lengths, Grand Theft is second by a nose, Made to Order is third by two. Time for one and ⅜ mile, 2:11 and ⁴⁄₁₀ seconds.

EIRIE *explodes in a joyous frenzy. He grabs* LONNEGAN *by the shoulders and shakes him.*

EIRIE. I won! I won! You hear that! I won 15,000! You hear that!

*Yeh,* LONNEGAN *heard that.* LONNEGAN *shakes loose, grabs his coat and heads for the door.*

*Ext. Alley—Day*

*He finds* HOOKER *waiting for him outside.*

LONNEGAN. Tell your friend I'll have the money here by post-time tomorrow. We'll take the first race where the odds are 4-1 or better. And make sure I can get to that window this time.

HOOKER. How am I gonna do that?

LONNEGAN *(coarsely).* I don't know, figure something out.

LONNEGAN *storms across the street to his waiting car and drives off.* HOOKER *relaxes into a smile. He's already figured something out.*

*Cut to*

*Int. Sleezy Diner Across from* HOOKER's *Apt. Bldg.—Evening*

HOOKER *sits at the counter finishing a plate of meat loaf.* LORETTA *is down at the cash register, leaning on the counter, looking idly out into space.* HOOKER *glances over at her every once in a while to see if she might be interested in striking up a little conversation. She's not. He finishes his meal and comes down to the register to pay his bill.*

HOOKER. Meat loaf, apple pie and a cup of coffee.

LORETTA *(ringing it up).* Sixty-five.

HOOKER *gives her a dollar. She goes to the register for change.*

HOOKER. What time you get off work here?

LORETTA. 2:00 A.M.

HOOKER. You doin' anything tonight?

LORETTA *(handing him his change).* Yeh, sleepin'.

HOOKER *figures that's enough of that. He pockets his change and starts out the door, when suddenly he stops short.*

*Ext. Street*

*Across the street in a doorway is the silhouette of a man. It's* COLE. *He's pretending not to look at the diner, but* HOOKER *isn't fooled.*

*Int. Diner*

*He goes back to* LORETTA *at the register.*

HOOKER. You got a back door to this place?

LORETTA. No. What's wrong with the front?

HOOKER *(urgently now).* Look, I don't have time to mess around. There's somebody out there I don't need to see. You got a fire escape or anything?

LORETTA. No.

HOOKER. All right, do me a favor.

Go into the bathroom, open the window and wait for me there.

LORETTA. What the hell for?

HOOKER. Just do what I tell ya and everything'll be jake.

*Cracks of concern begin to appear in* LORETTA'S *marble.*

LORETTA. What does this guy want?

HOOKER *(evenly)*. He'd like to kill me.

LORETTA *just looks at him a second. Realizing that this is no joke, she turns and walks slowly but steadily to the bathroom.* HOOKER *waits until she's out of sight.*

*Ext. Street*

HOOKER *goes to the front door and steps outside.* COLE *looks up at the sound of the door.* HOOKER *makes a big show of spotting him, and runs back into the diner.* COLE, *his cover blown, draws his gun and races across the street in pursuit. Arriving just in time to see—*

*Int. Diner*

HOOKER *go into the bathroom, he charges in after him, only to find the place empty. He goes quickly from stall to stall, on the chance that* HOOKER *might be hiding in one of them.*

*He comes to one that's closed, and seeing a pair of woman's legs under the door, rejects that, and moves on to the next one.*

*We cut inside the stall to reveal* LORETTA *sitting on the toilet with her skirt hiked up. Right behind her, crouched on the back of the seat, is* HOOKER.

COLE *has finished his rapid inspection now, and having found nothing,* *looks around for* HOOKER'S *probable escape route. He sees the open window and climbs out to find himself in a small air shaft, from which he knows* HOOKER *could not escape.* HOOKER, *seizing the time, bursts out of the stall and runs back out through the diner.* COLE *sees him, but too late to get off a shot. He climbs back in the window and gives chase.*

*Ext. Street*

*We pick up* HOOKER *barreling down the street with* COLE *a hundred yards or so behind.* HOOKER *makes a sharp cut into an alley, and we see immediately that it's a hopeless dead end. Inexplicably, he makes no attempt to run back out.*

COLE *draws up and cuts into the alley, anticipating the kill which should be easy now. He prepares to sight down his victim, when suddenly he realizes there is no victim in sight.* HOOKER, *miraculously, has vanished.* COLE *scans the alley frantically for some trace of him. There are no windows or doors at the street level. Not even a drain pipe. Just brick wall. It's impossible.* HOOKER *has disappeared into thin air.*

COLE *slams his gun into his shoulder holster with a curse, and starts back out of the alley, when all of a sudden he stops in utter terror. His mouth drops open and he chokes out the words:*

COLE. Salino, hey look. I didn't mean to move in on. . . .

*Before anything else can come out, two bullets rip into his chest. He falls to the concrete, coming to rest on a manhole cover, which we notice is slightly ajar. We:*

*Cut to*

*The Sewer Pipes*

*beneath the manhole. We see* HOOKER *making his way through the slop, having gained another reprieve, but unaware that with two down, there is still one to go.*

*Cut to*

Int. HOOKER'S *Apartment Building—Evening*

HOOKER *comes in the front entrance and goes to the elevator, one of the old-fashioned kind with the iron grid on the inside. He's still a little rattled and waiting for the elevator is making him restless. It finally arrives, and he steps inside, closing the grid behind him. As he starts to push the button for his floor, he realizes for the first time that he's not alone. He looks to the corner to find* SNYDER, *holding a gun on him. This time there's not much doubt that he'll use it if necessary.*

HOOKER. Hey there, Snyder. Long time no see.

*Cut to*

Int. *The Abandoned Warehouse—Evening*

SNYDER *brings* HOOKER *into the crate room where* SPECIAL AGENT POLK *and the other agents are waiting.* POLK, *as ususal, has his coat off, revealing his shoulder holster.*

POLK. Hello, Mr. Hooker. Special Agent Polk, F.B.I. . . . *(shoving a chair over to him).* Have a seat.

HOOKER *remains standing.*

POLK *(ignoring it, drinking from a cup).* You want a drink or something?
HOOKER. No.
POLK. We want to talk to ya about Henry Gondorff.

HOOKER. Don't think I know him.
POLK. Well give youself a couple seconds, crumb. You wouldn't wanna lie to me. Lt. Snyder here says you done a lotta confidence work in his town.
HOOKER. Lt. Snyder doesn't know shit.

CAPT. POLK *almost laughs, but he checks it.*

HOOKER. You got nothin' on me.
POLK. We'll get it, and if we can't, we'll just make it up. Grand larceny, extortion. *(with special emphasis)* counterfeiting, anything you want.

HOOKER *says nothing, but it's not from defiance now. He's beginning to get the picture.*

POLK. Look, I got nothin' against you, but you're in trouble here. All you gotta do is tell us when Gondorff's gonna play his chump. We come in at the string, make the pinch, and you walk out free as a bird. No questions, no court appearance, nothing.
HOOKER. No.
POLK. You've already done time twice, and judges don't like three time losers. You wanna sit in the can for forty years, startin' tonight?
HOOKER. I'll make parole.
POLK. Like hell. You won't even get a review till you're seventy.
HOOKER *(softly).* I'll chance it.

POLK *pauses for a moment, then seems resigned.*

POLK. Okay, if that's the way you want it. We might even provide you with a little company on the way up the river. That wife of Luther Coleman's—What was her name, Snyder?
SNYDER. Alva.

HOOKER'S *head snaps up and he regards* POLK *with veiled loathing.*

POLK. That's it. Alva Coleman. Quite a grifter in her time, I hear. Snyder says he's got quite a dossier on her. Nothing major by itself, but put 'em together and it could add up to a lotta years.

HOOKER. You stink, Polk.

POLK. C'mon, don't be a sap. It's not her I want. I don't care if you're too dumb to save yourself, but there's no sense draggin' everybody else down with ya. *(pause)* It's all over, Hooker. You can save me a lotta trouble, but I'm gonna get Henry Gondorff whether you help me out or not.

HOOKER'S *thoroughly whipped. He sits down for the first time.*

HOOKER *(softly)*. Will you wait until the chump is played?

POLK. Hell yes. We don't care about the mark. He deserves what he gets.

HOOKER *(with heat)*. I mean completely played. Until he's beat and the score is taken. You come in before we beat him and I'll kill him. You'll have a tough time explaining that, won't ya.

POLK. All right, Hooker, but you take it on the lam, and we'll shoot you down on sight.

HOOKER *(barely audible)*. Just as long as I get to finish the play.

*Cut to*

*Int.* GONDORFF'S *Room—Night*

GONDORFF *and* HOOKER *are playing gin rummy and drinking.* GONDORFF *makes little comments as he plays, but* HOOKER *is quiet and withdrawn. The carousel is not in operation and a heavy silence hangs over the place.*

GONDORFF. What's the matter, kid? You're not sayin' much.

HOOKER. Just a little nervous, that's all.

GONDORFF. Luther always told me to bite my toenails when I got nervous. You see yourself doin' that and you realize it ain't worth it.

HOOKER *smiles feebly.*

BILLIE *appears at the door.*

BILLIE. Things are a little slow tonight, Henry. I wanna open the round for the girls.

GONDORFF *takes out a set of keys and tosses them to her. She leaves to go start the merry-go-round.* GONDORFF *settles back into the game.*

GONDORFF. Take it easy, you won't lose him now. We had him 10 years ago when he decided to be somebody. Believe me, I've seen enough to know.

HOOKER *(softly)*. How many guys you conned in your life, Henry?

GONDORFF. Two or three hundred I guess. Sometimes played two a day when I was in Shea's mob. We had it down to a business *(pause)* 'Course Chicago was a right town then. The fix was in. The dicks took their end without a beef. All the Wall Street boys wanted to make investments for us. Even had marks looking *us* up, thinkin' they could beat the game. *(pause)* Yeh, kid, it really stunk. No sense in bein' a grifter if it's the same as bein' a citizen.

GONDORFF *chucks his cards on the table. He's through for the night.*

GONDORFF. I better do some packin'. I'm gonna be a hot number again after tomorrow.

HOOKER. Then why you doin' it?

GONDORFF. Seems worthwhile, doesn't it? Maybe it's just for the cave-in on Lonnegan's face when we put in the sting.

*That's good enough.* HOOKER *gets up to leave.*

HOOKER. Henry.
GONDORFF. Yeh.
HOOKER *(apologetically).* I appreciate your stickin' your neck out. I wouldn't have asked ya if it weren't for Luther.
GONDORFF. Ain't nothin' gonna make up for Luther, kid. *(pause)* Revenge is for suckers. I been griftin' 30 years and never got any.

HOOKER *just nods and walks out the door.*

*Int. Carousel*

*We follow him past the Carousel which is now full of giggling prostitutes in various stages of undress. Their childish frolicking is charming from a group usually so jaded, but it's lost on* HOOKER *tonight.*

*Cut to*

*Ext. A City Street—Night*

*It's late now and the street is deserted save for an occasional derelict or streetwalker on her way home from a night's work. We pick up* HOOKER *coming down the street toward his apartment building. He walks slowly, almost reluctantly, as if he didn't care whether he ever got there or not.*

*As he nears his building, he notices* LORETTA *coming out of the diner across the street. He stops and watches as she looks up and disappears into an adjacent building that advertises rooms for rent. After a few seconds, we see a light come on in one of its second story windows.*

HOOKER *just stands there a second, debating with himself, trying to figure out a reason for doing what he's going to do anyway. We follow him* across the street to LORETTA's *building and:*

*Int.* LORETTA's

*He goes up the stairs to the room where the light came on. He passes a couple of derelicts on the way. He knocks twice and* LORETTA *answers in her bathrobe. She is more than a little startled to see him.*

LORETTA. Looks like he missed ya.
HOOKER. Yeh, this time anyway.

LORETTA *notices an old busybody peeping out at them from her room across the hall.*

LORETTA. Good night, Mrs. Hillard.

MRS. HILLARD *quickly closes her door.*
HOOKER *(shuffling a little).* I, ah . . . thought you might wanna come out for a while. Maybe have a drink or somethin'.
LORETTA. You move right along, don't ya.
HOOKER *(with more innocence than confidence).* I don't mean nothin' by it. I just don't know many regular girls, that's all.
LORETTA. And you expect me to come out, just like that.
HOOKER. If I expected somethin', I wouldn't be still standin' out here in the hall.

LORETTA *looks at him carefully. She knows it's not a line.*

LORETTA *(with less resistance now).* I don't even know you.
HOOKER *(slowly).* You know me. I'm just like you . . . It's two in the morning and I don't know nobody.

*The two just stand there in silence a second. There's nothing more to say. She stands back and lets him in.*

*Cut to*

*Int.* GONDORFF'S *Room—Night*

A record spinning lazily on an old phonograph. We hear Robert Johnson's "Come On In My Kitchen." GONDORFF is sitting up in bed, with his hat on, lost in thought. BILLIE is curled up asleep next to him. There's a packed suitcase next to the bed. BILLIE wakes up and turns over a second.

*Cut to*

*Int.* GONDORFF'S *Room*

BILLIE. C'mon Henry, knock off. You've done everything you can.

GONDORFF nods his agreement like a zombie and goes right on thinking.

*Cut to*

LORETTA'S *Room*

HOOKER and LORETTA are asleep against each other, their bodies illuminated every few seconds by the light from a neon sign across the street. We dolly to the window and move in on another window in the building next door. There's no light on in it, but we can discern the basic outline of a face behind the curtains, which are slightly parted to afford a view of HOOKER'S room by a black-gloved hand.

"I said come on in my kitchen 'Cause it's gonna be rainin' outdoors."

*Music ends.*

*Fade out*

*Fade in*

THE STING

*Fade out*

*Fade in*

*Int.* LORETTA'S *Room—Morning*

We open on HOOKER in bed, the morning sun streaming in on his face. He awakens slowly, looks at the ceiling for a second and, remembering last night, turns to the side to find that LORETTA is no longer there. Still drowsy, he gets out of bed and looks around the room for a note or some evidence of her continued presence. He opens an empty closet, then opens empty drawers. Finding nothing, he suddenly hits on another possibility, and looks in his wallet. The money is still there. Almost disappointed, he slumps down in a chair, as the harsh reality of what will happen this day floods back in on him. Music begins and we:

*Cut to*

*Int. An Unknown Location—Day*

We see the black-gloved hand opening a small wooden box. Wrapped inside is a shiny black revolver, at this point in two pieces. The hand reaches in and takes them out.

*Cut to*

*Int. The Sleezy Diner—Day*

HOOKER is poking at a plate of waffles and sausage. The waitress on duty is not LORETTA and HOOKER has noticed.

*Cut to*

*Int.* GONDORFF'S *Room—Day*

GONDORFF is standing in front of the bathroom mirror, putting on his tuxedo. He goes to his dresser, pulls out a very small gun and tucks it in his cummerbund.

*Cut to*

*The* GUNMAN'S *Room Again*

The hand swirls a pipe cleaner inside the barrel of the revolver and *picks some lint out of the chamber. He then screws the barrel onto the body. This is all seen in closeup.*

Cut to

HOOKER'S *Room Again*

HOOKER *now has his tuxedo on. He takes two small rubber bladders out of a drawer and puts them in his pocket.*

Cut to

*Int.* LONNEGAN'S *Suite—Day*

LONNEGAN *paces nervously around the room, looking at the clock. Obviously waiting for something, he's getting extremely impatient.*

Cut to

*The* GUNMAN'S *Room Again*

*We watch the hand carefully loading bullets into the chamber of the revolver.*

Cut to

*Int. The Carousel Building—Day*

GONDORFF *emerges from his room carrying his suitcase. He stops and looks up at the mezzanine where* BILLIE *is standing. They smile sadly at each other and give a simple wave, having done this too many times to get sentimental about it now.* GONDORFF *walks out of the building.*

Cut to

HOOKER'S *Room Again*

HOOKER *is busily stuffing all his possessions in a paper bag, lumping clothes with food, records and toilet articles.*

Cut to

LONNEGAN'S *Suite Again*

LONNEGAN *goes to the door to admit* FLOYD *and two assistants, one of whom carries a large brief case.*

LONNEGAN *takes the brief case to a table and opens it. Inside is a half million dollars in cash.*

Cut to

*The* GUNMAN'S *Room Again*

*We see the hand putting a silencer on the revolver. The* GUNMAN *puts the revolver up to his eye to check the alignment and for the first time we see the face that goes with the hand. It is fully as menacing as we had imagined: Broad, flat nose, thick cracked lips, narrow eyes and cauliflower ears.*

Cut to

HOOKER'S *Room Again*

HOOKER *is on the phone now.*

*Int. Warehouse*

*We see that he's talking to* CAPTAIN POLK. SNYDER *listens also.*

HOOKER'S *Room*

HOOKER *finishes the conversation, hangs up and goes to take one last look at himself in the mirror. Finding everything in order, he grabs up his sack of possessions and leaves the room.*

*Ext.* HOOKER'S *Apartment*

*We pick him up emerging from the building, and follow him around the corner to a secluded alley which he generally takes on his way to the store. As he walks along, he notices* LORETTA *coming toward him from the other end. She's wearing a coat, obviously on her way somewhere. As she comes closer, we move to reveal the* GUNMAN *appearing suddenly in the alley behind and to the right of* HOOKER.

*Ext. Alleyway*

The GUNMAN *quickly takes out his revolver, braces it in the crook of his hand, and takes careful aim.* LORETTA *sees him. The* GUNMAN *fires.* LORETTA *falls dead on the asphalt.*

HOOKER *spins around in confusion. The* GUNMAN *moves quickly toward him.* HOOKER *starts to back up but the* GUNMAN *stops when he gets to* LORETTA. *He kicks her over to reveal a gun under her body.*

GUNMAN. She was gonna kill ya, kid.

HOOKER *is stunned. He can't believe it.*

GUNMAN *(dragging the body over behind a trash can).* Her name's Loretta Salino. Lonnegan's people set her up in the diner. C'mon, let's get outa here.

HOOKER *wants to stay and try to figure it all out, but the gunman drags him away.*

*Cut to*

*Int. The Abandoned Warehouse—Day*

POLK, SNYDER *and several federal agents are busy putting on their shoulder holsters, and checking their weapons.*

POLK *(to* SNYDER). We got a tip that Gondorff's playin' for some New York wheel. As soon as we're inside, I want you to get the guy outa there as fast as possible, before the reporters show up. We can't afford to embarrass any big shots.

SNYDER *nods.*

*Cut to*

*Ext.* LONNEGAN'S *Hotel—Day*

LONNEGAN, *carrying the brief case personally, is seen getting into his* limousine. *Four assistants get in with him.*

*Cut to*

*Int. The Store—Day*

GONDORFF *enters the store carrying his suitcase. Several of the boost are already there.* GONDORFF *clasps his hands to generate a little enthusiasm. He's obviously up for this one.*

*Cut to*

*Int. A Taxi Cab—Day*

HOOKER *sits in the back seat with the* GUNMAN *right next to him. He's still very uneasy with this man.*

HOOKER. She coulda killed me last night.

GUNMAN. Too many people coulda seen ya go in her room. She was a professional. Used to work in the Dutch Schultz gang.

HOOKER. Who are you?

GUNMAN. Gondorff asked me to look after ya.

HOOKER. How do I know you're tellin' the truth.

GUNMAN. Don't have much choice, do ya?

*We go to* HOOKER. *No, he doesn't.*

*Cut to*

*Ext. The Abandoned Warehouse—Day*

*We pick up* POLK, SNYDER *and the other federal agents coming out of the warehouse in their white skimmers, and piling into cars.*

*Cut to*

*The Store Again*

NILES *is busily spreading "boodles" all over the cashier's area.* SINGLETON *checks his microphone. It works fine. He checks it again.*

*Cut to*

LONNEGAN *in His Limousine*

*He holds the brief case in his lap, his fingers tapping lightly on it.*

*Cut to*

*The Store Again*

HOOKER *and the* GUNMAN *enter and go over to* GONDORFF, *who breaks into a wide smile.* HOOKER *returns it half-heartedly, still ill at ease about what has happened.*

*Cut to*

*The F.B.I. Cars on Their Way*

*There are four or five driving in a column.* SNYDER *and* POLK *ride together in the back of the lead car.*

*Cut to*

*Ext. The Drugstore—Day*

LONNEGAN'S *limousine pulls up outside, and the bodyguards pile out.*

*Cut to*

*The Store Again*

GONDORFF, HOOKER *and the others waiting, the tension expressed in their faces.*

*Int. The Drugstore—Day*

LONNEGAN *sits tensely in the usual booth. He keeps both hands firmly planted on the brief case. The phone rings and* LONNEGAN *goes to it. Music ends.*

VOICE. Place it on Syphon at four to one.

LONNEGAN *hangs up with the look of the financial killer. Four to one odds is more than even he could have hoped for.*

*Ext. Street*

*We follow* LONNEGAN *across the street and into the store. The bodyguards remain outside.*

*Int. Store*

*The store is buzzing with activity. Money and booze are everywhere. The sheet writer and the boardmarker can hardly keep up with the action.* LONNEGAN *walks quickly to the betting line and finds to his relief that there's only one man ahead of him. The man puts $25,000 on King's Image.*

LONNEGAN *steps to the window, swings up the brief case, and opens it for* NILES *to see.*

LONNEGAN *(straight-faced).* Five hundred grand on Syphon.

NILES *is struck dumb. He's never seen that much money before.*

NILES *(playing the flustered clerk).* Hold on, I'll have to get the manager.

NILES *goes and returns with* GONDORFF.

GONDORFF. What's the problem?
NILES *(pointing to the brief case).* He wants to put a half million on Syphon.

GONDORFF *looks at the money a second and then looks up at* LONNEGAN *like he's gotta be crazy.*

GONDORFF *(uneasily).* I can't lay that off in time. We lose a bet that big, it could break us.
LONNEGAN *(challenging).* If ya win it could make ya, too.
GONDORFF *(to* NILES). What are the odds on Syphon?
NILES. Four to one.

GONDORFF *looks at* LONNEGAN *long and hard.*

GONDORFF. A half mill on a four to one shot. You're dumber than I thought, Lonnegan.

LONNEGAN. You're more gutless than I thought.

*The words "Last Flash" are heard on the speaker.* GONDORFF *looks at* LONNEGAN *with utter contempt. He turns to* NILES.

GONDORFF *(chopped)*. Take it.

NILES *hurriedly writes out a slip for 500,000 dollars.* LONNEGAN, *allowing himself a sly smile, picks it up and retires to a nearby table. He flashes a little okay sign to* HOOKER *who acknowledges it with a nod.*

CALLER. Ladies and gentlemen, this is Arnold Rowe, your caller for the San Antonio Handicap at Pimlico in Baltimore—A mile and ¹⁄₁₆ for three-year-olds. And they're off.

LONNEGAN *takes a deep breath and leans forward in his chair, the larceny boiling in his veins.* HOOKER *looks to* GONDORFF. GONDORFF *gives him the "office."* HOOKER *has to smile.*

CALLER. And around the first turn it's King's Image by a neck, Syphon is second by one, Key to the Vault third by one half, followed by Mr. Moonlight, Red Ridge, Moneyman and No Charge.

*Unexpectedly,* KID TWIST *bursts in through the entrance. Barely able to control his enthusiasm, he hurries over to* LONNEGAN'S *table and sits down next to him.*

TWIST. Sorry, but I just couldn't wait. Did everything go all right?

LONNEGAN *(motioning for him to keep his voice down)*. Take it easy. Everything's all right. I put it on Syphon, on the nose.

TWIST *(in utter horror)*. On the nose! I said place. Place it on Syphon. That horse is going to run second.

LONNEGAN *looks like he's just been stabbed. He vaults over the table to the teller's window and grabs* NILES.

LONNEGAN. You give me my goddam money back! You hear me? There's been a mistake!

NILES. I'm sorry, sir. The betting's closed.

LONNEGAN *begins to shake him violently.*

LONNEGAN. You give me my money back. There's been a mistake, do you hear me?

GONDORFF *leaps to* NILES'S *aid when suddenly there is a crash at the entrance door, and* POLK, SNYDER *and eight federal agents burst into the room, guns drawn. The place falls silent except for the loudspeaker, the members of the boost afraid to move.* GONDORFF *and* NILES *look at each other wondering how this could have possibly happened.*

POLK *(motioning to* HOOKER*)*. All right, Hooker, you can go.

HOOKER'S *eyes go to* GONDORFF, *who looks back at him in utter disbelief, the betrayal raging in his features.* HOOKER, *unable to meet his gaze, lowers his head and starts to walk out. Almost unnoticed, there's a flash of movement at* GONDORFF'S *belt. A small gun. A shot.* HOOKER *clutches his back and falls dead on the floor, the blood spurting from his mouth.* POLK, *reacting instantly, pours four shots into* GONDORFF, *who goes down in a heap. Pandemonium breaks loose. The members of the boost race for the door.* LONNEGAN *is totally stunned. First he lost his money and now he's involved in a murder.* SNYDER *rushes over to him.*

SNYDER. C'mon. We gotta get you outa here.

*Ext. Street*

SNYDER *drags him through the crowd and out onto the street where an F.B.I. car is waiting. His bodyguards have long since fled at the sight of the F.B.I. men.*

LONNEGAN. My money's back there.

SNYDER. We'll worry about that later.

SNYDER *gets in beside* LONNEGAN, *and the car speeds away.*

*Cut to*

*Inside the Store Again*

*The pandemonium has now ceased. Those who could escape have; the rest are lined up against the wall in frisking position.* GONDORFF *and* HOOKER *lie on the floor dead. The loudspeaker drones on.* SINGLETON *is still calling the race from his booth, apparently oblivious to what's happened.*

CALLER. And the winner is King's Image by four lengths, Syphon is second, by two, Moneyman third by two and one half. Time for 1 and 1/16 miles, 1:21 and 2/10 seconds.

POLK *walks slowly over to* HOOKER'S *body and bends down.*

POLK. He's gone.

HOOKER *opens his eyes and slowly drags himself up off the floor, spitting out a little rubber bladder, filled with blood, that he's had in his mouth.*

GONDORFF *does likewise.* NILES, TWIST, SINGLETON *and the rest of the boost begin to laugh and shake hands, as do the Federal Agents.*

GONDORFF *(to* POLK). Nice con, Hickey. I thought you were Feds myself, when you first came in.

HICKEY. No problem, Henry. Snyder went for it all the way. *(laughing)* You shoulda seen the rag he lit under Lonnegan.

GONDORFF *turns to the others.*

GONDORFF. Okay, let's take this place apart and get outa here. You can get your splits from Eddie at Boudreau's tonight.

GONDORFF *walks over to* HOOKER, *who's wiping the blood off his face and hands.*

GONDORFF. You beat him, kid.

HOOKER *(softly).* You were right, Henry. It's not enough . . . But it's close.

GONDORFF. You wanta wait for your share?

HOOKER. Naw, I'd just blow it.

GONDORFF *nods, and walks slowly behind the bar. He comes out with his suitcase in one hand and* HOOKER'S *paper bag in another. He throws the paper bag to* HOOKER, *who stops by the door. The* EIRIE KID *is standing there.* HOOKER *gives the "office" to* EIRIE, *who beams and gives it back.*

*Ext. Alley and Street*

HOOKER *and* GONDORFF *leave. We hold on them, two ragtail grifters again as they walk off down the street and disappear around the corner.*

*Fade out*

*THE END*